# The Dartnell

# Public Relations

# Handbook

**DARTNELL** is a publisher serving the world of business with business books, business manuals, business newsletters and bulletins, training materials for business executives, managers, supervisors, sales representatives, financial officials, personnel executives and office employees. In addition, Dartnell produces management and sales training films and audio cassettes, publishes many useful business forms, conducts management seminars for business men and women and has many of its materials and films available in languages other than English. Dartnell, established in 1917, serves the world's whole business community. For details, catalogs, and product information, address: DARTNELL, 4660 N. Ravenswood Avenue, Chicago, Illinois 60640, USA—or phone (312) 561-4000.

# The Dartnell Public Relations Handbook

Robert L. Dilenschneider
Dan J. Forrestal

With a Special Section on the Health Care Field

**THE DARTNELL CORPORATION**
CHICAGO · BOSTON · LONDON

## OTHER DARTNELL HANDBOOKS

Advertising Manager's Handbook
Direct Mail and Mail Order Handbook
Marketing Manager's Handbook
Office Administration Handbook
Personnel Administration Handbook
Sales Manager's Handbook
Sales Promotion Handbook

Copyright 1967, 1979, 1987
in the United States, Canada, and Great Britain by

THE DARTNELL CORPORATION

all rights reserved
Third Edition, Revised 1987
Second Printing, 1989

Library of Congress Catalog Card
Number: 87-71012

ISBN 0-85013-159-6

Printed in the United States of America by Dartnell Press, Inc., Chicago, Illinois 60640

# Contents

*Picture sections follow pages 424 and 616*

# Foreword

One of the most important trends in recent years has been the integration of public relations into the marketing mix. No longer do corporations view it as a separate, narrow-objective tactic, a tactic that is isolated from other marketing activities. Today, most marketers understand that public relations must be linked with other marketing disciplines. They recognize that the planning and implementation of a public relations program must harmonize with overall marketing objectives.

That recognition is what makes this new edition of the *Public Relations Handbook* so important. Authors Robert L. Dilenschneider and Dan J. Forrestal appreciate marketing's role in public relations. They explore the myriad ways public relations can be used as a marketing tool. Writing from both agency and client perspectives, the authors provide practical information, illustrated by case histories.

Public relations has multiple marketing applications. Corporations can use it for everything from issue management to strategic planning to image enhancement. They can coordinate PR efforts with promotions and advertising to improve trade relations. Or they can launch financial relations programs that can support initial public offerings, orchestrate security analyst meetings, and communicate sensitive merger and acquisition information.

Public relations, like all marketing disciplines, has become a field of specialists. Just as the old advertising generalist had given way to specialists in direct-response advertising, business-to-business advertising, and the like, public relations now breaks down into many areas of expertise.

You'll find public relations agencies that focus on special events. Others bill themselves as financial PR strategists. Within corporations, you'll find communications' employees who are responsible only for internal newsletters, brochures, and magazines; others are media relations experts. This increasing specialization facilitates interaction between public relations and other disciplines, which respond positively to this new breed of specialists. A corporate marketing director, for instance, welcomes the PR professional who understands trade relations; that marketing director feels comfortable including the public relations person in planning as well as in implementation.

In this book, the gamut of specialized PR activities are covered. An especially timely section concentrates on health-care public relations. More so than ever before, hospitals, HMOs, and other health-care organizations are aggressively marketing their services. Within this marketing mix, PR has become a key component. What that component entails is discussed as it relates to this field.

In the 1980s and beyond, corporate communication and PR agency executives must understand their marketing roles. It is no longer enough for them to be great release writers or to establish terrific media contacts. Today and in the future, they must understand how their skills dovetail with those of other marketing professionals. How can they best work with a market research department or firm? How can they contribute to the sales department's efforts to open up new channels of distribution? How can they maximize the impact of the ad agency's new campaign?

There is a strategy here that didn't exist—or at least, was not common—a decade ago. Public relations professionals must be prepared to deal with a staggering variety of people, issues, and subjects.

This excellent book contains information to help prepare the public relations practitioner to meet the challenge.

—GEORGE LAZARUS
Marketing News Columnist
*Chicago Tribune*

# Introduction

Only eight years have elapsed since The Dartnell Corporation published its Second Edition of the *Public Relations Handbook*. However, the appearance of this Third Edition is by no means premature. Much new material has been assembled by the authors, Robert L. Dilenschneider, president and chief executive officer of Hill and Knowlton, and Dan J. Forrestal, public relations consultant of Forrestal & Associates who formerly was director of public relations for Monsanto Corporation. Much of it relates not merely to small details that needed updating but to the sweeping changes that have come over the theory and practice of public relations. This industry (or business) is still not far out of its formative years, and only in the past decade has it grappled with some fundamental issues in its own development.

Meanwhile, its growth has been rapidly accelerating as a consequence of the "information revolution." Everywhere people have been challenged by the need to know, as they have confronted options and choices had they never had or even heard about before— exotic new investment forms, gaudy new consumer products such as home computers and videocassette recorders. To be a conscientious citizen today one has had to master at least the rudiments of such matters as the technology of the space shuttle, the safety factor in nuclear power plants, and gyrations of the dollar in international money markets. Whoever it was that said, "knowledge is power," could have added, "and you can't survive without it." Ironically, a major Wall Street scandal of the 1980s involved trading in *inside information.*

Vast stores of data accumulated in computer memories and have been spewing forth from machines that seem to operate at the speed of light. Corporations now had continuing relations with a number of different "publics": their stockholders, investment banks, consumers of their products, suppliers of raw materials, the communities they were established in, government regulators, and environmentalists and other concerned groups. The penalty for neglecting any of them could mean corporate death.

Eliminating the technical barriers to the ever-rising volume of information exchange has not been a particularly serious problem. The innovating hardware of telecommunications has pretty much kept up with the demand. On the human side, however, there were large obstacles yet to be cleared away. On the surface, the right to know seemed absolute and indisputable, but when you got down to details, difficulties loomed. It wasn't just the mania, endemic in Washington, for classifying everything "top secret." In private business and nonprofit organizations as well, there wasn't much enthusiasm for disclosing delicate matters. Accordingly, the powers-that-be holed up in their fortresses behind their moral certainties, and a junior public relations person was assigned to keep the wolves at bay.

The picture has changed remarkably fast. The Freedom of Information Act has lived up to its grand name by prying open the federal archives, and officialdom has suddenly become very available and quite talkative. The President's cabinet members clamor to be interviewed on the morning talk shows. Top corporate executives have been stepping off their pedestals to speak their minds—and sometimes do some listening too. It was a time of opening up; even the Russians had a word for it, *glasnost,* which became the theme song of the Gorbachev regime.

It was an auspicious time to have a job that emphasized gathering and elucidating information. At its best, public relations embodied a dual job—first, sorting out and comprehending the economic, financial, and social pressures that affect the performance of the client organization and second, keeping the world-at-large familiar with and favorably inclined toward that same client. As Bob Dilenschneider says in this *Handbook* (see Chapter 3, page 35), "Public relations people who are at the top of their jobs learn that all targets are moving targets, and that therefore the nature of the work and the exercise of good judgment require ceaseless renewal of information and insights."

Many public relations people, no doubt, still spend their days doing traditional chores—grinding out routine press releases, composing banquet speeches for serious executives, preparing copy for the annual report. How different is a day in the life of someone at the cutting edge of the business, which may start with organizing a presentation to defend the company's performance before an audience of security analysts, then explaining to a business magazine writer how the company's new electronic product works.

Today's public relations arena has no place for hacks. In the past, the PR jobs had often gone to newsmen who welcomed the chance to bolster their retirement funds. They usually had good news sense and wrote clear prose, but they lacked the kind of style that might have added distinction to the message. Gresham's Law was operative here, and the more imaginative and ambitious younger men and women moved in and took over. Inevitably, they began thinking of public relations as a desirable lifetime career.

That thought led quickly on to the notion of declaring it a profession. It might not matter much if some ambitious young people wanted to be thought of as members of a professional group, but "credentialism" would rear its ugly head. Trouble results whenever professional status is used to exclude potential new members. They might be required to obtain licenses, or maybe pass a test (just as budding lawyers must pass their bar examinations). Lawyers are a relatively homogenous group. Public relations embraces many different functions that would not fit comfortably under one roof. A way to get around that would be to establish more public relations schools around the country like the schools of journalism that have sprouted on so many campuses. As a matter of fact, a good many journalism graduates never see the inside of a newspaper office; they wind up in public relations.

The really serious concern is not how to ensure an adequate supply of young public relations people, but to determine how educationally fit they are for the job. The authors argue commendably that the best schooling for a career in public relations is a sound grounding in the liberal arts—history, sociology, psychology, literature, and political science—augmented perhaps by courses in economics and corporate finance, business law, and business organization. Regardless of what intellectual competences a person may bring to the job, the human quality that is most vital is a veneration for truth. Uncompromising, unwavering honesty is, of course, desirable in its own right, but there are several reasons it should be stressed in public relations. In public relations work, particularly, personal reputations are at stake, and what the public will tolerate least of all is lying. Nixon's Presidency collapsed not because he approved the bugging of a room in the Watergate building but because he—and the aides who managed his public relations—played fast and loose with the truth. Similarly, in the case of the Iranian arms deal during the second Reagan administration, it was the deviousness of the participating officials that hurt the most.

Another reason its veracity must be kept above suspicion is that public relations is a comparatively young industry. The memory of its unsavory forebears, the "flacks" and "press agents" who would flinch at nothing to get a client favorable mention in the papers, lingers on. To this day, when a too obviously favorable profile of a public figure appears in print, the cynical reaction is: "They did a PR job on him."

In exalting truth, care should be taken to distinguish it from objectivity. A public relations firm is not obliged to take a polygraph test with every statement it makes. It is in the business of promoting or selling an elusive commodity—a favorable public impression of its clients, which, among other things, might be a person, a grocery product, a political party, or a controversial cause. A PR professional cannot be expected to approach his or her assignment with a vacant mind. To each case the professional brings a set of judgments whose acceptance needs to be won. What is not defensible, however, is for there to be a concealment or distortion of known truths for the sake of desired outcomes.

Regard for the truth had been the implied issue that long divided public relations from the press. Journalists gave the impression that they were the anointed guardians of the First Amendment while the PR people were always flirting with venality. Four decades as an editor of a business magazine have convinced me that that's a lot of nonsense. Aside from a few cranks who tried to bar the way to the executive offices and monopolize the interviewing or demanded to see unedited versions of our article, PR people were most cooperative and helpful.

The fact of the matter was that the journalists looked down on the PR people, critical of the way they did the work; *real* reporters ripped their stories out of the throats of reluctant witnesses and did not sit in cushy offices reading books. Action reporting was all right as long as journalism confined itself chiefly to crime and politics and war. But it was no way to cover more complicated, technical subjects that required help from the experts.

Around the time OPEC first jolted the world with its oil-price shock, there was a surge of demand for explanatory reporting of business economics and finance—areas in which nonspecialist news people were woefully weak. The deficiency was soon corrected as able younger reporters, sensing where good salaries were, shifted over. At the same time, the journalists swallowed their pride and went to the public relations offices for help.

Thus did the information revolution forge a new alliance, an alliance that benefits the best practitioners of both disciplines and their audiences.

—ROBERT LUBAR
Retired Managing Editor
*Fortune*

# About the Authors

Robert L. Dilenschneider was elected president and chief executive officer of Hill and Knowlton, Inc., on March 4, 1986. He is a member of the firm's board of directors.

Dilenschneider joined Hill and Knowlton in 1967 in New York, shortly after receiving an M.S. degree from Ohio State University. He received a B.A. degree from the University of Notre Dame. In 1978 he moved to Chicago to organize the firm's National Division, opening more than 15 offices and building the operation from 50 employees to the current 600.

At Hill and Knowlton, Dilenschneider's responsibilities have covered a variety of fields, ranging from major corporations and professional groups to trade associations and educational institutions, and included dealing with regulatory agencies, labor unions, consumer groups, and minorities, among others. He has directed communications activities during the U.S. Steel/Marathon merger, the Kansas City Hyatt disaster, the Three-Mile Island accident, and the Bendix/Martin-Marietta takeover, and participated in communicating the redevelopment of assets in numerous companies—from the high tech business to heavy industry. He has also personally counseled six of *Fortune's* "10 Toughest Bosses."

Dilenschneider is a member of the Chicago Association of Commerce and Industry, the Steering Committee of the Founder's Council of the Field Museum of Natural History, the Public Relations Society of America, the Economic Club of New York, the International Public Relations Association, the Wisemen, the Advisory Board of the New York Hospital-Cornell Medical Center, and the U.S.-Japan Business Council. He is a former member of the board of directors of United Charities of Chicago and the board of the Council of the City of New York. He received New York's

"Big Apple" award in recognition of his contributions in making that city great.

Dilenschneider is widely published and has lectured before scores of professional organizations and colleges, including the University of Notre Dame, Ohio State University, and New York University.

Dan J. Forrestal has been a public relations counselor of Forrestal & Associates, with offices in St. Louis, Missouri, since 1974, when he took early retirement as chief public relations executive of Monsanto Company. He has provided public relations appraisals for a wide variety of corporate clients, the most recent being General Motors Corporation, Detroit.

Forrestal joined Monsanto Company as assistant director of the Industrial and Public Relations Department in January 1947, becoming director of public relations in 1958. During his 27½ years at the multinational corporation, many of the company's programs and publications received national recognition. In 1974 he received two major national awards, the American Academy of Achievement Award for Excellence and the Golden Anvil Award from the Public Relations Society of America (PRSA).

A native of St. Louis, Forrestal started his career on the *St. Louis Globe-Democrat,* and over 19 years served in various capacities: sportswriter, music columnist, feature editor, war correspondent, and assistant managing editor. In overseas assignments in 1945 and 1946, he represented the North American Newspaper Alliance syndicate and the Columbia Broadcasting System.

Forrestal served as national president of PRSA in 1957 and as chairman of the Public Relations Seminar Committee in 1967. In 1984 he was listed among "the 40 leading public relations professionals in the world" at a New York dinner observing the 40th anniversary of *Public Relations News,* a publication distributed to 91 nations.

Forrestal currently serves as a member of the President's Council of St. Louis University, of which he is an alumnus, and on the advisory board of St. John's Mercy Medical Center in St. Louis County. He is a member of Sigma Delta Chi, the Harvard Club of New York City, and the Board of Governors of the Saint Louis Club in his home city.

He was coauthor of the 1967 and 1979 editions of Dartnell's *Public Relations Handbook.* He recently authored books based on the 75-year-history of Monsanto, *Faith, Hope and $5,000,* and on the 75-year history of the A. E. Staley Manufacturing Company, *The Kernel and the Bean,* both published by Simon and Schuster. In 1981 and 1982, Forrestal was editor of the *V.P. Fair Magazine,* published in conjunction with the St. Louis area's largest single civic observation. He has been a frequent contributor of articles in national business and professional journals.

During a twenty-year career in communications, David B. Williams has developed wide-ranging expertise in public relations, publications, and advertising. A former editor for the major medical publisher C. V. Mosby & Co. and *The Journal of the American Student Dental Association,* he has a special interest in health and medical topics.

Williams is currently public relations manager for Kiwanis International, serving as the organization's spokesman on various matters of national interest, including membership. He has played a key role in the recent Kiwanis public service campaign to support First Lady Nancy Reagan's efforts to combat school-age drug abuse. The Kiwanis promotion has garnered more than $12 million in public-service space and air time.

A respected writer and editor, Williams has authored numerous magazine articles and contributed to several books in the areas of science, management, communications, and public relations. His communications work has brought him such honors as the George Washington Medal from Freedoms Foundation and recognition in *Who's Who in America.*

# Acknowledgments

I am delighted to have this opportunity to thank and congratulate the authors and editors responsible for Parts 1, 2, and 3 of the Third Edition of Dartnell's *Public Relations Handbook.* Hill and Knowlton has always been extremely proud of its relationship with the *Handbook,* long regarded by all members of the profession as the industry bible.

In particular, I would like to thank the many Hill and Knowlton professionals who took time out from their busy schedules to share with us their knowledge of the profession. Each of their individual contributions is outstanding. Taken as a whole, their work demonstrates a remarkably broad knowledge of an increasingly complex business. It is a credit to these professionals and, I believe, their company that their writing fully conveys the accumulated wisdom of a public relations firm in its 60th year of industry leadership.

The Hill and Knowlton staff who contributed to this edition of the *Handbook* undoubtedly first learned their craft with the assistance of earlier editions. It is thus entirely fitting that the next generation of public relations practitioners will benefit from the experience and knowledge contained within this new compilation.

— *Robert L. Dilenschneider*

As author of the internal public relations section, Parts 4 and 5, of this *Handbook,* I have tried to practice what I preached: to stress how important it is for the so-called listening process to prevail. As a result, my narrative is alive with contemporary comments and examples from a broad range of communicators who were initially contacted with the simple question, "What's going on?"

Particularly since so many of the nation's employees have been caught in the discomforts of corporate belt-tightening, job insecurities, and widespread unrest, the role of internal communications becomes all the more urgent as the eighties begin to wind down. Communications can enlist support, understanding, and productivity by efforts to inform and to "level with" those in employee ranks.

In light of the immensity of the problem, I contacted almost 100 public relations colleagues—including many longtime, respected friends—soliciting their ideas, their experiences, their recommendations. The feedback was heartening. So many wanted to help in order to underline the validity of the practice of public relations as a business function.

There have been a few exceptional participants whose identity merits mention. My intrepid and long-suffering secretary, Frankie Spriesterbach, has been a vigilant and diligent heroine. Mary W. Wilson, director of the Public Relations Society of America Information Center in New York, has been a skillful bird dog whenever elusive information was otherwise unfindable.

The International Association of Business Communicators also provided assistance, adding an important dimension to the book. Also, the Public Relations Foundation for Research and Education gave first-time-ever permission for use of the most recent Foundation lectures. Gathering up the material and spearheading the effort to obtain permission from his Board of Trustees was Don Bates, New York public relations counselor serving as the Foundation administrator. When approached for his help, Bates's response was "OK. Right away." And he added, "It's for a good cause." Such sums up the total experience.

*—Dan J. Forrestal*

PART 1

# Public Relations: An Overview

Robert L. Dilenschneider

# Chapter 1

# Public Relations in the Modern World

Public relations, as we know and practice it today, is a product of the twentieth century. As a business, it had its origins in the first third of the century. Its pioneers were men like Ivy Lee, Edward L. Bernays, Pendleton Dudley, John Hill, and Carl Byoir, who thought of themselves as in the business of "publicity" or "corporate publicity." Only later did the term "public relations" come into general use. Whatever it was called, the activity filled a need.

Ivy Lee, as much as anyone, can be regarded as the founder of modern public relations. Lee was a financial writer who saw that big business and the press were at odds with one another and who felt that better communication could and should be established between them. The press agents of the day—it was 1904—had a reputation for insincerity and, furthermore, were usually more oriented to entertainment than to business.

Lee set himself up as a new kind of publicity man. Using his own experience as a newspaperman and the knowledge he had gained of business and industry as a financial writer, he would try to bring about better communication between business and the press. He insisted that his clients deal frankly with the press, being open about bad news as well as good, and issue only truthful information. He sent to newspapers a "Declaration of Principles," which said:

> This is not a secret press bureau. All our work is done in the open. We aim to supply news. This is not an advertising agency. If you think any of our matter ought properly to go to your business office, do not use it.

Our matter is accurate. Further details on any subject treated will be supplied promptly, and any editor will be assisted most carefully in verifying directly any statement of fact.

Ivy Lee's most famous client was John D. Rockefeller, and the job Lee accomplished in changing the public perception of "the world's richest man" from that of a cold, grasping tycoon to that of a warm, friendly philanthropist remains one of the classic examples of successful public relations.

## The Communications Link

John Hill, the founder of what is now Hill and Knowlton, told in *The Making of a Public Relations Man* how he happened to go into business. A newspaperman who had become an editor of a steel industry trade publication, Hill wrote that "one of my jobs was to handle news about industrial companies, most of whose officials had no use for newspaper reporters and no desire to give out any news. Those who had news to report did it with incredible ineptitude. It was clear to me then that most companies had need for help in the area of press relations."

Hill further related that industry executives would complain that the press was hostile to them. His answer to the executives was that the press sensed their own hostility, and that what was needed was more openness and frankness—in other words, better communication. That, succinctly expressed, is the essence of public relations.

Ivy Lee, John Hill, and the other public relations pioneers were all "publicity" people, who later became known as public relations counselors. One of the first industrial companies to set up a public relations department as an internal staff function was E.I. Du Pont de Nemours & Co. The company, which started out as a maker of gunpowder and explosives, had diversified following World War I but was still generally viewed as a munitions manufacturer. That perception wasn't helped when occasional explosions occurred and the company, like many other corporations, refused to give out any information.

After the establishment of a company news bureau, however, Du Pont began to turn itself around in the eyes of public opinion. It adopted a policy of honesty and openness, even encouraging inspections by the press and public to demonstrate that it was far more than a munitions maker. The success of the news bureau is evident today, as Du Pont is recognized as a major producer of "Better things for better living, through chemistry."

## Public Relations Is Universal

It is only in the twentieth century that public relations came to be codified, formalized, and practiced as a profession. Actually, however, it is as old as the human race. Every organization, institution, and individual has public relations whether or not that fact is recognized. As long as there are people, living together in communities, working together in organizations, and forming a society, there will be an intricate web of relationships among them.

The good will of the public is the greatest asset that any organization can have. A public that is well and factually informed is not only important; without it, an organization cannot long survive. Therefore, the starting point for good public relations in any organization is the development of sound policies that are in the public interest. Public understanding and approval must be deserved before they can be earned.

## What Is Public Relations?

Despite all this, however, public relations is notoriously hard to define. There is no universally accepted definition, perhaps because public relations is actually a composite of many different elements—research, media relations, product publicity, graphics, public affairs; it is all these disciplines and more. What draws them together is a common focus. From this can be derived a broad but accurate definition of public relations as the use of information to influence public opinion. Public opinion is the ultimate power in a free society, and the role of public relations is to ensure that the public has the information it needs to make informed decisions.

The decisions may include whom to elect to public office, which securities to invest in, which international trade liaisons to establish, or which product or service to buy. Or more subtle decisions may be involved, adding up to favorable attitudes. Such attitudes are vital to the institutions and organizations of a free society, and to none more so than to business and industry, which can operate only at the will of public opinion.

It is clear, then, that:

1. Anything not in the public interest is an unworthy cause.

2. Prestige and good will are invaluable assets of any institution.

3. An organization or institution has a clear responsibility to provide information and interpretation that are truthful and realistic, because public distrust may be due to lack of information.

## Expanding Role of Public Relations

Public relations, as we have seen, began as "corporate publicity." But it soon became apparent to both public relations people and management that there was a much broader role for public relations to play. Business had had bitter experiences and had suffered serious reverses as the result of actions that had not taken into account the public interest or the effects on public opinion. Management began to see that the public interest had to be considered when important decisions were made.

Management itself started the trend toward raising public relations to the policy level and giving public relations people responsibilities in the policy-making area. Until recently, however, relatively few public relations people had moved up to the policy level partly because, perhaps, the number qualified to do so was limited. Today, there has been an increasing number of public relations executives who have taken their places on management teams and who are fully qualified to do so. It is not unusual to find the senior public relations executive of a corporation—often called the director of corporate communications or something similar—with a high corporate title, such as vice president, senior vice president, or perhaps even higher in the corporate structure.

This is a continuing trend. There is still room at or near the top for public relations people who are able, as a result of their education, experience, and knowledge of business, to observe and interpret public opinion, to help make management decisions, and to plan and carry out programs that will gain and maintain public understanding and support. Management today realizes that in making even routine decisions, the impact on public opinion and the resulting consequences can be of tremendous importance.

A company making such a commonplace decision as one to change the price of a product, for example, at one time would take into consideration only the costs of production, the prices of competing products, possible reactions within the trade, and legal considerations. But today, other factors must be taken into account—public and consumer attitudes, the possible reactions of labor and of government to the price change, and the reactions of the financial community.

Once the decision has been made, public relations skills are called into play to announce the change so that it is clearly understood by all the "publics" that will be affected by it. These skills will include expert writing, careful planning and scheduling, and consideration and care in serving the special needs of the news media through which the announcement will reach the public.

## Growth of Public Relations

During the 1940s and 1950s, public relations underwent a period of tremendous growth, which continues today. The initial period of growth was stimulated by the following:

- Increasing government regulation of business and industry, and a perception on the part of many that government was increasingly making itself responsible for much in society that had previously been the concern of individuals or of the private sector—for example, care of the poor and the aged.

- The growth of organized labor in numbers, in political clout, and in legislative gains.

- A higher level of education and of social concern among the public, giving rise to such social movements as civil rights, environmentalism, consumerism, and the like.

- Increasing recognition by organizations and institutions of all kinds, including government itself, of their dependence on public approval and of their need to communicate.

Today, much of this has changed. The 1980s have seen increasing deregulation of business. At the same time, some government agencies—the Securities and Exchange Commission (SEC) in the United States may be one example—

that were once seen as antagonistic to business, are now generally regarded as helpful. Organized labor, though still highly visible and vocal, has lost much of its strength in numbers and no longer can be viewed as a political monolith.

Such social movements as environmentalism, consumerism, civil rights, and the like have, on the other hand, continued to grow and have become enshrined in public agencies at all levels of government. And new ones, such as feminism and antinuclear activism, have been born and have gained tremendous strength.

## Widespread Use of Public Relations

In recent years, an ever-increasing number of organizations have felt the need to promote public understanding of themselves and their causes, and have put to use the techniques of public relations—notably, skill in dealing with the news media—in order to do so. Public relations has, therefore, increasingly been recognized and used not only by business and industry but also by the proponents of most issues, interests, and causes in American life.

During the 1960s, Bert C. Goss, then chairman of Hill and Knowlton, Inc., cited six evidences of the increasing role of public relations in management. Some of his statements were simply factual, others prophetic. His six points were as follows:

1. Public relations now constitutes an integral part of the operations of business—and there will be increasing emphasis upon good public relations by business in the future.

2. Public relations today operates as an arm of business management—and the future public relations practitioner will have to be thoroughly familiar with modern business procedures as well as the skills of communications.

3. Public relations executives—because of the pervasive influence of the functions they perform—will continue to move in large numbers into positions of responsibility in American business.

4. Increasingly greater emphasis will be placed on the acquisition of highly trained professional talent, on the development of better methods, and on the use of modern research in the practice of corporate public relations.

5. Public relations in the future will devote a greater portion of its efforts to the problem of winning understanding and support from the intellectual leaders of the nation—who, through their teachings and writings, are able to influence the minds of millions.

6. Public relations as an organized function will continue to expand internationally as business and communications and political ties between nations increase.

In his fifth point, Goss may have overestimated the influence of "the intellectual leaders of the nation," by which he seems to have meant the academic community. He apparently did not foresee that these leaders would increasingly seek to influence minds not so much through their teachings and writings as through their adoption of the techniques of public relations.

## The Public Defined

Public relations practitioners recognize that there is no such thing as one homogeneous "public." Not only do we live in a pluralistic society; we also live in a complex one in which each one of us may be, at the same time or at various times, an employee, a consumer, a stockholder, a member of an industrialized community, a voter, a parent, or a member of any of several other groups.

Often, the comprehensive term "the public" may be used to denote different groups, rather than the entire populace. Therefore we speak of "publics" rather than of "the public." From the point of view of business and industry, the major publics that need to be addressed include the following:

- **Employees.** Good public relations begins at home, and employees are part of the business "family."

- **Stockholders.** They are the owners of the corporation—the "capitalists" whose investments provide the funds with which corporations are founded, maintained, and caused to grow.

- **Communities.** The areas in which the corporation maintains offices, factories, or service facilities. The people of the community are the corporation's neighbors, whose friendship, loyalty, and support it needs.

- **The news media.** These comprise all the means of public communication—print, electronic, satellite, computer networks, and others that are constantly being developed and restructured as technology continues to improve and audiences become more segmented.

- **Government.** At all levels—federal, state, and local—government, as "the voice of the people," has the power to tax, regulate, and in one way or another supervise the operations of corporations under its jurisdiction.

- **The investment community.** In particular, the people and institutions that analyze and evaluate the performance of corporations, and both invest themselves and make recommendations to others based on their findings.

- **Customers.** The ultimate consumers of the corporation's products, whose good opinion is vital to the continuing success and growth of the enterprise.

For any given enterprise this list of publics may be longer or shorter. For example, a corporation that sells its product only to other corporations is likely to have only a few customers, but one whose products include food or household supplies, for example, may have literally millions of them.

For organizations other than corporations, target publics will be defined differently and will depend on the makeup, purposes, and goals of the organization. Labor leaders, hospital managers, foundation heads, college presidents, administrators of charitable, research, or benevolent organizations, and others will define their primary audiences—their publics—in the light of their own objectives, problems, and needs at a given time.

Candidates for elective office and heads of government are perhaps the only persons for whom the public means everyone within their jurisdiction who is or may possibly become part of their constituencies.

Depending on the field of interest of a given institution, other audiences may be of paramount importance. These may be, for example, college-educated women, or ethnic groups, or teenagers, or a particular professional group such as doctors or lawyers. The basic difference between public relations for profit-making organizations and that for not-for-profit groups (discussed in Chapter 18) is one of goals and audiences, not one of technique.

Most organizations, upon launching a public relations effort tend to concentrate first on those identifiable categories of people who are often referred to as "opinion leaders." These are the people or groups who are admired by others, and who tend to be believed in. What they do, say, write, or express opinions about actually forms public opinion. And often, the decisions they make are critical to the fortunes of the companies or other organizations that communicate with them.

# Chapter 2

# Public Relations and Social Change

The twentieth century has been marked by tremendous social, economic, political, technological, and other changes in America. The century opened in what was still the Victorian age. Shortly thereafter, however, major upheavals began to occur that have changed the nation itself and the lives of all its people.

The first quarter of the century was marked in one way by the first World War, in another way by the appearance of such major inventions as radio, the automobile, and the airplane, and in still a third way by the beginning of the era of Prohibition. The second quarter saw the stock market crash and the coming of the Great Depression of the 1930s, the three-plus-term presidency of Franklin D. Roosevelt and the New Deal, World War II, a postwar economic boom of unprecedented proportions, the growth of organized labor, major population movements from the farm to the city and from the city to new suburban areas, and the dawn of the nuclear age.

The century's third quarter brought perhaps the greatest changes of all. It opened with the Korean Conflict, and followed that with the shattering and demoralizing effects of a long, disillusioning war in Vietnam. The violence of the Vietnam war spawned violence at home. National leaders, President John F. Kennedy and his brother Robert, and civil rights leader Martin Luther King, Jr., died at the hands of assassins. Not only was one president of the United States murdered, but another, Lyndon B. Johnson, was forced to end his political career as a result of his support for the war, and still a third, Richard M. Nixon, resigned his office in the face of an impeachment threat.

The years between 1950 and 1975 were marked also by unrest virtually everywhere in American society. These were the years of the civil rights movement, women's liberation, the revolt of young people against the "middle-class values" of their elders, the sexual revolution, and many changes that tended to come about violently rather than by evolution. But this same quarter-century brought the jet plane, the age of space exploration and the landing of men on the moon, the development of new means of communication such as television and satellites, the emergence of the computer, and numerous other changes that are continuing in this final quarter of the twentieth century.

## With Change, Public Relations Grows

When President Roosevelt launched the New Deal in an attempt to bring an end to the Great Depression, business felt threatened, as the government put into place restrictions, regulations, and regulatory bodies that had never before existed. And with each of the many social changes that followed, new circumstances brought change in the relationships between the business community and the larger society of which it was a part. Changed relationship brought about a greater use of public relations.

The years following World War II were marked by the development of new industries, new materials, new processes, new devices, and new ways of thinking. Plastics, electronics, nuclear fission, computerization, synthetic fabrics, chemicals, and new medicines and diagnostic methods are but a few of these. And in each instance, there were problems of public understanding and acceptance that had to be dealt with by the effective communication of information.

## The Spread of Education

One of the unexpected effects of World War II was a tremendous upsurge in higher education. Before the war, there was only limited opportunity for young people to go to college, particularly during the depression, when family incomes were low or nonexistent. But the so-called GI Bill of Rights, stemming out of the war, made it possible for veterans—there were millions of them—to get a college education or trade school training at government expense.

Later, these veterans formed families of their own and wanted higher education for their children, and there gradually evolved the situation we see today, where a college degree is often seen as the passport to white-collar jobs everywhere in American society. The college rolls were further swelled as the civil rights and feminist movements accounted for more minorities and women enrolling at universities. As a result of the spread of higher education, each new generation—as consumers, as workers, as voters, as citizens—is more highly perceptive, more particular, more discriminating, more thoughtful, and more articulate than any preceding generation.

## The World Grows Smaller

In 1927, the world marveled when Charles A. Lindbergh flew an airplane across the Atlantic. Twelve years later, in 1939, regular transatlantic flights began. In the 1950s, the development of jet-powered aircraft made overseas flights much faster and more frequent, and by the 1970s supersonic jets cut flying time still more.

Television, although it was invented before World War II, did not begin to come into its own until the 1950s. Since then, it has become an almost universal medium for news and entertainment, and the conquest of space and the launching of communications satellites have made television, telecommunications, and facsimile transmission instantaneous and worldwide.

The resulting shrinkage of the world helped focus American attention on the international scene to a greater extent than every before. International trade, the growth and economic and political significance of transnational corporations, the emergence of the Third World as a political power, the ever-present tensions between East and West, the formation of the European Economic Community—all these and more created both problems and opportunities for governments, labor, schools, the corporations involved, and, of course, the public.

## Civil Rights

Since the middle of the century, America has been characterized by social ferment, and few institutions have been unaffected by it. Beginning in the late 1940s, the country moved toward a new awareness of the need to bring racial and other minorities in the population into the main stream of civil and economic life. In 1948 the Dixiecrats bolted the Democratic Party and ran their own presidential slate along racial lines. However, the momentous Supreme Court decision in the case of *Brown v. Board of Education* in 1954, outlawing racial segregation in schools, marked for most Americans the beginning of the civil rights movement.

In the years following, television for virtually the first time played a major role in the mobilization of public opinion. It showed violent confrontations between blacks and whites, with escalated emotions on both sides. It chronicled bombings of schools and churches attended by blacks. It pictured in graphic detail attacks on blacks by white police armed with clubs and water hoses and accompanied by menacing dogs. It allowed millions of viewers to take part vicariously in "freedom marches" in parts of the deep South.

As a result of the widespread media coverage, civil rights came to the forefront among American priorities. Millions demanded that the outmoded and unjust system of "separate but equal" schools for blacks and whites be done away with forever and that true integration be established. This demand for school integration led naturally to movements for equality in housing, economic opportunity, and every other facet of American life. It led also to demands for equality by other groups in our society. Movements for women's rights, gay rights, senior citizens' rights, and even animal rights had their genesis in the civil rights movement.

## The Environmental Movement

The movement to preserve and protect the environment—water, air, wildlife, physical features of the landscape, the oceans, and the earth itself—had its roots in the conservation movement that began in the nineteenth century. But the accusation that mankind—and perhaps particularly America, and perhaps even more particularly American business and industry—was polluting the environment and was in danger of destroying or permanently harming it began to come to the surface of the American consciousness in the 1950s.

As with other public issues, several circumstances came together to bring the environment to the fore as a matter of major concern. One was air pollution—the smoke of factories and the emissions of the automobile, the quantity of which had skyrocketed, began to cause alarm as dangerous to the health of individuals and potentially destructive of the environment. Another was the emergence of peaceful uses of atomic energy, first seen as a boon, later as a creator of dangerous radiation that contained the potential for major disasters. Still a third was the publication in 1962 of Rachel Carson's book *Silent Spring*, which warned of dangerous quantities of insecticides in the food chain and of their adverse effect of wildlife.

All of this led to stringent federal, state, and local laws and regulations, to the creation of environmental protection agencies at all levels of government, and to a new distrust of business and industry on the part of many Americans.

## Consumerism

Beginning in the 1960s, a number of circumstances came together to create, for the first time, an organized consumer protection movement in the United States. Attempts on the part of the government to protect the public from unfair trade practices had been make long before—antitrust laws and the creation of such agencies as the Federal Trade Commission, the Food and Drug Administration, the Securities and Exchange Commission, for example, date from earlier years.

But the major impetus for the beginning of an organized consumer movement was perhaps the publication, in 1965, of Ralph Nader's book *Unsafe at Any Speed,* which not only made Nader the most prominent "consumerist," but also led Congress to enact legislation controlling the design of automobiles. Subsequently, laws at all levels of government set new standards of safety for many products, new requirements for disclosure of the costs of credit, and new regulations of many kinds. A U.S. Office of Consumer Affairs was established in 1971, and the Consumer Product Safety Commission in 1973. Today, large consumer organizations are active at local, national, and international levels.

Much of this activity—legislation and the creation of new government agencies in particular—drew strong opposition from business. Eventually, however, the new consumer thrust became generally accepted, and business reacted by improving warranties, handling complaints more satisfactorily, inspecting products and instituting better quality control, and in general adopting a more open public relations stance.

## The Women's Movement

The civil rights movement of the 1950s and 1960s gave rise, as has been noted, to movements for equality on the part of other groups in American society. Most notable of these, perhaps, has been "feminism," the demand of women for full equality in all phases of life and work.

The issue of women's rights dates back to the nineteenth century or even earlier, but its first proponents were not taken seriously by a society that remained strongly male-dominated. Women did not gain the right to vote in the United States until enactment of the 19th Amendment to the Constitution in 1920. But the serious and widespread attempt to gain full legal and economic equality for women began around 1963, sparked by the publication in that year of *The Feminine Mystique,* by Betty Friedan, who three years later founded the National Organization for Women.

Since then, the women's movement—despite the failure of the Equal Rights Amendment to achieve ratification via state legislatures—has brought about profound changes in American society not only in business but in all aspects of life including marriage and the structure of the family. It seems likely that no other part of the civil rights movement has had so great an impact. And, of course, public relations has been called upon to help business meet the challenges these changes present.

## Government Regulation

The inauguration of the "New Deal" by President Franklin D. Roosevelt in 1933 marked the end of what might be called the era of *laissez faire* economics. Between that time and the present, the regulation of business by the government has grown enormously. And despite the deregulation of some industries such as the airlines in the 1980s, the American economy remains to a great extent a governmentally regulated one.

In the decade between 1963 and 1972—that is, during the administrations of Presidents Kennedy and Johnson—29 major bills were enacted that either established new regulations and government agencies to enforce them, or extended the powers of already existing regulatory bodies. This range of legislation was so broad that it affected virtually every industry in one way or another.

These actions not only greatly increased the statutory obligations of business. They also made the federal government one of the most important audiences for the messages that business felt it essential to communicate.

The result was the emergence into the foreground of the element of public relations known as government relations or public affairs. Congress, the regulatory agencies, and the administration became so important to business that many of the largest trade associations moved their headquarters to Washington, public relations firms opened offices there, and lobbying began to be regarded as one of the functions of public relations. At the same time, public-interest groups representing consumers, environmentalists, and many others were established in Washington.

The Occupational Safety and Health Act, the Consumer Product Safety Act, and the Equal Employment Opportunity Act are only three of the important pieces of legislation affecting business that were enacted during the 1963-1972 period.

Business had always been the primary user of public relations and the largest employer of public relations people. Growing government control over business practices, products, policies, and activities brought about a far greater exposure of many companies to potential unfavorable publicity or official criticism. And business had to try to shape proposed legislation into workable concepts. All of this required a new and often higher degree of public relations judgment and skill.

## Energy

The term "energy crisis" came suddenly into general use in October 1973. A boycott by Arab oil producers cut off much of the flow of imported oil. Shortages of gasoline and fuel oil developed quickly. Petroleum prices soared. Motorists lined up at service stations, sometimes waiting for hours to get less gasoline than they felt they needed.

The boycott lasted through the winter and was finally called off in March 1974. But things did not return to what had earlier been thought of as "normal." Energy shortages remained, prices stayed high, and Americans could never again take for granted an unlimited supply of energy.

The boycott thus taught a painful but worthwhile lesson. It convinced Americans of the necessity to use available energy sources thriftily and to seek new ones. Solar, geothermal, and other forms of natural energy began to be investigated with a vigor and thoroughness that had previously not been shown. Formation of a U.S. Department of Energy made the subject a national priority.

Government and industry had to reconsider some environmental restrictions that had been imposed earlier without regard to the availability or cost of fuel—the burning of coal and of high-sulphur oil, for example. The greatly increased cost of all petroleum products, which contributed to the high inflation throughout the economy, changed completely the economics of the many industries that depended on energy or on the fuels that produce it. And the high cost of energy touched all sectors of the American economy, even affecting the lives of individuals and families and their modes of living, travel, and dress.

Since few goods or services are so universally used as fuel in all its forms, energy problems became a preoccupation of the American people and a continuing problem for every company or organization that produces fuel or electricity, or uses it in significant quantities. And public relations has played a major role in meeting the public demand for information about the subject of energy.

In addition, the entire energy industry was in the spotlight, and corporations in the industry were impelled to disclose much more information about themselves and their activities than they had in the past. This helped cause other parts of the business world to adopt a more public stance and therefore to upgrade the quality of their public relations functions.

## Generalists and Specialists

The preceding discussion has touched on some of the events, developments, movements, and trends in the American society and economy that have brought about the growth of public relations from an almost incidental, peripheral service to an almost universal function, as common to most organizations as legal or accounting services.

Until the 1950s, public relations was a business carried on by generalists. A qualified practitioner—usually, as we'll see in the next chapter, a person with experience in the news media—could and would confidently tackle virtually any assignment. Assuming the person had sound judgment and an adequate knowledge of the company's or client's business, the public relations practitioner could counsel management intelligently, because the range of problems encountered fell within limits familiar to anyone with a modicum of experience. And if something new arose, research would show how others had acted in similar situations.

The public relations practitioner expected to handle publicity, crisis situations, financial public relations, speechwriting, media relations, and community relations. Sometimes, the practitioner headed the organization's internal communications as well. But each advance in duties, and each new development in business and industry, brought new demands. The experienced, capable generalist in, for example, retailing faced major problems if he or she moved into a high-technology field such as electronics, computers, or aerospace. And the old pro who headed public relations for a utility company had the same problem if management decided to move into nuclear power generation.

For these reasons, the public relations field began to open up in the late 1940s and the 1950s to people with technical backgrounds in addition to the skills generally recognized as being necessary for public relations work. There was much talk of the need for people who could "translate technical jargon into English," but it was not that simple. The public relations executive had to master at least those aspects of the organization's technology that were relevant to the public. And, when it came to the detailed work of producing news stories, speeches, and other forms of communication, people were needed who could understand the technology without lengthy study. This was perhaps the first time that a major change in society itself called for a new kind of specialization in public relations.

There had always been some degree of specialization, however. In the 1930s and 1940s, most public relations directors worked singlehandedly—although the largest corporations might have on their staffs, in addition to a director of public relations, a speechwriter, an editor of employee publications, and perhaps a specialist in product publicity. But these were more divisions of effort than true specialties as such.

As society increased its demands on established institutions, however, further specialization became essential. Consider, for example, financial public relations, which has changed greatly in the past quarter-century or so. At one time, financial public relations consisted almost entirely of getting out annual and interim reports and standard press releases, and preparing for an occasional appearance before a group of security analysts. Today, it has become far more sophisticated. It may involve conducting a takeover attempt, or defending against one; maintaining a vigorous program of shareholder communications; dealing with and surveying analysts and other financial decision makers, counseling with management on strategy, and dealing with the growing number of media that serve the financial community.

In addition, financial communications today are subject to complex and rapidly changing requirements of the Securities and Exchange Commission and of the stock markets themselves. Court decisions have made it clear that public relations people issuing such communications are responsible for their accuracy and legality, and are subject to civil or criminal penalties if standards are not met. The public relations practitioner who has access to information before it reaches the public is legally defined as an "insider" and must therefore not act on that information.

Obviously, this is no place for a generalist. Financial public relations today requires specialists who are intimately familiar with corporate finance, accounting, management policy, and the legality of any financial relations activity.

In other areas of public relations specialization, the legal implications are not so great, but special expertise is equally important. For example, matters of health are at issue in many controversies over the environment, consumer matters, and industrial safety. At the same time, medical science moves rapidly ahead into whole new areas such as nuclear diagnostics, biotechnology, and the like, becoming ever more complex in the process. It has always been difficult, and is becoming more so, to become an instant lay expert in any aspect of medicine, and the controversies that develop tend to be technical, prolonged, and sensitive. The company suspected of endangering the health of the public, the community, or its own work force has to deal with the problem in a factual, detailed, technically correct, and credible manner. Its statements, data, presentations, and claims must withstand the scrutiny of medical experts, science writers, and regulatory authorities.

Few public relations generalists are qualified to function effectively in an area such as this without the aid of specialists. As the world grows more complex, so does the work of business and industry, and so also does the job of the public relations professional.

Only the largest organizations, however, such as units of the federal government or major corporations, find it practical to maintain a high degree of specialization on their public relations staffs. Over the years, therefore, the tendency of corporations, trade associations, and other institutions has been to rely on outside counsel for the specialized public relations help they need. Some public relations counseling firms specialize in one or two areas, such as financial public relations or product publicity. But the larger firms try to include most of the specialties of public relations within one organization.

## Toward Diversification

Public relations has thus become far more diversified and all-encompassing than it was in its early days, and it has opened up to people of more varied backgrounds and talents. It has constantly stretched the minds and capacities of the men and women who have worked at it long enough to qualify as veterans—some of whom have remained generalists while others have developed fields of specialization.

The changes in public relations practice reflect the changing nature of society over the greater part of the twentieth century. One important change remains to be noted here, and that is the growing sophistication of the public, resulting in a need greater than ever before for public accountability. This accountability may be mandated and policed by government, or it may be a voluntary effort. Whichever it may be, it calls for experienced judgment of the public implications of management decisions—the effects not only on such directly interested parties as employees, stockholders, and regulators but also on disinterested outsiders. And it calls for clear and expert use of the techniques of public relations and communication.

As a result, most business executives now recognize the need for their organizations to practice public relations professionally. Public relations is as common today in voluntary groups as it is in labor unions, hospitals, and other nonprofit organizations, and in business and industry, where it originated. Unfortunately, however, many organizations do not practice good public relations at the point where it is most needed—the point of decision. The manager who decides or acts without thorough consideration of possible public reaction is in danger of making serious mistakes.

Consider, for example, the case of a company that approached a major new investment in what it considered a thorough manner. It planned to build a high-rise apartment building that any community would be proud of. One major decision, the choice of a site, required extensive study. There must be enough open space, proper subsoil conditions, appropriate zoning regulations. The area must be convenient to transportation, schools, churches, and stores. The design of the building itself must be compatible with its surroundings.

Ultimately, with the help of architects, engineers, and community planners, and after discussions with officials of target municipalities, the management purchased a site. But there had been no consultation, at any point, with the company's vice president of public relations. He came into the picture after the architect's rendering and the engineering plans were ready for submission to the town council, which would make the project public. Everything was right about the project, except that the people living near the site organized bitter opposition to it. They were outraged at the prospect of an apartment building in an area of one-family homes, adjacent to a school.

The opposition was so heated and so well organized that the corporation had to back down and abandon the project, which had been carefully planned—but not carefully enough—at great expense. The company had created a public relations problem where none had existed, and a potentially profitable undertaking stood on the books as a dead loss. Asked later what he would have advised, if he had been consulted in advance, the public relations vice president said:

"Naturally I'd have done a quiet survey of residents in the neighborhood. If their opposition to a high-rise had surfaced, as it probably would, I'd have advised finding another site where no such opposition existed."

Although he was not brought in on the planning, the problem of handling the community uproar fell within his province. As he knew, and as his management belatedly learned, the better use of public relations is to steer clear of problems rather than work at their abatement.

It is this function of public relations that is still too often overlooked, in spite of the quite remarkable growth of the specialty. The reasons why this may be so, and what professional public relations practitioners can do about it, are covered in chapter 16.

# Chapter 3

# The Public Relations Professional

As pointed out in a previous chapter, public relations is notoriously hard to define, and in fact, it never has been defined to the complete satisfaction of everyone. One reason is that the field covers a large number of functions that are embraced by the term "public relations." Another is that too many people appropriate the term for their work, even though it may not fall into any category of public relations that a true professional would recognize.

Fund raisers, for example, often call themselves public relations people because they use some of the techniques of public relations, such as newsletters and publicity. And, of course, there are all kinds of marginal publicity activities that are often referred to as "pubic relations" but that lack the scope that seems necessary to justify the name. Influence peddlers of all kinds use the term, as do some entertainers, tour guides, and even door-to-door sales people. The loose or abusive use of the term has blurred its meaning, so that people outside the field are often genuinely confused as to just what it is that a public relations person does. And there is no authority that can make a definition and enforce it.

Another reason for the difficulty of definition was implied by John Hill in his book *The Making of A Public Relations Man*. While he was writing particularly of the counseling aspects of public relations, his words apply to any executive in the field:

> In my early days in public relations, the work was concerned chiefly with press relations. Since then it has come to cover a wide range of activities bearing upon all phases of communications. ...In my view the basic role of the public relations counsel is to give *counsel* to his clients, based on wide and varied experience. But, it may properly be asked, counsel on what? Public relations counsel are not lawyers. They are not management engineers. They are not sales specialists. They are not labor relations experts. They are not scientists. They are not certified public accountants. Then on what do they counsel? Curiously enough, the recommendations for which they are asked may impinge on any of these fields.

In another context, Hill said that public relations counseling refers chiefly to the client's external relationships with society. Insofar as that implies a definition, it is a very broad one—but a broad definition is needed to comprehend all of the activities that public relations people undertake today. The public relations practitioner is a person with certain requisite skills, employed in particular ways. These particular skills, and the ways in which they are used, can be easily defined. We call them many things—publicity, release-writing, speech preparation, internal communications, for example. They are some of the routine processes of the public relations function, and their performance requires special aptitudes or abilities in addition to certain personal qualities that endow these skills with their value to the organization.

Beyond the fundamental skills, the public relations practitioner has a most important function, which is advisory in nature. It is the elusive function that distinguishes the true public relations professional from another person who may have the skills of communication but who somehow never successfully makes the move into public relations. Many an excellent writer, editor, or radio/TV news person has crossed the line into public relations from the media but has failed to become a competent public relations practitioner.

One highly competent newspaperman, when he joined a

public relations firm, abandoned his lively, breezy, highly readable style of writing for a heavy, ponderous prose that he thought better suited to the serious subjects with which he was dealing. Another kept his journalistic writing style but proved unable to deal directly with clients in an advisory capacity. A well-regarded magazine writer with many published articles to his credit assumed that the objectivity he had cultivated would be a liability in public relations work and tended to write one-sided documents that were often an embarrassment to his company and its clients.

For some people, failure to make the grade in public relations may be a matter of self-identity or career orientation. The public relations person is required, without ever losing personal objectivity, to identify with the interests and policies of the organization. A person who cannot do this is not going to be successful in public relations and will be better off in another endeavor.

Few come fresh out of college or from another career fully equipped to serve as advisers to management. To do so requires a thorough understanding of the total functioning of the organization, its management style and policies, its corporate culture, its internal organization, and even its internal politics, as well as its problems, opportunities, goals, and strategies. Only when this is accomplished can the public relations practitioner call into play the special judgment, the "sense of public relations," to advise about the organization's human relationships. But it is this advice, no matter on what level of the organization it is given, that lifts the practice of public relations out of the mere management or operation of a communications program. And it is the *quality* of such advice over time that usually determines how highly the public relations function and its practitioners are regarded in the organization.

In the study of public relations, as in its practice, this advisory function is too often overlooked. But it is precisely this function—the ability of public relations people to help establish sound management policy—that is at question in the never-ending debate over the status of the function and its practitioners, particularly in industry. Who, if not the public relations person, will assume the responsibility of answering the social and public opinion consequences of a policy, plan, or course of action?

## The Public Relations Career

The late Kerryn King, formerly senior vice president of Texaco, Inc., and president of the Public Relations Society of America, described a typical career path in public relations in a speech he gave at Ball State University in 1985. His description is worth quoting at length:

> Public relations as it is practiced today presents to the beginning practitioner a lifelong series of challenges, and a lifelong opportunity to grow as experience and knowledge increase. ...Each new practitioner is going to recapitulate, in his or her career, the history and growth of public relations itself.
>
> Young people just coming out of accredited public relations curricula...tend to think of public relations as the application of basic communications skills. On their first job, they are likely to find themselves handling press releases, most likely in the area of product publicity. They may also be called upon to write for house organs, to script video news segments, and to do similar chores.
>
> This is the basic groundwork. It is not what public relations is all about. But it lies at the heart of everything we do, and it provides the basic training that all of us must have. It remains at the heart of our work, no matter how far we may move ahead as practitioners. ...
>
> After a year or two spent in this way, learning the fundamentals of public relations practice, the young practitioner may move into a minor supervisory role. He or she may begin also to specialize in some particular phase of the business, such as financial relations or community relations. ...
>
> Then, after five or six years devoted to learning well two or three specialties, and to becoming skilled in the management of specific functions, the practitioner begins to move into the more demanding aspects of the public relations business. He or she now becomes a part

of middle management and must direct staff operations. At this stage, if they have not already done so, practitioners must learn both the planning and budgeting processes, and must see to it that plans and budgets mesh. In addition, they need to learn the important function of research and evaluation.

Let us then look at the practitioner who has mastered the fundamentals, gained expertise in the activities most important to the organization, and demonstrated ability to manage, plan, budget, research, and evaluate. At this stage, this practitioner has also learned a great deal about the business, industry, or other type of endeavor in which he or she works, and can "talk shop" with people from other departments—whether they are in manufacturing, marketing, or the legal or financial departments. Practitioners who have progressed this far, mastering every step along the way, are now ready to take their place in the ranks of top management. They must, however, perceive their role as being active participants in the formulation of public policy—and not as merely passive technicians ready to go into action only if and when the chairman, president, general counsel, or chief financial officer pushes the button.

This is a crucial point. One of the major problems with public relations in the past—and I am happy to say that it has become less of a problem today—is that the public relations practitioner has been looked upon as merely a communicator, as one who carries and transmits a message that has been formulated by someone else. That is a very narrow view, and it has been fostered by public relations people themselves. If we look upon public relations simply as communications, and upon ourselves as simply communicators, then we cannot blame others ... if they see us the same way.

King's final observation here reflects the findings 20 years earlier of a study of management attitudes toward public relations made by Robert W. Miller, formerly of Columbia University and later of American University and the American Heritage Foundation. Through questionnaires and interviews, Miller elicited the views of the presidents or chairmen of more than 200 large corporations. Fewer than a third of these executives said that their public relations vice presidents or directors were drawn into principal policy discussions and policy formulation.

The reasons, as spelled out in the Miller report:

In many cases, the chief executive officer seems to be critical of his own public relations people. He feels that too often the individual's background and training is not as broad as it should be for the work. The main criticism is that the public relations man is skilled in writing and in publicity-getting techniques and mechanics, but that he is not as useful to the firm as he should be, because he lacks an understanding of the overall economic picture and of the total corporate situation.

Yet, Miller found, "Most chief executive officers reported that public attitudes are a vital factor in determining their corporation policies."

## Times are Changing

Since Miller made his study in 1965, public relations has undergone tremendous changes. It is a far more complex and sophisticated pursuit. And it is no longer the almost exclusive domain of veterans of the news media who have "gone over to the other side." Today, young people by the thousands—men and women alike—are making public relations their first choice for a career. By contrast, most of the older practitioners were at the outset less interested in public relations as a desirable career than in the greater income or job security they hoped to find.

The older generation had to keep pushing at the frontiers of public relations, and they did more than any other group to bring the business into widespread acceptance. They had to do it the hard way, finding and setting their own standards, learning how to use opinion research, learning how to be of value to their managements, searching constantly for new approaches to problems and new techniques, seeking lessons in both successes and failures. In effect, many of them had to write—and rewrite—their own job descriptions as they went along.

For most of the members of that older generation, learning the trade and mastering economics and the principles and practices of management was a form of on-the-job training. Some of the old-timers flunked out. Others rose to the top public relations spots in their organizations, but never achieved the depth of understanding to serve as part of decision-making management.

Those who succeeded in truly becoming part of management—or outside counselors with the trust of management—set standards that became goals for all other practitioners. Today, however, the world has passed beyond the point at which middle-aged or elderly public relations people can be fully effective, unless their careers have been continuing exercises in self-education. Nobody realizes this more clearly than the public relations veterans themselves, and that is why they have encouraged young people to prepare more fully and pointedly to become effective practitioners.

Older leaders of the public relations profession have led the moves to support professorships or departments of public relations in colleges, have provided scholarships and internships, and have themselves become lecturers and adjunct professors at leading business schools. They were the founding members of the Public Relations Society of America and its predecessor organizations, which have sought to establish professional standards and a code of ethics.

These older public relations practitioners, and the younger ones who have been increasingly supplanting them in recent years, know that public relations is more than a professional exercise of communicating information and points of view. It is the principal means by which any institution accommodates itself to a changing world and to what is perceived as the public interest—a perception that is itself constantly changing. Some administrators who do not have public relations training or experience are innately sensitive to the pulse of public opinion and automatically consider it in arriving at important decisions. But many are not, and it is these decision makers who need the continuing guidance that only a public relations professional with good and experienced judgment can give.

## Public Relations Sense

There are no formulas for the development of good judgment, or "public relations sense." It begins with an intuitive or acquired understanding of psychology and a familiarity with sociological phenomena and history. The public relations practitioner relates this knowledge to what is learned on the job, making connections between the employer's policies and actions and the reactions to be anticipated from the publics affected by them.

In time, the practitioner develops an ability to predict that is pretty reliable. He or she can anticipate what kind of reaction is likely to be caused by a given action—among the media, employees, shareholders, community ncighbors, or other important groups. The practitioner is always keenly aware of the way variables can alter such predictions and will raise questions, propose alternative courses, and seek to minimize risk and maximize opportunity.

The true public relations professional avoids rote thinking and often has to use diplomacy in dealing with managers who think bad news can be softened with optimistic words, that a matter of great concern to the organization is automatically newsworthy, or that any important public is monolithic or unchanging. Public relations people who are on top of their jobs learn that all targets are moving targets, and that therefore the nature of the work and the exercise of good judgment require ceaseless acquisition of new information and new insights.

This kind of judgment is, of course, the product of a successful public relations career, rather than a prerequisite for entering upon one. Yet any young person thinking about devoting his or her life to public relations will want some assurance that the potential to develop along these lines is there before a career commitment is made.

## What Kind of Person Does Public Relations Need?

There are no stereotypes among public relations practitioners. There are no fixed criteria on which to base a judgment that this or that person should go into public relations. You used to hear young people say, "I like people, and therefore I should be in public relations." That, of course, is nonsense—if only because almost everyone likes people.

There is no uniform opinion about the personal qualities, desired education, and experience needed for a public relations career. Some believe that formal education in public relations or communications is indispensable. Others reject that and look for people with much broader educational backgrounds. Some feel that specific kinds of experience are necessary. Others say that there are only three prerequisites—brains, a sound education, and intellectual curiosity.

One public relations veteran with a good track record for spotting young people who have turned out to be first-rate practitioners says, "I'm completely open-minded about educational credentials or past experience. What I look for are signs of life, for interest and enthusiasm—not necessarily about public relations, but about *something*. I try to get people talking—about football or music or politics or anything at all—so I can see how their minds work. You'd be surprised at how many young people seem to have no interests or enthusiasms at all."

## The Educational Background

It seems likely that the best educational preparation for a public relations career is a sound liberal arts education. Often, the liberal arts student comes out of college with a good educational basis in science and the humanities— history, psychology, sociology, English and American literature, and political science. This leaves gaps, however, which the aspirant to public relations should fill by taking some additional courses—in economics, corporate finance, business law, marketing, and business organization, for example. An MBA degree is usually not considered a prerequisite, although it may be desirable to acquire one later on.

For the newcomer or aspiring newcomer to public relations, it is important to gain an understanding of local, national, and world political forces and of the social pressures affecting the American as well as the international scene. This is not necessarily acquired in a classroom, particularly since these forces and pressures are constantly changing. Mastering at least one foreign language is an additional plus. And, of course, it is as necessary for the public relations man or woman to write competently and clearly as it is for the accountant to calculate accurately. This is a fundamental and universal requirement. And in addition, he or she must have, or must quickly gain, both a knowledge of graphics and printing and an understanding of the ways in which the media gather, process, and produce news. This is the beginning.

The question is, of course, whether valuable undergraduate years should be spent in learning professional or "vocational" subjects, when knowledge of other things, not easily acquired after college, may be even more important over the span of a career. Courses in which one learns to write news releases, for example, prepare a student only for the very opening stages of public relations work, not for the difficult and demanding phases of the work that are essential to success.

A student's writing ability can be sharpened in many ways without professional courses—by working on the school paper, by taking postgraduate courses or an advanced degree, or by serving an apprenticeship with one of the news media before coming to public relations. The undergraduate years provide an opportunity to thoroughly explore literature, political science, psychology, history, and the physical sciences—subjects that will help produce a rounded individual and will form the foundation for continued reading and understanding. Some public relations and journalism courses are moving away from emphasis on the nuts and bolts of work skills in response to the needs of business and the media for people with greater depth in the humanities and social sciences.

The problems we have to deal with today tend to be complex and far-ranging. They require a breadth and range of understanding by anyone who works in public relations, and, more and more, a lot of knowledge of a few subjects on the part of specialists. The knowledge requirements are so great that public relations firms have instituted almost continuous learning programs for their professionals.

Some people in public relations have found diminishing value in media background for a public relations career. Such a background is no longer considered indispensable, as it once was. Yet it remains true that media experience—particularly newspaper experience—is valuable because it provides training in writing and because it requires quick analysis of facts, accurate reporting, discipline under deadline pressure, and rapid adjustment to changing situations—all of great value and use in public relations work. Moreover, it is helpful to have been on the other side to gain appreciation for the problems and pressures of the media.

Young public relations people with the greatest potential always exhibit a lively interest in people, events, and actions. They have insatiable curiosity and a high energy quotient that lead into a number of activities that are not necessarily related to school courses or working life. Public relations people have to be more energetic, more alert, and more reflective than the average person. They need to take a second look at every conclusion they come to, yet they also need rapid perception—the ability to understand a situation or a thought quickly and to assess it for its meaning in the context of their work.

What this adds up to is a quick and wide-ranging intelligence, coupled with a genuine interest in being in the middle of whatever action is going on. The work is not easy. Most public relations people, right from the beginning, are under pressure much of the time. They have to go on until any given job is done, so there is little room in the business for people who want a nice, orderly 9-to-5 routine. That makes the energy factor important.

## Business or Profession?

Public relations took its place long ago as an arm of management and is widely accepted in nearly all lines of organized endeavor. But it is not yet a profession, although it is often referred to as such. It cannot properly be called a profession until strong standards of ethics, qualifications, and performances can be applied to and observed by legitimate practitioners. With these standards, there must be effective means of policing them and ways of distinguishing clearly between the legitimate and the illegitimate practitioner.

The leader in the move toward professional standards has been the Public Relations Society of America, which made a major move in that direction when it adopted an accreditation program. The society already had a code of ethics governing the behavior of its members. Its membership, however, constitutes only a fraction of the number of public relations people practicing all over the country. These nonmembers range from highly capable executives in many fields of endeavor to partially qualified and part-time people who must be looked on as public relations practitioners. Unless standards ultimately can be applied to non-PRSA executives, "professionalism" can have no real meaning.

The benefits of professional status for qualified practitioners should be great. It would afford management a much better judgment criteria in selecting public relations executives and counsel. It would ensure that required standards of experience and ability have been met. It would mean that a sharp distinction could be drawn between ethical and capable practitioners on the one hand, and the few opportunists who frequently use the public relations title to cloak questionable operations. And it would make it easier for qualified professionals to offer their services to prospective employers or clients.

The PRSA accreditation program falls short of establishing public relations as a profession but it will continue to be a boon to those who meet the strict accreditation standards worked out by the accreditation board. This board is made up of public relations executives of advanced status and with long successful careers. The least that has been accomplished thus far is the establishment of qualitative values for the public relations business.

Meanwhile, it is worth noting that the code of ethics of PRSA is being observed by virtually all the society's members. Only in a few cases has any member transgressed the code badly enough to bring on censure by the society. This speaks well for a business whose stock in trade is resourcefulness and imagination in meeting the broad spectrum of requirements.

How or when it will be possible to establish the required standards of professionalism for the practice of public relations remains to be seen. There is little sentiment for government licensing and regulation of public relations, nor does it yet seem feasible to establish the kind of self-regulation so effective in other professions, such as accounting and law, which are strictly governed by their own national associations. Much will depend on whether, and to what extent, business, industrial, association, and institution management are inclined to rely on accredited public

relations executives, and the relative caliber of performance by those accredited individuals.

## Opportunities and Rewards

Over the course of a career, the intangible rewards of
working in public relations loom larger, because the tangible rewards tend to level out about even with other business
specialties. These intangible rewards vary with the individual, of course, but there are some that most public relations
people could probably agree upon.

Almost everything that public relations people do is on
behalf of, or subject to the approval of, top management.
Their work is of consequence, and therefore calls for regular association with the people in the organization who
make the decisions. The newest staff member, assigned to
research and write even a simple release, usually must interview or talk to somebody high in the organization to get
the facts, and then submit copy for review and often for a
personal critique.

At more advanced levels of operations, most public relations people deal with department heads, plant managers,
and officers on a regular basis. On matters involving communications, at least, the public relations person is usually
consulted as one having the special knowledge and a talent
that is uncommon in most organizations. And at the highest level, the practitioner actually participates regularly in
deliberations over policies and actions, and is able to influence the course of events.

Throughout a public relations career, the practitioner
has an inside view of the organization, and an association
with the decision makers that makes him or her one of a
privileged few. Often, the rigid departmental lines of communication mapped out on organization charts for most
white-collar workers in a big organization simply do not
apply to the public relations representative, whose work is

usually interdepartmental. When confined to a single plant location, department, or division, the practitioner's scope of activity is still broader than most. But almost always the public relations representative works, at least part of the time, with whoever is the top boss.

To many, this is challenging and rewarding. And outside the plant or office, the public relations person tends "to meet the most interesting people"—the world of the media, government officials, community activists. This too is stimulating and rewarding.

## Being on the Inside

Everybody likes to be an "insider." Public relations people automatically are, because they are the link between what is happening inside and the vehicles of communication that will tell others about it on the outside. Often, these events are significant and newsworthy—strike situations, important business developments, controversies of public interest. Even the preparation of a speech that helps shape policy may be a form of participation in events.

There are other ways in which experienced public relations executives take part in policy formation. The most important role that a public relations executive can play is that of management counsel—analyzing the public consequences in planning or reaching policy decisions. Top executives call for public relations counsel as readily as they do for legal, accounting, engineering, or technical opinions.

In some large corporations—and today, in smaller ones, too—it is often a public relations executive who first articulates the organization's public policies. A growing number of public relations practitioners are specialists in the sense that they concern themselves exclusively with policy matters. Reporting to their chief executive officers, they may turn anywhere in or outside the company for information and opinions on issues and developments that may affect the company. Then they help put on paper those statements, speeches, responses, or proposals that become the public expression of top policy. To the seasoned veteran of public relations, added zest is given to being an "insider" because his or her opinion on what to do with regard to communication, at least, will have some effect on how the event is perceived by others. And with the respect and trust of management, the professional may have an influence on the event itself.

## Professional Satisfaction

Writing professionally is a discipline that, once mastered, offers endless rewards to the public relations worker. Working within confines imposed by the nature of the assignment or the aims of the organization, he or she still finds room for self-expression.

For most men and women in the field, the scope for expression is wide—much wider than that offered in any of the news media. The public relations writer must not only adapt to newspapers, magazine, radio, television—to all the media—but in time will probably also write position papers, speeches, programs, presentations, brochures, reports, and even advertising copy. He or she may be required to produce periodicals or brochures as well as write them, and even handle sensitive management correspondence. Most of this is under deadline pressure and brings forth the highest professional effort from anyone who really cares about writing.

To become a real professional, capable and confident, is to know the kind of pleasure that comes only from self-realization. This applies not only to the tools of the trade, of which writing is the most common, but to all aspects of the public relations business. The accomplished professional begins to use the expertise developed with skill and certainty that bring recognition and appreciation within the organization, and often outside it as well. Radio, television, satellite communications, and other forms of new technology have brought new dimensions to public relations for those with the ability to communicate effectively through these newer media. More and more, there has been a tendency for public relations representatives to serve not only as the unnamed and invisible spokespersons behind the news, but also as acknowledged spokespersons before the TV camera and radio microphones.

## Other Rewards

Because of the nature of their work, public relations people often enjoy a degree of freedom from routine that is not the lot of others in the organization. They may, and often do, put in long hours, and they are constantly fighting deadlines, but their work is far from dull or repetitious. There are always new challenges that vary with the changing aims and circumstances of the employer. Public relations people are oriented both to news and to problems—ensuring at least an occasional change of pace, and, at times, whirlwind changes.

Professional associations, designed to provide practitioners with opportunities for self-development and contact with others in the field, are available to generalists and specialists. There are many local groups comprised of practicing public relations people and press clubs that accept public relations people as nonvoting members. National societies, many with local chapters, foster professionalism and knowledge, usually along lines of related interest.

Public relations people can vie for prizes, honors, or awards by entering their work in competition. Many organizations have awards programs, among the best known being the Silver Anvils granted annually by the Public Relations Society of America and the Golden Quills presented by the International Association of Business Communicators, both for noteworthy programs, and the *Financial World* magazine awards for outstanding annual reports. Recognition that can be important to their supervisors and themselves is available to public relations people who remain alert to opportunities.

# Chapter 4

# The Public Relations Field

There has been marked and rapid growth of the public relations field in the past quarter-century. Virtually every organization and institution in the United States now has public relations as one of its formal functions, usually organized into a full-scale department. And, increasingly, the same is true of institutions elsewhere in the world.

Change is a fact of life, and the pace of change in the U.S. and in the world has accelerated greatly in the years since World War II—particularly in the period from around 1960 to the present. The increased speed and volume of public communication has figured prominently in the growing velocity of change, and that has made public relations essential to any organization or group that is concerned about public opinion.

To arrive at the reasons for this, let us first consider what may be called the basic or generic functions of public relations. Public relations deals with the transmission of facts, but it is nevertheless, by its nature, self-serving to the user. For this reason, it needs to be analyzed in some detail. The generic functions of public relations are to educate, to disseminate news, and to advocate.

## Education

Many public relations programs have no other object than to inform the public of certain facts. In very recent times, for example, programs have been undertaken under the sponsorship of government agencies and private groups to spread information about the dangers inherent in the use of mind-altering or addictive drugs.

For a number of years, one organization in the pharmaceutical industry has devoted its entire public relations effort to publicizing the safe ways in which to use medicines and to keep them out of the hands of children. The content of the program is factual, positive, educational, and noncontroversial.

Widespread ignorance of business economics among the general public is generally acknowledged. Over the years this lack of knowledge has been confirmed by hundreds of public opinion polls. Business people have long felt that if more people understood how business really works—for example, how it is financed, how it produces earnings, how those earnings are distributed, and how they are used— then antibusiness sentiment, which the same polls also show to be widespread, would decline. They feel too that this public ignorance has been exploited by some politicians and some of the news media, to the detriment of business and at great, but hidden, costs to consumers.

For this reason, hundreds of large corporations and trade associations have made economic education a major objective of their public relations programs. They have certainly done this in their own self-interest. And yet such programs have to deal in economic data and theories that have authoritative support. To the extent that they have been perceived and accepted by the public, these programs have been educational.

The educational function of public relations is real, and it is far more commonplace than many would expect. It touches on many areas. The Cereal Institute, for instance, has for years supplied the public with scientific information about nutritional breakfasts. More recently, individual manufacturers of breakfast foods have been doing a great deal to educate consumers about the health benefits of their products. The Edison Electric Institute distributes materials on the conservation of energy, as do the American Gas Association, the American Petroleum Institute, and many individual companies. Safety is a major theme in the programs of scores of corporations and trade associations.

Insurance companies and their trade associations specialize in informing the public about health problems of all kinds, about fire and accident prevention, and about security for people's homes, cars, boats, and trailers. Institutions in the financial services industry often feature personal money management in their programs. Dozens of magazines carry lists of free booklets published by business organizations. These booklets are factual and helpful and provide a real service to consumers. Their sponsors hope, of course, that these educational efforts will contribute to their own reputations as good corporate citizens.

Industry has long been a major contributor of teaching materials to schools. These materials are ordinarily prepared under the supervision of qualified committees of educators, and information must meet rigid educational standards. Commercial identification is kept to a minimum. These materials, usually in the form of audiovisuals, often provide explanations of industrial processes and they help young people to develop an understanding of facts, principles, and processes that is a genuine part of their education. Admittedly, companies and industries are helped too, for these are self-serving programs that earn benefits for the sponsors by creating benefits for the users. But because schools are under no obligation to use these additions to the standard curricula, they must have educational value.

The educational function of public relations is not confined to commercial enterprises. Almost every kind of organization engages in it: federal, state, and local government agencies; educational institutions; nonprofit associations; and organizations of the professions.

## News

Disseminating newsworthy facts about the organization and chronicling events as they occur are important functions of public relations. Facts are by nature neutral, though they can be distorted and used to mislead. They are used neutrally in any public relations program that is properly and ethically conceived and implemented. Any public or private organization that misuses facts, distorts them, or conceals them risks the loss of credibility, as do the individuals involved in massaging the facts.

Many believe that the most certain way for a company or another organization to establish and maintain credibility is to refuse to varnish or to hide facts. Those who are evasive or misleading usually accomplish just the opposite of what they are attempting to do. For example, in the early days of the airline business, overzealous employees used to paint out the company name on the wreckage of planes involved in crashes and would do whatever else possible to hide the facts from the media. With few exceptions, the truth eventually came to light, either through the investigative efforts, rumors begun by eyewitnesses, or the revelations of disgruntled employees. This produced two stories, the accident and the cover-up. The airlines soon learned to cooperate fully with the media, even going so far as to fly reporters and photographers to the scene. That didn't eliminate the negative publicity about the event itself, of course, but it did help get the full story to the media faster and more accurately and, therefore, out of the papers or off the air much sooner. It also predisposed the media to look more favorably on positive news emanating from the airlines.

Many corporate, associate, and institutional managers and public leaders jump at the chance to trumpet good news to the skies but try to lie low when the news is bad. This tendency is often simply a manifestation of most people's unfamiliarity with the customs and attitudes of the news media. But it is also the understandable human desire to escape the painful experience of negative publicity and the criticism and embarrassment it can bring.

Every effective public relations practitioner has learned to face the dilemma of dealing openly with bad news. An organization's reputation with the print or electronic media is only as good as its day-in, day-out performance in passing along information, good and bad. Editors throw away handfuls of news releases for every one they use. They would not be competent to do their jobs if, in judging two stories of comparable news value, they didn't select the one from the more respected source.

There was a time when corporate public relations people were judged largely on the volume of favorable clippings they were able to garner for management's gratification. Good publicity can, of course, improve an organization's standing with important audiences and may help sell products or ideas. It is, therefore, still diligently sought by most public relations departments and brings certain benefits.

But the issues of importance to business and to all other institutions these days transcend what used to be thought of as "good" or "bad" publicity. Today, the organization that is not completely candid and open is automatically suspect. No public entity, whether inside government or out, is conceded more than a limited right to privacy. A refusal to respond to questions, sometimes very tough questions indeed, is generally interpreted to mean that there is something to hide, and therefore raises suspicions. The public relations person who does not understand this, or who is consistently overruled by higher management in adopting an open stance with the media, has a serious problem.

It takes a great deal of skill to respond fully and truthfully while conveying management's point of view in a constructive way. The public relations person needs the ability to serve simultaneously as counselor, advocate, and "witness for the defense," in response to the media's role as prosecutor and judge.

Media people tend to be ambivalent toward the public relations function, particularly if they've had the unpleasant experience of dealing with unprofessional practitioners. Reporters and editors assume that the public relations representative stands for a special interest to begin with. They are, therefore, prone to skepticism, and the only way to overcome this attitude is to establish a record of honest and open dealing.

It is wise for the public relations person responsible for handling an organization's relations with the news media to recognize how important the news media are in shaping an organization's reputation, and to serve as an intermediary between media and management not as a one-sided "promoter." This function does not relieve an organization's leaders of direct contact with the media. A spokesperson, although he or she should have access to top executives and officials and should represent their interests, cannot replace them.

However, the need for direct communications between the press and an organization's executives should be evaluated by the public relations representative in the interest of efficiency for both company and media and, once initiated, should be monitored and managed effectively.

Despite management's views to the contrary, as far as the media are concerned, the only function of public relations is to serve them. This can be done to their satisfaction only by a policy of prompt and full disclosure. While a limited, but carefully defined amount of information on business activities and performance must be disclosed under regulations of the Securities and Exchange Commission, publicly held companies that are public relations-oriented promptly disclose any events, changes, or developments that might be newsworthy, whether or not each event individually contributes to the organization's self-interest. This kind of full-disclosure policy produces a positive effect on a company's position in the public eye compared to other companies that are similarly situated. It works equally well for all business and public sector organizations.

## Advocacy

Most public relations men and women are, at least in part, advocates. Some, usually those representing special interest groups, are advocates pure and simple. The role of advocacy in public relations is the most easily perceived by the media and, of course, by adversaries. This perception tends to blur in their minds the distinction between the educational or news-handling roles of the public relations professional and his or her undisguised championship of a cause. It is the source of much of the animosity toward public relations, much of the misunderstanding, and at least some of the mudslinging.

Unfortunately, too many shady operators, whitewash experts, and make-a-buck opportunists palm themselves off as public relations people. Where honest misunderstanding of the true public relations function already creates difficulties, the depredations of such people reflect poorly on the entire craft. If this situation is ever to be corrected, it must be done by sincere professionals who in their own minds are clear about the distinctions in these responsibilities and who can make them plain to others.

Most of the advocacy activities in public relations are so clear-cut as to need no explanation. The public relations person who helps prepare testimony before an investigating commission or legislative committee—or who helps publicize it—is so obviously espousing a point of view that everybody recognizes the fact.

A company and its employees engaged in a controversy of any kind are going to want to advance their cause and do so vigorously. This is just as true for a union, an environmental group, a government agency, or a religious sect as it is for a business. Often, books and articles are written, and speeches given, with the contents chosen and worded for the very purpose of advancing a cause. This too is advocacy, and nobody will mistake it for an impartial recitation of revealed truth.

Advocacy is both an affirmative activity and a defensive one. A corporation acts affirmatively, for example, when it takes a stance for or against a legislative act. It is being defensive when it responds to an accusation. There is no question in such situations about the position of the corporation's public relations representative. He or she is an advocate.

Yet in these instances, the ethical public relations man or woman is under the obligation of doing two things: 1) staying with the strict and verifiable truth in any facts employed for the purpose, and 2) indicating directly or indirectly when a personal opinion is being set forth in anything written or said.

Society's interests and priorities are subject to dynamic change. Such change rarely takes place unless it is espoused, or advocated, in such a way as to attract the support of influential groups of people or to form a consensus within the public. In a democratic nation, where institutions exist at the will of the people, the institution that fails to foster good will is flirting with extinction. The advocacy function of public relations is one of the means, and perhaps the principal one, by which institutions work to win the approval of the electorate and, in some cases, to bring about the better nation they envision.

## Increased Role of Government

Despite a trend toward deregulation and a diminution of government's role in the 1970s and 1980s, the influence of government in the U.S. remains far more pervasive than it was prior to World War II. At various levels, undertakings that used to be private are now public, in the sense that they are supported by public funds or are subject to government controls of one kind or another.

The active exercise of governmental power over so many institutions is a principal cause for the spread of public relations practice. The significance is not hard to find. Behind every important new act or extension of government there must be at least the tacit consent of the electorate, and many federal and state legislators will not act without that overt approval. This makes it almost mandatory for every organized group within American society to attempt winning public support for its views on specific issues and for its general philosophy. The tremendous expansion of public relations activities by government entities is manifest evidence that even federal, state, and local administrations must continuously strive to justify their policies, programs, acts, and expenditures.

And, of course, all institutions of any size that disagree, or that feel threatened by such views, have to publicly advocate their own alternatives. Thus the growing role of government has greatly spurred the practice of public relations.

The only way to get a social movement under way or to change public policy is to enlist the interest and emotional involvement of masses of people. The means of achieving that interest and involvement is, of course, public relations and lobbying. In this form of activity, a helpful attention-getting device is to find scapegoats and to attack them vigorously. So from the outset of all the social movements, the use of public relations techniques, if not the practice of serious and well-rounded public relations, has been required in two ways: To get the movement off the ground on one side, and to oppose it on the other.

One consequence of the increased political and social activism of the past 25 years has been the elevation of public relations considerations in the minds of decisionmakers, as well as the growth of the specialty itself. Another consequence is that the student or well-educated young man or woman can now seek a career in public relations with greater certainty that one will be found in the field of choice. Business and government once absorbed the great majority of new entrants because that's where the jobs were, and it didn't make much difference whether the aspiring public relations professionals were technically and emotionally fitted for these fields. People do better in a congenial work environment that engages their spirits as well as their minds and skills. The committed consumerist might not want to work in an uncongenial business establishment, and an entrepreneurial spirit might feel stifled in a bureaucracy. In an era when public relations has been adopted by virtually every kind of institution and organization, the practitioner's horizons are nearly infinite. The chances of matching a career with one's most cherish interests have been vastly improved.

Professional public relations activities are undertaken in all major segments of society. The following list is by no means complete but is intended to illustrate how broad the spectrum of public relations is.

**Business and industry.** Manufacturing and service organizations of every conceivable kind exist in nearly every commercial center of the U.S. and major cities abroad. Despite recent cutbacks in many U.S. industrial companies, large corporations still generally have both corporate and divisional public relations staffs in several locations and therefore a layering of personnel, permitting them to employ more people entering public relations than is usually the case with organizations that have small, centralized staffs.

**Agriculture.** National and regional organizations of farmers, and of investor-owned or cooperative marketing and supply organizations, and dairy products associations, employ public relations people and lobbyists.

**Trade and industry associations.** There are thousands of business associations, at federal, state, and regional levels. Some (The American Petroleum Institute or the toy manufacturers associations, for example) represent companies within a single industry. Others (The National Association of Manufacturers, chambers of commerce) represent companies from many industries. The largest of them have public relations representation not only at national headquarters but also at key sites elsewhere. The biggest concentration is in Washington, D.C.

**Travel and tourism.** Public relations looms extra large in this major subdivision of industry. Cities, states, and nations depending upon tourism employ public relations people as do sizeable transportation companies, large hotels and hotel/motel chains, resorts, tour packagers, and travel agencies.

**Nonprofit organizations.** Public relations growth in this huge field has been especially rapid. Public hospital communications, for example, have grown so extensively that practitioners have formed their own organization. Employing public relations to good effect are environmental, consumer, and feminist groups; ethnic improvement organizations; libraries; museums; orchestras; civic and service clubs; youth groups like Boy Scouts and Girl Scouts; and many others.

**Education.** Colleges and universities, local school systems, regional and national educational associations, organizations of teachers and professors, school principals and administrators, and government education bureaus have provided another large field of growth for public relations people in recent years.

**Government.** The federal government employs thousands of public relations people and spends well over $1 billion each year for public information services. Because of the many titles given public relations people by different agencies, this figure is probably an underestimate. For example, virtually every senator and representative has at least one public relations assistant, though few may be identified as such by their titles. Yet the federal total may be equalled by the thousands of public relations men and women employed by states and their agencies, county governments, and municipalities. This is another big and growing field.

**Labor unions.** No reliable figures are available, but virtually all national unions employ public relations staffs or use counsel, or both, as do many state and local councils.

**Professional associations.** Most organized professions (like the American Medical Association, American Institute of Certified Public Accountants, and others) are heavy users of public relations talent at their headquarters. There are equivalent state organizations that also make extensive use of the public relations function.

**Politics.** Perhaps the most up-and-down field of them all, which tends to peak at campaign time and fall off at other times, is politics. Public relations people are employed by candidates, political parties, and elected officials. Much of this work is part-time, but often leads to full-time jobs on the staff of elected officials or in other government positions. It is a field in which many make a living, and one in which unpaid volunteers can get a start.

**Organized sports.** Practically every professional sports team requires public relations people, as do the leagues and other sports organizations. At some colleges with large sports programs, athletic directors employ publicity people who are not on the university public relations staffs. Some opportunities exist with private or municipally owned stadiums, resorts, or clubs and with companies producing sports equipment.

**Media.** Newspapers, magazines, book publishers, book clubs, large radio and television stations, networks, syndicates, and motion picture producers are large users of public relations talent, particularly in publicity and promotion.

**Public relations counsel.** There are counseling firms that specialize in some of these fields, including business and industry, trade and tourism, labor unions, politics, and sports. Others make no such distinction and are prepared to cover them all. Opportunities for beginners in counseling firms are limited by both the economics of the business and the necessity to provide clients with experienced judgment and expert services. Newcomers to public relations are well advised to gain experience first, if their ultimate aim is to form or join a counseling firm.

What do public relations people do in all these diversified fields? The quick answer is that the thrust of their work varies greatly. In subsequent parts of this handbook, the major specialties of public relations are broken into their components, examined in some detail, and illustrated with case histories. That's the long answer.

The important thing about this breakdown is that it groups organizations that have similar public relations goals. Any public relations program must be put together for a specific purpose or purposes, generally called objectives. This leads the discussion back to the matter of management policy again, for whatever policies are adopted for an organization determine the objectives of the public relations program.

Here's a hypothetical illustration: It is the policy of an agricultural association to maintain exemption of buffalo herders from the minimum wage bill. An objective of its public relations program will be to oppose any legislation proposed to the contrary. A strategy of the program will be to examine proposed bills in the House and Senate for any hazard to this policy, and if such a bill does surface, to oppose it. The program contains tactics by which the association will carry its case to the legislators, inform its members of the hazard, and mount an effort in opposition to the bill.

However, an agricultural union has established the policy that all farm and range workers should be covered by the minimum wage bill. An objective of its program is to convince Congress to make such a provision in the law. The program provides for drawing up a model bill, finding sponsors for it, and making a public case in the media to bring pressure on Congress to pass it.

These differences in policy establish for the two organizations competing objectives that lead to wholly individual programs which we might define as defensive and aggressive. Yet both will rely on their ability to communicate facts and points of view effectively; they will use some of the same techniques in pursuit of their objectives; they will share some audiences, competing for sympathy and support. They will seek out "grass-roots" support from their quite different constituencies, and they may differ a great deal in the forcefulness and credibility of their stories.

Note too that one side of this issue (the union) has an emotional appeal and at least a superficial appearance of logic that will automatically win some public support. But the other side will have to rely on dry, factual, and probably economic information devoid of human interest. This is often the case in confrontations that involve industry or any of its components and other kinds of adversaries. It is one of the reasons public relations on behalf of business organizations is difficult and demanding work.

This hypothetical example is, of course, a great oversimplification to illustrate a point: Effective public relations programs are pragmatic, purposeful, and goal-oriented. They derive from business objectives or other broader organizational goals. Public relations also requires commitment on the part of the practitioner. It is doubtful that the public relations representative for the union in this case could change sides comfortably, even though similar skills are involved. If a career is, as the dictionary defines it, "progress or general course of action of a person through life. . .," then the person who works under one philosophy while holding another, is certainly a candidate for ulcers and possibly for the psychiatrist's couch.

People differ not only in their approaches to politics, other interests, and the role of government itself but also in their talents and professional interests. For the student or the novice, therefore, a look at the differences in approach and emphasis among the groups cited above may be worthwhile.

**Business and industry.** This is a field in which every aspect of public relations is intensively practiced, and the only one in which financial relations looms large. Corporations have many constituencies: employees, shareholders, communities, consumers, suppliers, and all the layers of government.

**Agriculture.** For most elements of the vast agricultural establishment, federal policies and, to a lesser extent, state policies of all kinds have a great impact on individual decisions. This fact makes public affairs the aspect of greatest importance to organizations in this field. Yet urban ignorance of farm and food economics requires a continuing public education program.

**Trade and industry associations.** Public relations objectives in this area are quite similar to those of their corporate members and dues payers, but with significant differences. Pricing is outside their purview and, therefore, so are most aspects of marketing, except in the generic sense. Financial relations is not a concern for an association, although industry economics clearly is.

While individual corporations can and usually do adopt policies on everything affecting them, the objectives of associations usually cover only those matters on which there is membership consensus. Thus they tend to confine themselves to those public or legislative issues broad enough to affect entire industries. Trade and industry associations have many important functions beside public relations, such as establishing engineering standards, collecting important data, providing educational services, and the like. But in many—and perhaps most—of them, public relations is a key activity, and it is based on the old American principle that "in union there is strength."

Associations speak for aggregates of companies and people. Moreover, they are once removed from the direct commercial interest of individual companies and product lines. These attributes provide a certain acceptability to industry spokespersons that is often difficult for individual company spokesmen to achieve, particularly on a national or grass-roots basis. Often, particularly on controversial public or legislative issues, an association can mount a public relations effort that uses corporate executives as spokesmen, not only for their own companies but also for the industry as a whole.

On such issues, associations tend to take the leadership in public affairs activities whenever there is a strong consensus of their constituencies, but they are helpless to act when no such consensus exists. Yet associations rarely preempt the roles of individual members in public relations/public affairs. They add an overall and often persuasive force to the efforts of individual member companies that may differ sharply on some aspects of nearly every issue.

Large associations have a continuing public relations function quite unrelated to the crises that arise from time to time that must be treated with urgency. This continuing activity usually consists of at least three distinct operations:

• They regularly compile industry data which become the basis for corporate and government planning and, of course, for news in all the media.

• They carry out strong national programs of education in economics, product use, safety, conservation, and other subjects.

• They conduct or support major research projects in public opinion and other areas of interest which help to shape the nature of their public relations programs.

Such organizations value and use great amounts of writing talent for publications, publicity, speeches, legislative statements, bulletins, and other projects. Exposure of public relations practitioners to an industry at the association level is excellent experience for those who aim ultimately at corporate public relations within that or a similar industry.

**Travel and tourism.** In this field, the name of the game is marketing, expressed through public relations as publicity. Large corporations in the travel field (airlines, for example) practice the full range of public relations and public affairs, but throughout the field the principal function is to lure visitors, guests, or passengers. This is done by a consistent program of publicity, special events, tie-in promotions with manufacturers, brochure preparation and mailing, etc. It is a good field for public relations people with lively imaginations, who are good writers, have a good eye for photographic possibilities, and have a penchant for travel.

The need for crisis communication skills in travel and tourism has, unfortunately, become more pronounced in recent years, as a result of heightened media coverage of natural disasters, along with incidents of terrorism against tourists.

**Nonprofit organizations.** Such organizations are as varied as is business and industry, and linked by little more than their noncommercial character. Each is engaged in its own vision of service for the public good. The Sierra Club, as an example, finds it in a vigorous program to preserve wildlife and the natural surroundings. The Urban League finds it in a national program to wipe out racial discrimination. Nonprofit hospitals serve their communities, and museums, the life of culture. The Boy Scouts and Girl Scouts provide educational and character-building activities for children and young adults.

This diversity provides opportunities for public relations men and women to seek public service within a field of interest. In many nonprofit organizations, fundraising is the major, or at least one of the most important, functions of public relations, and publicity would run almost neck and neck with it.

**Education.** In general, the main objectives of public relations at higher levels of education are to: 1) raise the esteem of the institution through publicizing the achievements of its staff, 2) attract well-qualified students and faculty, and 3) encourage financial support.

Elsewhere in the educational establishments, the objectives vary with the nature of the organization. Except for colleges and universities, which for the most part have national or international constituencies, most problems are dealt with primarily locally and secondarily throughout the state. Public relations for a school board, for example, is essentially community relations. Associations of educators have public affairs representation in Washington and in at least some of the states.

To function at any of these levels in education-oriented public relations requires a true dedication to and a considerable knowledge of the field of education. Indeed, it would appear that the majority of education-oriented public relations practitioners are former teachers, people who studied to be teachers, or activists who have become familiar with the field from Parent-Teacher Association work. A public relations practitioner at the college level, especially, is usually required to have a degree. Writing skill, the ability to popularize the technical or abstract, and good judgment are more important than teaching qualifications.

**Government.** Public relations is generally known as public affairs or public information in government agencies, and with good reason. The staffers of most such agencies are—or at least need to be accepted as being—in the position of disseminating straightforward, unadorned facts and data. Congress is one of those organizations in which the term public relations is not usually acceptable. The federal government alone is the largest fact amasser and fact dispenser in the nation; the Government Printing Office may be the largest publisher in the country, and various agencies of the federal government probably circulate as many periodicals as the ten largest magazine publishers combined.

Not all of this, by any means, funnels out to the public. But the part of the information stream that is expected to make news, or that touches on government policies, nearly always does. So there is an enormous base of positions in nearly every nook and cranny of the federal government for public relations people who are equipped to evaluate, process, and disseminate news. To a lesser extent, the same is true in all but the smallest units of government below the federal level.

Americans are acutely aware of public relations in government at the highest level, The White House. Every pronouncement of the presidential press secretary or members of his staff is examined for its policy implications. Yet, throughout the government hierarchy, there are public relations executives who not only disseminate policy matters to media and public, but are in a position to counsel on policy decisions. Their titles vary greatly.

While the majority of information specialists in government are devoted to the information and education functions of public relations, advocacy is also part of the job. Governments, particularly incumbent administrations, are under the same impulse as industry and other institutions to justify, even to "sell," policy and decisions to the electorate, perhaps even more so.

The public has the option of taking direct action by throwing the politicians out from time to time, while it has only indirect power over other institutions through its patronage or lack of it.

The public relations person inclined toward public service or dedicated to a political philosophy represented in government can find excellent career opportunities in civil service or appointive positions. Governments use all varieties of creative talent, and public relations people, at least in federal service, can expect to earn incomes at least on par with those in private industry, except at the highest policy levels. For the beginner, experience in government public relations, including the armed forces, is an excellent background from which to make a career move.

**Labor unions.** Labor unions espouse their causes through public relations, lobbying, and sometimes overt political action. Internal communications in national unions are highly professional. Some large locals and councils employ public relations people for both internal an external communication. Policy counsel in some unions is in the hands of outside public relations advisers specializing in the field. To practice public relations on behalf of organized labor requires a commitment to the aims and methods of the movement.

**Professional associations.** Until recently, most groups of professionals have operated under strictly interpreted rules of ethics that have inhibited advocacy public relations activity. This is certainly so of architects, engineers, public accountants, lawyers, doctors, and probably of others. Painful controversies have prodded some, like the medical and accounting professions, to take much more open stances with the public. Even before controversy erupted, most associations maintained educational programs, using the services of qualified public relations practitioners. This is a large and growing field for public relations people.

**Politics.** There is usually a public relations person or team that plays a major role behind every major political appearance, rally, or other event; behind every speech, commercial, or print advertisement; behind every candidate, in fact.

For people with an all-consuming interest in the political process, or a total dedication to a political philosophy, this is a natural field. This interest can be discharged on a part-time or volunteer basis by nearly anybody with the requisite public relations skills, for candidates are always hard up for both help and funds. And campaigns—it doesn't matter for what office—are always organized from the neighborhood up, which means that many more public relations people are needed than are available.

Some of the public relations policy-makers in government get there through service in politics. But such positions, if they are not covered by Civil Service, are always threatened by a reversal at the polls.

Volunteering for a political cause is not a bad way to start for a beginner, or for a more mature person thinking of a career change, to gather experience and the evidence of competence—in the form of speeches, brochures, releases, for a job in another branch of public relations.

**Organized sports.** This field of public relations is almost, but not totally, preempted by former sports reporters for the news media who are deeply steeped in every aspect of the sporting personalities, history, traditions, and fine points of the game. Colleges offer the best prospects for beginners.

**The media.** In many respects, public relations problems of large and influential newspapers and television networks are the same as those of other types of corporations. They, therefore, require the same kind of careful public relations programming and staffing.

Beyond this, however, most elements of the media depend upon publicity in other media for several things: 1) marketing—to sell books, improve audience rating, or increase circulation and advertising; 2) to increase prestige and awareness among the public; and 3) to get the benefit of "third party" endorsement, or an implied credibility of the network, station, or publication that is contained in coverage of its stories in another medium.

When, for example, a newscaster starts his broadcast with "Early editions of the *Daily News* revealed today," it is obviously a coup for the *News* as an enterprising paper. Likewise, when the Monday newspaper says, "The Secretary of State said yesterday in an exclusive interview on CBS...," that network has the same sense of accomplishment.

The formidable obstacle for public relations on behalf of any of the media is that they are competing with all others, yet must find the hook to make their publicity attractive enough for the competition to use it.

The fact that the print media cover television and review books and motion pictures only intensifies the competition, since space for such material is minimal, considering the volume of television programming and the production of books and films.

It is a good field for imaginative publicists with a keen sense of news and feature values and a knack for presenting them in compelling fashion for each of the competing media.

# Chapter 5

# Essential Functions of Public Relations

If public opinion is to be fully and accurately informed, it must have access to, and trust in, authoritative sources of information. In the case of a corporation or other organization, the most authoritative source is the head of the organization—the chief executive officer (CEO) or the equivalent.

Whatever is said by the CEO will be viewed both inside and outside the organization as the final word on the condition of the organization and on where it stands on a given issue. There are always some, of course, who question the accuracy of the CEO's facts and there are always those who disagree with the CEO's opinions, interpretations, and forecasts. But when the CEO speaks for the organization, his or her words are viewed as coming directly "from the horse's mouth."

Therefore, the chief executive officer of any organization should always be its most authoritative and credible spokesperson. Yet all sizeable organizations have other representatives: officers, plant managers, department heads, specialists of all kinds. The closer any of them comes to one-on-one discussion with people important to the organization, the more believable and convincing he or she is likely to be. As opposed to spokespersons, those who actually make policy cannot only speak their own minds but they can also respond personally to the reactions of those they speak with. That is why in so many instances and programs public relations people insist on the personal participation of the CEO.

Obviously, however, the CEO cannot be brought into

person-to-person interchanges with the thousands or even millions of people who comprise potential audiences. We sometimes forget that the use of public relations techniques for the function loosely called "communications" is no more than an attempt to do indirectly what the executive is unable to do in face-to-face discussion. Putting out releases, appearing on television, and making speeches are necessary substitutes for personal conversation, but they are not nearly as effective.

Each substitute has its own limitations. The listener out there may be hostile, skeptical, or even unwilling to hear what is being said. One of the challenges of public relations is to find the best, most workable ways of bridging the gap between the reality and credibility of the personal contact on one hand, and the impersonal, structured output of communications directed to groups, rather than to individuals, on the other.

## Spokespersons

In any large organization, one of the first questions of public relations is: Who speaks for us?

A corporation, a trade association, a service organization, an educational institution, a professional society, and a government body all face the same spokesperson problem. Each must have many spokespersons, because the responsibilities of the chief executive usually prohibit the expense of an inordinate amount of personal time to acting as spokesperson. The President of the United States reserves the role for matters he considers critical to the interests of the nation or of his political party. On his behalf, cabinet members and the heads of regulatory agencies, commissions, and other government entities and the President's press secretary and press officers of each federal department and agency speak authoritatively for the functions included in their portfolios. And most of them in any administration will "speak with one voice" by following either the party line or the policy direction laid down by the President. Failure to do so has cost many high appointees their jobs.

The distinction between the top spokesperson for the administration and others at lower levels is directed by the form of governmental organization. The same may be true in institutions such as corporations, universities, public service groups, trade associations, and others. But this does not come about automatically. The matter of who may speak on behalf of the organization, and what restrictions are placed on the subject matter or the media to which each has access, must be clearly understood throughout the organization.

In public relations the word "spokesperson" does not necessarily refer to someone who speaks directly. Spokespersons are those to whom any statement is attributed, as for instance in a news release. Although spokespersons may not necessarily write the statements in the releases quoting them—or, for that matter, the speeches they deliver—they nearly always review and approve any statements attributed to them before dissemination.

Typically, in a large company the chief executive officer will preempt the role of speaking on matters of corporate policy and actions taken by the board of directors or of financial matters, on major appointments or changes at the highest corporate levels, and on any specific topics considered sensitive. The CEO may reserve the spokesperson role in all communication with shareholders. There are endless variations of such responsibilities. In organizations with both a chief executive and a chief operating officer (COO), the two may divide between them the role of highest spokesperson, based on the functions for which each takes primary responsibility.

Below this level, in most large organizations, spokespersons have a more restricted role. Within general policy guidelines, they are free to speak on matters involving their functions. In a diversified corporation, for example, one officer may head all the activities within each line of business. If the corporation has four lines of business, there are four spokespersons. Officers are the ranking authorities within their own sphere, but none is in a position to speak for the others. Further down the line, a district manager, a plant manager, a product manager, and a state manager may have similarly restricted spokesperson roles pertaining only to that part of the organization for which their positions and knowledge qualify them to speak. All must understand the boundaries within which they are permitted to be the voice of the organization.

This may sound as if every organization is wrapped in red tape or laden with prohibitions. But that is not at all the case. Defining the spokesperson role is necessary to ensure that the organization is consistent in what it says and that it is dealing with all its publics correctly and authoritatively. A plant manager thousands of miles from headquarters may be the correct and authoritative spokesperson about smoke emanation from the plant's stacks, but is hardly in a position to explain to the local newspaper or television audience why the board of directors voted a stock split. The difference between the *limitation* of the spokesperson's role and its *positive functioning* is the organized effort of a public relations department to put the materials of communication in the hands of all spokespersons.

While plant managers or division heads cannot make the decision that the company will invest $100 million in new environmental controls, they can certainly repeat the information once the decison has been made public by the top corporate spokesperson. Furthermore, they can explain the significance and/or effect of this corporate decision in terms of the unit or units for which they have responsibility, the employees of these units, and the communities in which they are located.

The audiences that any organization seeks to reach tend to grow smaller and closer as the rank of the spokesperson moves down from the top. For example, the person in charge of the large Smith Jones Company plant in Pensacola, Florida, is the trusted voice of that company in that city. To most of the city's residents, the local plant manager is much more an authority on the company than its chairman, who is off in some distant part of the country. Indeed, it is likely that most Pensacolans perceive the Smith Jones Company as being that particular plant rather than an enormous corporation spanning the globe. So, on a Monday, the public relations person at the Pensacola plant may distribute a release to local and state news outlets in which the company chairman announces the decision to spend millions at its many plants to improve environmental controls. On the same day, or even later in the week, the Pensacola plant manager speaks before the chamber of commerce, telling how much is being invested in the Pensacola plant and, in some detail, what improvements are expected to be made. Which of these stories makes bigger news in Florida? Certainly the latter.

The assignment of authority and limitation of the spokesperson must take into account the differing interests of the news media. Organizing the formal spokesperson role in any big public relations operation is a fundamental requirement, yet it is not a bar to enlisting large groups of nonexecutive employees to speak for the organization, contradictory as that may seem.

In many instances, employees have concerted their efforts to support employers during controversies or hard times. This is a reversion to the truth universally recognized in public relations: There is no really satisfactory substitute for the give-and-take of personal interchange between senior executives and the media. But it is essential to understand that when this employee-spokesperson technique is used, it must be done under special conditions:

- The story to be told need not be simple but it must be uniform, and the people chosen to tell it must have the right qualifications to do so.

- The subject must be of universal interest.

- Some form of control is required to ensure that the employees engaged in the effort perform as planned and do not transcend the limited information roles assigned to them.

It should be clear that the careful assignment of the spokesperson role is not an inhibitory act, nor is it a matter of rating the importance of communications, level by level. It is more akin to putting up a framework in which to hang a program of communication so that the organization can deal coherently with all its important publics.

## Communication Strategy

Public relations people and the executives to whom they report often have only limited control over their communications. A response to a newspaper reporter on deadline may have to be brief and incomplete due to the time restrictions the reporter faces as the publication approaches press time. A release may say exactly what its originator wants it to say, and in precisely the way it can best be said, but its interpretation is mostly out of the organization's control once it leaves the office. Sometimes in interviews the right questions are never asked, or the executive being questioned may be ambiguous or misunderstood. Poor writing and clumsy talk promote misunderstanding. The act of communicating is only half of a transaction; the reception or perception of what is communicated is the other half. Most public relations people have seen with dismay how imperfect the perception often is.

This limited control puts a premium on quality in communications. Clarity and simplicity in language are keys to effective communications. Logic in the sequence of ideas is another key, as is the clean and evident organization of any written material. The best written communications do not leave the reader with unanswered questions or objections because of omission. Questions and objections should be anticipated in the planning of written materials answered in the writing. Why?

- This method makes one-way communication more meaningful than it would otherwise be; it approaches the ideal of personal interchanges.
- It tends to disarm possible critics.
- It bespeaks the organization's desire to be forthright, thorough, and honest in the acknowledgment of problems or disagreement.
- Side-stepping an obvious question raised by a new policy, for example, makes an organization look insensitive at best and evasive at worst.

Some of the most effective communications have been disseminated in the form of questions and answers. A good example is a booklet published several years ago by the Air Transport Association (ATA) as part of its economic education program. The ATA had sponsored a national study that revealed widespread misunderstanding of airline operations and economics. Each major fallacy it found in this study led to a question in the booklet (Example: "What are the airlines doing to eliminate noise near airports?"). The questions were answered factually and concisely. The booklet, "Questions people ask about airlines; Answers you can give them," was distributed by the millions to in-flight passengers by airlines members of ATA.

The Q-and-A technique is, of course, a special one that is not adaptable to all communications. In this case, it was selected as the most direct and hardest hitting approach to communicating a number of important but not closely related facts with brevity and impact.

Even the most affirmative things said in a public relations program often have negative aspects that should be anticipated. An electric utility has good news: It is going to build a new generating station. This will help meet the needs of a growing population. It will create jobs, reduce the danger of brown-outs, and perhaps attract new industry. Good news, indeed, but if the company tells its story this way, it will leave a lot of questions unanswered. What, many will want to know, will be the environmental effects? Others will wonder whether the new plant will require installation of long-distance transmission lines, and if so, where they will be located. The community nearest the plant will find some residents pleased and others perplexed. Will the project bring an influx of temporary construction workers, gouge the countryside, and create noise and dirt, offsetting the economic benefits?

In all probability, the company cannot prevent an outcry from environmentalists, if they see reason for alarm; nor will it solve community problems that may arise when construction begins merely by anticipating and covering these subjects in its news anouncement. But the utility will allay some fears, prevent some questions, and avoid some antagonisms by such foresight. Moreover, it will impress some who are exposed to the announcement that the company is dealing honestly with problems.

Making a general announcement of this sort is only the beginning of a communication program that will take different forms and may go on for years. One of the company's first considerations must be for the differing interests of its specific audiences.

Employees will want to know, "What significance does this have for me?" The financial community and shareholders will be critically interested in how the new facility will be paid for and what effect new financing may have on the company's stock price, dividend policy, and its current and future profitability.

The community where the plant will be built will need continuing communications geared to its special interests in the project. Utility customers will want to know how they will be affected. Certainly there will be local, state, and possibly federal units of government that must be kept informed. All these audiences are important to the long-range well-being of the company, and the public relations practitioner should discern the need for tailoring communications to each of them. Typically, he or she would probably consider:

- Distributing a "fact sheet" on the project at all executive levels of the company. This will enable managers to talk intelligently about the new plant in conversation and to respond to questions that may come from employees or others.

- Preparing a major story on the subject for use in the company's internal publications.

- Designing, if the project will have a major financial impact on the company, a special communication to shareholders, which will also be distributed to securities analysts, bond-rating agencies' portfolio managers, officers of the company, and others in the financial community. If the project is not significant enough to justify a special communication, full details may be included in the next quarterly earnings report.

- Preparing a comprehensive program of local communications, to be carried out over time, if the project has major impact on the community. How extensive this should be will depend upon an estimate of the probable reaction.

- During construction of nuclear generators, some companies have estabished field offices near the plants, staffed full time by professionals capable of conducting an ongoing educational program. In other cases, the community job may be handled by local speeches, interview sessions, releases, advertisements, and other methods.

- Establishing special communications with customers to underline the new plant's benefits for them. Such communications, as a rule, include bill stuffers, posters, and brochures for display and dispensing at business offices, and print, radio, and television advertising.

Why all these separate communications? Why not wrap up the entire story in a single document suitable for everybody? A complete answer is not simple. In fact, the public relations department may compile a single comprehensive document buttressed with data in great detail. Such a document, often known as a "background memorandum" or "position paper," may be used by the staff as its principal source for all communications and answers to questions. It may even be passed to media people interested in such a compilation.

Normally, however, a communication like this is overwhelming for audiences who really want to know, "What effect will this project have on my life?" It is not as if they were eager to immerse themselves in it; indeed, many who should be interested are often indifferent. The purpose of tailoring communications for specific audiences is to serve the company's interests, to earn appreciation and support, to win acceptance of its policies and activities, to moderate

criticism or to abate anticipated attacks, to maintain its
credit and financial markets, and to enchance the desirability of its stocks and bonds as investments.

All of this requires deliberate and unremitting effort to
communicate with the different audiences in terms that are
acceptable and interesting to them.

## Subdivision of Public Relations

Like the term "public relations," the nomenclature for
the many different branches of the business can be confusing. Press relations, media relations, and publicity are
sometimes used interchangeably and sometimes to make
distinctions. Consumer and customer relations could be the
same but are different. Public affairs is usually employed
synonymously with govermental relations, but by some it is
meant to encompass all public relations activities and concepts.

Some organizations now eschew the words "public relations" altogether, because of the frequent misuse of the
term. They may call their function "corporate communications," "corporate relations," "corporate affairs," or something else. But when they break the overall function down
into natural components, the terminology usually reverts
to generic use, such as "community relations," "shareholder
relations," and the rest.

There is a tendency among some in public relations to
add the word "relations" to any particular audience and
thus seem to create specialities that do not, in fact, exist.
The real distinction between the general practice of public
relations and a specialized practice is not related so much to
the audiences encompassed as it is to the different techniques used or of the special knowledge required. Public affairs (or governmental relations), for example, is a genuine
specialty, principally because it requires an encyclopedic
knowledge of the processes of government and the intrica-

cies of politics, not because politicians or bureaucrats are so much different from say, environmentalists.

Most public relations departments are smaller than their directors would like them to be, and only a relatively few are large enough to offer full-time specialists. Typically, trade associations, corporations, or nonprofit institutions may have a single governmental relations representative in Washington. Multi-plant manufacturing companies may have one "communicator" at each major plant location to handle both internal communications and community relations.

Double assignments on a public relations staff is common, with the result that the great majority of public relations people automatically gain experience in most of the field's subdivisions. The professional assigned to cover an event for the employee newspaper in the morning may be planning the annual report at lunch and writing testimony on proposed legislation later in the day. Thus, in a single day, he or she uses skills in three markedly different ways to meet the needs of as many different public specialties.

Where specialization reaches its occupational peak is in public relations consulting firms. The nature of consulting is to confront, over and over again with many clients, the kind of problems any single client organization experiences only from time to time. This makes specialization economically expensive for a small staff serving one organization exclusively, but possible for a consulting firm with several clients.

From a practical standpoint then, most public relations people have to identify the distinctions between the major specialties if they are to apply their skills and judgments intelligently, as their work assignments vary. All these specialties are covered in some detail elsewhere in this book, so the listing that follows attempts merely to point up their distinguishing features.

## Financial Relations

This is a specialty peculiar to corporate America and is rarely, if ever, practiced by other institutions. Its use is spreading among corporations in other countries. It is the means by which investor-owned firms regularly report operating results and other information to the shareholders, the financial community, and the public. Certain disclosures and practices are governed by law, creating a large area for informed judgment. Financial relations is a major means of carrying out corporate strategies of consequence, sometimes involving heated public competition for the support of individuals and financial institutions.

It is a field calling for a broad understanding of business law, economics, and corporate finance. Most public relations techniques are involved in a financial relations program. The media in this field are the specialized financial press as well as reporters for business sections of daily newspapers and some radio and television programs. Practitioners usually work closely with top corporate officers, lawyers, and accountants; and must therefore have those qualities of knowledge, judgment, and tact to function effectively in this milieu.

## Public Affairs

This function is any organization's foot in the door of government. The public affairs representative monitors developments in the legislative, executive, and judicial branches of government, alerts management when developments are deemed important, and counsels on how to react. Public affairs practitioners channel the flow of information, suggestions, or requests from organization to government, develop relationships within government, and help form and carry out information programs related to pending legislation or regulation. In some organizations this may involve lobbying.

## Internal Communications

This is the only branch of public relations in which the employer has complete control over most of the channels of communications. The subject of employee relations has been so extensively studied over decades that a special body of knowledge has accumulated, complete with theories of communication applicable solely to this field. While much of public relations practice is developed to serve media outside the organization, internal communication requires designing and producing the company's media, which may include the full array: newspaper, magazine, films, television, audiovisual instruction materials, booklets, and others. (See Part 4.)

## Community Relations

Each community is both a microcosm of the nation and an individual entity. The techniques and programming used in community relations at a company plant may be mirror images of the firm's national effort, adapted to local conditions and carried out on a more personal basis. The community is where the large impersonal organization assumes a local face, and many public relations activities can approach the nature of personal interchange. This can be good or bad, depending upon the performance of the organization and the disposition of the citizens.

Where the large corporation experiences its most stubborn environmental problems—for example, in Washington—the plant finds them in its own backyard in the form of complaints from neighbors. The practice of community relations often involves having organization officials participate in community affairs for the opportunity of personal contact, exposure of the company story through speeches, slide presentations, films, plant tours, and other opportunities to personalize and thus humanize the organization.

## Publicity and Marketing Communications

Publicity is more properly considered a technique of public relations than a specialty of its own. It is used in all branches of the business. But when it is considered in any organization to be an aspect of marketing, the subtle change in objective transforms the press relations, or publicity function, into one related to sales rather than policy. Even so, the talent required for marketing communications usually resides in the public relations department. In a corporation, marketing publicity is akin to the fund-raising publicity often considered a public relations function in nonprofit organizations.

Publicity is a potent force in marketing because people are more inclined to believe what they read or hear in an editorial context than to accept the same information in advertising. To undertake this kind of communication requires a strong marketing orientation.

There is a special skill in discerning what it is about a commercial product or service that can be made interesting to the media in the form of news, features, or visual attractions. It requires a detailed knowledge of potential media and their criteria for acccepting or rejecting such factors. In some cases, technical experience or education may also be required.

The marketing communications specialist works toward objectives that quantify sales quotas, profitability, and advertising investment. He or she is part of a business-oriented team, required to think and perform more as salesperson than strategist. In addition to product publicity, professional effort may be required to handle motivational communications with the sales staff, prepare materials for dealers, and establish tie-in promotions with retailers and others.

## The Specialists

The foregoing branches of public relations can be considered specialties mainly because the functions are different, not because the audiences differ. If every audience addressed were to designate a specialty of public relations, it would take another book to list them.

The great changes in society that have led to the rapid growth of public relations in recent years have required a good deal of specialization by people in the field, but not necessarily the development of new forms of public relations.

Environmentalism is an excellent example. This movement gave rise to widespread fears about the degradation of the modern world. It resulted in legislation, new governing bodies at all levels, and new concerns over public and occupational health and safety. This, in turn, has led to further legislation and regulation. The environment is an emotional and scientific subject and, in many respects, it is a subject of controversy. Because it's a pervasive subject, the environment has to be dealt with at every level of public relations: financial relations, public affairs, community relations, employee communications, and, in some cases, marketing publicity.

No new branch of public relations has evolved to deal with this vast subject. New public relations people capable of mastering all the facts of the subject have certainly been required, and their special knowledge is applied across the entire field of public relations.

To keep abreast of developments in such a broad sphere requires a major effort. It calls for continuing study of scientific and popular literature, attendance at conventions, convocations, seminars, and colloquia, and acquaintance between one group of environmentalists and media people who are covering the subject regularly. Only specialists can do this adequately. To some extent, the same is true of other national or worldwide developments. Special knowledge to begin with, and a continuing effort to keep on top of the field, often requires specialization. Depending upon the employers' interests, this specialty may be in the fields of health, education, the consumer movement, the world food crisis, or urban problems. It's not just a matter of knowing what is going on but also of interpreting it in terms of the company's interests and counseling top management on the organization's posture and program.

There is no indication that the trend to specialization will slow down. More and more public and governmental concerns are being affected by the incalculable growth of knowledge that makes all but the simplest human relationships more complicated than ever. The functions of public relations are not likely to alter radically—not in the near future, at least. But the ability of public relations professionals to carry out these functions effectively will require greater and greater access to that growing fund of knowledge and, therefore, a higher degree of specialization.

# Chapter 6

# The Role of Research
# In Public Relations

Public relations research is the study and analysis of the "other" side of communications—not the writing or the work of the publicist, but the listening, the observation of past facts or present perceptions of them.

Public relations is only as good as the research that underlies it. Nothing creative in public relations can happen in the blind—in other words, without context or unaddressed by history, facts, or assumptions. It is becoming increasingly true that the degree to which a public relations firm or department is research-driven is the degree to which it is on the cutting edge of communications.

Public relations, by definition, depends upon its "public" to have a relationship. It depends upon a repository of information in the minds and hearts of the target audience, to which it adds or reorganizes that which is already known. Research defines what information may be missing and how existing information, from the perspective of the receiver, can be credibly reorganized. It does this by studying the information a sample audience has already absorbed and evaluated, and then observing, through interviews, how the target sample handles new information or reorganizes old information.

Research is of strategic importance in public relations. Research helps public relations target information to strike responsive chords and to produce credible effects in its targeted audiences.

Public relations research can be broadly classified into

two categories: factual research of published information and public opinion research. It is the study of the listener, watcher, or reader who makes up the "public" the practitioner "relates" to.

Factual research can produce clues. Opinion research can produce hypotheses. When processed by the creative mind of a publicist, such clues and hypotheses lead to effective campaigns. This process is no secret. Even before the advent of modern science, Western thought had begun to analyze facts and to hypothesize about how additions or alterations in the presumed facts would change behavior. Today social sciences and computer technology have taken this process to a level at which any junior researcher can analyze patterns a trillion times more complex—and simplified—than those available to Aristotle. The demand today, therefore, is that the researcher be at least as creative as the communicators, the publicists, and the advertisers.

## Factual Research

Reading may be as important a function to a public relations practitioner as writing. Much of the practitioner's world involves accumulating, evaluating, classifying, and synthesizing information and ideas.

To work at their best, public relations men and women must have easy access to such minimum reference tools as a good dictionary, a thesaurus, an atlas, at least one almanac, a compendium of governmental statistics, and a library at the end of the telephone.

Even the smallest public relations department or counseling firm needs a reference library and some method of culling useful information from newspapers and other periodicals. To keep current, practitioners must be exposed to the press and other daily media important to their organizations as well as to specialized trade or professional publications. This creates a flow of reading matter that must be monitored, studied, clipped, and filed.

In any public relations organization of more than a few people, a librarian quickly becomes a must, even if the person cannot devote full time to this task. Few busy public relations practitioners have the time to read all the publications crossing their desks. Somebody has to scan many of them to clip out those items the professional ought to see and may want to route to others. This is an important form of public relations research.

Once someone has been designated as reader and clipper, that person is usually asked to dig facts out of standard references for articles and speeches. Somebody asks, "What was the population of Michigan at the last census?" or "What was the gross national product last year?" Presto! A research facility is born that may, in time, save many valuable hours of professional time each week in a public relations department or counseling firm.

Few public relations activities can be accomplished without some element of literature research. Matters of economics, legislation, public policy, and competitive circumstances can rarely be dealt with in stories, speeches, annual reports, pamphlets, or advertisement without reference to authoritative sources outside the organization.

Larger corporations, trade associations, and public relations firms tend to maintain libraries staffed with professionals. In some organizations, there is a substantial department to conduct research. At the world's largest public relations firm, for example, what is now called Research and Information Services began 30 years ago as a small library and internal clipping service staffed by one young woman. It is today a department of 20, headed by a senior vice president and performing a service for the firm and all its clients that continues to grow in importance.

In a large department, researchers do much more than

simply clip articles and monitor newswires. Research projects constantly flow into such a department and can range from requests for reference-book information to quite elaborate and sometimes difficult undertakings. For example, one consulting firm research department was recently asked to provide an account executive with a summary of U.S. policy changes toward the Middle Eastern nations over a 30-year period, and to do it within 24 hours.

This department has provided public relations practitioners with such esoteric fare as detailed histories of the tin can and chewing gum industries. Similarly, an insurance company planning a 50th anniversary celebration researched America in the company's founding year, covering such matters as clothing styles, customs, newspaper headlines, popular songs, and major events. For a major industrial company, researchers ferreted out information about the sources of income of every art institute and state arts council in the United States. This information helped build a case for heavier financial support for the arts by federal and state governments.

The reasons for citing such assignments is twofold: To indicate 1) how sophisticated and detailed such research has become, and 2) how essential it is for a public relations operation to be backed up by a professional research capability. Such research makes researchers a part of the public relations team.

## Establishing a Research Capability

A small public relations department or counseling firm that wants to establish a research capability with limited funds needs the minimum reference works previously mentioned. Others of value would include the Congressional Directory, the federal government's Monthly Catalogue of Publications, and *Who's Who in America*. If the organization is a business and can afford to, it should also join the

New York City-based Conference Board and get it's publications.

Experienced researchers advise acquiring indexes rather than additional reference volumes. With indexes and a good public library nearby, a researcher can get just about everything needed. If there isn't a good library in the community, information is generally available from libraries elsewhere by telephone or mail.

A business-oriented organization might wish to acquire such indexes as the *Business Periodical Index, Reader's Guide to Periodical Literature, Public Affairs Information Systems Bulletins, Funk & Scott Index to Corporations, The New York Times Index,* and the *Biographical Index.*

## Opinion Research

There are vast data banks that can tell researchers and public relations people almost anything they need to know about the American public. Information in these data banks covers:

- Demography: The United States census.

- Demography and market behavior: Donnelley Marketing Information Services.

- Market behavior and media habits: A. C. Nielsen for television, Arbitron Ratings Company for radio, and Simmons Market Research Bureau for print.

- Market and media behavior relative to lifestyles, attitudes, and opinions: Values and Lifestyles (VALS) and custom surveys.

There is so much opinion research available today that, before commissioning a new study, the practitioner should ask, "Does the information exist already?" It probably does. Advances in computer software enable researchers to use these data banks as if they were a single, integrated system. Software programs have been developed that break up, or segment, each group of population into definable groups on a national, state, or local basis, allowing them to be analyzed with regard to buying habits, political beliefs, or any of the other types of behavior in any of the data banks. One of the most sophisticated of these databanks is ClusterPlus, a joint software product of Simmons and Donnelley. It isolates 47 definitions of Americans, or Clusters, by 64 factors, all tied to the neighborhoods in which more than 86 million households can be found.

For example, those people who are most opposed to nuclear power are in "Cluster 17." This cluster also has the highest index of videocassette recorder ownership. Members of the group tend to be young, politically active achievers with children in grammar school; both parents work; their favorite television program is "Hill Street Blues" and they are early AM radio news listeners; they think of themselves as "up and coming"; they are neoconservative; and so on, with ClusterPlus identifying them by a wide range of other definitions and factors. Using the ClusterPlus system, the members of Cluster 17 can each be contacted via telephone or mail, or information can be directed to them through advertising and news story placements in the specific media they read, listen to or watch.

Variations in this kind of software are being used by virtually every major communications and research company for a variety of purposes:

- Definition of strategy.
- Development of segmented messages.
- Identification of media best used in particular circumstances campaign.

The results of customized opinion surveys involving attitudes and opinions about a given subject, corporation, or issue can be matched against data in the major data banks through ClusterPlus or other software systems. In this way, the researcher gains the value of all the information stored in those great data banks plus the specific value of the information gained in the custom survey, and can project the results over much more specific groups of people with greater accuracy.

This phenomenon is unique to the American marketplace. It exists nowhere else. In Japan, France, the United Kingdom, and Germany, where similar data banks are currently in various stages of development, the private sector cannot access nearly as much information about individual households as it can in the United States. This unique situation means that a large public relations firm can produce entirely new research products based upon integrated data bank information. Here are some actual examples developed by Strategic Information Research Corporation (SIRC), the public opinion subsidiary of Hill and Knowlton:

- A college and university recruitment program that specifically identifies students the college should encourage to apply for admission.

- A niche-marketing program for financial institutions that identifies prospects for financial products and aids in siting of branches.

- A program to stop ballot initiatives by conducting an electronic search for invalid voter signatures.

- A "look-alike" duplication program that can take any set of people—by demography, market behavior, media habits, lifestyle, and attitudes—and create a "look-alike" listing of similar people. For example, such a program can create a list of people who resemble municipal-bond holders in every way *except* that they don't yet own municipal bonds.

The system has applications limited only by the imagination of the researcher. For example, merging companies often conduct shareholder and customer surveys to measure the effect of the merger on share price or product preferences under the new identity. The data banks can, in some cases, supply a national sample of public opinion, including comparative subsamples of each company's shareholders and product users, a list which would be impossible to attain through a custom-designed survey without incurring enormous costs.

## Professional and Ethical Concerns

A public opinion researcher must be aware of why a poll or survey is contemplated. When a survey is conducted for purely public relations purposes—that is, to generate information that can be disseminated to the news media as part of a publicity campaign—then the researcher must follow professional and ethical procedures to avoid criticism aimed at the survey's objectivity.

Almost all of the well-known public opinion polling companies in the United States are owned by media outlets ( a newspaper, a television network, or a large communications company), so matters of ethics are paramount, especially in the reporting of poll findings. Procedures on how polls for specific purposes can be accomplished without pronounced bias or loss of objectivity have been agreed upon among the members of the World Association for Public Opinion Research.

Of the custom surveys conducted annually by public opinion research companies for public relation or marketing purposes, only a small percentage are for publications. Most are for strategic use; that is, they are used to design communications strategies, not to be a story in themselves. These proprietary strategic surveys, and the processes leading to them, are described in the following section.

## Strategic Surveys

Public relations programs can be designed to reach targeted segments of the population in the same way that advertising campaigns are tailored to reach specific segments. They are often targeted to diverse groups, or publics, at the same time. For example, the focus of a new product introduction for a computer manufacturer could be on any combination of senior management, data processing supervisors, or line employees; attorneys, bankers, or financial managers; editors or writers at business and trade publications; government executives, legislators, or regulators involved in trade regulations that would prevent overseas competitors from importing a certain product; community leaders near the plant where the product will be produced; and many other groups. In devising the program, the existing attitudes of these groups toward the company, its products, and its competitors need to be evaluated.

Segmentation of the sample for study is the first step in developing a public opinion survey. How one goes about the survey depends upon whether the researcher is seeking owners in the group who would want a free tape on the product, or qualitative findings, such as how exciting members of the group find the new product's styling. In the first case, one uses such quantitative methods as random or quota sampling, structured interviews, or controlled interviewing processes. The subsequent data can then be analyzed statistically to relate the sample (say, residents of Des Moines) to the universe of study (for instance, owners of VCRs).

Typical techniques for carrying out quantifiable surveys include the telephone interview, the face-to-face personal interview, and the self-administered, mail-back poll. The latter technique is especially useful for internal samples (employees, shareholders, or customers), where a response rate of 60 percent or more can be expected if the survey is implemented correctly.

The telephone has become the principal interviewing medium, even with highly specialized groups (one might say *especially* with highly specialized groups), because Americans actually provide more information over the phone than they do in face-to-face interviews.

Contrary to the claims of those who say "I'd never answer that question," most Americans are willing to share information with people who really need it. Any experienced telephone interviewer will tell you that the difficulty is getting people to stop talking, not getting them to respond.

Even rather small samples of respondents can be quantified. For example, in the case of a shareholder vote on a merger, acquisition, or other serious corporate issue, one can interview the hundred largest individual shareholders of the company and the portfolio managers in the major institutions holding that company's shares and then predict the outcome of the vote with as much accuracy as one can predict a close election.

Even as few as 20 interviews of a given group can be useful in formulating public relations strategies. For example, in 1986 a food company shareholder used shareholder surveys to assess the chances that a merger would be rejected, and then later surveyed employees to help find areas of consensus in an effort to end a major strike. Research helped a toy company evaluate the possibility of a consumer demonstration against a product and gave a brokerage firm the information it needed to affect the outcome of the debate over tax reform.

## Marketing Communications Research

In marketing communications, custom surveys can be matched against information in major data banks to identify specific target audiences, messages that will generate the best response from those audiences, and the most suitable media. The information from such surveys can help in every aspect of a communications campaign: Developing brochures or direct mail pieces, producing videotapes, developing publicity, setting up a news bureau to place stories with the media, training sales people, improving dealer relations, refining telephone sales pitches, and evaluating feedback to measure the campaign's effectiveness.

## Focus Groups

Public opinion researchers often use videotaped focus groups to measure the qualitative effects of material or messages on members of a target audience. Research shows that human response to information—talk about the news, gossip about a product, rumors about something new—is just as important in comprehending information or forming attitudes as the content of the information itself. The stimuli can be advertising, news stories, or direct communication. Therefore, the important thing to learn about such stimuli is the kind of interactive conversation or talk they tend to create.

What stands up? What is not credible? In terms of such stimuli, awareness is not as important as credibility, because credibility is what gets passed on in interaction with others. A carefully selected focus group can sometimes tell whether a particular group of stimuli—advertisements, sales pitches, booklets—are going to achieve their objectives.

## Content Analysis

Content analysis is a research technique borrowed in part from politics and in part from academia. In this technique, radio, television, newspaper, and magazine stories are rated as if they were people responding to a public opinion survey. As a first step, a questionnaire that gets to the heart of a particular issue or subject is developed. Stories covering that particular issue or subject are then "interviewed" and the answers are processed by a computer. The findings show what is being reported, where, to how many people, over what period of time, in which media, and how the coverage changes over time.

Content analysis provides answers to several questions. Do the trade papers carry the most comprehensive stories? Is negative criticism sourced and quoted? What falls out when the story shrinks to 30 seconds on television and what remains? Do the themes of the public relations campaign appear more, or less, frequently as the campaign is expanded.

This is a useful tool for finding out what happened in a publicity campaign, a product introduction, a media tour, a merger period, or a crisis. In contrast to other surveys, it can be extended into the past or future. For example, to see how 1984 content analysis came out against 1985 and 1986 analyses, the researcher needs only to assemble a comparable number of stories from 1985 and 1986 issues of the same media and study the current data.

## Measuring Public Relations

Measurement of communications campaigns is an elusive business. It becomes impossible when the focus used is solely on the individual at whom the campaign is targeted. Communications researchers have been aware for years that the typical person cannot report the source of information accurately, no more than a person can tell exactly how, in a conversation with others, the information was used to form an attitude or how the attitude that was formed subsequently affected the person's behavior. However, just because the typical person cannot report what caused a change in attitude or behavior does not mean there were no stimuli that caused that change, or that their impact cannot be measured.

For example, tracking polls and content analyses can demonstrate the effect of news and advertising on political behavior. The results of such polls can then be verified on election day. Such techniques have been used since the early 1970s to predict shifts of up to 60 percent of the electorate during a short period of intense news coverage and advertising. These techniques can also be used to measure the effect of publicity. Content analysis can show what goes out, who in the media used it, and who in the media's audience ought to have heard it; a survey can then show who actually heard it and, more important, who believed it. Other responses—requests for information, shareholder votes sales, coupon usage—can show what actually happened, in terms of actions that can affect a company's bottom line.

Corporate America increasingly asks for measurement of the effectiveness of communications and they are going to get it through research results. Research can tell a public relations firm or department how to start and can later show whether the objective has been achieved.

Research provides tangible understanding, based on documentation, that gives a substantial basis for the direction of almost any public relations venture. Authoritative studies can project reactions, analyze specific market segments, illustrate the effects of similar projects approached in dissimilar ways, and merit the confidence and respect of all media by offering reliable and expertly prepared material for public attention.

## A Case in Point

A few years ago, the lead industry fell victim to several convergent forces that jeopardized existing and future markets. They included the following elements:

- Health concerns about poisoning from paint and leaded gasoline that unsettled public acceptance of other uses of lead.

- Public confusion about lead as a toxic substance.

- Emotional and sometimes biased statements by environmentalists that usually went unanswered by the media.

Research established that the public was generally misinformed and unaware of lead's capabilities, advantages, and economic attributes. The research also identified specific public relations opportunities in which the industry's position could be presented in a positive fashion.

By identifying new information and unused aproaches rather than attempting to disprove existing opinions, the research opened public relations avenues and provided insight into the specific concerns of targeted demographic groups.

Another case in point illustrates how research enabled a major corporation to guide marketing direction for a new, sophisticated, and specialized micro-microcomputer.

Honeywell, Inc. used the research to validate its faith in the micro-microcomputer and market it accordingly. Honeywell developed a major technological change from the standard analog gauges and valves that monitor pipelines, boilers, flow lines, levels, and pressures in a petroleum refinery. Cost of the micro-microcomputer was about double that of older-technology models.

Research determined the selected public relations audiences and benefits of the product through surveys and interviews with instrumentation engineers, purchasing personnel, and senior management at a representative sample of large and small refineries.

Research also defined five specific beneficial areas of interest, as follows:

- Labor savings in terms of fewer man-hours required for maintenance and modernization.

- Energy conservation in steam generation.

- More accurate measurements of oil flow into and finished product from the refinery.

- Reduced inventory costs.

- Rapid return to operation following shutdown.

It was determined that labor savings and speedy operational resumption would overcome price-based resistance and the most salable benefit to senior management was lower inventory cost.

In another case in point, a racetrack manager wanted to develop a list of potential patrons who were not currently racetrack fans. Research analysts recommended that the racetrack develop profiles of its attendees in terms of sociodemographics and life-styles and then create a list of look-alikes who could be the target of a communications marketing campaign.

Twenty thousand auto license numbers were collected from the track's parking lot and cluster-coded, and the attendees home addresses were mapped. The preferred fans were selected by cluster. Track managers were then given 20,000 names and addresses of people who were look-alikes of the original set of preferred fans. A direct-mail promotion was used to attract the look-alikes to the track. Feature stories were sent to media that reached the selected profile of potential track attendees, and targeted advertising was also used.

To measure success, researchers went into the parking lot on another race day and again collected auto license numbers to see if the new fans sought in the promotion were actually in attendance. A comparison between the "handle" of the track before and after the promotion, laid against the old and new numbers of fans, enabled track managers to measure cost-effectiveness of the campaign down to nickels and dimes.

# Chapter 7

# Working with the News Media

Getting desirable news and feature coverage in the media is an essential function of public relations. Known as successful media placement, this is much more than a mechanical process; it is something of an art. Practicing this art requires a multitude of talents: a flair for creativity, an eye or ear for the interesting or unique story, an understanding of the media, and a solid knowledge of the company, issue, or product being presented to the media as newsworthy.

Just getting an organization's or individual's name in the newspaper is pointless if that exposure has no other goal than gratuitous publicity. Having a good idea or "hook" is important, but even more important is the ability to put the "media plan" into effect, to follow up with contacts, and to create tangible results.

## Research and Planning

Media placement begins with research. The successful practitioner is constantly on the lookout for something that sets his or her company, client, product, or service apart from the rest of the pack. What is the company's expertise? Is it a trend setter or on the cutting edge of technology? Have significant developments in the field made it newsworthy? What makes the firm's activities more interesting than those of its competitors? Furthermore, which of these possible news elements will translate most effectively into a story that will help achieve the overall communications goals?

## Selecting the Right Media

When the public relations practitioner is confident of the objectives of the program and the themes or ideas to be presented, it is time to identify the appropriate media to approach. There are several reliable media directories available, and at least one can be found in most public libraries. However, it makes sense to go beyond these standard directories. Careful thought and research can reveal a variety of specialty publications and electronic outlets that may enhance and enlarge the scope of media exposure.

When a media list is developed, it makes sense to verify that an editor or reporter is still with a television or radio station or still covering the same topic or beat. Media people tend to change jobs frequently.

## Making the Pitch

Whether he or she is trying to set up an interview, publicize a service, or promote a product, the public relations practitioner usually approaches the media first with a carefully crafted and succinct pitch letter and then follows up with a phone call. Some practitioners make "cold" calls—calls with no prior letter. Such calls, however, are generally limited to late-breaking, newsworthy events and work best when the caller or organization is well-known to the media.

## Exclusivity

The public relations practitioner should be prepared to deal with requests for exclusivity. This means different things to different people. The practitioner must clearly understand whether an editor is asking for an across-the-board exclusive (i.e., the story will be discussed with no other outlet) or just an exclusive within a geographic area or field of interest.

## News Kits

Since public relations practitioners work with electronic as well as print media, it makes sense to avoid such outmoded terms as "press releases," "press kits," and "press conferences" in favor of "news releases," "news kits," and "news conferences." No one wants to alienate the all-important electronic media by implying that print (i.e., press) is the only game in town.

One of the most important tools in dealing with the media is a media information or news kit. The material in the kit should be factual, accurate, well-written, and attractive.

Items that may be included in the kit are as follows:

- News release.

- Question and answer sheets.

- Fact sheets.

- Glossy black and white photographs (with identifying information attached to each print).

- Color film clips or slides for television (also clearly identified).

- Color transparencies, with suggested captions, for magazines or newspapers printed in color.

- Logo sheets.

- Maps.

- Charts and graphs.

- Pertinent reprints.

- Speeches.

- Biographical information on individuals mentioned in releases.

- Newsletters.

- Company magazines.

- Brochures.

- Annual reports.

- List of sources to contact for additional information.

In this day of multilingual population centers, it makes sense to consider the need for bilingual or multilingual media information kits and news conferences.

Once the information has been gathered and written, ancillary materials produced, and kits assembled, how is this information to be distributed? Delivery is generally determined by the timing of a news conference, the lead time needed for scheduling interviews, the importance of particular media, and the geographical distances involved. The public relations practitioner has several options: regular mail, overnight mail, special messenger, personal delivery (by the practitioner), or special newswire (such as P.R. Newswire or Businesswire). Radio stories may be transmitted by telephone, and major news may be distributed by satellite to television stations.

## Training Spokespersons

Having a spokesperson who is comfortable with the media and cool and collected in a crisis is important, but few executives are born with these talents. Today, it is a well-accepted practice for corporate spokespersons to receive special training in handling interviews and confrontations. Such training is widely available from public relations firms as well as from consultants who specialize in working with speakers and spokespersons.

## The Media

Public relations practitioners sharply differentiate between the print and electronic media. Nearly everything about them is different. A story that merits a thousand words in a daily newspaper may get 200 words in a weekly news magazine, 60 seconds on television, and ten seconds on radio. Skilled practitioners take advantage of these differences to tailor their information to the requirements of each medium. They see the differences as opportunities rather than obstacles.

It is essential that the practitioner study all the media closely. This volume must confine itself to categories and generalities, which are certainly important, but the practitioner must deal with specific and clearly identifiable differences.

## Print Media

Print media include newspapers, Sunday supplements, magazines, trade publications, newsletters, employee communications, books, and other printed material. Each has its own style and format requirements and readership.

**Newspapers.** Newspapers are by far the most widely read of the print media. According to industry sources, 1,651 dailies and 6,857 weeklies were published in the United States in 1986. While the physical size (tabloid versus standard) and circulation of newspapers may differ, content is generally similar. Most daily newspapers group their pages into international, national, local, and sports news sections. In addition, the larger papers normally run special sections covering such topics as lifestyle, business and financial, and entertainment news.

Because newspapers report mainly on events of the previous day or the same day, depending on whether they are morning or afternoon publications, they require information that is timely. In a few large cities, both morning and evening papers are published, in some cases by the same publisher, in other cases independent of one another.

Most daily newspapers use photographs from a wide range of sources: staff photographers, photo services, and public relations practitioners. Glossy, black and white, 8-x-10-inch photos are preferred. Many dailies now run color photos. They are very selective, however, in their use of such photos, and a check with an editor before submitting color photos or transparencies can be a wise investment of time.

Weekly newspapers differ from dailies in several ways. Generally they have fewer sections, are not as concerned with being on top of the news, are more localized in their coverage, and tend to treat news from a feature standpoint, often going into more depth than a daily newspaper does.

Probably the greatest difference between the two, from a public relations practitioner's standpoint, is the limited staff running a weekly newspaper. While dailies, for the most part, have specific editors for individual sections of the newspaper, one editor may be responsible for several sections in a weekly. That means a weekly paper editor may have less time to consider outside material, but because he has a small staff, or even no staff for news gathering, may be more receptive to good material from PR people.

**Sunday supplements.** Supplements, whether locally produced by newspapers or provided by a national source, generally are published on weekends. *Parade* and *USA Weekend* are two well-known national supplements. Supplements are essentially feature oriented and tend to keep to topical events. They do, of course, run information of an "evergreen" nature as well. A key point to remember in working with national supplements is the rather long lead time, six to eight weeks, under which they operate in developing their features.

**Consumer magazines.** Consumer magazines offer tremendous opportunities for the public relations practitioner. More than 1,500 consumer magazines are published in the United States. Most are targeted to specialized audiences. Unlike the handful of general interest magazines, consumer publications zero in on particular subjects, such as sports, business, computers, health and fitness, food, and travel.

Timing is important in approaching magazines because of the wide range of publishing dates and the differing deadline requirements: weekly, monthly, quarterly, and semiannually. The best advice in dealing with any magazine is to check with the editors on their needs or to submit queries before investing substantial time in story development.

**Trade publications.** Here again many different publications cater to an equally large number of different interests. There are 90 different categories of trade publications, accounting for 4,500 books. These publications cater primarily to the needs of specific segments of business and industry. Virtually every industry and occupation is covered by at least one trade publication.

With such diversity comes an equal diversity in requirements and needs. The needs, of course, are based on a publication's readership.

**Special note.** The key to working with the print media, considering the vast number of newspapers, magazines, or trade papers, is a good working knowledge of the requirements of the publications. It is essential to know the media. A good public relations practitioner must pick up recent copies of the publications and study them: determine the editorial treatment they give subjects, which subjects are emphasized more than others, who the columnists are, who the editors are, how they treat photos. It pays to have this kind of information in hand before approaching publications. It is especially counterproductive to propose a story that is the same as or very similar to one recently used.

## Electronic Media

There are two main categories of electronic media: television and radio. Each has its own structure and subdivisions.

**Television.** Television is the most influential medium in terms of its impact on large numbers of people. More than 1,200 television stations in the United States operate under license from the Federal Communications Commission and, for the most part, are independently owned. The notable exceptions are the handful of stations operated by each of the commercial networks: ABC, CBS, and NBC. The Public Broadcasting Service encompasses 314 additional stations across the country.

Cable television is a quickly expanding broadcast medium. Currently 7,300 cable systems serve 19,000 communities in the United States. Cable satellite networks, such as Cable News Network and Financial News Network, provide increasingly high-quality programming available only to cable subscribers.

Adding to the burgeoning numbers of television outlets are "superstations" like WTBS in Atlanta and WOR in New York, local independent stations that are distributed nationwide via satellite.

All television stations produce some of their own material locally, and some initiate virtually all their programs.

However, hundreds have network affiliations, and most station managers use packaging services that syndicate programs, movies, and other features. Most stations also subscribe to one or more of the principal newspaper wire services, which provide national and international news specially packaged for radio and television.

In dealing with television, public relations practitioners distinguish sharply between ideas for network television and those for local stations. Network television is rarely interested in a subject without national appeal, while television stations are rarely warm to an idea, story, or project that lacks local or regional interest.

Because television is a visual medium, it seeks out stories with visual impact. Television producers try to avoid "talking heads." In planning for television publicity, practitioners look for a story with dramatic or, at the very least, interesting visual qualities. Without something eye-catching, an idea has little chance of making it to the television screen.

Time is another important element. With few exceptions, news shows do not give a single story more than one minute; 20 seconds is about as much as can be expected for a product-related story. On the other hand, talk shows can provide from five to 20 minutes for a specific subject.

Most local television stations have one or more news assignment editors who sift through the day's events and determine which stories to commit camera crews to cover. Talk shows are planned by a producer or designated talent coordinator. The public relations practitioner should have a good working knowledge of the specific show or newscast targeted for publicity: format, time-frame, type of guests, point of view. This knowledge permits a story to be positioned properly so that it has the greatest possibility for acceptance.

Network programs are considerably different from local ones. In publicizing a news story, the public relations person almost always deals with a program's producer. This producer decides whether a specific story will become part of the newscast. Networks, which are basically a collection of independent stations, do not have their own film crews to cover events. They rely on the stations that comprise the network to provide material for newscasts. Therefore, on a fast-breaking story, the public relations practitioner may work with a local assignment editor as well as with the network's news coordinator.

In some instances, locally covered news is judged to be of national importance and is passed to the network by the local station through an electronic feed. This feed is much like a wire service in that locally originated material is sent to the network, which, in turn, passes it to stations across the country. These stations then have the option of including the story in their broadcasts.

**Public broadcasting.** The Public Broadcasting Service offers fewer opportunities for publicity coverage than the commercial networks. Issues, rather than products or events, get the greatest play on Public Broadcasting stations.

**Radio.** There are more than 9,800 radio stations throughout the United States: more than 4,800 AM, 3,800 commercial FM, and 1,200 noncommercial FM. Radio provides more frequent news coverage than any other medium. The deadline for newscasts can be every half-hour throughout the day. The primary opportunity for publicity in radio lies in the great number of talk shows that interview guests. Radio stations cover a wide variety of interests: business, general news, entertainment, hobbies, work. Contacts for talk shows are the shows' producers, while news goes to the station's news director or assignment editor.

The time available for each story on radio newscasts is even more limited than on television, while talk shows can be much longer. A number of shows run three or four hours and provide up to two hours for a guest to be interviewed.

## How to Reach the Media

There are literally dozens of techniques for generating media interest. Each has benefits and drawbacks.

- **Written release.** A news release commits a story to paper in the style acceptable to the media for which it is intended. Some general news stories are written one way for newspapers and another for the electronic media. The release may be a single copy for a particular news outlet, or it may be reproduced by the hundreds for broad distribution.

- **Interview.** When the subject matter is important enough, when questions that must be answered by an authority will arise, or when publicity for an individual is the goal, interviews may be necessary. There is no way of categorizing interviews; they will follow the interviewer's interests and may often stray considerably from the orginal subject. Often, for the electronic media, they are recorded at length, but only one or a few short segments actually go on the air. Print media interviews may last for extended periods, or reporters may return time and again for further information or viewpoints. Thorough preparation can help a spokesperson handle difficult, even hostile questions with confidence. Similarly, providing the interviewer with background information on both the spokesperson and the topic can help keep the interview squarely on target.

- **News conference.** News conferences, at which a number of media representatives cover an event or an announcement, should be reserved for especially newsworthy events. In deciding whether to hold a news conference, the public relations staff must ask, "Can the information be disseminated as effectively in any other way?" If the answer is *truly* no, then a conference is in order. A basic checklist of activities and due dates includes site selection, refreshments, audiovisual equipment, speeches, invitations, media lists and confirmation calls, press materials, staffing, run-through, and devil's advocate questions. This list, expanded and refined to include specific details relative to a particular situation, can go a long way in helping to make a news conference successful.

- **Satellite news conference.** In urgent or exceptionally unusual situations, satellite communications make it possible for companies to take their message directly to television stations throughout the country or around the world. Such electronic news conferences have been used in takeover fights, product recalls, mergers, and disasters. Providing the television stations with a telephone number makes it possible for broadcasters to call in their questions just as if they were present in person at the news conference. The company sponsoring the news conference can control the geographic areas being reached, limiting the conference's impact to the areas or countries in which it does business.

- **News briefing.** A news briefing can be used when a company does not have hard news to report but can provide interesting background information or its views on a particular issue. The briefing permits an exchange of views or in-depth questions. Media representatives are receptive to this approach because they can decide whether to participate, knowing in advance no hard news will be announced but that the background might be helpful in future stories.

- **Editorial board meeting or roundtable.** Sometimes a business leader or spokesperson will meet with the key editors of a publication to discuss the company's or industry's plans and prospects. Such meetings give the spokesperson an opportunity to influence future editorial opinion and to provide editors with solid background information. Such meetings usually do not generate immediate media coverage nor are they expected to.

- **Media tours.** Media tours (i.e., sending a spokesperson or public figure to several cities sequentially to speak with as many reporters as possible) can be effective ways to target a message to specific geographic markets. Lead time of six to eight weeks should be allowed for setting up a tour. This allows for scheduling the spokesperson for television and radio talk shows (which need this lead time) as well as for interviews with the local newspapers. Since such tours typically involve a number of cities, the spokesperson should be prepared to relate the subject matter to each city. Tie-ins with local retailers or plant operations are helpful in establishing local news angles. (Remember, local media respond to news with local impact.) Before a media tour, the spokesperson should be thoroughly rehearsed to deliver key messages as well as to become comfortable with various interviewing techniques used by the media.

- **Case histories.** Case histories, or success stories, are often publicity stimulators, particularly for trade publications, whose readers are generally interested in how other companies in their industry have solved problems, initiated new sales or marketing approaches, or originated new operations. Often the case history is based on a satisfied customer's explanation of how it has been helped. Such stories are genuinely informative and are quasieducational, as well as promotional.

• **Editorial color page.** Some practitioners, especially those publicizing food products, provide newspapers with camera-ready copy and artwork or photography. For example, a food company might distribute an editorial color page featuring a recipe story and full-color food photography. The color page is distributed to newspaper food editors for use in their sections or as the section's front-page feature. A color page should feature good quality photos and interesting copy.

• **Video news release.** The tremendous demands upon local television news camera crews to cover events almost preclude coverage of any but the most newsworthy stories. A video news release can make it easier for stations to cover a story. Keyed to a special event or trend, the video news release can provide wide exposure for a company's product or service in a 60- to 90-second piece of videotape. This "clip," featuring the company's message in the context of a news story, can be distributed to television stations across the country.

A video news release is distributed in one of two ways. It can be transmitted by satellite to up to 600 stations around the nation that have on-site satellite dishes. Stations are alerted in advance of the distribution time and content of the release. They then have the option of picking up the release for use in their regular news programming. A second method is by mailing the release on 3/4-inch videotape to a specific list of television stations, such as the top 100 markets in the country or in a particular geographic area. This form of distribution is especially effective if the release is appropriate for a specific region. When using the direct-mail approach, the public relations staff must keep in mind that more than the videotape can be sent. To catch the attention of the program director or assignment editor, creative practitioners use off-beat packaging and include related press materials. For a St. Patrick's Day promotion for Lender's Bagels, for example, a videotape was sent in shamrock-decorated wrappings along with green bagels and a press release describing Lender's annual green bagel giveaway.

- **TV slide kit.** The television slide kit provides a less expensive alternative to a video news release. This kit includes a script, slides, and various props that a broadcaster can incorporate into a program, most often a talk show. The skill lies in designing the kit so that it has broad appeal, even to broadcasters who are addressing themselves primarily to local topics.

- **Special radio opportunities.** Many independent radio producers offer a service whereby a company can buy time for informational features on regularly scheduled programming. These segments, which can range from two to 30 minutes, are then distributed to local radio stations that contract to air the programs.

- **Radio actualities.** A radio actuality is a prerecorded feature. The radio "feed" can be distributed to a limited number of stations by telephone, or nationwide by satellite, through a network service such as the AP/UPI Radio Network or National Public Radio. It can be a scripted version of a press release being distributed to newspapers over a wire service or perhaps a short, scripted message about a topic of general interest that relates to the company or product.

- **Radio interviews.** More than 500 radio stations across the country conduct interviews over the telephone. This provides an excellent opportunity to use a spokesperson in a cost-effective manner. The public relations practitioner can use such interviews to target information to specific kinds of audiences or geographic areas.

- **Radio trade-for-mention promotion.** Many radio stations are open to company-sponsored contests. The company generally develops a contest, such as daily trivia questions, or a promotion concept that involves listener participation. The company provides prizes, which may include its product, at no cost to the station. The radio announcer opens the contest to listeners who call in to win a prize. In exchange for the contest materials and prizes, which attract listeners to the station's regular programming, the radio station agrees to mention the company as the sponsor of the contest each time it is aired.

- **Media alert.** For media representatives to cover an event, they need to be aware of the "what, when, where, and why" well in advance. This information can be distributed quickly in a one-page summary of these facts. To target a particular media group that is not readily reached through distribution of the "one-paper" over a news wire service, it's a good idea to send the media alert by mail or messenger. This also provides an opportunity to package the alert with eye-catching press materials. If the media alert is targeted to the city desk, feature, business, or photo editors, it can be distributed to them directly through one of the commercial wire services, such as PR Newswire or Businesswire. Once the alert is distributed, it's important to follow up by telephone.

- **Backgrounder.** Backgrounders are documents that cover an entire subject area in an easy-to-read form. They are particularly useful in developing feature stories because they provide the media sufficient detail on complicated subjects. For ease of reading, the backgrounder should be written in journalistic style. It can run 20 pages or longer and may be printed or reproduced from typewritten copy.

- **White papers.** These are similar to backgrounders. The difference is that white papers focus on a company's position, and the reasons for it, concerning a controversial subject. Both white papers and backgrounders have long lives and are designed as reference pieces rather than news generality releases.

- **Photograph.** A photograph should tell a story with as little reliance on text as possible. Captions or cutlines should fully identify any individuals, things, or actions depicted. Every photo submitted for editoral consideration should be clearly marked, usually by an adhesive label on the back, with the names and affiliations of the subjects, and a contact name and telephone number for more information. Generally speaking, the media will give short shrift to photographs that are not first rate. Photographers who supply photographs to wire services can often be used on a free-lance basis to cover a company-sponsored event with the understanding that they will attempt to place the photo and caption with one of the wires.

The task of working with the media can be capsulized in a few key phrases:

- Discover and create a unique and salable story.

- Target the audience or audiences.

- Pitch the appropriate story to the appropriate media with finesse and honesty.

- Know how to use spokespersons. Make sure spokespersons are well prepared.

- Clearly identify an available person who can be contacted for more information.

# PART 2

# Public Relations
# In the Marketplace

Robert L. Dilenschneider

# Chapter 8

# Financial Public Relations

Financial relations has experienced an extraordinary growth in recent years. Probably no segment of public relations has grown faster. Several factors have contributed to this phenomenon, among which are the following:

- The increasingly intricate and constantly changing body of rules dealing with public disclosure set down by the Securities and Exchange Commission (SEC), stock exchanges, and other regulatory bodies.

- The increasing number of mergers and acquisitions and changing attitudes toward the use of high-risk, high-yield money.

- The profound changes in the basic structure and dynamics of the investment market.

- The growing importance of institutional money managers and the widening sophistication of individual shareholders.

- The recognition by corporate management that effective financial communications are essential to a company's future ability to raise capital, to grow, and to stay independent.

Before 1890, corporations generally went their laissez-faire way, with little regard for the public consequences of their actions. Passage of the Sherman Antitrust Act marked the beginning of the end of that era. By 1914, with the Clayton Act in effect and the establishment of the Federal Trade Commission authorized, it had become evident to many leaders of business and industry that public opinion was a powerful force that had to be recognized and accommodated.

The roots of financial public relations as it is practiced today, go back to the early 1930s. In the wake of the stock market crash of 1929, and with the nation languishing in the deepest economic depression it had ever endured, Congress passed two laws that set strict new standards for those issuing or trading in stocks and bonds. These laws were the Securities Act of 1933 and the implementing Securities Exchange Act of 1934. As a result, corporations were required to file detailed registration statements with the newly established Securities and Exchange Commission. They also had to provide current information by publishing annual reports. The new rules also limited insider trading and spelled out other rules to better ensure fair markets.

Underlying the Securities Act was the theory that everyone—small shareholder, broker, insider, and institutional investor—should be put on a more or less equal footing in terms of the information used in making an investment decision. To accomplish this, the rules required prompt public disclosure of developments that could affect the price of a company's stock.

In recent years, Congress, the SEC, and the courts have interpreted, expanded, revised, and occasionally confused the original statutes. Today, the practice of financial public relations is a highly specialized, demanding craft, and one which requires experience with, and respect for, the complexity of the prevailing legal requirements. But the basic principle of disclosure of important news promptly and to a broad public remains central to the subject. Public relations people, who have access to inside information and who are responsible for transmitting material information to the media need to understand the rules of financial communication.

## First Test

The first and, until recently, best known lawsuit to test and develop the disclosure laws was brought by the SEC against a corporation then called the Texas Gulf Sulphur Company. The SEC charged that various company executives, including officers, directors, and employees, used inside information (i.e., information not previously disclosed to the public) about copper ore discoveries in Canada to purchase company stock at low prices before informing the public.

The case was based on SEC Rule 10b-5, which says that no stock trader may use any scheme to defraud or "make any untrue statement of a material fact or . . . omit to state a material fact." This rule had been on the books since 1942 and had been tested in only a handful of prior cases.

The Texas Gulf Sulphur case dragged on through several courts in the late 1960s and into the 1970s. It is hard to overstate the controversy and debate that it raised in corporate and legal circles. The various decisions tended to raise as many questions as they answered and courts are still elaborating on the reach and meaning of Rule 10b-5.

The Texas Gulf Sulphur case focused intense attention on when, where, how, and to whom a company should report development. It put financial public relations on the firing line. The consequence of distributing news to a limited group or of leaking information became crystal clear: a lawsuit by regulatory authorities or individual investors who did not get an even break on the new development.

Numerous books and articles on the Texas Gulf Sulphur case and on Rule 10b-5 have been written. They deserve study by a student interested in pursuing a career in financial public relations.

## Disclosure Rules

As a direct result of the Texas Gulf Sulphur case, the New York Stock Exchange (NYSE) revised its rules on timely disclosure. Two passages in the NYSE's looseleaf "Company Manual" are worth reproducing here because they summarize some of the basic patterns of conduct expected of corporations. They read as follows:

> A listed company is expected to release quickly to the public any news or information which might reasonably be expected to materially affect the market for its securities. This is one of the most important and fundamental purposes of the listing agreement which the company enters into with the Exchange.... A listed company should also act promptly to dispel unfounded rumors which result in unusual market activity or price variations.

> News which ought to be the subject of immediate publicity must be released by the fastest available means. The fastest available means may vary in individual cases and according to the time of day. Ordinarily, this requires a release to the public press by telephone, telegraph, or hand delivery, or some combinations of such methods. Transmittal of such a release to the press solely by mail is not considered satisfactory. Similarly, release of such news exclusively to the local press outside of New York City would not be sufficient for adequate and prompt disclosure to the investing public.

> To insure adequate coverage, releases requiring immediate publicity should be given to Dow Jones & Company, Inc., and to Reuters Economic Services.

> Companies are also encouraged to promptly distribute their releases to Associated Press and United Press International as well as to newspapers in New York City and in cities where the company is headquartered or has plants or other major facilities.

> A copy of any such press release should be sent promptly to the attention of the company's Exchange representative.

In the 1980s both the volume of insider trading and the number of cases brought to court have increased. In four years of the early 1980s, the SEC took action on more cases than it had in the preceeding 32 years. Among those charged in insider cases in the New York area, according to *The New York Times,* were stock brokers, investment bankers, securities lawyers, and other Wall Street market professionals, plus a dentist, a taxi driver, a police officer, and a *Wall Street Journal* reporter. The penalties for those getting caught were made more stringent. The Insider Trading Sanctions of 1984, for example, allowed courts to impose fines of up to three times gains instead of simply requiring offenders to give up their profits. The government's late 1986 case against arbitrageur Ivan Boesky netted fines reportedly exceeding $100 million.

For all that, any clear-cut definitions of what constitutes insider trading remain elusive. In its latest sanctions legislation, Congress skirted the issue by simply applying the sanctions to those found guilty of insider trading. Under Rule 10b-5, it remains unclear exactly what is required for conviction. Lawyers indicate there should be both a breach of fiduciary duty and a misappropriation of information. However, under another SEC regulation, Rule 14e-3, legal experts say that anyone trading on inside information, no matter how they have acquired such knowledge, may be prosecuted.

In 1980, the Supreme Court in *Chiarella* v. *United States* found that an "outsider" (here, an employee of a financial printing firm) was not criminally liable for trading on inside information. The court reasoned that the employee, who invested based upon information concerning pending tender offers from materials to be printed, was not a company "insider." The court observed that he had not directly misappropriated the information from the companies, and that no relationship of trust and confidence existed between the transaction parties.

The SEC did, however, successfully institute a civil suit to force the employee to give up, under pressure, the profits he had realized.

In response to the Supreme Court's ruling in *Chiarella*, the SEC instituted Rule 14e-3. This rule requires that *any person* who obtains information about a tender offer from either the bidder, issuer, or any of the principals or employees of either entity must either publicly disclose this information or abstain from trading in shares of the company to be tendered. Further, no one may pass on such information to another, where it is reasonable to foresee that the person who receives the tip will act upon it, in violation of Rule 14e-3.

Although the purpose of Rule 14e-3 was to confer liability upon people who successively receive a tip and then traded upon material inside information, the Supreme Court in 1983 in *Dirks* v. *SEC* narrowed the scope of the rule. In *Dirks,* a brokerage analyst received information from a former company officer that the company's assets were vastly overstated as a result of corporate fraud. The analyst investigated the allegations, which were corroborated by company employees; company senior management, however, denied any wrongdoing.

Neither the analyst nor his firm owned or traded any of the company's stock, but throughout his investigation, he openly discussed the information he obtained with clients and customers, some of whom sold their holdings in the company. The price of the company's stock fell, and the SEC filed a complaint against the company.

The SEC found that the analyst was guilty of violating antifraud provisions of the securities laws, including 10b-5. The Supreme Court, however, overruled the Court of Appeals to find instead that whether a person who receives a tip is under an obligation to disclose or abstain from trading is determined by whether the insider's tip constituted a breach of the *insider's* duty to act in confidence. This breach of duty depends, in turn, upon the personal benefit the insider receives from the disclosure. There is no breach of duty to the shareholders without an improper purpose by the insider, and there is no derivative breach on the part of the person who receives the insider's tip without a breach committed by the insider.

The Supreme Court thus held that the analyst had no duty to abstain from the use of the inside information that he had obtained, and there was no resulting violation by him. He had no preexisting legal duty to the company's shareholders. Furthermore, the company's employees, as insiders, did not violate their duty to the company's shareholders by their disclosures to the analyst.

The employees were motivated by a desire to expose fraud, received no monetary or personal benefit from their disclosures, and did not intend to make a gift of valuable information to the analyst. The insiders therefore committed no breach, so there was no derivative breach by the analyst. In essence, the *Dirks* decision has taken the SEC out of the business of bringing actions against "remote tippees."

One of the continuing problems in financial public relations is the gap between theory and practice. The kind of news distribution described above by the New York Stock Exchange will put news into the hands of many people. But it clearly will not put news into the hands of absolutely every investor.

There are enormous conceptual and practical problems when news is released to the papers but not actually published, when it is sharply edited as is the case with most earnings reports, or when it contains inaccuracies through omission or mechanical error.

Likewise, there are problems when news is carried by The Dow Jones news service but not by Reuters, when different editions of the same publication carry different versions of a story, or when a reporter seeks additional information on his own initiative in connection with a material release.

The variations in problems that can occur are nearly infinite and far beyond the scope of this chapter. New developments on the subject occur frequently. Probably the best way to keep abreast of the law in this area is to read periodical business publications or consult with a securities lawyer on difficult questions.

## Growing Problems

A number of special corporate problems include proliferation of raids and takeover attempts; the evolution of many companies into conglomerates and multinational corporations, with all their attendant complexities; turbulent economic conditions worldwide; and the spawning of special interest groups demanding special attention of corporations in public meetings.

Moreover, business today must have more capital to expand and grow. But the number of individual investors who can provide that capital cheaply by buying company stocks or bonds has steadily decreased over recent years. Nowadays companies must look to the far more demanding and sophisticated managers who control the investment strategies for the billions of dollars in pension and mutual funds, insurance companies, and in other large pools of capital.

Public relations people with a high degree of knowledge of corporate financial matters are playing an increasingly important role in helping companies raise capital through their ability to deal with these demanding investors. For the institutional investor, unlike the individual investor, the question of loyalty to a particular company is rarely if ever raised. Over the past two decades these institutions have become increasingly competitive with each other, constantly seeking the highest return on their investments compatible with the lowest risk. Even when companies perform well and produce outstanding results, institutional investors may sell their stocks, preferring to take a profit and reinvest it in other stocks that they regard as undervalued.

Future demands on the public relations practitioner will be even greater, for the laws and regulations governing corporations and their securities continue to grow more numerous and complex. Changing accounting regulations also are requiring financial relations people to have additional expertise.

Dealing with the labyrinthine subtleties of financial public relations obviously is not a game for the amateur. Mistakes can be devastatingly costly both in terms of dollars and credibility lost.

Apprenticeship under the tutelage of someone who is experienced probably is the best method of learning the twists and turns of the perilous road of financial public relations. Many public relations firms and individual counselors specialize in financial public relations today. They can be of immeasurable value to a corporate public relations person whose familiarity with such matters may be limited. Colleges and universities also offer courses that are helpful to a person interested in expanding his or her knowledge of the field.

## Objective of Financial Public Relations

The objective of financial public relations is not only to inform but to interpret issues of substance for both the investor and the corporation. The investor wants relevant information about the condition of a company so that knowledgeable decisions concerning the investment attractiveness of its stocks and bonds may be made. The company, on the other hand, needs a real sense of the mood of the investor if it is to foster and maintain a healthy market for its securities.

In essence, the basic rule for promoting investor confidence is that a company through its public relations practitioners keeps the investment community, and particularly the security analysts, informed of both short- and long-term prospects and developments on a timely basis. Or as *Business Week* once warned, "Hell hath no fury like a surprised analyst."

A company's financial "publics" are a diverse lot: individuals trading in the stock market; current stockholders; stockbrokers; professional security analysts; financial institutions such as insurance companies, mutual funds, bank trust departments, and pension funds; government regulators; employees; and the business press. Each audience is reached in a variety of ways, some broad and overlapping, others sharply focused.

A company's primary means of communicating with investors, large and small, are its annual meeting, annual and quarterly reports, and required news releases on material events. Unfortunately, this is as far as some companies go in their financial communications programs. The majority, however, recognize the value of taking additional measures to stimulate investor interest.

Too many companies launch financial relations programs with scant awareness of the attitudes and opinions of the many groups they hope to inform. Management's view of itself may differ sharply from an outsider's perception. In-depth surveys of security analysts, individual shareholders, or financial editors often turn up unexpected problem areas. Armed with a carefully done survey, a company can do a far more effective job in communicating with its various publics.

### The Value of Credibility and Integrity

Flimflammery has no place in a sound financial relations program. Investors must be convinced that they are receiving the fullest information possible and that the company's integrity is unquestionable.

Uncertainty about a company's prospects can hurt its market price. But often, uncertainty only reflects a lack of knowledge on the part of the investor, a matter that can and should be corrected by providing information about a company's true condition.

Unfortunately, some practitioners have taken credit for raising stock prices above reasonable levels by employing high-flown promotional efforts. This has sometimes been possible in rising, speculative securities markets. But eventually investors measure a company's promises against its performance. When the gap is too wide, the price drops, sometimes precipitously. The company then has apparently lost credibility with the financial community. Credibility, once lost, is difficult to restore.

A certain amount of unpredictability always exists in the practice of financial public relations. A company's prices can take an adverse turn despite an admirable public relations program. Depressed industry conditions in general, for example, can hurt the individual company stock price even though the company's outlook is auspicious and its financial communications exemplary. Similarly, a company with a not-too-promising future and below-par financial communications may be pulled along with a rising stock market.

Peculiar external circumstances also influence stock prices. A chemical company that makes pesticides, for instance, may well enjoy a rise in its price should the Midwest become overrun by corn borers, for investors will be quick to recognize that the epidemic could mean rising profits for the firm.

## Legal Requirements

The Securities and Exchange Commission's Rule 10b-5 prohibits an individual or a group from taking advantage of "material information" affecting a security that is not generally available to others. Numerous court opinions and SEC interpretations have gone far in spelling out what constitutes "material information." Nevertheless, gray areas still exist that sometimes cause corporate managements and financial public relations people to worry over whether something is material, and if it is, when and how it should be made public.

In a case involving Merrill Lynch and Douglas Aircraft, the court set forth three conditions or "tests" which the Commission considers necessary to establish liability under 10b-5. The conditions apply both to "insiders" who come into possession of information in the course of their business activities, and to people who receive information from an "insider" or third party. The tests are stated as follows:

> We consider the elements (necessary to establish liability for insider trading) to be that the information be 1) material and nonpublic, 2) that the tippee, whether he receives the information directly or indirectly, know or have reason to know that it was nonpublic and had been obtained improperly by selective revelation or otherwise, and 3) that the information be a factor in his decision to effect the transaction (in the security of the company involved).

The broadened scope of the disclosure regulations has induced many companies to develop statements of policy for officers, directors, and employees to ensure compliance with the law. Financial public relations people can frequently be helpful in working with management and legal counsel in preparing such statements.

The spirit of the disclosure rules and the objectives of financial public relations are akin: securing the broadest, most timely dissemination of information important to investors. Practices that best satisfy the disclosure rules, therefore, are also generally the best financial public relations.

## Specific Situations Requiring Disclosure

Both the New York and American Stock exchanges have developed guidelines to help publicly held companies determine the types of information that generally are material and require disclosure.

Those most often encountered are:

1. Negotiations concerning acquisitions, mergers, or joint ventures.

2. Stock splits.

3. Plans for an exchange of stock or a tender offer.

4. Changes in dividend rates or earnings; declaration or omission of dividends.

5. Calls for redemption of a debt issue.

6. New mineral discoveries.

7. Annual and quarterly earnings.

8. Unfavorable news materially affecting a company.

9. Financial forecasts.

10. Additional financing (debt or equity) plans.

11. Change in management or in the control of a company.

12. Bankruptcy or Chapter X or XI proceedings.

13. Defaults on debts or contracts.

14. Write-offs.

15. Change of accounting methods.

16. Disputes with suppliers or customers or significant litigation.

17. Initiation of a program to purchase the company's own shares.

18. Important acquisition or disposition of properties.

## What To Tell a Reporter

After more than two years of discussion, a clear consensus is developing in court decisions and SEC rulings about when and how a company may disclose merger discussions. Also clarified have been the circumstances under which a company has an obligation to correct or update such disclosures.

In a recent case, the Court cited the SEC ruling In re *Carnation* and other cases to find that a company could refuse to comment on its share price rise. However, once it opted to comment, it was obligated to do so truthfully. The Court observed that the company's statement that "no negotiations" were occurring would be understood by the average investor as an absence of contacts of any kind and therefore require correction as events changed. The Court also noted that a company's silence following its denials of negotiation discussions was not the same as a silence following a lack of comment.

According to some experts on financial disclosure, the Court's assertion that a company has the option of refusing to comment at all about merger discussions seems to clarify the SEC ruling in In re *Carnation*. The decision validates the informal practice of many companies of saying "no comment" in all such circumstances.

At the same time, however, it is clear that companies choosing to comment on or respond to an Exchange or regulatory inquiry must do so truthfully, acknowledging that discussions are taking place.

A comment asserting that the company is "aware of no reason" that would explain market activity in its stock *is a comment*. If the company, in fact, *knows* the reason for the market activity but denies its awareness, it has made a false comment and is probably liable.

## Isolating Target Groups

The efforts of any corporate financial public relations program are aimed primarily at reaching two key groups: 1) individuals who buy and sell stock for themselves, and 2) professionals who make the investment decisions of institutions, or advise institutions or individuals.

Individual investors include:

**Stockholders.** Obviously, they are important because a company wants them to hold, rather than sell their shares. Moreover, their attitudes toward a company may influence others—friends, neighbors, or relatives—in making investment decisions regarding a given stock.

Stockholder loyalty also pays off when a company must repel a takeover attempt, seek backing for management proposals that require stockholder approval, or call for support when critical legislation or regulatory issues are pending. In many cases, stockholders may also be company employees or members of a company's plant community.

**Other individual investors.** People who are "in the market," who buy and sell stock regularly, are particularly important. A company needs them to ensure a liquid market for its stock and to achieve a wide distribution of stock ownership. Many companies make efforts to cultivate the individual investor to counterbalance the trend toward the concentration of large blocks of stock in the hands of a few owners, such as financial institutions. Surveys by the New York Stock Exchange and others suggest that the number of individuals who invest in stocks is declining.

The professional investors include:

**Investment analysts.** These are professionals whose business is to analyze companies and their securities and to make detailed investment recommendations. They are often called security analysts or simply analysts. Analysts may be employed by brokerage houses or independent research firms providing clients with investment counsel. In many cases, analysts supply information to, or themselves work for, banks, insurance companies, pension funds, or other financial institutions.

**Financial institutions.** These are organizations that invest funds for which they have fiduciary responsibility. The list includes insurance companies, mutual funds, bank trust departments, and pension funds.

Such institutions are an important investing influence because they buy and sell securities in volume and thus have more of an effect upon securities prices than most individual investors. Moreover, many individual investors tend to pattern their own buy/sell decisions on the actions of institutions, thus magnifying the total impact on the market.

Obviously, the degree of interest any institution may have in a particular stock depends on its assessment of the corporation's management capability and its prospects for earnings. This is a major reason the institutions are such important audiences for financial public relations programs. When an institution buys or sells a large number of stocks, and does so all at once, the effect on the price can be sharp.

Another reason for close attention to institutions in financial relations is that they have the ability to sell blocks of stock—large volumes—when this is disadvantageous to corporate management. The block may be sold to an unfriendly person or company trying to gain control of the corporation or interested in securing a position on the board of directors. Financial institutions with large holdings in a company sometimes intervene directly in the affairs of the company to the detriment of other stockholders. They can do this because of the voting power the large stockholding gives them.

At the very least, large holdings of stock by institutions means that there are fewer shares available for day-to-day trading in the stock market so that relatively small transactions may have an exaggerated impact on the price movement of the company's stock.

For all these reasons, one common objective of many financial public relations efforts is to increase the number and geographic distribution of small individual investors in a company's shares. While a company cannot control who buys and sells its shares, it can take steps to bring the stock to the attention of the kinds of investors it would like to own its shares.

**Stockbrokers.** "Registered representatives" trade for and advise individual and institutional investors. While brokers will use data developed by their own firms' research department, they may also gather information and analyze investments themselves.

## Financial Public Relations Tools

Some of the basic tools used in financial public relations to communicate with the investor audience include annual reports, quarterley reports, annual meetings, special stockholder meetings, and special stock holder communications.

- **Annual reports.** Issuing an annual report is a requirement for nearly all public companies. How far a company goes beyond the essential legal requirements in reporting on the preceding year is a matter of choice. The annual report is generally considered to be the single most important communication a company issues during the year. A candid account of important events, an explanation of the company's goals and business philosophy, sufficient operational and financial detail to satisfy the most demanding investors, crisp writing and attractive graphics all play their part in presenting a company's message to a broad range of readers beyond the stockholders for whom the report is primarily required.

The SEC has widened its requirements for the annual report. The challenge for the financial public relations person is to meet the basic requirements and, at the same time, create a readable and informative document that avoids excessive legal language and interprets the company's performance and goals in a way which will build interest and credibility in the minds of investors.

The importance of the annual report can hardly be stressed enough. More and more individual investors are analyzing stocks on their own and wish they could rely more heavily on annual reports in doing so. In The Hill and Knowlton 1985 Annual Annual Report Report, 83 percent of the individual investors interviewed reported that they analyze stocks strictly on their own or that they weigh a broker's advice with their own analysis before investing. Forty-three percent of the individuals said they invest exclusively on the basis of their own analysis.

Richard E. Cheney, chairman of Hill and Knowlton, says, "These findings show that the annual report is a golden opportunity for companies to reach individual investors, but that many managements are missing it. Companies need to answer more directly in the annual report what they are doing for their shareholders. They also need to tell their stories in a way that doesn't require a graduate degree in engineering or accounting to understand."

Individual investors questioned annual reports'

believability. A New York investor said, "To put it simply, companies need to be honest in their annuals. They rarely are."

Fifty-two percent of the individual investor sample agreed with the statement, "I often distrust what management tells me in the annual report." Eighty-two percent of the individuals agreed that annual reports often play down bad news or hide it in the back of the report.

Hill and Knowlton's 1986 survey found that annual reports now rank sixth in importance as a source of investment information.

- **Quarterly reports.** Exchange-listed companies must release quarterly results to the press. There is no requirement for a company to mail quarterly reports to stockholders. Nevertheless, most companies find it in their interests to do so. A number of companies have found that they can transfer a good deal of the communications burden of the annual report to the quarterlies by publishing through the year. The trend continues to be toward more frequent and more timely communications with shareholders.

- **Annual meetings.** The managements of many companies view the annual meeting of stockholders merely as a legal requirement that must be endured. If planned properly, however, the annual meeting can be an important forum for management to brief stockholders, other investors, and the media on recent developments and on the outlook for the firm. Some companies take the additional useful step of informing all stockholders of what went on at the annual meeting by mailing out a special post-meeting report. The post-meeting report is often combined with the first quarter report.

- **Special stockholder meetings:** A number of companies interested in cultivating their current stockholders as a key investor audience have begun holding special stockholder information meetings apart from the required annual meeting. At these meetings, management gives a presentation on new developments and answers stockholders' questions. Frequently regional meetings are held in areas of greatest stockholder concentration.

- **Special stockholder communications.** In addition to quarterly and annual reports, many companies find it beneficial to communicate with stockholders through special letters and other means. These special communications need not be issued according to a regular schedule, but can be sent whenever there is a new development to report or when management has an important message for stockholders. For example, the company might want to give shareholders the text of an important speech a member of management has made or bring a favorable article about the company to the stockholders' attention.

## Meetings with Security Analysts

Meetings with security analysts are central to most financial public relations programs. The purpose of the meetings in every case is to familiarize security analysts and the media with developments at the company.

The meetings take several forms. They may be sponsored by a Society of Security Analysts. The largest of these societies is in New York City. However, there are more than 30 societies with their own meeting schedules scattered across the country in large metropolitan and financial centers. It is generally necessary to schedule these meetings several months ahead.

The members of societies follow different industry

groups. Naturally, all the analysts who concentrate on a single industry—steel, for example, or forest products companies—have common interests. In many large cities, analysts who follow the same companies have created informal clubs called "splinter groups" because they operate independently within the main society. These splinter groups hold their own meetings for the companies they are most interested in.

Finally, a company may wish to hold its own meeting with security analysts and invite any analysts who have expressed an interest in learning more about the company.

Most companies today have assigned one person either full- or part-time to talk with analysts who call or wish to visit the company. This person may be a member of the public relations department but more frequently is assigned to the treasurer's department. Whatever the assignment, he or she must coordinate the financial public relations effort to ensure that the information flowing to analysts and to the investing public is the same in content and objective.

Fewer places change at a faster rate than the financial community where mergers and acquisitions are commonplace and the formation of new institutions an everyday affair. With $16 billion a month flowing into mutual funds, securities analysts and funds managers can and do jump ship at the ring of a phone. According to *Forbes* in its annual survey in 1986, aptly entitled "The Maddening Multiplicity for Funds," there were then no fewer than 1,339 mutual funds.

Keeping track of which analysts do—and, even more important, should—cover a particular company takes time. Increasingly, in-house investor relations executives are turning to the larger public relations firms to help them reach the institutions that matter most when it comes to buying their securities. This can be done either by arranging individual meetings or by making presentations before groups of analysts.

Both candor and detailed operating and financial data are essential for effective analyst presentations. The information should also be presented in a form that makes it easier for the analysts to do their jobs quickly and well.

Above all, the company must be careful to avoid surprises in its financial communications. Unexpected lower (or higher) earnings, dividend cuts, and the failure of an apparently healthy operation are examples of surprises. There is an old saying that "Wall Street hates surprises." The reason is clear. Since analysts have the responsibility for following a company, a surprise means that they have not been doing their job as well as they should. A surprise also means either that management has not been as aware as it should be of problems at the company or that the company knew the facts but concealed them.

In any case, a surprise piece of news can hurt the company's reputation in the financial community. It bears repeating that credibility is difficult to build and once lost is doubly hard to regain.

## Other Activities for Reaching Professional Investors

In addition to in-person and group meetings, other forms of communications are suitable for reaching the professional investment community. They are as follows:

- **Research efforts.** In developing or evaluating a financial public relations program, it is best first to learn something about attitudes toward the company. A useful procedure is to conduct an objective opinion survey of individual shareholders, security analysts who follow the company or its industry, and institutional investors. The findings of the survey then serve as a factual foundation to help formulate the goals for the financial public relations program.

- **Analyst tours.** Many companies invite groups of analysts on tours of their facilities. Analyst tours are particularly effective in cases where the opportunity to view operations firsthand adds to the analysts' depth of understanding of the company or the industry. New facilities or new production processes offer special tour opportunities.

- **Financial fact books.** In their work, investment analysts must assemble and analyze data on companies as the basis on which to draw conclusions and prepare recommendations. To obtain a reservoir of basic data, they often turn to information sources that can often go beyond the message of the annual report. A company can make the analyst's job easier by providing a specially prepared fact book presenting all the basic information of greatest importance.

- **Supplemental material.** To keep development at a company before the analyst, as well as to provide pertinent, updated information, many companies send their supplemental materials, such as significant news releases or reprints of articles having a bearing on the company.

- **Publicity.** The value of publicity should not be overlooked in financial public relations planning. The subject is covered in the next chapter.

## Preparing for Takeovers

The growth in takeovers—both hostile and friendly—has increased at a rapid clip, so much so that by the mid-1980s many began to wonder if enforcement of antitrust legislation by the Federal Trade Commission and the Justice Department belonged to another era. Corporate takeovers are of two types, but the demarcation lines keep blurring as savvy raiders continually add new wrinkles.

In *tender offers,* an individual, company, or group offers to buy shares from another company's stockholders at a premium price above the current market price. A tender offer also may come from a company's own management in the form of a leveraged buyout, often with issued shares being exchanged for high-yield, high-risk bonds.

In *proxy contests,* the adversaries vie for control of a company by seeking to replace some or all of the members of the board of directors with people who share their ideas for the company's future.

Whereas there used to be a distinction between tender offers and proxy fights, by the mid-1980s it has become increasingly apparent that these really were alternative strategies to attain the same end. As long as Wall Street has the funds and appetite, it appears that changes in corporate ownership will continue to occur at a fast clip.

To keep their raiders at bay, defending companies are resorting to increasingly complex stratagems. Among them are the following:

- Open market purchase of their own shares. Carter Hawley Hale, the department store group, bought more than half its outstanding common shares in the open market during a seven-day trading period. This unusual response stood up under court challenges by both the raider—The Limited, Inc.—and the SEC.

- Launching a self-tender as part of the defensive efforts. Facing a takeover by Northwest Industries, Pogo Producing Co. launched a self-tender that was upheld in court, even though, as the court noted, one of the principal purposes of the self-tender was to defeat a partial bid for Pogo.

- Threatening to sell the crown jewels—the defender's best assets—before the raider can take control. Such a ploy is by no means certain to succeed as the courts have ruled both in favor of and against such sales.

Most public companies have put in place a variety of defenses, including staggering the election of directors and fair-price provisions that seek to guarantee that all shareholders (not just large holders or the first to respond to an offer) will receive the same "fair" price for their shares. While it is true that invariably what carries the day is the value placed upon the outstanding shares, there is an important role for public relations specialists to play before that valuation is reached.

In a speech to the Financial Executives Institute, here's how a veteran of takeover contests during the past three decades, Richard E. Cheney, described the role for public relations in any takeover or proxy fight:

> Public relations is essential to the routine communications surrounding any tender offer, proxy fight, or leveraged buy-out, friendly or unfriendly. In connection with such transactions, there are often dozens, sometimes scores, of releases to be prepared and distributed, dealing with significant events in the course of the offer—such milestones as the commencement of the offer, litigation, court decisions, the end of the proration period, Hart-Scott-Rodino developments, charges, and countercharges.
>
> Often, the company's inside public relations department is very good at news dissemination insofar as routine corporate developments are concerned. But in the high-pressure atmosphere of a proxy fight or tender offer, it simply doesn't have the manpower and the experience of dealing with lawyers and investment bankers to be as effective as it is under ordinary circumstances.
>
> At a minimum the financial public relations practitioner will be involved in:
>
> - Preparing and issuing press releases and answering reporters' questions.
> - Preparing letters to shareholders in connection with the offer.
> - Preparing paid advertisements for newspapers setting forth management's side of the story.
> - Securing appropriate publicity.

In addition, some public relations agencies have moved into the information agent role, providing street-name holders (those who keep their stock in the broker's name and who aren't identified in the company's shareholder records) with all key information on the offer. The agency also may send key documents, such as complaints and court decisions, to the arbitrage community, which plays a key role in the modern takeover battle.

Tender offers and proxy contests both come under close regulation of the federal securities laws. These laws affect what may, and may not be said, what *must* be said, and the clearance and timing of communications. In recent years, the rules governing tender offers have been made even more strict to protect stockholders from being stampeded or cheated.

To function effectively in tender or proxy contests and to avoid lawsuits, a financial public relations practitioner must have a firm grasp of all the applicable regulations.

## International Financial Relations

Capital markets have been increasing in number on the international scene. Due in part to the buildup of large dollar deposits in foreign central banks in Europe and Japan, many of the larger American companies are working actively to establish markets for their stocks internationally. For example, companies have been listing on foreign stock exchanges and publishing their annual reports in foreign languages. These measures also help ease the way for obtaining financing from foreign banks. Companies periodically visit institutional investors and financiers in Europe and Japan. Such efforts will probably be increased in the future as overseas capital markets become more important.

## The Future of Financial Public Relations

The securities markets and the economy continue to undergo fundamental changes that affect investor attitudes. Factors such as negotiated commission rates, energy scarcity and environmental concerns, and demands for greater social responsibility by business are part of the changing investment scene.

At the same time, American business must raise more capital than ever before to build new productive capacity. After a few fallow years, corporations in the mid-1980s again found they could tap into a rich stream of funding by coming to market with new equity issues. These new equity financings can only succeed to the degree that business is able to get its story across to the investor, and the degree to which investors trust the companies.

Financial public relations probably appears static and unchanging to outsiders. However, quite the opposite is true. Few areas of public relations change so rapidly. There are numerous fads in the practice. One example was the trend toward elaborate and costly annual reports, which occurred in the late 1960s. Today, annual reports may look less expensive but contain far more solid information. Today there is a renewed interest in finding economical and efficient means to reach stockbrokers directly. It is too early to tell where this interest will lead.

In addition, the underlying rules of financial public relations—and there are many of them—can change dramatically. Each court decision or new rule from the SEC alters to some extent the way in which financial public relations is carried out. There is under way now a long-term review of the entire conceptual basis of disclosure that is sure to alter significantly the practice of financial public relations.

Against this background, then, the best guidance one can offer is simply to keep as current as possible with new developments and to examine each seemingly routine financial public activity to make certain that it is helpful and relevant.

With business and financial relations spreading to ever-broadening horizons, the challenges and situations that develop pose new opportunities for public relations involvement.

While only a few years ago, it seemed that business and financial relations were limited to annual or quarterly reports, personnel, or product developments, today's practitioner is confronted with complexities that can be downright mind-boggling.

Public relations people have contributed to the solution of board room problems as divergent as investor skepticism; a corporate name change; recovery from bankruptcy; restoring analysts' support; propping up sagging employee morale; helping a new and relatively unknown business raise public funds; and assuaging fears about the largest corporate bankruptcy in history.

## Some Cases in Point

A case in point was the growing concern of investors about the earning potential of companies in biotechnology. A spate of acquisitions and mergers resulted in very powerful competition for Cetus Corporation, which is involved in the application of genetic engineering and health care products. Desirous of becoming a biotech leader, Cetus initiated an investor relations effort to establish the credibility of its new management, and to position itself as a leader in cancer research and as a dominant presence in the pharmaceutical industry. It also wished to expand market sponsorship and ownership of its securities.

Taking its case to the financial community, Cetus made presentations to 19 groups of analysts and portfolio managers. It also participated in one-on-one meetings with 29 investment firms in key markets. Concurrently, senior management met with financial medical and science writers. Within a year, Cetus was repositioned as a world leader in biotechnology and esteemed in the international pharmaceutical market. Its institutional sponsorship increased by 65 percent; "market makers" doubled to 44 percent and diversified to new geographic regions; trading volume leapt 466 percent and Cetus' stock price tripled to a new high.

In another instance, management at Consolidated Foods Corporation came to believe its name no longer communicated the nature of its business and had lost its appeal to the financial community. Research substantiated that companies known by brand names received higher price-to-earnings ratios and stock market evaluations.

A public relations task force, backed by comprehensive research, recommended that Sara Lee, a Consolidated Foods brand name projected the desired characteristics: quality, stability, strong marketing, and other connotations that appealed to consumers. With management and shareholder approvals, new graphics, media kits, multilanguage videotapes, and individual letters (answering the most frequently asked questions) were distributed throughout six countries where the company operated.

A pair of special events dramatized the changed name. At the New York Stock Exchange, brokers and traders received painters' caps, lapel buttons, and tie clips bearing the new name and trading symbol. A flag, emblazoned with the symbol, flew outside the Exchange. In Chicago, the company entertained officials of the Midwest Stock Exchange at a breakfast that featured products of the company's Hillside Farms and L'eggs divisions. More than 300 publications, reaching approximately 75 million people, reported the change, and the company's price-earnings ratio increased from 9.5 to 15. *Fortune* magazine applauded the company and its improved reputation.

Another good example concerns Navistar. After International Harvester Company completed the sale of its beleaguered agricultural equipment manufacturing unit, the company sought guidance in establishing a new corporate identity. Navistar International Corporation was selected as the new company name. In addition to changing its name, the company wanted to introduce a financially healthy "new" company, promote its management in the medium and heavy truck market, and rebuild weakened employee morale and management support.

Navistar was introduced simultaneously to all of the firm's 15,000-plus employees around the world via live satellite transmission from Chicago. Production lines to every plant were halted so that employees could be a part of the historic moment via large-screen video. Smaller company facilities were equipped with loudspeaker systems to receive audio transmission of the announcement. In addition, toll-free telephone numbers enabled retirees and off-duty employees to listen as well.

Immediately after the employee announcement, a news conference was held at corporate headquarters. Supplementing these major activities were several additional events:

- Local media briefings in plants throughout North America.

- A video news release transmitted via satellite to television stations nationwide.

- AP and UPI audio feeds to more than 1,900 radio stations.

- A new corporate capabilities brochure.

- A new annual report, reflecting the name and identity change.

- Two 90-second video programs for employees.
- A stockholders' meeting to "officially" announce the corporation's new name.
- A meeting with key financial analysts and a ceremony, held on the floor of the New York Stock Exchange, to mark the first Navistar stock purchase.

The Navistar public relations program was a full-scale undertaking that produced maximum impact on a broad range of audiences. It was coordinated, in both content and timing, with a national advertising campaign, and organized in secrecy that was maintained until the day of the announcement. Although the success of the program was obvious, the reward for the public relations counselors came when the Navistar executives said it was "the best communications program" the company had ever done.

This is but one example of media relations in action. Most campaigns are narrower in focus; but the size of the program does not diminish the importance of the effort.

After the former parent company of Toys "R" Us struggled through a complex bankruptcy that dragged across four years, and the toy maker emerged as an independent company, it sought to establish rapport with its investor group, the financial community, the media, and the public. A public relations program was developed to communicate Toys "R" Us stability and individuality with the company's shareholders, bankers, real estate developers, suppliers, and customers. The following were:

- The company's continuous profitable growth despite the bankruptcy of its former parent.
- The unchanged management that included founder-chairman Charles Lazarus.
- The loyal customer base.
- Its merchandising strategy.

The consistent message netted positive results. Within four years, Toys "R" Us stock climbed from 3 to 30 and was split twice. Management was frequently invited to address broker-sponsored symposia on the retail trade, and the company became a retailing favorite, with institutions owning about 70 percent of its common stock. Less than three years after its rebirth as an independent company, Morgan Stanley investment brokers underwrote a $50 million issue of convertible debentures for the company.

When Lorimar, producer of top-rated television shows—Dallas, Knots Landing, and Falcon Crest—went public, it gained little stock market recognition. Investor perception was also blurred by its acquisition of the Kenyon & Eckhardt advertising agency.

A three-pronged investor relations program was developed following a series of strategy meetings with Lorimar management. The program aimed at the following:

- Promoting greater awareness of the company and its American Stock Exchange (AMEX) listing.

- Educating analysts on the company's potential.

- Reaffirming management's strength through business page coverage.

Media coverage reiterated the three objectives.

Arrangements were made for corporate officials to meet with the investment community at eight locations to explain its move to the AMEX. To preclude OTC market-maker dumping and softer market pricing, Lorimar informed all 151 analysts, 600 key brokers, and 534 institutions of the reasons for its move to the AMEX. At the time of the listing, which was announced with appropriate fanfare, management met with 86 analysts at five presentations. The quarterly and annual reports were redesigned to tell management's story forcefully.

Within 12 months, Lorimar's price-earnings ratio rose from 11 to 20—more than double management's original objective—and the shareholder base grew 43 percent. The number of institutional holders doubled. Wall Street coverage of Lorimar doubled to 17 reports, fueling a net gain of $11.4 million in investments in contrast to an industry loss of $48 million. When a year-old company in a relatively new, unknown business needed to raise public funds, its problems were compounded by the fact it had yet to produce a profit and could offer prospective shareholders only the promise of the future.

Research showed neither major money management organizations nor leading retail industry security analysts had more than casual knowledge of the warehouse merchandising business and Denver-based PACE Membership Warehouse, Inc. Prior to its initial public offering, PACE acted to take the usual step of distributing an intentionally modest annual report. The report served its purpose of describing PACE, its financial position, and its growth prospects. About the same time, PACE's management was introduced to market makers in key cities. Media kits and appropriate financial information were channeled to all media. The unorthodox approach resulted in the leading retail industry securities analyst featuring PACE in his report on the new industry, even though PACE, at that point, was still privately held.

When the initial public offering (IPO) was made, media coverage was extensive. The IPO included a million more shares than the company's underwriter expected. Institutional investors gobbled up 75 percent of the original offering. PACE's unusual approach paid handsome dividends.

# Chapter 9

# Business and Financial Publicity

When public relations first became a business early in this century, the lion's share of the day-to-day activity centered on press relations, as the principal means of reaching the masses was the nation's newspapers.

Many a seasoned veteran will admit that most crucial problems—whether consumerism, investor relations, or a sensitive issue that might affect a company's reputation—involve discussions, many meetings, much soul-searching, and elaborate programs. However, nothing *happens* until the matter reaches influential audiences.

This can be particularly true of business and financial media relations. Companies need visibility in order to be understood and accepted, and one of the most efficient and least costly ways to gain this visibility is through publicity. Two elements are usually necessary for successful business publicity: a substantive matter and a news peg. The substantive matter is fairly self-explanatory: It should be of significance to the ultimate reader, listener, or viewer. The acquisition of one company by another is usually sufficiently important; the fact that the company is celebrating its tenth anniversary is not.

A news peg is the reason for the story, the "hook" on which it is hung. For example, the profile of a company, although interesting, may not be newsworthy unless some event happens within a certain time frame. If the president is elected to chairman and chief executive officer, this could provide a peg for a corporate profile on the company. Another peg would be going over the billion dollar sales level for the first time.

The business daily most large companies like coverage in is *The Wall Street Journal.* Next comes *The New York Times.* The reason is simple: These are the two most widely read newspapers by the decision-makers on Wall Street and in Washington, and the two that day in and day out most thoroughly cover what's truly important in business affairs. But even with their greatly expanded news coverage, the *Journal* and the *Times* cannot report every piece of news generated by the business community. Far from it. On most days these papers end up with several pages of stories left in overset.

## Growing Media Interest

Fortunately for both publicists and business people, media interest in business and economic affairs has grown over the past two decades. Advertisers have learned that business publications are excellent vehicles for carrying a broad range of messages. As a result, there are many other publications and increasingly more broadcast outlets that will take such stories.

High up on any national media program should be the *Dow Jones* and *Reuters* news services, with their links to the investment community and almost all leading publications, as well as the Associated Press and United Press International news wires. With national circulations, for example, there are *USA Today; Investors Daily;* the *Journal of Commerce,* redesigned by its new owners, Knight Ridder; and even an import, the *Financial Times* of London.

More specialized and interpretive coverage is given by the weekly *Barron's; Business Week;* and the *Economist,* another import from England; and by the bimonthly *Fortune* and *Forbes* plus the monthly *Dun's Business, Institutional Investor,* and *Financial World.* Other print possibilities include the newsweeklies *Time, Newsweek,* and *U.S. News & World Report,* although these tend to concentrate more on broad-gauged, economic trend stories with mass appeal than on specialized news of interest only to business people. For smaller companies with interesting stories describing how they achieved success and fortune, there are *Inc.* and *Venture.*

Regionally, most local newspapers, with the *Los Angeles Times, Washington Post, Chicago Tribune,* and *Miami Herald* in the vanguard, have expanded their business and economic coverage, often devoting to it a special section several times a week. Not to be overlooked are the specialist regional publications such as *Crain's New York Business* and *Crain's Chicago Business,* plus a number of glossy monthlies, such as *Manhattan, Inc.,* which feature the human side of business leaders. Opportunities for editorial briefings are available with top editors at all the leading publications, provided executives have something noteworthy and provocative to say.

An equally important change in business journalism in the mid-1980s was the growing realization among broadcast executives that what worked and sold advertising in print would do the same in television and radio. Led by the cable industry, and aided by their newly found ability to generate graphics that enhance the presentation, a plethora of television shows devoted to business, financial, and economic affairs began emerging. Such shows include the MacNeil/Lehrer Report and the Nightly Business Report on Public Broadcasting, Cable News Network's Money Line and Pinnacle, and day-long business and stock market reports on Financial News Network. Not to be outdone, the major networks have begun to present business news shows of their own.

## Work with Bureaus

Some specifics will be helpful. It's best to work with the nearest bureau of *The Wall Street Journal* if a company is located outside New York. One of the unwritten rules is that headquarters won't try to scoop the hinterlands. Story ideas should go to the bureau chief or another contact there.

Something many people in investor and public relations forget is that *The Wall Street Journal* and Dow Jones are two separate entities under the same umbrella. Appearing on the ticker (the Dow Jones wire service, also called the "broad tape") does not ensure *Wall Street Journal* pickup. One way to stimulate appearing in print as well as on the DJ wire is to phone people on the *Journal* responsible for certain news categories to let them know a story in their bailiwick is on the ticker so that they can be on the lookout for it. In most instances, the Dow Jones item will be directed to them, but if they are alerted beforehand they can start to make plans.

Say a news release is in the field of banking. A public relations staff member reads the story, usually in the form of a news release, over the telephone to the proper person at Dow Jones. It appears thereafter on the ticker. The public relations person then phones the banking editor of the *Journal* to let him know of the ticker story. The editor may ask a few questions. In most instances, he'll simply express his thanks and ask where a contact can be reached if there are any follow-up questions. Chances are fair the ticker story will be printed in some form by the *Journal*. The availability of space, of course, will be one of the deciding factors.

It is usually not a good idea to call a story in to *The New York Times*. If a story has been transmitted over *PRNewswire* (the national newswire service that transmits releases to news media and financial institutions for a fee paid by the organization issuing the release), it will be read. If it has made the Dow Jones wire, chances are it will be read again. There is no harm in sending a back-up copy of the release by hand, if the firm is in New York, but sending a messenger with a release has some built-in negatives. There are the security provisions at a newspaper that frequently prevent the messenger from getting into the news operation. Hand deliveries can sit for some time before they arrive at the desk of the person for whom they're intended. In the case of *The Wall Street Journal,* all hand deliveries are automatically moved to one main desk unless they're marked "Personal and Confidential" for a particular individual.

## Offer an Outline

For a more in-depth, feature story, it's always best to outline the idea on paper, direct it to the person responsible for the particular news category or one of the editors, then give it time to be read. If the public relations staff doesn't hear by phone or letter, it's acceptable practice to call at a time when the publication is not "closing" (approaching the printing or broadcast deadline) to discuss the story and get first-hand reaction.

One publication that does not leave a public relations staff hanging is the Sunday business section of *The New York Times.* If the story idea hits paydirt, the staff normally receives a phone call. If it doesn't, the busy but interested editor normally sends a courteous note explaining why not.

*Business Week, Fortune, Barron's,* and *Forbes* all have their special approaches. Suffice it to say that if the public relations staff has news, it has a ready audience in the editors of *Business Week.* And although it is a general business newsmagazine competing with TV and with other publications, it has a very special audience composed primarily of business people.

A quick look *Business Week*'s masthead (the publishers information and list of personnel at the front of the publication) shows there are plenty of people to contact about story ideas. In New York the best contacts are the 20 or so department editors, who are specialists on such topics as management, money, energy, and information processing. They have a large say about what goes into the magazine each week, always subject, of course, to final approval by the six top editors.

For firms outside New York, the best starting point is the *nearest* bureau. The next best step is to write a brief story outline and direct it to the department editor closest to the company's basic business line, following up a week or so later by phone.

## Working with Fortune

*Fortune* still follows its own paths to business news. Ideas are generated by the staff, and editors and reporter-researchers do much of their own digging, but there is a growing interest in story ideas from the outside. Several dozen corporation stories are published each year (not all as flattering as some companies might wish them to be), and there are management stories and corporate profiles on colorful business personalities.

There are *Fortune* editors in cities across the U.S.— Washington D.C., Chicago, Dallas, Menlo Park (outside San Francisco), Pittsburgh—who have time to listen to story ideas.

There is still time, too, for *Fortune* editorial luncheons, a time-honored format for conversation between editors and top executives. *Fortune* likes to initiate these, although a public relations professional can always make suggestions. Clear ground rules about on or off-the-record comments must be agreed upon because the ultimate aim by *Fortune* is to turn the meeting into material for articles that may range far afield from the platform sought by the executive. The *Fortune* editors want innovative management stories that are of interest to the magazine's readers. It even provides a column, *Other Voices,* that is devoted to the unconventional, provocative, and contrarian views of business executives.

In line with their "management story" concept, one editor explained that "if your company or client has come up with an unusual and really innovative way of compensating executives, this might not be a corporation story, but it might be the springboard for a story on executive compensation. We like to hear about your ideas."

One of the stories often neglected is the industry story, in which a company is setting a trend in its industry or perhaps benefiting from a trend. The public relations staff should let *Fortune* know on an exclusive basis for an initial period, and the chances of getting coverage can be good.

## Ideas for Barron's

When it comes to *Barron's,* the editors say they have a "singular view about any prospective story. It must be news; it must say something fresh; there has to be a point to it." What the magazine prides itself on most are thoughtful analyses on which readers can, in part, base investment decisions.

Individual company stories can get a strong play in *Barron's.* Consistently most of these articles deal with companies on the upbeat. But *Barron's* does not shy away from writing the obits for high fliers that have been forced down to earth.

Many of its articles are generated in-house, but it draws a greater number of its basic story ideas from two prime functions: reading and talking. Says one editor: "Apart from countless press releases, annual reports, market letters, industry studies, we get close to 100 trade publications—from *Aviation Week* to *Variety,* and a few from abroad such as the *London Mining Journal* and believe me, they are read. We

159

also do a lot of talking—to people on the street, to presidents and financial executives, to economists, to government officials. I once figured I speak in the course of the year to no fewer than 500 company representatives.

## Aiming at Forbes

*Forbes* likes to think its editors and writers are drama critics who take up where newspapers and newsmagazines leave off. "We render criticism, favorable and unfavorable, and sometimes mixed" is the way one senior editor puts it, adding, "We want to know who's helped and who's hurt."

*Forbes* prides itself on being concise and pungent and along the way has gained a reputation for being "unlovable." It tries to be as factual as possible but at the same time express opinion: Is the company good or bad? Has its management succeeded or failed?

*Forbes* is primarily interested in significant events or trends in big companies that affect performance. The editors still lean toward companies with a volume of at least $100 million because of anticipated high reader interest and high volume of shares to be traded. But increasingly it seeks out personality pieces on how entrepreneurs have made their fortunes for the "Up-and-Comers" section. *Forbes* now has a bureau office in major U.S. areas as well as a Pacific Bureau and a European Bureau. These bureau chiefs and reporters will listen to story ideas.

The magazine is not hostile to public relations people unless its reporters encounter difficulties. One shouldn't hide when a call comes from *Forbes*. A reporter can always talk to a firm's competition, people on Wall Street who know the company, and others who might possibly do a company harm. In the long run, a story with both pluses and minuses is a lot more believable than a fan magazine piece. And what characteristic is more wanted on the corporate scene than believability?

## Wire Services

While the Dow Jones wire service is devoted exclusively to business and financial news, three other services also cover such information: the Associated Press (AP), the United Press International (UPI), and Reuters. The most accessible for business news is Reuters; the AP and UPI are more concerned with general news.

Reuters, although far smaller than Dow Jones in this country, insists business news be transmitted to it simultaneously with Dow Jones. If the public relations staff slights Reuters, it can expect a knuckle-wrap or worse—the staff's next approach being ignored. One of the best opportunities for public relations people with Reuters is their "Talking Point" wherein an executive can discuss his company or industry and see his views come over the Reuters ticker in banks and brokerage houses.

The public relations staff must ensure its idea is solid before approaching AP or UPI. The business staffs of both are lean. Their prime concerns are Wall Street and the effect of federal regulatory agencies on business. Their time is strictly limited for corporate information, with one exception: the genuinely good business feature, especially if it indicates a trend. The results can be rewarding. An AP or UPI story may be picked up by hundreds of newspapers.

## Radio and TV

Many people in public relations tend to overlook radio and television when trying to publicize business and financial news. Until recently, broadcast coverage was scant but, as noted above, this is changing. From the early morning to the late night shows, stories about business can no longer be ignored by broadcasters. This must be kept in mind, especially if a story has the kind of visual impact required by television. In addition, the public relations staff must always be sure company executives are fully trained in the correct ways of handling broadcast interviews, which have their own approaches and often differ widely from interviews with the print media.

## Local Interest

If a story is genuinely strong news, it will frequently be moved by the news wires to the major newspapers. But there are times when the interest will be primarily regional or even local. What is good for the *Chicago Tribune,* the *Boston Globe,* the *Atlanta Constitution,* or the *Los Angeles Times* may not be what is good for *The Wall Street Journal* or *New York Times,* which are national in scope.

Before the public relations staff approaches regional publications, it must be certain there is a good reason. A new plant opening in Akron, Ohio, is a rationale for zeroing in on the *Akron Beacon Journal,* but it may mean nothing to other publications.

## Making Contacts

The public relations staff must stay in close contact with the people who write business stories. "I overheard a discussion that went something like this," reported a veteran publicist, "One man speaking was the communications vice president for one of the top *Fortune* 500 companies." The incident was reported as follows:

> "We've changed so much during the past five years," he said. "There was a time we had to live with newspapermen, but fortunately we've advanced to the point where 90 percent of our activity is involved with strategy. Company statements speak for themselves."
>
> He reminisced about the press agentry aspects of his early days. "I don't think that today I know a single editor by his first name," he said proudly.
>
> One week after this conversation the chief executive officer of the company represented by this man was spotlighted in a major magazine

in a piece that tore the company apart. No sooner had the smoke lifted when a nationally read newspaper published a series of articles that seriously damaged the company's reputation.

Trading of the company's stock was halted. Irate shareholders' letters poured into the executive suite. Wire services hummed with the unhappy news and into the living rooms of most American homes tumbled the story of the big bad company. The company now wonders if it can move its annual meeting from New York to East Overshoe.

In both cases, the company had been offered the opportunity for interviews and backgrounders. But believing it was "above it all," the opportunities were turned down. The media then turned to security analysts, other companies in the industry and even ex-employees for information.

This situation is not all that isolated. In "letting company statements speak for themselves," the public relations staff had tried to operate divorced from the reality and the necessity of that old-fashioned function we have been examining: press relations. In their efforts to become strategists, they had dropped the ball.

## Working with the CEO

It is not too difficult to trace how some corporations have reached this impasse in their corporate policies and communications activities. The typical corporate chieftain has worked long and hard to reach the pinnacle. His background is finance or sales, engineering, or law. He has a head that seeks the pragmatic solution, that is impatient with the esoteric. He spends much of his time with people who are his subordinates, or his paid consultants, and he can easily become isolated from the world outside his organization. To some who run our corporations, public relations is something to be "put up with," intangible activities run mostly by people who have the ability to make their speeches sound good and their annual reports reasonably palatable. The real possibility of a crisis of instantaneous communications—when five unfavorable lines in *The Wall*

*Street Journal* can seriously hurt a $500-million corporation—is, in some cases, just beginning to get through to the corporate consciousness.

Human nature, training, and experience being what they are, there may be a subtle built-in antipathy between top executives and their public relations people. However, as the organization's conduit to the outside world at large, the public relations person must ask the tough questions first—if no one else inside is willing to, he or she must poke holes in management's arguments to ensure they are credible and persuasive.

## Better Understanding

CEOs deal with the developing new breed of communications-public affairs strategists—men or women who not only understand the media but have a grasp of economics; can read and understand the balance sheet; know their way around Washington; and can fathom a problem and see it in its full context of legal, governmental, social, and economic ramifications—and they come to recognize public relations as a vital aid to management. But although the smart CEOs see the necessity of the concept, they often do not yet see around them the public relations people who can strategize and implement it. Why else have some companies turned to lawyers to supervise their public relations departments?

CEOs themselves are changing, too. They know increasingly that the corporation is not a fiefdom unto itself, that it must stand up to scrutiny of the business and financial media, of protesting shareholders, of determined and ambitious legislators, of organized consumers and environmentalists, of employees who realize the company cannot exist without them.

The newspaperman or woman or broadcaster has changed as well. No longer is the newspaper office staffed by friendly souls who will take a release and slap a headline on it. Bernstein and Woodward brought down the White House, and many a newspaper reporter now has at least one eye on the Pulitzer Prize. The other eye is on the front page, where more and more business news appears.

No longer will you find that a newswriter is a graduate of the publication's morgue. If not a Neiman Fellow at Harvard, he or she at least may have earned one graduate degree or written a book. And financial writers are increasingly adept at analyzing complex corporate finance matters.

## Honesty as a Policy

Of the many tasks with which the business publicist is faced, the primary one is to present the best face of the company, association, or client. The best face is the honest face. The public relations professional must comply with full disclosure requirements, present the financial and corporate facts without frills or unnecessary footnotes, keep up with the deadlines, and never varnish the truth. The practitioner who does this will be a reasonably satisfied and quite competent public relations person.

But it is not always that easy. What is full disclosure? How can a firm avoid confusing footnotes on such complex matters as LIFO, fully diluted earnings, and foreign exchange transactions, when lawyers and accountants often can't agree? Can you always be absolutely certain that what crosses your desk is absolutely authentic when acquisitions are hovering in the background, steeped in frustrating but necessary mystery, or when the board room door suddenly opens and someone says, "Get this on the wires immediately!"

The public relations person doesn't want to be merely a conduit between the executive suite and the media. He or she doesn't want to have to say superiors are "traveling and can't be reached" when that means they're somewhere between the lobby and the executive dining room. We all have to live with the facts of life and no one is more aware of that than members of the press. Here is a little practical advice. Publicists should:

- Try to expose their top people to the media.

- Keep the company or client updated on the rapidly changing backdrop to the increasingly important world of business and financial media relations.

- Stay on top of the constant changes in regulations coming out of Washington.

- Use press conferences sparingly, but expand the use of the editorial briefing.

- Expunge all traces of puffery from written materials.

- Respect deadlines as if they themselves were the business editors.

- Try to keep more than the organization in mind while performing everyday duties. Respect the fact that consumers, regulators, and reporters have matters other than your company on their minds.

The public relations staff should give high priority to face-to-face meetings between the company chieftains and editors, writers, and publishers who help shape and inform the public mind. The CEO and his advisers may be a bit gun-shy because they have been burned in the past by distortions or omissions. If they stay in the closet, however, they'll pay a price. Falsehoods and conjectures thrive in a vacuum. As the catalyst, the public relations professional must bring the corporate and media minds together so that trust and confidence can flourish.

## A Specific Instance

A company some years ago was continually described by one of the newsweeklies as "sickly" and "ailing." Customers were wary, shareholders disturbed, employees dubious, security analysts skeptical, editors cynical. A great deal of the malaise could be traced to repeated quotes from an unflattering series of articles published by a powerful magazine. A casual discussion with the magazine's editor disclosed that as the final copy arrived on his desk, he would insert disastrous adjectives. "You can't convince me that company is well-managed!" he said.

As a consequence, the public relations counsel arranged a meeting between the editor and the corporate leader. The editor's staff peppered the CEO with tough questions. He never flinched. Every corporate rock was lifted. Realization dawned on the editor and his people that here was a man knocking himself out to put the whole company together. Within a month, the magazine published one of its longest corporate profiles about the company. It read almost like advertising copy. In due time, all the negative elements changed. This CEO still says, "That story was the turning point!"

## Calling a News Conference

Some public relations people believe a news conference should be called whenever there is "news." One who falls into this trap will become the boy who cried wolf too often. The editorial briefing or backgrounder could be the answer. This technique allows matters to be aired, questions to be pinned down, and the media to be kept abreast of new developments without the circus atmosphere—and the responsibilities—of the press conference. Before the public relations staff calls a news conference, it must ask one question: "Is this the best approach in this area?" Other techniques are more effective in most cases, although not nearly as gratifying to the egos of those who like to make announcements in the spotlight.

Finally, not a line should emerge from a company that is not a fact, as best the public relations staff can determine.

# Chapter 10

# Corporate and Trade Association Public Relations

The term "corporate public relations" (CPR) has often been misunderstood or assigned a low level of strategic priority because it is general in nature and appears to refer to no particular element within the organizational framework. The tendency on the part of bottom-line-oriented managers to regard corporate public relations as a luxury, or an amenity, is now, for the most part, a thing of the past. Events and attitudes have altered the business climate over the past 20 years, and today top executives in virtually every industry recognize that no aspect of a company's public relations program is more vital to long-term stability and growth than its efforts in the area of corporate affairs. In effect, through the need created by rapid change, corporate public relations has redefined and asserted itself.

Corporate public relations differs from other public relations disciplines in that it does not support *directly* any of a company's specific operational functions, such as marketing, sales, promotion, customer relations, or financial and investor relations. Each of these other functions deals with a carefully focused or technically precise set of circumstances and objectives, and each is ideally supported by a public relations program targeted at a well-defined audience. Corporate public relations, on the other hand, is concerned with the company as a whole, with its identity in the public mind, and with the way in which it is perceived by many audiences as a supplier of goods and services, as a well-managed enterprise, and as an active and responsible citizen of the community. In many respects, it can be said that the purpose of corporate public relations is the creation and maintenance of a reputation that is greater than the sum of its parts. To confine the role of corporate public relations to such a lofty and all-encompassing ideal, however, would be to overlook both its value in policy and strategy development, and its essential place in the shifting world of competitive, social, and political reality.

## The Corporate Climate

Corporations, like people, exist in a complex environment with which they must interact and upon which they must ultimately depend for success and survival. The elements of the corporate environment are the media, the general public, customers, stockholders, educators, civic and political leaders, and trade and special interest groups. They are the air, earth, fire, and water that act upon everything a company does and wants to accomplish, and it is the primary goal of a corporate program to generate a business environment that minimizes obstacles and increases the effectiveness of individual divisions or units.

The absence of a corporate program will almost certainly impede the efforts of line managers and lead to the unnecessary and wasteful expenditure of time and energy on the solution of avoidable problems. While it is not possible to create a permanently perfect environment, or even to alter it at will, it is possible to use the elements to positive effect and to be prepared for those occasions when they present adverse conditions or a crisis in which the initials CPR take on new meanings. That is, in essence, what a corporate public relations program should be structured to do.

## The Working Level

Corporate public relations is more than an exercise in the philosophy of communications. It is, rather, the art and the science of perceptions. Pragmatically, corporate public relations should be viewed as a working tool with real applications at every level of the business organization.

First, and most fundamentally, corporate public relations serves as a two-way channel of communications. Just as the company's various audiences must have information in order to understand the messages directed to them by the company, so must executives have a steady flow of accurate and unbiased information upon which to base policy and strategic decisions. In the management process known in the military as the OODA cycle (observation, orientation, decision, action), corporate public relations plays a major role throughout: gathering information, evaluating conditions, recommending courses of action, and implementing decisions.

Nowhere is this function more obvious, or more important, than in the development of a company or an organization's position and direction. Positioning is the sum total of what an organization is, what it does, where it is going, and how it wants to be perceived generally and in relation to its component parts. It is not enough for a corporation to state its positioning in a clever slogan. Positioning is achieved through deeds. As with human beings, it is not what is said that counts, but what is done. Corporate public relations helps translate thought and need into action.

In the real world of a free society, all corporate decisions and actions are subject to review by the media, business, and consumer audiences, public interest groups, legislative bodies, and the competition. Advertising is a controlled form of communicating with those audiences, but it is not until policy, strategy, and performance have been weighed openly on the scales of public opinion that a corporate position or policy can be said to be operational. Corporate public relations is at the heart of this process, whether it involves the strengthening of an established positioning or the development of a completely new positioning made necessary by a change in corporate direction. In each case there are facts to be gathered and honestly assessed, policies to be structured, and messages to be communicated to key audiences.

Corporate public relations plays a major role in the identification of key target audiences and in the development of messages, both general and specific, that will build understanding, confidence, and support. Here the program can be divided into several basic areas of activity, each having to do with what can be described as an "audience category."

The first, and most obvious, is the news media. The others, of equal importance, are the customer, the investor, the employee, the community, and the industry or industries the company is part of. There is no formula for communicating with any of the audiences or subaudiences represented in these categories. The techniques—the news conference, interview, press release, backgrounder, feature story, profile, speech, company publication—are familiar. The basic tenets, however, tend to be forgotten too often and need to be reviewed periodically. These tenets are as follows:

- Communicate regularly, not only when there is something new to sell or when a problem develops. Plan the program so that it works year-round and capitalizes on important events, such as the release of financial statements, acquisitions, new product announcements.

- Be consistent. If the company positioning is valid, the messages that follow will fit logically. Keep the future in mind. Think of the corporate positioning and never jeopardize it for the sake of a transient need or temporary advantage.

- View the situation from the audience's perspective. Avoid the gravitational pull of the corporate ego.

- Be open and direct. Do not obfuscate. Avoid hyperbole. Let the facts speak for themselves.

- Do not deny access to further information once you have stimulated interest. If time is needed to get facts, say so, but don't ask for more than is reasonable.

- Be positive. Remember that people generally admire resiliency, respect honesty, and want solutions.

- Be interesting. Stimulate involvement. Encourage dialogue.

Corporate public relations can provide valuable support for ongoing programs in marketing and sales, production, and research and development by obtaining general or specific audience exposure designed to broaden receptivity to new messages through participation in community programs, the arts, and education. Another highly important function of corporate public relations is active participation in trade and industry associations to exert leadership and to derive the benefits of unity on major issues and information circulated among the members.

## Community Relations—A Decisive Factor

Community relations is public relations at the local level. In fact, community relations is where public relations begins, and it should be thought of as a specialized part of the whole. Community relations deserves special thought, planning, and execution, usually within the framework of the overall public relations program.

The most important requisite for a successful community relations program is the continuing interest and support of top management. Community relations specialists need management support in order to function effectively. They can maintain the needed support by performing their jobs well.

The benefits of a good community relations program can be significant. Good community relations can help in attracting competent clerical and technical people. It may also help encourage executive talent to relocate.

Good community relations can also foster the right climate for obtaining reasonable governmental decisions, from zoning ordinances to environmental regulations. Many companies have found that the strongest financial base they can have is the solid backing of a local stockholder community. Such a constituency can discourage corporate raiders and can sometimes be motivated to speak out on behalf of the company if their loyalty is developed by good performance and good communications.

Community relations is not, however, a one-way street. The community expects some benefits from the company. These include good jobs at fair pay; a willingness to shoulder a fair part of the local tax burden; a commitment to deal with local suppliers, where possible; contributions to worthwhile causes; employee time donated by the company to help in local causes; and so on. These involve business decisions, not communications activities. The company which is not willing to give these concessions or which gives them grudgingly will have a difficult time reaping benefits from the community.

## Beginning at the Top

Good community relations begins in the attitudes of management toward its employees, its community neighbors, and such other audiences as customers, stockholders, government officials, and educators. From management attitudes come policy decisions and actions. Effective communication is the responsibility of the practitioner, whose aim is to help achieve the understanding and support the corporate policies and actions deserve. The word "deserve" is important because if the company's policies and actions are wrong, the practitioner isn't going to be able to help the company gain much understanding and support.

Therefore, it is important that the practitioner make sure that top management is aware that actions speak louder than words. Certainly, it is no coincidence that all the successful pioneers of the profession have referred to this critical fact. Convincing the public that the policies and actions of the company are in the public interest is fundamentally what this business is all about.

## Community Relations Is a Personal Matter

In community relations the practitioner is communicating with fellow employees, friends, and neighbors. In this intimate environment it is best to "tell it like it is," in terms that various audiences understand. A successful community relations program demands deep involvement in community affairs, joining community groups, mingling and sharing with community neighbors. Involvement in community affairs is important for all levels of management, not just the public relations practitioner.

Invariably, companies that enjoy good community relations have many lines of friendly contact and involvement among all levels of employees and neighbors outside the company. The participation of a firm's people in the civic, social, educational, recreational, and religious activities of the community are essential in establishing a favorable climate. Conversely, if management neither lives in the community nor participates in community affairs, it is exceedingly difficult to gain any substantial measure of understanding or support for its decisions, policies, and actions.

Obviously, no two companies are precisely alike, and every community has its own special characteristics or environment. This means that the practitioner should have intimate knowledge of both the company and the community. Then he or she must exercise sound judgment and sensitivity in formulating a community relations program that is compatible with the community chemistry.

## Objectives and Target Audience

Once the public relations person has set objectives and defined the audiences, he or she can then consider the best way to reach the people. A good way to start is by thinking about the needs of the audience.

At this point, the practitioner may begin to choose from several sound underpinnings of community relations programs:

- **Open house.** One of the best ways to demonstrate friendliness and desire to be a good neighbor is to invite the neighbors in. Many companies have successfully done this over the years with open houses or various kinds of plant tours. Facility tours may be effective with specialized groups, but the open house is the preferred activity for employee families and their neighbors in the community.

  Whatever the extent of the open house, success depends on detailed planning and careful follow-through. Usually, this is best achieved by appointing a planning committee of persons whose departments are most affected by the open house. There should be top-level agreement on the messages and impressions to be conveyed to visitors: the company is a good place to work, makes quality products, is a desirable neighbor, is a leader in its field. It's best if the open house can be timed to coincide with a special company or community event, and top management should definitely participate.

- **Public speaking.** Good speakers are always in demand, and within any company is a good deal of information that will interest community audiences. Public speaking is one of the most effective forms of communication. The opportunities are numerous, and the potential benefits are well worth the time and effort required.

Even in small communities, the number of speaking opportunities can be substantial. Chambers of commerce, local and regional meetings of service clubs, professional and trade associations, schools and colleges, adult education classes, personnel associations, and industrial editors' societies are but a few of the platform opportunities.

As their numbers of qualified speakers and platforms increase, some companies organize their efforts into speakers' bureaus. If the activity is extensive, this is an advisable step to avoid confusion and ensure mutually satisfactory results. The speakers and their subjects might be listed in a folder or leaflet, which can be circulated among local clubs, associations, and civic and educational organizations.

- **Education cooperation.** Schools and local industries stand to gain mutual benefits from cooperative experiences. Educators recognize that there are many learning resources within the company, and the company will ultimately benefit from education programs that help young people develop into active, productive, well-adjusted members of the community.

   Education activities include opening plant or company facilities for student field trips; providing speakers or consultants to classes; furnishing samples of raw materials, products, and printed materials, providing assistance to vocational guidance counselors; sponsoring scholarships, donating materials or tools no longer needed by the company; and sponsoring community resources workshops for teachers.

- **Clergy cooperation.** It is recognized that the clergy is a vital force, striving constantly to strengthen the moral and spiritual fiber of the community. It is less well understood that the clergy also has constant concern for the economic welfare of the people. Clergymen will be interested in knowing more about the company and its employees.

  One way to get better acquainted with members of the clergy is to invite them to the facility for lunch or for a special tour of the facility. They should be added to the company's mailing list for selected publications that will furnish information on employees, wage rates, working conditions, employee benefits, and kinds of work and products. Top managers may encourage employees to participate in church activities and to invite the clergy to participate in special events at the company.

- **Community participation.** Active participation in community affairs is one of the most important elements of a sound community relations program. Management and employees at all levels should be encouraged to take an active part in all kinds of community activities—the more, the better.

  The company can begin to demonstrate its desire to be a good citizen in the community by maintaining an attractive plant; eliminating smoke, odors, and eyesores such as waste materials; helping provide educational and recreational facilities for use by the community as well as employees; buying and banking locally; and lending company personnel or equipment for community improvement projects.

Company personnel should be encouraged to become active in various service, fraternal, and professional groups; charities and governmental, church, and school activities. Many companies have received community appreciation for their support of such groups as Little League, Junior Achievement, Boy Scouts and Girl Scouts, YMCA and YWCA, 4H Club and Future Farmers of America.

## Policy Development

A good community relations program begins with establishing sound and workable policies in collaboration with top management. One such policy is to receive complaints in good spirit and to respond to them promptly. It isn't always possible to correct the condition that gives rise to a complaint. It is always possible to listen politely and at length to the complainer, and to respond with sympathy and understanding. The very act of complaining is cathartic, doubly so when the person receiving a complaint has a good ear and a soft shoulder.

When complaints are justified, management should always be willing to make reasonable adjustments. There may be no short-range alternative for cleaning out an industrial smokestack from time to time, although there ought to be a long-range plan to overcome the problem. When valid claims are made, there must be some way to compensate the complainer for them, monetarily or by other appropriate means. Such compensation does two things for an employer: 1) it acknowledges responsibility, a prerequisite for trust, and 2) it mollifies not only the aggrieved but the entire community. Again, these are not specifically communications matters, but they do have a distinct effect on public perception of the company. If, in addition, management can assure its neighbors, through the community relations apparatus, that it is working on— or even has within sight—a solution to the problem, it may make some new friends.

Adjustments like these, and concessions to hundreds of other valid complaints, are routinely made by corporate and plant managers because they are reasonable, because they are palpable evidence of good citizenship, because they are essential to the retention of good will, and, sometimes because they stave off an inevitable confrontation with neighbors or officialdom.

## Corporate Contributions

Corporate giving policy and its place in a company's public relations planning are receiving increasing attention in the 1980s—in seminars, periodicals, speeches, business conferences, and "how to" workshops.

What is corporate giving and what should it be? Is it charity in its simplest form? A marketing communications technique? An executive's discretionary perk? A government relations program? An employee fringe benefit or internal communications device? A waste of corporate earnings? A significant and sophisticated component of a corporation's communications strategy?

Corporate contributions programs have been used—and misused—in each of these ways at one time or another. Many corporations still do not understand the value of a giving program that is integrated into their overall communications plan. Often, they do not see any potential business value in making contributions outside the company.

Some senior management people think corporate giving is a necessary nuisance activity; something that's expected of them but not worthy of their time or thought. As a result, they make contributions in a scattershot manner, with no focused business-related purpose to their giving. This wastes dollars and the opportunity for positive visibility. The reason is simple: They are uncomfortable with the giving process.

## History Shapes Policy

To understand the current issues in corporate philanthropy, the activity must be placed in its historical context.

A corporation's ambivalence, its unbusinesslike behavior when making contributions decisions, has its roots in the evolution of corporate philanthropy in the United States.

Corporate giving is a uniquely American phenomenon. It began when basic Judeo-Christian concepts of personal charity were superimposed on the corporation, an economic institution that evolved in this century.

In the burst of industrialization after the Civil War, enormous personal fortunes were made and dozens of Horatio Alger stories were reported on the front pages of America's newspapers. By the early 1900s, when major American corporations were forming, they were the creation of individuals like Rockefeller and Carnegie, who personified their own companies. The early corporate giving was their private, individual giving taken public: personal charity in a new and emerging economic context.

It followed that the traditional values of personal charity (privacy, anonymity, giving to do good for others with no thought of personal gain) were transferred to the embryonic economic institution, the corporation.

The corporation, however, has undergone evolutionary change since the beginning of this century. It is generally no longer the embodiment of a single person. To be effective now, its giving must reflect the needs and concerns of the modern corporation's multiple constituencies: its many shareholders and those who advise them, its employees and plant communities, and its consumers in diverse markets.

The traditional values of personal charity—privacy and anonymity—are not appropriate primary operating principles for today's corporate philanthropy, although they still guide many corporate giving programs. Consequently, there is often tension and conflict between the private roots (values of personal charity) and the public nature of modern corporate philanthropy (where giving should reflect corporate goals and values while supporting nonprofit activity).

This conflict accounts for much of the confusion and lack of direction in many corporate contributions programs. Corporate giving often has no strategic policy driving the decision-making process. Giving is scattered and unfocused. As a consequence, the contributions program often has little or no credibility within the corporate power structure. It has no credibility because it is not being used in a way that adds value to the company's business. Corporate giving is being run on a personal charity value system, but evaluated and found wanting on the basis of a "bottom line" value system.

Today, as the federal government reduces its support for social and community programs that have been public sector responsibilities since the New Deal and moves even farther away from funding these programs, volunteerism and private sector responsibility are growing issues. There are, and will continue to be, conflicting viewpoints as to who is responsible for what and how much.

In this climate, corporations have a major public relations opportunity. With careful evaluation of their contributions programs they can make their charitable dollars work for the donor company as well for the nonprofit recipient.

## Today's Role for Corporate Contributions

When a company makes a contribution, it creates the opportunity to establish or reinforce its corporate identity, to sell its products, to increase its credibility, to soften or neutralize criticism of its goods or activities, to enhance its stature with elected and appointed officials, and to generate favorable opinion with new or existing audiences.

Corporate giving today should reflect a company's goals,

its values, and its constituencies. An effective and well-planned philanthropic program should be guided by a sensitive application of the rules of the marketplace. Rather than being shaped by the individual values of charity Americans are taught as children, it should be a strategic business decision.

## What Is Strategic Giving?

Strategic giving is a well-defined plan of contributions policies and objectives integrated into a complete corporate communications program. It is a giving plan that lends support to a company's marketing strategy, enhances a company's image among its constituents, and favorably positions a company's executives, its products, or its services.

Each company has its own personality, audiences, and needs that should be reflected in a corporate giving program. The number of nonprofit institutions and programs seeking funds is enormous. In this diverse field, it is possible for a corporation to define areas of interest and to fund projects that will carve out a unique giving personality for the company.

How can corporate contributions be used in a positive, nonexploitative way so that the function earns credibility with corporate decision-makers and important outside audiences? Here are some ways:

- *As a marketing communications technique:* Giving can be carefully associated over time with organizations whose constituencies mirror the corporation's markets for a specific product or service. Giving can be used to expand markets for an existing product or to introduce a new product to a tightly targeted audience. Corporate giving is an elegant, extremely cost-effective way of reaching exactly the right market segment while doing good at the same time.

- *As a business-building and public-affairs technique:* Corporate executives can be positioned effectively through their personal involvement with nonprofit organizations to strengthen existing client relationships, to develop new business relationships, and to create or strengthen positive impressions of the corporation and its executives held by elected and appointed government officials.

- *As a component of employee communications programs:* Giving can be used to improve morale, to build a sense of affiliation with the company, and to instill pride in employees. The employer can organize employee volunteer and community relations programs. Company-created recognition activities can include "sweat equity" contributions, where the employer recognizes and "matches" an employee's volunteer work with a cash contribution to the employee's charity keyed to a formula based on the number of volunteer hours contributed.

- *As a vehicle to generate public support and positive opinion with a national audience hostile to the company's business:* Contributions can communicate strong, positive messages about a company in a context that gives the message third-party endorsement. The inherent credibility of the message as a contribution is much greater than an equivalent dollar expenditure for paid advertising pleading the company's case. Classic examples are public television programming supported by big oil companies and major museum exhibitions supported by cigarette manufacturers.

## The Public Relations Professional and Contributions Policy

The practitioner has an opportunity to refocus what is often a reactive, scattered, and untargeted giving process into a functional, visible, and effective contributions program. He or she can integrate gift-giving into overall communications and marketing plans so that philanthropy reinforces specific corporate objectives.

The public relations professional can help shape giving policy and contribution choices so they communicate the right messages about the corporation to carefully targeted audiences. Contributions decisions should be viewed as communications decisions.

Either in an agency setting or as part of an in-house corporate staff, the practitioner can facilitate the growth of healthy corporate/nonprofit organization relationships by:

- Defining reasonable, attainable objectives to be achieved by the giving program.

- Suggesting logical steps to achieve them.

- Asking the right questions of both corporate management and nonprofits seeking funds.

The corporation and the nonprofit organization often have different value systems and different perspectives on the same situation. The practitioner needs to understand both sides and to serve as a translator, when necessary, to make the relationship work.

The corporate contributions decision maker needs to ask several questions: Who do we want to think well of us as a result of our giving? Knowing we can't support everything, what kinds of projects make the most sense in the context of our business (locally, statewide, nationally)? Association with what kinds of nonprofit organizations will work best for us? With which audiences do we want to be visible? What messages and what kind of positioning will be most effective for our company and management?

## How To Build an Effective Program

The first element of an effective program is building credibility internally. The practitioner should:

- Actively seek and select projects that will create a clear, prominent, charitable giving profile for the company. Look for projects and programs in which a mutually beneficial relationship can be developed, where "the fit" is right; don't wait for them to come to you.

- Restrict the bulk of contributions to identifiable specific projects (from a children's hospital Christmas fair to underwriting a museum's gift shop); special events (anything from a community health day to a ballet gala); or productions, exhibitions, and publications (from an annual report, to a leaflet on poison plant tips for parents, to a performing arts company's marketing literature).

- Give to groups that are, by their nature, highly visible to constituencies of importance to the donor company (or that can be made visible) rather than to general operating support or endowment funds.

- Keep track of successes and keep management informed of them. If an underwritten activity receives press coverage, "thank you" letters, or recognition from government officials or from others important to the company, circulate the information. A contribution that works has a positive impact on the bottom line.

A second key to building an effective program is management involvement. The active involvement of senior executives is an important component in building credibility for the contributions program. The practitioner can use contributions activity over the course of time to position management with key outside audiences. This is not a chip trade among chief executive officers, in which the game is "I'll buy a table for your charity and you can buy one for mine," but is rather strategic placement for the benefit of the donor company and executive as well as of the nonprofit institution.

Inside the corporation, management involvement gives the clear signal that the contributions program and nonprofit activity are part of the company's business strategy. Outside, active management concern builds trust and esteem for the company and its leadership with the audiences directly involved. Reactive, "knee-jerk" giving with no management presence indicates to those seeking financial support a lack of corporate and management concern and awareness of the world outside. Often, these organizations have key corporate, government, and financial community leaders on their boards.

## Building Credibility Externally

Size, consistency, and continuity of corporate giving are some of the key factors in building credibility with the boards, donors, and other important audiences of the recipient organizations.

After a nonprofit recipient is selected, the donor corporation's public relations staff should take steps to ensure that the company:

- Gives an amount that's large enough to underwrite a project, be visibly helpful to the organization, and provide visibility for the donor.

- Is not a gadfly donor, giving here one year and someplace else the next. It takes time to build identification with the recipient organization and appreciation for the donor company in the minds of the target audience.

- Supports the gift using the firm's publicity and marketing expertise. As appropriate in a given situation, use advertising, bill stuffers, window cards, public service announcements, or press releases.

- Ensures that both sides in the underwriting arrangement have a clear understanding of each other's values, needs, and priorities. Know the expected amount of press support, recognition, and advertising.

- Deals with questions of visibility and recognition on a case-by-case basis. What works in one situation may not in another.

## Project Selection: Good and Bad Choices

How can the practitioner make the right choices to develop an effective contributions program? How does a donor firm tread the line between haphazard anonymous giving that eliminates any benefit a corporation might derive, and behavior that is so relentlessly self-serving that it jeopardizes the integrity of the recipient organization as well as the donor's public profile?

Nine basic kinds of corporate giving, good and bad, are evident today. Any corporate gift may involve more than one of these attributes. Some are counterproductive, even potentially harmful to the donor; some appear to be effective for both the donor and the recipient. The line between good and bad is often a matter of degree rather than kind. The types of giving are as follows:

- *Reactive giving* responds in a nonplanned way to requests from outside the corporation. The contributions are usually nonstrategic, unrelated to the corporation's business or its image, and scattered among many recipients without coherence. From a business perspective, this is invisible and dysfunctional giving.

- *Location giving* involves donations to causes in communities in which the headquarters or plants are located. These may be either scatter-shot or effective.

  A good example: Over a period of years, a toy manufacturer gives to the same three institutions in its headquarters city. The company underwrites specific projects for children: one in the arts, one in health, and one in education. It supports the gifts with advertising and with mailings to local audiences that are important to both the manufacturer and the recipient organizations. The chief executive officer of the company serves on the Children's Hospital Board of Trustees.

  An ineffective example: About one-third of a national food company's contributions are given through its subsidiaries and plants, but without any relation to priorities set by the company or the company foundation. Recipient organizations change from year to year, depending upon who asks first. Contributions are doled out as very small unrestricted gifts in response to outside requests until the pot runs dry for the year.

- *Safe giving* to traditional, prestigious, established, and noncontroversial causes will work fine if the gift is restricted to a project and receives proper public relations support. However, corporations often give to these organizations but don't target the gift to a specific purpose. They give simply because the organization has grants from, and therefore "the seal of approval" of, established nonprofit funding sources such as the National Endowment for the Arts or the Ford Foundation.

- *Me-too giving* occurs when a corporation feels it must be seen along with others, for instance, on the local arts center's roster of corporate donors. It doesn't give enough for targeted visibility, just enough to be a name on the donor list. The contributions officer fears the firm must be marked "present and accounted for." A gift to the same organization, but earmarked to a specific and visible project, would more effectively use the dollars.

- *In-house giving* is philanthropy used inside the corporation as a perk for employees. Matching employee gifts to causes they care about and personally contribute to is a commonly used method.

    Philanthropic programs can also be used as a morale builder. The corporation communicates its charitable activities through a company newsletter, thus making employees proud to be a part of the company.

    A more active application would be a company-sponsored volunteer program, with various employee recognition devices (pins, newsletters, recognition luncheon, media placements) and the "sweat equity" matching program described earlier.

- *Good Samaritan giving* occurs when a corporation sponsors needy or worthwhile causes that do not provide it with visibility and which do not serve a corporate business objective. Examples include skills training and high school equivalency education for teenage mothers by an investment banking firm or food contributions to senior citizens' homes by a heavy industry manufacturing corporation.

    In some instances, this may be turned into effective local giving. In some others it is charity in the personal, anonymous mold described earlier. Should a corporation's management wish to include some purely charitable giving in its contributions plan, that's fine. But it should be a defined and limited part of the program done by decision, not by default.

- *Effective market-driven giving* is related to a marketing strategy or an overall corporate goal. This may be done in a time-limited and project-specific manner or in the context of a long-term, multiyear strategy.

For example, in a three-month period, a national credit card company donated a penny to the Statue of Liberty project for every credit card transaction and $1.00 for each new card issued. In this way, $1.7 million was raised for the cause while card use rose 30 percent and the number of new cards issued rose by 15 percent. The corporation supported this contribution with a massive national advertising campaign and by mailing "stuffers" to card holders.

Another example is a home and business computer maker, which has donated hundreds of computers to school systems throughout the country over the last few years. Over time, the company has carved out by far the largest share of the school market for its product and has built consumer base for the future at the same time.

- *Excessive market-driven giving* occurs when a corporation's quest for visibility for its giving is so self-serving that it could potentially backfire. This may begin as a solid, creative program, but crosses the line from innovative to tasteless. For example, some food coupon promotions prey upon the customer's guilt or anxiety about loved ones to push products, such as a coffee advertisement featuring disabled children in wheelchairs toasting marshmallows around a campfire, with copy indicating that the manufacturer will donate one dollar to send the afflicted children to summer camp for each coffee coupon redeemed. A cookie manufacturer tried to play on people's emotions by offering to mail packages of its product to homesick members of the armed forces, if a serviceman's family sent in three proof-of-purchase seals.

- *Creative market-driven giving* happens when a corporation either actively designs a philanthropic project or responds to a good program and develops its components with the nonprofit organization, creating a "win-win" situation.

Among examples of this type of giving was the creation and funding of Public Television's Masterpiece Theatre in the early 1970s. Without major oil company support, these classics would have been impossible for public television to produce. The project served the corporation's strategy to enhance its reputation with upscale audiences and soften criticism from ecology interest groups.

Another example involves a champagne producer that built a relation with a prestigious opera company and an identification for its product with the opera's board, donors, and audiences over a period of years. The company first contributed its product for use on stage in operas where champagne is important to the story. It then extended the relationship to include underwriting special benefit evenings and the use of its products at all the opera company's important, high-visibility dinners.

A bank created a corporate and foundation consortium in its home city to revitalize the public education system from preschool through high school and received an enormous amount of civic recognition and positive visibility. Bank executives viewed the decline of the educational system as a decline in the quality of the labor pool and a potential danger to the local economy. Over a five-year period, the bank took a leadership position in generating funds and expertise to work on the problems. Groups from a number of other American cities have come to the bank to learn how to set up the program in their communities.

As corporate philanthropy takes on increasing importance in this country, charitable giving can and should be a tremendous communications asset to a company. It will be if the giving program is designed and implemented to reflect the company's goals and to communicate the corporation's important messages to its chosen audiences. The public relations practitioner is the essential catalyst in this process.

## Trade Association Public Relations

Trade associations and professional societies differ markedly, not only from corporations but from each other, in their structure, purpose, and operations. Associations, however, are not-for-profit organizations whose income derives from membership dues or contributions, and whose expenditures are normally devoted to advancing in various ways the industry or profession they represent.

In a sense, any trade association or professional society is basically a public relations organization. Ordinarily, however, it is not perceived as such by either its members or its executives, who for the most part do not have professional public relations backgrounds. However, such an organization is constantly concerned, on the one hand, with relations among its own membership, and, on the other, with relations with the various publics affected in one way or another by its industry or profession. So a great deal of its work is devoted to public relations in the broad sense.

A current dictionary defines a trade association as "an association of merchants or business firms for the unified promotion of their common interest," and this will serve as an adquate working definition. Virtually, every business and industry in the United States has its own trade association. Some are very small; others are huge. For example, the National Association of Retail Druggists has 32,000 members, the National Association of Retail Merchants nearly as many.

Frequently a business organization, even a small one, holds memberships in several trade associations. A company with several product lines, for example, may belong to associations representing each line, as well as to one or more general associations, such as the National Association of Manufacturers. It may also hold memberships in local, state, or regional associations as well as national groups. Furthermore, some of the associations to which it belongs may themselves be members of larger associations, for there are trade associations of trade associations.

A primary function of an association is likely to involve the monitoring of favorable proposed legislation affecting the industry or profession it represents, active support of favorable proposed legislation, and active opposition to negative or hostile legislative proposals. Obviously, this may take place at the local, state, or national level, or at any combination of them.

The association may conduct a lobbying effort, and it may try to involve as many of its members as possible in contact work with legislators in their own and in other areas. Coordination of such work by the association staff is essential if a truly effective effort is to be mounted and maintained throughout the industry.

Public relations and public affairs work will certainly play a major role in this effort. Its function is likely to include preparation of background memoranda, position papers, membership information bulletins, and, of course, publicity concerning the issues involved.

An association or professional society may offer a wide variety of services to its membership, and in most of them the public relations staff will play an important part. Membership services may include:

• Regular newsletters.

• Special "flash" news bulletins.

- Statistical data.

- News releases on industry matters to be distributed locally by members.

- Maintenance of a speakers bureau.

- Development of generic speeches.

- A wide variety of research functions.

- Marketing guidance.

- Standard-setting for the industry or profession.

- Codes of ethics.

This list could be extended greatly because each industry and profession has its own specific needs which its association or society attempts to meet. Some associations perform so many services and provide such a large flow of information to their members that they find it necessary to provide members with periodic summaries of their work. This is a good idea, since it is usually helpful to remind members of the numerous services they are getting in return for their dues.

Since the membership is perhaps the most important "public" that the association staff must deal with, considerable attention must be paid to membership communications. A number of types of such communications have already been mentioned, but some need to be treated in somewhat greater detail at this point.

If the association or society exists, at least in part, for the purpose of providing its members with *technical or professional information,* all such communications should pass through the hands of the public relations department to ensure that they are pertinent, concise, well written, and understandable, and also to determine whether they contain anything of publicity value. This scrutiny by public relations people leaves aside, of course, the question of the accuracy of the information, a matter with which public relations practitioners may not be competent to deal. They must, however, seek out confirmation of factual accuracy if they have any doubts. If they do not, the media regulators, legislators, consumers, and others are likely to do it for them.

It is often part of the association public relations function to prepare brief summaries of technical papers for periodic issuance to the membership, as a means of ensuring that the papers have been received and noted, and also as a means of reminding the membership of the service that is constantly being provided. These summaries are often distributed to trade publication editors, college faculty, congressional staff members, regulators, and others.

Public relations staff members must also be prepared at all times to respond intelligently and helpfully to members' requests for aid and information. Whether or not association staffers can help a member with a public relations problem is often a delicate matter of association policy. The general principle is that the association exists to serve all its members, and therefore cannot always accede to individual requests for aid, except in providing advice.

It is necessary and desirable for an association to determine the state of public opinion concerning the industry or profession, and it is natural that this function be delegated to public relations professionals. Public opinion surveys are useful not only to the industry as a whole, but to individual members who can put the information gathered in them to use in their own advertising, marketing and other programs. And it is more economical, as well as more practical, for the association, rather than individual members, to conduct comprehensive surveys.

In addition to comprehensive surveys, there may be other research in which information is gathered from specific segments of the public—for example, the news media, government officials, or consumers.

The public relations staff of an association or society is likely to play an important part in connection with the group's meetings and conventions. It will certainly be expected to publicize them, and, depending on the size and nature of the group, it may be called upon to do considerably more.

Public relations people, whether or not they are involved in such details, should play a part in the overall planning of meetings and conventions. Press coverage will have to be arranged, and proper planning for this includes a voice in selection of the site. Provision of adequate press facilities, for example, might play a part in determining whether or not a convention should be held outside the continental United States.

At the convention itself, the major functions of the public relations staff will be to operate a media room. It's important that reporters are provided with opportunities to interview speakers, association leaders, and prominent members. Public relations also provides the media with the working conditions, materials, and facilities they need, and ensures they have full opportunity to take part in all convention activities, including entertainment. New techniques, such as the transmission of news and feature material to television stations by satellite, can be used to good advantage when conventions deal with information of interest to the general public.

It should be clear that in a trade association or professional society the role of the public relations director and staff can and should be a large and comprehensive one. To be sure, in small associations, few of the specific activities mentioned in this chapter may be necessary or appropriate. In large associations and societies, however, tasks and activities may go beyond the outlines provided here.

In many instances, associations retain outside public relations counsel to supplement the work of the internal staff. Public relations directors usually welcome the aid provided by outside counsel in solving problems and carrying out assigned tasks. A public relations counselor will have had broad experience in a number of different industries and can bring that experience to bear on a particular problem. Furthermore, this provides an objectivity that is sometimes much needed, since an outside counselor is not subject to the same pressures as those felt by the association staff.

Learning to work effectively with an agency counselor usually produces fresh thinking and excellent results, while failure to do so will waste time, money, and effort.

## Outlook

The world of business is becoming more complex each day. Multinational corporations are serving the needs of the global village. Competition and technological development are intensifying and accelerating. Information has become a form of capital, and the future belongs to the company that interprets it and uses it to open new fields beyond the reach of obsolescence. Deeply involved in this adventure, as part of the management team responsible for converting information into knowledge and objectives into results, is the corporate public relations professional. The work itself—touching on science, medicine, technology, law, politics, the arts, and the lives and aspirations of individuals and nations—is as unlimited as the challenges and opportunities it presents.

Corporate and association public relations is the connecting link between a company's or association's policies, position, and aims and the various people it addresses. The company's or industry's image is reflected by its objectivity and capability to anticipate events, developments, and trends that can present either an opportunity or a problem relating to public perception.

## A Case in Point

When the management of RCA sought to enhance its position as a leader in electronics technology and scientific research, a comprehensive communications program was formulated. It centered on a series of approximately 300 speaking engagements over a two-year period. The program allowed corporate spokespersons to address selected, diverse audiences.

Newspaper, magazine, radio, television, and other interviews were arranged to coincide with speaking dates. The spokespeople were trained in public speaking and media confrontation, and speeches and publicity material were prepared. A steady flow of local and national news coverage about RCA's electronics technology and scientific research resulted.

Another case in point illustrates how F.W. Woolworth perceived, planned, and publicized its 100th anniversary as a peg upon which to build a national awareness program.

Management's objective was to emphasize Woolworth's position in retail history and the company's growth, as well as to instill pride in its rich heritage among employees and suppliers. A year-long flow of information, spiced by special events, focused public attention on the corporation throughout the year.

Local and national press kits were prepared and distributed. Company backgrounders, a centennial information guide, four television newsfilms (which were seen by more than 16 million viewers), radio feature stories, and a 20-minute documentary film were among the other products used. A corporate history was prepared for shareholders, opinion leaders, libraries, members of Congress, and other appropriate groups.

Special events were woven through the anniversary year. They included ceremonies at corporate headquarters, and these events were enhanced by a replica of an early store and the nostalgic performance by Eubie Blake, a noted ragtime pianist who plugged sheet music in Woolworth stores at the turn of the century. Other events included a centennial celebration for 2,500 long-time suppliers, displays of turn-of-the-century merchandise at museums and antique fairs, unveiling a plaque on the site of F.W. Woolworth's first store, and mention of the anniversary's significance into the Congressional Record. Governors of three states issued proclamations recognizing Woolworth's civic, economic, and other contributions.

News stories appeared prominently in all the nation's leading newspapers and magazines in conjunction with network and local radio and television coverage. This case in point emphasizes the value of anticipation and careful planning in successful corporate public relations.

Often an important step for a company in establishing its position in the market is one that does not involve its product directly, or even at all. Corporations frequently use public relations to make a statement about the kind of companies they are by venturing into a relationship with an activity which of itself connotes a desired image.

For the Merrill Lynch stock brokerage firm, the venture began with a relatively small project involving the Metropolitan Opera. The corporation approached the opera in 1981 with an interest in underwriting a project with a contribution only in the area of $10,000 to $25,000. Its interest was confined to this amount because it perceived the Metropolitan Opera as a New York City organization and what Merrill Lynch really sought was visibility with target audiences elsewhere. However, public relations executives convinced Merrill Lynch that its view of the opera company was incomplete. As a matter of fact, eight of the firm's most important markets happen to be in the cities that the Met visits on tour.

The result was that the two organizations combined to develop a program under which Merrill Lynch became the first corporate underwriter of the Met's annual spring tour. The combination proved ideal because the audiences the Met attracted in these eight cities were composed precisely of the same people whom Merrill Lynch regarded as their prime business targets in those cities. Moreover, the tour established Merrill Lynch more firmly with local opinion and social leaders in the tour cities.

Each year since 1981, the investment company has followed through in each city on the tour with a series of events designed to create visibility and contacts for local Merrill Lynch people. Among the events used were opening night parties; seminars with artists, local donors, and the press; and luncheons with local board members, donors, audience members, and the media. These events provide opportunities to entertain existing clients and meet potential clients in relaxed, nonbusiness circumstances where Merrill Lynch is the "star." Additionally, attendance by the press allowed for spontaneous coverage of recognition and appreciation for the firm's contribution.

In another case in point, the Mazda Motor Corporation also turned to the arts for an association that carried a message. In this case, the vehicle was the Grand Kabuki, the famed, traditionally stylistic Japanese theater form that was being presented in the United States. Mazda appeared in connection with presentations in New York, Washington, and Los Angeles, reinforcing in each city the carmaker's message primarily with a different type of audience.

Unlike public relations efforts related to Mazda auto plants in the United States, the Grand Kabuki tour relationship was not expected to generate large amounts of media exposure for the company. It was, however, seen as a way of opening doors and changing or improving Mazda's image among a very select group of highly influential people. The program showed Mazda not only as an efficient and valuable member of the U.S. economy but also as a responsible member of society, contributing to all members of a nation in which it operates.

In New York, the group that was entertained consisted primarily of business, cultural, and social leaders. In Washington, the group included U.S. governmental administrators and legislators, with the media, auto industry representatives, and members of the Japanese diplomatic corps also present. Los Angeles lured the most varied group, including leaders from the city government as well as leaders in business, culture, and the media.

In each city, Mazda invited its guests to attend a reception and the opening night performance of Grand Kabuki. In all three locations, meetings were held between Mazda executives and governmental leaders, key experts in the field of economics, and the media. The net effect was to increase in the minds of these key individuals overall awareness of the Mazda Corporation and of its financial commitment to the U.S. market.

A positive public relations program also proved beneficial for a major trade association. When Congress passed a provision requiring banks to withhold 10 percent of all interest accrued to all accounts as part of a tax reform package, it was not debated as an individual item. The provision was buried in the sweeping reform proposal, and the American Bankers Association (ABA) feared its group would be blamed by the public for the new regulation.

Research determined that most people were unaware of the proposal. Bankers were concerned about possible customer reactions to withholding portions of interest payments, and news media were indifferent to the proposal's ramifications. The research also showed that if withholding was to become a public issue, it would require a special effort by the American Bankers Association to stir the awareness of the man on the street.

Three phases were developed for the public relations program. They included involving local bankers to explain the withholding provision and to encourage customers to register disapproval in letters to Congress, publicizing the bankers' opposition, and spurring repeal of the legislation.

A kit, which outlined and explained the issues and appealed to all special interest groups, was supported by local and national publicity. All the ABA's efforts were backstopped by regional agency offices, which also arranged 219 local interviews during a critical four-month period.

The withholding provision was repealed 13 months after its approval by Congress. The leading proponent of the withholding provision capitulated and suggested the Senate retain the ABA for any future grassroots public relations effort. No doubt, his tongue was in his check, but his point proved the case for a good public relations effort.

# Chapter 11

# Industrial and Labor Public Relations

Over the course of the past 40 years we have seen a significant change in the strength of the organized labor movement in the United States. U.S. Department of Labor statistics show that in 1985 only 18 percent of the American work force was represented by a union, while in 1945, 31.5 percent belonged to a union.

This lessening of union influence occurred for many reasons, but there is no doubt that the changing face of the U.S. economy is a major factor. Heavy industry, the traditional stronghold of the organized labor movement, is being eroded by foreign competition and adverse exchange rates. The professional and service sectors of the economy are growing, but these areas, for different reasons, have been resistant to unionization.

What do these trends mean to American managers and to the public relations professionals who work on their behalf? Do they mean that the pressure has lessened, that it is no longer necessary to try to communicate management's messages to unionized employees?

The answer is no. In an atmosphere in which employees represented by unions may feel increasingly embattled, management must redouble its efforts to communicate fully and honestly. To do anything less is to ensure that the classic adversarial relationship between management and labor, the "we versus them" attitude that prevents true communication, will continue even more intensely. The consequences, to employer and employees alike, can be drastic when the very survival of the business may be at stake.

A vivid way to appreciate the labor communications challenge facing American business today is to contrast the economic and management-employee environments of the recent past with those of the present. Before the late 1970s, the watershed years for change, the American economy was generally healthy. Companies grew because profitability was a function of production capacity. Foreign competition was limited; unions were stable or were increasing their memberships.

Internal communications tended to be from the top down, with employees receiving very little information about the state of the business. Instead, companies let union leaders tell workers about the issues, which the unions naturally were inclined to define narrowly, in terms of wages, benefits, and work conditions.

The "we versus them" posture prevailed. Employees had little to say about company decisions. While management may not have been loved, it was generally respected. The primary contract issue was usually the size of the wage and benefits increase because the consumer would pick up the costs of the final agreement.

So much for the old days.

## Labor Communications in a Changed Environment

Now, in the latter half of the 1980s, the situation has changed. The face of the American economy has altered radically. Basic industries such as steel, aluminum, and rubber, suffering from shrinking profit margins, have increasingly found themselves unable to invest the capital necessary to update aging facilities and equipment and to maintain their work forces at the wage and benefit levels that were possible when it seemed that economic expansion could go on forever. As a result, many companies have been forced to make permanent layoffs or to close down unprofitable operations. Waves of mergers have further reduced the employee ranks.

Even in industries or businesses in which unions remain a powerful force, conditions have changed. Industry bargaining has virtually disappeared, putting increased pressure on companies and union locals. Employees are unhappy with management's performance. Supervisors are caught in the middle between the company management and the union.

How about management-employee communications? Many companies are telling their employees less, not more, about the firm's true condition. The unions, meanwhile, have learned their lessons well. Typically, they have become much more sophisticated in their communications, making full use of the many media outlets available to them, media which many companies choose to ignore.

## Communications, Productivity, and Survival

The business climate has changed for all companies. External and internal forces have combined to increase the need for productivity improvements, cost reductions, and greater efficiency. The need for employees to participate in making contributions to a company's future strength has never been greater.

But labor-management relations and communications for many companies haven't improved, despite the fact it has become increasingly clear that how Americans manage their businesses has a direct impact on productivity. Furthermore, a key component of management style is how employers talk to their employees. How effectively are corporate leaders handling internal communications?

Not very well, according to surveys of thousands of employees by the Opinion Research Corporation (ORC). For example, the ORC reports that no more than four in ten employees at any organizational level, including middle managers, feel that their company is doing a good job of informing them about what is going on in the business.

How would employees like to get their information about the company? Clerical, hourly, and managerial employees all answered that they would choose to receive information from their supervisors and from group meetings with management. They *don't* want to have to rely upon the "grapevine."

How, in fact, were most of the surveyed employees obtaining their information? From the grapevine, the ORC was told, and, after that, from company publications and bulletin boards. Few employees named supervisors or management meetings as purveyors of information about the company, the state of its business, and the issues confronting it. In short, employees seem to be saying that their companies are not keeping them well informed and that their senior leaders are not willing to talk to them or to listen to them.

These finds are no surprise when one understands how companies have approached internal communications. Traditionally, they have been reluctant to talk directly to employees about major issues facing their industry. Management will talk about such matters to the media, to stockholders, and to analysts—with varying degrees of candor, to be sure—but not directly to employees.

Typically what management will say in its internal communications program is both trivial and unfocused. The usual company newsletter also lags behind and is often contradicted by the "grapevine." This reluctance to speak directly to employees about major issues frequently applies to companies without unions as well as to those with them. Employees at nonunionized firms are often as much in the dark about company matters as their unionized peers.

In today's economic environment a company wants to increase productivity, reduce costs, remain competitive, grow, increase shareholder value, or merely survive. Its communications objective is to have employees understand, believe, and support the company's position and understand that the business environment has changed. It cannot succeed if it clings to an outmoded style of communications, if it is still "we versus them" in its approach to employees, and if it rarely attempts to address workers fully and honestly.

## A New Communications Strategy

Is there no way out of the tunnel of futility that exists when senior management fails to keep channels of communication open? Must the public relations practitioner just stand on the sidelines and watch valuable economic entities be weakened or destroyed by avoidable conflicts?

Fortunately, there is a way out for both company and employees. The answer lies in creating and implementing a new labor communications strategy, one no longer frozen into the outmoded "we versus them" posture. This new strategy has four elements.

First, it calls upon a company to gain control of its own communications. It requires a company to open lines of communications with its employees in two directions: from the top down and from the bottom up.

The communications must include face-to-face meetings as well as publications. For employees to feel the need to contribute to the company's future, they must believe their contribution involves more than financial concessions. Face-to-face meetings with top management provide the opportunity for senior leaders to detail efforts to improve the company's position and to prepare for the future. Face-to-face meetings are the best means of communicating that management has a plan, and for company spokespersons to develop credibility with employees. A sophisticated employee communications program must be created on a long-term basis, well in advance of a crisis, and it must be pursued with the same professionalism and expertise as the company's other future-oriented activities.

Second, the new labor communications strategy calls for consistent and factual messages in external and internal media. The bad as well as the good news must be told. And the company must discard strident rhetoric if it wants to gain trust and respect among its audiences.

Third, the company must establish themes that emphasize the interdependence of the company's fortunes and the employees' livelihoods. It must select broad issues that are evident throughout the industry, not narrow, self-serving ones. The themes can create a foundation for ongoing communication.

With these themes, a company is using nontraditional techniques to reach its employees. It is telling them about the rigors of competing in a world market. It is telling them that the markets and driving financial forces of companies and industries have changed, permanently. It is telling them that management is striving for stable growth and increased earnings in a difficult and overcrowded market. It is telling them that it has a plan to survive and prosper in this new environment. It is telling them it wants employees to participate in the decision-making process. It is telling them that with their help the company has a future and that there is light at the end of the tunnel.

In doing all this, the company is identifying or creating issues upon which the company and its employees can stand together, thus diluting or eliminating the classic "we versus them" attitude.

Fourth, the new labor communications strategy focuses on defined and targeted audiences. They include, of course, nonsupervisory employees.

But the key communicators to those employees must be

front-line supervisors. Top managers of the company must undertake a program to train these supervisors in their new roles as the primary communicators. The supervisors should be trained in effective techniques of communicating with employees and in answering their questions regarding the company and the industry. In addition, a system must be established to provide answers to questions beyond the supervisors' expertise so that they can return quickly to an employee with an answer.

Management must then meet regularly with the supervisors to brief them on the latest developments within the company and the industry. This will enhance the credibility and effectiveness of the supervisors and their ability to act as communicators as well as barometers of employee attitudes. This makes it possible for supervisors to know what's happening before other employees come to them with grapevine news.

The strategy also recognizes the value of other audiences, including third parties, in influencing employees. These third parties include the families and friends of employees, the community, the media and industry-watchers. Publications should be sent to the homes of employees. Company executives should periodically brief community leaders, or take them on tours of the plant.

Finally, by cultivating the media, a firm is taking a wiser position than when it says little or responds with "no comment." After all, employees get their news from television, radio, and the press. They are likely to believe a report about the company when they hear it on the evening news.

The fifth point about the new labor communications strategy is that companies must anticipate differences of opinion. There is no guarantee this strategy will always produce unanimity among employees or the community, but a company that is tolerant of these differences has a better chance of winning public opinion than one that bristles at them.

The new labor communications strategy can help companies survive.

## Nontraditional Issues: An Emerging Challenge

Up to this point, the discussion has concerned examining industrial and labor communications within the context of traditional issues: how management does or does not communicate with employees about the company, the state of its business, wage and benefit issues, and so on. Public relations professionals, however, must remain alert to the challenges presented by issues that have not always been regarded as subjects for labor communications. In order to serve fully a company's needs, it is necessary to identify and develop communications strategies to meet these new issues as they emerge.

One such issue, substance abuse in the workplace has emerged as a central concern in the mid-1980s. Hill and Knowlton is a leader in exploring the nature of this problem and outlining communications strategies to deal with it. The agency's approach to developing and implementing substance abuse policies serves to suggest how other nontraditional issues may be addressed as well.

Statistics about widespread substance abuse in the workplace and articles about its serious implications for employee safety, productivity, employer liability, employees' rights to privacy, and a host of other complex issues have appeared often in the media over the past few years. Substance abuse is a problem for which there is no single answer or easy solution, yet one that more and more companies are facing as they attempt to develop policies to deal with it. But it is precisely because the issue is so complex, and because the implementation of employee testing is so emotionally charged, that a well-thought-out and effectively administered communications program is critical to any organization's effort to establish and employ a substance abuse policy.

Each company has to consider and evaluate the characteristics of its business—type of work force, geographical location, and so on—in order to develop a practical and viable policy. Although substance abuse has become a national dilemma, no single policy can be expected to work in every situation. Nevertheless, some communications guidelines are applicable, whatever the specific provisions of a company's policy.

## Substance Abuse Communications Programs

After carefully considering all of its ethical and legal ramifications, a company can create what it believes to be a fair and workable substance abuse policy. Why is a communications program necessary?

To begin at the most basic level, why shouldn't the company simply announce that, as of a certain date, all employees will be expected to submit to drug testing and let it go at that? The answer, simply, is that *acceptance* of the policy and of related actions to implement it is crucial to its success. Acceptance must be earned by creating a climate of persuasive communication. Persuasive communication requires clear and frequent explanation of the policy. This will lead to employee acceptance of it and employee commitment to its success. Simply announcing an action is not the same as persuading employees of its necessity and desirability. Faced with the sudden imposition of drug testing, most employees—quite understandably—would be likely to react with anger, fear, or other hostile emotions.

For example, a few months ago employees of a certain newspaper were up in arms over reports that the publisher was considering a drug-testing program. There were even stories that drug-sniffing dogs were to be sent into the newsroom. The publicity was both unfortunate and incomplete. In fact, it came at just about the time the publisher had been planning to announce a comprehensive drug and alcohol abuse program for all of its employees. Although this program would have benefited everyone and had been in preparation for more than a year, it had to be delayed while tempers cooled.

Another example, again involving a publisher, illustrates the advantages of advance planning and of controlling information. In this case, the publisher eventually was able to institute a tough and effective drug-testing program with little opposition. The publisher's first step was to consult other companies about their drug programs. That research suggested a few cardinal rules:

- Secure a guarantee of support from top management.

- Obtain medical and legal advice.

- Put policies and procedures in writing and develop a communications program.

- Train managers, especially supervisors, in the operation of the program.

Before the program went into effect, management initiated a variety of communications. A letter with a copy of the policy was sent to each employee. Articles explaining the program were printed in the firm's two house organs. Copies of the material were sent to all unions representing the firm's employees. Finally, employee unions were given an opportunity to discuss the policy.

## Reaching All of the Audiences

Let's assume you understand the necessity for communicating your policy and its implementation to all employees and the unions as a condition of its success. Are these two groups the only audiences?

No, others are involved. Also to be considered are those who influence or are influenced by your employees. For example, Company Y, which has a large number of operating locations nationwide, gave its plants the option of testing applicants and certain high-risk employees with critical jobs. Before the firm launched its program, communities in which the plants are located were briefed about the company's objectives and purposes so there wouldn't be any surprises.

A complete list of audiences might include employees, families, union associates in other locals, community opinion leaders, media, customers, and suppliers. The applicants who are asked to take the drug test also are a very important audience. It is important for applicants to be comfortable with the program. If a company develops a bad reputation, its recruiting efforts will suffer and the best employment prospects may pass it by.

Companies that already have communications programs in place should examine them carefully for credibility. How well are the messages received? Are the communications vehicles respected, or do they always take second place to the grapevine?

Does the company have a good relationship with the media, or is it either unknown or misunderstood (which frequently results in negative stories)? A preliminary audit will determine the effectiveness of a company's communications. If there are deficiencies, repairs should be made before embarking on a drug abuse program.

Obviously, among the most important audiences, and the one that must be reached first, is employees—from management to hourly workers. Communicating with employees should be looked upon as an opportunity to promote unity. Management's messages should stress that "we are all in this together." It is important, however, to remember that employees at different levels need different kinds of information, and messages must be tailored to these different needs. These messages can:

- Dispel any notion that the drug-testing program is punitive.

- Emphasize the positive aspects, especially that the program is designed to enhance the overall performance of the company.

- Address the individual, pointing out that the company is concerned about his or her welfare, which is important to the welfare of the company.

In order to reach the individual and enlist support, communications must also involve employees' families. It is necessary to illustrate that drugs are a genuine problem in the workplace, that nobody is immune, and that strict measures are required to control the situation. For a drug-testing program to succeed, it must be understood and supported by the workers and their families.

Information must emphasize that effective procedures are essential when pinpointing drug offenders, not just to catch the offenders, but to protect the jobs of innocent workers who can be seriously affected by drug abuse. Equally important is the need for support from union leaders. They should be brought into the confidence of top management before any general announcements are made because their members will turn to them for confirmation and clarification of the firm's message.

When the word gets out that a company has launched a drug-testing program, it also will have an impact on community leaders and the media. Unless communication with these publics is handled carefully, the impact could very well be negative. Almost immediately, serious questions and concerns will be raised among each of a company's audiences regarding the possibility of serious trouble at the firm. If customers and suppliers are not informed first, business could be badly damaged through rumors and allegations.

That's why it is important to have a communications plan that touches all bases, including community leaders, customers, suppliers, newspapers, television, and radio. If all have a clear understanding of what a company is doing, it will be a plus for its image.

## Establishing Effective Communications Vehicles

Any substance abuse policy communications program, in other words, must address multiple audiences. How does one reach these different groups reasonably quickly, efficiently, and cost-effectively, and yet ensure that the necessary climate of acceptance is created?

Once audiences have been identified, the next step is to develop a white paper that defines the key messages to be communicated. This will bring consistency and understanding to the program. The white paper will also anticipate problems and remove inconsistencies. Once the white paper is formulated, it is time to choose the best methods of reaching the target audiences. There's no better starting place than sending to the employees and their families a letter that spells out the objectives and procedures of the program. It is a good idea to send with the letter a list of questions and answers about the key components of the testing plan. This should be followed by a meeting with the employees. A senior company leader should explain the program and provide an opportunity for questions and answers.

Among the employees, priority should be given to briefing supervisory people and union leaders so they will be prepared to deal with questions from the work force. Keeping these groups well informed reduces the risk of misunderstanding. These letters and meetings should be reinforced with stories in company newsletters and other house organs. Videotape is also an effective way of reaching employees, especially when hundreds or thousands are involved and they work at many locations. Video gives top management a chance to deliver its message in a way that is personalized and meaningful.

Probably the best way to approach community leaders is through one-on-one meetings and letters. It is important for them to understand why the program is being instituted because they are key opinion-makers in the community. When possible, bringing third parties—impartial sources who look favorably on your objectives—into the plan can strongly reinforce the message with all audiences. This step can be achieved through talk shows, guest editorials, and op-ed pieces that define the drug abuse problem and deal with solutions.

Last, but of equal importance, are the news media. They must receive background information on the program through written materials and interviews with key company executives. Good media contacts and the resulting coverage afford the company a chance to reach anyone it may have missed through other channels. Drug testing may very well be among the most controversial actions a company will undertake in the mid-1980s. Few other issues demand such a solid communications strategy.

## The Future of Industrial and Labor Communications

Current industrial trends indicate that it will become increasingly important to develop and maintain effective communications with employees. It is obvious that foreign companies, often subsidized by home governments, will continue to be forces in markets long dominated by American companies. In addition, a growing number of domestic companies are using technological advances to automate production, thereby reducing long-term costs. Minimills and similar smaller production facilities are becoming more and more prevalent. These trends underscore the need for companies to reduce costs in order to compete in an evolving market.

In all likelihood, senior management will be forced to continue to ask employees to share the sacrifices necessary for a company's survival. But employees will not make continued contributions if kept in an information vacuum. Employees must be regularly briefed and updated with regard to the direction in which management intends to take the firm and how it plans to ensure the company's competitiveness. Workers' cooperation will be essential in implementing the often difficult tasks which lie ahead for most companies.

In addition, the American labor movement is becoming increasingly sophisticated and innovative in its efforts to organize workers and achieve the demands of current members. Although there has been a significant decline in union jobs in the traditional, basic industries, unions such as the United Food and Commercial Workers and the Service Employees International Union have proven extremely successful in organizing workers in newer, service-oriented industries. Many of these workers traditionally were not represented by bargaining agents—for example, white-collar workers who are increasingly seeking union support.

Because of new marketing and organizing techniques and the involvement of the AFL-CIO to coordinate multiunion organization and information against new targets, it can be expected that companies will need to provide a great deal of information as employees ask questions about what is in their best interests.

New issues, such as those associated with drug testing, will continue to emerge in the area of industrial and labor communications. While it is impossible to predict at this point what they will be, it is possible to conclude that effective communications will be crucial to management success. The desire to improve productivity and efficiency will require that employees understand and support company actions. This support can be achieved only through effective two-way communication up and down the organization's hierarchy.

When trouble comes to companies in the form of labor strife, they become aware—sometimes painfully and for the first time—that they are faced at that moment with public relations problems, both internally and externally, which must be faced and managed for survival.

## A Case in Point

Continental Airlines discovered that it had to maintain the confidence of its traveling customers in the face of charges by its workers that their strike was making Continental flights unsafe and that it was preventing the airline from fulfilling its schedule commitments. Trouble came to a head during July 1983, when negotiations between the airline and the International Association of Machinists and Aerospace workers (IAM) broke down. A strike was called for August 12 after the IAM demanded a 35 percent wage increase against Continental's offer of 20 percent, provided there were productivity improvements.

Public relations was called in even before the strike deadline. Research undertaken immediately established an interesting set of facts: the IAM was traditionally unsympathetic to company problems; the media coverage strongly indicated a strike was likely; other airlines' management had traditionally maintained silence during strikes. In addition, strikes traditionally caused drastic declines in passenger business because of uncertainty regarding safety and schedule reliability. Therefore, even though Continental might have been doomed, efforts to pursuade union members to influence their leaders toward reconciliation began at once. At the same time, the airline's management determined it would continue efforts to fly regardless of whether a strike was called.

Thus, while still working to avert a strike, public relations people began to position the company for continued flying. The media was made aware that the company was confident of its ability to maintain service despite a strike, and attempts were made to discredit, even before they were made, any union efforts to claim that a strike would make flying unsafe and unreliable.

Among the public relations preparations was the development of information kits for use by spokespersons including Continental's managers in 108 cities; the establishment of a hotline for managers about to be interviewed; the gathering of statistics on other airlines' labor positions in support of Continental's position; the setting up of press rooms in Houston, Denver, and Los Angeles, the airline's hub cities, each with direct links to operational command positions and the company's senior spokesperson; the training of regional managers and spokespersons; the preparation of an open letter to the flying public; and the establishment of procedures for controlled dissemination of information to media and the routing of releases to travel agents.

When the strike occurred, efforts concentrated on maintaining passenger confidence, stimulating the return of strikers, and defusing safety questions. Accessibility to the media was the top priority, which meant assuring reporters that key spokespersons were available for numerous one-on-one interviews and for regular briefings, and operating press rooms around the clock. Continential used a spokesperson-city manager network to monitor media coverage and identify new issues.

When Hurricane Alicia struck Houston on the sixth day of the strike, it suddenly became necessary to also set up alternate communication systems. The result of the airline's efforts was that media coverage generally reflected the positive aspects of Continental's position and the effectiveness of the union attacks was substantially reduced.

The general public was also influenced positively. Passenger load levels, which had stood at 57 percent the week before the strike, actually climbed to 58 percent in the first week and then followed normal seasonal levels, averaging almost 57.8 percent during the month of August despite intensive picketing and even verbal abuse of passengers by strikers. Continental made a temporary cutback in the number of its flights but returned to 90 percent of pre-strike flight levels after the first week. By September 1, the airline was fully operational.

In another case, the Samsonite Luggage Company found it had to communicate with its nonstriking professional employees to assure them of their safety and also with their striking employees to acquaint them with the facts of labor negotiations.

Even before the strike began, it was clear from past history that it would be vigorous. For one thing, the United Rubber Workers had been quite effective in gaining public sympathy for other strikes; for another, the union was facing job action situations with other companies and obviously was eager to show muscle in dealing with Samsonite as a warning to the others. It was also a matter of record that the union had in the past encouraged sabotage among its members in plants where it had lost strikes.

The public relations effort began by training Samsonite officials for their roles as public spokespersons. At the same time, the media effort began with the preparation and delivery of press kits crammed with background information, which then and later would be used by reporters as basic reference. The Samsonite spokesperson presented himself at the offices of press editors as well as television and radio news directors, establishing himself early on as the source of information available at all times.

For office workers and other professionals not on strike, meaningful reassurance of their safety and the importance of their efforts was made plain. At the same time, the company made clear publicly that it was concerned about the welfare of employees on strike—that it still considered these people part of the group. This included letters to the strikers informing them of the company position and keeping them advised, but it did not stop there. There were a number of small but meaningful gestures showing the company's concern for the strikers. At one point, when television reported pickets shivering over makeshift fires, the company immediately supplied the pickets with tents, coffee, doughnuts, firewood, and portable toilets.

The result: When the strike ended, workers returned with a minimum of resentment even though they had been forced to accept a wage and benefit cut. Violence on the picket line, and later sabotage on the assembly line, were avoided. The company once again enjoyed cordial relations with union representatives.

# Chapter 12

# Public Relations for Professional Service Firms

A trend is taking place in the field of public relations, reflecting both the recognition of public relations as an important management discipline and the fact that American business has become, to a great degree, service-industry driven. This trend is toward the increasingly pervasive use of public relations practices and techniques by professional service firms, which until a decade ago either ignored or disdained public relations as a real option to help them grow and go forward.

Today, professional services firms are beginning to use the full range of communications techniques to support their recruitment and practice development efforts. In several professions, the use of advertising is limited by ethical or cost-benefit concerns. On the other hand, public relations techniques—such as publicity, printed materials, publications, speaking platforms, seminars, and internal communications programs—can be adapted to the needs of any firm in any profession. Public relations can be used to perform the following functions:

- Attract the attention of potential clients and tell them about the firm's capabilities.

- Help retain and expand relationships with existing clients.

- Maintain awareness of the firm and its accomplishments among those who refer business to it.

- Cross-sell services between clients of different practice areas.

- Explain internal policies and career opportunities to employees and job candidates.

- Motivate professional and support staff to achieve better morale and greater productivity.

A professional service firm is any organization that exports the expertise of its professionals to create a value for its clients, which can be individuals, corporations, trade associations, or governments. Firms engaged in management consulting, law, accounting, architecture, engineering, interior design, executive recruiting, medicine, dentistry, and communications all fall into this category.

## The Professional Services Environment

Professional service firms can be distinguished by their labor intensity. As Roger Schmenner of Duke University observed in the *Sloan Management Review,* service firms require "relatively little plant and equipment and considerable worker time, effort, and cost."

Beyond the hallmark of labor intensity, professional service firms have certain special limitations that also make them stand apart. For example, there are legal restrictions on what lawyers and doctors can say about their practices that do not apply to most other kinds of organizations. And many professional service firms deal with highly sensitive and proprietary information regarding their clients, and this imposes major restrictions on their actions for reasons of client confidentiality and trust.

The marketplace has never exhibited as much demand for professional services as it is doing in the 1980s. The level of demand has created some giant firms in a number of professional sectors, such as law, management consulting, public relations, and advertising. With such obvious demand and success, why are professional service firms now turning to public relations? Although there are many factors contributing to this trend, the most significant is the fact that the dynamics of the professional marketplace have changed and that the forces of economic reality have created a new era of competition in all professional disciplines, with all that competition implies.

Professional service firms in virtually all arenas of expertise have been forced to deal with cataclysmic changes in the way they get business, the way they do business, and the way they keep business. Paul Bloom, who wrote "Effective Marketing for Professional Services" in the *Harvard Business Review* summed this situation up by stating that "not very many years ago, professionals could count on their reputations and country club contacts to obtain a steady stream of clients or patients. Today though, lawyers, accountants, management consultants, architects, engineers, dentists, doctors, and other professionals must do extensive marketing to maintain and build their practices."

In this relatively new competitive environment, public relations has become a necessary part of the management mix for many professional firms. A cursory review of the pressures on today's professional service firms quickly reveals why public relations has become so accepted over the last several years. Consider these factors:

- Major users of professional services—large corporations, associations, and government bodies—have increasingly turned inward to fulfill service needs previously found outside the organization. New departments have been created and staffed to deal with everything from legal matters to strategic planning to management consulting. Virtually no discipline has escaped the trend toward internal staffing, even considering the major restructuring that has been going on in corporate America over the past decade. The impact of this change is broad. Competition for professional projects has spread and now often includes the internal staff as well as external competitors. Professional firms are forced to create specialties, or niches, where internal staffs are weak, in order to be considered for the special work that is available. Professionals within the service firms have to be more on the cutting edge than ever before because of the increasing sophistication and capabilities of purchasers of professional services.

The "Old Boy Network," which worked so effectively for generations, has to be exchanged for the "Professional Decision-makers Club," a far less elite but currently far more powerful group.

- Until quite recently, members of the professions were held in high regard by most of the American public and the business community. However, in more recent years, a serious erosion of professionals' credibility has occurred and the high esteem once automatically enjoyed by most professionals now has to be earned. Phillip Kotler and Paul Bloom described this phenomenon in their book *Marketing Professional Services* in the following way:

  > Substantial numbers of people see lawyers as ambulance chasers, accountants as tax loop-hole finders, architects as avant-garde elitists, and dentists as overpriced mechanics. Influenced by unflattering portrayals of professions in the media and best-selling books, clients have become much more likely to question the judgment of professionals or to offer strong complaints. Consumerism has struck in the professions, taking the form of malpractice suits and other overt challenges to professionals of all types.

- Professional services in the 1980s are marked by their profusion rather than their scarcity. Competition in many professional sectors has heated up as more graduates in law, medicine, architecture, and business school enter the professional marketplace. As these professions become overcrowded, competition becomes an economic reality which must be dealt with directly. Since most professional service firms have not been equipped or staffed to deal with the business side of their marketplace, they have, of necessity, had to turn to outside specialists to lead the way. Because public relations as a discipline cuts across so many areas critical to professional service firms—marketing, crisis communications, materials development, recruitment, practice development, internal communications, special events, and general image development to name just a few—it is readily apparent why public relations has been sought as a major resource by professional service firms.

- In the past 10 years, most of the professional, state, and federal laws and regulations that restricted soliciting, advertising, and certain kinds of promotions and activities for many professional service firms have been eased or entirely eliminated. The impact of this broad easement of restrictions has been to intensify the rapidly increasing competition among professional firms. As Kotler and Bloom put it, "While some restrictions remain, professionals are essentially free today to promote their services however and wherever they want, as long as they do not make any deceptive or misleading claims. This newfound freedom has sparked a wave of intensifying promotional and competitive activity in most of the professions. Many professional service organizations are finding that their survival hinges on being able to compete in this new climate."

- Finally, because of all of these factors, print and broadcast media have become intensely interested in chronicling what is transpiring on the professional services front. Consequently, an entire industry of reporters, columnists, special trade publications, and even television programs has been created from the need to inform the public of developments in the various professions. The scrutiny of the media has put professional service firms under the microscope; the coverage that results can have a major impact—either up or down—on the future revenues of the firms. For this reason, professional service firms are turning to public relations counselors for counsel and guidance.

The professions have begun to embrace public relations. The trend is clear. However, the acceptance is by no means universal; even those professionals who have pioneered the use of public relations are often unwilling to discuss their ground-breaking ventures outside the confines of their own organizations.

That professional service firms are seeking advice, counsel, and help in implementation from a variety of outside consultancies comes as no surprise when one considers that the service sector of the American economy has been the fastest growing sector in the last several years. For the most part, the needs of these firms closely parallel the needs of all growing organizations, from both an internal and an external perspective.

Professional service firms have clients they need to serve better; employees they need to depend on to get the job done; outside publics upon whom they are dependent for good will and credibility; potential clients with whom they hope to develop business; organizational and communications problems with which they have to cope; business and trade media professionals with whom they may have to interact; and, perhaps most important, competitors from other professional firms who are also trying to get their arms around the same limited marketplace. If this sounds familiar, it should, because it's the story of every growing, competitive American corporation—and, as it turns out, it's the story of most professional service firms as well.

There is at least one very real difference, however, between other organizations and professional service firms that skews how professional service firms deal in the business world and with public relations. This difference is the real "product" of professional service organizations: their people. Unlike all other types of organizations, professional service firms have only one kind of tangible, substantive asset, and this asset is made up of the professional men and women who bring creativity, integrity, and specialized skill to solve their clients' problems. For those who spend significant time working with professional service firms, it is clear that the "people" factor puts a very different perspective on both what is done in a public relations sense and how it is done.

## Recruiting

Recruiting is among the most critical investments that a professional service firm makes. Firms are challenged to improve their recruitment practices, while at the same time they face fierce competition. Today, investment bankers, law firms, accounting firms, and other professional firms as well as corporations all solicit the same select cadre of students.

The individuals whom the firm recruits will not only perform the current work, but also provide its next generation of leadership. Consequently, the cost of selecting the wrong people can be extremely high. In addition to the opportunity costs related to the use of time during the hiring and training process, hiring professionals whose style and skills do not match the firm's needs can create a negative reputation for the company and compromise its ability to hire qualified candidates in the future.

Nearly every professional services firm's recruiting program has three objectives:

1. To attract more of the top students from selected schools.

2. To make more efficient use of firm resources— practitioners' time and firm expenses—in the recruiting process.

3. To increase the visibility and enhance the reputation of the firm at selected schools.

A fourth objective should be added, which is particularly important when bringing associates or partners into the firm above the entry-level:

4. To match applicants' skills and style with the future needs and style of the firm.

## Factors Influencing Students in Making Decisions

One specific case in point involving what influences law students in making decisions to join law firms can be used as a basis for better understanding the recruiting process for professionals in all disciplines.

In 1983, Hill and Knowlton surveyed second-year law students after they had accepted or declined a particular firm's offer. These interviews were conducted with students and faculty from law schools at the universities of Chicago, Michigan, Wisconsin, Minnesota, and Virginia, and North-western, Yale, Stanford, and Harvard universities.

This research showed that the most important factor affecting a candidate's decision about a firm is the applicant's impression of the firm's associates and partners. While the overall reputation of the firm in the general and professional communities was an initial influence, students' reactions to the firm's on-campus interviewers largely determined their perceptions of the firm and the likelihood that the student would accept future interviews.

The research also showed that other students provide another credible source of information about a law firm. Law students obtain this information from personal contact, the grapevine, and reports filed by summer clerks about their experiences with various firms. Summer associates make their assessments of summer programs based on the personal attention, training, and development they receive as well as perceptions about new associates' opportunities for client contact. Summer associates, who gain experience in a broad range of work and who have opportunities to work with a number of partners, quickly circulate this information through the grapevine.

From this research, it can be inferred that some common assumptions are not true—for example, that it is more important for a recruiter to have attended a particular law school than to be a good communicator. The rule that underlies the extensive social activities conducted with summer associates must be reexamined in light of the findings that assessments are based upon personal attention, training, and development. Finally, in view of the importance of the grapevine in a firm's recruitment program, the firm must be certain that it has a clear picture of its reputation on key campuses.

Two other cases in point illustrate effective use of public relations practices in recruitment.

When a midsize Minneapolis law firm experienced difficulty hiring qualified new associates, it enlisted the help of a public relations firm. A series of surveys and interviews were conducted with second- and third-year law students, applicants who had chosen other firms, the firm's own first- and second-year associates, and law school faculty. The results showed that the firm gave less information about itself to its candidates than did competing firms. Also, the firm's interviewers were given low ratings by those who were interviewed. Associates often said they chose the firm despite their initial impression because the firm's summer program had a good reputation and young associates they spoke with unofficially seemed satisfied with their jobs.

The public relations counselors recommended that the firm broaden its recruitment efforts and make them more attractive by preparing recruitment-oriented literature, providing interview and presentation training for recruiters, and arranging off-the-record sessions between candidates and specially chosen associates. In addition, a 60th anniversary celebration for the firm was organized, and key publications—such as *The American Lawyer*—were contacted to propose feature articles on the firm's progressive compensation system and unusually young practice leaders. These efforts enhanced the law firm's appeal among students trying to differentiate between many apparently similar firms.

With its recruiting system revamped, the firm retained three new associates and five summer clerks from prestigious law schools. The acceptances reflected the firm's improved presentation, screening, and candidate feedback monitoring program.

A much larger firm, with 175 attorneys in offices in three states, was also concerned with recruiting high-caliber, law school graduates on a wider basis. Following a study of all aspects of the recruiting process, the firm instituted a program that:

- Concentrated recruitment at fewer, more-desirable law schools.

- Instituted procedures for screening and responding to unsolicited inquiries from law students.

- Reorganized the manner in which students were invited to and accommodated during interviews, in order to dramatically differentiate the law firm from its competitors.

Descriptive literature was prepared about the firm, its areas of practice, history, benefits, and office locations. Spokespeople for the law firm were briefed and trained for recruiting and follow-up procedures streamlined for quicker response. Pleased with initial results, the law firm continued the program through subsequent seasons. Clearly, improving a firm's success in the recruitment process becomes increasingly important as the costs of recruiting escalate. Some firms estimate the cost at between $25,000 and $30,000 for each successful hire, and in excess of $15,000 for those who are required to be visited, but who do not accept offers. This investment is substantially increased by the rising salaries offered to professionals entering the practice.

What can a firm do to communicate with students in a manner that encourages the right students to join a particular firm? Here are just some of the steps a professional service firm should consider:

1. Organize the recruiting system so its communications to candidates are efficient and responsive.

   The firm's recruitment committee should help to shape the firm's definition of itself, set policies on recruitment, and oversee their implementation. All of these elements involve public relations issues or effects. Typically, a well-run recruiting committee would be responsible for:

   • Drafting guidelines for the firm's interviewers.

   • Compiling a list of questions students are likely to ask, and when possible a suggested answer to each, and drafting sample questions for interviewers to ask.

- Developing a series of key points to stress about the firm.

- Selecting the schools where the firm should recruit.

- Selecting the best mix of executives for on-campus interviews.

- Identifying future practice development needs of the firm.

- Matching the applicants with the appropriate members of the firm for in-firm interviews, both to take advantage of students' special areas of interest as well as to avoid redundance with internal interviews.

- Determining how offers will be presented and timed.

2. Prepare interviewers to be as effective as possible.
   Interviewers, both on-campus and in-house, should be thoroughly prepared to anticipate and answer questions and to be knowledgeable about all areas of the firm. This planning will ensure consistency among interviewers while avoiding duplication.

3. Prepare quality materials that highlight the distinctive features of the firm and its geographic location.
   The firm may want to consider using a recruiting resume that brings out its flavor and unique aspects. The resume should be tailored to emphasize those qualities that separate it from other firms and to highlight practice specializations. Some firms have included perspectives from associates working in specialized areas who present their perception of the firm and their responsibilities.

In 1984, two firms—New York's Shearman & Sterling and Miami's Shutts & Bowen—pioneered using video presentations as a tool for attracting students. The Shearman & Sterling piece used firm members to present the firm to students who view the tapes at selected law schools. The Shutts & Bowen production sells the city of Miami as a place to work and to live.

4. Take advantage of special opportunities to find and keep top graduates, particularly those with local ties.

   Senior firm members are most likely in a position to see or hear about particularly capable students. They should be encouraged to use feeder systems from schools, academic competitions (like moot court or design competitions), participation in seminars or courses, or contacts with faculty members to develop these special opportunities.

   Firms should recognize that most graduates are likely to practice near the school from which they graduate or near their hometown. Therefore, firms should consider paying greater attention to the top alumni of local graduate schools and those with preexisting ties to the area who are attending graduate schools away from home.

5. Review summer programs.

   A well-planned orientation at the beginning of a summer or internship program will be appreciated by the summer associate or intern as a solution to the frequent lack of organization among these programs. Throughout the program, a feedback system should be used. This may take the form of an "ombudsman," or of a project-by-project review by the supervisor. The summer experience should conclude with an exit interview that covers the mechanics and interaction aspects of the summer program as well as general information about the firm's reputation, its recruiting skills, and the attractiveness of the work experience.

6. Raise the visibility of the firm at selected schools.

Because students are most likely to interview at those firms that they consider to be prestigious, and because all of a firm's communications activities contribute to the creation of prestige, it may be useful to consider recruiting as a secondary objective of all public relations activities.

## Internal Communications

Traditionally, internal communications at professional services firms were primarily limited to management discussions held by the senior partners. These policy discussions shaped the future of the firm, but were rarely communicated directly to its members. Instead, the policies developed became the largely unspoken credos of the firm and were passed from generation to generation.

This elitist process was effective as long as there were no challenges to the time-honored seniority system and while the professions engaged in limited competition. However, in the past decade, younger professionals sought to become part of the process. These younger professionals brought to the profession a series of questions and challenges based upon their exposure to business and marketing:

• What are our growth plans?

• How will we achieve them?

• How are we going to compete in the marketplace?

• To what degree will compensation relate to contributions made to reaching these goals?

When these questions were not answered clearly or suitably, the new generation urged changes in the firm's structure to allow participation in these discussions, or they left the practice.

Internal communications plays a central role in the development and communication of a firm's policy. In addition, it is vital to ensuring that the company meets its business objectives. An effective internal communications program can prepare a firm to handle crises; effectively integrate new professionals, departments, or entire firms; and provide the foundation for cross-selling initiatives.

The growing size of professional services firms has also awakened management to the need for coordinated plans of internal communications. No longer can all professionals meet in a conference room or over lunch. With members of professinal firms in offices around the country or the globe, questions and concerns of those within the same firm are no longer homogeneous.

Professional services firms are beginning to recognize the need to establish coordinated programs of internal communications. Often, these programs become the impetus for developing shared values and goals. Top management must determine whether growth is desirable or whether the firm's members should endeavor to become specialists or generalists before it can communicate its policy on these issues.

## Firm Retreat

A common method of building shared goals and values is a firm retreat. This can be an effective way to begin the internal communications process. For a retreat to be successful, it must have a clear objective. A series of discussion areas should be defined prior to the meeting. Among appropriate topics:

- The firm's strengths and weaknesses.

- What the company stands for.

- An analysis of the competition.

- Where the firm wants to go.

In order to maximize the benefits of the discussion time, these topics should be divided among group leaders who research the subject, develop proposed recommendations, and prepare approaches that will facilitate group involvement. Leaders should identify whether background information, such as revenue information or comparative data, is needed and compile this information in advance.

## Action Plan

The internal communications effort cannot begin and end with the retreat. These planning sessions should conclude with the development of an action plan that defines specific activities. Follow-up may include a series of regularly scheduled meetings (by department, or by the firm as a whole), an internal newsletter that reports on departmental activities, an informal luncheon series with presentations of case studies by practice groups, or team-building exercises.

Internal communications can ensure that a crisis of confidence is avoided, both among professionals and their clients, when professionals leave the company. This communication is also important when two or more firms merge.

Here is another case in point: A long-established architectural firm had developed its practice in two areas with relatively limited forecasts for growth. The firm's younger professionals challenged the existing management to adopt an aggressive program of growth that would increase their opportunities. The firm resisted and a number of senior associates and young partners left the firm, leaving the older partners shaken and other younger professionals questioning their future. The firm recognized the need to coalesce around clearly defined and generally accepted growth objectives. Doing so required the firm to launch a practice development program that radically changed its prior reliance on a few "rainmakers." Now, all professionals are expected to play a role in the firm's growth and be measured on their performance. The company developed a policy and reinforced it through a series of internal meetings and memoranda that showcased the success of practice developments efforts.

## Handling a Crisis

A crisis may include the departure of a partner, the loss of a major client, the firm being named as a defendant in a lawsuit, or a member of the firm being accused of professional impropriety. When these events occur—and some crisis occurs at every firm at some point—the instinctive response of a professional services firm's management tends to be to "circle the wagons." The senior members of the firm often believe that reducing the flow of information is the best way to minimize the potential for damage.

Managing a crisis, however, requires the rapid dissemination of accurate information. For a professional services firm, which thrives on integrity, this information flow is particularly important. Consider two alternatives:

- Alternative A: The firm answers no questions, not even internal questions. Its members are called by their clients, and because they have no official information, they can only speculate.

- Alternative B: The firm distributes to all professionals and the support staff a statement that provides its response to the issue. Company employees are encouraged to limit their responses to client inquiries to the information included in the statement. (All media inquiries are handled by a central source.)

Alternative B produces consistent information and minimizes speculation that can lead to defections by the firm's employees and its clients. Disseminating accurate information requires one additional step. As soon as the information can be updated, it must be. The firm will not benefit by having once correct, but now erroneous, information in circulation.

## Addressing Firm Expansion or Restructuring

The merger of two or more professional firms has become fairly commonplace. An increasing number of firms are acquiring practice areas or entire firms in their home cities or offices in other cities or countries. They can benefit from the experience gained in the corporate sector where such mergers take place more frequently than among the professional service firms.

The firms should begin by assessing where they have differences and where commonalities exist. This analysis should include questions of practice area strength, governance, style, client conflicts of interest, and compensation structure. This internal assessment must reach throughout each organization to associates, to paralegals, to clerks, and to support staff.

Once the internal perceptions of the merger are defined, the firm can explain the new organization, first internally and then externally. It should strive to define its objectives: how the practice "fits," what strengths can be leveraged, what weaknesses can be overcome. Interaction between management and staff is very important in building internal confidence. It may be appropriate to hold a series of meetings among departments or to hold meetings of the entire firm that directly address the difficult questions. These communications should be formalized through an internal publication that regularly presents updated information on the merger along with the answers to commonly asked questions. Typically, this vehicle will be a newsletter, but a videotape that reinforces the personal relationship of top management to professionals at all levels may be a preferable alternative, if it is produced in a professional manner. (People's reaction to anything on television is strongly influenced by the sophistication of modern broadcast programming. Amateurish or overly long in-house videos fail because they lack impact and credibility.)

Often, the move to implement internal communication begins with a crisis at the firm, but should be just as important on an ongoing basis. The internal awareness needed to encourage cross-selling between practice areas or disciplines is an important reason to implement such a program.

## Materials

Materials about the firm do not take the place of effective one-on-one communications. However, they can play an important role in reinforcing contacts and expanding knowledge of the firm, its capabilities, and its character. For example, an employee may make a presentation to a group of prospective clients. After the presentation, he or she can hope they remember the firm's name and its areas of practice. Or, the presenter might distribute a brochure, resumé, or another printed piece that covers a special segment of the firm's practice.

During the recruitment process, the firm may wish to establish a foundation for its campus visits by providing background information that distinguishes it from its competition. One approach might be to distribute a recruitment brochure, or the company might consider developing a videotape about the firm or the city in which it is located. As an additional follow-up to preliminary contacts, or as an "added value" to clients, the firm might consider publishing a newsletter that provides timely updates on important subjects. Newsletters can also be important cross-selling vehicles as they highlight a variety of practice areas, in some of which the client or prospect may lack knowledge of the firm's involvement.

## The Company Brochure

Often, professional services firms begin their inquiry about starting a practice development effort by considering whether to produce a brochure. While a brochure or other materials do not substitute for an overall practice development program, such products can play an important role in positioning a firm. Here again, a variety of editorial and design techniques can be used. By using a narrative approach and design style that reflect the essence of the firm, its qualities as an aggressive, entrepreneurial group can be emphasized. Or using a different approach, the firm can highlight its long history and solid corporate reputation. A brochure can also be useful in profiling certain practice areas among a firm's capabilities. For example, for a firm known primarily for its consulting to health-care companies, the inclusion of a section in a brochure about its consulting services to high-technology firms can raise the visibility of this other specialty.

A printed or videotaped piece that provides a broad overview of a firm can expand the present clients' understanding of the organization's breadth and depth. When used in this way, these can be effective tools for cross-selling the firm's capabilities by educating the firm's specialists on their colleagues' capabilities, and giving them something to use with clients and prospects.

A case in point is provided by a relatively young law firm specializing in complex patent and trademark litigation that needed to be perceived as solid and experienced. A brochure was developed that stressed the attorneys' backgrounds with government agencies and other firms, while the firm retained the distinctions of entrepreneurism and client service that distinguished it from the competition. A photographic cover, with the firm's name in gold-leaf carved in green marble and action-oriented four-color photographs accompanying the text were used to dramatize the energy of the firm in the context of solidity.

Recruitment is another use for such a brochure. However, the firm should consider whether the message it conveys to potential clients is the message it needs to communicate to prospective employees. It may be more appropriate to develop a separate piece for recruiting or to include a special insert to students in a pocket at the back.

Creation of a successful brochure requires agreement within the firm about what, exactly, the firm is. At its root, this is a business strategy and firm governance issue, not primarily a communications question. Partnerships being what they are, producing a first brochure can be a difficult episode for a firm that lacks either strong, central management or a clearly defined business strategy. Both are needed to set the emphasis on characteristics and practice areas represented within the firm as a whole. Such emphasis, based on the importance of certain qualities and the potential for practices, must be determined before practice development goals, and the communications objectives to reach them, can be set. A brochure is only one step in an overall communications program, albeit a visible one.

To be effective, the brochure should:

- Reflect the firm's perception of its culture.
- Help position the critical practice areas and capabilities.
- Respond to questions and issues of importance to the firm and its clients.
- Use design and editorial copy that support an overall theme and tone for the firm.

- Be written with the client's point of view in mind

A profile should not:

- Attempt to tell everything about the firm to everyone.

- Be bland, in order to avoid making any statement about the firm's personality.

- Succumb to being written in technical jargon or lose substance by being written and edited by a committee.

- Be considered the only necessary communications vehicle suitable for all audiences and situations.

Once the firm determines what role the brochure will play in its marketing efforts—whether it will be mailed, handed out in mass distribution at speeches and conferences, and/or used with selected, present clients—a decision must be made about the format and style of the document. The classic format for a brochure that resembles a corporate annual report is a bound publication of 8, 12, or 16 pages with or without photographs.

Flexibility and a more dynamic presentation may be preferable in some cases. An alternative format might be one that includes removable sections describing different aspects of the firm. These could be used together or separately, along with other sections that provide an overall description of the firm and its philosophy. Other sections might include names and backgrounds of partners, special cases, and pro bono activities. This approach may make more business and economic sense for a diverse or growing firm.

## Newsletters

Newsletters offer a regular means of communicating with active and inactive clients, referral sources, and others. In addition, a newsletter can help expand awareness of the firm's areas of expertise and position it as a thought leader by presenting issues not considered elsewhere. It can also help to differentiate a firm from its competition by presenting a unique consulting approach, analyzing recent decisions and issues related to the profession, highlighting the professional leadership of a company's members, and informing readers of the firm's approach to providing value-added service.

Before a firm begins to produce a newsletter, it should consider that regular, informative, and meaningful pieces require a substantial commitment of resources is required. These publications are costly to produce in terms of professionals' time invested in gathering, writing, editing, and overseeing production. In addition, mailing lists must be constantly updated.

After considering the pros and cons of newsletters, a firm should look at whether alternatives exist. For example, a series of monthly mailings in letter format could briefly address timely topics covering various aspects of the firm's practice. Or, it may be appropriate to publish a series of specialty newsletters that address separate practice areas. If a newsletter provides the best opportunities to highlight a firm's breadth of experience, the firm should:

1. Develop a design format and name for the piece. The newsletter design should present an identity consistent with the firm's letterhead, business cards, and other written communications, but be sufficiently distinctive from other mail received by the readers. A larger size, off-white paper, or distinctive masthead can provide this difference.

2. Establish an editorial policy. The firm should decide on editorial content by subject matter and maintain the topics in all issues. For example, the firm may want

to have one section on recent decisions that affect the profession, another on relevant business issues, and a third on recent speeches and articles written by employees.

3. Establish an editorial committee and editor-in-chief to oversee the editorial policy. This person will be responsible for maintaining quality control over the publication and should assign editorial committee members to develop stories and news items.

4. Develop a comprehensive mailing list that includes present and former clients of all departments of the firm. Careful consideration should be given to the seniority of individuals included to ensure that the editorial policy of the newsletter is consistent with their information needs.

Periodically, the firm should conduct a readership survey to determine appropriate areas of interest for content, as well as to address issues such as style and frequency of distribution. Follow-up mailings to nonrespondents can be used to enhance response as well as to build interest in the newsletter. Further, this research can provide insights into the overall interests and needs of the firm's clients.

## Company Resumé

The resumé is a relatively standard piece of "literature" used by professional services firms. It normally highlights the firm's practice areas and provides examples of significant clients. Often, it concludes with the biographies of the principal partners of the firm.

In many cases, firms use the same resumé for many years. If this is true, it should be reviewed regularly to determine whether it conveys an accurate impression of operations and reflects present areas of practice. If the firm's health-care consulting practice has expanded, it may be more appropriate to segment this specialty into subsections covering services for not-for-profit providers, for-profit providers, and medical products suppliers. The key is to define the firm's capabilities from the client's point of view, describing capabilities in relation to their benefits, not the processes involved. Problem-solving, opportunity-enchancement, cost-effectivess, and similar results measurements must be emphasized.

## Video

Video marketing is a relatively new technique among professional services firms. As such, it presents an opportunity to substantially distinguish a firm from its competition. At the same time, for many firms, this technique could be perceived as unusually aggressive.

Several audiovisual approaches are or could be used to communicate information about a firm. Here are some approaches:

- A video on the firm and its specialties could be a "talking" representation of its brochure. In order to take the greatest advantage of the visual impact of the medium, a videotape should show examples of a firm's product or services, or show its staff in action. It also might be appropriate to interview the firm's clients to include their comments. The video could explain the company to prospective clients and recruits. If it includes information on billing and other processes, it might be a useful introduction to the firm for both new clients and new employees.

- A video on the city in which the firm operates could be an important element in the recruiting process. A firm in a smaller city may want to develop a video that highlights the life-style benefits that its location offers. This video could include comments from civic and business leaders who would provide an direct endorsement of the city and an implied endorsement of the company.

- A video that highlights the firm's expertise could serve as a video newsletter. This offers an opportunity to showcase the firm's expertise while presenting its members as effective counselors. It could be developed as a quarterly product that is distributed to clients or used for special situations when a development in the profession warrants a longer discussion about an issue.

## Special Project Development or Services Pieces

At times, the firm's individual departments may want to provide specific information about their services without including general firm background. Most often, this occurs when a cross-selling opportunity is identified for an existing client or when a prospect has general knowledge about the firm but lacks specific information about one of its specialities in a relevant area.

A descriptive piece on a single service or function provides in-depth information only about that particular practice area, or it might describe a series of practice areas in relation to a specific industry. A firm may determine that it needs services pieces on each of its specialties, each major industry it serves, or each geographic area in which it does business. For example, if a law firm with a sophisticated litigation practice wanted to build its reputation as a firm that understands entrepreneurial companies, a services piece that highlights its capabilities in relation to that market segment could be useful. In order for the communication to reach its maximum potential, it should include case studies that highlight the firm's experience and success with these clients (if permitted), or hypothetical scenarios and profiles of key members of the practice that specify their qualifications for working with entreprenurial companies.

## The Annual Review

The annual review provides a synopsis of the firm's achievements during the year. It offers an alternative to revising the overall brochure, and at the same time it presents current information.

For example, the review might provide photographs of award-winning advertisements produced by an ad agency or investment banking firm. It must be timely and avoid being redundant with the overall brochure.

## Other Communications Techniques

Public speaking opportunities have long been used by professionals seeking new clients and greater prestige among their peers. Reproducing a speech and mailing it to members of the audience and other prospective and existing clients and business referral sources serves to reinforce both the message of the presentation and spread it further. The more important the speaking platform, the more impact a speech reprint has, but even remarks given to a small or less prestigious organization can be leveraged through a well-produced and distributed reprint.

Most organizations line up their speakers four to eight months in advance. Most business groups arrange their outside presentations through a member designated as "program director" or something similar. Professional and trade associations can be reached through their executive director, or advice can be obtained from the organization's public relations office.

The professional education seminars or similarly named events run as part of many conventions and trade fairs give professionals an excellent opportunity to reach their target audiences with a speech or workshop. For example, the high-technology practice group of a leading accounting firm regularly presents start-up financing ideas to attendees of COMDEX and similar trade shows. The entrepreneurs who attend these lectures often turn to the firm's local office for additional advice, which is initially provided free of charge. A relationship is established that can, with continued effort, turn into business for the firm that will grow as the entrepreneur's company grows.

Not all new business leads generated through speeches and workshops have long payoff periods. A tax attorney speaking to a local business group during late 1986 on the subject "What You Can Do To Keep the New Tax Bill from Hurting Your Bottom Line" would have been very likely to come away from the meeting with a pocket full of business cards from potential clients whose questions were too complicated to answer when they were raised at the event. Some of the follow-up calls would almost certainly lead to business relationships.

Workshops on a topic of significant concern to a target group can be proposed to associations or to trade show sponsors, or they can be put on independently by the professional services firm. Because this can be a very effective avenue for new business opportunities, firm-sponsored seminars have proliferated to the extent that the potential attendees are frequently overwhelmed with invitations. Colleges and universities, profit-making seminar organizers, and professional associations all compete with the professional firm for seminar and workshop attendees.

An added difficulty in producing firm seminars is the assumption made by potential attendees that an event sponsored by a single firm is an attempt to sell them something. This is generally a fair assumption, and the resistance it creates can be overcome by several means. First, having speakers from outside of the firm featured in the program gives the impression that a viewpoint broader than the firm's own will be represented. Second, it can be very effective to bring in a professional firm from another discipline or specialty as cosponsor (if you are a lawyer, invite a management consulting firm to be cosponsor, for example). This has the added benefit of spreading the costs. Third, firms can approach a local university, trade association, business publication, chamber of commerce, or another organization to serve as host or cosponsor. This adds credibility, especially among alumni, members, subscribers. An added benefit of this approach is the ready availablity of mailing lists from the cosponsor or host. The use of such lists should be negotiated in advance.

Another alternative is to propose a half-day seminar in conjunction with a local university or business school executive education program. These programs are often held during the summer months and are coordinated by either a full-time administrator or a faculty member.

All speeches, workshops, seminars, and similar activities are opportunities to expose local business media and regional and national professional publications to the firm's expertise and message. Either by inviting reporters to events or by turning speeches or presentations into articles, the firm gets extra mileage out of these practice development opportunities.

# Chapter 13

# Public Relations in Marketing

Marketing communications is a rapidly growing aspect of public relations that is becoming a vital part of corporate and product promotion programs. Marketing public relations specialists are called upon to assist in the introduction of new products or services and to help reposition old products or services to stimulate sales that have gone flat. Marketing public relations also comes into play with corporations, trade and professional associations, and even countries that want to build positive public attitudes.

The goal of marketing communications is to build awareness and enthusiasm among audiences that are important to success. The ultimate objective is to increase visibility to such an extent as to make the product or company a household name. Today, as the needs, interests, and buying habits of different segments of the population become more thoroughly analyzed and defined, marketing communications programs can be targeted to very specific audiences such as upscale teenagers, senior citizens who can afford foreign travel, or college-educated working women.

Marketing public relations opens for the practitioner a world in which cleverness, superior ideas, and the ability to create attention-getting events can make a competitive difference. It is not by chance that some products appear on national television while others do not. Stories or publicity material involving consumer products tend to be looked on askance by the news media as highly commercial. Unless they are presented in so interesting or entertaining a way that the very idea outweighs any commercial bias, such stories will not win space or time in the media. The public relations man or woman charged with promoting a product or service recognizes that the essential challenge is to persuade the media to accept a story idea or event as being of general interest.

A mystique can be built up around a product, a company, or an idea through careful marketing public relations. For example, the Cabbage Patch Kids craze began with a well-orchestrated public relations program. Those toys were hot items long before advertising and other promotional activities went into play.

In most cases, marketing public relations happens in conjunction with a number of other activities designated to raise awareness. Advertising campaigns, sales promotion, merchandising, and couponing are all part of the mix of the techniques used by the marketer. These elements working together can create broadscale awareness for a product, service, or company.

## The Role of Publicity

Publicity, sometimes called "media relations," is fundamental to all public relations, but it is the very heart of the marketing function. There is no marketing public relations without it. Media are the conduit used by marketing communications specialists to reach key audiences.

In Chapter 5, we discussed the various kinds of media. In this section, we will discuss these media from a marketing viewpoint and describe the different approaches to them. A knowledge of the media and a mastery of communications techniques do not make a marketing publicity professional. Public relations is an "idea" business that requires clear and, when possible, original thinking, followed up by superior communication of the thought.

Since the media almost automatically resist anything

that smacks of marketing, this branch of the business requires that the practitioner employ an uncommon degree of inventiveness and sensitivity. Anybody qualified to practice public relations should be able, on occasion, to develop a good marketing idea and plan. But it takes a special kind of mind to hang in there year in and year out, doing an effective marketing public relations job.

The first step is to determine whether a story has consumer implications. Does it have broad appeal? If the answer is "yes," then the practitioner can continue to select media and apply techniques described in this chapter. Is the story highly visual? If so, perhaps a video news release is the way to go. Is it truly newsworthy to a wide variety of media? Perhaps a press conference is called for. Is the subject of interest in certain markets and not in others? Maybe a media tour makes sense. It is obvious that every story must be viewed independently.

## The Trade Press

Trade publications are important in marketing public relations. Survey after survey through the years has confirmed that in business, people rely on trade publications for information.

A survey conducted among Wall Street financial analysts and portfolio managers, by Strategic Information Research Corporation, showed that 22 percent of these experts rated trade journals as their most-relied-upon source of information. In another survey, government officials said trade publications were their leading source of information; while at the state level, trade publications were a close second to direct contact with company spokespersons.

Where other media—newspapers, magazines, radio, and television—confine business to a small portion of their total content, each trade paper devotes 100 percent of its space to the field it covers. From a trade paper, the reader expects, seeks, and gets news and information on products, people, materials, processes, markets, plants, services, equipment, trends, and governmental actions, concerning an industry or profession.

The American trade press began with the *Philadelphia Price Current* of 1783. It reported wholesale commodity prices and marine information to merchants and shippers. Today, the trade press serves the entire spectrum of business activity. It covers all industries and professions and also includes specialties such as export and import, finance, government, merchandising, and religion. It's virtually impossible to find a substantial field that isn't covered by one or usually several trade magazines—from *Advertising Age* to *Welding Journal;* from the *American Drycleaner* to *Traffic Management.* There are trade books for accountants, designers, engineers, maintenance men, managers, purchasing agents, researchers, sales representatives, and public relations people.

On a geographical basis, there are trade papers that circulate internationally, like *Automobile International;* nationally, *Engineering News Record;* regionally, like *Western Fruit Grower;* within one state, such as *Virginia Pharmacist;* or even a single city, *Chicago Purchaser.*

While most trade magazines are monthlies, others are published weekly, biweekly, bimonthly, or quarterly. A few are published daily. The readers of these publications want information, and public relations people can help supply it. The following directories provide lists of trade magazines:

*IMS Directory of Publications*
IMS Press
426 Pennsylvania Avenue
Fort Washington, Pennsylvania 19034

*Bacon's Publicity Checker*
Bacon's Publishing Company
332 South Michigan Avenue
Chicago, Illinois 60604

*The Standard Periodical Directory*
Oxbridge Communications, Inc.
183 Madison Avenue
Suite 1108
New York, New York 10016

*Standard Rate & Data Service*
(Business Publicaton Edition)
3004 Glenview Road
Wilmette, Illinois 60091

*Ulrich's International Periodicals Directory*
R.R. Bowker Company
205 East 42nd Street
New York, New York 10017

*Working Press of the Nation*
Volume II—Magazine Directory
The National Research Bureau, Inc.
Division of Information Products Group
Automated Marketing Systems, Inc.
310 South Michigan Avenue
Suite 1150
Chicago, Illinois 60604

The best way to start preparing and placing trade publicity is by becoming familiar with the journals that are pertinent to a company's business. Public relations staff members should study recent issues to see precisely what material they publish. Each trade journal normally has its own sections, departments, columns, and features. Some magazines carry only brief new product items; others publish articles and features; still others lean to the technical side. Some magazines are staff-written and accept nothing from the outside, but these are interested in following up good story leads. Most journals accept releases and articles, but some incorporate the data into broader stories that cover an entire industry. And then there are those that depend entirely on publicity material.

In many cases, an editor will provide the public relations department with a printed schedule of subjects the magazine will emphasize over the coming year and information as to which issues are buyer directories or market-data annuals, and which are based on the industry's yearly convention. Special issues provide good opportunities for placements because editors need more articles to balance heavier advertising. Some out-of-town magazines also have local correspondents with whom public relations people can work in placing a story.

## Using Publications

Publicity should not be limited to periodicals of one specific industry. For example, a release on a new grocery product will obviously be of primary interest to *Progressive Grocer, Supermarket Business,* and similar publications. However, with modification or the addition of extra details, the release may also have appeal to packaging, food processing, and even institutional magazines.

These publications offer opportunities for much more than standard news releases. Even when there is no news, there are possibilites for features, industry roundups, "how-to" stories, case histories, technical pieces, forecasts, trend articles, and speeches. When there is news, it doesn't necessarily mean product news. Stories can be based on developments in design, research, materials, processes, plant construction, equipment, applications, finance (trade papers are read by security analysts), and markets. Management interviews can be arranged for editors, plant tours can be set up, and panel discussions can be reported.

Trade publicity can also be organized as a continuing campaign. Following an initial news release, the publicists can create a more comprehensive version of the story for the one or two magazines that can do the company the most good. Weeks or months later, the publicists can begin placing case history articles describing the success of the product, process, or development.

There's even a way to almost guarantee results. Nothing is more frustrating to a public relations person than to research and write an article only to discover that nobody wants it. One way to avoid this is to "presell" the story before preparing it. A public relations staffer should tell the editor what it is he or she has in mind and then get suggestions on how to tailor the piece to the exact needs of the publication. If the story idea is really important to the readers, the editor may consider making it a cover feature. Nowadays, this usally means the public relations staff will have to provide a color photograph good enough to merit front cover use.

Photographs are just as important as a well-written story and a good headline. Trade magazines usually use black-and-white shots, but they have to be good. If color pictures are available, the editor should be alerted. Some major publications use color on inside pages.

For anything but a straight news release, it's best to include with an article, a letter that briefly outlines the contents, and the reasons why readers would be interested. The editor needs to know whether it's a complete exclusive or just an exclusive in the magazine's field. The editor will take a week or so to review the material before making a decision.

## Working with Editors

News conferences are also used to disseminate news to trade magazines, especially for occasions like a plant opening or a tour of a new reserach and development facility. Deadline dates vary widely, and the editor of a monthly won't be overjoyed if a weekly competitor gets the same media kit at the same time. This problem of fairness becomes more critical when reporters from daily newspapers are invited to trade press conferences. Ideally, the trade publications should get the news far enough in advance so that everyone can break with the story on or about the same release date. Each editor should be given the opportunity to obtain additional information to differentiate that publication's version of the story from those published by the competition.

In addition to unfair timing, trade editors have other pet peeves.

- One is a story that doesn't stick strictly to news and facts or offer some reader service. It gets routed quickly to the wastebasket. Publicists should take care not to promote and or mention a client or product too frequently.

- Another peeve is the failure of publicists to keep "exclusives" truly exclusive. This isn't conducive to lasting relationships.

- Editors in Canada don't take kindly to articles that aren't "Canadianized" in some way. Quotes from the company's Canadian management and discussion about its Canadian plants, distributuors, and customers make the story more interesting to audiences in that country.

- A final peeve is the impatient publicist who keeps calling the editor to get news of a story. Most trade magazines are monthlies whose editors work several months in advance. A good many editors assemble material for a specific issue and don't look through it until they're actually working on that issue.

## Getting Value

Let's say the public relations staff has done everything right. It has prepared fact-filled articles, taken excellent photos, and arranged for multiple-page placements. The job isn't complete, though, if the staff isn't merchandising these results back to the company or client.

Trade placements make excellent promotional material for sales people, distributors, and dealers. Most magazines will produce a large quantity of reprints at a reasonable cost. These reprints can be used in customer and prospect mailings that serve as "door-openers" for sales follow-up. On sales calls—which, according to studies, cost an average of $131 each—sales people can be armed with folders containing an array of placements, to complement "party line" company literature.

In merchandising publicity results, it's a good idea to state the circulation and describe the importance of the readership to the company. This information can be obtained from the Business Publication edition of *Standard Rate & Data Service.* Trade publicity articles frequently result in inquiries from readers and these, too, should be reported to the company for follow-up.

In getting copies of placements, experienced public relations people don't relegate the job to a clipping service. Clipping services seem to function best when they're on the lookout for broad coverage. When it comes to catching a single placement of a story in a specific magazine (unless the firm subscribes and the public relations staff reviews every issue), it's best to contact the publication's circulation department and request a copy or tear sheet after publication. A piece of publicity may be bumped to make room for late news. Chances are it will appear in a future issue. Incidentally, a good way to cement a relationship with an editor is to pass along any industry news you may have picked up when researching a story.

## Wire Services and Syndication

Virtually all the daily newspapers in the U.S., with a combined circulation of 60 million readers, subscribe to one or more of the wire services and buy features from syndicates. These are desirable targets for publicists because their material receives good coverage in newspapers throughout the country. Also, credit lines such as Associated Press (AP), United Press International (UPI), and Newspaper Enterprise Association (NEA), give stories a certain prestige value among editors. In addition, newspapers pay for the services, whether they use them or not; so they get their money's worth only when they publish the material. The wires and the many syndicates are in fierce competition to produce good stories. Competition keeps the quality high, and that builds acceptance at the newspapers.

Almost any story carried on the two major wire services—Associated Press and United Press International—will reach more newspaper readers than a story carried any other way. The wires want hard news as early as possible, and each wants it no later than the other. They don't expect exclusivity in news stories, but they do expect promptness and simultaneous receipt of the news.

Publicists must distinguish between AP Newsfeatures and UPI Features on the one hand, and the AP and UPI wires on the other. AP Newsfeatures and UPI Features operate separately from their related news operations. Although a large segment of the feature material is moved daily on the wires, much is also distributed by mail. These feature services are actually in competition with their own news wires as well as with rival syndicates.

Syndicated columnists historically have been carried widely because they provide a convenient way for newspaper editors to run a spectrum of political, social, and business opinions. This is especially true in these times of inadequate staffs and increasingly complex news. More and more editors rely on columnists to explain national and international news, economics, and social trends while their own reporters—especially on medium-sized and small papers—stick to local and regional news.

In recent years, the tendency to cut news space because of rising costs has sharply reduced the use of secondary or marginal stories. The syndicated column, however, has survived the "news-space recession" because of its low cost to the newspaper publisher. This is best illustrated by a statement attributed to Art Buchwald: "You can fill half the paper for less than it costs to pay a copy boy. It's the cheapest form of editorial copy there is." For the most part, columns are used on a regular basis in a fixed spot in the newspaper's format.

The syndicates must have their stories on an exclusive basis. Editors also insist that both sides of a controversial subject must be given equal treatment to avoid offending the varying editorial policies of subscribing newspapers. They also want each story tailored for their particular syndicate. Thus, the practitioner should first submit a story idea to a syndicate editor by a memo, letter, or phone call. If the editor is interested, he or she will tell the practitioner to develop the feature along specific lines or will assign a staff writer to develop it.

There are more than 340 syndicate feature services listed in the *Annual Directory of Syndicated Services*. Most, however, are limited to comics, columns, and specialized subjects such as crossword puzzles, child care, and Hollywood. Others, such as the *New York Times* news service or *Wash-*

*ington Post-Los Angeles Times* news service, distribute only material that is published in their newspapers.

There are actually just a handful of syndicates that can handle general news features on a daily basis. They are AP Newsfeatures, UPI Features, Newspaper Enterprise Association, North American Newspaper Alliance, Women's News Service, Enterprise Science Service, King Features, Editorial Research Reports, and Copley.

## Special Needs of Electronic Media

Competition for network television time is fierce. A survey taken several years ago showed that each network news program screens 100,000 feet of film a week from all sources, of which less than *2 percent* is aired.

The approach to television publicity can begin with the understanding that unlike newspaper reporters, television news people are apt to be generalists. A newspaper reporter is usually assigned to a "beat" and builds up a great deal of knowledge of that area. The electronic news people, however, cover a broad range of news, although sports and weather usually command special broadcasters. There is much more need for publicists to provide background information and briefing to electronic media than to print media.

**Broadcast interviews.** A company's top managers have to be better prepared for broadcast interviews. They must understand that their interviews are going to be edited down, making it important for them to be brief and to the point. Generally, executives sound more natural and believable when they speak in their own words rather than memorizing responses. Still, they should be rehearsed and schooled in the art of news program interviews.

Various agencies now offer day-long training sessions

involving a variety of mock interviews by experienced broadcasters. Video replay can be an excellent teaching device in this kind of training. The need to localize a story for radio and television is greater than in newspaper publicity. Networks are looking for stories of national interest, while individual stations want stories with a strong local element. A newspaper can vary its mix of local national news each day; while a television or radio station usually sets aside specific amounts of time for local and network news.

**Talk shows.** Talk shows and call-in shows on radio are excellent opportunities for marketing publicity. The show hosts are interested first in entertainment and next in helpful advice. A spokesperson who combines both and adds the ability to localize a basic story is usually well accepted.

Any television interview or appearance on a talk show or news program is far more effective if it includes something visual. A two- or three-minute film makes a guest more interesting, and a demonstration, even on a cardboard model, is far better than a talking head.

**Other marketing opportunities.** Programs need props, and it is possible to place a commercial product as a prop into a television program (or a Broadway play). At an athletic event, for example, it might be possible to have some of the principal competitors interviewed on television while sitting in a certain car or sipping a specific beverage.

Just as there are syndicated columnists for the newspapers, so there are syndicated television and radio programs. These services supplement the networks by providing "feature" programming at a relatively low cost. Slide and script releases are used by the smaller television stations. One service, North American Precis Syndicate, Inc., periodically sends scripts and slides to a group of 300 television stations, with reportedly excellent results.

## Sponsored Films

Another way of reaching television audiences is through a film sponsored by a company or client. These generally run from three to five minutes, but are sometimes long enough for a 15-30-minute program. In most cases, the film is used as a filler—when sports events end earlier than expected, for example. Distributors of film to television as well as to many other outlets include Association-Sterling Films and Modern Talking Picture Service. These services charge according to the size of the audience they create through multiple distribution of the films.

Just as marketers can use print placements to help support sales efforts, they could also turn broadcast publicity into marketing tools. For example, cassette tape recordings of product "plugs" or executive interviews on radio or television can become effective desk top audio tools in the prospect's office, as can filmed highlights of television publicity activity.

There are numerous possibilities for merchandising publicity results. A trade association for a major food industry produced what many constituents called its most intriguing annual report ever: a magazine format that illustrated editorial and consumerist challenges, together with the association's aggressive, multimedia response. In this case, clippings played a role in demonstrating the value of the particular association to its members, as well as the overall value of publicity.

Favorable editorials, convincing rebuttal of an accusation, reports of executive meetings with the media—these and other evidence of progressive corporate policy can also be used effectively at stockholder meetings, directors' sessions, and distributor conventions.

This calls for good planning and follow-through: the economical use of clipping services (given specific instructions on what to look for ), orderly filing of results, and the use of successful publicity in other aspects of the marketing communications program. Neatly kept but never-merchandised scrapbooks become just that: scrap.

## The Special Event—Making News Happen

To the marketer a special event is an off-beat measure to create news. Its form is limited only by the imagination. Its aim, in most cases, is pure publicity, although sometimes a special event may serve several purposes.

A special event may be as simple as a new-product introduction in an unusual setting or as complex as an around-the-world race. It may be glitzy or sober; it may aim for wide or narrow media appeal; it may involve tie-ins with other organizations or require the collaboration of a number of elements of a single industry to make broad a point in which all have a joint interest. The special event is often costly because of the nature of the activity itself (sponsoring a golf tournament, for example), or because of the manpower required to plan and operate an intricate occasion, such as an open house at a large manufacturing plant.

A special event that will probably live in the memory of many Americans is the 100th birthday celebration of the renovated Statue of Liberty on July 4, 1986. From the mammoth fund-raising efforts for Lady Liberty's facelift to the three-day unveiling extravaganza involving top celebrities and senior political figures from the U.S. and France, this was a public relations effort at its finest.

The Statue of Liberty renovation and unveiling was itself a special event for hundreds of American companies that found ingenious ways to use the occasion to contribute something of their own flavor to the celebration and, in the course of doing so, to call favorable attention to their own marketing aims, services, or products.

To one commercial enterprise, a special event may be a fashion show; to another, sponsorship of a mobile museum exhibit. Pharmaceutical companies go to great lengths to exhibit at conventions of physicians with displays that both make news and carry a selling message.

## Attracting the Press

Whether it's a news conference to introduce a new product, or an open house to unveil a planned facility, the special event affords an opportunity to heighten media interest. Properly run, the event, with company officials face-to-face with the press, can dramatically promote both that which is being introduced and the people behind it, their longer-range corporate goals, and public benefits.

The key word is "special." The important thing to keep in mind when planning a special event is that you are dealing with a method of communication, a means to a publicity end. It is not a social affair or an occasion that has inherent value other than communicating to others. Unless you have something tangible to show to the press, community leaders, and other affected publics, unless there is a newsworthy point to make, the cost might be better invested in other communication activities.

The best way to determine newsworthiness is to determine the communication objectives. Once that objective has been clearly defined, the practitioner can then plan the event to make certain that every element of the press conference or plant tour will help achieve those objectives. In planning, there are certain fundamentals that must be covered. For example:

- Be sure there is enough money, enough time, and enough staff power to get the job done right.

- Make sure the right people attend: editors and commentators; public officials who know and understand the objectives; distributors and dealers in decision-making marketing positions. Don't depend on one letter of invitation; follow up personally and follow through after the event. And don't mix editorial "apples" with trade "oranges." Tailor separate events for news gatherers and customers. Their needs are usually *not* the same.

- Thoroughly brief the company's participants. Work out ahead of time what will be said (keep it terse and factual). Anticipate every tough question. A special event is supposed to be a newsmaker, not a surprise party for your executives.

- Spell out every assignment, from transportation and refreshments to visitor registration, tour guides, and press kit. Assign every activity to a responsible individual or team. Then prepare a "what-if" backup plan for each function.

- Incorporate in press kits only what will explain the product, service, facility, or company. Photos should "work" in that they demonstrate function, benefit, dimension. Use question-and-answer outlines, speech summaries, and key-point fact sheets to help the busy writer or commentator prepare the story.

## Creativity a Must

All of this does not mean that a special event, however carefully planned, should be dull. In fact, the medium can indeed be part of the message, if the planning is creative and the event is designed to underscore the basic point. For example, a news conference held to acquaint consumer editors with a new odor-fighting insole was staged at a Japanese restaurant, with the shoes-off ritual deliberately tied in with the new product. The shoes-off news conferences gave the writers a clever news peg on which to hang their stories, and many of the stories resulting from that briefing incorporated the novelty of the event itself.

Suppose, for instance, a local casting foundry has as its goal the wish to show the community that it is a good place to work; that health and safety take high priority; and that it manufactures useful, high-quality products. Now suppose it decides to hold an open house. If the foundry is of sufficient size and importance in the community's economy, it may be possible to spice the event by enlisting the mayor to issue a proclamation saluting the foundry for a variety of reasons such as its efforts on behalf of air and water pollution control or its steady growth, which has provided dependable employment.

The local foundry may hold a planned tour for employees' families, an in-house conference with local educators on a subject of mutual concern, or a community open house. Many firms prefer to time special events to observe an anniversary, announce an important expansion or modernization program, or to reveal recently completed expansions or improvements to the public.

Any business that installs pollution control equipment in or outside the plant has a special event opportunity. Before-and-after photos, the costs involved, and community benefits to be derived should be emphasized. All these help demonstrate that the company cares about its people and its community—that it is a desirable neighbor.

All aspects of an open house—housekeeping, signs, exhibits, worker practices, physical conditions, and visible quality control practices—should be geared to achieve the company's objectives. While not difficult, these events require thorough planning, follow-through, and time. On the day before the event, news media should be given a preview of the tour. This will enable them to give your event the coverage it deserves.

## Other Techniques of Marketing Communications

**The marketing mix.** As mentioned in the introduction to this chapter, marketing public relations is one element of an awareness-building program that might include advertising, sales promotion, and other techniques. This section discusses other aspects of marketing communications that sometimes involve the marketing public relations specialist.

**Planning a meeting.** The specialist can be of invaluable help to his or her marketing and sales colleagues, if the purposes of the meeting or seminar are to communicate rather than to simply "glad-hand" prospects.

Once again, it is important to establish clear-cut meeting objectives and dynamic strategies to reach those objectives. Thus, the session might become a real seminar—with emphasis on third-party endorsements by "visiting" engineers or a panel of university faculty members and "ideas-in-use" tie-ins with the product or service. On the other hand, if the product lent itself to a store's merchandising program, the "visiting experts" could be retailers who would comment on the need for such a product.

The actual meeting place can be important, too. If appropriate, the session could be held in a plant meeting facility near the production site, or aboard a plane in which a new passenger feeding system has been successfully tested. The purpose is not to distract from the information process, but rather to underscore the positive values to be presented. One company, for example, converted hotel meeting parlors into supermarket meat departments. They had various cuts in plugged-in coolers to show how a new retail meat identity code system, including colorful point-of-purchase materials, would help retailers move more product and make shoppers happier.

Wherever possible, what the company wants to sell should be shown in use, or at least in a stimulating setting. This can be done by on-site usage or by means of film, tape, or other audiovisual devices.

The alert publicist should not overlook the promotion opportunities inherent in such meetings and seminars in the form of photo-and-text stories for trade publications, including the customer's own employee newsletter.

One other opportunity should be stressed before leaving this subject: the opportunity for the customer to ask questions and to exchange ideas with the meeting organizers. Far too many meetings and seminars are structured to allow plenty of time for speeches and self-congratulation, and too little for the kind of interchange which the same marketing people seek in a one-on-one call.

**Trade shows and direct mail.** The marketing public relations person is obviously part of the team in planning and running such meetings and seminars. Not so obvious is the role of public relations people in marketing through trade shows, direct-mail solicitation, point-of-purchase displays and other techniques.

These are areas for specialists, people with highly developed talents in such fields as exhibit design, and for production companies, direct-mail houses and advertising agencies. Yet oftentimes the work of such specialists is the product of ideas originated by public relations people, or supervised by them and, in some instances, both conceived and executed by them. The marketing public relations specialist, as part of the corporate team, has the opportunity to work in all these areas.

*Trade shows:* The trade show is the modern descendant of the village marketplace and the medieval fair. In recent years its value has come under attack. Its proponents point to a continuing need for a coming together of marketers and buyers to examine wares, to allow prospects to compare carpeting products and their sellers on the spot. Its opponents cite increasing costs of exhibiting, time taken away from "regular" business activities, and the fact that a show may draw prospects from only a 200-mile radius even when it is advertised as a "national" exposition.

The point is that *both* the proponents and opponents have a case. Whether to participate in a trade show is a matter for each individual company to decide, depending on its particular marketing strategy. A new product will probably make exhibiting worthwhile—*if* it is showcased properly, *if* advanced word is passed to prospects, and *if* a publicity program is executed to bring the product to the attention of trade editors and local business reporters.

Six basic points govern trade show planning and execution:

- Find a good creative exhibit builder who is familiar with the trade show and who also knows the way around the labyrinths of exhibit hall management. Develop with the builder a concept that does *not* bring in the kitchen sink (unless you manufacture them); then let the builder work out the proper design.

- Make sure the sales people who will staff the exhibit are well briefed, that they have sufficient information material, that they know how to refer press inquiries, and that they are prepared to handle more than their own favorite customers.

- Alert trade and local business press to the event *if* you have something important to announce. Once you're on the scene—and you should be if you want to be certain that the communication job is being covered—get to know the staff assigned to the media room.

- Keep the media room supplied with handouts; more important, keep tabs on who is coming from the media and when they are expected. Trade shows are, if nothing else, visual and busy. Alert local TV station assignment editors.

- Retain a photographer to shoot not only the record picture of your exhibit but also newsworthy photos that can be offered to the trades or, if there is enough consumer interest, to one of the local newspaper business editors.

- Seek tie-in platforms at the show, such as a "convention daily" published by one of the trade publications, a speaking opportunity at the show for a key executive, or interviews with local media.

*Direct mail.* Of all the tools employed by marketers, perhaps nothing is more competitive for the attention of today's busy homemaker or business person than direct mail. Many an expensive mail campaign, involving long hours of creative effort, finds itself lost in the "junk mail," and gets pitched into the waste can.

Forget it, then? Not if you realize that quite a few people—ranging from large mail-order houses to enterprising individuals selling everything from pet rocks to sunflower seeds—are making a very tidy living on direct-mail inquiries *alone.*

There is a catch here, though. Successful mailers know what they're about:

- They build careful lists of prospects, constantly weeding out, adding on (from yet other lists depending on the audience), and working out their demographics according to the product, the time of year, and other variables.

- They usually do not depend solely on direct mail, but use rifle-shot advertising in specific-interest publications.

- They work year-round, rather than on single-shot campaigns.

- They develop sophisticated message approaches based on what people *want* to read on an envelope or in an opening paragraph. (Are you a recognized firm? Are you offering something useful as well as merely free? Can you offer a product or service at a saving? Do you have information that is immediately helpful so that further reading time will be rewarded?)

One peculiarity of direct mail is that, in many instances, once a prospect is captured by a particular mailing—especially if it promises more useful information to come—he or she is likely to anticipate further mailings. This follows the psychological premise that everyone anticipates the arrival of the next installment in a serialized story, assuming it's a cracking good story in the first place.

The degree of reader involvement is important here and depends on what kind of action is required. If, for example, a Congressman asks his constituents for their opinions on a provocative issue, chances are the response will be reasonably heavy. But if a marketer wants to sell a product by mail, the offer generally should be based on as little reader effort as possible, such as an easy-to-handle coupon or order blank.

If the purpose is not to solicit a direct sale by mail, but rather to provide product or service or corporate information that may induce a customer to listen to a sales agent, then some of the specifics will change, but the basic principles still apply.

There's no law that says a mailing must be sent out in a standard envelope or look like every other mailing. Successful mailings have been made sealed in steel cans, with part of the message (and the address) on the can label. Others have consisted of minifilmstrips in throwaway paper viewers. Still others have taken the form of a message to the boss wrapped around a single rose for his secretary or a wall poster whose commercial message was simply the name of the creator of the inspirational lines or eye-pleasing art.

Yet another technique involves preparing a fact folder that comprises the first in a series of mailings on a particular subject such as a tourism destination. The folder contains initial background materials, plus the promise to send more specifics as they are developed, and the suggestion that the handy, file-drawer-sized folder—perhaps appropriately tabbed for quick identification—be used to contain the remaining mail pieces. Information, organization, continuity, anticipation of use—all work together to help make direct mail more than just "junk."

**Education programs.** There are many opportunities for the business sector to transmit to elementary, junior high, high school, and college students not only valuable knowledge about *things*, but equally valuable positive perceptions about *business itself.*

Students are not, however, captive audiences, nor do education administrators breathlessly await paper or film handouts from the business community. They do welcome carefully thought-out classroom materials which emphasize, in the *student's* language, usable facts, and which provide fresh insight on the subject.

An educational package can take a variety of forms: grants-in-aid; study outlines; reference books, brochures, and photo collections for library use; films, tapes, and other audiovisual aids; guest lectures; facility tours; on-site "inform" programs; and combinations of all of these.

Regardless of form, there are fundamental considerations that any acceptable program must reflect.

- A knowledgeable education information specialist or committee should be involved in the preparation of the package. Frequently, teachers and administrators are available during after-class hours as consultants.

- The subject, and its treatment, must be aimed at the proper audience. What interests a college sophomore may be too sophisticated for a seventh-grader. The program should get to the point quickly and not waste limited class time.

- A teacher's study plan and reference bibliography should be included along with the student's material. Motivating the instructor will enhance the success of the entire program.

- Programs should talk *concepts* and spark *ideas* rather than provide a commercial in disguise. They can explain an industry's positive impact—present or potential—on the student's life, show career opportunities, and, if appropriate, point out the benefits others have received from the product or service.

- A program should be planned sufficiently ahead of the school year—at least six months—to allow time for evaluation and curriculum scheduling.

**In-store merchandising.** The average supermarket carries more than 10,000 different items on its shelves. No wonder the point-of-purchase (POP) industry influences billions of dollars in sales, as manufacturers compete for the eye of the typical shopper who, according to *Progressive Grocer,* spends less than 28 minutes per store visit.

Dump displays, end-aisles, shelf talkers, counter-toppers: these and other units compete for the impulse sale, and impulse sales account for as much as 70 percent of the final ringup at the checkout counter, depending on which study you read. But there is one statistic that even the point-of-purchase makers ruefully admit is valid. Roughly 80 percent of all the colorful, hard-hitting displays sent to food, drug, and mass-merchandising outlets *never reach the floor or are gone almost before the customer sees them.*

This is an extremely expensive symptom of what the merchandiser faces: largely untrained and uncaring store floor personnel; pilferage; constant demands by the retailer's regional supervisor for "fresh," ever-changing display set ups; the plethora of manufacturers' "deals" that prompts merchandisers into short-life scheduling of each display.

Is there a cure? Probably not a complete one; but to eliminate point-of-purchase materials would be as foolish as continuing to make the basic mistakes that lead to so high a nonuse rate.

Properly conceived and placed, point-of-purchase displays can indeed boost impulse sales, help introduce new items, achieve mutually profitable tie-in displays, and, by their very existence, aid the manufacturer in getting better product facings. Surveys of retailers reveal several key points to keep in mind when planning point-of-purchase materials:

- Develop new materials in concert with retailer merchandisers. Find out their needs and test concepts before going to production.

- Plan POP displays as "umbrella" merchandisers. Using your product as the pivot, provide the means by which other, noncompeting products can also be displayed in a natural tie-in (e.g., soft drinks and picnic supplies; tuna with mayonnaise and salad fixings; sun tan lotion with beach supplies; a new fishing reel with other tackle equipment). Space is at a premium in any store.

- Create a theme that the store can use. Again, put the tie-in umbrella to work, rather than a narrow "buy me" approach.

- Provide managers with illustrations of display ideas, emphasizing tie-ins. Managers love new concepts, especially if they don't call for a lot of display-building and maintenance time.

- Develop similar illustrations or brochures, stressing product merchandising advantages and *ongoing* tie-in opportunities, for the men and women manufacturers usually overlook—the regional supervisors who are the people primarily responsible for keeping displays up, taking them down.

- Provide trade publications with a photo and brief description of new POP displays before placing the materials in stores. Showing the display in action—even if simulated—increases chances of obtaining supportive publicity.

## Case in Point

The mechanism of a multicity media tour aimed at reaching a specific audience with a message was the mainspring of a marketing case in point: People over the age of 60 were the specific target of this information campaign, conducted by United Airlines. Research demonstrated that 40 percent of Americans in this age group took a trip within the domestic United States during 1985 and that most of them chose to fly when they traveled.

Accordingly, United Airlines created a senior citizens travel club called "Silver Wings Plus" with certain benefits for members. The hope was to enroll approximately 250,000 persons in the club and the challenge was to differentiate it from similar organizations.

The public relations program was built around Betty Lowry, who had retired after serving 37 years as a United in-flight attendant. During her service to the airlines, she not only had logged an impressive number of hours but also had served many famous travelers, including President Dwight Eisenhower, General Douglas MacArthur, and Eleanor Roosevelt.

Lowry was named president of "Silver Wings Plus" and official spokesperson for the club. She was dispatched on a media tour of U.S. cities that were chosen on the basis of their high concentration of senior citizens.

She appeared on national television shows, such as "PM Magazine" and on many regional television and radio stations. Lowry also handled innumerable interviews with travel editors of major daily newspapers and magazines. In her appearances, Lowry gave details on the club and also offered special tips for older travelers, packing hints, and other helpful ideas.

In the same vein, a booklet entitled "Senior Travel, No Better Time" was put together for United Airlines. It contained the same sort of information. Lowry offered this booklet during her public appearances, and it was also available free of charge on request. Press kits including the booklet, and information on "Silver Wings Plus" and its benefits, the club, the spokesperson, and the subject of travel by older persons in general, were distributed to travel editors and other media people throughout the country.

Simple statistics indicate the results. Within six months, "Silver Wings Plus" enrolled more than the target membership.

A special event was the keystone of another case in point. The assignment was to publicize the opening of a bagel factory, of all things, in Mattoon, Illinois, of all places. The payoff included a front-page story in the *New York Times* and media coverage that reached an estimated 15 million people.

Bagels, traditional Jewish rolls with holes in the middle, most commonly have been associated with the east coast, especially New York City. However, Lender's Bagel Bakery constructed a new plant, with the capacity to make two million bagels a day, in Mattoon. The Illinois community (pop. 19,055) was previously known as the "buckle on the corn belt," and many local citizens had never tasted a bagel.

The objectives of the public relations campaign, therefore, were to introduce the product and the plant to the local population as well as to attract national attention to the new and unlikely "Bagel Capital of the World."

Keying the event to the off-beat character of the product, public relations people put together the "World's Biggest Bagel Breakfast."

A table 1,000 feet long was set up on Mattoon's Main Street and the entire town—as well as print and electronic media from all over—was invited to join Lender's for a free breakfast of bagels, cream cheese, coffee, and orange juice.

The event on a Saturday morning drew a crowd of 7,000, including a number of media people, state and local political figures, and the general population. Adding to the gaiety of the festivities were bagel games and prizes, "bagel songs" played by the local high school band, and bagel window displays, signs, and decorations. The event not only attained the national publicity its hosts sought, but it also started the new plant on a warm, friendly footing with the community.

Incidentally, the "World's Biggest Bagel Breakfast" is now an annual event.

# Chapter 14

# Specialized Marketing Communications

Certain industries call for specialized techniques in marketing communications. Attention will be focused here on some of the more prominent industries: travel and leisure, food and beverage, "life-style," general consumer goods, entertainment, sports, and health care. Business-to-business communications also require specialized treatment and will be discussed in this chapter.

## Travel and Leisure Public Relations

Tourism today is the largest industry in the world. It makes a major contribution to almost every country's economy. The worldwide number of travelers and tourists is now nearing the four-billion mark; Americans alone spent over $22 billion traveling in foreign countries in 1984.

This means, of course, that there are many opportunities in travel and leisure public relations, a field in which a wide range of groups—airlines, cruise lines, hotels and resorts, country destinations, and tour operators—are all competing for a piece of the total tourism pie. They need good, creative public relations to help them distinguish and enhance their product.

The traveling public spends a considerable amount of time planning vacations. It is not unusual for a trip to represent a family's single largest expenditure in a year, and it is important that the right choice be made. People need information to help them make a decision, and they gather this from a wide range of sources. The dispersal of positive information by a variety of public relations techniques is therefore critical.

Often, a vacation destination has an image in the minds of the public that results from many factors unrelated to travel. In this age of international communications, the news media constantly report on countries around the world, and not always positively.

Travel public relations deals with both positive and negative perceptions. The work for most travel destinations or services is a combination of generating positive publicity and counterbalancing any negatives. In the travel business, many outside factors, both man-made and natural, must be dealt with. These may include airline disasters, acts of terrorism, strikes, local health problems, earthquakes, or fires. Public relations plans are required to cope with all these possibilities.

Another problem often faced in tourism public relations is the disparity of marketing concepts. Some foreign companies attempting to tap the lucrative American travel market view it in terms of their own foreign public relations perceptions. Often these perceptions must be changed before they can make inroads in the American arena.

Most important, however, is the fact that tourism by its very nature is a cooperative venture. No one travels in order to sit in an airline seat or a hotel room. Once travelers arrive at their destinations, they visit and experience restaurants, beaches, museums, and all the other places that make a vacation a rewarding experience. Thus, public relations may have one primary message—publicity for a destination perhaps—but it also has many "secondary" messages concerning hotels, resorts, and airlines, all of which contribute to the proper promotion of the destination. Without including these, the destination's publicity efforts may be ineffectual.

**Selling travel.** The selling of a travel product, with the exception of hotels and airlines for the businessman or woman (who more often than not is interested primarily in the utilitarian aspects of both), often involves a variety of emotional appeals to a variety of consumers, all of whom have been dreaming of that all-important, two-week getaway from the rigors of everyday life. For the honeymooner, the appeal may be romance; for the outdoor man or woman, adventure; for the senior citizen, serenity.

Since travelers have such varied interests, they choose vacation destinations for a variety of reasons. Thus, a travel promotion must publicize as many aspects of a destination as possible in order to be successful and to increase the popularity of the vacation spot among a variety of potential travelers.

An article in a woman's magazine about the superb shopping in Hong Kong, for example, helps raise travelers' awareness of that city as an interesting vacation destination. A media tour of food editors to Hong Kong publicizes the cuisine of the city as much as it does the city itself. An article on the safety of women traveling alone, in which the concierge of a Hong Kong hotel is quoted, has substantial positive publicity value, not only for the hotel but for the entire colony of Hong Kong. Each of these ideas, while taking a different tack, helps promote, publicize, and increase awareness of Hong Kong as an attractive vacation destination among travelers with varied interests.

Equally important for the public relations practitioner in travel and tourism is the necessity to build, enhance, and publicize reliability and credibility. Because tourism is an industry that is rife with consumer complaints on everything from poor restaurant service to lost luggage, it is important that a destination or travel-related company be perceived as helping prevacation dreams become reality. Few travelers want to chance their annual vacation and savings on a destination or hotel where potential problems may outnumber the potential for pleasure.

As in other areas of public relations, a variety of tools can be used in marketing travel and tourism. In fact, imagination and creativity are the only limiting factors. Here is an overview of various methods that can be used.

*Print media.* Many publications publish travel and leisure-related articles. In addition to weekly travel sections in newspapers throughout North America (over 600 newspapers currently use color photography in these sections, a figure which attests to the importance subscribers place on travel information and articles), several travel and leisure publications run articles on destinations, hotels, restaurants, and other holiday topics. These include *National Geographic Traveler, Travel & Leisure, Signature,* and *Travel-Holiday,* among others.

In addition, many regional and city magazines—*New York, Sunset, Philadelphia, D, Los Angeles,* and a host of others—publish monthly travel columns that offer further opportunities for promotion. A large number of other publications include travel articles in their regular monthly features. These include many home magazines *(Better Homes and Gardens, House Beautiful);* senior citizen publications (*Modern Maturity, 50 Plus*); travel newsletters *(Entree, The Hideaway Report, Travel Smart)* and special interest publications (those published for campers, yachtsmen, archaeology buffs, scuba divers). Good, evocative color photography is an important tool for use with the print media.

Guidebooks also offer good promotional possibilities, as do the many freelance writers who often write articles for several publications. Many travel editors and writers are members of The Society of American Travel Writers (SATW), and the organization's directory can be helpful in putting one in touch with reliable authorities who are receptive to article ideas.

Like other fields, the travel industry has trade publications that feature news of interest to travel agents and wholesalers (the agent is the person who actually sells the trip to the customer; the wholesaler puts the tour together and sells it to the agent). Among these publications are *Travel Weekly, Travel Agent, Travel Management Daily,* and various regional editions of the *TravelAge* publications. These feature items of interest to agents—rates, fare changes, and other information that affects the industry—rather than consumer-oriented material concerning the beauty and history of a particular resort or area.

Some major consumer magazines, such as *Esquire* and *The Atlantic,* also publish special annual travel sections. Others, such as *Sports Illustrated,* through its popular annual swimsuit issue, offer a substantial amount of publicity for the destination where a special article is photographed. Material provided to publications should always be colorful and highly descriptive.

*Radio and television.* Radio and television can also be used effectively to promote a travel destination. Television coverage can include travel segments, not only on local shows, but also on cable and nationally syndicated programs such as "PM Magazine" and "Evening Magazine." But the public relations professional seeks other outlets as well.

In the case of Hong Kong cited above, the public relations agency with the account also pursued a variety of other television programs to reach its target market of upscale travelers, including vacationers, business executives, and professionals. To accomplish this, the agency staff interested producers of several popular shows to send film crews to Hong Kong. The coverage that resulted include "60 Minutes" (a segment on a wealthy Chinese businessman); a top network soap opera (their location shoot resulted in five weeks of daily exposure); and segments on several other popular series such as the "Love Boat" and "Dallas." To augment this coverage, travel-oriented and life-style video news features were also produced and sent by satellite to 300 stations across the U.S.

Radio provides additional opportunities. In addition to using life-style segments, some stations are interested in spokespersons who are available as talk show guests or as experts for soft news pieces. Although there are few radio travel shows scattered about the country, some larger stations have the ability to do on-the-scene broadcasts from various holiday locations.

*Special promotions.* Staging special promotions helps to raise the profile of the travel spot. Creativity is the key to successful promotion, and one should look beyond the travel media to obtain extensive positive consumer exposure. For instance, department stores such as Bloomingdale's and Macy's in New York, Neiman-Marcus in Dallas, and others throughout the country at times host promotions that highlight a particular country. Large shopping malls often do the same for destinations, hotels, and restaurants. The obvious benefit is direct consumer exposure in important target markets. Travel trade shows, special travel agent promotions, and agent seminars can also help bring a message directly to the industry.

Larger special projects have the potential to be even more effective. When the Mexican resort of Ixtapa desired to attract more visitors to its Pacific shores, it hosted the "Battle of the Network Stars," a two-hour, celebrity-filled, prime-time special on network television. In addition to the network crew that attended the taping of the special, representatives from other television and print media were invited to attend and to interview the celebrities who were participating. Despite the considerable logistics involved in the overall production, the resort derived extensive publicity from the show. In addition to the more than 20 million viewers who watched the special when it aired a few weeks after taping, the resort also gained a great deal of exposure in newspapers, on other TV programs, and in subsequent reruns of the show.

*Media familiarization tours.* Whether one is dealing with print or electronic media, the most common means of promoting tourism coverage is a media familiarization trip. To the travel editor as well as the news editor, "seeing is believing." Media tours for editors and writers usually consist of small groups of five to 10 people. Logistical requirements for such trips—development of press releases and press kits, hotel and airline reservations, development of itineraries—can be time-consuming, but these steps are necessary to ensure the success of the project.

Although travel editors receive literally hundreds of invitations to travel all over the world, they must be selective as to those they accept to ensure that their articles continue to reflect the interests of their subscribers. The primary tasks of the public relations professional organizing a media tour is to be familiar with an editor's needs, to suggest a variety of article ideas to those invited, and, most important, to target the trip to appropriate publications. Successful public relations executives don't pitch a mountain climbing trip to an editor who writes exclusively for senior citizens or a cuisine trip to an editor of an outdoor or adventure publication. They know publications' markets, the interests of their subscribers, and which story angles to suggest to an editor. Finally, in developing their list of invitations, they do not invite writers from competing publications to attend the same familiarization trip.

*Trade relations.* Public relations can play an important role in winning the support of the travel trade, particularly the travel agent, who provides advice upon which vacationers often base their plans. Therefore, any comprehensive public relations program will always include provision of information to agents. Seminars for travel experts can provide an effective way to impart this information.

## Food and Beverage Publicity

For public relations professionals currently working with food and beverages, the market is ripe. Food is the subject of the 1980s and will no doubt continue to be in the next decade. Americans are obsessed with food—its look, taste, health value, and preparation—as never before in our history. And competition among food and beverage suppliers reflects the public's frenzy for food.

Public relations professionals are faced with the question of how to penetrate a very popular but very competitive publicity market. Trend data can be used as a basis for developing strategies and approaches for clients. This supplements consumer research with analyses of its own, such as regular studies of food and life-style pages in newspapers to determine the kinds of materials that are being sought and used by the nation's editors.

Careful analyses of both industry-specific and broad-based research is paramount to developing a marketing communications program. Coupled with creativity and a keen sense of timing, the public relations practitioner is armed with all the tools needed to distinguish one company's product from another.

## Life Style Public Relations

Public relations in the home furnishings, fashion, and beauty industries involves products and services that rely heavily on trade and consumer media support, activity at trade shows, and special events. Because of the visual nature of products, photography and audiovisual materials that position these products in an environment compatible with current style trends are important in putting the story across.

As an integral part of the marketing communications mix, public relations plans follow marketing objectives, target audiences, and product distribution channels in establishing strategies and tactics, creating messages, and selecting media. Specialized publications and broadcasting programming, which retailers and consumers consider authorities in their fields, provide many media outlets for home furnishings and beauty and fashion product information.

Fashion editors of trade and consumer publications are arbiters of style and taste, and stories appearing in trade publications can have a significant effect on retailers' buying decisions, making the media powerful in communicating to specific audiences.

## General Consumer Goods Publicity

Public relations is becoming an increasingly important part of the marketing communications mix for consumer goods. It can help a brand cut through the "message clutter" of today's advertising and establish a priority position in the consumer's mind. Public relations creates a positive selling environment by shaping a brand image, creating awareness, and establishing credibility for paid messages.

While an effective public relations program can contribute to the success of almost any marketing campaign, there are particular opportunities in packaged goods marketing. Areas where public relations can make a difference include:

- New product introductions.

- Product reformulations.

- Parity product entries.

- Revitalizing the image of an established brand.

- Support for brands with limited budgets.

- Motivating trade and sales force.

- Legitimizing advertising messages.

As more and more brands begin to include public relations activities in their marketing mix, the competition for editorial attention grows. This is particularly true in the area of packaged goods, where there are no "dedicated" media—unlike food, fashion, and health products, where there are numerous publications and regular columns that focus on these topics. As a result, a product's manufacturers have become exceptionally creative about their public relations efforts, often typing their message to an existing "news hook" by means of a sponsorship (a sports or arts activity, for example) or a community event.

Another recent trend is for a firm to use public relations to promote a product's in-store promotion. By turning such a promotion into news, the company not only creates awareness, but also generates excitement that motivates participation both at the trade and consumer levels.

## Entertainment Publicity

The role of marketing communications in the entertainment field is to build an audience. The audience is one of the most measurable components of public relations since it can be directly calculated by counting the number of tickets sold, by rating the number of A.C. Nielsen or Arbitron listeners, or by counting the number of records purchased by music fans.

The entertainment field is also one of the oldest and most maligned areas of public relations since its heritage can be traced to the mid-1800s, an era that gave birth to carnival barkers and traveling showmen who used publicity stunts to attract attention for their performers. Today's professional public relations practitioner relies on more sophisticated techniques. Campaigns are usually divided into three stages: building anticipation about an upcoming entertainment program or product; familiarizing the audience with the performer; and enticing the consumer to buy a ticket, view a performance, or purchase a prerecorded tape or record.

The technique of building anticipation about an upcoming performance gave our language a new cliché: the "behind the scenes" story. Publicists invite the news media to cover the filming of a movie, the preparation for a TV show, or the development of a stage act in the hope of getting pre-event publicity about the product. Other methods of building anticipation include "sneak previews," press releases announcing the start or completion of filming or rehearsals, and background feature articles on the producer, writer, or director of the production.

Familiarizing the potential audience with the performers is a key to creating audience empathy and identification with the characters in the plot or the entertainers on the stage. People who recognize the names of the cast are far more likely to base their purchasing or viewing decision on a performer's past successes. The role of publicists is to remind the audience of the performer's reputation for quality entertainment or to foreshadow the potential for a great performance in the new show or record. Today's "star system" is the outgrowth of years of public relations maneuvering in this field.

Enticing the consumer to take action (buy a ticket, view a show) is a combination of impulse buying and heightened awareness for the upcoming performance. The emphasis of this publicity is on the date and venue for the performance, or the availability of the tape, record, or film of the production. The lead time for such publicity is in direct proportion to the popularity of the entertainer. In other words, the greater the chance that the ticket decision is an impulse decision, the more likely it is that the publicity will be more effective the day or week of the event itself. On the other hand, pent-up demand for the ticket, record, or tape generated by earlier public relations efforts lessens the need to rely on this stage of the publicity campaign.

Critical reviews of the entertainment and high-profile "opening night" or "premiere" events are two examples of the public relations techniques used to support this phase of the campaign. However, the public relations practitioner is at the mercy of the critics if the preview or premiere performance is lackluster. Many publicists circumvent this risk by relying on exploitation of the cast's previous successes or by focusing instead on the topical issues involved in the plot, song message, or performance.

With today's more sophisticated audiences and wider array of entertainment choices, the role of public relations in the audience-building process is more complex and targeted than ever before. What used to be a huckster's art is now a well-calculated craft based on consumer motivational techniques and audience segmentation. The art of entertainment now relies on the business of public relations and the science of marketing communications.

## Sports Marketing

Sports marketing is to public relations what a hurricane is to meteorologists: unpredictable, but capable of generating a tremendous amount of activity when the right combination of elements exists. With the emergence of a wide variety of professional sports, public relations professionals have discovered another outlet to help their clients market products and services.

Typically, sports marketing entails spending a significant amount of money to sponsor a particular event that matches the demographic target of a company's product. The amount of money required depends on the degree of exposure desired. This type of involvement often leads to brand exposure through on-site signage or identity with the event itself, such as R.J. Reynolds' sponsorship of the NASCAR circuit, now known as the Winston Cup Series.

While mainstream sports sponsorships are not difficult to find—hundreds of event organizers are constantly soliciting monetary support from major corporations—targets of opportunity often arise which deviate from typical sports promotion ventures.

## Health Care

America's health-care bill in 1985, according to federal government statistics, exceeded $425 billion. Despite extensive cost-containment initiatives on the part of both employers and the government, the rate of annual increase in health-care expenditures, though dropping below the double digit rates of the 1970s and early 1980s, continued to exceed the general rate of inflation. The nation, moreover, by 1985 was spending a greater percentage of its GNP on health care than such "welfare state" economies as Sweden or Great Britain.

In this environment, the practice of health-care public relations has both flourished and evolved rapidly in sophistication and impact. If any one factor differentiates the current milieu for health-care public relations from that of earlier decades, that factor is surely *competition*.

- For-profit hospitals and health insurance companies have grown stronger, appealing to the cost-containment preferences of employers and the federal government.

- Nonprofit hospitals and health insurers (such as Blue Cross and Blue Shield) have responded with more aggressive marketing and public relations activities.

- Research-based pharmaceutical and medical device companies have used public relations to create increased consumer recognition and "pull through" of new, patent-protected drugs and devices formerly promoted primarily to physicians, pharmacists, and hospitals.

- Generic pharmaceutical companies and many drug store chains have responded with communications programs designed to promote the therapeutic equivalence of their less-costly products.

- Medical research institutes, voluntary health organizations (such as the American Heart Association and American Cancer Society), and major university hospitals have developed more sophisticated strategies for attracting media attention and financial support.

In essence, the traditional concerns (complexity of subject matter, lack of in-depth media coverage) that have always differentiated health-care public relations from other areas of practice have been intensified by contemporary economic pressures and competitive forces. These conditions have called forth new skills and created increased rewards for specialized health-care public relations practitioners.

Factors that traditionally separate the work of the health care public relations person from the generalist include:

- The need for a grounding in scientific method and medical terminology.

- The ability to translate specialized medical language on at least two levels, from the specialist professional to the generalist professional and, further, to lay audiences.

- The lack of sophistication (though this is less a problem than in the past) and breadth of responsibility of medical and science reporters in the consumer media.

- The limitation of time and space allowed for science and medical news. (In 1986 alone, both *Science Digest* and *Science 86* magazines folded, leaving only *Discover, Omni,* and the venerable *Scientific American* as outlets for extended stories on science and medicine for lay audiences.)

That these factors are still present in the increasingly competitive environment places added pressure on the health-care public relations practitioner, and makes the field increasingly challenging and lucrative for well prepared young professionals. (See Part 6 in this *Handbook.*)

## Business-to-Business Marketing Communications

Business-to-business marketing is a communications process between one business and another in which the first wishes to sell its goods or services. It includes manufacturers or marketers of business equipment—office products and services, factory equipment or systems, for example— where the product's user is another business. It also includes programs that provide marketing support throughout the distribution process—specifically, to the seller's sales force, distributors, and wholesalers, as well as dealers, retailers or agents.

While many of the techniques used in general public relations are applicable, the main difference is that business-to-business communications is targeted to a specific audience while consumer public relations is generally a mass communications effort. Like any specialized process, business-to-business communications has specialized elements: media, audiences, and messages that differ from those that deal with the mass consumer market. Trade publications, sales meetings, training programs, trade shows, dealer newsletters, and business media all play a part in the targeted process of business-to-business communications.

## Application of Marketing Techniques

While marketing generally is perceived as an aggregate of functions involved in moving an item or service from a producer to a consumer, its application to public relations frequently aims at building awareness of a specific interest.

A case in point is the L'eggs minimarathon for women, which was born as a novelty in 1972 when jogging was budding. The first 10-kilometer race attracted 78 women and was unusual enough to attract widespread media coverage. During the next 10 years, interest escalated and the race regularly attracted approximately 5,000 women.

By 1982, media coverage centered on the sports pages for about two weeks prior to the race and for one or two days afterwards. Although women are the only market for L'eggs hosiery, the coverage was appearing on male-oriented newspaper and magazine pages and on television and radio sports programs. The generous support L'eggs was providing was not being communicated effectively to its target audience: women between the ages of 18 and 40. The public relations program shifted emphasis accordingly.

Prerace publicity, prepared and placed months in advance, was directed towards life-style news sections and radio and television programming that appealed directly to the target audience. While sports page stories continued to precede the minimarathon, announcements, public service messages, updates on entrants, photography, and feature stories aimed at women also earned attention.

Increased media support and general interest were reflected in sales spurts during the months prior to and immediately following the minimarathon. About 60 percent of all publicity was national. More than 67 million impressions were received by women from other than traditional sports coverage, and year-round commentary established the L'eggs minimarathon as a benchmark of competition for women runners.

Another case in point of effectively building public awareness about a product concerned a new compound for treating duodenal ulcers. For nearly six months in 1983, the U.S. pharmaceutical arm of the British-based Glaxo Group tried to impress the advantages of Zantac upon prescribing physicians. Zantac had proved to be superior to its major competitor in clinical healing rates and lessened drug interactions. The introduction was greeted with skepticism by the medical press and changes in physicians' prescribing habits were slow. In January 1984, following research analysis of the medical and consumer markets, three objectives were established:

- To build public awareness of ulcer disease and its consequences.

- To position Zantac as superior treatment for duodenal ulcers.

- To establish Glaxo's identity as a major ethical pharmaceutical company.

Zantac's effectiveness and lessened interaction were stressed in promotional campaigns directed to consumer and medical audiences. All media were used, emphasizing Zantac's rapid relief of pain, reduced risk of drug interaction, and low side-effect profile. When Zantac's availability in injectable form for use in hospitals was announced, a co-ordinated news campaign positioned the medication prominently in all media.

Results were impressive. Public service announcements (PSAs) generated more than 900 million impressions from broadcasts by more than 60 television channels. The radio PSAs were aired by more than 300 stations. A brochure about peptic ulcers prompted 30,000 requests. A media tour featured physicians on 45 radio talk shows, and news reports reached about 18 million people.

By August 1985, Zantac had leapt to third place among U.S. prescription drug sales, and Glaxo had climbed to tenth place on the Pharmaceutical Data Services ranking. Those are but two examples of specialized marketing communications.

Illustrative of the broad range of communications avenues opened to specialized marketing are the diverse audiences that can be targeted. Tourism promotion, for example, can be enhanced by unique exotic and ethnic nuances. New products and production processes, special events anniversaries, and other such opportunities provide fertile ground for public relations creativity.

Such was the case with the State of Alaska. Usually perceived as barren, snow-covered, and desolate, Alaska has many attractions—rugged beauty, primitive art forms, colorful frontier history, and individuality—that had been overlooked or unknown by most Americans.

To tell its story, a promotional strategy centered on a cohesive media blitz. More than 50 specialized writers and broadcasters were guided to some of the state's most attractive, little-known places. Copy as well as still and newsfilm photography files were updated and visuals distributed to every major media outlet in a continuing publicity campaign. Kits, literature, and special events—such as displays of Alaskan art in the Capitol in Washington, New York's Grand Central Terminal Colorama, and San Francisco's airport—backed up the informational flow.

It had been conservatively estimated that a free brochure would attract 10,000 requests; it drew 25,000. A newsfilm, which was monitored, had an audience in excess of 16 million. Features about Alaska in major daily newspapers increased by 35 percent. Travel industry officials reported more bookings than ever before in the state's history.

Tourism to Mexico was promoted in like fashion until September 19, 1985, when a major earthquake occurred. Although its effects were concentrated in Mexico City and the resort of Ixtapa, graphic media coverage of the damage and rescue operation created the misconception that the entire country was devastated. Tourism came to a halt. It was feared that Mexican tourism, a vital segment of the nation's economy, might not recover for years.

Within three hours of the tragedy, public relations counsel established a command post to serve as a clearing house for information to the news media. Information received from hotels, airlines, and ham radio operators was channeled to appropriate outlets. Television interviews with BBC, CBC, ABC, and CNN provided a visual perspective to the situation. Details of accommodations were forwarded to 1,600 key travel agencies throughout the U.S. and Canada.

Honest, concise communications, including news of Mexico's recovery, reassured the travel trade and its consumers that tourist facilities remained intact. By December 1985, tourist arrivals had returned to the levels that were standard before the earthquake.

Another aspect of tourism was presented in research that showed many travelers viewed Hong Kong as only a stopover enroute to other Asian destinations. A public relations agency was retained to correct the misconception. A comprehensive media campaign, designed to highlight Hong

Kong's blend of modern services and ancient culture, was developed. Its target audience included upscale travelers, business executives, and professionals. The objective was to generate first-time and repeat visits of a minimum of four days.

Concentrated attention was directed toward television, and coverage included a segment on CBS's "60 Minutes" as well as location shooting for CBS's "Search for Tomorrow," "Love Boat," and "Dallas." Seven days of travel features by Steve Birnbaum on CBS radio and coverage on "PM Magazine" reached hundreds of millions of viewers.

Cover stories and photo spreads in several major magazines were supplemented by feature pieces in major newspapers around the U.S. No fewer than 13 video news features were beamed by satellite to 300 selected television outlets. They were timed to coincide with the Chinese New Year celebration. Special events, such as the Dragon Boat Races, shopping mall displays, a major contest promotion, and galas featuring Hong Kong's cultural aspects kept awareness at a high level.

Results of the five-year program are impressive. The number of visitors to Hong Kong from the U.S. now exceeds the number of travelers from Japan. The Hong Kong Tourist Association reported an increase of more than 15 percent and a 93 percent per-capita spending increase by these visitors.

Specialized marketing faces an especially difficult challenge in the case of alcoholic spirits because FCC regulations prohibit advertising on radio or television and consequently disinterest by these media.

When sales of Courvoisier Cognac declined, public relations experts were requested to develop a program that would increase consumption in a nontraditional cognac market. Broadcast publicity was specifically the client's objective.

Since cognac is a flavor enhancer, the Courvoisier Culinary Classic, a cooking competition for amateur gourmet cooks throughout the U.S., was created. The agency retained Paula Wolfert, a respected cookbook author, to serve as a spokesperson for the event and to make a media tour to promote it. She was prepped with on-camera skills before visiting Los Angeles, New York, New Orleans, and Chicago. During interviews she plugged the Courvoisier Classic, including entry details, and her tour reached radio and television audiences totaling more than 16 million. Eight television shows, eight radio interviews, and more than a dozen newspaper feature stories, not including a wire service feature distributed to 700 other papers, led to more than 5,000 entries in the competition.

Courvoisier used specialized marketing to reach a previously unexploited market: the amateur gourmet.

Similarly, the objective was to have consumers taste the product when Dairymen, Inc., a cooperative of dairy farmers, introduced Farm Best aseptically packaged milk. The unusual product received considerable attention when it was introduced in 1983, but sales failed to reach projections two years later and public relations counsel stepped in to help market the product in a dozen states along the eastern seaboard.

While aseptically packaged fruit juices had experienced great growth, the American public was cautious about milk that did not require refrigeration. Despite early publicity that Farm Best contained no chemicals and was bacteria-free, consumers were reluctant to try it. With a shelf life of six months, the unrefrigerated milk was truly a convenience item.

A network of sampling opportunities was created at heavily trafficked locations, and more than 500,000 people were surveyed after they tasted it. The unfounded objections were quickly overcome.

Taking a product to the people can be done in more than one way. When Fleishmann's developed a new yeast called RapidRise that cut in half the rising time of fresh bread, public relations theory was employed to develop a dramatic nationwide introduction.

The solution was a multicity satellite teleconference. It originated in New York and was beamed to six cities: Chicago, Atlanta, Seattle, Los Angeles, Denver, and Dallas. Regional offices delivered invitations in shopping bags that contained freshly baked miniature loaves of bread. More than 300 media representatives attended the seven-city teleconference, and questions were answered by a two-way audio direct line. Bread was baked at the New York location.

A 45-second newsclip was forwarded to 400 television outlets immediately after the teleconference, and a radio release was distributed to 2,000 stations. Newspaper features appeared in all major marketing areas and the significant measurable result of the media blitz was that Fleishmann's reported 80 percent distribution of the new product within six weeks of its introduction.

Coordination media focus was also directed to promotion of cellular phone service in selected metropolitan areas when early forecasts overestimated initial demand. GTE Mobilnet attributed consumer hesitation to high costs and perceived expensive service costs.

When specialized public relations marketing was introduced, both national and localized publicity was generated. Videotapes, brochures, newsletters, media interviews, sponsorship of special events, and other attention-getting promotions sparked local market awareness and positioned Mobilnet as an industry leader. The specialized marketing created interest and demand, which Mobilnet willingly satisfied.

Marketing to a particular segment of an industry requires public relations finesse to promote a product in a highly competitive trade. For example, while DuPont, the inventor of nylon, had long been the recognized leader in carpet fiber, the company began to lose its market share as well as retailer awareness and interest.

Research showed retailers relied heavily on floor-covering trade publications for credible market information, and public relations efforts were responsible for increasing retailer awareness of "Antron" and demonstrating its quality, performance, and style.

Third-party endorsement and dramatic photography were the focal points for communicating the message to trade publications. Special displays were arranged for trade shows and as a source for editorial support. Case histories were cited and quoted, and special promotions were developed as background. During the program's first year, more than 200 stories and photos were placed with leading publications, and DuPont research determined an overwhelming gain of 60 percent during a nine-month period.

The program expanded to include consumer editors, particularly for women's magazines, and life-style editors of key newspapers. A newsfilm was prepared for cable television and was shown by nearly 75 stations during a six-month period.

Explaining complex technology, such as Eastman Kodak's introduction of its new disc camera and film; spicing Spic and Span's 60th anniversary celebration; coordinating a one-day promotion that enlisted 5,000 volunteer runners; or helping bring a new product to the store shelves—each involves specialized marketing.

Techniques may differ, budgetary limitations may eliminate many possibilities, and timing can warrant serious consideration. Yet, creativity, coordination, and careful planning generally ensure successful specialized marketing.

# Chapter 15

# Environmental and Occupational Health Issues

Few subjects are of more concern to the public, the government, and industry than those in the environmental and occupational health fields. The growing need for programs and communications in these areas has brought increased demands on the professional talents of public relations men and women. And the rapid rise of interest in these fields has opened additional opportunities for rewarding careers in these new public relations specialities.

Because there are some similarities in these specialized areas, a number of companies and public relations counseling firms originally assigned these functions to either a single department or a particular individual. However, as these fields continue to grow in size and complexity, the tendency has been to develop specialists in each of these public relations areas.

## The Rise of the Environmental Movement

Although some forward-looking individuals were concerned for the environment as far back as the 1940s or even earlier, the public in general only became aware of the problems in the 1960s and early 1970s. Since the mid-60s, the environmental movement has grown from a small band of scientists, a few government officials, and a handful of conservationists to a movement that can marshal the support of nearly everyone from the Boy Scouts to Congress. The passage of far-reaching federal and state legislation and of local laws regulating air and water pollution, toxic waste disposal, noise, land use, and hazardous substances has had an enormous impact on the activities of business and industry. Few, if any, major decisions regarding plant operations are made by top management today without serious reflection as to how those decisions may affect the environment. Indeed, for major projects environmental impact studies are now required in many jurisdictions before work may be officially approved.

With the rise of public and industrial concern for preserving the environment, a need developed for public relations people with special skills. They were needed to interpret environmental developments to industry, to counsel on the public relations effects of proposed industrial actions, and to communicate industry's accomplishments or responses to criticism.

The rise of this public relations specialty was so rapid that it caught a number of people in the field unprepared. Many were not prepared either by education or experience to understand or handle the complex issues involved.

Those who did become involved discovered that the subject could not be easily isolated. The environment had many ramifications and was closely related to other socioeconomic problems. Public relations professionals quickly discovered that while general public relations knowledge was helpful, textbook techniques and standard procedures would not always work. As a result, new approaches to problems and adaptations of proven communications techniques have been developed to deal with this complex, dynamic subject.

## A Career in Environmental Public Relations

Because they still are growing, the fields of the environment and occupational health offer excellent opportunities for students seeking careers in public relations. Although in the earlier years of the environmental movement it was impossible to "learn on the job," a basic education in science is almost a prerequisite today.

Writing ability is of particular importance in environmental public relations. A communicator in this field must be able to translate intricate scientific subjects into simple laymen's language.

A review of the broad educational requirements for a career in general public relations, as outlined elsewhere in this book, would be helpful for a young man or woman interested in the field of environmental public relations. Additional courses in the physical sciences, statistics and, if available, a course in science writing would be extremely valuable.

## Dealing with Environmental Problems

The reactions of businesses facing environmental problems, like those of individuals, differ widely. The range can run anywhere from a complete denial that an environmental problem exists to partial agreement with the stand of environmentalists who are criticizing the company. Most company positions, however, usually fall somewhere in the middle.

A review of the policies of a number of companies that are successfully coping with environmental challenges shows that in almost every case top management has placed a high priority on environmental considerations. The environment has a place in top policy ranking with raw materials, manpower, capital equipment, sales, profits, and taxes.

A public relations practitioner may be faced with a single, well-defined environmental problem, or with a number of related or unrelated problems. For example, environmental problems include:

- Air pollution.

- Water pollution.

- Solid waste disposal.

- Land use.

- Noise pollution.

- Energy crisis.

- Toxic substances released to atmosphere.

- Radiation.

- Pesticides.

- Toxic waste transportation and disposal.

## Key Audiences

Professionals working in the environmental area are likely to be dealing with a number of different audiences:

- Company managers from the top executives to first-line supervisors.

- Employees both salaried and hourly.

- Community leaders.

- Government officials at national, state, and local levels.

- Scientific and academic groups.

- Environmentalists and citizen's groups.

- Specialized and general media representatives.

To keep important audiences informed about a company's or an industry's environmental problems and what is being done about them, booklets, newsletters, slide presentations, and motion pictures are used.

American Iron and Steel Institute, in an attractive booklet titled "In Quest of Cleaner Air and Water," told of the steps the steel companies were taking to safeguard these two natural resources. The Society of the Plastics Industry prepared a pocket-size booklet, "Answers to Questions You Are Asking About Plastics and the Environment," which was widely distributed within the industry and to interested outside audiences.

Because many people confuse a sanitary landfill with the old-fashioned town dump, Browning-Ferris Industries prepared a booklet for residents in an area where it proposed the sanitary landfill. Among the questions it answered were: what is a sanitary landfill, and what makes a sanitary landfill acceptable? Boise Cascade Corporation, in a comprehensive communication program on the timber supply in Idaho, pointed out that if the U.S. does not want to face a wood shortage in the future, it must make proper use of its natural resources today. Following the theme "Trees Are Renewable," Boise Cascade used printed materials, films, slides, filmstrips, radio tapes, and exhibits to bring its message to diversified audiences. One of the highlights was a traveling exhibit van called "Forest U.S.A."

## Reaching Specialized Audiences

While printed booklets, films, and slide presentations usually are effective in telling a company's environmental accomplishments to a general audience, many companies use a different approach to specialized groups. For government officials and bodies of scientists, teachers, and environmentalists, many companies rely on face-to-face meetings wherever possible. These may be informal discussions with small groups or full-blown formal presentations to larger audiences at seminars and symposia. Questions are usually encouraged to ensure productive discussions.

In communicating with scientists, several fundamental points should be kept in mind. It is necessary to have a message that is of interest to the scientist, not just to the sponsor. The information must be complete enough to answer fundamental questions of interest to scientists. In addition, the door should be left open for two-way communications with scientists who have a deeper interest in the subject.

Several effective ways for communicating with the scientific community have been developed:

- Publication of scientific materials in appropriate journals.

- Letters to the editors of the journals.

- Advertisements in scientific journals.

- Articles in the semiprofessional press.

- Direct mail to well-targeted groups.

- Seminars, symposia, and other scientific meetings.

- Personal visits to selected scientific leaders.

Dealing with the environmental press requires the use of all the talents the public relations professional has. As Darden Chambliss and Daniel J. Walsh, two communications executives from the Aluminum Association, stated in an article in a special issue of the *Public Relations Journal,* three basic rules are followed by those who have been successful in this area:

1. Know your editor and know his book. The turnover in people and publications is far faster than most so this rule applies with triple force.

2. Know your subject matter. In this fast-changing area, you'll hit some editors who know so much about the subject that you will feel stupid. But you will also hit others so naive that you will have the task of helping them to catch up fast.

3. Know what the news is. This follows from the items above, but it's not as obvious as it sounds. The news used to be "how dirty things are." Now it's a far more complex story about the methods and cost of cleaning up: what works and what doesn't; what costs will do to inflation; the effects on foreign competitiveness on the energy crisis. Sensible environmental writers are asking penetrating questions that go far beyond the holding tanks.

## Working on an Environmental Problem

Although there are typical environmental problems, each has its own unique aspects and must get individual attention. Yet there are some routine steps many professional communicators take when they begin working on an environmental project. These include:

- Marshaling all the available facts on the situation. One of the ways this is done is through a public relations environmental inventory. This tailormade checklist is essential for developing a sound environmental public relations program.

- Establishing an early warning system so that the company is not caught by surprise by restrictive legislation, by publication of a critical report by an environmental group, or by some other action that might affect the company adversely.

- Preparing ready-to-use, in-depth background materials on all sides of environment problems.

- Establishing contacts with appropriate governmental, academic, environmental, and scientific groups.

- Setting up a procedure to answer criticism immediately and forcefully.

- Telling the positive environmental actions of the company over and over through every means available.

One of the pioneers in environmental communications is Carl Thompson, former executive vice president of Hill and Knowlton, Inc. As founder and director of that firm's Division of Scientific, Technical and Environmental Affairs, he observed many industry and company environmental programs in action. In an article in the *Public Relations Journal,* he explained that in companies and industries that have taken the leadership in solving environmental problems, he's found that successful communicators many times find themselves:

- Helping develop and carry out an environmental inventory.

- Keeping attuned to all major happenings on the environmental front, particularly to anticipate those developments that may affect the company or its products.

- Goading management to see the realities and priorities in the environmental areas. One way this is being done is through the preparation and publication of a corporate environmental policy statement. This may be as brief as a few paragraphs, such as that of American Cyanamid Company, or as comprehensive as Bethlehem Steel Corporation's 18-page report detailing the company's position toward the environment.

- Collecting, analyzing, and interpreting available facts in environmental areas that may affect the company to assure that company officials are informed.

- Preparing informational materials on matters that may be coming in line for public attention unexpectedly, and keeping these updated with sound, supportable facts.

• Being prepared as a matter of policy to challenge sensationalized attacks.

• Keeping employees informed of company environmental programs and plans, and particularly of their role in such plans and programs.

• Establishing the company's reputation for credibility in the environmental area by deeds as well as words.

• Calling readily on experts for help and assisting them in communicating technical stories. Scientists mean what they say, but they can't always say what they mean in words the public can understand.

• Demanding strict accuracy in all corporate materials relating to the environment. Ideally, all major points in company communications should be supportable by scientific documentation.

## The Environmental Crisis Team

When an environmental or occupational health crisis strikes a corporation, all too frequently the company is ill prepared to manage the situation in an effective manner. In recent years, however, the concept of the crisis management team has rapidly found favor in many corporations. To the extent that such teams can be put together in quiet times and then rehearse their roles in simulated crisis situations, the company enhances its chances to come out of a crisis with its reputation and business intact.

Generally, an environmental crisis team consists of specialists in several disciplines who must address a variety of questions throughout the course of the crisis:

• Medical—How bad is the problem? What are the short- and long-term health consequences?

- Technical—How do we fix the problem? What do we need to do to make sure it doesn't happen again?

- Government relations—What likely actions will federal, state, and local regulators and legislators take as a result of this problem? How can we work with them to limit the negative impact on the company?

- Financial relations—What will be the impact on our stock and general financial condition?

- Customer relations—How will our customers and suppliers react to this situation?

- Legal—Who is likely to sue us? How strong will their case be?

- Employee relations—How does this affect our employees? Can they be a source of support for the company during the crisis?

- Community relations—How will it affect our relations with the communities in which we do business?

- Public relations—How can we most effectively communicate information about this crisis to all of the audiences important to this company?

The critical element in the effective functioning of an environmental crisis management team is making sure that all the potential negative impacts on a company are thoroughly discussed before deciding upon a course of action. Permitting only legal considerations to dominate the company's response or lack of response, for example, frequently can have long-term negative effects on the credibility of the company.

The role of the public relations professional on the crisis management team is perhaps the most important of all because communicating the company's positions and actions in all of the areas described above to all of the company's critical audiences actually defines the corporate response.

## The Use of Outside Consulting Firms

When a corporation or an industry is confronted with a sudden or unexpected environmental or occupational health crisis, it has been almost automatic in recent years for the company or industry to seek out the temporary assistance of an outside public relations consulting firm with broad experience in handling such issues. While most of the larger agencies have at least one professional with environmental crisis communications experience, only the very largest can afford to maintain staffs sufficient in size to handle more than one environmental or occupational health crisis at a time, or to pay the top salaries that experienced environmental crisis communicators demand.

The reasons given by companies for going "outside" in time of crisis are varied, but the following are the most frequently mentioned:

- If an environmental crisis has national or international implications, most corporations have insufficient manpower in their public relations departments to deal with the sheer magnitude of the internal and external communications required. It would not be unusual, as in the case of a major national issue such as the recent dioxin/Agent Orange controversy, for an agency to have from 50 to 200 professional and support people involved, at least to some extent, on a monthly basis, assisting the client with the problem. Essentially, no corporation is equipped to handle such a massive workload internally.

- In most situations, the public relations staff of even the largest companies has had minimal or, at best, limited experience in dealing with the communications aspects of an environmental crisis. The outside consulting firm, on the other hand, can bring many dozens of man-years of experience in dealing with numerous similar situations to bear on the client's problem.

- Even where the corporation's public relations or public affairs specialist has an extensive background in environmental communications, the "second opinion" from the experienced outside consultant frequently helps to refine or produce a superior communications approach to the issue. In other cases, upper management in effect demands that the company's specialist receive the concurrence of outside experts on the solution(s) selected before proceeding with a particular line of action.

In recent years, another rationale has emerged as a frequent reason for retaining outside consultants in the heat of an environmental or health-related crisis, and that is simply to help the company's experienced specialist convince his upper management to recognize and respond responsibly to the problems facing the company. More often than is healthy for the reputation and credibility of American industry, corporations have reacted emotionally to accusations against them by environmentalists, health officials, or regulators. They have blamed the media for its coverage instead of dealing with the errors of distortions of their antagonists. They have accused environmentalists and members of Congress of being set on destroying the free enterprise system. And, at least in one instance, they have labeled the majority of American religious groups as dupes of the international Communist conspiracy. Such visceral reactions more often than not hinder the public relations professional in dealing with the substantive charges being leveled against his company, and he must spend most of his time defending management against its own ill-chosen words and opinions.

According to experts in the field, most corporations under fire for alleged environmental or occupational health problems are at least "somewhat guilty as charged." Helping a corporation recognize this fact, when it is true, and then assisting it in dealing with the realities of its situation provide the most significant benefit that an outside consultant can bring to an embattled client.

## The Liability Morass

That America has become a society prone to engage in lawsuits over the past decade can come as no surprise to anyone. Multimillion-dollar liability awards and multi-illion-dollar lawsuits (as in the case of the Bhopal victims) are common today and are increasing as a major problem for American industry and, indeed, world industry. Regardless of the validity of plaintiff's claims, the asbestos industry is the single most-obvious example of an industry that has been effectively destroyed by the lawsuits brought against it. Proven effective drugs also have been taken off the market, not because they have been shown scientifically to have harmful side effects but because of the threat of multimillion-dollar awards that *might* be granted by juries swayed more by emotion than by reason.

This "liability morass" has created enormous problems for the public relations professional. On the one side is his or her responsiblity to explain the facts of the situation to the wide variety of audiences that is important to a corporation's continued reputation and success. On the other side are the lawyers, both corporate and outside counsel, who feel that any discussion of the issue could jeopardize an upcoming case, or, perhaps, generate one. In many recent situations this fear of litigation has rendered corporations mute in the face of hysterical attack by their accusers.

The questions to the public relations professional, as well as to the corporation for which he or she works, is whether there is any way to discuss an environmental or occupational health situation under the threat of actual or potential litigation. A number of corporations have found ways around the "liability morass." While their approaches may not work in every situation, it is far better for a company to seek ways to communicate on a health issue rather than to take the more comfortable "we cannot comment on that because the matter is under litigation" route.

In recent years a major drug company and a major chemical company (both involved in extended litigation) determined that they could discuss generically the health effects of their products without discussing the specifics of the cases under litigation. For example, the Dow Chemical Company committed nearly two dozen of its top scientists to an extensive media contact program to discuss the human health effects of dioxin (an unintentional contaminant in certain company-produced herbicides). Under litigation was a class action suit by more than 20,000 Vietnam veterans who claimed that they had suffered various ailments as a result of their exposure to Agent Orange, which was a defoliant manufactured for the U.S. government by a number of chemical companies, including Dow.

Since dioxin was the contaminant in Agent Orange that had allegedly harmed the veterans, Dow was able to discuss the human health effects of low exposure to dioxin (essentially zero, according to the medical profession) without relating that discussion specifically to the pending trial. In short, by discussing the dioxin issue generically, they were able to deal with the Agent Orange case without addressing it specifically.

In the case of the drug manufacturer, it was being sued in a highly publicized and emotional trial in Florida. It responded by preparing an extensive background paper on the known medical research on its product. The paper was distributed widely to reporters (both print and broadcast) who might be covering the trial. The intent was not to discuss the specifics of the case being tried, but to provide reporters with a factual basis against which to judge the arguments against the company.

Many other companies, in order to circumvent their entrapment in the "liability morass," have adopted similar strategies.

Since there appears to be no end to the litigation problems facing corporate America, the public relations professional will continue to be faced with the challenge of discussing issues while at the same time avoiding compromising the company's legal position. It may be the ultimate challenge to public relations for the rest of this century.

## Working with the Media

In the midst of an environmental or occupational health crisis, the general media—both print and broadcast—constitute an extremely critical audience for the company under fire. Not only will most of the corporation's other important audiences obtain much, if not most, of their basic information on the issue, particularly in the early stages, from the general media, but the media represent the company's most viable conduit for rapidly disseminating its side of the story to the outside world.

Perhaps even more important, the company's reputation with its various audiences will rise or fall depending on the skill with which it handles its media relations during the crisis. If the firm is perceived as acting humanely and responsibly in light of the problems it has caused, the general reaction will be positive. If, on the other hand, it is perceived as not being in control of the situation, or if it tries to hide obvious guilt behind a barrage of legalese, the long-term damage to the company can be severe. Some basic ground rules for media relations during an environmental or occupational health crisis apply.

- Tell the truth at all times, even if it hurts. It is far better for the company to disseminate additional "negative" information on an issue than to allow its opponents to be the first to "spread the news." In this way, the company is able to position the new information to its own best advantage rather than being a mere reactor to information disseminated by others.

- There is no information vacuum in a crisis. If the company does not tell everything it knows when it knows it, someone without the facts will make them up to satisfy a persistent reporter.

- Establish a rapid approval mechanism for clearing responses or new developments. Nothing destroys a company's ability to deal effectively with a crisis than having to tell a reporter, "I'll get back to you on that by tomorrow morning," when the reporter has a half-hour deadline.

- Work to establish the company as the major source of information, both good and bad, on the issue.

- Because credibility is a critical factor in an environmental crisis, whenever possible use scientists as the company spokesperson. A reporter is more likely to believe the corporate medical director when he tries to explain the health implications of a toxic spill than he would the head of public relations. This means, of course, that the scientists must be trained in talking to the media, both print and broadcast.

- Whenever possible, have interviews conducted one on one with reporters and in person. If you want reporters to believe that you are not polluting the world, they have to "see it in your eyes and hear it in your voice."

- Avoid press conferences as a means of disseminating information, unless you have something positive to report. This, of course, can prove impossible in a breaking story situation.

- React humanely to an environmental or occupational health problem. The world doesn't want to know how much it is going to cost the company to clean up a problem or how much production is going to be lost; it wants to know how the company feels about the people it has harmed and what it is going to do to help them.

- Keep in mind at all times that the media are not your enemy, but can be an effective conduit for getting your side of the issue out.

## Meeting Occupational Health Issues

One of the newest public relations specialties, occupational health, has emerged from growing government control over employee health and safety. Although good communications have long been important in motivating employees to follow safe work practices, occupational health has only recently become a subject of major concern for communicators.

Limiting exposure to toxic materials in the workplace is not new to either industry or government. The Walsh-Healy Public Contracts Act of 1936 established threshold limit values (TLVs) for occupational exposures to many substances. These TLVs have now been integrated into new and tougher regulations applying to all industries.

The passage of the Occupational Safety and Health Act of 1970 and new laws controlling the level of exposure to toxic materials have put new emphasis on the need to communicate effectively with employees on health and safety problems. The multitude of new industrial chemicals coming on the market every day adds to industry's need to tell its story effectively to a variety of audiences.

Because of highly publicized cases such as the polyvinyl chloride scare of the early 1970s, public awareness of occupational health problems has grown vastly. Substances long taken for granted are now regarded with greater skepticism.

## Specialized Skills Needed

Communicating in this field calls for highly specialized skill. The communicator usually must interact with scientists and physicians who often speak in a language almost incomprehensible to the layman. While the communicator, obviously, is not expected to know as much about the subject as the expert, there is a certain minimum knowledge required to ask the necessary questions.

For a communicator wishing to specialize in occupational health, a background in science is essential. Advanced courses in chemistry and biology and a general knowledge of medicine are helpful. The ability to read and understand technical papers and to put the subject matter into laymen's language without changing the meaning or emphasis is of prime importance.

## Need for Industrial Communications

The companies that rate highest in relations with their work force have followed a policy of keeping employees informed not only of the accomplishments that have been achieved in health and safety but also of the problems that still remain to be solved.

If employees don't get the facts from their company, they

can and do get them from other sources such as unions, government agencies, activist groups, or the media. The result may not be to the company's advantage. For example, a chemical company involved in the discovery of a previously unknown occupational hazard took the position that the less the employees knew about the problem the better. In a Senate subcommittee hearing, the company heard one of its own employees accuse it of deliberately concealing the facts of the situation from its workers. The accuser learned about the problem in the press and from a high union official who came to the plant and told the workers what was going on.

## Audiences in Safety and Health

Production employees are most affected by occupational safety and health hazards. Therefore, they are the number one target for the company's communications. Other important audiences include:

- Company management and supervision, from the corporate officers to the first-line supervisors.

- Appropriate government agencies at the federal, state, and local levels.

- Scientists, including doctors, researchers, and the academic community.

- Union officials at the national and local levels.

- Community leaders in areas where the company has plants.

- Science writers, as well as the press and electronic media.

## A Basic Communications Program

Few special techniques have been developed to tell a company's story to its various audiences because occupational health and safety communications is a relatively new public relations specialty.

A typical company program might include the following basic activities:

- Analyzing the company's current communications activities on a plant-by-plant basis to see how they can be improved or more closely focused on occupational safety and health matters.

- Setting up a monitoring system to alert the company to any information on these subjects being released by the unions, governmental agencies, or activist groups, and to topical news appearing in the media.

- Developing a quick-response technique for rebutting erroneous information put out by others.

- Preparing booklets, newsletters, posters, speeches, background memoranda, white papers, fact sheets, and other materials for communicating with employees and other important audiences.

- Planning seminars and preparing seminar materials for informing upper-, middle-, and lower-level management, including supervisory personnel, of the company's occupational safety and health situation and the need for and suggested methods of communicating with employees.

- Setting up a plan for an effective procedure for handling a crisis situation, such as the discovery of a new health hazard among the company's plants or an unfactual adverse story in the press. Such a plan could call for coordinating press, employee, and governmental relations efforts to assure a balanced assessment of the situation by all interested parties.

Business and industry must comply with laws regarding safety and health, which are enforced by a dozen or more governmental agencies. In addition, organized labor, the media, and the Occupational Safety and Health Administration are striving to educate workers as to their rights under the law as the hazards to which they are exposed are accelerating. The need for communications by specialists in occupational safety and health is therefore becoming more and more important, even for companies that have no serious current problems.

Sewer sludge, industrial chemicals, fluorocarbons, and saccharin were among the more controversial issues of the past decade. Doomsayers warned of catastrophe and an apprehensive public teetered between panic and ignorance.

It often seemed that misinformation was reported more sensationally than factual explanation. While the U.S. in particular, and the world in general, became aware of these issues, the need for precise information became evident.

## A Case in Point

In 1975 the Milwaukee Metropolitan Sewerage District began supplying digested sewage sludge, called AGRI-LIFE, to farms in rapidly urbanizing southeastern Wisconsin. The sludge, a by-product of waste-water treatment, is valued by farmers as a soil conditioner but viewed by uninformed nonfarmers as a threat to health and environment.

Nonfarming residents were annoyed by the odor and truck traffic and were afraid the sludge would contaminate groundwater. Misinformation disseminated by local activists went unchallenged until 1983, while public opinion mushroomed. Deliveries of AGRI-LIFE dropped 20.6 percent from 1982 to 1983.

Public relations counsel was retained to counter the misconceptions and fears that existed and to help stop, or repeal, ordinances that threatened distribution of AGRI-LIFE. A program was designed to alleviate or alter nonfarming citizens' perceptions. It included participation in town meetings, media interviews, establishment of a 24-hour Citizens Advisory Committee as a source of information and recommendations to the community, educational displays at five county fairs, and continuing consistent communications. By 1985, AGRI-LIFE was being delivered to six communities where it had not been previously available. These communities had considered ordinances against AGRI-LIFE, but they refrained from adopting them. No new sludge ordinances were adopted.

When trichloroethylene was found in ground water near Roscoe, Illinois, the county health officer recommended that residents drink only bottled water and the EPA advised boiling all water before it was consumed. Trichloroethylene is a suspected cause of cancer, and it is used as a cleaner by Warner Electric Brake & Clutch Company in production of automobile parts. It is used to scrub off grease from machine parts before they are painted.

A toxicologist from the Illinois Attorney General's office began investigating area industries, including Warner. While investigations of the possible cause for contamination continued, Warner Electric was not targeted by the media as a source of the problem nor was it implicated, even though a disgruntled former employee had written letters to the media accusing the company.

This was because Warner had responded at the first alert in a positive way, clarifying its position. With open, timely communications, Warner spokespeople were trained and responded to media inquiries. An audiovisual presentation explained the company's controlled use of the chemical and its industrial and waste treatment facilities. The media was invited to the presentation and toured the plant for first-hand observations.

A consulting firm, expert in chemical waste, was retained to assist in testing the company's potential as a cause for the problem, and its findings were presented to the public. Concise, honest statements concerning the company's investigation and cooperation with state officials were made promptly whenever appropriate. The forthright action by Warner Electric prevented editorial speculation and rumors, and it allayed public concern in a volatile situation.

Such was not the case when charges, based on computer findings rather than scientific research, that fluorocarbon propellants were threatening the earth's protective ozone layer ignited a wave of public fears in 1975. The media concentrated on the threat of possible skin cancer and other negative aspects of the story.

A major producer of fluorocarbon propellants engaged public relations counsel to initiate a communications program that would propose better balance to the reporting on the issue.

Public relations professionals recommended a well-defined focus on scientific research and distributed findings to the media. A personal letter from the chairman, explaining that research was under way to determine answers to questions posed about propellants, was sent to all customers. A periodic newsletter followed, reporting new findings and activities in the political area. The newsletter, initially aimed at customers, also was circulated to newspeople and government officials. Concurrently, background papers for science writers and educational literature kept media people updated on new findings.

Federal, state, and local government actions; media reporting; and all scientific developments were monitored. Teams of company spokespeople and researchers were trained in media interview techniques and publically discussed the situation. A company group visited 25 cities and conducted more than 200 media interviews during a four-month period.

A special response team, including a scientist, a corporate spokesman, and a public relations professional, was developed to reply to breaking news stories as they developed. The group could produce a statement and release to the wire services within 30 minutes after a newsbreak occurred.

The public information program functioned for four years. During that time, alternate materials and systems were developed and introduced and public concerns lessened because of the balanced reporting on the issue. In many instances, newspapers altered their editorial positions in recognition of the fact that the risk involved in taking the time for the additional research was reasonable.

Less-than-complete scientific study similarly ballooned the case concerning saccharin out of proportion. The U.S. Food and Drug Administration on March 9, 1977, announced its intention to ban saccharin from foods, beverages, medicines, and other products because it was suspected to play a part in causing bladder cancer. The FDA pronouncement was based on Canadian tests with rats in a laboratory.

Within days, an ad hoc group was formed among members of the industries using saccharin. Believing the ban was unwarranted as a matter of scientific and public policy, the ad hoc group enlisted public relations counsel to mount a scientific, legal, legislative, and communications effort to delay the ban while developing a more balanced view of the issue.

Two basic techniques were used to communicate the focus on public sentiment in favor of the flavoring:

- Concentrating informational efforts on the studies and statements of scientists, medical authorities, and other credible third-party sources, rather than on industry spokespersons.

- Stimulating and assisting citizen groups—such as those concerned with diabetes, heart disease, and weight control—to make known their views to the media, members of Congress, and other groups.

Extensive research and documentation were the sources for a continuing informational program about saccharin: its uses, history, benefits, and positive alternatives. Special events appealed to special interest groups, and monitoring and response systems enabled the clients to reply quickly to FDA statements and distorted media reports.

Barely nine months after the FDA's original announcement, the President signed into law a bill mandating an 18-month moratorium on the ban to allow additional study. When the initial vote on the moratorium was before the Congress, only 30 of 535 members voted against it. The moratorium remains in effect today.

# Chapter 16

# Crisis Communications: Dealing with the Unforeseen

Crisis and controversy can strike any organization, regardless of its size or line of business. For management and communications professionals alike, the rule is: Anything can happen.

No organization with the remotest chance that its regimen could be upset by surprise happenings should fail to keep at least one eye open for the unexpected. Whether this be accident or disaster, labor difficulties or a strike, political or public attack, or a temporary reverse in financial affairs, public relations professionals must work hand-in-glove with management to anticipate what can go wrong and to develop efficient means to respond when it does.

Crisis communications, or crisis management, is the newest discipline in public relations and perhaps the most challenging because to be effective it draws on a number of public relations capabilities. And while it usually comes into play only after the unforeseen has occurred, crisis communication ideally is forethought, a preventive measure for responding swiftly and responsibly when a crisis strikes. It's now part of good business.

Recent years have seen refinements in the methods and techniques of this specialty, as well as increases in the number of companies that have crisis communications programs in place. Railroads and airlines for years have had public relations procedures for handling serious accidents, and companies in virtually every industry have followed suit, designing communications plans patterned to fit their own potential exposure to calamity. The crisis communication program is an integral part of the effort to minimize the scope of the disaster, for in making sure everyone knows exactly what to do if a crisis occurs, guesswork and improvisation are reduced.

By accepting that they could one day be accountable in a crisis, top executives have ordered development of appropriate communications programs, as well as periodic review and revision of the company's existing plans. Indeed, a survey conducted after the 1985 Bhopal chemical disaster found that a majority of America's largest corporations were taking measures to deal with crises that might affect them. This is crisis management at its best: preparing in advance, knowing whom to call and which buttons to push, but hoping the plan will never be called into use.

No organization can expect to be immune to events that engage public attention, affect key constituencies, and arouse emotions. Whatever the problem—a chemical spill, a financial irregularity, a plant closing, a product boycott— it presents a severe communications challenge before, during, and after the instance. Three simple questions can put the crisis communication planning process into context:

1. Before disaster strikes, the public relations staff should ask, "What if...?" and outline proper response logistics for every contingency.

2. When the crisis occurs, the staff should ask, "What now...?" and proceed with the plan. If there isn't one, the organization should bring in outside crisis experts immediately.

3. In thinking about the aftermath of the problem, the staff should ask, "What next...?" and work to rebuild the confidence of affected constituencies while trying to attract new ones.

## What If...?

Developing a crisis communications program has four key ingredients:

- **Farsighted management.** It is the job of an organization's leadership to know the territory, its downside risk factors, and how to communicate quickly and effectively with the key internal and external publics. Management should make certain that the company anticipates and addresses in a plan all of the potential mishaps of the company's operations, and it should assign responsibilities in accordance with the outline.

- **Professional communications assistance.** In an actual crisis, the flow of information must be flawless. Both management and its communicators will need the right information to achieve this goal. In putting together and organizing the material and in managing communications, public relations professionals play a vital role. In order to develop an adequate crisis communication plan, the company's public relations staff needs ready access to management and the experts who know the problem. Once they know how management evaluates the risks facing the organization, the company's public relations staff can outline mechanisms to keep all constituencies reasonably informed of minute-to-minute developments.

- **Experienced communications counsel.** A crisis should not be a training ground for the inexperienced. Because both emotions and managment pressures run high when a crisis strikes, the objective viewpoint and broader experience of specialized communications counsel can help the company in crisis to quickly marshal its resources and control the damage. These agencies work frequently with companies in trouble and bring added strengths to even the most professional in-house communications staffs, with which they must work closely.

- **"What if" exercises.** These are mental fire drills, but their purpose is not only to rehearse a disaster response. These exercises also will help management and the communications staff to anticipate contingencies that could affect the organization and to create rational communications responses. What if one of our corporate jets crashes in the middle of the night? What if a tanker blows up? What if one of our key executives commits suicide? What if our product is tampered with? What if...? You get the picture: Each "what if..." should have a response.

## What Now...?

Even for all the planning and practice that go into designing effective crisis response programs, none will ever be perfect. No organization can prepare for every contingency, and for many there are no particular risks that are not shared by the population at large. For them the best bet is a general disaster plan that could be used to answer the question "What now...?" and which details procedures to be followed in whatever emergency may befall.

Points to remember when a crisis strikes are:

- **Accept that it is a problem.** This is the most difficult step. Assessing the potential consequences requires sensitivity to public opinion and a feel for the future. Management must be able to take the reins quickly and guide the firm through a difficult period, realizing that the company will remain in the public spotlight for some time. Effective communication to and from management should facilitate this crucial step.

- **Gather the facts.** It is vital to let the public know immediately that you are dealing responsibly with a crisis and that you will convey essential information as it comes to light. Yet, in cases of disasters, controversies, and scandals, the impulse all too often is to try to hide the facts—or worse, to rush out an announcement or disclaimer before all the facts are known. The best procedure is to gather available facts immediately and to open the lines of communication to the public. Never go beyond the known facts until more are at hand. Only when the situation's full magnitude is known can proper conclusions be drawn and conveyed.

- **Throw all available resources into resolving the problem.** To give good direction in a crisis, management needs to be aware of its resources and know how to use them. Management must know how the communications contingency plan works, the roles of the persons involved, and the capabilities of outside assistance. Senior leaders also should work closely with communications staff counsel and listen before giving direction.

- **Maintain an open flow of information once you know the story.** Media covering a crisis story often are urgent and insistent, firing barrages of questions and demanding quick answers. The temptation to respond on the basis of personal feelings, theory, or supposition is strong, but it never pays. As more information is gathered, management will be able to evaluate the available data, to share them as appropriate with media and other key audiences, and to give enlightened direction to resolve the problem effectively.

- **Establish a pattern of disclosure about the issue.** As reassurance that the company is acting responsibly and is in command, the media and other key audiences should be kept informed of all developments during the crisis, as well as after it's over. It's better for the company in the long run if, from the outset, it takes control of what's being communicated, volunteering information on its own terms. The company's image rebuilding process begins with the first public announcement about the crisis, and the value of setting a precedent here cannot be overstated.

## "What Now...?" Checklist

Although crisis communication plans differ, some procedures are common to virtually all of them. Based on its years of experience working with clients in this area, Hill and Knowlton has developed a checklist for help in preparing a basic disaster plan. It answers many "What now...?" questions and can be used in preparing a generic plan to handle virtually any kind of emergency.

1. **Alert corporate communications immediately.** The company's communications staff should be informed of the crisis immediately. Corporate communications, the link to management, should have all known details in hand before advising senior level officers. These include:

   - How, when, and where did the problem begin?

   - What are the financial, legal, human relations considerations?

   - What's happening now?

   - Have outside agencies been called in for help?

   - Are there injuries or deaths? Are people in the surrounding area safe?

   - Have families of the injured or dead been notified? Who's in charge of keeping the families informed?

- When will the situation be cleared up? What additional help is necessary?

- When will additional facts be available?

2. **Establish emergency alert procedure.** Division leaders, plant managers, and supervisors should be drilled on reporting crisis emergencies to the corporate communications department. They must be instructed not to speak for the company except on those occasions when they are designated to do so.

3. **Establish centralized spokesperson.** The switchboard operator and all of the company's employees should know that they are to refer all questions to the corporate communications department for routing to the designated spokesperson, who must have full knowledge and understanding of the material to be communicated.

4. **Determine the facts.** Corporate communications staff and authorized employees at the crisis site should confer and determine what facts are known, prepare a short statement, and inform the media.

5. **Establish a press corps station.** All media arriving at the scene of the emergency should be directed to a safe place at which they can learn the situation and receive periodic progress reports.

6. **Provide communications assistance to the media.** Typewriters, telephones, and additional staff assistants should be made available to members of the media.

7. **Log information released: track questions received.** Assign a member of the communications staff to keep track of when each announcement was made, what questions were received, and who asked them.

8. **Don't release information prematurely.** Names of victims should not be released to the media until the families have been notified by someone from management. Also, don't minimize the effects of an unfortunate incident; your company will not only appear callous but you may also create legal problems.

9. **Don't speculate.** The cause will become apparent as more facts become known; let the experts (police, fire department, etc.) determine what happened. Speculative statements have a tendency to come back and haunt the company that issued them.

10. **Correct false information.** The media has sources other than the company itself: the police, the fire department, on-the-scene witnesses. Whenever possible, in statements and interviews, address possible misconceptions of the event and provide the facts.

11. **Control camera crews.** Photographs tell a story in graphic terms. Think ahead, and be on guard for camera crews whose work could misrepresent the story.

12. **Keep information flowing.** Update the media as often as possible, but only when there's something to say. Release only accurate information and correct previously released information that's known to be erroneous.

13. **Ask "what next?" and plan follow-up coverage.** As soon after the crisis ends as possible, offer to discuss the incident and what it means to the company and its constituencies: the community, employees, etc. A full-scale communications program to keep people informed of postcrisis developments should be considered.

## "What Next...?"

Just as there's no telling what crisis or controversy might strike an organization, there's also no way to know how long a problem may persist. Even though the actual incident may be readily contained, lengthy investigations may ensue, lawsuits may affect the company's finances for years afterward, and reference to the matter on the public record may continue for some time. Because of this, good crisis management also deals with the aftermath of the crisis, rebuilding the company's image in the public mind.

Sometimes a negative situation provides the well-prepared organization with an opportunity to impress both the public and the media with its good planning and efficiency. As mentioned above, the company's image rebuilding process begins with the first public announcement about the situation. While certainly not to be considered the calm in the eye of the storm, asking "what next...?" is key to taking responsible action throughout the ordeal because it forces management to keep an eye to the future.

Aggressive candor is imperative in a crisis situation, and being forthright has better long-term implications for the company.

It's essential for a company in trouble to take the initiative in going to the public with bad news without waiting to be asked. Companies may argue that a delay is desirable because they don't know everything they should know to provide a comprehensive news announcement. But they run the risk of getting caught up in a rumor mill that will bring reporters' calls. The reporters still won't have all the information they would like, and management will find itself in the embarrassing position of responding to searching questions instead of volunteering information on its own terms.

When it's thinking like this, the company is already on the comeback trail before the story even hits the papers.

But it's not only media that the company should be concerned with; all parties affected by the company's business and by the crisis at hand need to be kept informed of what has happened and what it means to them.

In the wake of a crisis, the company should maintain communication with every audience vital to its well being—customers, suppliers, shareholders, creditors, employers, analysts, trade and general media, legislative and regulatory bodies—updating them on developments in the postcrisis period.

This time of rebuilding brings an opportunity to reinforce the company's strengths among existing constituencies, broaden its exposure to new groups, and increase its following in other areas. For instance, if a public company's stock price takes a beating because of a negative incident, Wall Street analysts may continue recommending the stock if they believe management handled the incident responsibly. Similarly, previously skeptical analysts may be enticed to take another look.

## Crisis and Energy Affairs

The energy business has been the subject of more crises and controversies in recent years than perhaps any other industry. As technology becomes more advanced, the potential for crisis naturally increases; the more sophisticated the equipment, the more room there is for error. Topics such as Three Mile Island, the energy crisis, and multi-million-dollar rate increases from new power plants have engaged the public's attention and aroused its emotion as never before.

While it may not have been possible to predict or prevent these crises, there are many ways in which companies could have prepared for them and minimized their effects.

Numerous factors make the establishment of an effective crisis communications program particularly difficult in the area of energy affairs. Inflation and deflation, critical shortages (especially in fuels), environmental constraints, consumer unrest, and cost pressures for repeated rate increases all represent severe financial threats to the energy business.

Yet, in a survey of appointed or elected officials serving on public utility commissions in 32 states, respondents admitted that communicating their position to the public is difficult. In the energy industry, there has long been a piecemeal approach to dealing with communications problems. Within an electric utility, for instance, those concerned with rates have tended to proceed independently of those in engineering planning; those concerned with customer relations have tended to proceed independently of those who deal with technical aspects of customer service, and, perhaps most important, those concerned with broad management policies have tended to proceed independently of those charged with communicating such policies.

Following is a diagnostic procedure consisting of a series of steps to aid energy companies in anticipating crises:

**Media monitoring.** Careful monitoring of the media should be conducted to determine whether any misinformation about the company is being conveyed. It is crucial to stay on top of the media since false statements are almost impossible to remove once they become part of the "news chain," and because one erroneous statement tends to build upon another.

**Networking and marshaling resources.** In the strategy known as "networking," a company builds bridges with its adversaries, be they special-interest groups, government agencies, or politicians. The parties then can meet each other at the halfway mark rather than confront each other belligerently should a crisis arise. Besides coming to terms with adversaries, it is important to line up allies, or marshal one's resources. Whether these allies are customers, suppliers, bankers, or lawyers, the company must determine who will best be able to help with particular issues.

These strategies are particularly crucial as energy affairs communications activities are becoming almost adversarial. The pattern is now well established. At the local level, activist groups are successful in building a nucleus membership. They then choose an emotional issue for purpose of a media event and are often successful in achieving extensive local coverage.

Using this as a base, an effort goes forward to enlist widespread support. Groups such as the Council of Churches, Sierra Club, Public Interest Action Foundation, Environmental Action Foundation, Consumer Utility Board, and Common Cause become involved at the local, state, and national levels. Energy businesses are also challenged by a growing number of consumer agencies and advocates, including the public interest research groups supported by the Nader organization and the Consumer Federation of America. These forces combine to represent a strong network of national, state, and local organizations moving aggressively on major issues.

**Scenario development.** This is probably the most important component in preparing for a crisis. The strategy involves anticipating all possible crisis scenarios. Some people find the notion of scenarios development futile, for the same reason they object to preparing for an interview. This objection is not valid. When preparing for a newspaper interview, some executives say, "We can't anticipate because a reporter can ask us anything under the sun." The truth of the matter is that the reporter can change his adverbs or change his nouns, but there's a finite number of questions a reporter can ask, and the public relations staff must prepare for them.

**Audience identification.** After potential crises have been identified, a firm must consider what audiences will be affected. The energy industry has numerous audiences with which to contend.

## Reaction to Crises

Crises are seldom planned, but reaction to them should be. A clearly defined procedure, established in written policy, should be implemented within moments of the determination that a situation has reached its critical phase. A designated spokesperson, supported by knowledgeable associates at a central location, should be the singular source for all information pertinent to it.

Such was not the case when the shuttle Challenger exploded nor when the nuclear reactor at Three Mile Island malfunctioned and threatened to emit a harmful level of radiation. While the Challenger tragedy erupted in a ball of flame seen by millions of televiewers, the Three Mile Island incident simmered for about a month before the plant finally was shut down.

Early in 1979 the Three Mile Island nuclear reactor failed to cool properly. No one knew exactly why. There was no official spokesperson and speculative news stories were breaking from diverse sources in Washington, Bethesda, Harrisburg, and Middletown. Panic and controversy followed and because the general public was sorely lacking in background knowledge about nuclear power issues, the sometimes conflicting reports fueled rumors, guessing games, and general confusion.

The credibility of Metropolitan Edison, caretaker of Three Mile Island, was shattered. President Carter's visit to the site restored a semblance of calm. The decision to designate Harold Daneton of the Nuclear Regulatory Commission as spokesman helped unravel the tangled lines of communications and a public relations consulting firm was requested to help develop a detailed emergency public communications plan.

Contact between public utilities representatives, the state, county, and local leaders was established. Public briefings and community meetings in several locations helped explain to the public exactly what happened. An observation center at Three Mile Island was upgraded as part of the public information program and a forceful public education program was launched. A media relations group at Three Mile Island arranged plant tours and briefings and provided the public with up-to-date information on the plant's daily status.

On a larger scale, four key groups were created by the nuclear power industry as a direct result of the Three Mile Island incident. They were as follows:

1. The Nuclear Safety Analysis Center was created to investigate the accident, to also evaluate all information, including technical lessons learned, and disseminate findings to the industry across the U.S.

2. The Institute of Nuclear Power Operations was formed by the electric utility industry to establish benchmarks for excellence in the operation of nuclear plants and to share operating experiences thoughout the industry.

3. A mutual insurance organization was established to supplement the Price-Anderson Act by helping utilities cover the costs of replacement power resulting from a shutdown.

4. A public information group, the Committee for Energy Awareness, was created to inform the public about nuclear power generation.

Three Mile Island was a landmark incident because of

the shortcomings it demonstrated in the area of effective public communications. The establishment of a coordinated communications program helped overcome many of the fears that existed in the mind of the public. The lack of a defined policy was the basic fault.

In sharp contrast, another disaster provided a well-prepared energy company an opportunity to demonstrate its planning and efficiency. In 1974 a fire in a gas well owned by Pacific Gas & Electric Company produced a conflagration, with flames climbing to 300 feet. Its roar could be heard a mile away and there was danger of an explosion.

Realizing that news people would soon be on the scene, the gas company established a news center and ground rules to protect reporters from possible injury. The news center served as the hub for all coverage. On the day that water was to be pumped into the burning well, through a relief well, reporters and photographers were transported to a special news location where they could safely see and record the action. The cohesive action by Pacific Gas & Electric earned the American Gas Association's highest award for public relations achievement.

A company's response to crisis should be planned with a certain flexibility. It is possible for a crisis to arise within a crisis and this was illustrated in the case of the Marble Hill nuclear power plant.

Public Service of Indiana, operator of Marble Hill, had been targeted by public officials and consumer groups following its announcement that it planned to halt construction on the plant.

A public relations consulting firm was retained to assist the company in educating key audiences about the reasons for the action. One of the major components of the plan was to help Public Service of Indiana gain approval for a rate increase. Among the actions taken to reach this objective were:

1. Development of messages from opinion surveys and focus groups conducted with customers.

2. The launching of a direct mail effort that used bill stuffers to educate customers and identify company supporters.

3. The calling of meetings with major business and economic development organizations to obtain support.

4. Explanation of the direct mail program to growing audiences.

In the midst of the program, the crisis within a crisis cropped up when a piece of legislation was introduced in the state senate that would have prohibited utilities from recovering any of the costs of uncompleted power plants. The bill was introduced on a Friday. The senate was scheduled to recess the following Thursday, four working days later.

This crisis was resolved with establishment of a telephone bank message directed towards supporters.

By Tuesday, the computer tape of about 9,000 supporters, identified through the direct mail phase, was matched against telephone company tapes and approximately 7,200 numbers were located. The phone bank message was prepared and callers were hired and briefed on the issues. By Wednesday, the phone bank was operative and 5,500 individuals were reached. By Thursday, 40 targeted state senators received a total of 3,000 telegrams from constituents who combined to convince the senate to defeat the proposed bill.

There is but one way to deal with crises. Response and reaction should be concise and honest, and transmitted to everyone concerned as quickly as possible.

## A Case in Point

In 1982 the JWT Group, Inc., a communications holding company, discovered a serious financial irregularity in its television advertising syndication unit. The development would force the company to restate its earnings for four prior years and write off $30 million. The firm's public relations strategy was: Tell the full story clearly and consistently to everyone who should know.

Almost immediately, major clients were telephoned by the chief executive officer and told they would receive details, as they became known. While auditors and legal counselors examined the situation, the public relations staff alerted the New York Stock Exchange, assembled and distributed background materials to analysts, the media, and the company's office managers around the world. More than 5,000 shareholders, 1,000 clients, and approximately 8,600 employees in 150 offices in 32 countries were apprised of the situation.

Because of the simple, forthright strategy, several analysts reaffirmed their "buy" recommendations, since they predicted the stock price would drop on disclosure of the story and a bargain was at hand. Coverage during and following the crisis was fair and accurate because of open communications. Even the initial reaction by the media was positive, praising the thoroughness with which the JWT Group ensured reporters' understanding of the complexities involved.

Clients were supportive, understanding that they could face a similar crisis at almost any time. Banks more than doubled JWT Group's line of credit and, after an understandable sag, the company's stock recovered and climbed to a new high within a matter of months.

JWT's professional approach contrasts with the muddled manner in which the National Aeronautics Space Administration reacted to the explosion of the shuttle Challenger in 1986. The chronology of the tragedy tells the story.

The spaceship blew up at 11:40 AM. More than an hour later, NASA announced it would hold a press conference at 3:00 PM. It was twice rescheduled, and finally at 4:40 PM spokesman Jesse Moore had little to say other than to confirm what millions of people had seen on television five hours earlier.

He could have made his statement—all but the fact that a search showed no signs of survivors—well within the 20 minutes directed in NASA's disaster contingency plan. Because of its delay, NASA demonstrated it had lost control of the crisis. By failing to heed its own contingency plan, the agency did itself a disservice.

As the Presidential Commission appointed to investigate the cause of the disaster would later determine, there were indeed communications problems at NASA. The investigation uncovered cost overruns, flaws in the agency's decision-making process, budget, and personnel problems. NASA's "trial by the media" was grueling.

It is likely that negativism toward NASA would have prevailed in any case, regardless of the public affairs office's lack of decisiveness. Frank Johnson, a former director of NASA's public affairs office said, "You need to have clear, crisp procedures which aid in making decisions in the event of crisis. When line management tries to improvise, you have to pull back and say, 'Hey, we have a policy. It's designed to happen this way.'"

These are important words for all crisis management professionals to heed—because anything can happen.

PART 3

# Public Relations:
## Special Considerations

Robert L. Dilenschneider

# Chapter 17

# Public Affairs and Governmental Relations

If "go into plastics" was the advice of a previous era, the inside word for the coming decade is *issues:* "Go into issues, my boy." No profession possesses greater opportunity in this regard than public relations, which in the years ahead will shift its emphasis from products, people, and corporate promotion to issues communications.

Public relations will experience a metamorphosis in the coming years, shedding old misconceptions, acquiring new responsibilities, and garnering an increasing amount of power, prestige, and pay. Issues such as environmental standards, product liability, consumer protection, tax policy, and energy resources will occupy corporate attention just as keenly as does market share today.

Until recently, business appeared unaware that rules of the free enterprise system had changed. It behaved as if it were still operating in the economic and political atmosphere of the Eisenhower administration. In the latter half of the 1970s, business began to realize that government decrees were severely limiting corporate freedom by restricting a host of traditional management prerogatives, from new plant openings to product development.

It will be important to business to appreciate the nation's political and social agenda, an agenda that ultimately could cost corporations billions of dollars in taxes or lost opportunities. But that which is a danger to business is often an opportunity to public relations professionals.

In the decade to come, the role of public relations will be

to guide top management in making the primary corporate commitments. Public relations will not only be an early warning system but an integral part of the entire corporate planning process. It will provide advice on how company decisions will fare in the social and political milieu of the outside world and how such decisions may be more favorably accepted by the public and the government. It will be vigilant to changes in society that might impinge on the corporation. Public relations outside the Washington area will increasingly resemble the issue-oriented approach that has been the norm in the capital for 20 years.

## Public Affairs and the Policy-making Process

In Washington, D.C.—the societal, political, and communications nexus of America—interests that span the globe are beating a path to the most sought-after people on earth: American voters. From within the U.S., Americans are accustomed to being courted by merchandisers and politicians. Now, from all over the world, American citizens are sought after for their dollars, opinions, taste preferences, political sympathies, and support.

Few internationals—or Americans, for that matter—recognize the uniqueness of the U.S. system and how it works. Affecting trade policy, reaching markets, influencing foreign policy, and even being heard can either be an enormously complex undertaking or elegantly simple, depending on how one approaches the American system.

Those who would change U.S. trade or foreign policies should take their cases directly to the people. In this country, the real power on these issues resides with them. The public must be convinced. Without consensus, the President and Congress cannot endorse great change. Americans as well as foreigners tend to lose sight of the fact that much of American policy simply mirrors public opinion. There is nothing more frustrating for a lobbyist after making a convincing, airtight case, than to hear a Congressman say, "You have all the arguments, but if I go with you, my constituents will send me home."

What makes this process seem inscrutable to outsiders is that the catalyst to public opinion, the gatekeeper to the American consensus machine, is the free press. To most internationals, the press is a four-headed hydra: one part missionary, one part door-to-door salesman, one part vigilante, and one part executioner. And the four parts seldom are equal.

The American system of media-fired public opinion and policy-making can be summarized as follows: To move our government, get to our people; to get to our people, get to our press. The media moves the message to the people. The people move the government. Then, and only then, the policy shifts. That's when America moves.

America stalls when the public is inadequately informed. For instance, today the Midwest is home to some of the strongest protectionist sentiment in the country, and at the same time the region is the largest beneficiary of U.S. world trade dollars. A tremendous contradiction, which in the long run is very destructive, exists between the region's dependence on agricultural exports and the protectionist sentiment echoed by bumper stickers that proclaim, "Let them eat their oil; we'll burn our wheat!"

Who should communicate this contradiction? Understandably, American industry is not going to do it. And the U.S. government does not have the ability to do so; the United States Information Agency is prohibited by law from spending a penny within the United States. This task must be left to foreign companies and governments. But how are they going to succeed at communicating if they do not fully understand the weave of opinion, influence, and power in the U.S.?

The American press and its freedom, the U.S. public and

its power: these are the two most important dynamics in our policy-making system. Those who understand the workings of these forces and the relationship between them are able to make a significant impact on the U.S. policy-making process.

It has been said that democracy presupposes that it is better to count heads than to break them. However, the success of a democracy depends not only on an awareness of what is in the heads of a nation's citizens but also on a knowledge of how the information gets there. Does it come from comic books and sit-coms, the evening news, or a college education? Is it the suggestion of the boss, the advice of a neighbor, the mouthings of a relative? To answer these questions, it is necessary to travel to the headwaters of public opinion and consider the source of most of America's information: the news media.

It is a truism that "the mass media may not be successful in telling us what to think, but they are stunningly successful in telling us what to think about." The media set the agenda. Like it or not, our press provides the indisputable "menu of choices" from which issues are selected.

In addition to setting the agenda for the public discourse, the influence of the media on policy making has grown steadily along three major coordinates. The first is America's mass purchase of television receivers and our subsequent total reliance on this medium. The second is the advent during the 1960s and 1970s of bias in journalism as a fully accepted institutional and commercial imperative. The third is the development of new communications technologies that will permit message senders to target and penetrate American homes as never before, thus allowing the media to participate more directly in the policy-making process.

The most significant and fundamental development in U.S. politics since the advent of universal suffrage has not been the rise or fall of philosophies or a swing from liberal to conservative. It is the establishment of what Theodore White dubbed, "The Reign of TV."

In 1950, 4.4 million homes boasted television receivers. The next 10 years witnessed an explosion of television purchases. During some weeks in the 1960s, no less than 10,000 people a day bought their first television sets! By 1960, 45 million homes in America had TVs; by 1980, the total had climbed to 80 million homes, as close to saturation as is statistically possible.

American life has been altered to fit the tube. Legislators and policy-makers may receive much of their information from print journalism. They also may attend briefings and personal meetings with the well informed. But the vast majority of Americans get their information from television news. More Americans watch any one of the major network news programs than all the readers of all U.S. morning newspapers combined. This development has revolutionized the business of lobbying. It no longer is possible for a lobbyist or politician to ignore the impact of constituent pressures at the grass-roots level arising from the evening television news.

As the media's power to form public opinion increased through the proliferation of television, many observers recognized a noticeable drift away from what we always had believed to be the three most important principles of good journalism: accuracy, balance, and fairness. For decades, "getting the story and getting it right" were the watchwords of the journalist's profession. By the end of the 1970s, it seemed that this ethic was in danger of shifting to "getting the story and using it right" to affect changes in policy. In fact, responsible voices today charge that the press is attempting to "micro-manage" U.S. foreign policy rather than to report on it.

As part of this tendency, American *journalists now have*

*the freedom to interpret the news.* Editors encouraged the trend. Owners of media outlets go along with it because it has proved good for business. This interpretive approach to journalism certainly can cause reasonable disagreements and not a few major showdowns among reasonable men and women. Yet it is important that we guard against listening to those who subject anyone from the press to a loyalty oath. We must understand press problems and constraints as well.

Creed Black, president ot the American Society of Newspaper Editors, observed, "The press has replaced the hippies as the public's scapegoat for its animosities and frustrations." Black notes that being made a scapegoat for bad news is an "occupational hazard because newspapers are performing better than ever in their watchdog role." Black makes an important point. The numbers of those who say they want a fair press, when what they really mean is that they want a favorable press, are legion.

The truth about press bias, like all realities, is complex and certainly does not fit neatly into any one ideological category. Many times, the real bias lies as much with the observer as it does with the reporter.

Nonetheless, reporters do operate from personal biases, which often do color their reporting. The evidence cited in a set of attitudinal surveys published in 1981 by Professor Robert Lichten of George Washington University and Stanley Rothman of Smith College confirms that U.S. media elites tend to think and vote liberal.

The survey polled 240 journalists and broadcasters at some of the most influential media outlets in the country, including *The New York Times, The Washington Post, The Wall Street Journal,* and *Time Magazine.* Eighty-one percent said they thought U.S. economic exploitation contributed to Third World poverty. Despite hundreds of billions of dollars in foreign aid from the U.S., only 25 percent said the West had helped the Third World. Twenty-eight percent said the U.S. needed a "total overhaul."

The most prevalent bias in news reporting grows out of the structure of the news gathering and reporting process itself. What drives the media business is the driving force for all business: competition. What animates this competition is the economic and marketing imperative to make the news interesting, even sensational. Making an economic "summit" interesting is an art form that can go awry, sometimes understandably.

The system rewards generalists to practice "parachute journalism" around the world, jumping into wherever the action of the moment may be. Today, Beirut. Tomorrow, the Great Wall.

Further, there is a shallowness and sensationalism in the news. Never mind if a reporter is short on information. If the material is sufficiently sensational, it will be judged newsworthy. An afternoon's interview, with all the necessary shadings, complexities, and qualifiers, will be reduced to 25 seconds.

Finally, reporters naturally seek sources who seem disinterested. Those with no economic or political interest or who seem "morally" above the fray are prime candidates. People with the most facts, a business leader, say, or a government official, are assumed to have ulterior motives, whereas uninformed protestors are perceived as disinterested and hence, "reliable."

The rapid pace of technological development has completely changed the face of the communications industry and promises to affect our politics as thoroughly as the invention of the home television receiver. The ability to speak directly to the American people is possible as never before. The rapid proliferation of cable systems and direct satellite broadcasting (now to stations, soon directly into the home) will make the concept of a "wired electorate" a reality.

Of particular significance is the interactive cable network. Despite the short-term difficulties experienced by this system, it may be utterly revolutionary in its impact on U.S. policy. Interactive cable technology gives consumers the ability in their homes to shop, bank, vote, and communicate their views directly to their representatives. Interactive cable will soon make it possible for a printout of tens of thousands of constituent opinions on a particular issue to be on a lawmaker's desk within a day of requesting this information.

Influencing public opinion will no longer necessarily be a matter of going through the national media as intermediaries or final arbiters of which stories are told. The technology to take stories directly to the people is here, and it is becoming politically imperative to use it. To ensure that power remains with the people of this country, where it rightly belongs, we traditionally have relied upon sacred beliefs and constitutional safeguards. We now also may enlist technology, a powerful new democratizing force.

Those who wish to influence the American policy-making apparatus, if they are to be effective, must understand this technological revolution, above all. In the future, Americans will "get the story and get it right," from a score of sources, and they will continue to provide the consensus that animates U.S. policies around the globe.

**Washington news corps.** The Washington news corps is the largest and most influential in the world. There are relatively few glamour figures among this group, but collectively the news corps has unique access to the process of government and an eager worldwide audience for its records and views. Despite the large number of the capital's media representatives, reporters usually have far more news leads than they can possibly cover.

Few of them have much time for parties and the cocktail-party circuit. Much more important are individual associations with the people they cover, write about, and work with, including friends in public relations. As a class, these correspondents and reporters must be versatile, energertic, self-starting, and productive writers. In a town where there is tremendous competition for the top story, reporters must have an editor's skepticism as well as a writer's enthusiasm.

By and large, they are industrious workers who have to develop tremendous flexibility to handle widely varying stories. They are in Washington by choice and, for most of them, for the length of their professional lives, if they have anything to say about it.

They welcome pertinent input from public relations people. Whether in initiating a new story with fresh information and ideas or rounding out an in-progress piece, many often depend, at least partly, upon the public relations people they know, to flush out or update their story or outline. Thus the professional public relations person must maintain a reputation for honesty and reliability if he or she is to enjoy entree to the press.

For example, during a period when the government was considering ending a years-old helium conservation program, a counseling firm represented the private contractors involved in the program. The firm organized an information program that included staging two helium seminars. From them came scientific papers on new energy technologies such as helium-cooled high temperature reactors, superconductive electric power transmission systems, and magneto-hydro dynamic power generation. Years later, as landmarks of progress, these papers are still being quoted. The working press of Washington came to regard the counseling firm as a basic information resource in this area of energy research.

Every kind of journalist can be found in Washington.

Some like to be called correspondents—newspaper, magazine, television, or radio. Others prefer to be known as just plain reporters. There are writers, commentators, columnists, photographers, pamphleteers, newsletter writers and editors, authors, and consultants.

Their exact number is uncertain, but it approaches 4,000. There are approximately 1,200 members of the Congressional Press Galleries (open only to printed daily publications), 625 more in the Television-Radio Galleries, another 777 in the Periodical Press Galleries, and 308 in the Press Photographers' Gallery. Facilities for all these are maintained in both the House and the Senate on the gallery floor above the legislative chambers. The news galleries also handle press credentials and arrangements for covering political conventions. The White House also has facilities for accredited correspondents and photographers.

The role of the presidential news conference has grown in recent years. In the 1940s, presidential news conferences were held comfortably in the Oval Office with reporters arranged around the president's desk. In the 1950s, they moved to the Indian Treaty Room of the Executive Office Building, then to the first televised conferences in the State Department auditorium, and, more recently, to the spacious East Room of the White House. As one can see on TV, they are now heavily attended and glamorous events.

**Local and national press.** In addition to this group, more than 1,000 reporters, editors, photographers, and others make up the news, editorial, and photo staffs of the two Washington daily newspapers, the *Post* and the *Times,* plus the staffs of Washington-based publications like *U.S. News & World Report, Broadcasting Magazine,* Bureau of National Affairs publications—*Science Service, Congressional Quarterly*—and other research publications such as *Editorial Research Reports* and *National Journal*. Added to these are trade journals and scores of suburban news publications that reach into the vitals of community affairs.

Include also the burgeoning broadcast news staffs of networks and local radio and television stations, as well as the independent film and news feature production services that have sprung up to serve the broadcasting industry. Add also at least several dozen reporter-writers for the numerous newsletters and business information services published in Washington. And finally, tag on the free-lancers specializing in some field or other, those who are writing anything from novels to nonfiction books, and even a few who shuttle from press to government and back to independent public relations consulting.

Add them all together and you've got the mix of Washington journalism for the public relations professional: a lot to choose from, and a complicated lot to cultivate and know.

**Washington bureaus.** Washington news bureaus, like Washington correspondents, have proliferated through the years. The bureaus come in all sizes, from one person to United Press International's staff of 115 to the Associated Press's 145-person staff.

Typical large bureaus maintained by out-of-town newspapers include the Newhouse National News Service, Hearst Newspapers, *Los Angeles Times, Chicago Tribune,* Copley News Service, Gannett, *Wall Street Journal,* and a score of others. Among the periodicals, large Washington news organizations are maintained by *Time, Newsweek,* McGraw-Hill, and *U.S. News & World Report.*

Radio and television networks also maintain full staffs to report and process Washington news, over and above staffs of their local affiliate stations. So do the surviving movie and newsreel organizations, and film-making enterprises, that satisfy the need of business and industry to project their comments and arguments on television by means of videotape and film. Senate and House members also have their own television and radio studios to produce newsfilm and tapes.

News and feature syndicates maintain Washington bureaus, but generally these are small operations. Several of the better known columnists work out of their homes, using the syndicate's address as a mail-drop or transmission point.

Foreign press associations, newspaper and other publications also operate news bureaus of varying sizes, and these concentrate largely on diplomatic and economic matters. Typical of these are Agence France Presse, Mainichi Newspapers, Reuters, and Tass.

A large number of bureaus are of the one-, two-, or three-person variety. These are maintained largely by so-called special correspondents. Often the correspondent is an independent contractor, providing Washington coverage on a local-angle basis to smaller publications that cannot afford full-time correspondents of their own. Other bureaus provide similar news service to one or more smaller papers.

These special correspondents frequently represent a specific area of industry interest, for example, cotton, tobacco, or oil. They often become first-rate outlets for the public relations practitioner. They're busy and they like to be helped, so providing them with a worthwhile story or idea is a real service to them.

**The Washington dailies.** The city's daily newspapers—the *Washington Post* and the *Washington Times*—provide readers with perhaps the broadest collection of national news columns published in any city in America. However, the natural emphasis on politics and government affairs creates a news-space problem particularly with business stories that have no local angle. The space for financial news, apart from stock-market quotations, is usually so limited that it does not give the business editors much room for anything but a localized story.

If there is any general rule for the public relations staff to follow in working with the Washington news corps, it is to do everything possible to put the reporter in the position of knowing the organization's side of the story. If the reporter is provided all the useful background materials available and is kept updated from time to time, at least he or she has no excuse for not knowing.

**Working with Washington media.** The difference between media relations elsewhere and in Washington is worthy of notice. The great majority of the press and electronic media people at the capital are not local; they represent services that are national or international, or media whose audiences are elsewhere.

The size and diversity of this group present unusual opportunities to public relations people, but the concentration on government and political issues also sets limits on what can be done. Except for the strictly local media, the only stories of real importance in Washington relate to the interaction of government and the rest of society. Even in the local media, the Civil Service beat often creates more news than the police department, and business developments that may rate major headlines in other big cities may be cut down to a paragraph on page 53 in a Washington daily.

Even with all the unique characteristics present in every public relations program, some common methods can often be applied on behalf of an organization to help the public understand and take action on issues clouded by misinformation, political rhetoric, self-interest, and public apathy. These methods include the following:

- *Make the issue public.* Get the facts out and understood. If the issue is truly one involving the public interest rather than a cloakroom fight between lobbies, public officials will be encouraged to stand up and provide support—or else will have to justify their opposition before the voters.

- *Enlist the help of experts.* There are many people, well-known and respected for their accomplishments in other fields, who, if they knew and understood the issue, might be induced to rally to a cause. Their testimony, based on fact and presented in the public interest, adds credibility and depth far beyond that which can be accomplished by an organization's spokespersons alone.

- *Recruit allies.* A group's goals normally affect more than just its members. They affect suppliers, manufacturers, consumers, workers, and financial interests, all of whom may be represented by still other groups. Many of these can be counted on to be vocal and persuasive once they are brought to understand the problem, its broad ramifications and its effects on their interests.

A good general rule is, "If you can't build a convincing case that what you want is in the public interest, forget it." Government issues are rarely decided on objective merits, but "on the basis of their political implications and their interplay with public opinion." Public relations, to be successful in Washington, *must* take this into account.

## Lobbying: Access and Hard Work

A glance at the press these days somehow makes it appear that the major concern of Americans is an increase in advocacy in the nation's capital. Reports speak darkly about the rapidly growing power of the lobbyist, about an "excess of access," about the "tidal wave" of government officials who have turned to private practice for profit.

But access, the ability to reach decision makers on behalf of private clients, is Washington's most perishable commodity. Misuse it and you lose it. And continuing access, the ability to be heard over the years, involves more than temporary fame or power. Access is an earned, essential raw material for the lobbying process, but it is vastly overrated as a finished product all by itself. No dam ever was built, no publicly funded program saved, no vacancy filled, and surely no lobbyist's success assured solely on the basis of access.

After all, people whose job requires what we now call access are really conduits through which clashing attitudes reach decision makers. A state legislature anxious to meet the challenge of toxic-waste disposal ought to hear the views of environmentalists as well as those of industry. When voting on foreign aid, Congress ought to know the positions of other governments on key issues affecting America's national interest. Access aids the process because it enlarges the discussion.

Access may open a door—once—or ring the telephone on the Cabinet officer's or senator's desk—once. But access alone is without value to the professional to whom lobbying is more than an afternoon golf game with a crony. Washington's best consultants, those who have served clients with skill for many years, may not agree on the best formula for a complicated campaign. They will agree, however, on what causes access to fade fast.

Whatever their past positions, however close to power they once were, lobbyists know calls will go unanswered if issues are misdirected to a Cabinet officer or legislator when an assistant secretary or staff aide would have been more appropriate, if pleas are not backed by an understanding of the issue and its place on the political and economic agenda, if inaccuracies stand uncorrected, if competing claims are improperly presented or overstated, or if the lobbyist's clients are taken to a busy office just to show they can get in.

The successful lobbyist is a prism, refracting a client's need into a series of basic, attractive messages designed to get the attention of decision makers. Combining expertise with access over the years creates a credible voice.

Lobbyists cannot just yell "More!" or "Now!" or "Never!" in the ears of influential and accessible friends and hope to succeed. They can, however, provide the best information in a reasoned context, match client needs to public interest, bring experience and expertise to the table. If the lobbyist does all this, he or she will find access slowly evolving into something of real value: credibility. But credibility is earned over the years, not conferred by having been "the former Deputy Director of Almost Everything that Matters."

The formula for successful client representation is a far cry from the picture often painted in the press of access-laden influence peddlers moving with almost hypnotic effect through the government, twisting public policy to individual self-interest by trading on their most recent jobs. A lobbyist is only as good as the credibility of his last presentation, not his last title.

Today, many public officials are moving to private practice. What current reports do not reflect are the obstacles faced by those unwilling to put in the time and effort to develop expertise and credibility. For those who do, the raw material of instant recognition can be refined into a lifetime of access. For the rest, access will evaporate without doing them or their clients any good.

The question of how a lobbyist goes about the job has

been answered by George M. Worden, vice president of Hill and Knowlton, in a piece titled "Working with Congress." It is one part of a five-part monograph on Washington public relations published for the Counselor's Section of the Public Relations Society of America. Here are excerpts.

There is no textbook on how to work with the Congress and there will probably never be one. Exercising the right of petition as guaranteed by the First Amendment to the Constitution is anything but an exact science.

A certain methodology has developed, however, which generally, but not always, applies.

The basic constituency when one works with Capitol Hill are the 535 men and women who make up the House of Representatives and the Senate of the United States. Whatever issue you are supporting or opposing, it is unlikely that you will have to deal with all 535 of them.

Fortunately for us and for them, the Congress works by the committee system, so your immediate universe is sharply reduced. Let's say you are interested in a general business issue. Bills are introduced in the House and the Senate and then referred to committee. In the House the committee might be Interstate and Foreign Commerce. This committee is made up of 43 members: 24 from the majority party, 19 from the minority.

On the Senate side, the Commerce Committee is comprised of 18 members: 11 from the majority party, seven from the minority. Your immediate audience then totals not 535 but 61 in both houses.

That represents just the members. The people who make the wheels go round are the committee staffers. The Senate Commerce Committee staff, from director to the most junior staff counsel, totals 35. The House Interstate and Foreign Commerce Committee has a professional staff of 23. The bill you care about will be assigned by the staff director to one or more members of that staff.

One more group of behind-the-scenes movers and shakers are the people who work for the congressmen. You don't have to know all the people in all the offices, but you do have to find out who, if anyone, in these offices is assigned to the issue or bill you care about. Don't ask to see a member of Congress if you don't know him or her. Work with the staff; they'll more than likely be able to tell you what the member is thinking about. If they don't know, they will find out.

Now your bill, the one that will make or break your company or your industry, is beginning to move along. The first thing you need is a written statement of your position, why the bill is good or bad, the economic impact it will have on particular states and Congressional districts.

So you start on your rounds having brief meetings with Congressional and committee staff members, and now and then with members of Congress, leaving behind your background memo and at the same time doing a head count on how the committee vote might go.

After you have covered all these bases and have a reasonable feel of how the issue is developing, there is a third force you should consider: the news media assigned to the Congress. In both the House and Senate, there are press galleries. Take a supply of your background statement to the superintendent of each gallery. Where there is individual state impact, call attention to it.

You have now made all the standard opening moves. The middle game is beginning.

The bill you care about is now scheduled for hearings. There are hundreds of days of hearings. An average work day when Congress is in session may have as many as 12 hearings in each House, with 25 witnesses on subjects ranging from atomic energy to boundary inspections, consumer product safety to preservation of baby seals.

In addition to what they can assimilate directly and personally, members of Congress must rely heavily on information developed through the hearing process.

Since your bill is very important to you, it will probably be decided that your best spokesman should appear as a witness on your behalf when hearings are held.

There are some ground rules regarding hearings. They are subject only to the rules of Congress. Rules of evidence and procedures in a court of law do not necessarily apply.

The appearance of your witness before a Congressional committee is not lobbying, so he or she does not have to register or become concerned with lobbying regulations.

Here's a brief checklist of things to do before your witness appears:

1. Monitor hearings of the committee involved. See which members show up and what kinds of questions are being asked. Identify your friends and your foes.

2. Prepare as concise an opening statement as you can. If you have detailed back-up material, have that submitted for inclusion in the record.

3. Remember, committee members can interrupt at any time.

4. The person testifying is sitting in front of and below the committee. It is a lonesome place. Have in mind the value of two other representatives, maybe a technical authority and your counsel, as flankers. This is reassuring and often helpful. The witness should introduce these colleagues. They may speak, preferably on signal from the witness.

5. The fact that only two or three Congressional committee members appear does not indicate a lack of interest. Congress is a place where multiple demands are made on one's time. In any case, the staff members will be on hand, and they are the experts on your issues.

6. When one takes the stand before a committee, there are four immediate audiences:

   • Committee members: Those who aren't there will read the transcript.

   • Reporters: Sitting at tables right behind you, they may put what you say before the public.

   • Committee staff: Typically this group will include lawyers, economists, and whatever other specialists the issue requires, from agronomists to political scientists. Be assured that they have done their homework.

   • Your associates: Interested observers and opponents, they sit in the hearing room.

Following the hearing, you should get your witness's statement around to the offices of all the committee members, whether they were there or not. This is a precaution. Better two statements in an office than none.

Then, you should think about broadening the horizon a bit. If this hypothetical bill will be all that good or bad for your industry, someone else has to care about it too. Will the bill hurt or help another area of the economy? Will it have an impact on the farmer, for example? If it does, then every member of Congress from a farm area should be included in your direction if you show how the bill will hurt or help the farmer. Tell the farm organizations about it, too. Similarly, if the bill will eliminate jobs or restrict expansion, consider labor audiences. Enlist the support of the appropriate unions and advise Congressmen from heavily industrialized districts that provide large labor constituencies.

By now, you will have found the Congressmen who are completely for you, and you know the ones who are against you. Your mind should then turn to the "gray area." The Congressmen who are on the fence or who really don't know much about the issue.

You will often hear the comment, "I usually follow Senator Smith on that kind of issue." This means the first senator knows that Senator Smith is an authority, and he or she usually votes the same way. So, unless there is a pressing reason not to, your senator will go along with Senator Smith.

When a bill reaches the floor, many members follow their party leadership. In each of the two bodies, there are majority and minority leaders plus whips and assistant whips who, once a party has taken a position, are supposed to mobilize all, or as many as possible, of the members of that party to vote a particular way.

You will need to know what the party position is on your bill, but if it is primarily a local or technical issue, members will look to the committee rather than to the party whips for guidance.

Another dimension of lobbying to consider is Congressional terms of office. In theory, at least, the House represents the people, the Senate represents the nation. However, House members are no sooner elected than they are running for office again, two years is a very short time. They are particularly sensitive to what the folks back home have to say. Senators, who have six year terms, are a little slower to react, but it must be remembered that one-third of the Senate is up for re-election every two years.

One must use the utmost discretion and care in generating grass roots reaction.

The advertisement in a newspaper extolling an issue and urging readers to "Write your Congressman" is an overused gambit that can do as much harm as good. The canned barrage of letters which all say the same thing—or even worse, coupons mailed to Congressmen—just aren't the answer.

Almost every member of Congress has a district or state office open year-round and staffed by a trusted lieutenant who is in regular touch with his or her principal.

If you have a stake in a state or district, for example a manufacturing facility, brief your plant manager by phone or letter, send your background memo and your witness' statement, and ask that a personal visit be made to the state or district representative, explaining exactly what the bill means to the city or state and why the local member of Congress should vote for or against it. Mobilize other natural allies to do the same thing: the Chamber of Commerce, the union, a prominent minister, local suppliers to your factory. Have your plant manager ask to see the member of Congress on his or her next trip home. This is the most effective and productive way of attracting attention to an issue. The member of Congress may weigh the mail, but he listens very carefully when his district representative speaks.

If this is your first Washington assignment, there are a few reference documents you will need. The *Congressional Directory* lists all members with their biographies, committees, and subcommittees, and it also includes names of members of the media accredited to the Congressional press galleries. A valuable adjunct is the *Congressional Staff Directory*. This is privately printed, and it contains the names of all the staff members and a number of staff biographies. The *Congressional Record*, which comes out daily when Congress is in session, is a must. Copies of bills are available at the Senate and House document rooms.

The question of whether or not to register as a lobbyist will probably come up, and there isn't a simple answer. If you are "providing information," you probably don't need to register. If you are attempting to influence legislation, you *must* register. If there is any question, it is safer to register. Contact the Secretary of the Senate and the Clerk of the House of Representatives for appropriate forms.

This is a brief summary of an area in which some people spend their entire lives. Don't presume to become an instant expert. There is no such thing. Just as you have it all worked out that the whole thing is going your way, it turns out that the other side has been working too. Suddenly on the floor of the House or Senate, a member rises with an amendment which guts your bill. He is supported by a leading member of the other party. Your supporters are caught by surprise, a quick vote is forced and you are beaten! It can't happen? It just did.

One point cannot be stressed too heavily. At all times be both courteous and businesslike. All the people you will be seeing work long and hard, so take as little of their time as you can.

## Tips for Effective Congressional Relations:

- It is always best to make contact with a member of Congress through a constituent.

- Learn which member represents the district in which your plant or corporation is located. Establish a good rapport with the member of Congress or staff members.

- It is always easier to see a member of Congress in his or her district. Make plans to invite the member out to the plant or company for lunch with some of the staff when he or she is in town. Or, arrange for the plant manager to visit the member of Congress when he or she is in the district.

- Strengthen the company's legislative affairs department. Know which Congressional committees are important to the company and which Congressmen play key roles in these committees.

- When the company is a member of an association, use the association to help reach the industry's goals. For example, if an association is sending a letter to Congress, a participating member company should send the letter to the member of Congress of its own district for a more effective response.

- Choose a friend or associate of a member of Congress to send correspondence stating the company's position on an issue.

- Produce a well-written letter, preferably on one page. Make an effort to state your position clearly, interestingly, and amusingly, and speak to a broader perspective. Write it in plain English.

- Don't write anything you wouldn't be willing to read in the newspaper.

## Four Basic Types of Letters

The types of letters a Congressmen receives from a corporation or business association can be grouped into several categories:

- A letter from a corporate officer who lives in the member's district. This is usually given a personal response from the member of Congress and noted as good input. It is far better to receive a letter from a plant manager in the district than from the president or chairman of the board located in another state.

- A letter sent from within the state, but not in the district. It will probably be handled by the staff and noted, if not directly answered.

- A letter sent from the corporation's headquarters, not within the district or even the state. Most attention is paid if the member of Congress is actively concerned with the issue. It may not be answered, even if it is an active issue. However, it will have a certain amount of input.

- A letter from out-of-state, on an issue with which the member of Congress is not directly concerned, will be noted but probably not counted as input.

While these tips apply more to the House of Representatives than to the Senate, the rule of constituent priority is no less applicable in the Senate.

## Legislative Analysis and Monitoring

Skillful legislative monitoring and analysis provide one of the best methods available for keeping an organization informed and up-to-date on any congressional actions—bills, hearings, investigations—that will affect its interests, either directly or peripherally.

Some organizations have one overriding interest, such as trade legislation, tax law changes, or environmental and health issues. Others have a number of less dramatic but continuing concerns that must be watched for when Congress is in session.

Those who work in Washington quickly acquire a specialized knowledge of the legislative process, and it is easy to forget that the rest of the nation generally has a vague memory of an eighth-grade civics course to draw on when trying to understand how Congress works or what makes a bill become law.

This means it is sometimes easy to impress people in another part of the country, simply by tracking a recently introduced bill to its home in a subcommittee or obtaining the names of additional cosponsors of that bill. While these small tasks can be very helpful, it is a mistake to believe that the public affairs practitioner has a direct pipeline to Congress or is infallible when it comes to predicting the actions of the House or Senate.

Legislative analysis and monitoring are more complex than simply attending hearings and reporting on what took place, although attending key hearings and knowing which hearings *are* key is part of the job.

Becoming adept in legislative analysis and monitoring means first knowing how the House and Senate function, which committees and subcommittees are concerned with what issues (committee titles are sometimes misleading), and understanding the intricate system that causes several different committees to have a voice in the same issue.

It is necessary to understand the concerns of the chairmen and members of the many committees, and one should know at least the basics about their constituencies. Does a certain representative or senator come from an area of high unemployment? Is acid rain a major concern for another? Does a key member represent a district in which aerospace industries are located, so that defense contracts (and, therefore, the defense budget) are of special interest to him? These are some of the factors that must be known and weighed when preparing legislative analysis.

It is also necessary to establish good contacts on the staffs of the various House and Senate committees, as well as on the staffs of the members of Congress. This takes time. However, it is more important, and more realistic, to develop a working relationship with these staffers, who do much of the preparation and planning for hearings, than with the members of Congress.

Committee staff members are valuable sources of information because it is their job to prepare for hearings, plan agendas, and schedule witnesses. Finding and cultivating contacts among staff members, whether on committees or on members' staffs, can't be done with one phone call. It can't be done at all if the wrong approach is used. These people are busy and sometimes impatient, and they appreciate straightforwardness in conversations with them.

They will want to know, particularly before a public relations practitioner has become established with them, why one wants to know certain information and on whose behalf. Generally, an open answer, tempered with discretion, will satisfy them. It's a mistake to say "I can't tell you" or "That's confidential." It's also a mistake to ask for information or plans that one knows to be confidential or to press them for answers they're not ready to give.

Sometimes the practitioner hits a stone wall; the information he or she wants is simply not provided. Relaying this back to the person who originally requested the information can be difficult, for a common non-Washington response to a refusal from a Congressional or federal source is "Tell him I pay his salary and I want an answer." That's a good way to end all further contact.

The public relations professional must not become a nuisance with any contacts that he or she has established. One shouldn't call for information that can be found elsewhere and shouldn't take it as a sign of inefficiency if a hearing is suddenly canceled or, equally annoying, is announced without prior warning. Capitol Hill staffers have demanding jobs and work long, hard hours. It is understandably frustrating to be dealt with curtly or denied needed information, but patience and persistence will help in these situations. The first responsibility of these people is to Congress, not to a public relations person.

It also is necessary to develop a good knowledge of regulatory agencies and how they work. Their higher-ranking members frequently testify at Congressional hearings, providing information and agency positions on specific issues. Washington abounds in agencies, both independent and tied to the various departments. The U.S. Government Manual for 1985 lists 56 of them, and their concerns range from the stock market to the environment.

The Environmental Protection Agency was established to allow "coordinated and effective governmental action on behalf of the environment." The EPA's recommendations and actions can impinge on such areas as factories, automobiles, clean water, asbestos, pesticides, and other environmental interests. All of these issues have been matters for Congressional concern and hearings.

An example of an active and important agency is the Food and Drug Administration, which is a part of the Department of Health and Human Services. FDA decisions affect such matters as pharmaceuticals, over-the-counter preparations, cosmetics, food additives, food labeling, food contamination, artificial sweeteners, cosmetics, and a host of other matters, all of which interlock with congressional interests.

There are 13 federal departments: Agriculture, Commerce, Defense, Education, Energy, Health and Human Services, Housing and Urban Development, Interior, Justice, Labor, State, Transportation, and Treasury. In order to produce fully informed analyses, it's necessary to know the functions of these departments and their subsections, as well as how their actions may ultimately affect specific organizations.

Fortunately, it is generally easier to obtain information

from government agencies and the various departments than from Capitol Hill. It sometimes takes several attempts to find the right person in the right department, but that is a by-product of large staffs and highly specialized functions, not a policy of keeping information back from those who need it. In fact, the amount of information available in Washington, for anyone with patience and tenacity, is amazing. And each helpful response, each source name learned, is another addition to a file of personal contacts.

Much of what one may need from an agency or department already exists, in the form of charts, reports, statistics, or press releases. It is sometimes possible to have a practitioner's name added to a mailing list for some of these materials; for others, one can simply call and request them.

There are basic and valuable print information sources for keeping abreast of what the various House and Senate committees have scheduled. The *Congressional Monitor,* which is printed daily when Congress is in session, lists each day's hearings plus those scheduled for the future. When possible, it also lists the slate of witnesses. It is important to check this every day; some hearings may be profitable for a public relations person to attend. It's also a good idea to scan the *Congressional Record,* which covers the day's events on the floor of the House and Senate (the *Record* does not cover committee hearings or meetings). Frequently a member has made a speech, or had a statement read into the *Record* on a matter that may be of interest. The *Congressional Record* is printed overnight and delivered the following morning.

It's also a good idea to pay attention to the news conferences or briefings that are a daily Washington event, at least when Congress is in session and the city is alert and active. Some of these adhere to rigid rules, and only working media are admitted. Even so, it is almost always possible to get a copy of the material distributed simply by calling the contact telephone number listed in the announcement.

Other news conferences are open to all comers. Perhaps one of the many consumer interest groups has an announcement to make on the subject of its concern. It could be air bags versus seat belts, an attack on an artificial sweetener said to cause health problems, or a concern over the possible toxicity of children's crayons. Special interest groups also present their views at events like these, dealing with such issues as imports that jeopardize American jobs, water cleanup issues, or the closing of a steel mill. These briefings are held in Washington to draw congressional and federal attention to the issues involved. The public relations staff should pay attention to them whenever they touch upon the interests of its organization or a client.

Clear and detailed reports on hearings are essential to monitoring and analysis. Knowing in advance who will testify is important, but it is not always possible to verify this until almost the last minute. Arriving early allows one to get a good seat (some hearings are packed, and latecomers must stand for hours) and to get copies of the witnesses' prepared statements. A tape recorder is useful if one is sitting near the front of the room, but good notes are essential. Hearing transcripts are not available for weeks, and sometimes months, so they can't be relied upon as a backup.

During breaks at the hearing, a discreet conversation with others attending can be useful. Naturally, everyone is playing the same game, which is to find out why others are there and what their interests are without revealing their own concerns. Still, one may hear a provocative opinion or learn something new that can be of help.

When writing a legislative analysis, it's best to avoid stating flatly that one thing or another will happen, because there will be too many imponderables along the way. One should present the views and *likely* actions of the key players, and should detail any subsurface conflicts or interests that come up. Opinions should be accompanied by buttressing reasons and data as well as an alternative scenario, so as to give the full range of possibilities. The analysis should also cover possible future courses of action that may be taken as a result of current congressional actions.

The major points for doing legislative analysis and monitoring are:

1. Be thoroughly familiar with the interests of your organization or client and any peripheral issues or actions that may affect them.

2. Know the steps a bill must go through before it can become a law.

3. Know who the chairman and members are for each committee dealing with matters that concern you. Know their interests and constituencies.

4. Establish good relationships with committee and Congressional staff members.

5. Attend all key hearings and news conferences affecting your interests.

6. Know the functions of the federal departments and regulatory agencies. Monitor their actions.

7. Be prepared to write fast and well, against tight deadlines to keep your organization or client informed.

## Public Affairs and Government Relations —At the State Level

The turbulent period of the 1960s marked the beginning of major, structural changes at all levels of government, particularly at the state level. These changes have continually challenged business to attain higher levels of awareness and responsibility.

In the first half of the twentieth century, business paid little attention to state legislatures. Washington was where the growth in government was occurring, a process that accelerated dramatically following the election of Franklin D. Roosevelt in 1932. Roosevelt's New Deal programs centralized more power than ever before in the nation's capital.

By the early 1970s, the face of state government began to change. Like the federal government 30 years earlier, state legislators were becoming more activist. The very measure of that activity is striking. From 1961 to 1985, the number of pieces of state legislation introduced annually more than tripled, rising from 60,000 to almost 200,000. Four notable reasons explain the increase in activity in state government:

- Emergence of the "new politics," which has been defined as a process of campaigning outside of and around established parties and structures.

- A partial reversal in revenue flow from Washington back to the states. The revenue-sharing program begun during the Nixon Administration provided billions of dollars to the states. The Reagan Administration, however, effectively halted this effort, through its "New Federalism" policy. This involved the transfer of funding obligation for programs to the states in exchange for increased autonomy in the management of those programs.

- Growth of a new anti-Washington populism, a theme used during the presidential campaigns of both Jimmy Carter and Ronald Reagan that decried the growth of a federal government that was unfeeling and removed from the interests of the population.

These factors led to an important conclusion by astute public affairs people: State government would have a greater impact on national policy.

Whereas in the 1950s there were probably no more than a few hundred state administrative agencies, by the mid-1970s the number was in the thousands. Each agency brings to every legislative session its own agenda of bills to be introduced. The ideas presented in this legislation spread rapidly from one state capitol to another.

To handle the heavier work load, state legislatures are meeting more frequently and for longer sessions. Legislatures that once held 60-day sessions now meet for 90, 120, or even 180 days. In many states, when the sessions end, interim committees continue to work year round. In more and more states, Florida and Minnesota for example, interim committees act with full authority and are prepared to take legislation directly to the floor on the first day of the next session. In others, there have been significant procedural changes: more committee roll calls, more public hearings, and fewer executive sessions. All these measures are designed to open up the lawmaking process in ways that reduce the certainty of outcome by diluting both external and internal pressures and attempts to control the direction of proposed legislation.

Another vehicle for bypassing the legislative process is the initiative or referendum. Now effective in 23 states and the District of Columbia, the initiative allows any individual or group to have an issue placed on the electoral ballot simply by collecting a sufficient number of valid signatures.

**Evolution of public interest advocates.** Tied in closely with the proliferation of state agencies and increased legislative activity has been the rapid evolution of the new special interest groups or "public interest advocates." These groups are often concerned with consumer or environmental issues and work to provide a check on business and industry.

Unlike their progenitor, the Populist Party, special interest groups aim to influence the content of government decisions without organizing to gain office. Notwithstanding their aura of legitimacy and wholesomeness, advocates may often assume an uncompromising position on issues.

Public interest advocacy has spurred the movement for greater openness in government, particularly at the state level. A number of these groups have had significant impact on the decision-making process and on the guidelines for the creation of many new state agencies. Most of these agencies and commissions are created to fit today's social conditions and to serve the "public good."

Leverage of public interest advocacy in state capitals has been increased by the noticeable disintegration of traditional party loyalties. This has been particularly evident in recent elections, as members of both parties often seek to avoid being associated with the unpopular policies of their national counterparts. It appears the role of the orthodox political party has been transformed from that of leader to that of adviser, from a body commanding loyalty to one merely recommending action.

**New breed of activist legislator.** Somewhat related in concept to the independent voters are the so-called new breed of state legislators. They are better educated, more articulate, and less likely to bend to pressure from party leadership. They also represent a far greater demographic spread, with far more women and minorities holding office. Many are trained as lawyers, and some come from small business, but an increasing number look to elected office as a career.

Generally, the new legislators are more activist, with a

more direct concern for their constituents. This acknowledges that their basis of support is largely outside the party. The independence of the new breed of legislators is often related to the relative strength of the party system in their states. In states with strong party affiliation, the endorsement may provide the cushion of victory and will be won only in return for future loyalty. However, there is an increasing trend, even in old-line party states, to shun the party and run as an independent Democrat or Republican.

**Building a government relations program.** The huge increase in state governmental activity has created a range and complexity of public policy issues that require new and more active forms of business participation in the decision-making process. How does business get more involved before it gets ignored or left out? Business can become more effective at the state level by beginning to evolve a new style of government relations.

Corporations are going to have to treat state government relations with the seriousness and planning devoted to their federal efforts. The "good old boy" network for lobbyists that involves lunches, banquets, small favors, and remembrances may never be replaced, but it needs to be supplemented with modern political techniques, such as state-of-the-art constituent targeting, coalition building, and a grass roots organizing program. Given the size and complexity of state government today, we have reached the point at which knowing the right person is not enough. The margin of victory is often a demonstration of broad public support for an issue.

Public relations practitioners must consider a few important reminders:

- The complexity of issues and the proliferation of individuals and organizations addressing them complicate the job of the legislative liaison. Every lobbyist must have a procedure to gather and process information as well as the ability to use the tools of technology to supplement personal contacts and instincts.

- Planning has assumed greater importance. The effectiveness of a public affairs campaign is closely associated with the ability of a company or group to gather solid intelligence and set priorities. Success requires preparation, judgment, and the ability to assess and draw on all the resources available.

- In every public affairs effort the following items should be included:

  1. A strategic plan, managed by a central coordinator, but with the approval of senior operating management.

  2. A legislative support system that includes a media relations plan and a grass roots organizing plan.

  3. Supporting materials: i.e., position papers, research documents, third-party documents, and other important information.

A broad-based public relations approach often is the appropriate remedy when a problem arises out of the public's perception of a particular situation or from legislative efforts that create a problem. In such cases, the remedy takes on the method of effectively assembling and disseminating correct information to the public or to the legislature.

## Case in Point

A case in point arose in a midwest state where three major utilities found their economic survival threatened when a well-intentioned but unrealistic, energy-related initiative was placed on the state ballot.

The proposal, put forth as being in the public interest,

would have eliminated the automatic rate adjustment clause in the utilities' charters and required full "cost of service" hearings for each rate adjustment request made by a utility. Moreover, it would have limited a utility to making only one such request at a time.

The net result of such an initiative would have been to throttle business operations of the utilities to such an extent that both major bond-rating agencies, Moody's and Standard and Poor's, warned that passage of the proposal would threaten the bond ratings of the electric companies.

It was noted that the average length of time required for a rate hearing in that state was 14 months; hence the rule would have forced utilities to wait more than a year for funds to make up for outlays and thus would have forced them to borrow additional funds and incur unnecessary interest expense. All this, of course, would have to have been passed along to industrial and residential consumers in the form of higher energy costs. Higher unemployment and service cutbacks were also possible outcomes.

Not only were these dire results not apparent to the public, but a poll in the spring of an election year indicated the initiative was extremely likely to pass. At that time, sentiment was rated at 78 percent "yes" and only 16 percent "no" with another 16 percent undecided. To stave off impending disaster, it was necessary to change public sentiment among the approximately 3 million voters who would go to the polls in the fall.

Specifically, the need was to convince the voters that there was a better way of doing things—specifically, that a referendum drafted by the companies, passed by the state legislature, and placed on the ballot in competition with the initiative was this better way. Under election rules, the referendum would take precedence over the initiative if it received more "yes" votes.

Working with the state's news media presented both a problem and an opportunity. Reporters generally were found to view any information coming directly from the utility companies with skepticism. The first task, then, was media relations. The media was at once made aware of the existence of an independent coalition of people and organizations. The campaign was launched with announcements at several regional news conferences, personal briefings for media in the state's 20 major cities, and the preparation and dissemination of background information on the proposals to 500 outlets.

From Labor Day to Election Day, media awareness was constantly focused by a variety of means, including the formation of regional committees of civic, business, and, importantly, labor leaders in favor of the referendum; the use of more than 15 regional spokespeople for the campaign, including such prominent individuals as the president of the state chamber of commerce, the president of the state AFL-CIO, the president of the Michigan Farm Bureau, the Senate Minority Leader, and the House Majority Leader; editorial board briefings with spokespersons; an actuality feed service, giving weekly statements by spokespersons to more than 250 radio stations; bylined editorials by prominent spokespersons; scheduling spokespersons for radio, television, and print interviews.

Along with this, an "Allies Network" was set up. This was a statewide coalition of business, labor, agriculture, civic, and religious leaders and organizations. Their members were recruited intensively and their activities were publicized throughout the state and locally, through personal contacts from the utilities' boards of directors, small group meetings, speeches to local business and community groups, resolutions and announcement press kits for the endorsement of local and regional chambers of commerce, and the use of "canned" feature articles not only in the utility companies' publications but in the employee publications of other companies allied with the campaign.

A speakers bureau with 12 regional coordinators was set up, and preparation included a sample speech, orientation sessions for speakers, and a 10-minute slide show to accompany speakers. That the campaign was taking hold became apparent during the last days of October when polling showed 90 percent of the electorate had recalled hearing or reading about the referendum.

Of 41 daily newspapers, more than 30—representing 90 percent of the state circulation—printed editorials favoring the referendum or opposed to the initiative. More than 1,500 separate news items had run by November 1, and by the final week, spokespersons had conducted more than 100 radio and television interviews and newspaper editorial board appearances.

The speakers bureau accounted for 363 appearances before civic and professional groups with more than 13,000 community leaders present at these talks.

On Election Day, more than 3.1 million citizens voted. The results:

|  | Yes | No |
|---|---|---|
| Initiative | 1,472,442 | 1,431,884 |
| Referendum | 1,670,381 | 1,131,990 |

Since the referendum had the most "yes" votes, it carried the day, a relatively close final result but a stunning reversal of public attitude since the spring.

Another striking case in point involved public health. Specifically at stake was the continued use of DPT cc, which has been used in the United States for more than a half-century as a major method of preventing diphtheria, whooping cough, and typhoid fever. Most states and municipalities require children to be vaccinated before they enter school.

Despite the vaccine's success, however, a number of parents' groups had been formed—usually at the instigation of attorneys—to attack the vaccine, citing certain side effects of the pertussis fraction of the vaccine, which had been recognized and accepted for years. In fact, the filing of lawsuits had driven out of DPT vaccine production all manufacturers except Lederle.

A public relations program then was devised to demonstrate the continued need for the vaccine to suppress these three diseases and to use this information with Congress to obtain legislation that would put a cap on liability awards. The general aim, of course, was to establish that the greater public good requires the vaccine despite the acceptance of lesser risks, while at the same time acting to mitigate those risks.

Accordingly, an extensive background paper was developed noting that epidemics of whooping cough had broken out in at least two countries where widespread use of the vaccine was abandoned, and also noting the preventive nature of the vaccine and detailing steps under way to develop improved vaccines. A video presentation also was prepared for pediatricians along with other materials concerning the side effects and their mitigation. Presentations on the DPT subject were made to appropriate Congressional leaders and in hearings.

At this writing, this is not a complete case story, because the program is ongoing. However, a bill to eliminate DPT vaccinations in the nation's most populous state, California, has been defeated and Congressional reaction has been encouraging.

In a legislative case in point (also discussed in Chapter 16), Public Service of Indiana ran into economic danger after it halted construction on the Marble Hill nuclear power plant. Legislation was introduced in the state Senate that would have prohibited utilities from recovering any of the costs of uncompleted power plants. What is more, there was tremendous time pressure since the bill was introduced on a Friday and the Senate was due to go into permanent recess the following Thursday.

First, a computer tape of supporters was identified through the direct mail program (about 9,000 names) and compared against telephone company tapes to find approximately 7,200 phone numbers. A phone bank message was prepared, and callers were hired and briefed. These callers reached more than 5,500 people. On Thursday, the final day of the session, 40 targeted state senators received some 3,000 telegrams from constituents.

The bill was defeated in committee.

Passage of an election proposal was the target in another case in point, this in Sacramento, California, where voters had petitioned to be transferred from the Pacific Gas & Electric Co. to the Sacramento Municipal Utility District (SMUD). In fact, it was necessary that two ballot proposals, labeled "G" and "H," both pass for the change to be made.

The campaign in favor of SMUD focused on voter information, emphasizing to the electorate SMUD's good track record in managing its development and its success in keeping generation costs down by the use of nuclear power. Voter turnout also was crucial, since the case of lower electric bills seemed strong and backers might not bother to vote.

Public relations methods included use of a press backgrounder, two direct-mail pieces to go to registered voters, and a speech for use by local businesspersons and others at civic meetings and rallies.

The turnout was strong and measures "G" and "H" passed by wide margins.

Rallying of public support behind the improvement of education was the task in the State of Georgia in 1983 after a blue-ribbon citizens group formed by the governor recommended sweeping reforms and a step-by-step program of implementation and funding called the Quality Basic Education (QBE) Act.

The crisis had been easy to define: Educators were leaving the profession and decrying the system; parents were pleading for better educational opportunities for their children; business leaders were warning that the state's educational system would not only deter new businesses from moving to Georgia but would lead to the departure of some already established firms.

Public relations was enlisted to create public awareness of the problem and translate that awareness into passage of the QBE Act.

A 28-member coalition of prominent citizens was formed into a committee called Georgians for Excellence in Education, which visited editorial boards and media in major cities, held 14 QBE Days at the state capitol, made approximately 200 speeches and appearances, and raised funds for fees and expenses. Flyers, booklets, buttons, bumper stickers, and lapel pins were produced and distributed. Governor Joe Frank Harris made a seven-city, "whistle stop" tour, and legislators in opposition were sent counter-argument letters.

The media response was overwhelming in volume and more than 90 percent favorable. The result: QBE was passed unanimously and virtually intact and signed into law in April 1985. Over $1 billion in new money was appropriated for QBE.

In a California case in point, the use of plastic pipe would have been limited by proposed legislation that was being backed by special interests who were spreading misinformation on the subject.

On the counterattack, a "Plastic Pipe Information Bureau" was set up to contact every significant media outlet in the state to correct this misinformation, and a major news conference was held in Los Angeles, covered by three wire services, eight television stations, 16 newspapers, and 11 radio stations. In the Los Angeles area alone, this conference reached a total audience of 4.5 million.

The legislation was defeated.

Chapter 18

# Public Relations for Nonprofit Organizations

Nonprofit institutions and organizations throughout the United States enrich the lives of millions of Americans through programs in the arts, education, community service, health care, and research.

The nonprofit sector is an essential part of our society, but one that is coming under increasing financial pressure with each passing year. Particularly vulnerable are those institutions whose activities lie beyond the basics of health, housing, and welfare: the performing and visual arts, museums, libraries, parks, botanical gardens and zoos, and historic preservation programs.

## Institutional Public Relations

For the nonprofit institution, making a persuasive case to its audiences about what it is, what it does, and why its activities are important, exciting, helpful, or enriching may make the difference between an empty theater or a full one, a busy library or a deserted one, a deficit or a year in the black. For nonprofits, getting the story out effectively to the right audiences may ultimately make the life or death difference for the organization.

Often, nonprofits are running so hard just to survive that no one asks the difficult questions essential to formulating institutional public relations policy and strategy: Who *are* our audiences? Are we reaching all of them and with the right messages? How are we perceived by the media? Do they even know we're here? What do donors and potential donors think of us? Local government agencies? The local community? Who is our competition? What's our audience-building strategy over the next three years? Our board-building strategy? Our fund-raising strategy?

The practitioner must ask all these questions and work closely with the board, the management, and the staff in developing a communications program that reflects the answers. Much more than in the corporate sector, the communications professional in the nonprofit organization must be the catalyst for internal dialogue and the leader in communication policy formulation.

After the strategy sessions and the setting of objectives, the practitioner must:

- Develop and place stories about the institution on a timely basis over the course of the year. Aim to encourage attendance or use of the facilities and raise the level of awareness and the esteem in which the organization is held by its target audiences. This activity, in turn, supports the organization's fund-raising efforts with individuals, corporations, foundations, and government agencies. Appropriate outlets for an organization may run the gamut from national prestige magazines and network television shows to community or ethnic newspapers, local bank or shopping center newsletters, school display cases, and utility bill "stuffers."

- Survey current donors and users of the institution and find out what they like and dislike about it, what they know, and what they don't know. Develop an external communications plan that reinforces the positive elements while it educates and builds awareness and attempts to neutralize the negatives.

- Ask questions and listen. Wonderful "pearls," stories that will help the organization, frequently turn up this way. The archivist or librarian, the volunteers, the subscriber of 40 years' standing, or the employee who's worked with the group for several decades may give the practitioner the exact peg needed to get an important message out to a specific audience.

## Public Relations, Contributions, and Donors

In the current economic climate, the number of nonprofits seeking contributions far exceeds the resources available. In this competitive environment, nonprofit public relations and fund raising are most effective when interrelated.

Many arts and cultural organizations have become fairly sophisticated in working with donors. They know who "their people" are and are learning ways to cultivate and retain them. But they frequently need to develop a clear institutional public image that will tell their story and make the organization attractive to the uncommitted. A public relations program that includes specific activity to support the institution's quest for major donors is crucial.

## Public Relations and Corporate Giving

Cultural organizations must attract new donors with the means to sponsor programs, productions, exhibitions, and special events with substantial gifts. These high visibility projects that by their nature appeal to specific market segments are ideal for attracting corporate underwriting.

The practitioner may often be in a better position than the fund raiser to describe a project needing funding in terms that make sponsorship attractive to the potential corporate donor; to formulate and present a realistic sponsor recognition plan to the corporate donor; and to deliver recognition (in the institution's materials and in the media) that is appropriate and effective for both the donor and the recipient. These are public relations functions rather than fund-raising functions, but the practitioner and the development staff must work in close coordination to achieve success.

A few examples will illustrate some of the problems cultural institutions encounter when seeking corporate support and the ways in which creative public relations work can be of help.

- A museum needs a grant to underwrite a photography exhibition that will be sent on a tour of other museums after the initial exhibition. The museum's curatorial staff people are enthusiastic and describe all the exhibit's artistic and aesthetic merits to the prospective corporate donor. They don't mention the size of potential audiences, the location of tour museums in relation to the corporation's major markets, a publicity plan for the exhibition, or the potential for preview parties and client entertaining. The museum public relations staff must present the program in business terms that illustrate its attractiveness and usefulness to a corporate sponsor.

- A midwestern ballet company with a large membership has a year-round program of social events, seminars, backstage activities, newsletters, and a lounge for donors' use during performance intermissions. Some of the company's board and major individual donors are the very visible social leaders of the city. The ballet's major benefit dinners (two each year) are underwritten, but the company absorbs the costs of the member perks program as part of its fund-raising expenses. Many of these smaller projects (needing smaller gifts) would be of interest to financial service firms, local department stores, perfume, and luxury goods manufacturers. The ballet company public relations people need to position these activities as vehicles capable of giving a corporate donor visibility and social and business contacts for gifts provided.

- Throughout its season, a national opera company spends a substantial amount in fees for specially trained horses, dogs, cats, and donkeys that appear in its performances. The cost is absorbed as a production expense in the annual budget. Properly presented, with a good donor recognition plan, it would be a valuable underwriting project for a pet-food manufacturer. The opera's financial and operations people may not look at the company's activities and operating expenses and see them as special projects to be packaged for corporate support—with built-in public relations opportunities for the right donor.

- In each case, a communications program developed and explained in business terms can make a persuasive case to obtain support for the artistic product.

## Public Relations, Earned Income, and Audiences

Competition for earned income and audiences—whether the audience is composed of ticket buyers, library or museum patrons, or historic preservation group members—is fierce. Effective programs to retain existing audiences and to attract new ones are vital. Many of the techniques described in the chapter on specialized marketing communications apply in designing marketing communications for the nonprofit organization. The "new techniques to reach new audiences" are particularly appropriate as are "market segmentation techniques."

## The Practitioner as Internal Communications Catalyst

Given the needs of the nonprofit institution, public relations, fund-raising, and marketing are most effective when interrelated. A communications strategy designed to respond to the different but overlapping activities in these areas will provide maximum mileage for every dollar spent.

However, given the nature of most nonprofit institutions, the development and marketing staff and the public relations staff (when there is one) rarely work in harmony, applying their varied skills to a unified institutional strategy. More often than not, they clash or don't communicate much at all.

Within the nonprofit institution, the practitioner has an opportunity to be the link to integrate aspects of marketing and development through media support of their programs. The marketing staff must sell tickets or increase use of an institution's facilities or services. The development staff must reward major corporate and individual donors with press visibility and stimulate interest in the institution among the uncommitted to expand the donor base. The public relations practitioner can assist both by creating and maintaining dialogue within the institution and generating effective publicity outside it.

In the years ahead a nonprofit organization's ability to communicate—to tell its story persuasively—will be closely linked to its ability to survive. It's a tough and exhilarating assignment for the public relations professional.

## College and University Public Relations

Vital educational institutions are essential to the well-being of our nation. Today, however, higher education finds itself in a situation of challenge and flux. Demographic changes are altering the university landscape, as the number of college-age students declines. Increased competition for students and resources is forcing colleges and universities to become more businesslike in their operations.

To remain competitive, universities have to realize that,

organizationally at least, education is also a business and that they must market themselves properly to meet increasing competition. The demographic, economic, governmental, and attitudinal changes will tax the ability of many institutions to thrive and even survive over the coming years.

Carefully developed strategies of communication and marketing, therefore, become important factors in how a college fares in the new environment. A good public relations program creates a favorable climate for a variety of essential activities, from fund raising to student recruitment.

**Objectives.** A successful public relations effort must be carefully planned. What are its major goals? What does the institution hope to accomplish? Is the school planning a major fund-raising campaign for a recruitment drive? The program developed will be shaped by the answers to these questions.

Public relations is essentially a communications function charged with showing the college in the most favorable light to its significant publics. In the past, its main task was to generate news. Now, however, public relations must be tied in with marketing: It must support marketing goals and dovetail with marketing strategy.

Only in recent years has the term marketing been applied to education, and it is still a term that meets with some resistance in the academic community. This sensitivity, however, is more a question of the term than the process, for colleges have always been involved in marketing. Every time an admissions officer sends a prospective student a brochure, every time a college holds an annual reunion, every time a college president makes a speech, marketing has taken place: Someone has been informed, or persuaded, or influenced.

Today, however, marketing is increasingly widespread

and the process itself is more consciously pursued. Responding to a real, or anticipated, decline in the demand for their services, many institutions of higher education are undertaking a serious review of their goals, priorities, and strategies. Marketing, called now by its real name, is today becoming an accepted, respected, and essential function at colleges and universities.

In broadest terms, the overall goal of a public relations effort is, therefore, marketing. Within this framework, however, a college may have any number of specific objectives. These might include:

- Increasing national visibility for the school.

- Increasing visibility in key regional areas to support the recruitment effort.

- Gaining recognition for faculty research or publications in a particular department.

- Creating a "context of visibility" to support a major fund drive.

- Develop a more extensive alumni relations program.

Public relations, through a well-developed communication strategy, can greatly enhance all of these undertakings.

**Target audiences.** The audiences for any public relations effort must be carefully defined. Does the institution want to reach prospective students and their parents in key regional areas, or is the emphasis on increasing visibility among state legislators? If a fund-raising campaign is being planned, key target audiences will include potential corporate donors.

Among the audiences to be considered are prospective

students, alumni, legislators, corporate leaders, foundation executives, parents, faculty, high school guidance counselors, and the general public.

**Elements of communications strategy.** Once the key target audiences have been defined, a strategy for reaching them must be developed. Various channels of communication may be considered, including the media (national, regional, and local), direct mail, special events, and speaking engagements.

A good college public relations program might include a strategic assessment survey, a marketing plan, a media relations campaign, special events, and speaking platforms.

**Strategic assessment surveys.** The first step in developing a public relations plan is an extensive fact-finding effort.

Fact finding is an important process, not only for the information developed but also for the opportunity afforded to all those involved—faculty, administrators, trustees, students, and alumni—to participate in the promotion process.

The data-gathering phase can take place through distribution of a questionnaire or through interviews with various campus spokespersons. Areas to be covered include: perception of the school's image among its various internal audiences, key themes to be addressed, outstanding programs, and notable faculty. In addition to information gathered from these interviews, any institutional reports, including accreditation studies, long-range planning documents, and case statements, should be reviewed. This information will provide themes and topics to be highlighted in the media campaign.

Another facet of the fact-finding effort is a publications audit—review of the college's printed material to see if it reflects a central message and the institutional goals. All publications, whether recruitment pieces or development brochures, should reinforce the main themes. This material should also be studied with the target audience in mind: What mailings does a particular audience receive? It may be determined that alumni receive too many fund-raising requests and not enough information on current institution programs and activities.

**Marketing plan.** Now that the word marketing is used openly on campus, many college advancement functions—whether public relations, publications, alumni relations, or planning—are done within a marketing context.

The essence of marketing preparation is looking at the institution's strategic situation and breaking it down into component parts. First of all, this means being clear about what the institution is: a liberal arts undergraduate school, a large research university, a community college. Secondly, it means having a clear understanding of what its goals are: to increase enrollment, to become better known nationally or in a specific region, to raise the academic qualifications of its existing students, to increase corporate contributions for research. A concise mission statement can then be drawn up.

The plan's third aspect is an understanding of the larger context in which the institution exists. This includes knowing competitors, knowing existing strengths in the marketplace as well as points of vulnerability, and having a sense of likely future direction. The public relations staff should study trends and statistics concerning the education environment and see how its college fits in.

With this background, a plan that includes the basic communications strategy can be developed. It is important to reexamine the plan annually and revise it as necessary, based on both internal and external changes.

**Media relations campaign.** The competition that colleges face for students and funds exists for media attention as well since scores of colleges and universities have awakened to the importance of marketing, in general, and effective media relations, in particular. Positive media attention provides important third-party validation for an institution's programs and activities.

Based on the background research and the marketing plan, a strategy can be developed for an ongoing visibility campaign designed to reach the key target audiences with appropriate themes and topics. In putting together a media campaign, an institution can concentrate on the national media, if possible, or on the local and regional media when the interest of national reporters is difficult to engage.

Regional media exposure frequently stimulates interest nationally. In addition, by focusing on areas with a significant concentration of alumni or from which new students are drawn, communications efforts in target cities can provide visibility support for goals in recruitment, fund-raising, and alumni relations.

In implementing a media campaign, it is helpful to find out what types of stories are of interest to various editors and writers. Smaller papers, for example, are frequently interested in news about local students. An ongoing program of home-town releases may, therefore, be an important component of the media plan. Larger papers and big-city dailies are generally more issues-oriented. An informal survey of education writers and editors in the institution's targeted region can help determine what is of interest to them. Such a survey frequently serves as the first step in the process of press cultivation.

In addition to education-oriented stories, a successful media relations program will draw on campus-based experts in a wide range of fields. For example, a science professor may be called upon to comment on an environmental issue, or a political scientist can develop an op-ed piece dealing with a key current-affairs topic.

In order to help position its faculty as a major resource for the press, a college public relations staff should put together a list of experts the media can call upon. Listing faculty and key administrators and their areas of expertise, the directory should be sent to newspaper editors in the surrounding area.

In approaching the media, it is important to maintain accurate and up-to-date mailing lists, targeted to the appropriate audience. A press release on a campus art exhibit, for example, should not be sent to education editors at major national newspapers.

The value of positive media exposure can be greatly reinforced by secondary dissemination. Reprints of significant articles can be sent to alumni or prospective students. Videotapes of appearances by faculty or administrators on local or national television can be shown at alumni gatherings or fund-raising meetings.

Information dissemination on campus is important as well. A special bulletin board in the library or in another prominent spot on campus will keep the college community informed of press coverage. Major articles can be sent regularly to key administrators or department heads. This helps generate enthusiasm and support for the institution's programs.

In summary, three steps should be taken in the development of a successful media relations campaign:

1. Clearly position the institution based on its mission statement and marketing plan.
2. Present it to the media for third-party endorsement.
3. Follow through with secondary dissemination of the media coverage to targeted audiences.

**Special events.** Another important element of the communications strategy is a well-conceived, carefully planned special event that can focus a high level of awareness on an institution.

Carried out in conjunction with an ongoing program of media relations, a special event provides intensity and a sharper focus of attention, and generates increased press interest in the college. The event can be planned, for example, around the dedication of a new facility or program, the announcement of a research discovery, or the celebration of an anniversary or development occasion.

Specialized press that may not be part of the institution's ongoing media relations program frequently can be called upon for special events. Scientific or technical editors can be approached with a research discovery or opening of a new science or engineering facility. Society editors might be the appropriate press contact for a fundraising gala or alumni benefit.

Securing the involvement of prominent alumni and guest celebrities can greatly enhance the newsworthiness of an event. Holding a press conference is another way to attract the interest of the media. The conference can announce a faculty research discovery, the opening of a new campus facility, a major policy decision, or any other significant happening.

**Speaking platforms.** Another very effective method for extending the college's reach to a broader audience is to arrange speaking engagements for the president and other leading college spokespersons. Appearances before the press, business groups, or community organizations can greatly enhance the school's visibility. Opportunities can also be arranged for the president to provide testimony for congressional hearings. By addressing the business community or press on important issues, the president develops a reputation as a spokesperson and the college becomes known as an important information resource.

In the same way, faculty can be positioned as spokespersons in their own areas of expertise.

## Public Relations Support for Fund-raising

The fund-raising arena has become an increasingly crowded one. Record numbers of public institutions are now entering this field, which has traditionally been dominated by private colleges.

With this increased pressure for scarce resources, the "context of visibility" becomes increasingly important for long-term fund-raising success. The public reputation of an institution, regular exposure through the media, and the regard in which it is held within corporate and foundational communities are all tremendously important factors in being able to set and reach monetary goals.

A minimedia campaign, with its own target audiences, objectives, and themes, can be developed in support of a major fund drive. Paralleling the college's ongoing media campaign, the effort would focus attention on the special programs and activities for which funds are being sought and concentrate on key regions targeted for the fund drive. Campaign spokespersons would be identified and speaking platforms sought.

Appropriate printed material would also be developed to support the campaign, with the case statement being the primary document. It outlines the objectives of the campaign and defines the institution in a way that appeals to its target audience. In making a case for the institution, this statement lists its strengths and unique qualities. It also clearly positions the college among its competitors. In addition to its primary purpose as an approach to prospective corporate and foundational donors, it can be drawn on in developing media strategy as well.

The case statement and related material should be part of the institution's overall communications strategy. The school's overall audiences also would include targets for the fund-raising effort, such as corporate prospects, foundations, and potential alumni donors.

In the context of today's competitive education environment, public relations assumes a greater importance than ever. Educational institutions frequently find themselves on a "slippery slope" where doing nothing means falling behind. Small schools must gain some degree of national recognition in order to expand recruiting efforts. Large public universities must reach out to new constituencies and solidify relationships with others, including alumni, as they begin to develop a fund-raising base.

The needs of an institution of higher education can best be supported through a businesslike approach to public relations, fund-raising, recruitment, and alumni relations.

Colleges must take a lesson from the corporate world on how to remain competitive in a tough marketplace. Although part of the nonprofit sector, schools must begin to operate in the manner of for-profit organizations in terms of defining their positions in the marketplace, clearly differentiating themselves from their competitors, coming to a realistic appraisal of their strengths and weaknesses, and taking advantage of appropriate public relations and marketing techniques.

Assistance in developing and implementing public relations programs is available from the various education trade associations. The Council for the Advancement and Support of Education offers a full schedule of programs, seminars and workshops in fund-raising, marketing, media relations, alumni relations, and other facets of institutional advancement.

From time to time, public relations is called upon to provide service in the public sector. In some cases, it provides the means of mobilizing the public to find ways to do something the public generally desires but would otherwise probably fail to accomplish.

## A Case in Point

Never was this phase of public relations more dramatically presented to the entire world than in the summer of 1986 when America celebrated the restoration of the Statue of Liberty, a symbol of so much of what the nation stands for. That the statue will continue to lift its lamp beside the golden door in New York harbor for at least another century is due in large measure to efforts conducted on behalf of the statue by public relations practitioners.

In 1980, federal engineers discovered, to their surprise and shock, that the Statue of Liberty was in such a bad state of disrepair it was unlikely to be open for public visitation when its 100th birthday rolled around in 1986. After nearly a century's battering by wind and storm, the statue's rivets were missing by the hundreds, its torch was crumbling because of water leakage, and pieces of it had even been found washed up on the nearby New Jersey shore.

President Reagan took the first step in the restoration process when he established the Statue of Liberty-Ellis Island Commission, a federal government advisory group that studied the restoration of both the statue and nearby Ellis Island.

The commission created the Statue of Liberty-Ellis Island Foundation, Inc., a private organization dedicated to raising the $230 million needed for the restoration, which would be conducted under the supervision of the National Parks Service. Chrysler Corporation Chairman Lee A. Iacocca, who had been named chairman of the commission, became chairman of the foundation as well.

Public relations had to carry almost the entire fund-raising load for the first year of operation. Fund-raising goals were met and surpassed and the first stages of a highly successful, five-year public relations campaign took place. (Advertising support was added in the latter years and contributed strongly to the overall success of the program.)

Research produced an enormous amount of material from public and private records, and this was communicated to the media along with new and old photographs. By the end of 1983, the first year of operation, the statue campaign was firmly in place with the nation's media and was receiving their full support.

As the work of restoration progressed, the public relations effort produced a series of important events designed to draw media attention: the raising of the 300-ton scaffold, the removal of the statue's battered torch and also the seven points of its crown, the construction of an entirely new torch and flame and its emplacement, and the removal of the scaffold. News release followed news release, announcement after announcement; media representatives were sought and accommodated. A torrent of publicity rallied public support from every part of the country.

From the start of the campaign until July 4, 1986, the period during which the statue and Ellis Island restoration fund-raising was under way, more than 150,000 newspaper stories were printed. Not even a conservative estimate of the project's exposure on radio and television is possible, but millions of viewers and listeners were exposed to the fund-raising publicity over and over again.

In late 1986, the foundation announced that a total of $294.4 million had been raised. That not only far surpassed the original goal but also covered all of the additional improvement work later added to both projects. Although the Ellis Island project is not scheduled for completion until 1992, it's already paid for in full—as was the statue restoration—thanks primarily to the donations of American citizens and corporations.

A somewhat different case in point involved public relations on behalf of the 1984 International Games for the Disabled (IGD). This Olympic-style annual competition was held in Nassau County, New York.

The games have no permanent organization to draw on, and little help for the opening of a public relations campaign existed. In addition, research disclosed that the American public, while sympathetic, viewed such events more as "recreational therapy" than true sports and also confused this two-week event with the Special Olympics, a recreational event for mentally retarded children.

The public relations effort, therefore, aimed first at establishing the identity of the IGD as a sports event and differentiating it from the Special Olympics, then sought to obtain national publicity for the event, thus leading to public acceptance.

To establish, on a smaller scale, the same kind of excitement that precedes the Olympic Games the public relations program included press briefings, public service television announcements featuring professional football players and other nondisabled athletes, electronic media kits providing material for 500 television stations, stories on past accomplishments of star disabled athletes, and coverage of site preparation. During the contests, public relations augmented the strong media coverage already attracted by providing a sports news service, including prewritten stories for the athletes' hometown papers, photographs, and video footage.

Initially having very little material to work with, public relations professionals created a worldwide awareness of the International Games for the Disabled and the capabilities of the athletes who are physically challenged.

# PART 4

# Internal Public Relations

Dan J. Forrestal

# Chapter 19

# Internal Public Relations: An Introduction

Internal public relations revisited: these four words appropriately describe this section of the *Public Relations Handbook*, inasmuch as the author of this section, Dan J. Forrestal, has returned to revise and update material he presented in Dartnell's predecessor handbook published in 1979.

The new narrative is more than a refresher that brings yesterday's communications strategies into contemporary focus. It signals "a new ballgame." Granted, the software and hardware of traditional communications efforts within an organization are included in the interest of completeness, but the similarity stops there. Actually, the new challenges of the real world approaching the twentieth century's last decade are becoming so overpowering that an analysis of yesterday's communications strategies alone would not suffice.

What are the new challenges? They abound dramatically in the software, or content, of today's employee communications. They literally reverberate in the high-tech hardware of the modern computer/electronics era in which a microscopic silicon chip can take over the job of keeping score on the events of a kingdom.

Although Dartnell's 1979 *Handbook* was perceptive enough to point out the incredible consequences of emerging technology on the preparation and distibution of employee communications, scant but specific mention was made of laser beams, satellites, and microwaves. There are

significant differences between then—less than a decade—
and now. Some of the plainly visible signs on the horizon include the following overall circumstances:

- A stimulating new array of humanity's high expectations.

- A world beset by anxieties and eager for credible communications offering reasonable reassurances.

- A new set of values in the marketplace.

- A new demand for ethics and morality in the ranks of
  business and political leadership.

- A revitalized American work ethic for employees,
  young and old.

- An unprecedented sense of compassion for the welfare
  of others.

- A louder, more incessant questioning—"What's going
  on?"—among all echelons of employees.

The business sector is particularly visible in the headlong
rush toward renewal. When in 1970 Alvin Toffler surveyed
the economic scene in his book *Future Shock*, he described
the work structure of the nation as "archaic, tailored to the
needs and accomplishments of an industrial revolution
long since past." "Industrial revolution," once the theme
song of the American economy, is being rapidly replaced by
the upbeat tempo of what John Naisbitt calls "the information society" in his book of the eighties, *Megatrends*.

What are some of the telltale trends of the new era?
What fundamental changes are involved? What transfor-
mations are being encountered at the job site?

Using the previous edition of the *Public Relations Handbook* as a point of departure, it can be observed that the
emerging new culture on the American business scene has,

for example, triggered new relationships between labor unions and employers.

The new culture has spawned a revolutionary lifestyle of having both husband and wife in dual roles of breadwinners in millions of households, changing child care centers from a cottage industry to a thriving business and making take-out foods and frozen entrees the popular nourishment of the era.

It has made tabletop computer systems progenitors of a cult and has added videocassette recorders, telephone answering machines, and other convenience appliances to liberate busy individuals everywhere.

It has put word processors in a position destined to have 20 millions users in the United States alone within the next several years.

It has taken the old board game Monopoly and made it a harbinger of corporate takeovers and mergers in unprecedented numbers—with revolutionary consequences.

It has turned thumbs up on jogging and aerobics and thumbs down on cigarettes and cholesterol.

And it has been sensitive enough to underline that the more high technology takes over, the more there is a need for the human touch.

In the new high-tech arena, the employee may have a new kind of coworker. On the assembly line, if that coworker were asked a question the response might sound mechanical inasmuch as it may be on tape. The coworker's eyes may have a special electronic sort of sparkle. In actuality, the coworker is the newest robot in the plant, welding more efficiently than welding was ever done before.

Remembering that the iceman never returned after being upstaged by the refrigerator, does the businessperson have apprehensions about the mind-boggling changes that are bombarding him or her? Is he or she sufficiently resilient to survive on the shaky terrain of a strange environment? Can the businessperson cope in the new maze of fiberoptics? The answer is "Yes" to all of the above, thanks to human ingenuity that, perhaps ironically, was initially responsible for creating the new technological puzzlements of a revolutionary society stressing service industries more than manufacturing industries.

The puzzlements will dart in and out on the pages that follow. And the solutions will unsurprisingly and frequently involve the role of internal, two-way communications.

# Chapter 20

# Employees Come First

Employees, of course, make up the internal public that is so crucial to the well-being of an organization.

Among employees one finds senior executives plus second- and third-level managers; then comes a wide assortment of subordinates assigned to administrative, functional, and operational responsibilities. There are also employees at so-called staff levels—in law, in advertising, in finance, in data processing, in public relations—plus, of course, the so-called hourly rate employees who make it all hum.

Work places include the plant and the office in rural, suburban, and right-in-the-middle-of-town settings. The mix includes large corporations and small companies, centralized and decentralized. There is the clustered organization with all employees at a single location as well as the widespread organization with divisions, plants, and offices scattered all over the nation and, in some cases, in other parts of the world.

The millions of employees who serve in any of these circumstances have—in addition to being employees—one thing in common: each is an individual. Each awakens to a work day in which he or she will bring to the job an individual personality, ability and skills, experience, heredity and background, dreams and goals—as well as frustrations.

Too often, for the sake of convenience and habit, people are largely regarded as members of groups. No harm is done by such thinking as long as one does not lose sight of the fact that each person is a unique individual with a sense of dignity and nobility and a desire for personal fulfillment.

Important as they may be, are employees the only inhabitants in a company's internal realm?

How about stockholders? Although they may be considered by some as "members of the family" in corporate life, stockholders are for all practical purposes outsiders rather than insiders.

How about retirees? Despite their 9-to-5 affiliation with the organization in earlier years, alumni and alumnae must be viewed as part of an external constituency. They are in a gone-but-not forgotten classification. It is bad manners and bad business for a company not to keep in touch with its pensioners, where a substantial amount of loyalty continues to repose. Many corporations publish newsletters directed to former employees, some of whom have found it difficult to adjust from "belonging on Monday" to "being cut off to fend for themselves on Tuesday." Such newsletters for retirees often accompany pension checks. Particularly in light of so many early retirements—forced or otherwise—that have enlarged the lists of alumni in recent years, it seems more prudent than ever for companies to stay in touch with men and women who served them in the past.

As August A. Busch, Jr., of Anheuser-Busch Companies, Inc., once remarked while recognizing the importance of his organization's former employees, "They're all still beer drinkers, aren't they?" Which means: idealism and pragmatism can be served simultaneously.

Management, personified by the chief executive officer (CEO), is a constant influence on the corporate scene. Inescapably, the CEO is the MIP (most influential person) aboard. Even when the CEO isn't specifically mentioned during a discussion of some public relations effort, he is still *there*. Even when he is somewhere out of the country, his presence is felt. His continuing influence is well recognized. His leadership style has a way of reminding colleagues of his viewpoints whether he is in the building next door or is many thousands of miles away.

Roger B. Smith, General Motors Corporation chairman, is an ideal example of a CEO creating an influence in the world's largest company. Are employees the number one constituency at GM? When he was asked this question recently, he said, "We've become rather adept in dealing with multiple constituencies simultaneously, but allowing no offense to any audience I would have to say that employees are unquestionably the most dominant single group for our corporation. They're the heartbeat of our enterprise."

Particularly in public relations, the role of top management is crucial. Indeed, many corporation chairmen and presidents regard themselves as the principal public relations officers of their organizations—and their job descriptions often say so. Both morale and morals are in their care. Their companies' reputations are a major part of senior officers' concerns. Public relations is conceptualized as a "way of life" and a "manner of behavior." Yet in the functional sense a public relations department serves not only as advisor to management but also as the internal and external "communications machine" for the organization.

In actual practice, the specialty skills of various functional groups converge at the doorstep of executive row because that's where policies are born and major decisions are made. Those policies and decisions determine—among other things— the way employees are treated in their role as the crucial core of a company's existence.

Are employees treated well because they merit a considerate attitude? Or because the CEO is a humanitarian? Or because of employees' contributions to productivity?

As America proceeds toward the nineties, productivity has become a word used over and over by businessmen struggling to hold down costs and maintain earnings during a time of economic stress and intense competition. Most businessmen had long since learned that there is a relationship between productivity and morale, and that there is also a relationship between morale and internal communications.

A cynic would say, "Companies communicate with employees chiefly for the purpose of productivity and efficiency." Such an observation represents an insensitive attitude. There are many companies, probably most, that are dedicated to effective internal communications not only for pragmatic purposes but also for human purposes. Despite the dehumanizing specter of robotics, some companies have extended a stronger-than-ever effort to communicate internally because they view their employees as human beings who should be treated as such.

Certain companies like to boast about the high morale of their workers. It is not uncommon for a corporation CEO to say, "We run a happy ship." Of course, the fact that a person says so doesn't make it true. However, it is of some comfort to know that even in the most dehumanizing factories, the meanest boss in the world has a conscience.

"I'm a bottom-line man," the hard-nosed general manager of manufacturing will boast—and by bottom line he means the final, magic line on the financial statement that shows net profit or loss. This declaration of rugged self-esteem is often voiced in an effort to impress. It can be interpreted to mean, "I respond to the principal demands of my responsibilities within the profit system, and I am not tempted by the siren songs of frivolous side issues."

Astute bottom-line people don't talk this way, and, for the most part, don't think this way. They realize that the shortest and most enduring road to the best bottom-line results involves the establishment of an environment in which employees will want to do their best. It is not just a digital world even though it may sometimes seem so.

How, you may ask, can one appraise the true role of management insofar as importance of employees is concerned? To gain an insight, find an answer to this question: To what degree does management communicate effectively with, and listen to, its employees?

Inspirational heroes are hard to come by: they are people of extraordinary character and stature whose careers are exemplary, whose achievements in the public interest are outstanding, and whose lives involve the pursuit of high purpose. Edgar Monsanto Queeny (1897-1968) was such a person. He was the only son of John Francis Queeny, who founded Monsanto Company in 1901. Edgar Queeny was the initial sponsor of his St. Louis-based company's public relations program in the mid-thirties, when his duties encompassed marketing and advertising. Subsequently he became president and board chairman. In 1939, he wrote the following for his company's Organization and Procedure Manual:

> The company's public relations program seeks to identify with Monsanto that which in an individual would be good morals and good manners. So-called good public and employee relations will be determined by the way we treat our employees, by the way we treat our shareholders, by the way in which all or business and community contacts are handled. In other words, whether we accomplish our purposes, or fail in their accomplishment, will depend on the way we do things, and the way in which our corporate character is interpreted and identified.

Following is another sample of Queeny's business philosophy, expressed in an editorial he wrote in 1934 for his company's internal publication, *Current Events*:

> The affairs of every corporation are inseparably linked with the interests of employees, shareholders, and customers. These three groups constitute a tripod on which a corporation rests. It is the job of management to see that each receives fair and considerate treatment.
> Every Monsanto employee has a stake in this business. He has a

right to expect management to do its utmost to assure the permanency of his job and to compensate him in accordance with his contribution to the company's welfare and progress. He has the further right to expect safe, sanitary, and congenial working conditions. In return he must give an honest day's work and undivided loyalty.

On pages later on in the *Handbook*, readers will encounter a myriad of adventures involving employees. In most instances, the examples will demonstrate communication in action or not in action. Much of the material will pertain to the internal activity in large corporations and institutions, but the lessons can be applied easily to smaller companies.

The internal sound and fury within General Electric are essentially the same as the hustle and bustle within Suburban Bakery. People are motivated in essence by similar ambitions, desires, hopes, and longings for fulfillment. Management motives are generally and universally the following: profitability, efficiency, service. These goals are equally a challenge at General Electric and Suburban Bakery.

As an organization grows, the problems become more complex and the curse of impersonality looms larger. At General Electric people discuss interpersonal relationships. At Suburban Bakery people talk about "getting along with each other." Same thing! At both GE and the bake shop, the reasons for keeping employees informed are about the same, differences in organizational size notwithstanding.

The *objective* of an internal communications program represents a consideration meriting thought at this juncture, keeping in mind that communications are a means and not an end in themselves. Too often, specialists in the communications business are tempted to regard communications as the moon and the sun and the stars, becoming unduly concerned with their form and appearance. They are so captivated by both the message and the medium that the objective is frequently hazy, if not forgotten altogether.

Professional communicators will even go as far as to cherish awards received for having produced the best employee magazine, revelling in those proud and professional moments when such things as words and pictures seem like the end of the rainbow, which they are not. They are no better than the information they effectively impart and the understanding they bring about. They are, in fact, sterile in themselves if not directed toward the achievement of a purpose.

"What is the objective?" This chapter and those that follow will keep coming back to this question.

The objective of an internal communications program should be the creation of an atmosphere of understanding and merited support, of coordinated interchange, of high morale and high efficiency. These objectives are towering and reasonable at the same time if considered in the light of "let's set our standards high and see to what degree we can reach them." A shortfall is not only permissible but also recommended if encountered in pursuit of a lofty goal; it is frequently simply a temporary halt as one tries to advance.

In such a setting it is appropriate to look more firmly at the objective of high morale. High morale among workers in a business organization is not a negotiable commodity. As any director of personnel will attest, it cannot be written into a labor contract. Nor can it be ordered by fiat or ordained by policy. It must be earned.

Despite its importance, high morale is often difficult to identify, elusive to quantify, and impossible to arrange for. Morale is a condition. The dictionary calls it a "mental state." High morale can, almost singlehandedly, break production records; it can precipitate and accelerate ingenuity, cause synergism, and intensify loyalties.

Anything with such magic must, one might say, be the secret weapon all organizations would like to possess. And there are companies abounding in positive management policies and attitudes, which unmistakably establish and nourish a state of high morale.

The creation of high morale involves an extra dimension, which is sometimes not sufficiently felt nor understood by the busy business executive bred on digits alone. An executive skilled at examining a complicated financial situation, for example, is not necessarily sensitive to those subtle ingredients that go into the making of high morale.

A humanistic approach is essential, of course; a desire for that happy ship is also essential. Even so, high morale will not necessarily follow. However, the likelihood of its emergence and continuation will be there. In contrast, if the humanistic approach and desire for high morale are not intensively present, forget about that happy ship.

Some cynics have said the average blue-collar employee works eight hours a day solely for the purpose of take-home pay. The cynical caricature of workers appears as follows: "They can hardly wait for 5 PM, at which time they check out of a life they hate and return to the outer world of freedom, family, friends, recreation, and contentment. They endure the dispiriting existence of what they don't want to do in order to be able to afford to do what they want to do."

Positive-thinking observers of the business scene believe that workers *can* find a measure of fulfillment in their jobs, *can* find circumstances of satisfaction and challenge between 8:30 AM and 5:00 PM. And morale, good or bad, is often a crucial element as the worker looks over his shoulder after a long day at the plant or office. Low morale can be fatiguing; high morale can be invigorating.

# Chapter 21

# The Attitude of Management

Public relations in its conceptual sense means a way of life, a manner of behavior, striving for an image and, inevitably for a reputation. In its function form, public relations focuses heavily on the planning, preparation, distribution, and evaluation of communications.

There is no uniform definition of public relations. It means so many things to different organizations and different people that one simple definition such as "analyzing problems and shaping solutions" is too broad to have real meaning. Further, such a sweeping definition can also apply to the work of people in other specialities who also analyze problems and shape solutions.

Public relations can best be defined as an attitude of management. For example, if a corporation's president wants to keep employees informed—both for pragmatic and human relations purposes—a way will most definitely be found. If this president's communications specialists in the public relations department do not follow through with effective programs in keeping employees informed, the president most likely will import some new employees who will carry out his wishes. In other words the president's desires will be fulfilled.

What if, on the other hand, the corporation's president has little interest in keeping employees informed? Such a president may say to his communicators, "Let's see how little we can get by with." Or, worse, he may regard employees as chattel and take the view that "we pay them well; if they don't like it here they can go somewhere else." Professional communicators working for such an employer will have a rugged row to hoe. If they are not able to persuade him away from his short-sighted ways, they will be handcuffed by his "attitude," which is the key word.

Even in situations where the employer has an enlightened attitude about communications for employees, there is one more ingredient that is needed: upwards communications, which will inevitably shed light on employee reactions.

Sometimes officers who are lower down on the corporate ladder are in a position to have substantial influence on communications. Perhaps a vice president in charge of production is affecting the life or death of certain internal communications efforts. Maybe the local plant manager's attitude is hampering or helping the efforts. There are also instances where a local personnel manager's attitudes can have a positive or negative influence, particularly on local communications. And, of course, there are a great many examples where a public relations director's attitude will have a definite effect on what traffic is set up in communications pipelines to and from employees.

It is satisfying to report that there are encouraging examples of public relations directors' having beneficially influenced the attitudes of top executives by demonstrating that the company is 1) out of step; 2) missing the boat in terms of opportunities for employee loyalties and support; 3) failing to achieve a sufficient esprit de corps; and 4) lagging in productivity partly because signals aren't clear and employees are demoralized. And it is not infrequent for a company to be persuaded to have a better attitude and do a better job after learning of the progress made by a competitor who has instituted more enlightened internal communications practices.

The difference that attitude can make is demonstrated in the story that follows.

The vice president of administration should probably never have been put into his new slot. Granted, he possessed certain credentials: experience in matters of production, substantial administrative responsibility, reliability, trustworthiness, diligence, honesty, steadfastness, and frugality. However, this officer had little imagination. When running the corporate bases, he never strayed more than a small step from any bag. An engineer by training, he led a digital, slide-rule life. One day he found himself pushed up the corporate ladder and given a more spacious office, a more important title, a larger salary, and greater responsibilities. In fairness to our hero, it should be said that he had not asked for the advancement. His superiors were to blame for the circumstance that forced this square peg into a round hole. In his new position he had administrative responsibility for several corporate staff departments of an East Coast multidivisional food manufacturer, including the public relations department.

The new vice president had never had even 10 minutes worth of experience in any aspect of public relations; moreover, he had no sensitivity for the subject. Yet, "by golly, I'm determined to get things straightened out" was his approach. In an effort to sort out the priorities of his public relations department's external and internal program, the vice president decided he should step in and decide "what's important and what's not."

He called in his secretary and dictated a memo. Among other things, the memo solidly placed certain kinds of public relations activities in a "top priority" category and others in a "secondary priority" classification. In other words, this wizard decided on his own, and without consultation with anyone else, to separate the wheat from the chaff by official edict. He put the whole area of employee communications in the secondary priority category. He was, to be sure, a cost-control-above-all sort of fellow to begin with

Caterpillar Inc., Peoria, Illinois, produces monthly tapes, targeted to its employees, featuring a variety of guests and covering topics like competition, marketing programs, and cost reduction achievements. This photograph is a black-and-white reproduction of a four-color picture that appeared in Caterpillar's 1986 Annual Report. It shows Caterpillar Chairman of the Board George Schaefer (right) and President Pete Donis being interviewed for an all-employee videotape by Joyce Schrock of Employee Information Division. Reproduced with permission from Caterpillar Inc.

This photograph was published on the cover of a special fund-raising issue of *Discovery YMCA,* an internal periodical for 63,000 volunteer members of YMCA boards of directors and 11,000 professional staff. It won an Award of Excellence for Anthony Ripley of YMCA of the USA in the 1986 Gold Quill Awards Program of the International Association of Business Communicators. The photograph, taken in Africa by Chicago free lance photographer David Barnes, records a time of famine, displacement, drought, and death in Africa. With some 22 African nations having YMCAs, the International Division of the YMCA of the USA sought support for a five-year fund-raising drive to help African Ys. Reproduced with permission from the YMCA of the USA.

McDonnell Douglas Corporation, which has some 100,000 people working in aerospace, computer systems, and finance, firmly believes that recreation and fitness make for well-rounded employees who are more productive. To that end, it maintains active recreation offices at each plant that coordinate a variety of events, including "Run for Fun," an annual event taking place on United Nations Day weekend. This photo was taken at one of these events to capture a moment that communicated the human emotion of joy, of people having fun. It won an Award of Excellence for Keith Skelton of McDonnell Douglas in the 1985 Gold Quill Awards Competition of the International Association of Business Communicators. Reproduced with permission from McDonnell Douglas Corporation.

A four-color version of this photograph adorned the cover of a special
annual report that commemorated the merger of The Bank of California,
the West's first incorporated banking institution and eighth largest bank
in California, with The Mitsubishi Bank, Limited, the 12th largest banking institution in the world. The goal of the photo was to portray the concept of the similarities and differences of the two merging organiza-

tions, brought together in a positive, artistic, and strong statement. The photo, also used in a poster, won an Award of Excellence for Joelle Yuna of The Bank of California, San Francisco, in the 1986 Gold Quill Awards Program of the International Association of Business Communicators. Reproduced with permission from The Bank of California.

To help employees identify with and become acquainted with their newly restructured company in the wake of the divestiture of the original AT&T and Bell operation companies, Bell Communications Research Inc. produced a special edition of *Bellcore News,* an employee publication. Featured in this issue were photo essays on Bellcore employees, shown in their work environments. This was one of the photos in the series, which won an Award of Excellence for Bonnie L. Henson of Bell Communications Research in the 1986 Gold Quill Awards Program of the International Association of Business Communicators. Not only did the portraits of the workers appear in print; framed photos are also proudly displayed in Bellcore offices. Reproduced with permission from Bell Communications Research Inc.

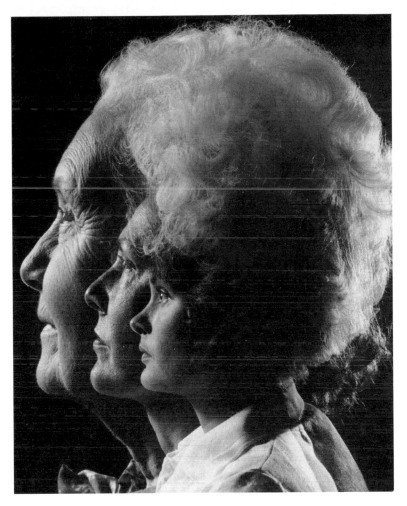

Depicted here are three generations of women—daughter, mother, and grandmother—to illustrate "The Womens Health Connection," a network of health programs and services for women unveiled at the Methodist Hospital, Omaha, Nebraska. The photo appeared in *Pulse Beat,* a quarterly distributed to customers, physicians, employees, donors, community leaders, patients, and the media. It won an Award of Merit for Gini Goldsmith of the Methodist Hospital in the 1986 Gold Quill Awards Program of the International Association of Business Communicators. Reproduced with permission from Methodist Hospital, Omaha, Nebraska.

*Life in the Bike Lane*

This photograph appeared on the cover of *Burnettwork,* an employee publication for the Leo Burnett Company targeted to 1,600 employees of the company in the USA, top management in 38 Burnett offices around the world, clients, press, retired Burnetters, and potential employees. Photographer George Kufrin took the picture of a Burnett account director, one of the many Burnetters who come to work under "people power," bicycling to work. The mission of the photo was to say, "spring is here," and to illustrate a short feature on the company's rental facility for bikes. The photo won an award of excellence for Joan Kufrin of Leo Burnett in the 1985 Gold Quill Awards Program of the International Association of Business Communicators. Reproduced with permission from the Leo Burnett Company.

and probably reluctant to put anything into a top category requiring attention and expenditures. Downplaying the importance of internal communications was the unkindest and most unfortunate cut of all.

When asked the why of his action, he explained that internal communications programs and especially programs requiring printed materials "are really no more than a compromise supplement to the day-to-day, eyeball-to-eyeball communication between supervisors and the workers."

Fortunately the tenure of the new vice president of administration was short-lived. The harm he could have done through his negative attitude toward internal public relations was thus minimized. He wound up back in operations, where he came from and where he belonged.

Nevertheless, his beliefs were something to be reckoned with during his administrative tenure. Actually, his negative bias regarding the function of public relations was an attitude he would carry wherever he went. Yet the harm he could do in an operations post was relatively small when compared with the overall damage he might have done had he remained in a broader administrative position that encompassed public relations.

Quite often, attitude is forged not only by knowledge or lack of it, and by feel, intuition, habit, and judgment but also by political circumstances within a company. A second- or third-echelon corporate officer will sometimes find it convenient to construct an attitude to fit the whims and pleasures of the chief executive officer. If, for example, the CEO is a compulsive string-saver, this can and will affect the attitudes of those immediately below him on the organizational chart.

Consequently, even though the second- and third-echelon executives may appreciate the importance of internal communications, they may find it imprudent to express their true feelings under the circumstances. However, in an encouraging number of cases, more and more companies are persuading their managers at all echelons to show courage for what they believe in; stick to their convictions; hold on to their principles—at least until they're voted down.

There were numerous instances in the mid-eighties when drastic cost-cutting became commonplace in many companies and staff reductions were often prevalent. Despite turbulent economics and widespread belt-tightening, many companies continued to reaffirm the importance of internal communications. Undergirding such resolute faith in employee information was a growing and positive attitude of management, recognizing the bedrock basic urgency of internal communications programs.

During the days when Professor Ralph M. Hower was conducting exciting classes in administrative practices at Harvard University's Graduate School of Business Administration, he relished recounting his "telltale evidences" of management attitudes. He would exclaim, "Show me a management which really, truly, honestly, actively endorses a comprehensive program of employee communications and I'll show you a company which also abounds in other merits." He regarded employee communications not simply as a supplementary option in an otherwise astutely managed company but as a basic essential—so essential, in fact, that its presence or absence was, by his reckoning, "telltale evidence" in itself.

Professor Hower would also inquire, "Does management mean what it says or does it simply give lip service to internal communications?" Fortunately, one hallmark of enlightened management has more and more veered in the direction of always keeping employees informed. With such a situation prevailing, Professor Hower's lip service apprehensions quietly fade away.

Chapter 22

# Effectiveness and Credibility

The extent to which communications programs "pay their freight" obviously depends on how much attention they receive from their targeted audiences. As far as internal programs are concerned, the following questions need to be asked: How much understanding do they bring about? Do they offer credibility? Are they engendering employee support? Do they achieve their sponsor's objectives? In short, how effective are they? As management wonders about such questions, it hopes to find hard answers and not mere guesstimates or partisan evaluations.

Most companies are not in business to publish magazines, newspapers, newsletters, or brochures; nor are they producers of motion pictures, videotapes, or bulletin board announcements. Such media, when used for the purpose of informing employees, are only the vehicles, the devices, the conveyances to deliver the company's message.

Each vehicle is different, each with special strengths and limitations. There is no 100 percent effective vehicle that carries all messages to all employees. Life is simply not that simple.

How about the commonly and widely used interoffice memo?

It would be impossible to estimate how many millions of interoffice memos make up the daily traffic in business organizations. Granted, an increasing number of these memos are distributed via electronics and by a wide assortment of sophisticated methods throughout the nation's business community, often saving both cost and time. Yet crusades to cut down on mountainous paperwork is still more of a promise than an achievement. Despite incinerators, shredding machines, recycling, and landfills, paper disposal continues to be a nightmare.

With the projected increase in population and corresponding increase in the number of workers, additional interoffice memos will surely be generated. The consensus among office systems experts seems to be that simple interoffice memos from one employee to another will remain essentially the same—individually prepared—but that memos to multiple recipients will be further automated, perhaps using equipment still to be invented.

Routine individual memos, of course, are not normally in the province of public relations or of any other department. Professional communicators within an organization are concerned mainly with written, oral, and visual communication for groups.

The eternal questions with which public relations professionals are faced are: "What medium is best for this message?" and "What message is best for this medium?"

Marshall McLuhan, Canadian scholar and author, created a few shock waves with his book *The Medium Is the Message: An Inventory of Effects*. His analysis demonstrated that, indeed, the communication vehicle is a form of communication in itself.

There is—pre-McLuhan and post-McLuhan—an ample body of evidence that suggests the medium, or vehicle, communicates beyond whatever the message itself might be. When the President of the United States is about to deliver an address to the nation on television, the waiting audience anticipates, "We may not know what he's going to say but we assume it will be something important or else he would not have commandeered the television networks tonight." When an employee of a corporation receives a letter in the home mail from the corporation's president, he or she will probably think "Even before I read this I know it's something special because the president of my company uses letters to employees' homes only on the infrequent occasions when there is something significant or urgent to transmit."

One may not agree entirely with McLuhan that the medium is the message, but the medium is, nonetheless, a tip-off about the content and importance of the material involved. The late Pendleton Dudley, eminent public relations counselor in New York, once commented: "One doesn't send a love letter by third-class mail." Third-class mail is a form of communication in itself. It says, "I'm not a high-priority matter" even before the envelope is opened.

Appropriateness and effectiveness, then, are the keys in matching the right medium with the right message.

Within a business organization, there is another important consideration: "Who should get this message?" Sometimes the medium's distribution is so controlled that the "who" is automatic. If, for example, all employees get a company magazine, the answer to "Who sees this message?" is obvious. Or is it? All employees get the magazine. But do they read it?

Where the target of an internal communication is not clear, here's a tip-off. Whenever something happens within a company that merits consideration for passing along or sharing with others, there are three questions to ask:

1. Who is affected?

2. Who is interested?

3. Who is involved?

People sensitive to public relations instinctively and habitually ask themselves these questions whenever anything occurs. The answers to one or more of these questions will suggest where the information should be dispatched.

The questions seem to be similar, but they're not. Each has a slightly different shade of meaning.

Media selection is a more complex task than simply determining the target. The selection of the right vehicle depends on many elements, including communicators' experience and judgment, as will be seen in various examples in subsequent chapters.

It may be helpful to look at some of the more popular communications media and examine their advantages and disadvantages. First, let's look at the element of immediacy: How quickly do we need to communicate?

There are at least three transmission devices that have the quality of immediacy—live radio, live television, and, of course, the telephone. Delayed radio messages and videotapes on TV, assuming the recipient is aware of the time that has lapsed, have a lesser flavor of immediacy. "It happened" is not quite so powerful as "it's happening."

Motion pictures still are effective in the business world. They can involve action, speech, drama, graphs, diagrams, color, sound effects, and music. They are multisensory in nature, with the potential of having high impact, informing, instructing, and motivating. Equipment needed for projection of movies is normally more cumbersome than easy-to-use videotapes. Other disadvantages of motion pictures include captive audiences in dark rooms, cost, and rigid format (once the film is set in motion, it cannot easily be stopped, restarted, or rerun for purposes of audience discussion).

Slide presentations lack the advantage of motion, but they are as easy to edit as a motion picture is difficult to edit. Slides are also easy and economical to produce. Their popularity seems certain to endure.

Live presentations depend largely on the skills, personality, experience, and even the mood of the person doing the presentation. A man who has great rapport with his audience on one night may be cold the next night. Yet, even the best presenter can do only so much with words. Quite often, he'll need a blackboard, a flipchart, an overhead viewer, or a carousel tray full of slides to augment his presentation.

The printed message is probably the most common form of internal communication—in company magazines, brochures, newspapers, and newsletters. A major drawback of the printed word is its low sensory impact. Also the company magazine is in constant competition with all the other reading material laying around. On the other hand, printed material has tremendous retention value. The message is there, to be kept as long as desired, to be read and reread, filed away and referred to later. It can be enduring, almost permanent.

When brief announcements need to be transmitted quickly and simultaneously, the bulletin board may be the solution. If the company has distant outposts, the solution may be the telex, or, if available, the satellite relay. If a chart or photo is part of the message, facsimile by one of the variety of systems is available.

If confidentiality is a consideration, many companies use envelopes marked "Confidential," "Restricted," or "To be opened only by the addressee." Some corporations—like governments—even have the capability to send various kinds of telecommunications in code, to be unscrambled only by the intended recipient.

Giving wings to words is a daily challenge, particularly in large corporations with multilocation plants. Keeping employees informed in the right way at the right time is part and parcel of the challenge. The task is never ending, never completed. Tomorrow is always another day with new news to move along, new explanations to provide, new policies to promulgate.

There will always be the recurring question: Are the company's internal communications effective? That question can be pinpointed further: "Do they hit or miss the mark?" and "Do they accomplish their purpose?"

Alas, some senior executives say they are too busy with more important matters. They don't have time, they say, to trace and track the effectiveness of their internal communications efforts. In the absence of negative information, they assume all is going well.

Yet, increasingly, many managements will demand evidence of results. They will ask their communications specialists for proof and for evaluation. Since they're paying for results, they quite properly feel they deserve some evidential playback.

Total proof—tracing all the way to the so-called bottom line—is elusive. But some proof of effectiveness is not only achievable but should also be standard operating procedure. The ideal situation is this: A hard-nosed chief executive officer will delegate authority to a professional and experienced specialist (such as his public relations director) and will place faith and trust in the specialist and let him or her run with the ball. This is the high road to communications effectiveness if—and only if—the specialist merits that faith and trust.

Invited to participate in a Conference Board study on the reputation and credibility of the business a few years ago, Charles H. Sommer, Monsanto board chairman, wrote a frank letter to the Conference Board that mentioned the business system's "disinclination to be informative due to unreasonable fear of criticism." He further stated: "Business can constructively respond by putting its communications planning in the hands of people experienced in doing this sort of thing." His analysis then went on to decry "too much one-sided advocacy: too many pious platitudes; too much self-interest."

Let's focus on key points in Sommer's comments. To

begin with, Sommer recognized the need for putting communications planning into the hands of people who know what they're doing. And whereas he may have had both external and internal communications in mind, it is quite obvious that effectiveness cannot be achieved in employee communications if too much selfish advocacy is the rule of the road, if too many pious recitations pop up in the plant newspaper, or if too many one-sided overtures are the regular tune heard by the troops. Indeed, credibility is difficult to achieve if employees feel they are subjected only to sweetness and light.

# Chapter 23

# The Discipline of Planning

To challenge his public relations director, the chairman of a multinational chemical company once inquired: "What would happen if all of a sudden all of our public relations programs were wiped out? As a consequence, we would save at least several million dollars a year. What other consequences would there be?"

"You've got to be kidding!" the public relations director responded. "There must be validity in what we're doing if for no other reason than all of our competitors are communicating like mad. Isn't that a bit of justification in itself?"

"Not necessarily so," said the chairman. "By just saying 'Everybody's doing it' doesn't make things right. I don't question our need for big, fat manufacturing or marketing budgets, considering the tangible results, but I do wonder how we can justify our payroll, programs, and other expenditures for an 'unprovable item' like public relations."

Pity the poor public relations chieftain, even when the chairman added, "Nothing personal, mind you." The public relations director felt disadvantaged to be confronted by such a high-noon challenge out of the blue. For better or worse, he responded as follows:

"You could axe your entire research program if you simply want to cut corporate overhead. You'd never seriously miss the research department for six months or so, but in four or five years you'd find it pretty lonely to be the only chemical company in the nation without fresh bursts of technology rejuvenating the corporation—not to mention keeping up with the times. Granted you'd be temporarily 'cash rich,' but you'd be technologically destitute and you'd find that the wellspring of progress had gone dry."

The PR chief came up with another example: "What if the safety department were wiped out? In the short term you'd never miss it, but in the long run you could be flirting with disaster."

The justification for research and safety functions involves some degree of faith. Business judgment, in the larger sense, is the key to allocating funds for such basic activities. Yet, even such fundamental, traditional specialities as research and safety may not develop a return on investment consistent with objectives cited during sessions of long-term planning. Which means: even such stalwart activities may encounter shortfalls. But how about the hard-to-prove specialty called public relations?

To have no public relations programs would be preposterous. The real challenge is posed by such questions, "What kind of public relations?" "What kind of employee communications?"

To answer these questions, planning—that fascinating and perplexing discipline—becomes "the only game in town."

How does a company plan for its employee communications effort? A total program is hardly ever planned from scratch. "Let's beef up or cut back on some part of the existing program" is the more common approach and cost control is usually at the core when reduced activity is ordained.

Theoretically, there is a way to wipe the entire slate clean and to start anew. It's called zero-based budgeting. If handled right, it's superb strategy. Management consultants are its most ardent champions. Typically, a management consultant will say something similar to the following to the public relations director at, for example, Ajax Foods, Inc.:

"Start with a clean piece of paper. Assume you have no staff, no programs. And between now and January 1, the burden is on your back to present an effective program that will make business sense. Do not assume that any projects, programs, or publications currently in existence will necessarily be maintained. Start from scratch. Pretend your department will come into being January 1 and that Ajax will need a communications program to enable it to achieve its business objectives. What kind of program should this be? What should it cost? What personnel requirements would be involved? What kind of employee communications would be required?"

Zero-based budgeting exercises can be constructive, particularly since they require a new look at everything. They are especially constructive when they are mounted in an environment of objectivity and integrity.

At some companies, the zero-based-budgeting technique has left a bad taste in employee ranks. A deeper look will show that these companies used the exercise as a device to slash costs regardless of the study's findings. They pretended, in their initial announcements, that a straightforward attempt would be made to bring a fresh analysis to current and future public relations needs. But this wasn't the whole story. The companies' managements had quietly decided, "Let's see if we can cut back on overhead costs and headcount by 15 percent, and let's use zero-based budgeting to bring it about." In some cases, the companies have given the exercise a more euphemistic name, such as "The Plans for Progress Program." Yet underneath the seemingly objective investigation lurked management's foregone conclusion that "as of January 1, we will have trimmed our sails, findings notwithstanding."

Not quite forthright, you might say and you would be correct. Employees quickly recognize a shell game. They know right away that "this is not really pure research; it's loaded research." How much more honest the companies would have been if they had said, "To achieve economic stability and remain competitive in the marketplace, we have to cut costs 15 percent and we will use the zero-based-budgeting technique among others to help us get there."

When introduced without camouflage, the technique can be extremely helpful. It can dust off the cobwebs of prior practices that no longer fit, reveal new opportunities, and bring fresh perspectives. And it can even redemonstrate the necessity of mounting effective communications efforts.

"What should internal communications planning encompass?"

Under the assumption that the objectives are approved by management, the corollary question is "How can we bring this about?"

Let's get a fix on how Ajax Foods, Inc., will look on January 1. It will be headquartered in Cleveland, with offices and a manufacturing plant producing canned and frozen food, plus a warehouse, and a research laboratory. There will be an Eastern Division headquartered in New York and a Western Division headquartered in San Jose, California. There will be two manufacturing plants and warehouses in the east and the same in the west. In addition, Ajax will have nine sales offices in the eastern region and seven in the western region. The divisions, each headed by a corporate vice president and general manager, will be autonomous, operating with minimum interference from headquarters. Ajax will have a total of 8,200 employees, about half salaried and half on hourly rates.

How should Ajax be communicating with these employees? What "tools" or media should be used? What will be the most effective way to keep the Ajax family informed?

There are numerous possibilities:

- A monthly newspaper for distribution to all.

- Three monthly newsletters—one for the headquarters location, one for all units in the east, and one for all units in the west.

- A management bulletin at irregular intervals— "whenever there's something appropriate to communicate"—for the 4,100 salaried employees.

- Bulletin boards for day-to-day announcements.

- A slide presentation to show to new employees.

- An annual management conference for the top 200.

- A special internal publication for sales representatives.

- Special bulletins on safety for employees in the plants and warehouses.

What systems, if any, should be established to ensure dialogue between management and its employees? There could be a suggestion box. Periodic Q. and A. forms for employees to fill out offer another possibility.

Then come the telltale questions: What are the objectives of the marketing staff? What are the objectives in the manufacturing area? To what degree are internal communications required in order to help achieve these objectives?

There are many areas to study. Eventually, a "proposed program" begins to appear—a program replete with such details as individual objectives, media by media; content and format and frequency; targeted audiences; methods for later evaluation; costs.

Costs involve such items as word processors and typewriters, photocopy equipment, cameras, projectors, and printing and typesetting services. Also to be included in costs are salaries, expenses, and fringe benefits of the people who will be planning the internal communications, collecting and clearing the material, and putting the material into words, photos, graphics, and motion.

How large a staff is needed? What professional competence is required? Which staffers should be located at corporate headquarters, which at divisional sites? Should the communications staffers in the field report to headquarters or to divisional management?

Then come other key questions: To what degree are the internal communications objectives and programs endorsed by corporate management? By divisional management? By manufacturing management? By marketing management? By personnel management? Such questions bring up the inevitable need for interfacing for the meshing of gears.

"A comprehensive zero-based-budgeting program is like tearing down a house, putting the bricks in a pile, and then building the house all over again," commented one weary vice president of public relations in the steel industry. "We've never done so much homework in all our lives. Nothing was taken for granted. No cow was sacred. Everything was challenged. We forced ourselves to ask, 'what are today's needs and tomorrow's needs,' We even asked, 'What would likely happen if we didn't have certain communications programs that we've grown accustomed to?'"

Orderly planning and implementation of internal communications functions can, of course, occur without going to such an extreme and sweeping inquiry. In most companies a review comes up at least once a year, when new budgets are prepared and when fresh and challenging scrutiny is the order of the day.

If proof must be reflected in the corporation's bottom line, this is a tough challenge for an internal communicator.

Sales departments can achieve a quota; maintenance engineers can trim costs—directly traceable to the bottom line. Less traceable but equally important are the results achieved in the never ending task of keeping employees informed for both business and human purposes.

Planning, programming, and staffing can be as important in a small company as in a relatively large organization like Ajax. In a small company perhaps only one person will wind up with the entire internal communications responsibility. In a smaller company it is possible that one person and a secretary would handle both external and internal communication. To such a tiny department—overloaded, to be sure, as it embarks upon a wide, new field—the following encouragement can be expressed: "Relax. There was a day when General Motors had a tiny communications department. Yours could be the start of something big. Don't be intimidated. Do the best you can. Considering the base you're starting with, look how easy it will be to double in size."

Some companies have programs worthy of the word "exemplary"—programs encompassing the A to Z of internal communications, programs that have been tested, finetuned, retested, and improved. Professional communicators in such companies are normally happy to share generic information with other companies planning to do a better job. Quite often, the easiest way to get help in planning, programming, and staffing is to bring in an experienced public relations counselor who is able to reach into a storehouse of knowledge and select those bits and pieces that apply best.

Planning, programming, and staffing are actually part of ongoing, continuous efforts at many of the nation's principal business organizations. As conditions change, communications machinery is adapted to keep pace. Nothing is more obsolete than the strategy for yesteryear's communication needs. If one would have to select an outstanding company that has always handled its internal communications professionally and effectively, it would be difficult to come up with a better example than E. I. DuPont de Nemours & Co., Wilmington, Delaware. Planning, programming, and staffing for internal communications have received top attention from DuPont's senior management for many years, as well as top attention from three former directors of public relations, Harold Brayman, Glen Perry, and Thomas W. Stephenson.

DuPont's internal communications have always had three primary objectives: 1) to keep its employees informed on the state of their company's business; 2) to reinforce their understanding of how the American business system operates; and 3) to establish a climate of cooperation "for carrying out whatever programs are needed to keep DuPont a winner in a highly competitive society."

When Charles B. McCoy was president of DuPont, he wrote: "Internal communications have a high priority at DuPont. Employees have a right to be informed. They should be told important news immediately, good or bad. The people who work for DuPont want to know what the enterprise is all about. They want a sense of involvement, want to be a part of the organization. Therefore, they need to know about current business problems, the company's stand on such matters as imports and pollution control, its views on issues of public importance. Employees want straightforward, honest, balanced information—not propaganda. Informed employees are better, more productive employees. They get more out of their work, and they do a better job for the company."

Caution needs to be taken with respect to staffing. Beware of the advice of a management consultant who steers the selection toward a broad-based manager per se rather than a PR professional. Just as a law department normally needs to be headed by an attorney and an accounting department by an accountant, public relations must be directed by a communications specialist. The "manager is a manager is a manager" theory is risky—especially when public relations is concerned.

This all seems so fundamental that one might wonder, "Who in his right mind would ever suggest assigning a person with no communications experience and no communications sensitivity to a public relations department, much less the leadership of a PR department, on the basis of only his general managerial skills. Such a suggestion might very well come from an insensitive management consultant who might be knowledgeable about the so-called larger issues of business but ignorant about such a side issue as public relations. The rationale for hiring a generalist is this: The generalist stays aboard long enough to have a passing acquaintance with public relations before advancing to a higher post in the enterprise. In its predivestiture past, the Bell system once made it a habit of bringing from the field noncommunications-related, high-potential operating people to take on the vice president of public relations job for a brief period before moving upstairs to senior executive positions.

Such a training-the-executive device often demoralized PR staffpeople who commented, "I'll never be eligible to run the department regardless of my qualifications." In the seventies the various AT&T-owned companies began to abandon the practice described above. One by one these companies correctly placed people skilled in the specialities of communications at the head of PR departments. The late Paul M. Lund and the still-very-active Edward M. Block, exemplary AT&T public relations executives, were the leaders in the movement to keep PR in PR hands.

# Chapter 24

# Decentralization

Professor Ralph M. Hower of Harvard Business School, referred to earlier, used to say, "Let's turn to a juicy subject," directing attention to centralization versus decentralization within the corporation.

"So the company is tightly centralized with a few senior officers and maybe a corporate executive committee calling all the shots," Professor Hower would say. "In its earliest years, the company operated from a single command post with a pyramid shaped organization chart. That was the normal management pattern to select. Then the company began to grow. It started to build plants and to establish sales offices in outlying geographic locations in order to offer faster service to its customers and in order to reduce the cost and delays of shipping products from a single location."

Freshly dispersed but still tightly centralized was the new format, which worked well for a time. Then came greater growth, progress, and change. The company introduced new products serving new markets. Inevitably there were additional plants and sales offices. Ajax, Inc., became a formidable presence on the business scene. Should it remain centralized with the headquarters staff directing all the operations? Or should the company be divided into several operating divisions, lifting a large burden off headquarters?

And that's precisely how decentralization was born in American companies across the land. Particularly in the period before World War II when large corporations found it advisable to split into more manageable segments, decentralization—a phenomenon of epidemic proportions—became the ideal solution for giant corporations. Alfred M. Sloan, legendary General Motors chieftain, led perhaps the most celebrated of all decentralization parades.

Out of all this came a pendulum that swung mainly in one direction—toward the wonders of decentralization. At times it seemed that decentralization was only a way station on the road to disintegration. "Is anyone in charge here?" was the question at those companies that had become so enchanted by decentralization that their infrastructure became diffused to the point of confusion. Management accountability was often difficult to discern, leaving employees scratching their heads.

However, the pendulum could also swing in the opposite direction. "Back toward centralization" seemed the natural solution to correct the free-wheeling abuses and alienations caused by decentralization. Backers of central control reasoned: "Now that we've tried going from centralization to decentralization to splinterization, let's go back to the orderly, comfortable, easy-to-comprehend system of letting corporate bosses call the shots."

Professor Hower continues: "The pendulum never stops. Once a corporation feels it is getting too loose, too decentralized, too scattered, too diverse, there is always a natural tendency to say, 'Let's tighten up a bit; let's fix responsibilities a little better; let's all salute a common flag.' Or words to that effect."

Then some years later the corporation once again feels constrained by centralized control. The pendulum swings back to decentralization. The cry rings out: "Let's be more mobile; let's take more risks; let's be less authoritarian—and let's be more democratic."

Professor Hower would also add, "The situation is always

in a state of flux. Going to extremes in centralization results in 'let's loosen up.' And later on when looseness causes its own set of proliferating and scattered problems, the balance once again leans toward the tightening bear hug of corporate control. Back and forth, back and forth. It will ever be thus—generally in small increments, but sometimes a company will restructure itself and completely reverse its field in its pursuit of a better-mousetrap-sort-of organizational format which seems more appropriate for the times." The point is plain: Nothing is ever static.

Very much affected and involved in corporate organization charts are the public relations and employee communications personnel whose activities are directly affected by "who reports to whom." In a large decentralized company, the director of internal communications may report to the corporation's public relations director or employee communications director or director of personnel

Considering that decentralization currently prevails in most large companies, how are internal communications programs faring? With attempts constantly being made to push responsibility and authority as far down the organizational chart as possible, where does the plant communicator fit into a decentralized structure? To whom does he or she report?

Usually the plant communicator reports to the plant manager. Being responsible for a package of purely local information programs at Plant A, the communicator should also feel somewhat involved in what's happening elsewhere within his company. Here are some elements meriting consideration:

1. If the local communicator prepares a bulletin board notice or plant newspaper story, is corporate headquarters affected by the consequences of such a purely local item? It may be. Indeed, unbeknownst to the local communicator, people at headquarters may very

well receive press inquiries triggered by the innocent little internal story at Plant A. It is conceivable, for example, that an item prepared for employee information at Plant A might conflict with an emerging new policy at headquarters. What should be done before the notice is posted or published? *Check it out.*

2. If the routine little item at Plant A might later reverberate negatively within the walls of sister Plant B, wouldn't it have been prudent to have found out about this possibility in advance? Allowing that the overall corporation probably has systems for safeguarding the proclamation of possible conflicting signals, what is the Plant A communicator's responsibility beyond Plant A's walls? *Check it out.*

3. Is the item of information being released at Plant A so local and innocent in nature that it cannot have any effect on any other part of the company? If the item concerns Plant A's softball team, isn't such news purely local and of no interest anywhere else? What if Plant A's announcement is about an injured worker during a plant accident that would be of interest to the personnel at headquarters? *Check it out.*

4. News can also flow from headquarters to branch plants. Is the communicator at Plant A alert enough to realize the importance of some corporate news to share it promptly with Plant A's employees? Also, is there an established system within the company to make corporate news instantly available to communicators at all plants? Employees should certainly learn of their company's news events via workplace communications rather than from television and newspaper reports. *Check it out.*

Thus, the local communicator is not simply a "word merchant" who handles information programs for local employees. He or she is a facilitator and a coordinator. Further, the communicator is a participant in team play in a system of sending and receiving information through communications pipelines leading to many units of the company. In other words, corporate concerns sometimes receive as much attention as parochial in-plant concerns.

Whereas in small or medium-sized centralized companies, the traffic patterns of internal communications are usually uncomplicated, in large decentralized companies rules of the road are needed to traffic the right information to the appropriate person and location with regard to strategy and timing. The individual communicator obviously has a substantial role to play, and when the communicator isn't sure, the safest solution is to *check it out.*

Chapter 25

# Communicating Globally

Multinational companies have developed highly sophisticated systems for internal communications. The day is already here when Ajax Foods can transmit information via satellite to an affiliate in Japan or send messages and data and graphics into the affiliate's computer— instantaneously and easily. The day is also virtually here when Ajax can afford economical two-way closed-circuit television for business sessions involving marketing people in Tokyo and in Chicago. They will be talking to, listening to, and seeing each other as though they were all in the same room. The technology is here. The implementation at an affordable cost/benefits ratio is around the corner.

Some multinational companies have established, at their headquarters locations, communications command posts that resemble the control rooms at the networks. Every possible kind of visual equipment is there, including electronic hardware that will lift numbers from a computer and on to displays and transparencies for projection and transmission; the same numbers can be rearranged and translated into charts, graphs, and tables. It has become possible for globe-spanning companies to virtually push a button to transmit data and graphics from headquarters to overseas offices for immediate study and discussion.

A company can be sophisticated and naive at the same time. It may be so fascinated with transmitting financial projections on its electronic toys that it forgets to do the simple things, such as alerting distant outposts when big news breaks at the home office. Using Ajax Foods as an example, its employees at remote locations around the world could agree with the philosopher who said, "Those who are farthest away are the first to be forgotten." Ajax may have only six employees in its office in Luxembourg, but "word from the home office" can be more important to them than it is to those in larger Ajax offices in New York and Los Angeles.

When Ajax once bought a half interest in a small manufacturing company in England, several procedures were established to enable British and American colleagues to keep in touch. Those intrepid Chicagoans who were dispatched into foreign service were assured, at a bon voyage dinner, "Tomorrow you will be gone, but not forgotten. We've set up all sorts of systems to make sure you're kept informed of what's going on at home."

At the start, Anglo-American relationships within Ajax were a novelty. People went out of their way to keep information flowing in both directions across the Atlantic. But as often happens, the novelty wore off. Later, Ajax bought out its British partner and took over 100 percent ownership. The overseas subsidiary grew and prospered. Meanwhile communications problems began to surface, and shortfalls began to materialize largely because "we've got a lot of loose ends to tie up and a lot of other things to worry about."

By the time the eighties arrived, Ajax could proudly state it had manufacturing locations in 11 countries and sales offices in 19 countries, with European headquarters in Brussels. More than 90 percent of the employees at foreign posts were nationals, with less than 10 percent being Americans sent overseas from the home office. Ajax was trying its diligent best to be a good citizen in the host countries where it operated by employing local workers.

In its earlier experience with Great Britain, Ajax headquarters had found it relatively simple to send company news to "the troops." The common language contributed to the ease of communication. Every once in a while the Chicago-based director of public relations would visit his British compatriots and see a Chicago-originated personnel announcement on the British bulletin boards. He'd chuckle to himself when he saw that the word "while" had become "whilst." In general, all went well.

However, complications arose when Ajax went into France, Luxembourg, Spain, Italy, Mexico, Canada, and Brazil. Company news could not simply be prepackaged in Chicago for posting and/or distribution in, for example, Madrid. There was the little matter of a different language. Equally serious were the problems of idioms in languages, customs, and differences in cultural orientation.

Moreover, there were different time zones with which to contend. Chicago-based Ajax was never any more than two hours different from any of its American operations. When it wanted to communicate with their overseas personnel, Ajax encountered vast differences in the time of day or night. If it wanted to alert offices around the world simultaneously about a newly elected corporate vice president, it found that "some of our people haven't gotten to work yet and others have already gone home."

Ajax's experience abroad typifies what many American companies that pioneered in foreign service have encountered.

At Monsanto Company, for example, internal communications in many languages have been the order of the day for many years inasmuch as Monsanto has employees in 43 countries, most of whom are nationals. In fact, Monsanto employees speak 26 different languages and deal in 42 different currencies.

When Monsanto started operations in a new plant in Ghent, Belgium, it saw the need to assign quite a few of its

American employees there, on a temporary basis, to ensure the establishment of important and proprietary knowledge in the manufacture of Saflex, a plastic sheet which serves as the layer between two panes of glass in the shatterproof windshield—or windscreen, as it is called in some countries.

Today the Ghent plant is as Ghentish and as Belgian as the picturesque, Holland-like canals that run through this colorful community an hour's drive north of Brussels. Monsanto knows—as indeed most American companies know—the value of having employees who are local citizens and the value of "belonging" in a community.

Monsanto makes a conscientious effort to keep a proper flow of information to and from all its worldwide operations. So-called corporate overview information is channeled regularly out of St. Louis to the various locations around the world. When the information is important or urgent, it is sent by a system known as Rush News Service to each location around the globe.

Rush News Service is simply a house name for a telex system that transmits important internal news to selected and assigned communicators at each location within and outside the U.S. If, for example, Monsanto elects a new board member, the news is transmitted rapidly in bulletin form to all worldwide locations by Rush News Service.

Such internal news arrives at day or night, depending on whatever the time is in the various parts of the world. Monsanto's headquarters in St. Louis has a list of the home addresses and telephone numbers of the worldwide communicators in the event it is necessary or desirable to send Rush News Service messages to homes—as, for example, over a weekend. Once the communicator in, let us say, Hong Kong receives the news at his office or at home, it is his responsibility to use his judgment in determining when and how the local employees should be promptly informed.

Of course, all of St. Louis-generated news does not move to all distant points by Rush News Service. The rule of thumb is this: If, in the opinion of St. Louis-based public relations staffers, the news is apt to qualify for use on any of the news wire services, that's sufficient reason to use Rush News Service. Once an item of information meets this qualification, out it goes. If all goes well, the bulletins should have hit their mark within an hour or two after the news is posted or otherwise distributed in St. Louis.

A principal objective is to avoid having a Hong Kong employee of Monsanto learn about important company news from any source other than Monsanto. Promptness and accuracy of information transmittal are highly important.

Occasionally, there may be a shortfall. A communicator may be ill and his secretary may fail to follow through. A message may be stalled in transit due to mechanical problems or delayed because of translation difficulties.

In Europe, Hill and Knowlton, Inc. (H&K) has contributed many communications services for Monsanto with the veteran Loet Velmans, a constant crusader for international public relations planning, providing scholarly counsel. During its early association with Hill and Knowlton, Monsanto sent both internal and external announcements to H&K's offices in Geneva, Switzerland, where retransmissions to various European countries were accomplished following appropriate translations. Later on, Brussels and London became the routing points for European retransmission.

The Monsanto system is not all glory, as the following recounting of an incident demonstrates.

Several years ago, a St. Louis-based public relations executive sat in the office of Michel J. Plaisier, manager of the Monsanto plant at Antwerp, in northern Belgium.

"How're things going?" the visitor asked Plaisier.

"Fine," he replied.

"Your public relations friends at headquarters worked pretty fast last month when we rushed you an announcement about the appointment of a divisional marketing director," the St. Louisan bragged.

"I know you did," Plaisier said, politely. "But why did you send our material by way of the European headquarters in Brussels for translation into Flemish?"

"What's wrong with that?" the visitor asked, quickly on the defensive.

"Well, whoever translated the announcement wasn't familiar with our idioms. By the time I saw it, the announcement said the new marketing officer of Monsanto 'lives with' his wife in St. Louis County. But the Flemish expression 'lives with,' selected by your Brussels translator, is one which the Flemish use only when referring to living with a concubine," Plaisier explained.

The visitor blushed.

"Relax," Plaisier hastened to say. "The Monsanto employees here in Antwerp understand these things. They've seen inappropriate translations before."

The visitor muttered a weak "Thanks, Michel" and decided there must be some better system to use in the future. He checked into the gaff and found that the important internal news had been handled with care in the German, Spanish, Italian, and French languages but had been given too little attention in Brussels when translated from English to Flemish.

There is now someone specifically assigned to local internal communications at each of Monsanto's locations in Europe. However, the differences between internal communications customs vary from country to country. At virtually all European locations one will find employees of many nationalities. A recent study showed that at the Luxembourg plant, employees have seven different "mother" languages. Since it would be cumbersome to put seven different announcements on the bulletin boards, German is used as the official language because it is the most commonly spoken language at that particular plant.

"Isn't the English language becoming more and more the standard, particularly within multinational companies that have American roots?" one might ask. The answer is "Yes, to an increasing degree, and particularly among so-called management employees." However, it is discourteous to ignore local customs and traditions, and inexcusably discourteous to be disrespectful of local language. Workers in all parts of the world look upon their language as more than a tool for reading, speaking, and listening; it also involves national pride.

For any company establishing a new foreign legion in any country, the most foolproof thing to do is to engage the services of a public relations counseling agency that is knowledgeable about the local customs. Being well-intentioned is not enough.

Sometimes an American company will get so caught up in the hectic scramble of high priorities it will forget to take care of that last, little detail 5,000 miles away. Several years ago a U.S. corporation decided to close down a factory in France that manufactured electric shavers, largely because the profit potential seemed limited. The American company distributed external and internal announcements, worldwide and simultaneously. It forgot to do one thing: to inform the two unions that represented the workers in France. The French plant manager had mistakenly assumed that "the home office could not possibly overlook something like this."

If announcements are placed on bulletin boards around the world their contents must be selected carefully. A bulletin board announcement suitable for all stateside locations would probably be unsuitable for all locations beyond U.S. borders even if all the "foreign" employees understood English. For instance, the words "import" and "export" mean diametrically the opposite in Europe and in the U.S. The words "domestic" and "foreign" (a word to be avoided in any event) have opposite meanings to employees in Europe and in the U.S.

A notable public relations counseling agency in Great Britain observes, "Over here an American public relations man or woman will find we're a mix of some samenesses and some differences—with the samenesses dominant." This means that the basics are the same in London as they are in Chicago. "Performance plus communication equals reputation" holds true on Regent Street as it does on State Street. Employees in Spain yearn for a sense of belonging just as employees in Peoria do—and a sense of belonging is unlikely, if not impossible, without an effective program of internal communications. Workers everywhere wish to be treated with respect, befitting their sense of dignity.

American companies will go to different lengths, expending maximum to minimum effort to get the corporate overview into the hands of managers from Scotland to Italy so that the managers can, in turn, relay company information to plant, office, and laboratory employees. Some American companies will send their magazines and annual reports to their brother and sister affiliates in Scotland and Italy, feeling such distant employees should not be discriminated against and should, instead, see everything that U.S. employees see.

This is a noble motive, but it presents problems. If magazines and annual reports are sent to Scotland and Italy by surface transportation, it will take several weeks for their delivery. If they're sent by air, a substantial expense is involved. Dispatching such material into Scotland presents no language barrier, but such is not the case when Italy—or most other European nations—is involved.

A number of "solutions" have been tried. When there are

a large number of employees in Italy, a complete translation of the annual report may make sense. However, if a company needs to publish several editions in different languages, the costs become formidable. In addition to language differences, there is the additional stumbling block of different monetary currencies: the American dollar would have to be refigured into liras, francs, marks, etc.

There are a few compromise solutions worth considering. A four-page summary insert in Italian is an accommodation, economical and not too time-consuming.

More important than U.S. publications being sent as a dividend to employees in distant lands is how the French plant, for example, communicates with its French employees. Most U.S. corporations with operations beyond U.S. borders naturally put more emphasis on encouraging effective local internal communications overseas than they do on exporting U.S.-produced corporate overview material. These corporations have found that decentralized communications sometimes produce the best blossoms when they are in a remote corner of the world—"away from the meddling home office."

# Chapter 26

# Oral or Written?

Which is more effective? The spoken word? Or the written (or printed) word? Advocates abound for both.

Those who favor the spoken word make a convincing case. The spoken word is fast. It is cheap. It is personal. It is persuasive. It is friendly. Especially when oral communication involves one-on-one situations, there can be an immediate exchange of viewpoints. Questions can be asked and answers can be provided instantaneously. Further, the spoken word has more warmth, more humanity. Even when someone is addressing a group, rapport can be developed. Explanations and clarifications can be solicited, if needed. Importantly, a speaker's rhetoric, personality, and style can be downright compelling.

On the other hand, those who are staunch in behalf of the written word have their own set of arguments to proclaim. The written word is the traditional and current language of business. It represents the most risk-free method of internal communication. If a company announcement contains information for 4 or 40 or 400 employees, the written word permits all 4 or 40 or 400 to see precisely the same language, without deviation. Further, the "hard copy" written word permits retention of information and later retrieval. Particularly when a company has promulgated new rules of the road, there is a very real advantage in having information, in memo form or newsletter form, available for leisurely examination.

So much for the strengths of both systems, which are

many. But there are pronounced disadvantages on both sides as well.

The champion of the oral word will suggest that the business system has run out of waste baskets and, despite the use of shredders and compactors, companies are buried in excess paper—with copy machines simply adding to the glut. Particularly at a time when corporations are trying to simplify and streamline, proliferation of memos and internal publications should be moderated. So say the oral advocates.

The champion of the written word can be equally critical of the opposition. It is alleged in this camp that looking back on the highways of the business system one can find that the principal causes of all the communications wreckage and many of the misunderstandings and much of the confusion and most of the mixed signals are, end to end, traceable to the fragile and transient nature of oral communications. Further, say the written-word folks, everyone doesn't hear things the same way and, indeed, research studies have shown that individuals in groups tend to hear things selectively, partially, and poorly. Put it in writing, the argument goes, and the message will be more complete and enduring.

So much for the various pros and cons.

In a comprehensive study done a few years back for Illinois Bell, it was learned that the company's foremen were resentful when they were advised their company wanted them to be "the front line of communications" in contacts with their subordinates. "You'd have to be a Philadelphia lawyer just to understand all the ramifications of federal regulations, state regulations, local regulations, and Illinois Bell regulations," was, in effect, at the core to foremen's apprehensions.

To put it simply, many of the foremen didn't have the ability and inclination to become spokesmen on complex issues affecting their subordinates. Illinois Bell's reaction was interesting. Instead of reiterating the tired old glories of so-called eyeball-to-eyeball communication within the troops, Illinois Bell decided to intensify its internal relations program by requiring its printed publication to carry a greater explanatory load. The study that the company sponsored suggested, "If a foreman can wind up a conversational session by handing an employee a piece of paper and by saying, 'Put this piece of paper in your pocket and take it home and read it,' much of the problem might be solved."

Especially when company information contains any technical or numerical data, it is prudent to have such data in black and white. "That's the way of minimizing hassles and confusion," the Illinois Bell study observed.

Despite the difficulty of finding objective and quantitative data on oral versus written, most senior public relations people seem to tilt strongly toward written material in "either-or" arguments but they also often take the safe and sensible course of recommending "a judicious mixture of both techniques" as the best solution of all.

When Myron Emmanuel gained national recognition for his expertise as director of employee communications for E. I. DuPont, he stressed the belief that "the printed word is irreversible and permanent and official, impervious to distortion." Yet he also underlined the need to explore the merits and demerits of both techniques in order to be sure which alternative would be more effective in various situations.

Here are a few corollary observations.

One time in a Fortune 500 company, all the officers and general managers and department heads were invited to the board room for a meeting—to be advised of new regulations concerning expense accounts, travel, and assorted perks. Everything was orally communicated. After a question-and-answer period concluded the agenda, those in attendance were advised by the chairman, "Go back and inform your principal colleagues so they'll all know the new rules of the game."

So what happened?

Some of the newly disclosed information leaked to people in several parts of the company before the day was out. Such leaked information wasn't necessarily accurate—but it was sparklingly fresh. The grapevine always moves fast!

Further, two of the general managers had to leave town on business trips immediately after the meeting. One advised his assistant to spread the word. The other was so rushed he decided to race to the airport and catch a flight to California. "I'll bring my people up to date when I get back," he said to himself. As things worked out, he didn't return to headquarters for three days. By the time he came back, many of his people were "in the know" through the grapevine—but not quite accurately.

This little anecdote suggests that the chairman probably thought a "bucket brigade" system of communications would work out nicely and that the various attendees would methodically pass along the new rules and regulations. But such confidence obviously did not take into consideration that all of the attendees at the meeting would not have the immediate opportunity to engage in the pass-along plan.

One of the department directors was at home with influenza and was unable to attend the high-level meeting. His number two man was invited to the meeting at the last minute, but he had to go downtown to give a speech. And, naturally, the unrepresented department wasn't brought up to date until much later.

Thoughtless lack of attention to detail on the part of the chairman? Perhaps. Overreliance on oral communications? Of course. Naturally, there should have been—at the minimum—a summary of the new procedures, in memorandum form, to supplement the oral presentation in the board room. In analyzing the episode later, the chairman took full blame and called the experience "a disaster."

Back when Henry Ford II was chairman of Ford Motor Company, an occasion arose when he was asked, "What qualities do you look for in potential employees?" He responded as follows: "For starters I'd list honesty, candor, good judgment, intelligence, and imagination—*and the ability to write clean, concise memos.*"

And it all comes down to the ability to communicate, to be articulate, and to be professionally precise in *both* written and oral routes.

In its finest form an oral presentation often needs the supplemental assistance of written material, and vice versa. In many situations, the "combo" package is ideal. Yet even for the "combo" package, it is helpful if the employee communications director appreciates the singular and characteristic pluses and minuses of oral plus the singular and characteristic pluses and minuses of written.

Even at office supply stores, the subject comes up regularly and routinely. Blocks of telephone reply forms, available at such stores, are frequently headlined by the advice, "Write It—Don't Just Say It." Yet in one recent example the form's headline read, "Avoid Verbal Instructions." The author meant "Oral," of course.

# Chapter 27

# Restructuring in the Mid-Eighties

"Restructuring" is a word that was practically out of sight in most dictionaries. In the mid-eighties it became a fad word and its usage became widespread as the symbol of radical organizational changes in corporate life.

In earlier years, corporations simply reorganized, making adjustments that involved 1) swings from centralization to decentralization and, less frequently, swings in the other direction; 2) new infrastructures to better suit the strategies of officers at the top; or 3) departures from some lines of business and entrance into others. In other words, companies shifted gears and responded to new business conditions.

Almost overnight, restructuring became the revolutionary symbol of a new era in which companies plunged into new formats in management, new organizational arrangements, cost containment, new marketing techniques, intensified government relations and—important to internal communicators—into new strategies in the treatment of employees and in the handling of in-house communications.

At the core of all this activity was the imperative to trim operational costs. With the nation's manufacturers freshly conscious of their vulnerability in global competition, with the cost-of-goods-sold at a disadvantage due to U.S. wage rates being so much higher than those in other parts of the world, and with trade wars proliferating against the Japanese, Brazilians, and others, the business community—

almost on cue—decided something drastic had to be done. And the big companies, especially, were ready to set the pace.

What had to be done? The popular answer was: restructuring across the board. And it seemed that all of a sudden change became the only constant on the nation's business horizon. Customers, stockholders, plant communities, and employees were all affected. Improved service and restrained prices for customers were objectives at the heart of the issue. Particularly when the rate of inflation was retarded, a wave of lower-cost products appeared upon the scene in many industries, heralding the joys of keeping America competitive.

As greater return-on-investment numbers began to appear—resulting, in part, from corporate restructuring— Wall Street flourished, albeit on a roller coaster pattern, in the wake of what was perceived to be a healthy reawakening and a determination to slow down spending spirals throughout the business system.

Plant communities were affected negatively and positively, depending on what they produced. In cases where aging manufacturing plants were closed, plant communities became negatively affected by unemployment. Where newly established and efficient plants materialized, plant communities became bustling centers of economic vitality.

Employees in the corporate ranks were the most affected constituency of all. Particularly at those thousands of companies that decided to go all out on the restructuring route, employees were hit by dismissals, job changes, revised compensation arrangements, furloughs, changes in benefit programs, early retirement plans, and other good-news-bad-news consequences. Plus, an unprecedented wave of mergers and acquisitions added to the gravity of the situation. Consolidations became routine!

The element of loyalty—two-way loyalty—sometimes

became an issue within corporations. Too often employees assumed, "I've been here for 30 years and my long-time contributions to the company's progress most surely entitle me to considerate treatment." Corporations, at the other end of the spectrum, asked, "Can we afford to reward mere loyalty as generously as in the past?" As a major story in *The New York Times* declared on January 25, 1987, the "new order of ruthless management scorns loyalty in favor of market leadership, profits, and a high stock price."

The fact of life in corporate realms is: Profitability is essential—above all. In this context restructuring, therefore, became a clarion call to the imperative of financial soundness. Furthermore, restructuring became not only the slogan but also the thrust that enabled a company to aim for greater profitability in order to operate in the long-term interests of customers, stockholders, community, and even employees regardless of the short-term internal aches and pains accompanying revolutionary adjustments.

Where do employee communications fit into the mix? "Explanations are crucial for employees" is the most obvious observation. Employees resent silence. When there are uneasy stirrings within a corporation, employees often have that sixth sense prompting them to wonder, "What's going on?"

Information is vital. Employees feel they belong only when they are taken into confidence; they want explanations—including management details on "the fix we're in and the financial setbacks we'll suffer if we don't undergo the discomfort of radical change."

The Conference Board recently reported that up to 10,000 corporations have restructured themselves during the past several years. Aside from the dramatic adjustments required as a result of corporate takeovers and mergers, the whole concept of restructuring has perhaps become the most dominant single influence in recent corporate history—with virtually no organization immune, directly or indirectly, to the consequences.

Employees who fully understand what's going on can be a company's most vital asset. In order to understand, they need straightforward information—in face-to-face meetings, in letters to the home from management and in internal communications of all types. Naturally, there always will be some resentful employees regardless of what they learn about the predicament of their employers. However, they will be more resentful if their need for information is not sufficiently respected. Therefore, a company's internal communications apparatus takes on greater-than-ever significance.

Towers, Perrin, Forster & Crosby, a prominent management consultant, pointed out in its *C & M* (Communications and Management) bimonthly publication, "Bad news takes good communication."

The seven most important things employees want to know about include the following:

1. Organizational restructuring, especially if the direction is from centralization to decentralization.

2. Management's insistence on quality.

3. The explanation for the incongruity of increased sales and depressed profits.

4. Payment of bonuses to executives of companies that are losing money.

5. Increased employee contributions to medical plans that have been redesigned to save the company money.

6. The real impact of automation on jobs.

7. The replacement of experienced employees by part-time or contractor workers to save the company money.

That word restructuring is significantly present in the first point listed above. What is management's response to employee complaints about restructuring? Management almost inevitably first mentions its responsibility for maintaining a healthy balance sheet "now and in the future." Sometimes management will say, "We owe it to our stockholders and, in fact, to those employees left after restructuring has been accomplished." Also heard is the hackneyed phrase, "We've had to bite the bullet," implying that trimming back has taken courage. And management may even go so far as to admit, "We grew too fat. We let costs go out of control. We've got to get lean and mean."

An example of how extensive the consequences of restructuring can become is Exxon Corp., the largest oil company in the U.S., which recently offered 40,000 of its 146,000 employees early retirement or bonuses if they resigned. Restructuring was at the core of the Exxon action in the wake of the collapse in worldwide petroleum prices. In Exxon's case there also were elements of both decentralization and centralization. As part of the overall strategy, Exxon announced the creation of a single central internal organization to manage the company's global interests instead of having six divisions in the United States and Europe in command. Of course, there was an abundance of internal communications at Exxon during the company's period of blockbuster news.

As suggested earlier, a company's reputation among its principal constituencies, including employees, is largely dependent on its policies, its products, its performance, its behavior, and its management—and its communications.

It's a new era, of course. In an effort to assure rappport with employees, Monsanto Company of St. Louis reinstated *Monsanto Magazine*, mainly for distribution to employees. Unsurprisingly, the need for restructuring was the theme of the introductory issue of the publication. Monsanto even went so far as to declare, "Like other American companies, Monsanto once provided an unwritten lifetime job commitment to employees." But that was long ago.

# Chapter 28

# The House Organ, a Hardy Pioneer

Prior to World War II, when many thousands of companies decided to have a printed publication for employees, the so-called house organ surfaced widely. Generally modest in raiment, plain-Jane in format, and low in cost, the house organ became the first universal entry in what was to develop into a rainbow array of assorted printed and audiovisual information programs across the business landscape.

As the prolific and inadvertent father of a torrent of latter-day spin-offs, the house organ gained quiet fame by demonstrating the advantages of communicating with employees. Thus, in its own humble way, the house organ helped facilitate the eventual arrival of fancier and more expensive internal newspapers, magazines, motion pictures, slidefilms, video presentations, ad infinitum—with employees as the target audience.

But if the house organ, per se, had been a legitimate pioneer, why hasn't its role been more appropriately celebrated? Why did it vanish down the hallway and never come back? To paraphrase Mark Twain, rumors of the house organ's decline have been greatly exaggerated. Thanks to the whims of nomenclature, today's house organ is probably called the company newspaper or newsletter, which is very much alive and healthy for its modern role in which its information-providing assignment has changed drastically. The organ's tune has been refined; its chords have been more professionally orchestrated. In sum, it has burst forth as a star soloist on its own. It has surely and slowly grown up.

As old-timers will recall, first generation house organs were strong on personnel news, new hires, wedding anniversaries, deaths, illnesses, bowling scores—plus reports of fathers and sons serving in the armed forces. Even joke columns! Hard news was hard to come by. Even such crucial subjects as the company's annual sales and earnings were often bypassed in favor of stories and photos of the plant picnic, the annual boat ride, the Foreman's Frolic at the local dance pavilion, and the Christmas party in the cafeteria for employees' children under 16 years of age.

The material wasn't always what you'd call substantive. "Think pieces," relating to government policies and other external influences on the company's performance, were rare. The one basic subject that was seldom forgotten—and is still around today—was the subject of safety. It has been said that if management ever wants a rallying point that will engender automatic support of union and nonunion ranks, of white- and blue-collar workers, in short of all employees, safety is that central cause that gets universal backing.

Those early house organs were not too unlike the weekly newspapers published in small towns. Their forté was local news. Occasionally the early house organs would contain a sprinkling of what the workers called "management propaganda." But in the main they were straightforward worker oriented, and quite plausible. Those house organs that dipped into "the grandeur of the high commend" did so sparingly—and they often picked up a flavor of being patronizing in the doing.

Reader interest, whenever it was measured, was encouraging, even in folksy columns called "Factory Facts," "Business Office Buzzings," and "Sales Slants." The word "sales," in particular, was important in those early days, destined to give way to the glories of "marketing" later on.

In the late eighties, you may have a hard time finding the term *house organ,* per se, but you'll not have too much trouble locating a broad range of assorted printed materials playing major roles in employee relations. The principal publications today are newspapers, ranging from the simple to the elaborate; newsletters, generally unadorned; and magazines, usually adorned—plus brochures, booklets, pamphlets, and other printed miscellany.

A small to medium-sized company will likely have a basic newspaper plus, perhaps, a few newsletters for selected groups of employees. A larger company will customarily have multiple newspapers, perhaps one for each operating division, plus newsletters for selected audiences and, quite possibly, a magazine.

Do such items pay their freight? Are they really needed?

It is helpful to keep in mind that company publications can be—and should be—the standard "sheet music" for employees everywhere. The corporate overview should be presented to employees regularly. In fact, *the most important stories that companies have to tell are often recited with the greatest effectiveness in internal publications.* Folklore notwithstanding, the big picture of American business is not regularly on the agenda in discussions between foremen and their subordinates.

It is true that foremen and other supervisors can do a splendid job in passing along work orders, in listening to subordinates' complaints, in motivating, in fostering productivity, and in explaining company rules and regulations. However, most foremen have neither the time nor the experience, much less the inclination, to be the informants for such topics as the company's attitudes on the environment, the company's view on the investment credit, the company's philosophy on research and development, taxes, balance of payments, foreign competition, and so forth. Corporate overview and company policy should appear *in print,* including the printed words in internal publications, for all to see—unhampered by interpretations of various supervisors.

The "sheet music" on corporate overview and the showcase for company policy is seldom contained in the foreman's oral interpretation. It is not even the "staff meeting." Day in and day out, the "theme song" is most reliably and consistently and accurately sung *in print,* including the printed words in internal publications, which have the saving grace of using the same language for all to see. And it is quite obvious, if not academic, that scattered foremen in dozens of locations will not use the same language in detailing the corporate overview to their subordinates on heavyweight, complicated, important issues.

This, then, is where the internal publication can draw its best bead. It can communicate factually, promptly, and effectively about the larger issues that in turn affect workers' jobs, workers' benefits, worker's challenges, and workers' opportunities. Actually, a blend of both oral and written is the real magic recipe for effective communications.

Characteristics of the principal types of printed communications for employees are interesting.

## The Newspaper

This is the most versatile and flexible medium of all. It lends itself to reportorial news, to columns of interpretation, to letters to the editor, to photos, to editorials. The company-sponsored newspaper automatically involves at least some semblence of credibility by the mere virtue of being a reportorial vehicle guided by the facts. It is tabloid-sized. It can be locked up on Tuesday and distributed (hopefully by mail to employees' homes) on Wednesday. It is usually black and white (despite the temptation to imitate dazzling, multicolored *USA Today.*) It is generally economical.

The internal newspaper can carry the same explanations of policy throughout the company's geography. Employees in Denver, Kansas City, Indianapolis, Philadelphia, and London will see precisely the same words when a company wants to make sure its objectives are clearly identified.

And while the appearance and format of a company newspaper are important, the crucial element is content. "What information does it convey?" is the principal consideration. Content is the cake; layout and format are the frosting.

The eager, young editor in the first few months may want to present a feature on Valentine's Day—and may be tempted to have the type set in the shape of a heart. This is a mistake; it is immature. But a good editor will "get over it." He or she will learn to devote most of the time to gathering information and writing crisply, not to visual tricks.

Further, an internal newspaper editor should study exemplary external newspapers—like *The Wall Street Journal* —to get a feeling for good writing. Does a local college have night-time classes during which basic journalism principles are taught? Such would be ideal.

## The Newsletter

This is the bread-and-butter, no-nonsense item that has constantly increased in usage. It is usually only two or four pages in length. It is normally nothing more than a string of paragraphs, with typography resembling words from a typewriter or, more currently, by a word processor. It is seldom heavily illustrated. The successful *Kiplinger Letter* is an external forerunner of countless popular newsletters. This time-honored "tipsheet" out of Washington, D.C., to which business persons have been subscribing for many years, is cast in a simple format for the purpose of moving fast and economically.

A large company will have newsletters distributed on

both a vertical *and* a horizontal basis. For example, a manufacturing newsletter is a vertical medium. It will go to
everyone in manufacturing, from the general manager to
the janitor. A "vertical" medium digs deeply into a given
function such as manufacturing or marketing or research.
Thus, "vertical" is an accurately descriptive adjective.

Consider also a management newsletter, a so-called
"horizontal" publication. It will go to all general managers
and their principal assistants; it will go to manufacturing
directors, research directors, and staff department directors. That's a "horizontal" assembly, with distribution
sweeping across various functions but sticking essentially
to parallel managerial echelons at all functions.

## The Magazine

This is the internal publication which packs the greatest
wallop. It can be comprehensive. It can be leisurely. It can
be entertaining as well as instructive. It can use essays and
interviews and feature stories and illustrations. It can be attractive in black and white and it can be dynamic in color.
For depth and breadth, an employee magazine is hard to
beat.

Yet alas a magazine can be costly. In recent years when
companies were finding it necessary to cut back on overhead expenses, the magazine stood out so prominently on
budget sheets that it invited reconsideration. Unfortunately, but understandably, many company magazines that
have been routed to business executives have had a glossy,
slick, fancy, and luxurious look, standing out almost as a
symbol of expense. Result: Some of the finest employee
magazines have been discontinued. Yet, happily, the pendulum is beginning to swing in the other direction. New employee magazines, better than ever, are beginning to appear. Many merit display on coffee tables in employee
homes. And when an employee recipient points to such an

item of pride in his living room, it is not uncommon for the employee to declare, "That's *my* company."

Yet, as attractive as a company publication may be, management will continue to keep one eye on appearance and the other eye on costs, particularly since the price of paper and printing and distribution are edging upward.

Are there any technological breakthroughs coming to the internal editor's rescue? One in particular stands out. It's called desktop publishing. This innovation is so revolutionary that a major story was found on page one of the business section of the January 12, 1987, issue of the *St. Louis Post-Dispatch.* The story said, "With a minimum investment of about $10,000 in computer equipment, you can publish your own newspaper or magazine. That's what desktop publishing is all about—putting together the hardware and software to do everything that typesetters and layout artists do, and for a fraction of the cost. And it all fits on the top of a desk."

Up until recently, the internal editor would write and edit stories and headlines and would put everything in a large envelope for delivery to a typesetter. Then the editor would bring in a designer or artist for a paste-up; then he'd send the bundle to a printer; then the finished product would be delivered to the editor for mailing or another kind of distribution.

Yet, it the new era, the editor with a flexible computer and word processor can forget about outside vendors and can produce all or most of the major elements himself via software disks made for the purpose. He can select type for text material and headlines. He can select charts and graphs and other illustrations. He can select the most attractive physical arrangements. In other words, the editor can become a designer and compositor, literally building a newsletter (or newspaper or brochure) or whatever from scratch. And all inhouse.

Naturally, internal editors will need training in desktop publishing, which requires special skills. Yet, importantly, substantial economies await.

Deborah Williams, editor of publication at St. Elizabeth Medical Center of Granite City, Illinois, speaks for many when she says, "Now that we're doing our own typesetting, we've cut out production time by more than half and quality has improved a thousand percent."

There seems to be a consensus that desktop publishing, while still in its infancy, is definitely here to stay.

# Movies and Tapes for Training

When a supersalesman named Frank G. Arlinghouse was at the helm of Modern Talking Picture Service, Inc., directing the distribution of nontheatrical films, he was convinced that 16mm films were "the standard format for the world and would always so remain."

"Would always so remain": Excessively bold words. In fact, any forecast foreclosing on the possibility of future change is perilous. Change is inevitable in an imperfect world and it is the catalyst of progress in human endeavor—including the speciality of audiovisuals.

Black and white theatrical films were, to be sure, the progenitor. Sound was added in the late twenties, permitting Al Jolson to sing "Mammy" in the pioneering classic, "The Jazz Singer." Then Technicolor came onto the scene in the thirties. And while motion pictures entered a triumphant new era in theaters, they were sparingly used in the plants and offices of American industry. They were too cumbersome to handle in nontheatrical settings, mainly because reels of 35mm film were bulky and the arc-lamp projectors were ponderous.

Realizing that motion pictures with color and sound had spectacular impact, a number of enlightened and opportunistic companies concluded that a broad new market could be created if their engineers could make motion picture projection equipment lightweight and easy to handle. In efforts led by Eastman Kodak Company, 16mm film was developed. Then came smaller projectors and cameras to provide economy and portability. Frank Arlinghouse called that era "the dawn of a new day: movies everywhere!"

Eastman's role in the 16mm pioneering days was to manufacture the film in great quantity. Along with Bell and Howell, Victor, DeVry, RCA, and others, Eastman also got into the business of manufacturing projectors, screens, lamps, and assorted accessories. A promising new industry flowered. Particularly in business organizations and schools, 16mm sound-and-color motion pictures became standard.

Before and during World War II, 16mm projectors took their place among rifles and boots and other equipment at literally every military camp in the nation. Training the troops was the mission. How to dig a foxhole had to be taught in a hurry. There were other "how tos" that needed to be conveyed: practicing hygiene, cleaning the barracks; writing home; enjoying C-rations; taking care of uniforms; respecting foreign cultures; administering first aid; showing respect for superiors. These were among the subjects that could be effectively depicted on a motion picture screen.

The training films prepared for the army, navy, marines, coast guard, and air force were, of course, the main fare for the 16mm projectors. However, those projectors were also capable of providing entertainment. Theatrical movies, transferred from 35mm to 16mm film, were also available at army camps, at air bases, and aboard troopships.

Because the military had been so successful in the use of training films, the nation's business establishment quickly discovered that Rosie the riveter, Pete the pipe fitter, Fred the foreman, and Jerry the Jeep-maker could benefit from the same kind of audiovisual guidance. By the time the nation's business community faced the tremendous postwar need for expansion, 16mm films were on their way to becoming the most dominant training vehicle anywhere. The day for audiovisuals in the workplace had dawned.

Were other kinds of communications vehicles in the running for training military and nonmilitary audiences? This is a question worth considering. Radio, widely known for its news reports during World War II, seemed inapplicable to training needs. However 35mm color slides and slide projectors began to appear. Ultimately the carousel-type projector simplified the matter of showing slides conveniently and quickly on fair-sized screens.

Sometimes slides were better than 16mm films for training purposes. While the time frame remained constant in showing a motion picture (a 20-minute motion picture always takes 20 minutes to show), a slide show, with narration built in or added on, could be paced—speeded up or slowed down—to fit the requirements of any given audience. Thus, a slide show can be keyed to an audience's ability to comprehend, with a single slide transparency being held on the screen as long as desired. The speaker could focus on controls of a lathe, on various switches, the safety shield, or any other feature, as desired. A single slide clearly showing a lathe assembly can be retained on the screen indefinitely—for examination, for understanding, and for questions from the audience. An inflexible sound motion picture cannot as readily be frozen on a single frame for audience convenience.

By most other yardsticks, the 16mm movie gained widespread acceptance and popularity. Here are a few of the reasons:

1. A 16mm film's narration, plus sound effects, are in synchronization with what the eye sees on the screen;

2. The presentation can be of virtually any length for uninterrupted projections;

3. The movie can pack a heavy dose of emotional appeal —up to Hollywood's dramatic standards, if desired.

Where does television come into the picture?

Arriving, as it did, in the mid-forties and proliferating quickly, television and its revolutionary consequences represented precisely what Frank Arlinghouse underestimated when he proclaimed that 16mm films would continue to represent the standard for the future. Those who shopped for a TV set in the mid-forties will recall that RCA's feature model came on the retail market at $375—with a 10-inch screen. In the set there were 34 vacuum tubes, each with a short lifespan. The repair man—unlike the storied Maytag repair man who is depicted as lonely, unwanted, and unneeded—became a frequent visitor at households with TV sets. Even though the TV owner may have purchased a repair service policy, it was small consolation whenever the little screen flickered, pitched, rolled, and finally blacked out. Such was the joy of pioneering.

Then came networks, color, and larger picture tubes. Kinescopes also joined the parade, representing television's first primitive reach toward program longevity. Kinescopes were direct film copies of electronic images, but they were—at best—fuzzy. "Like looking through a screen door," someone observed. They were an attempt to enable people to see eventually, via kinescope, a program which they had missed, at a later time—a convenience that has since been called "time shifting."

In the more recent era, there came the revolutionary development called videotape, which enabled spools of the magnetic tan plastic to capture TV images and sounds in high quality. Plus, in short order, color and low cost. Just as motion picture film had progressed by going from 35mm to 16mm (and to 8mm and smaller), videotapes imitatively went from 2-inch magnetic tape to smaller widths: 1 inch, 3/4 inch, 1/2 inch, and 1/4 inch. The art of miniaturization is ceaseless.

So the age of videotape, even prior to the age of home

computers, became the threshold for major technological advances. By the time the late sixties arrived, videotapes spawned new industries, new devices, new conveniences— and a new road to audiovisual programs for training, motivating, and educating employees.

Limited earlier by the small size of picture tubes in households, videotape—and, indeed, television itself— grew into more commanding proportions by projection-on- big-screen hardware. And videotape's principal offspring, the VCR (videotape cassette recorder), became an in- demand accessory throughout business and household locations of America. While television was a monumental invention, it needed videotape to give it wings. And VCRs gave it convenience.

There is more to come on the horizon as the videotape is being married to computers and to laser pickups of digital disks. Can the simple, little videotape cassette further revolutionize the world of audiovisuals and even challenge 16mm films for business use? Of course. The change is well under way. Here's a clue: Skilled staff members at Southwestern Bell Telephone Corporation, which has strong in-house capabilities, can discuss the need for a certain new training program this month and have the presentation ready to roll—from scratch—next month. They also can develop a tidy, persuasive, taped audiovisual this week and show it next week. Reviewing footage immediately after shooting is perhaps the biggest boon of all.

What's next on the horizon? Will the day ever arrive when a company officer will say, "For the moment, no new training material is needed?" That's unlikely.

It should be remembered that a training audience is not stationary. An audience is like a parade, with some members going around the corner and going out of sight while other marchers come into view. And those employees who have already been exposed to training programs will need fresh guidance when the inevitable new products emerge from the American business system.

Equally inevitable, there always will be new employees who will welcome the helping hand of training as they enter a wondrous new age of American industry's resourcefulness and ingenuity.

# Chapter 30

# Relationship Between Internal and External Public Relations

When is company information appropriate for internal use only or for external use only or for simultaneous release through both internal and external channels? When is the information inappropriate for release to any audience? The answer to these questions may be found in the scenarios that follow.

Let's assume the information is of little or no interest beyond the walls of the Ajax, Inc., headquarters office and plant. The news is that the back parking lot will be closed for repairs.

Employees, who are directly affected, will naturally be interested. As they encounter the information on bulletin boards or in the internal newsletter, they will wonder "Where will we all park?" Ajax already has the answer as it has made arrangements for alternate parking: the existing front and side lots but not the back lot will be available for parking, and overflow parking will be accommodated by a newly purchased lot across the street.

The employees may be inconvenienced, but only slightly. There would be confusion if employees were not alerted in advance, whereas a suitable explanation will bring order rather than disorder.

Does such information qualify for timely disclosure within Ajax headquarters office and plant? Yes, of course. However it does not qualify for use at other Ajax plants nor for external release. Such parochial information is, therefore, pertinent at one location and inconsequential elsewhere. It is of no interest to local newspapers and radio and TV stations.

Now for a slight variation, let's assume the parking lot will be closed to make way for the construction of a $5 million Ajax research center. Should such significant news be emphasized, featuring the construction project, for use within other Ajax locations? Indeed, it should. Should it be made available to appropriate external media? Yes, again.

Decisions on the distribution of Ajax information, therefore, depend largely on the potential significance of developments. If Ajax's director of public relations will ask himself, "Who's interested? Who's affected? Who's involved?" The resulting answers will identify precisely which internal and external audiences are not to be overlooked.

What if Ajax corporate management determined, "Let's announce the research center news internally only and not initiate any external distribution of the news until next month when we hire a contractor."

"Such a decision can be dangerous, as the news will surely leak. The local TV station and radio station and newspaper are likely to learn from employees or others that Ajax will have a major building project in the works. And if management—for reasons of its own—tries to stonewall external news inquiries, and thus encourage the news media to use fractional information based on rumors and on employees' random reports, the story will surface in the public media with something less than total accuracy. It is worth remembering that newspapers and other external media always prefer being tuned in on the fundamental facts in a breaking story and that editors will often turn to less reliable secondary and tertiary sources of information when they have been frozen out by primary (corporate in this context) information sources.

What if the company decided to release information externally only? This, too, can be dangerous. Ajax information released externally on Monday, for example, will probably reverberate through employee ranks on Tuesday, even if the information has not been formally approved for use on bulletin boards and in other internal media. And rest assured, the information will probably not be totally accurate as it makes its way through the Ajax grapevine.

Why does Ajax management want to withhold its announcement from employees in the first place? A mystery. Ajax management would certainly be remiss in not realizing that it is virtually impossible to successfully bypass employees. If given the opportunity, internal communications people would remind management of the first commandment of public relations: Thou shalt communicate with employees first, or at least on a simultaneous basis.

Granted, there are times when even the most sophisticated companies—General Motors, for example—will find it logistically difficult to make sure that employees gain access to newsworthy company information before they hear it on the nightly news or see it in the newspapers. It is a matter of record that General Motors spends many millions of dollars to promptly send news items in summary form to plants and offices around the world in order to tell the news to the family (employees) first, and to eliminate or, at least minimize, surprises.

Because external media operate at lightning speed, it is sometimes difficult for corporations to get their versions of events to scattered locations before the Associated Press and United Press International begin moving their stories electronically to the mass media. Despite this handicap, a company must make the effort to communicate directly with their employees. Even if they sometimes learn of company news from next-door neighbors, the fact that their employer makes a strong effort to keep them informed is morale-boosting. To repeat, management's attitude is crucial.

Strange as it may seem, companies will come up with unrealistic decisions in their efforts to control and limit their internal distribution of newsworthy information. A classic example follows.

"We are ready to issue an important, general news release announcing that Ajax has set an all-time record in earnings in the first quarter. Use the news release on headquarters bulletin boards but for God's sake don't telex it to our Texas City, Texas, plant manager because he is closing in on a new labor contract and doesn't want his union employees to think we're rolling in dough. Even if you do send the information to him he said he won't release it—at least not until he finalizes the union contract."

That's what corporate management decreed. When the stunned director of public relations learned of this unrealistic demand, he said, "To begin with, you can't build a fence around news. Once the information on record earnings gets out, the wire services will carry it broadly, which means the Texas City newspapers will play it—and probably play it big. Even if for some reason the Texas City media fail to use the information, or if they use it inconspicuously, our headquarters employees who see it on their bulletin boards will be sending forth the good news far and wide. And you can be sure when they're on the telephone to employees at Texas City, they'll be passing along the happy news."

The public relations director suggested, "Let me call the Texas City plant manager and see if I can't reason with him and point out our predicament."

Minutes later, the public relations director got on the phone and tried to reason with the Texas City plant manager: "Joe, you can't put blinders on your people. If all your employees and your union people, too, don't read about our record profits on your bulletin boards, they'll find out quickly by other means. You have posted financial releases on your bulletin boards before. If you try to hide the news on this occasion, your employees will wonder why. They will recognize your clumsy effort to squelch the news. And they'll learn the facts, anyway, and ask, "Who is Ajax trying to fool?'"

The plant manager was trying to bring peaceful settlement to a labor contract and to "avoid inflaming," as he put it, union negotiators who might escalate their demands if they learned about high corporate profits by reading the news on the local bulletin boards. However, reluctantly, the plant manager did finally decide to put the company's performance figures on his bulletin boards—but not until the next morning when he saw the information on the business pages of the *Galveston News* and *Texas City Sun.* Did he encounter some turbulence when he next met with the union negotiating committee? Yes and no. He did succeed in negotiating a new labor contract that was in line with his expectations, but he took a lot of kidding about his unfortunate effort to impose a news blackout on his bulletin boards.

Finally, when is company information inappropriate for internal or external use? This can pose a real dilemma for corporate management. Whether to speak out or be silent is often a sensitive subject, particularly in a company that has traditionally been frank and up front in its contacts with employees and other principal constituencies.

The question does not concern whether to discriminate between insiders and outsiders but whether to reveal anything at all under certain circumstances.

"We'd like to level with employees and outsiders in this matter but..." is often the rationale for a management fearful of negative consequences. "We ordinarily like to have our friends share in the news about the breakthroughs in our laboratories" is sometimes management's initial impulse, counter-balanced by cautions and by fears that certain kinds of proprietary knowledge—acquired in research efforts at great expense and truly a corporate asset—should not be carelessly broadcast for the ears of competition.

"When in doubt, be safe and keep a low profile" is often the advice of a supercautious law department whose attorneys will tilt toward nondisclosure; such conservative attorneys are sensitive to the fact that "telling employees and neighbors is like telling the world."

Indeed, determining the relationships and consequences of internal and external communications is an important, serious, day-to-day matter of judgment in companies large and small. Attorneys will say something like, "Don't give away the store." Public relations people, who are perhaps equally prudent, but not always seeming so, will counter, "Keep employees and other major constituencies fully informed."

Executives fret about such matters. Traditionally they listen to many of their functional specialists who bring varying viewpoints to the imperative of employee communications. In the final analysis, someone has to sort out and weigh the conflicting advice, someone who will ultimately say, "OK. I've deliberated on the evidence. A decision is necessary and I'm about to make it. Here's what we're going to do!"

Day in and day out, that's the way it is. And let it be hoped that the high cause of keeping employees and others informed gets a fair shake in the decisions of those in the upper echelons of corporate America.

# Chapter 31

# The Importance of Writing Skills

In 1986, Thomas R. Cath, DePauw University's director of career planning and placement, said the following: "Most employers I speak with (there are rare exceptions) are not terribly concerned with a student's major, although they like to see he did well in his chosen field. Virtually all of these employers are looking for individuals with outstanding written and oral communications skills."

For purposes of this *Handbook*, this chapter will focus on writing proficiency, without which the Ajax, Inc., internal newsletter would be seriously disadvantaged.

Although the newsletter editor will also have to know how to produce and distribute his informal, four-page, printed communication, which can be learned on the job, the primary challenge consists of having writing and editing know-how. How does the editor get along putting words on paper (or onto a word processor's cathode ray tube)? And how proficient are his colleagues, who help in the communications program? These are the key questions.

First, let's focus on the editor and his personal qualifications in setting forth information for all Ajax employees to see. An appraisal of the editor's competency can start by examining the nature and scope of his formal education. Did the editor do well in English and composition in college? Has he pursued studies in communications in night classes?

In the course of maturing, did he find enjoyment and not drudgery in communicating clearly, distinctly, and creatively? Did the editor develop the habit of remembering the small and simple basics of grammar? Did he discover the joy of learning, improving, reaching, and, importantly, reading?

The following paragraphs can be used to test the competency of a newsletter editor. Would the editor permit the following item to appear in the company publication as it appears?

> Ajax, Inc. announced today their spring line would not represent an advance in sales prices and thus will step valiantly into the fight against inflation, the nation's constant enemy.
>
> Simultaneously, the company opened its new sales office in Springfield, on Olive, which will be in charge of P. G. Wisdom, chief chemist who is the founder's son.
>
> We believe the new line will achieve great success in the marketplace.

The example is something less than a professionally written story. Actually, it's loaded with bloopers. As a reader of the *Handbook* how many mistakes can you find? To begin with, a company cannot announce "their" spring line; the correct pronoun is "its." *A singular noun requires a singular modifying pronoun.*

Still in the first paragraph, the writer has Ajax stepping "valiantly into the fight against inflation, the nation's constant enemy." Who says inflation is still a "constant enemy?" This statement is an opinion and not a fact, so it should have been attributed to an Ajax spokesman. If an officer of Ajax wants to say his company will make a "valiant" move and to refer to inflation as an "enemy" it is surely his privilege, but he has to be so quoted. Only facts and not opinions can go without quotes or without specific attribution in a news story.

The company opened its new sales office in Springfield the story reports. Which Springfield—the one in Ohio, Missouri, Illinois, or in any other state with a town of this name? And what is Olive—Street, Road, Boulevard, Lane, Drive, etc.?

The story says the sales office will be "in charge of P. G. Wisdom." In all likelihood, it is the reverse situation: Mr. Wisdom will be in charge of the sales office. Furthermore, P. G. Wisdom is identified as "chief chemist who is the founder's son." A comma—it's called the parenthetical comma—is missing after "chemist." The name of the founder should also have been included along with the mention of his son.

Returning to the first paragraph, it is guilty of inconsistent usage of "would" and "will." The writer would have done better by deciding which to use and by sticking with it.

The last sentence, "We believe the new line will achieve great success in the marketplace" has two problems. Again, this is an opinion and needs attribution to an identified spokesperson. Also, that word "we" is a first-person pronoun that has no place in a reportorial item if left unguarded by quotation marks and attribution to a spokesperson.

If the editor of the Ajax newsletter was guilty of composing such a story, one wonders can he write correctly and can he guide others to proper grammatical usage? There are any number of resources to help the editor: short-term refresher courses that will not only give instruction in basic journalism but will also provide wide range of professional guidelines.

The Ajax newsletter will not be the only beneficiary if and when a company decides to develop its own communicators and to place a premium on the art of being articulate. Obvious dividends would include the following:

1. Research department reports, for example, would no longer be cumbersome and formidable. They would begin with a summary sheet or two in the hope that all recipients would read the up-front synopsis and that

other readers might be brave enough to tackle well-prepared reports in their entirety. Just because research chemists aren't normally trained to communicate effectively with nonchemists doesn't mean that all communications efforts will be futile. No profession is immune from the need to make itself understood.

2. The cause of management spokesmanship is substantially advanced when a company actively encourages elucidation on "here's where we stand." There is a subliminal relationship between spokesmanship and leadership. And knowing how to write well and to speak effectively can be a powerful corporate asset at all managerial levels. Clear communication should not be optional; it is mandatory.

A company's determination to communicate effectively includes and transcends the efforts of the newsletter editor who, nonetheless, is the person expected to exhibit basic professional standards. As the communicator, that person should set a good example.

Will readers notice if the newsletter stories are fuzzy, inconsistent, poorly constructed, or worst of all, inaccurate? Of course they will, inasmuch as they are constantly exposed to well-written items in metropolitan newspapers and national magazines and will instinctively notice poor writing.

In this context, how to write well is an essential consideration for Ajax, Inc. With such a skill so readily achievable through study and practice, the newsletter editor can become a trusted, credible purveyor of information, helping to establish an atmosphere of understanding and support among all employee ranks within the work place.

# Chapter 32

# The Role of Bulletin Boards

Bulletin boards may be considered by some as unimaginative relics of the Stone Age, but they continue to proliferate in offices and factories across the country. Even IBM, purveyor of electronic and computerized devices of almost infinite variety, relies heavily on bulletin boards in information and motivational programs for its 400,000-plus employees.

In a recent *Wall Street Journal* article, Richard Dougherty, IBM's general manager of manufacturing and development at Research Triangle Park, North Carolina, commented on IBM's reward program and mentioned that "bulletin boards are covered with snapshots of workers getting a handshake or a bonus check" for excellent performance.

But, alas, too often bulletin boards are taken for granted. They are plain, traditional, and humdrum. Their appearance hasn't changed down through the years. Even Julius Caesar used bulletin boards!

In a business organization today the bulletin board is frequently horizontal, sometimes square, occasionally vertical, and always flat. Sometimes it even reposes behind a glass door, which can be locked. It can be a fancy, store-bought commodity featuring a cork surface and a stainless steel frame or a homemade device with a plain wooden frame made by the plant carpenter.

Things are affixed to a bulletin board with thumbtacks or with little magnets if the surface is made of metal. Yet glue or other adhesives are never used because of the transient nature of the materials affixed to bulletin board surfaces.

The bulletin board is actually a stage for a continuous show of "something new and different every day," albeit some items overstay and yellow with age, a chronic problem.

The location of the bulletin board may be anywhere; next to the president's office, in the company lunchroom, at the end of the hall. As to what appears on the board, there is variety: official edicts announced for the first time, safety suggestions, news of promotions, and occasionally non-work-related personal items, where permitted.

When Milton Fairman was vice president for public relations and advertising for the Borden Company, he commented, "Someone should do a serious monograph called 'The Care and Feeding of Bulletin Boards.'" Fairman took seriously the distribution of appropriate information to company-wide bulletin boards, sending what he called "newsflashes" promptly to all company locations.

Who is in charge? Who has the authority to post notices on the main office bulletin boards? These basic questions require consideration. Without a clear and restrictive answer to these questions, disorder and clutter are inevitable. Preferably, the responsibility for the bulletin board should rest on one, and only one, department at each location—probably public relations, personnel, or office management.

At outer locations, bulletin boards are normally recipients of at least two kinds of information: announcements from corporate headquarters and announcements of a purely local nature, prepared locally.

Rules of the road are needed to determine what goes on the bulletin boards and what doesn't. Here, again, there has to be a traffic cop—a single place for accountability, if order is to be achieved.

Some companies have four kinds of bulletin boards:

1. For the company's official business only—announcements, news releases, and the like.

2. For use by the union or unions.

3. For employee-generated postings.

4. For noncompany posters and government regulations and endorsed community events.

The third category, a catch-all bulletin board for employee-generated postings, is not a bad idea. There should be a system and guidelines for posting: what qualifies and what does not. All employees should, of course, be informed about those guidelines.

Even at a large headquarters installation of a big company, a single employee bulletin board may be all that's required for the third category, particularly if it can be placed at some convenient location for all to see, such as just outside the cafeteria. The most popular—and most read—items on such a bulletin board will resemble the want ad section in the newspaper. "Boat for sale," "stereo wanted," "1980 Volkswagen, make offer"—these are typical samplings. Some companies permit snapshots that advertise "vacation retreat on lake, available during August" and "basset hound puppies available." There may be invitations to join ride groups, announcements of bowling tournaments and lost-and-found information.

Not all companies are willing to allow employee bulletin boards, taking the position that non-work-related activities should not be promulgated. But some—and here's where the big problem lies—will permit occasional "personals" to go alongside official notices on regular bulletin boards. This is a frequently committed sin, which can be easily avoided by the expedient of having an extra and separate bulletin board for appropriate employee-generated material.

The employee bulletin boards require systemization. Rules on their use may be as follows:

1. Employees are not permitted to do their own pin-ups.

2. Employees are asked to send all material to Central Personnel, which will determine if the material qualifies—in accordance with established guidelines.

3. Central Personnel will do the posting.

4. Central Personnel will also do the unposting, which is as important as the posting.

Normally, an item should never be permitted to stay on a board for more than a week. Items should be dated or coded, so that there is no mistake about when they have gone up and when they should come down.

Let's backtrack to the official bulletin boards—the number 1 category for which there must also be guidelines. Naturally, if the president of the company wants an announcement posted on all bulletin boards, this automatically qualifies, no matter what the message is.

There should be spelled-out guidelines for community events in the number 4 category. Normally, United Way announcements qualify, as do Red Cross blood drive announcements.

How about posting a bulletin in behalf of the subscription drive being launched by the local symphony orchestra? If you say yes to this group, you may be approached by the opera guild, the community ballet, theater groups, and so on. How about posting the announcement for the local major league baseball team or the local professional football team? If you allow such commercial items to get onto bulletin boards, then why discriminate against the local movie house, restaurants, and health club?

In large companies where there are bulletin boards on many floors of many buildings, further controls are needed. Let's assume the accounting department hires a CPA fresh out of Harvard Business School. Where should the announcement be posted? It probably should go only on those sectional bulletin boards in the area occupied by the accounting department.

However, if John J. Jones becomes a new general manager of an important division of Ajax, Inc., there is a possibility of overkill by posting two items: 1) An announcement signed by the president stating "I am sure you will give him every measure of cooperation" and 2) a news release written in a more impersonal style, yet a document that contains essentially the same news without presidential personalization. Only one or the other should be posted.

For a limited number of company announcements, it is appropriate to have personalized official announcements from the president. But, for most announcements, the news release alone suffices. Even though the news release is primarily for external communication, it can serve a second purpose by being placed on bulletin boards.

All news releases should not be posted widely. In general, releases of probable interest to all employees should be posted companywide and others should be posted only where an interest is apt to be present. Here, again, guidelines are crucial.

Some organizations have a condescending attitude toward bulletin boards and allow them to become cluttered and unkempt. At one large hospital in St. Louis, giant posters monopolized bulletin board space so heavily that it was difficult to find the official announcements. In another instance, in a large food company's general offices, old announcements predominated so much that new items seemed to get lost in the maze.

Patricia Mottram, manager of public relations for Cooper Industries, Houston, recently prepared a proposal for top management regarding bulletin boards. Here was Mottram's thorough approach:

**Rationale**—Cooper Industries has improved communications at the corporate office with the initiation of the Cooper News and the Management Bulletin, and the expansion of the Management Newsletter. While these have been positive steps, a more timely means of communicating with employees is needed to supplement these media and to fill the information gap between publication dates. Bulletin boards would service this purpose effectively and inexpensively.

Bulletin boards provide employees with quick and accurate information. They are flexible and easy to maintain. And they allow management to communicate with employees easily, at any time. Since readers tend to view bulletin boards as straightforward notices of vital information, the boards do not suffer the problems of credibility that sometimes plague other controlled communication. Most important, they are read.

**Location** To attract maximum attention, bulletin boards should be in high traffic areas. At the corporate office, the most central location would be by the water fountains on each floor. Here there is sufficient room.

**Contents**—Materials commonly posted on company bulletin boards are:

*Personal News:* promotions, transfers, vacations, holidays, benefits, meetings, training programs, company-sponsored events, service awards, personal honors, community service.

*Activities:* company events; community events, especially those sponsored by Cooper; fund-raising campaigns.

*Company news:* new facilities, new products, reorganizations, historical events, management messages, company honors and awards, critical problems, newspaper clippings of articles concerning the company, its industry, markets or products; financial news, such as profits and sales. Plus general news releases, preferably prior to release to the media.

*Travel news:* roster of incoming visitors, travel tips.

*Photo captions:* of products, activities, employees. Where applicable, photos can be distributed companywide.

**Responsibility**—The publication coordinator will be responsible for the development and dissemination of corporate office bulletins, with the approval of the manager of public relations. Bulletins involving any other department will have that department's prior approval.

**Formats**—Bulletin boards will be selected based on the recommendations of the office interior designer. The bulletins will be produced on 8-1/2 by 11 paper with preprinted color headlines to categorize the information.

**Procedures—**
1. Any employee may request to have company-related information posted, but all information must be approved by public relations and posted on a standard form.

2. In general, bulletins will be posted at the same time daily. All bulletins will be marked with a post date and remove date. Two weeks will be the maximum time a bulletin stays posted. Bulletins will be brief and timely.

3. The deadline for submission of material to the publications coordinator will be noon each day for the following day's bulletins. After the bulletins are approved, they will be typed on preprinted forms and duplicated.

**Cost**—the biggest expense in starting a bulletin board program is acquiring the boards. Once they are in place, the program will be very inexpensive to run, involving only the printing of the forms.

Bulletin boards range in price from approximately $70 for a 4x6 cork board with wood frame to over $300 for a glass-enclosed board. To insure maximum control of the program, glass-enclosed boards are recommended.

A year's supply of forms could be printed at one time, at minimal cost. And, this cost would be offset by the reduction in the number of memos now distributed to all employees.

**Long-term objective**—Once implemented here at corporate headquarters, an effective bulletin board program could be made available to all plant locations, providing a fast, easy, and inexpensive way to communicate with all company employees.

Mottram provides a model that is comprehensive and adaptable in other company settings.

# Chapter 33

# Feedback

Too often public relations is cast only in the light of one-way communications to employees and other targeted constituencies, with infrequent attention paid to feedback. It is a fact of life that *two-way communications* are essential in all organizations regardless of their size.

"Let's fill the pipelines with information to be carried to employees on a continuing basis" may be the expressed order issued by top management, but such a strategy must be accompanied by a way of determining the effectiveness of the various programs designed to keep employees informed.

It is necessary to ask: Do employees regularly read the company newsletter or newspaper? Assuming the publication reaches employees at their home addresses, do members of the employees' family read it? Do they hold it in high regard? Do they feel it addresses itself to those issues representing the actual concerns of company personnel or, rather, does it seem to avoid sensitive topics and to concentrate on uninformative and bland subject matter?

Increasingly in a down-sizing era when business costs are intensely scrutinized, the editor of the employee newsletter is more than ever budgeting for feedback programs that make it possible to answer the question, "Do the results of the newsletter justify the expense?" Justify is a crucial word. "What would happen if we would simply kill the newsletter and use bulletin board announcements to keep the employees informed?" is the kind of worrisome consideration that materializes when a company decides to re-trench.

For better or worse, the belt-tightening environment of recent years has often led cost-conscious businesses to look with skepticism at information programs that heretofore had gone unchallenged. As a result, feedback efforts have recently proliferated on the national scene and evidence, both good and bad, has surfaced to permit evaluation and provide guidance.

There are many devices that can be used in pursuing feedback. "Do a survey" is the most immediate knee-jerk reaction. In a survey, attempts are made to find out what the employees really think, to get their reactions, to find some form of measurement, to establish a benchmark, to zero in on readership.

The newsletter editor who becomes defensive and merely postulates the theory that communications are mother-hood, per se, and should be encouraged rather than chal-lenged can easily be perceived as being uncooperative if he fails to harken to the cause of feedback. Yet, the editor who is a pragmatic realist will insist that systems should be promptly established for testing the value of the employee publication. Actually, the desire and necessity for proving the worth of the internal publication should represent a re-sponsibility that the editor fulfills with leadership and en-thusiasm. "My newsletter pays its freight and I am eager to provide demonstrable, objective, arithmetic evidence. It's part of my job." That's the way an editor should think.

Opinion research feedback, serving as a radarlike device, comes in all styles and sizes. It can be exhaustively compre-hensive or superficially short and abrupt, costly or inexpen-sive. It can be planned and implemented by internal personnel—perhaps the editor and personnel department staff—or can be turned over to a professional outside opin-ion research organization. The latter alternative is far preferable, as an outside organization would be perceived as being objective—and such a perception is crucial. No one wants a slanted survey with loaded questions or a research project that culminates in imprecise, incomplete, and unhelpful findings.

Planning is, as always, the key. In the process of determining the scope of employee research, fundamental questions are examined comprehensively. Such questions include: What does the company hope to achieve by publishing a newsletter? What kinds of information represent employees' interests and what kind are low on the list of preferences?

Other questions can also be posed: Should the proposed survey involve all employees? Should it be handled by mail? Should there also be supplementary interviews with some employees—person-to-person or by phone or both? If employees are asked to fill out survey forms, should they be asked to sign their names or given the option to remain anonymous? Should the yes or no format be employed to ensure easy tabulation of results, or should participants be encouraged to express opinions in their own words? Should the findings ultimately be made available to all participants or should they be restricted to limited distribution among upper echelon of the corporate infrastructure?

That anyone in search of structured information, regardless of the searcher's experience, can develop an effective feedback program is an erroneous concept. An inexperienced amateur attempting opinion research is not likely to succeed.

The services of opinion research organizations have become commonplace in the operations of many major corporations, even for an assignment as simple as sampling the readership of a newsletter. Indeed, because opinion research findings are sometimes questioned by skeptical company officers, it is comforting and reassuring to cite the credentials of those professional outsiders who plan and implement the strategic and mechanical details of the survey.

Focusing on benchmarks is a technique often used by professional opinion researchers. If, for example, newsletter readership gets a high mark for information on products but a low mark for information on the subject of plant safety, the scores are noted as follows: Ajax will post the score for safety as a benchmark, which means that Ajax will give more attention to safety information in the future, presenting it in a more interesting and more comprehensive manner than previously and Ajax will ask essentially the same questions in an opinion research project two years later. This is called tracking, which is an effective device.

"Let's be happy with the peaks but we should concentrate more on the valleys," the late Claude Robinson, founder of Opinion Research Corporation, Princeton, New Jersey, used to say. Then he would add, "Let's shore up those low scores."

Opinion research efforts every other year may be ideal in concept but may not be in the thinking of a company that has just been introduced to the discipline. Such an organization may not want to be committed to a benchmark now and comparative benchmarks later. It may simply want to be told, "Here are the facts considering employees' reactions today." Such an introductory, one-time effort is certainly better than no feedback at all.

Feedback programs have varied effects. They often are educational. Unsurprisingly, earlier guesswork on employee reactions is not always substantiated. But employee opinions, whatever they may be, do travel upward and receive management's attention. Happily, feedback programs not only serve their purpose of forcing the internal communicator to justify the existence of the newsletter but also to examine it for the purpose of improving it.

Questionnaires are often tested on small groups before all-out research projects are launched. "I don't understand question No. 14." "Please clarify question No. 18 so I can understand precisely what you want to know." Such comments from test groups can help sharpen the questions in a survey. Another technique involves the use of so-called focus groups that will be assembled to determine the issues and to suggest the subjects that will be included in written or oral research efforts. Such advance work pays off and increases the possibility that the survey will be on target.

The president of a St. Louis-based multinational corporation once suggested that the "evaluation of what should be evaluated" is the trickiest subject of all. He observed, "We can't ask questions about everything in the cause of feedback. A clean and attractive lobby makes a better impression on visitors than a rag-tag lobby. So let's not have opinion research on the obvious. Some things depend on judgment and do not require putting pro and con numbers on common sense."

The formal survey is not always the only way to go. The tried-and-true suggestion system can be an excellent feedback device even though it was not designed primarily for soliciting employees' ideas about using publications for the purpose of promoting efficiency, enhancing productivity, and fostering morale. Suggestion systems have been instrumental in saving billions of dollars through the simple expedient of capitalizing on employees' solutions to specific problems. Many companies reward their employees for constructive suggestions and do so with notable success. For example, IBM's "Speak Up" program paid employees almost $60 million from 1975 to 1984 for suggestions that saved the company $300 million.

Suggestion systems have an additional advantage: They bring to management's attention employee concerns beyond such matters as ideas for debottlenecking, saving waste material, speeding up production, and double-checking on quality controls. Almost as an unplanned dividend, issues A to Z in scope usually surface as part of the suggestion system process, shedding light on employees' curiosities, frustrations, and bewilderments, which are disguised as suggestions competing for rewards.

Employees are given a medium in which they can ask "Why do we do this and why don't we do that?" They can identify areas of concern by the very nature of their recommendations and queries: "Why don't we have hand lotion dispensers in our women's restrooms?" "Why don't we save electricity by turning off all the ceiling fixtures at night? People driving by must think we're wasteful." Neither of these suggestions were award winners, but management felt they merited answers, which were given to the employees making the queries. For the woman who asked for hand lotion, the answer was given that the office management department had been considering lotion dispensers for several months and was about to install such equipment companywide. The answer to the man suggesting saving electricity was that the clean-up crew needed the illumination. These suggestions may have sounded trivial to some, but they weren't to the participants. And management was wise enough to realize that.

Are feedback ideas generated through research studies and suggestion systems or any other means so conclusive that they demand immediate action? Not always, as the following example indicates.

When Organization Resources Counselors (ORC) Inc., did a definitive study for Lever Brothers Company, an earnest attempt was made to pinpoint employees sources of internal communications. The outcome appears on the following page.

|  | All Employees | Plants | Field Sales | Lever House | Research Center |
|---|---|---|---|---|---|
| Grapevine | | | | | |
| Word-of-Mouth | 59% | 48% | 45% | 69% | 79% |
| Bulletin Boards | 50 | 67 | — | 46 | 18 |
| *Lever Standard* | 48 | 49 | 51 | 53 | 43 |
| Annual Report | 31 | 32 | 32 | 28 | 19 |
| Supervisor | 32 | 17 | 83 | 43 | 56 |
| Union | 20 | 28 | — | — | 5 |

The interpretation of such results is as interesting and important as the findings themselves. First of all, there are some communications people who don't like to see the grapevine given a place in a survey because they feel that the grapevine is fast but unreliable and should not be tallied on the same level as more reliable media such as bulletin boards and the employee newspaper *Lever Standard.*

Nevertheless, the employees were asked to identify information sources, and the grapevine appeared in their answers. They were not asked to differentiate between the reliability or trustworthiness of grapevine versus anything else. Moreover, the grapevine is a hardy perennial that is here to stay. Communicators can counteract the unreliability of the grapevine by making the reliable sources of information so attractive that employees will give more attention to bulletin boards, to the internal newspaper, or to both. To be sure, rumor, scuttlebutt, and juicy tidbits will not be eradicated, but internal media can carry their load and not, through default, encourage the growth of grapevine items.

Here are a few other observations on the ORC study:

Note that bulletin boards and the internal newspaper have high marks at Lever Brothers overall but the employees at the research center have not paid much attention to the bulletin boards. What is the reason for this phenomenon? It became obvious that once a study was completed, *another study* was needed to interpret the results. In the case of the Lever Brothers survey, ORC not only guided the opinion research effort but also helped management explore the significance of the findings and helped close the gaps.

Meaningful feedback involves hard, long, but important work. There are no shortcuts.

# PART 5

# Internal Public Relations: Inside Stories

Dan J. Forrestal

## Satellites Link Distant Employees

A new era is upon us in teleconferencing, in internal employee motivational programs, and in the transmittal of sights and sounds to and from man-made outposts in outer space for growing array of corporate benefits. Responsible for all of this are satellites, or electronic "birds," as they are called by their perpetrators.

Considering that satellites sit out there some 22,300 miles away from the surface of the earth, there may understandably be a puzzlement in trying to relate the fruits of faraway technology to corporations preparing information programs for earth-bound employees. But hang in there. Companies are increasingly using the amazing capabilities of satellites to communicate to and from distant points and to concentrate on the question, "How can we capitalize on satellites' potential for corporate assignments whose limits we have never fully explored?" Corporations need to know what sights, sounds, and data can be best moved to great distances, at great speed, and with beneficial results.

While the use of satellites by the business world is increasing for the presentation of a growing array of special events and programs, the entertainment industry still occupies the role of the most familiar user. Shows on premium TV channels accommodating HBO, Cinemax, Showtime, The Movie Channel, and Cable News Network, to name but a few, are most often mentioned as regular programming fare made possible by satellites. Yet, a wide variety of spot and special TV programming is also so handled. An example is the Olympics, seen worldwide as the events occur. Further, *The Wall Street Journal* and *USA Today* are electronically transmitted during the dark hours of the morning to scattered printing plants around the United States.

Without satellites such wondrous achievements through the skies would be impossible.

Efficient laser beams, lightweight fiber optic cables, and other incredible developments are stirring a fresh revolution in communications transmission, but the heavenly birds 22,300 miles away are the most amazing and challenging creatures of all. And they have only just begun to stake out their promising role.

How, one wonders, did the phenomenal concept originate? In 1945, a British science-fiction writer, Arthur C. Clarke was, in effect, the inventor of the concept. In an obscure trade magazine called *Wireless World,* Clarke proposed an idea rooted in Sir Isaac Newton's eighteenth-century formulation of the law of gravity. Clarke suggested the establishment in the heavens of a fixed instrument that would be at a point just beyond the gravitational force of the earth. He suggested, "Why not catapult from the earth such an instrument, through rocket power, to a precise point 22,300 miles upward as its home base?"

From the start, Clarke referred to the proposed device as "a communications satellite in geostationary orbit" traveling around the earth once every 24 hours and, hence, remaining constantly stationary over any one point of the earth's surface. By staying in one position over the equator as if it were on top of a long flagpole, such a satellite would, Clarke declared, allow the earth's inhabitants to zero in on such a fixed object for the development of a revolutionary new branch of science. Clarke also observed that it would be possible to cover a little more than one-third of the earth's surface if beams would be transmitted from a single satellite. He further postulated, "If we could launch three equidistant satellites, we could have a worldwide communications system for all nations to share."

Arthur C. Clarke was no casual dreamer. Noted for technological plausibility in his early science-fiction stories on the exploration of other worlds and in his detailed descriptions of space travel, Clarke had already gained a unique stature. Later on, in the sixties, he collaborated with Stanley Kubrick, the motion picture director, to author the screenplay for the award-winning film, "2001—A Space Odyssey."

Have "Star Wars"-type authors turning out best sellers been prolific in discovering concepts of new scientific principles? If Clarke had not suggested communications satellites in 1945, would not the concept ultimately have occurred in the minds of others, especially those in the Soviet science community that has long been captivated by the wonders and challenges of outer space? Such questions are speculative. Clarke's vision, on the other hand, led to reality as his concept was enthusiastically accepted by the scientific community. In 1955, Clarke authored a more detailed proposal, sparking new interest and new inquiry.

Formalization came in 1962 from the United States with the passage by Congress and the signing into law by President Kennedy of the Communications Satellite Act. Comsat, a stockholder-owned corporation, was formed in the following year. Dr. S. J. Campanella, who is currently vice president and chief scientist for Comsat, and Robert W. Hunter, Comsat's director of public relations, have been helpful to the Dartnell project by outlining, in simple language, the highlights of a complicated and fascinating real-life investigative adventure.

In 1964 and 1965 there were two historic American launchings. The first involved the formation of joint venture, called Intelsat, with 11 countries for the purpose of developing a global commercial satellite system. The second entailed using rocket power to put a 3½-foot-by-2½-foot satellite called "Early Bird" into orbit. Both the organizational and the operational accomplishments were legitimate firsts. By early 1987, Intelsat's satellites and 180 international earth stations had developed a global network for transmitting and receiving microwaves carrying telephone, teletypewriter, data, facsimile, radio, and television communications. Comsat's ownership of Intelsat now is approximately 23 percent. Intelsat is responsible for nonmilitary satellite operations around the world, excluding the Soviet bloc organization called Inter-sputnik.

Comsat currently identifies its heaviest communications traffic as including 1) telephone and telex, 2) electronic data transfer, 3) facsimile transfer, 4) television programming, and 5) business meetings through teleconferencing.

Are costs high? The answer to this question lies in a comparison: For commercial transmission of live television across the Atlantic Ocean in 1965 via the pioneering Early Bird, the Intelsat fee was $22,350 for one hour. Since then the charge has been reduced almost 80 percent to $5,100.

Providing a larger dimension are the following items:

- A recent joint venture, modeled after Intelsat, is the International Maritime Satellite Organization (Inmarsat). It provides worldwide maritime communications. Nearly 7,000 ships and offshore facilities use Inmarsat services. Ships and rigs are normally equipped with an above-deck antenna that is automatically stabilized to maintain communications with a particular satellite.

- When Arthur C. Clarke recently spoke by satellite to a National Press Club audience in Washington, D.C., from his home in Colombo, Sri Lanka, he was asked on an audio channel if there were any important new trends in his branch of science. The father of the communications satellite concept replied by announcing the newly developed "earth station in a suitcase." Clarke described the invention of Comsat Tele-

Systems, Inc., as being actually two user-friendly suitcases containing a small dish antenna and all the other elements needed for transmitting an "uplink" to the nearest satellite and onward to virtually anywhere in the world. The earth station-in-a-suitcase is small enough to be checked as luggage on a commercial airliner or stowed in the trunk of a car.

- At the start of 1987, more than 170 nations and territories were interconnected by 16 Intelsat satellites on 1,800 direct antenna-to-antenna pathways. Uplinks and downlinks in such a network were becoming commonplace in a world where a few short years ago such accomplishment was unimaginable.

- Dr. Joseph V. Charyk, former CEO of Comsat, has been quoted as follows: "I think few among us ever imagined how mankind would change as a result of the 23-inch-high, 85-pound cylinder in the sky and its more than 100 successors. When Frank Stanton was president of CBS, he singled out the communications satellite for comment and said, 'The mountains have been leveled and the oceans have been dried up through an 85-pound piece of scientific jewelry transmitting a six-watt signal.'"

- What gives the celestial satellites their power beyond six watts? Answer: thousands of silicon solar cells up where the sun is bright. The outer skin of a new state-of-the-art satellite is covered with 16,852 solar cells providing 500 watts of power for an average life cycle of seven years.

- In view of NASA's problems with the shuttle tragedy early in 1986 and with the later failures in launching Titan and Delta rockets, will there be sufficient blast-off power at Vandenberg Air Force Base, California, or

Cape Canaveral, Florida, for sending new satellites into orbit via disposable rockets or other lift-off vehicles? The answer in part is that Comsat has a contract with NASA and both organizations are optimistic over the long haul. Also, Hughes Aircraft, long-time manufacturer of actual satellites, has disclosed a plan to develop rocket boosters by the early 1990s. Perhaps more to the point is that, in addition to the U.S., 23 (at the last count) other countries have successfully sent commercial communications satellites in geosynchronous orbit. Most of those countries have readily available satellite price lists today for global hopscotching of communications signals in case any customer wants to lease time for transmission to almost everywhere in the world. And don't overlook the 16 Intelsat birds still functioning up there.

Considering the triumph of the U.S. in having put the first man on the moon and the additional accomplishment of having launched the pioneering Early Bird satellite, the hiatus resulting from 1986 failures looms all the more tragic, as political, military, and business needs are forced to mark time, to some extent awaiting Comsat's return to a program of full activity.

Apart from political, military, and business requirements, a philosophical view also seems germane. Recently, when Irving Goldstein succeeded Dr. Joseph V. Charyk as Comsat CEO, Goldstein discussed the role of satellites in world culture. He said, *"Communications is the first step in understanding.* Potentially contentious differences can be kept from getting worse. Physical distance between nations alone no longer can be blamed for the birth of disharmonies. When, for example, billions of people view an Olympic Games telecast on their television sets, brought to them by the Intelsat system, there is the possibility that many of those people will feel some sense of the common connections of all humankind."

On a more pragmatic level, there is concern voiced by some observers regarding the financial fate of Comsat and its affiliated companies that, unlike NASA and other tax-supported enterprises, comprise a high-visibility corporation with 2,660 employees and with listing on the New York Stock Exchange. As any Comsat stockholder would attest, profitability is the name of the game, romance of the enterprise notwithstanding. It is natural for the stockholder to wonder: How have revenues been holding up?

Recent Comsat profit-and-loss statements have been modest but the long-term potential seems encouraging. Some interesting, business-oriented examples follow.

• In 1984, Comsat entered into a joint venture with Holiday Inns to provide a private, satellite-based communications network capable of linking 1,500 Holiday Inn locations nationwide. The network's early use involved transmitting in-room video entertainment but its capabilities—including and transcending entertainment—encompass the promising field of telecommunications. There is, of course, no problem in setting up satellite services enabling corporations to have sales meetings, for example, at multiple sites. Thus telecommunications provides a company with the opportunity to beam out a presentation to thousands of employees simultaneously or, if circumstances so dictate, to a few dozen or a few hundred colleagues scattered at diverse sites or assembled in one meeting place. In addressing the joint venture with Holiday Inns, Comsat has told its stockholders that "over a 10-year period, the network is expected to generate approximately $400 million in revenues."

- J. C. Penney Company, Inc., is another Comsat customer, having used satellites not only for employee communications but also in experimenting with a concept that would "bring the goods to the merchandisers rather than bringing the merchandisers to the goods." Consider this problem: J. C. Penney, which is divided into 54 districts and five regions, frequently sends out some 60 merchandising specialists who select women's fashions for their areas. Visiting New York and other apparel centers several times a year for stretches as long as two weeks, these traveling buyers and their shopping assignments represent a costly expense item. Yet their activity is crucial to Penney's ability to order appropriate apparel for each locale.

    Could not some of this out-of-town visitation be handled by satellite transmission enabling buyers to see the merchandise by remote control? This was the question that Penney's New York headquarters posed to a company called Private Satellite Network (PSN), which is in the business of packaging satellite programs to fit the needs of a customer. A pilot program, handled by PSN, was a sensible way to start. In the course of the first, experimental uses of the satellite system at 14 J. C. Penney locations, much was learned. "More close-up detail is required" was a comment from some viewers at the 14 locations who cooperated in judging the adequacy of the new system. "Cut down on the time required to view merchandise from afar and don't parade the new fashions for eight hours at a stretch" was another recommendation. The experiment continues. Later it may include buyers of men's and children's apparel and home furnishings. Particularly for merchandise that is sensitive to new styles and new trends, ordering by satellite holds great promise.

- Merrill Lynch, Pierce, Fenner & Smith, Inc., also used

the services of PSN after sampling the wonders of outer-space transmission when it linked its New York, London, and Bern (Switzerland) headquarters offices. Communications among employee groups and programs for potential customers have increased since Merrill Lynch became a user. The newest hookup involves a private television network for institutional investors. In addition, the globe-spanning organization has started a regular program called Action Line for some of its branch offices. The company paved the way as far back as 1975 when it established facilities to produce videotapes for distribution to all offices. A microwave dish now sits atop the company's downtown headquarters building. From there, signals are broadcast to PSN's uplink in New York's midtown area.

- Hewlett-Packard Company, headquartered in Palo Alto, California, is a $5 billion company whose 79,000 employees are dispersed at locations around the U.S. and in 70 foreign countries. With such statistics and with the need to check with staff personnel regularly, it is not surprising that Hewlett-Packard proudly calls itself "the first American corporation to hold regularly scheduled teleconferences," which it calls videoconferences, via satellite. Hewlett-Packard began its teleconferencing program by engaging the services of VideoStar Connections, Inc., of Atlanta, which calls itself "The Satellite Networking Company." Starting with extensive planning sessions back in 1981, Hewlett-Packard adopted the objective of communicating regularly with employees at 300 field locations. Management stated, "We are searching for better ways to train personnel and to communicate with widely dispersed divisions, subsidiaries, and affiliates." Currently, the company has two-way live video capabilities for small conferences involving several sites and has one-way live video—with occasional audio response for reaching thousands of employees at other receiving sites. Joseph Schoendorf, director of marketing for the California company's technical computers, recently recalled the excitement that prevailed when Hewlett-Packard produced a three-hour live program to introduce new products to British employees gathered at receiving facilities in London.

"Every 20 minutes we stopped the formal presentation to permit questions. We kept an open phone line between Palo Alto and London the entire time so there would be no delays," Schoendorf said. Reporting on the interest generated by this venture, the marketing director said, "That satellite conference was one of the most motivational experiences the London office ever had. Actually, that program was so successful that we decided to expand our next conference to Paris, Amsterdam, Geneva, and Frankfurt. I think a live satellite conference is probably the most effective tool I've ever used."Robert Knapp, program manager for training in Hewlett-Packard's corporate engineering department at Palo Alto, added, "Ultimately, our dream is to have a 'university of the air' that would devote one morning every two to four weeks to a particular subject of interest to our engineering force. The possibilities are endless."

• The VideoStar organization in Atlanta can point to some significant accomplishments in recent years, often using interactive (two-way) TV in its hookups. It broke new ground in 1985 when it used satellite relays to stage teleconferences for the Airline Pilots Association (ALPA) prior to a threatened strike by pilots, flight attendants, and mechanics. In meetings at the Odeum Center near Chicago, a total of 13,000 strike bound workers participated prior to the start of a month-long walkout. ALPA officers referred to teleconferencing by satellite as "a unification tool."

- More recently, VideoStar handled the details for Chase Manhattan Bank's gathering of 2,500 employees in eight countries for a live interactive sharing of perspectives by colleagues from around the world.

- In March 1986, VideoStar hooked together employees of 650 ComputerLand stores in the U.S. and Canada. In December 1985 Eastman Kodak Company used a three-hour satellite teleconference to train sales and marketing personnel in the operation and applications of new software products. Previously, these employees had been flown into Rochester for training. The time and money saved by communicating the new way was substantial. Point-to-multipoint teleconferencing is growing so rapidly that it is difficult to keep up with the big, new strides. Ultimately, employees and customers will be the principal target audiences.

In the field of internal communications, motivational programs and training sessions stand out most prominently as areas with potential. Here's an anecdote concerning pioneering days that may become memorable. Last year when a New York City police officer complained to VideoStar that its trailer was extending too far into Park Avenue, VideoStar engineers got hold of several hacksaws and in a short time they lopped six inches off the trailer rather than interrupt a downlink program in progress. Even in a new medium, teleconferencing by satellite, "The show must go on."

It would be unfortunate if some young man or woman flirting with public relations as a career, or currently at an entry-level position at a corporation or agency, would say, "What's the big fuss? How do relays by satellites apply to my little role in the scheme of things? How is my task as editor of a routine newsletter affected by glamour of teleconferencing?"

The relevancy of satellite communications might not be obvious, yet all who have employee communications in their daydreams will probably be star-gazing toward new vehicles for information. Indeed, those who study all channels of communications—from lowly bulletin boards to exotic electronic birds in the sky—will be nourished and rewarded for their curiosity by new knowledge and thirst to learn more.

It is easy to remember the early fifties when computers came on the scene for data processing chores and when a number of forward-looking people in business were opportunistic enough to decide to investigate, and to learn, so they would be ready for the new era. Similarly, when videotape was still a toy at Ampex Research's laboratories in Los Angeles, struggling to be sharper and clearer than kinescope TV copies, some pioneer-spirited business people decided to acquaint themselves with the emerging technology so they too would be prepared for the new era.

Perhaps the day will come when corporate newsletters will be directly supplemented by satellite programs, giving a new dimension to employee communications. Perhaps issues aired in internal print media on Monday will be explored in interactive teleconferences on Tuesday.

Clearly, satellites are the newest man-made stars in the firmament. Inescapably, despite their far-away distance, they'll take photos of the new Ajax office building going up at the corner of Fourth and Elm—through infrared or whatever new device comes on the scene. So-called spy satellites have already been reported in news media. Man's curiosity will always lead to fresh investigations, new information programs, more progress—hopefully with accord and unity predominating in each, new successive era. Indeed, communicators will be crucially needed in the forward years. (Note: Southwestern Bell Corporation's million-dollar TV extravaganza, beamed by satellite for employee gatherings at 57 locations, is discussed on the following pages.)

# Southwestern Bell Enters Divestiture

Despite enlightened anticipation and year-long prepara- tion, discombobulation prevailed in January of 1984 when American Telephone and Telegraph Company (AT&T) and its wholly owned subsidiaries set in motion the so- called divestiture plan agreed upon by the United States Department of Justice and the Bell System. Even business scholars who had braced for the anticipated shock waves were overwhelmed by the magnitude of the upheavel. Never in corporate history had such a mighty transformation oc- curred. Indeed, today reverberating consequences continue to be felt.

As will be recalled, AT&T and its 21 operating compa- nies, historic custodians of "more or less monopoly status," were suddenly supplanted by eight newly formed organiza- tions, namely the seven independent regional entities and a reconstructed AT&T. All seven regional entities confront- ed the opportunity of getting into any businesses they fa- vored. AT&T, on the other hand, ceased being Ma Bell and became a competitor-customer-supplier of its seven now- independent offspring, reducing the AT&T product and de- velopment mix mainly to long-distance service, computers, and Bell Laboratories.

More than a million employees of the old Ma Bell were affected worldwide. This narrative concentrates on only one part of the total epic, namely Southwestern Bell Corpo- ration, with headquarters in St. Louis and with 98,000 em- ployees in Missouri, Arkansas, Oklahoma, Texas, and Kan- sas. In the new era, Southwestern Bell's core group of services and products includes the local telephone business; Yellow Pages and Silver Pages directories in major cities, plus printing, graphics, and design services; mobile systems, including celular telephones and pagers; and a wide variety of telecommunications equipment for sale or lease.

What is it like to work for a company that was recreated by government decree? What toll did regrouping take? What personnel changes and organizational adjustments were required? What new opportunities beckoned on a new horizon?

Two classic examples, both in the area of employee communications, merit review. The first involved a live TV show that was seen simultaneously by 75,000 of the company's 98,000 employees in five states. Staged shortly after the divestiture became official, the show cost almost a million dollars to produce and was, the company said, the largest corporate broadcast in history. Entitled "Celebrate the Spirit," the production was beamed by satellite from Kiel Opera House in St. Louis to 57 locations, where employees saw the proceedings at auditoriums and in hotel ballrooms equipped with large-screen projection television—plus locally catered refreshments.

At the start of the performance, musicians and dancers were in place on the stage when a loud voice asked, "What do you do when a hundred years of tradition are overturned?" And the answer came loud and clear from the master of ceremonies, "What do you do? You throw a party."

And what a party it was.

VideoStar Connections, Inc., of Atlanta handled all the satellite transmission arrangements and local technical details and Creative Establishment, Inc., of Chicago handled the programming. The star and number one cheerleader of the pep rally was Zane E. Barnes, Southwestern Bell's chairman of the board, whose objective was simple: to create a unifying spirit and to help get the newly transformed company off to a high-spirited start. "A mere divestiture is not the end of the world" was the show's theme. Barnes intoned, "We're embarked on a great new adventure." Helping such a message resound was pops singer Crystal Gale, backed up by the Belltones (an employee chorus of 80), dancers, musicians, and assorted stage effects—all seen and heard live by employees in 57 cities.

Why did Southwestern Bell opt for a satellite spectacular? "Traditional media would never have worked" was the feeling in Southwestern Bell's public relations ranks.

The second classic example had less hoopla but it also involved communicating effectively with employees. It was a planning memorandum for a high-impact, liberally illustrated internal magazine that the company hoped would motivate, inform, and uplift all 98,000 employees throughout the five-state system. Entitled "A Post-Divestiture Strategy for Southwestern Bell's Corporate Magazine," the public relations staff's planning memorandum stood out—and still stands out—as Exhibit A in comprehensive craftmanship.

Proposing an annual budget of $529,000 for four issues a year, the planning document was not so much a study in the mechanics of communications but was, rather, a study on the likely effects and consequences of an all-out effort to keep employees informed on issues, problems, opportunities, products, services, policies, strategies, and general operations of a "Fortune Top 50" establishment.

The planning memorandum follows:

**Overview.** With different names and formats, Southwestern Bell has had a corporate magazine for nearly 80 years.

Over those years, the magazine has become the company's flagship publication. It is the only Southwestern Bell medium which reaches all employees, active and retired. It has earned high readership and many awards for corporate journalism.

Throughout its life, the magazine has reflected the basic characteristics of its corporate sponsor:

• A major company with strictly defined service area.

- Operating as a regulated utility.

- With (more or less) monopoly status.

*The fact that these basic characteristics change with divestiture signals the need for change in the corporate magazine's strategy and purpose.*

In a fluid environment in which employees hunger for information, the corporate magazine should lead in setting new values and directions.

Changes in the magazine's target audience, content, and design will help it assume this leadership role and support the corporation during transformation.

Throughout its history, the corporate magazine has targeted nonmanagement and first-level managers as its primary audience. The rationale was simple. A fundamental purpose of the magazine was to support service and policy changes. People in the target audience drove service quality and implemented policy.

*Today we face a new, compelling need—to promote entrepreneurial behavior in the corporation, risk taking, cost management, and aggressive leadership.*

The potential (or need) for entrepreneurial behavior does not reside in one neat demographic category. Entrepreneurialism is an individual quality that exists throughout the employee population, as clearly indicated in divestiture research. To nurture and promote its expression, the magazine should focus not on a particular segment but on those individuals everywhere in the organization who can help the corporation the most through their entrepreneurial behavior.

The *strategy,* then, is to focus the magazine on those who can most benefit the corporation—the Southwestern Bell entrepreneurs.

Our *objective* will be to help create a climate that promotes entrepreneurial behaviors such as risk taking and cost management. The objective, in short, is to motivate behavior which produces bottom-line results.

The corporate magazine's role in fashioning this climate or corporate culture will be to:

- Provide a clear sense of direction and corporate mission.

- Explain desired behaviors in concept and practice.

- Link individual and corporate self-interest in entrepreneurial behavior create "entrepreneurial heroes."

Of all media, the corporate magazine is most fitting for this role. It is well established as the company's showcase for value and policy elaboration. And its inherent advantages of format—color and large graphic display—suit it well for this task.

We will work with public relations planning to design research to measure performance. *If the magazine cannot be proven to be effective, it should be altered or discontinued.*

**Secondary audiences.** As in the past, the primary audience for the new corporate magazine will be employees, active and retired, of the entire corporation (including subsidiaries).

However, the new book's entrepreneurial focus would convey *important messages to external publics* which we could capitalize on at *extremely low marginal cost.*

The present relatively small external distribution (approximately 2,000) could be expanded selectively through offers to target audiences we consider appropriate.

This selective offer could take the form of a magazine with cover letter introducing the book and its purpose. The recipient would return a postpaid card to continue receiving the magazine. Annual follow-up tests would ensure that readers wanted to receive the magazine and that our dollars were well spent.

Additional benefits could be realized through personalized offers.

- For example, executive shareowners (holding more than a specified number of shares) could be offered the magazine by their designated contact.

- CR managers could supply lists for the magazine (following guidelines furnished by us) and sign personalized cover letters.

- Investor relations managers could do the same with financial community contacts.

**Content strategy.** Over the last decade the corporate magazine has become increasingly issue-oriented as the business has become more complex. Still, magazine content has reflected the reality of a wholly owned, regional company.

With this reality changing, so should the content of the corporate magazine.

Several points seem essential.

In addition to content changes suggested by the strategy of keying on entrepreneurial employees, the new corporate magazine should mirror clearly the company's new independence, Fortune top 50 status, and broadened horizons.

This does not mean that our regional base is ignored. It means the new magazine should adopt a broader scope and deal more with national issues. For example, it means the magazine should deal more with Wall Street and its influence on the corporation and employee shareowners. It means the magazine should follow more closely national issues—political, economic, and social—which affect our business.

In short, the *scope of interest of the magazine should reflect the broadened scope of interest of its corporate sponsor.* From the content alone, employees should perceive clearly that their business is a concern with national interest.

The implicit message in the new magazine's broader outlook will be that employees, too, should expand their scope of thinking.

In addition to an enlarged scope, the new magazine's content should be perceived as *information on which people can act.*

We will seek out opportunities to relate policy to clear action employees can take. And we will develop items that actively involve the reader. For example, self-appraisal tests, pieces to clip out and save, coupons to mail in for further information, and articles that solicit employee response.

In addition to adding perceived value to the publication, the intent of these action-oriented materials is to communicate the personal involvement in the corporation desired and expected from employee readers.

Finally, and obviously, *high credibility is essential* if content is to be effective. To strengthen the perception of credibility, we will work to develop a creative edge to content. Frank self-analysis, recognition of setbacks, and commentary by outside antagonists all could help achieve the credibility we need.

As difficult as self-criticism is in corporate journalism, the price for a credibility gap is too high. Also, productive self-analysis is itself an attribute of the entrepreneurial culture we work to create.

(Proposed content outlines for the first two issues of the new magazine will be submitted later.) The two basic areas the magazine will work to strengthen are:

• The positive perception of the company and its future.

• The positive perception of the employee's individual ability to contribute toward the company's goals and thereby achieve personal goals.

To build employee belief in these fundamental points, magazine content will deliver these messages:

- The company has and is developing the products and services to be successful in the marketplace, and top management has the will and aggressiveness to take advantage of market opportunities.
- The company is fully prepared to take intelligent risks.
- Cost management and the need to work toward being the low cost provider are essential to success.
- Service is as important now as in the past; individualized service is what marketing is all about.
- The company will continue to be an excellent place to work—due to its wages, benefits, job security, equal opportunity, and the availability of chances for advancement.
- There is an effective, systematic process for determining our course of action.
- There is a direct connection between individual success and corporate success.

**Examples of generic articles.** To develop the messages, certain generic articles will be used. Following are some examples.

Message:  The company has and is developing the products and services to be successful in the marketplace, and top management has the will and aggressiveness to take advantage of market opportunities.

Generic article:  Viewpoint pieces on entrepreneurial market plans by selected officers.
Interviews with corporate directors which demonstrate their personal strengths and their reasons for confidence in Southwestern Bell.

Message:  Cost management and the need to work toward being the low cost provider are essential to success.

Generic article:  Examples of demonstrably successful cost management practices and the individuals who conceived the ideas.

Message:  Service is as important now as in the past; individualized services is what marketing is all about.

Generic article:  Customer testimonials on our individual attention to their particular service needs.

Message: There is an effective, systematic process for determining our course of action.

Generic article: Description of the process and thinking that produced a major sale.

Description of the means by which strategic planners choose among market opportunities.

Message: There is a direct connection between individual success and corporate success.

Generic article: Profiles of fast-track entrepreneurial performers that demonstrate the link between individual and corporate success (and the link between entrepreneurial behavior and success). Coverage of incentive program award winners and description of their thought processes in producing award-winning ideas.

**Design strategy.** Over the years the Southwestern Bell magazine has won a number of design and photography awards. It has had a look of quality.

Still, much as with its content, the magazine has had a regional company look. Its design has been informal, relating to a particular story more than a total concept.

Just as the company becomes an independent, Fortune top 50 corporation January 1, the magazine, too, should be independent of past design and look like the publication of an aggressive, successful and well-planned business.

In practical terms, this means the new corporate magazine should have a more sophisticated tone and design. It means adoption of a total *design concept applied to all content.*

This change will be another message to employees that their corporation understands and seeks quality.

**Frequency of publication.** Budget constraints require an end to monthly publication in 1984.

We propose a *quarterly publication schedule in 1984.* If research results prove positive, this schedule could be stepped up to bimonthly in 1985. [Author's note: No step-up occurred.] In 1984, this reduced publication schedule should be positioned for what it is—one more effort to reduce corporate expenses. At the same time, the company's continuing commitment to employee information should be made clear.

530

**Budget—force and expense.** Recent cuts in the publications force and expense budgets will make the success of the magazine more challenging, but these obstacles can be overcome. However, it is imperative that its staff writers be among the department's most talented.

We have $529,000 budgeted for the 1984 magazine, per agreement with the states. This represents a 23 percent reduction from 1983.

**Summary.** After nearly 80 years, Southwestern Bell's corporate magazine still has a role to play in the communications mix, but a radically different one. As the corporation must change, the magazine must be transformed to meet entirely new needs.

This careful advance analysis of an employee magazine, with its new requirements, was a forerunner of the 1984 divestiture.

When the new publication comes into being, it will be appropriately named *Enterprise*.

# Boise Cascade Faces the Facts

Boise Cascade Corporation, headquartered in Boise, Idaho, is a forest products company producing paper, packaging materials, office supplies, and building materials. Noted especially for its management of timberland resources, the company has assets exceeding $3 billion. Its employee count exceeds 2,000. Thanks to Alice E. Hennessey, senior vice president of corporate relations, an insider's view of the corporation was made available for inclusion in this handbook, reflecting the no-nonsense attitude necessarily prevailing during the past several years when the economic crunch intensified.

Two items in particular are noteworthy: 1) an idealistic statement on employer-employee interdependence, and 2) a no-holds-barred letter from the chairman of the board.

The interdependence statement advances the hoped-for mutual commitments between the company and its workers. The statement follows:

The company has a responsibility to:

- Value the individual dignity, worth, and rights of our people.

- Recognize that each person has special knowledge and skills and brings to the job unique abilities and experience.
    Treat our people fairly and provide equal opportunity to all employees.

- Encourage our employees' initiative, challenge their individual capabilities, and build pride in the quality of their work.

- Provide our employees with the opportunity to work at their highest levels of performance and fill positions from within the company whenever practical.

- Encourage employees to help determine their performance goals and participate in the candid evaluation of their performance.

- Reward performance fairly.

- Provide training, promote continuing education, and support problem-solving attitudes.

- Maintain an atmosphere of mutual trust and openness.

- Promote knowledge and understanding of Boise Cascade, tell people how their work contributes to the company's success, encourage open communications at all levels throughout the company, and involve employees in work-related decisions.

- Encourage our employees to be good citizens, to participate in the democratic process according to their individual beliefs, and to work toward the improvement of their communities.

Each of us has a responsibility to:

- Perform to the best of our ability.

- Maintain the highest ethical standards in dealing with other employees, customers, suppliers, competitors, government representatives, the general public, and the company itself.

- Avoid any work related conflict of interest.

- Sharpen and expand our job-related skills and abilities.

- Take proper care of all company resources within our control, whether they're physical property, financial capital, raw materials, supplies, or important information.

With the economic crunch hitting corporations across the land, Boise Cascade was not exempted. It would be difficult to estimate how many organizations have been suffering economic ailments during the past few years. Because of external conditions over which the companies have little or no control, because of unrelenting domestic and foreign competition, and because of—or despite—restructuring or other internal adjustments, companies have been required to ask employees to understand and cooperate in sharing the sacrifices, and to work a little harder, longer, and better.

To be sure CEOs don't enjoy sending somber letters to their employees. Prompted, however, by their fundamental responsibilities to shareowners, many thousands of CEOs have found it necessary to "lay it on the line" in recent times.

John B. Fery, Boise Cascade's chairman and CEO, fulfilled his responsibilities—admirably—in the message he sent to Boise Cascade employees.

The following letter can serve as a model in the art of "levelling" under duress.

> To Boise Cascade Employees:
>
> I need your help in further reducing Boise Cascade's cost of doing business.
>
> As you know, conditions have been difficult in the forest products business since 1980; and more recently, conditions have also been becoming more difficult for Office Products Distribution and Consumer Packing. In recent years we have made considerable progress in cutting costs, but at the same time, our operating environment has changed. Boise Cascade and its U.S. employees must continue to demand that the U.S. government slash the federal deficit—thereby lessening pressure on interest rates, allowing the value of the dollar to come into better balance with foreign currencies, and dramatically improving our business climate as our products again become competitive. But the problems in our economic environment will not be corrected overnight.
>
> Therefore, we must improve the company's performance by operating more efficiently. We *must* intensify our efforts to *cut costs* if we're to compete successfully in this very tough economic environment. Success in our productivity improvement and employee involvement efforts has demonstrated that the best ideas come from employees closest to the day-to-day work of the organization. Therefore, each unit is encouraged to solicit ideas and suggestions from employees through our normal employee involvement processes as to areas where cost savings may be implemented and to promptly put into practice those ideas and suggestions with a constructive application. We need to lower our costs of producing, distributing, and selling our products and the costs of providing staff support for these activities. But we need to do this while maintaining our emphasis on providing high-quality products and service to our customers. We must have all Boise Cascadians working toward the common goal of dramatically lowering our overall cost of doing business. Here are some steps our management group has already decided we must take:

**Hiring freeze.** Effective immediately, a hiring freeze is being imposed companywide. When vacancies leave work that must be done, to the extent possible responsibilities will be shifted within that unit. When this is not possible, specific approval of the appropriate group or staff senior vice president, or the president in the case of the Transportation and Distribution Department, will be required.

**Streamlining operations and staff.** The company has made tremendous strides in the past few years in streamlining its organization, accomplishing its mission with fewer people and eliminating unnecessary or redundant functions. We intend to continue with this effort to achieve further efficiencies. We will do all we can through attrition, but there will also be selective reductions in employment levels throughout the company.

**Salaries and wages.** Numerous of the company's competitors have taken action to curtail, freeze, or roll back salaries of all or part of their salaried work force. In view of the salary actions being initiated by our competitors and others in American industry and considering the economic situation facing us, we anticipate there will be little or no upward adjustment of the salary range structure of our salary administration program for 1986. Because of the actions being taken by our competitors and considering the economic situation, we do not believe increases for salaried employees, including management and executive officers, other than to correct serious inequities, will be justified through 1986. Nevertheless, we are confident that our salaries overall will continue to be competitive and will compensate employees fairly. This is the underlying philosophy of our salary administration program. The compensation of our hourly work force also will be carefully reviewed in light of the specific competitive and economic situations facing each of our operations. Where high labor costs prevent us from competing effectively, we must move to bring the costs into line. Of course, we will honor all our collective bargaining agreements, but as those agreements are renegotiated, the company will seek wage rates, benefit packages and work rules that will be fair to our employees but which will permit us to be a vigorous competitor.

**Capital spending.** We have reviewed our capital program for 1986 and will reduce our spending to the extent practical. This step will help ensure that we maintain a strong and flexible financial position.

**Management of our fee-owner timberlands.** We are reviewing our silvicultural programs as well as the level of our annual harvest and will modify these to the extent practical in order to reduce the company's costs. This will be done after giving careful consideration to our long-term forest management needs.

**Training.** Some training activities will be curtailed for the immediate future. However, other training activities are even more important during adverse economic times. Therefore, training activities should be carefully reviewed, but those activities deemed of critical importance to the success of the unit or of the company should *not* be curtailed.

**Travel.** All employees are asked to carefully review travel plans and to curtail all trips that are not absolutely necessary. All other travel and entertainment expenses must be carefully reviewed and reduced to the maximum extent practical.

**College and university recruiting.** With a hiring freeze in place, our recruiting activities will necessarily be reduced. However, we do wish to maintain some relationship with those colleges and universities which are key to our future recruiting activities and our long- term success. In addition, it will be necessary to add some individuals with critical skills, even during this period of economic difficulties. But we will be visiting fewer campuses and doing minimal hiring.

**Information systems.** We will defer or eliminate information systems projects which are not critically needed or which do not have an immediate, attractive return on our investment in software and hardware.

**Trade and other association activities.** Membership in trade and other associations by the company or company personnel is being reviewed by senior management. Some memberships will be curtailed or discontinued. Our participation in some associations will be reduced. Employees are asked to limit as much as practical their attendance at meetings of those trade and other associations in which membership is retained.

**Contributions.** We recognize our responsibilities as a good corporate citizen of the communities in which we do business. Accordingly, we will continue to support the United Way campaign in those communities, to pay our pledges, to support some level of educational matching gifts, and to fund a minimal number of additional projects, but the overall level of our contributions program will be reduced to the maximum extent practical.

These are difficult times we face, but I have every confidence that if we carry out these measures with the dedication andenthusiasm that we're known for, we can improve the company's performance and competitive position. We *must* do this if Boise Cascade is to remain the vigorous company it is today. Your cooperations is essential, and I know I can count on you to do your part.

Sincerely,

(Signed)
John B. Fery
Chairman and CEO

# Dow Chemical Stresses Wellness

There's a thin line between corporate paternalism and corporate concern for the well-being of employees. Particularly in what the labor movement called the "union-busting days" of the thirties, many employers appealed to their employees with such declarations of dependence as, "We are all members of the same family."

The steel and coal industries often provided company-owned housing for employees. There was also a company store and, later, a credit union for those working in the mills and mines. In West Virginia, visiting preachers were brought in for Sunday services. A school for the workers' children and clinics for the whole family were established.

Regardless of dependence on paychecks, today's employees seem to prefer a judicious mixture of dependence and independence, whether they are unionized or not. Speeches in July 1986 at the Statue of Liberty confirmed this sentiment through references to freedom and liberty characterizing the blessings of a nation and reflecting the dignity and respect for workers across the land.

How far does a company go in reaching into the lives and homes of employees? Is personal privacy violated when a corporation reaches out to be benevolent, perhaps beyond need?

The health of employees is an area of concern for all. Does a corporation have the right to try to keep members of its workforce trim and thin and hale and hearty, and free from cigarettes, drugs, and alcohol? As long as a company doesn't try to impose unwanted wellness standards on employees and as long as health programs are primarily optional, the company is not meddling in the personal lives of their employees.

Dow Chemical U.S.A., Midland, Michigan, provides a constructive example. It has recently started the publication of a monthly newsletter for employees called *Up with Life* for the stated purpose of "promoting good health for Dow people."

The inquiry that appears below was extracted from a recent issue of Dow's newsletter. Employees were asked 10 questions about high blood pressure. (The correct answers can be found following the questions.)

1. How many Americans have high blood pressure?
   _____ a. One out of 24.
   _____ b. One out of 18.
   _____ c. One out of 12.
   _____ d. One out of 4.

2. What are the most common symptoms of high blood pressure?
   _____ a. Dizziness.
   _____ b. Headaches.
   _____ c. Heart palpitations.
   _____ d. No symptoms, usually.

3. If you have high blood pressure, how long will you need to follow your treatment plan?
   _____ a. Six months.
   _____ b. One year.
   _____ c. Until the blood pressure is brought down.
   _____ d. Throughout your life.

4. Uncontrolled high blood pressure can cause which of the following problems?
   _____ a. Stroke.
   _____ b. Heart attack.
   _____ c. Kidney failure.
   _____ d. All of the above.

5. Hypertension means—
   _____ a. Being nervous and high-strung.
   _____ b. Feeling very tense.
   _____ c. Having blood pressure that stays higher than normal.
   _____ d. All of the above.

6. Although high blood pressure cannot be cured, it can be controlled with—
    _____ a. Tranquilizers.
    _____ b. Garlic juice daily.
    _____ c. Medications, sodium (salt) control, and weight reduction.
    _____ d. More sleep.

7. How can you tell if your blood pressure is up or down?
    _____ a. By how you feel physically.
    _____ b. By your emotions.
    _____ c. By your pulse rate.
    _____ d. By having your blood pressure checked by a doctor, nurse, or other qualified person.

8. If you have high blood pressure you need to—
    _____ a. Take medications if the doctor prescribes them.
    _____ b. Get your blood pressure checked regularly.
    _____ c. Decrease the amount of sodium (salt) you eat and lose weight if you are overweight.
    _____ d. Do all of the above.

9. Once your high blood pressure medicine has brought your blood pressure down to within the normal range—
    _____ a. You can stop taking your medicine.
    _____ b. You won't need to have your blood pressure checked again.
    _____ c. You will still need to have your blood pressure checked again.
    _____ c. You will still need to take your high blood pressure medicine every day.
    _____ d. You will need to take your medicine only on days when you feel your blood pressure is up again.

10. Who should get their blood pressure measured?
    _____ a. Only persons with high blood pressure.
    _____ b. Everyone, at least once a year.
    _____ c. Only people under constant stress.
    _____ d. All of the above.

## ANSWERS

| 1. d. | 2. d. | 3. d. | 4. d. | 5. c. |
| 6. c. | 7. d. | 8. d. | 9. c. | 10. b. |

The major consideration for employers is to help employees—not to be a meddling Big Brother.

In addition to the quiz, the newsletter contained information on heart attacks, cigarettes, aerobics, cholesterol, and diets. It also had an anecdote about Arturo Toscanini, the legendary symphonic conductor, who once related, "When I was very, very young I kissed my first woman and smoked my first cigarette on the same day. Believe me, I have never wasted any more time on tobacco."

# 3M Hot Line Helps Media and Employees

The around-the-clock emergency hot line between Washington, D.C., and Moscow does not rely on brightly hued telephones, as Hollywood might like movie-goers to believe. Instead, it involves the use of automatic teletype printers at both ends. As suggested elsewhere in the *Handbook*, the printed word is more reliable than the oral word in official communications, and reliability is of crucial importance as far as the U.S.-Soviet hot line is concerned. U.S.-Soviet messages can be translated, encoded and decoded, scrambled and unscrambled. Yet if anything ever goes wrong, it won't be the result of a slip of the tongue because all messages—including regular, routine test messages—are for the eyes to see and not for the ear to hear.

Minnesota Mining & Mfg. Co. (3M) of St. Paul, Minnesota, is not trying to upstage hot-line technology but it is embarking on high-priority communications expertise to provide information speedily to journalists, financial analysts, and others, including 3M's vitally interested employees at hundreds of plant and office locations worldwide.

"The 3M newsroom is the pioneer public relations electronic information source," says David W. Klinger, director of corporate communications. He adds, "It's a computer-access source for new product information, financial news, breaking stories, and technology background—and for providing quick responses for anyone zapping in a question. The new service has kept busy ever since it was inaugurated as an interactive two-way data base."

Newsroom service is available night and day at no cost. The service may be accessed with any standard personal computer or ASC11 terminal equipped with a 300- or 1200-baud modem. Here are the categories on 3M's main menu:

1. System instructions

2. Breaking news

3. Corporate viewpoints and explanations

4. Specialty stories

5. International information

6. Feedback

7. Executive biographies No. 1

8. Executive biographies No. 2

9. Consumer products

10. Graphic products

11. Electronic products

12. Health care products

13. Industrial products

14. Information products

15. Traffic and safety information

16. Logging out

Nonemployees gaining access can ask to get a response on-line, by telephone, or by mail. The same basic computer printout will serve as the source in all responses for employees. Personnel at company locations will find that important general information will be automatically sent to them via the newsroom. They also will be able to send in their own specific queries.

Those who want to get access to the 3M newsroom, which means getting a free, confidential log-in number and password to see how it works, can call 612-733-4339 or 612-736-6420. It's a 24-hour service with peak usage occurring from

10 AM to 2 PM Central Time, when lines are apt to be the busiest. The 3M company is noted for inventiveness. Employees at all levels are encouraged to use their ingenuity. Lewis W. Lehr, who recently retired as chairman and CEO, said, "There has to be an environment here for innovation. We sometimes say to employees, 'If you're not making mistakes, you're probably not doing anything for 3M.'"

# First Chicago Considers Employees' Children

The First National Bank of Chicago, the tenth largest bank in the U.S., known simply as First Chicago, has two skilled communicators who add sparkle to the employee newspaper. They are Adrianne T. Hayward, manager of internal communications, and Diana Williams, editor, both of whom thrive on innovations. In recent issues of their publication, *First Chicagoan*, they have dealt with two interesting questions:

1. At the turn of the century what will college tuition cost for employees' children?

2. When outsiders ask, "Where does your bank stand?" on controversial issues, what answers do employees provide? Because "I don't know" is not an acceptable answer, the bank management accepts the responsibility to furnish pertinent information on a broad range of issues.

The story on tomorrow's tuition is a manifestation of thoughtful preparedness. It not only alerts employees with children to what they will be facing by the end of the century in college expenses but, importantly, it also reflects a caring attitude toward employees. In addition, it demonstrates the bank's emphasis on the importance of economic education. The story follows:

> When your kids are ready for college will *you* be ready? By 1999, four years of college tuition for your son or daughter could cost you nearly $30,000 at a state university and an almost unbelievable $80,000 at a private school. That's projecting an average annual inflation rate of 6 percent.
>
> And these figures are for tuition alone. They don't include such expenses as room and board, books, laboratory fees, clothing, transportation, and incidentals.

When the time comes, will you be able to afford the college education your child deserves? The answer is "yes" if you start putting
money away now under the new First Education Savings Plan. As little as $25 set aside each month can grow to more than $12,000 in 18
years.

You'll want to start with a free Education Savings Analysis that
projects tuition expenses for the four years your child will be attending
college and estimates how much you will need to save—bimonthly,
monthly, or in one lump sum—to meet those expenses. You can prepare your own analysis using the personal computers on the main floor
or in Executive & Professional Banking, IFNP-2. Or, you can pick up a
First Education Savings Plan brochure in one of the banking centers,
complete the "request for Education Savings Analysis" form, and send
the form to Maria Scumas, Suite 0137, 1ND-17. You will receive a detailed, computerized analysis of your needs. Once you've determined
how much you'll need to save to meet your family's education goals,
you can take advantage of two investment alternatives specially designed for the First Education Savings Plan:

A "zero-coupon" CD, a certificate of deposit with a guaranteed return and guaranteed maturity value you select. It's available in maturi-
ties ranging from 5 to 15 years, and depositors are fully insured by the
Federal Deposit Insurance Corporation up to $100,000. You can make
a single deposit whenever you wish.

The education Money Market Account, a First Money Market Account with some very special benefits like bonus interest and an opening deposit requirement of as little as $100. You can make periodic de-
posits to the account through payroll deduction.

Your other investment options under the First Education Savings
Plan are First Investment Series CDs, stocks and bonds purchased
through First Discount Brokerage Service, several Dreyfus-managed
mutual funds, and more. Depending on your needs, you may select a
single investment approach or a combination of investments.

You can even shelter a portion of your income from taxes while saving for your child's education. The Illinois Uniform Gift to Minors Act
allows you to establish an account in your child's name. As savings ac-
cumulate in the account, earnings will be taxed as income to your child
—who, most likely, will start out at the zero percent tax rate. [Note:
With the enactment of new federal income tax legislation, this overall
treatment is no longer the case. Consult the new tax law for changes.]
The investment becomes the property of your child, with you as custo-
dian. Setting up a First Education Savings Plan under the act is simple
matter of completing a short form. There are no fees for opening the

account and no monthly service charges. Whether your children are in diapers or at the bicycle and skinned-knee stage, it's never too early to begin preparing for the day when they'll be college bound. For more information on the First Education Savings Plan, see Mary Jo Downey, 1FNP-Plaza, or call ext. 7-1981.

The second innovation in the employee newspaper also exemplifies the bank's concern for its employees. Realizing that friends and neighbors will be asking employees, "What is your bank's position on this or that public issue?" and sensitive that employees are most comfortable when they are informed, the newspaper often publishes short items under the heading, "Where We Stand." Controversial and timely subjects on matters beyond the walls of the bank are, therefore, interpreted in line with whatever the bank's policies are apt to be.

Here are two examples as they appeared in recent issues of the *First Chicagoan:*

> The issue of South Africa recently has received a great deal of media, and some legislative, attention. This is First Chicago's position on business dealings with South Africa.
>
> We do not do business with the South African government or its agencies, and no such loans are now on our books. Private sector business is done very selectively, only for customers who subscribe to equal employment and affirmative action practices that prohibit discrimination against non-whites in South African facilities.
>
> In addition, the bank does not sell the South African Kruggerand gold coin.

The second example deals with lending to the Soviet Union. It reads as follows:

> First Chicago and a number of other major domestic and international banks have helped arrange two credit facilities for the Bank for Foreign Trade of the U.S.S.R.
>
> The First believes these credits are in the best interests of the United States, the Midwest and our bank. They will facilitate purchases of agricultural goods by the Soviet Union, and that should means income for hardpressed farmers, employment for people in agriculture-dependent industries in the Midwest, and assistance in improving the U.S. balance of trade deficit.

The laws of the United States permit the trade of nonstrategic items with the Soviet Union and Eastern Bloc countries because our nation benefits both economically and politically. And the financing of such trade goes hand in hand with the movement of goods between nations.

Each transaction First Chicago has entered into with the Soviet Union or other Eastern European nations has been fully consistent with American laws.

When it comes to pricing, the bank ensures that every transaction meets market conditions, as well as the bank's own rate-of-return objectives. This is the case whether we are lending to the Soviet Union or to businesses in the United States.

In summary, financial relations with the Soviet Union encourage exports from the United States, including those from the Midwest. This contributes to the strengths of the U.S. economy and the Midwest economy. And it benefits First Chicago because of our strategic emphasis on this region of the country.

# Anheuser-Busch Fosters a Sense of Pride

Not all companies delegate all public relations responsibilities to captive departments, which may or may not employ outside agencies to provide supplementary assistance. Anheuser-Busch Companies, Inc., the successful St. Louis-headquartered brewery, is notably unique: It has no in-house public relations at all and instead, farms out its public relations planning and implementation to an outside counseling organization—even going as far as having agency personnel serve as regular spokesmen for the corporation. Unusual indeed—and all the more surprising considering that otherwise Anheuser-Busch is among the most progressive, professional, successful, and resourceful corporations in the nation.

A recent *Fortune Magazine* survey of 8,000 executives revealed that the St. Louis brewery ranked near the top in the "most admired" category and was also placed near the top in "quality of management." However, Anheuser-Busch does *not* go outside for its *employee* communications programs. It fully appreciates that employees communicating with employees is the time-tested right way to go. Happily, the internal communications operations is refreshingly orthodox, reporting to Carl J. Bolz, the in-house specialist.

The internal communications lineup at Anheuser-Busch is comprehensive. It includes the publication of the following:

1. *The Eagle*—a bimonthly newspaper, in a large format, for employees and retirees. The circulation is approximately 40,000. The stated objectives of *The Eagle* include: Help avoid misinformation and rumor. Recognize outstanding achievements, particularly those demonstrating creativity and ingenuity of individuals, departments, plants and subsidiaries. Create an em-

ployee constituency that will support Anheuser-Busch Companies through legislators and on other public fronts. Foster a sense of pride.

2. *Newsbank*— a modest monthly that is sent to plant managers and to those employees who have the responsibility of producing plant publications. *Newsbank* aptly demonstrates the brewery's recognition of the importance of the "care and feeding" of scattered communicators.

3. *Focus On St. Louis*—a biweekly newsletter for all St. Louis area employees and alumni, with a circulation of 8,000. St. Louis is, after all, the traditional home of Budweiser, as well as the home of the brewery-owned St. Louis Cardinals baseball team, plus Busch Stadium, and the famous Clydesdales.

4. *Video Magazine*—a quarterly sent in cassette form to 60 locations with local communications coordinators scheduling dates, equipment, and rooms.

5. *Team Talk*—a magazine for wholesalers and their employees and the Anheuser-Busch marketing staff.

Despite its proficiency in all principal avenues of commerce, advanced by a gigantic advertising program, Anheuser-Busch is particularly noted for its aggressive and imaginative marketing, which can be traced back to 1860 when a soap and candle maker, Eberhardt Anheuser, had a daughter who married a German immigrant and brewery supplies salesman named Adolphus Busch. The Anheuser and Busch merger began auspiciously and continued unwaveringly on the road to success.

Today, Anheuser-Busch is not only the world's largest brewer but it is also the world's most diversified brewer, listing, in addition to baseball, the following in its product line: wine, containers, baked goods, frozen foods, snacks, baker's yeast, refrigerator cars, railway operations, real estate, and tourist theme parks in Tampa, Florida, and Williamsburg, Virginia.

## Gould Budgets for Print and Video

$M$omentum is the name of a slick, first-class magazine for employees published by Gould, Inc., to reflect its image as a dynamic electronics company. Headquartered in Rolling Meadows, Illinois, Gould was reborn and wanted to make known its capabilities, character, resourcefulness, and personality. Company Chairman Bill Ylvisaker charged the corporate relations staff to showcase the new image.

Consider the challenge the employee communications staffers faced. They wanted to come up with a solution that would do justice to their company, one that would match a Gould project in California's blistering desert in which 1,818 giant mirrors reflect sunshine onto a giant stainless steel boiler, towering 290 feet, with water turning to steam to spin turbines capable of generating 10 million watts of power—enough electricity for 6,000 homes. The programmable controls for the 130-acre electric generating station, called Solar One, are from a Gould subsidiary.

The communications staff, spurred on by encouragement from management, approached the assignment by starting with the fundamentals. Employee surveys were part of the strategy from the outset. As the result of the feedback, it was decided that the company would communicate with its employees through three periodical media.

One would be the glamorous *Momentum*. The pendulum had swung back to the use of a fancy corporate magazine, a medium that many other companies had shelved because of the economic crunch. When the communications staff was first given the challenge, no one championed magazines per se. But later, when the question was asked, "What would be the most effective, most commanding, most dramatic way to portray the electronic excitement of the 'new Gould'?"

the consensus—from the corporate relations staff and the ranks—was the old-fashioned employee magazine but in a new-fashioned form.

The quarterly *Momentum* magazine would go to 35,000 employees worldwide as well as to former employees. The other two means of communications would be a Quarterly News Network Video for all employees and a monthly newsletter mainly for those in the management ranks.

What would the new communication package cost? Here are some numbers:

The quarterly magazine was, of course, the most costly to produce and distribute. The cost for a single issue was $45,000, for a total of $180,000 a year for the four issues. Production, paper, and printing costs accounted for $136,000 photography and other services for $32,000, and distribution (bulk shipment to divisions for mailing) for $12,000.

The video program, also produced for quarterly distribution, came in at $20,000 per issue. The breakout for this sum is $10,000 for local shooting, $9,000 for production, and $1,000 for distribution. The yearly total added up to $80,000.

The budget for the monthly newsletter for management is $2,500 per issue for production, paper, and printing, plus $1,500 for distribution. The bottom-line total for the year is $48,000 for 3,000 issues per month.

The grand total for the package was $308,000. This figure does not include staff salaries, benefits, and travel expenses. The price tag may be too high for some companies, "less than a spill" for others, but for Gould, Inc., it was obviously the right price for the right package at the right time. Yet, alas, in recent months, parts of the program were adjusted and the total outlay was modified.

# Employees Voice Their Concerns at Deere

Deere & Company (better known as John Deere), headquartered in Moline, Illinois, is a class act. The company's custom colors of green and yellow on tractors and other equipment are a proprietary symbol of identification around the world. Despite the recent headaches and heartaches in agriculture, Deere has persevered in maintaining its standards. Further, it has diversified and broadened its product line, as exemplified by its new backyard lawn mowers that are as rugged as the largest tractors used on the farm.

Nevertheless, bad times have taken their toll on Deere, affecting its growth, payroll, employment rolls, and communications.

Chester K. Laselle, vice president of corporate communications, recently pointed out, "The *JD Journal,* Deere's corporate magazine distributed to employees, retirees, dealers, and a small number of opinion leaders, has won numerous awards for its content and design." Laselle also added that "economic conditions have forced us to reduce its frequency to only two issues a year and, therefore, we started a publication called *JD Update,* a newsletter which fills in the information gaps." Laselle also transmitted a proclamation from Robert A. Hanson, chairman: "A mainstay of any employee participation process is an effective communications system that transmits timely and credible information down, up, and across the organization. Whenever practical, business information should be openly shared. Employees' questions should be answered as completely as possible. This sharing of information provides the basis for better decision making and builds trust and commitment. In this way the ability of each individual can be realized to the mutual benefit of all."

"Are employee questions really addressed by management?" Laselle was asked. In answer, he sent a transcript of questions and answers that were recently transmitted on Deere's Waterloo, Iowa, computer network. The transcript, which is reproduced below, provides a close-up view of employees' personal concerns as well as management's response.

Q. In regard to Machine 2774, since the operator already lost part of his hand operating this machine, wouldn't it be a safer machine if Deere added a two-hand control and changed the cutting tool arrangement so the operator would not have to guide the cutting edge with his hand?

A. The pinch-point where the operator lost the very tip of his left middle finger has been eliminated. The whole machine is presently undergoing revisions.

Q. Why spend money for new equipment when we can't justify spending money to make our existing operation efficient on products we have been manufacturing for years?

A. During the next five years we see our current product volumes increasing only to 40 percent of the 1979-1980 level. We have been working to gain more efficiency at lower volume levels. Mainly, we need to find new products that will utilize our facilities and put people back to work. The business of getting into new axles is a good example. Such axles are currently being a product made by a competitor in Germany. If we'd go into this new business we'd produce employment for 50 to 60 wage employees.

Q. What are the specifics in regard to the joint agreement with Iowa State University regarding development of nondestructive auditing equipment for metallurgical qualification process?

A. We have come to recognize the need to provide our customers, both internally and externally, steel that meets their requirements consistently on a continuing basis. To do this, we need a method to nondestructively characterize steel properties, such as inclusions and internal soundness. As a result, the component works, Deere Technical Center, and the ISU Center for Nondestructive Evaluation have entered into an agreement to develop such a system. The component works has responsibility for the project.

Q. Our office is being overrun with fruitflies as the trash is being picked up only twice a week. I would like to know if this situation is going to be corrected. If so, when?

A. The schedule calls for trash to be picked up from offices on a daily basis. If there is a specific office or area of concern, this should be brought to the attention of the Department 03J supervisor. Employees are asked to be helpful in locating or relocating materials which should be removed for sanitary conditions.

Q. I would like to know why it is taking two weeks to insulate that hallway leading to industrial relations. It seems like that normally would be a two-day job by any other work area. Is there any justification for taking that much time?

A. The duration of the hallway insulation job was seven days, not two weeks. The craftsmen who worked on this job also completed five service-related activities in A, A-1, R3 and R4 while the insulation project was in process.

Q. Are there any plans for General Motors to buy any portion of the Waterloo operations?

A. No.

Q. On the bulletin board every once in a while, John Deere posts some tractors and garden tractors for sale. How does a person go about bidding on them? Right after that, there is a price for the product. Is that the minimum bid they will accept?

A. This equipment is available for viewing at the location stated on bulletin boards. To submit a bid, you must work with and through a John Deere dealer. The prices stated are minimum bids that will be accepted.

Q. I would like to know why the foundry is working overtime trying to build Pontiac blocks when Pontiac can't even build its own blocks.

A. The block being produced in the foundry is an entirely new product line for Pontiac. Presently, we are the only source, and we must meet our commitments.

Q. I was wondering why no maintenance, no electricians, no welders, and no plumbers got to see the slides on China like the production workers did?

A. Departmental information meetings and the subjects selected for presentation or discussion are the responsibility of department supervision. A person who has visited China has been requested by a few departments to provide information on the experience. This is not a subject being presented in general by any factory policy but is available on request from the responsible supervisor. Subjects for consideration need to be made known to your supervisor for departmental information meetings. Time limitations require careful selection of the more valuable and relevant information for each department.

Q. Why is an employee allowed to run a part-time business from his desk? For examples, Amway or Avon sales. This is costing the company money and the problem is being ignored by supervision.

A. It is inappropriate for employees to solicit business on company premises.

Q. Is there a company rule regarding taking a half-hour popcorn break in the afternoon?

A. If the question refers to a bargaining unit person, authorized break periods are spelled out in the labor agreement. Salaried breaks are taken on a reasonable basis. Further information is required to fully answer the question.

Q. If the contract is ratified in June, would this necessitate an extended summer shutdown? Also, with the current activity in the stock market, is there any reason for the wild fluctuation in the stock prices due to announcement of additional losses posted by Deere?

A. There are no plans for an extended summer shutdown at this time regardless whether or not the labor agreement is or is not ratified in June. We have no explanation for the fluctuations in stock prices.

Q. Would it be possible to put in a water fountain at the cafeteria so you could get water and ice with your meal?

A. Upon request, ice water is provided at the cafeteria at the price of 10 cents, which covers the cost of the cup.

Q. When is Deere going to market a ground radar speed control system and what kind of price tag will be on it? Will the new radar speed control be built here in Iowa?

A. The Tractor Works introduced a ground radar speed monitor (not control) system last summer and units are now being shipped. Prices range from $500 to $890 depending on features provided and instrumentation already on the tractor.

Q. What is the advantage of Deere being a member of the Trilateral Commission, or does the Deere Company deny being on the Trilateral Commission?

A. The Trilateral Commission, which Deere supports, is a non-governmental policy-oriented discussion group of about 300 distinguished citizens from western Europe, North America and Japan. Its purpose is to encourage mutual understanding and closer cooperation among these three regions on common problems. The Commission concentrates on food and agricultural issues, including the need for more market-oriented agricultural policies.

# Amoco Produces Booklet Worth Emulating

Consistency and professionalism should pervade written material, including employee communications. It is necessary to have guidelines on spelling, punctuation, capitalization, abbreviations, etc., so that there is uniformity throughout internal employee magazines, newsletters, and other vechicles of written communications.

Readers readily notice senseless sprinkling of punctuation marks, different ways of spelling the same word, erratic use of capitalization, an abbreviation of a word here and the same word spelled out there. Such inconsistencies detract from professionalism—and possibly even the authenticity of the message itself.

The solution is to have a stylebook, which many public relations departments custom-make for their own use.

Ideally, such a stylebook will not only provide guidance on generic fundamentals but will also indicate preferred usage of proprietary words such as company tradenames, nomenclature of divisions, titles, acronyms, and other miscellany directly applicable to the company's usages.

In the absence of a homemade style manual specifically tailored to the requirements of an individual corporation, the next best thing would be a published version such as The Associated Press (AP) Stylebook, which can be helpful to any editor or writer handling employee communications. Even routine bulletin board announcements should be prepared with conscientious care and consistency, using a stylebook as a guide.

Although the AP's frequently updated stylebook is primarily for use by its news service editors and writers worldwide, the book also raises revenues for AP and is available in bookstores.

James H. Mayes, director of publications for Amoco Corporation, Chicago, sent in Amoco's new booklet called "Writing Style —A Guide to Usage for Amoco Communicators," giving reprint permission to Dartnell. The booklet's introduction follows:

A syndicated newspaper columnist once wrote: "Why does everyone think he's a writer? I don't think I'm a plumber." He was writing in exasperation, for he had been all-too-frequently bombarded by unsolicited manuscripts from amateur authors. Each of them was eager to have his or her work reviewed by this journalist who aside from writing a column had been a reporter, drama critic, book reviewer, and author.

His point was that most people unskilled in the use of a wrench would at least think twice before attempting to fix a leaky pipe. But many people hesitate not at all before undertaking a writing assignment, even though they lack basic skills in using the English language properly.

Being a plumber is hard work, and being a good one requires thorough familiarity with the tools of the trade. So it is with writing. Like plumbing, it is hard work. And it, too, requires a thorough familiarity with the tools of the trade: grammar, spelling, syntax, punctuation, vocabulary—and style.

Style? Sure. Just as a plumber must often choose between two equally acceptable wrenches to get the job done, so must the writer. Some words have two or more spellings, *grey* and *gray,* for example, or *judgment* and *judgement.* In both of those cases, both are perfectly correct. But which one should we use? Should we capitalize *federal* when referring to *federal government,* or shouldn't we? Both uses are correct. Without some principles to guide us, we'll capitalize one time and lowercase another. We'll use *pipe line,* two words, in one place, and *pipeline,* one word, in another. We'll throw in a comma here and delete one there. Such things constitute a loud static that interferes with the message the writer is sending the reader.

So, this is a stylebook, tailored to company needs and designed for use throughout Amoco Corporation and its subsidiaries. This booklet is a departure in both substance and form from earlier versions. It has been expanded to encompass new usages, and entries have been alphabetized and cross-referenced for easy access. It also contains an addendum that includes writing hints, a glossary of frequently misused words, a page on how to mark copy for the typesetter, and a list of significant company and petroleum-industry dates.

This booklet cannot possibly cover all the problems of style you'll encounter. To address these problems, especially when you're writing for company publications and press releases, we follow the style of The Associated Press Stylebook and Libel Manual, which stipulates, for example, that *gray,* not *grey,* be used, except in *greyhound.* Other recommended general references include *Webster's New World Dictionary of the American Language,* Second College Edition; and *Elements of Style,* Third Edition, by William Strunk Jr., as edited and expanded by E. B. White. In cases where usage prescribed by these references differs from that stipulated in this guide, Amoco communicators should follow the style prescribed herein.

Some publications have made it a rule always to adopt the shorter version of a word when two or more spellings of the word are correct— *employe* instead of *employee,* for example, or *enrolment* instead of *enrollment, or judgment* instead of *judgement.* For the sake of consistency, however, Amoco communicators should use the preferred spelling of the word as presented in Webster's except where otherwise noted herein. So we make it *employee, enrollment,* and *judgment*—all versions presented first in Webster's, thus indicating the preferred spellings in Amoco's judgment.

Some words seemingly have more than one correct spelling, but actually one or more of the versions have not gained widespread acceptance and thus should not be used. For example, such spellings as *nite* (for night), *thru* (for through), *tho* (for though), and *dialog* (for Dialogue) are unacceptable.

English, especially as spoken and written in America, is a changing and dynamic language. The purpose of revising the Amoco guide is to keep our usage as current and correct and consistent as possible.

# Opinion Research Shapes Solutions

The role of opinion research in employee communications discussed in Chapter 33 and elsewhere in the *Handbook,* merits a spotlight of its own. To illuminate this important topic, Walter G. Barlow was contacted.

Barlow, president of Research Strategies Corporation of Princeton, New Jersey, is a dedicated student of research who is also a longtime observer of corporate public relations programs. He is familiar with the ins and outs both of communications and of testing communications. As far back as the mid-forties, Barlow was the protegé of Claude Robinson, legendary founder and CEO of Public Opinion Research Corporation (ORC). When Robinson died, Barlow was his successor at ORC and has since formed his own firm at a nearby location in Princeton.

In soliciting employee communications material from Barlow, the following question was asked: "Is it true that employees sometimes list oral dialogue with their supervisors as their preference but wind up actually getting much (or most) of their internal information from printed materials?" The answer to this question is among the findings in the following report from Barlow:

> As you can see, I have carefully masked the identity of three companies surveyed, as you would expect. All three, as shown in the tabular matter to follow, are major organizations, operating internationally as well as in the U.S. Company A is a major brand consumer products manufacturer. Company B and Company C are industrial. The three organizations have been chosen deliberately to give you a spread, and, importantly, to show that the basic tendencies in one tend to be found in the other two.
>
> Now, let's make some generalizations:
>
> 1. In each instance, the major differences between where employees get their information and where they prefer to get it is that

word-of-mouth goes up dramatically as a *preferred source*, particularly from one's immediate supervisor. Likewise, meetings of one sort of another tend to come up higher as preferred sources.

2. The company publication tends to come out on top as an *actual source* of information. And in all three cases, this form of print stays relatively high as a preferred source as well. Note that in the case of both Company A and B, letters from top management go up strongly as preferred sources. In short, print doesn't disappear by any means as a source of getting information, and I see video coming on strong as a major new means of combining the power of the personal touch with mass communication.

3. Note that in all cases, the grapevine suffers a precipitous drop.

4. In all three cases, the company publication, when separately studied through special questions about it, does very well. In the case of Company A, there were two points in time—about three years apart. Taking the data from the first survey, management introduced some major changes and approaches, and frequency and amount of readership both went up as a result. This type of trend research, incidentally, is part of how smart managers are beginning to make the most of their publication budgets.

Let me add a few ideas that may be useful to you in speculating as to where communications (and hence communications research) are likely to go in the near future. Here are some fearless (it says here) predictions for you:

1. There will be radically better coordination between down-the-line, word-of-mouth communication and what is carried in print and AV media. Today you sometimes wonder if those in charge of information distribution of both types are really working for the same company.

2. A better definition is needed of what communications are supposed to accomplish, particularly what issues to stress. Why and to what purpose is going to be demanded by top management. For a long time, communicators have talked as if they were really advocates, but ended up watering down what was communicated to the place where it produced more nice warm feelings than anything significant.

3. While systematic evaluation and tracking of communications effectiveness is still done by only comparatively few companies, such

companies are the leaders. Others will also turn to research, particularly when budget pressures get heavy. A communicator should fight for the research he needs to continue/change/kill any specific communications medium.

4. In that regard, communications, it seems to me, have very clear in-sequence objectives: To transmit information, to gain belief and commitment, and, above all, to result in action—either in changed attitudes or in behavior or both.

5. To assume that a communications program will succeed without appropriately tailored research flies in the face of what we now know. I think it's safe to say that the effective and successful communications program of the future will use research to 1) get there faster, 2) deliver more punch and, above all, 3) do it at reasonable cost.

And one last observation: In all the surveys we have conducted, particularly in what we are now calling communication audits, the place where company after company gets criticized is at the "listening" function.

Employees feel, to varying degrees in different companies, that management talks *at* them, doesn't really want feedback, ignores the creative talents hidden in everyone of us, and puts far too much reliance on corporate communicators for carrying the message. It's a great case of the medium being the message: If you communicate with me through impersonal means that allow for no interaction, that tells me you want to talk, but not to listen. It's a formula for communications failure which managers often aren't aware of, because they have no incoming date to tell them *where* and *why* they are failing. And now—the numbers:

## COMPANY A
## Sources of Information

| | Among the Places Where I Now Get Information | Where I Would Prefer to Get Information | Actual Versus Preferred |
|---|---|---|---|
| Company publications | 62% | 41% | − 21% |
| TV, radio, or newspapers | 60 | 16 | − 44 |
| The grapevine | 53 | 4 | − 49 |
| Bulletin boards | 45 | 34 | − 11 |
| Company newsletter | 43 | 38 | − 5 |
| Location or plant publication | 32 | 32 | 0 |
| Supervisor | 26 | 55 | + 29 |
| Company management letter | 26 | 28 | + 2 |
| Union publications | 26 | 22 | − 4 |
| Annual report to shareholders | 26 | 16 | − 10 |
| Union representatives | 25 | 28 | + 3 |
| Business magazines | 22 | 9 | − 13 |
| Letters from company top management | 20 | 42 | + 22 |
| Group meetings with management | 11 | 44 | + 33 |
| Group meetings with supervisor | 10 | 40 | + 30 |
| Videotape programs | 6 | 18 | + 12 |
| Visits by top management | 5 | 31 | + 26 |
| Slide presentations | 4 | 12 | + 8 |

## COMPANY B
## Sources of Information

| | Among the Places Where I Now Get Information | Where I Would Prefer to Get Information | Actual Versus Preferred |
|---|---|---|---|
| Corporate newsletter | 66% | 40% | − 26% |
| Local or plant newsletter or magazine | 59 | 44 | − 15 |
| Bulletin boards | 50 | 37 | − 13 |
| The grapevine | 50 | 6 | − 44 |
| Annual report meetings/ films/brochures for employees | 49 | 35 | − 14 |
| Supervisor | 45 | 66 | + 21 |
| Letters from local or plant management | 27 | 47 | + 20 |
| Group meetings with supervisors/management | 26 | 55 | + 29 |
| TV, radio, local newspaper | 25 | 19 | − 6 |
| Reports from headquarters | 22 | 33 | + 11 |
| Annual report to shareholders | 21 | 17 | − 4 |
| Letters from top management | 19 | 41 | + 22 |
| Slide/film/tape presentations | 18 | 30 | + 12 |
| Visits by top management | 10 | 27 | + 17 |

**COMPANY C**
**Sources of Information**

| | Among the Places Where I Now Get Information | Where I Would Prefer to Get Information | Actual Versus Preferred |
|---|---|---|---|
| Company publications | 76% | 46% | − 30% |
| The grapevine | 69 | 16 | − 53 |
| Immediate Superiors | 49 | 54 | + 5 |
| Memoranda from management | 44 | 48 | + 4 |
| Company magazine | 26 | 13 | − 13 |
| Supervisor | 24 | 56 | + 32 |
| Publications in my own office | 24 | 37 | − 13 |
| Business publications: *Wall Street Journal, Business Week,* etc. | 22 | 11 | − 11 |
| Group meetings with management | 20 | 48 | + 28 |
| Annual review | 16 | 10 | − 6 |
| Departmental publications | 10 | 22 | + 12 |
| Bulletin boards | 9 | 13 | + 4 |
| Electronic mail | 6 | 11 | + 5 |
| Videotapes | 6 | 10 | + 4 |
| Professional journals | 5 | 5 | 0 |

# Grumman Employees Fight off a Raider

Use skywriting for internal corporate communications? A few eyebrows may be raised at the suggestion. However, none other than the distinguished Grumman Corporation of Bethpage, Long Island, New York, received such an idea from its employees in response to a takeover threat.

Grumman is one of the nation's largest defense contractors, with sales exceeding $3 billion a year. It supplies the Army, Navy, and Air Force with military aircraft and support systems. Employees total 30,000 plus.

Some of those employees responded to the takeover threat by hiring—on their own—a pilot to fly an airplane towing a banner (certainly a first cousin to skywriting) with the message, "Beat 'Em Back, Jack." "Em" referred to the Dallas-based LTV Corporation, which tried to acquire Grumman via an unfriendly tender offer. "Jack" was John C. Bierwirth, Grumman's board chairman, who was cheered on by employees not to yield to the Texas firm.

Thus the takeover battle extended far beyond such typical sites as courtrooms, stock exchange floors, regulatory agencies, lawyers' offices, and Congressional corridors. The most partisan protagonists in the contest were employees, retirees, stockholders, families, neighbors, and friends of Grumman, all of whom wanted the company to remain independent.

The news of the takeover attempt came on September 23, 1981, when Paul Thayer, LTV Chairman, phoned Grumman to say that LTV was announcing publicly it was offering $45 a share for Grumman's stock, which had been selling in the low- to mid-50s.

Without delay, the Grumman board convened and unanimously voiced its opposition to the takeover bid on the grounds that LTV's acquisition would violate antitrust and securities laws. Chairman Bierwirth explained to employees that "if fewer than 50 percent of our outstanding shares are tendered, the takeover bid will have failed" and added that "about a third of our shares are held by workers' investment and pension plans."

"These plans are managed by employees who will look long and hard at how well their fellow members would be served by selling off Grumman stock," Bierwirth further declared, "Much of the remaining stock is owned by Grumman people who understand their future is worth more than a quick return on a block of shares. The proposed LTV buyout does not take into account a whole host of other factors that, in fact, make us worth far more than the $450 million price tag they've put on us."

Highlights in the Grumman adventure follow:

September 28—8,000 Grumman employees attend a rally at Bethpage and wind up deciding to participate enthusiastically in a wide range of activities aimed at defeating the "outsiders."

October 2—Employees collect $15,000 for ads and hire their own ad agency.

October 4—"No!" ads appear in Dallas newspapers and in Long Island's *Newsday*.

October 5—*Plane News,* the employee newspaper, announces it will issue daily bulletins to all locations for the purpose of keeping all workers up to date.

October 6—The contributions from employees are now sufficient to permit ad placement in the *Washington Post.*

October 9—The "Beat 'Em Back, Jack" message in the sky, sponsored by Grumman Data Systems employees, echoes widespread local sentiment.

October 10-11—Employees conduct a weekend telephone poll of shareowners, only 3 percent of whom say they would tender their shares to LTV.

October 13—The pension plan completes acquisition of 1,160,000 additional shares of Grumman stock.

October 13—Retirees chip in for a larger ad in *Newsday*.

October 14—U.S. District Judge Jacob Mishler grants a preliminary injunction, on both antitrust and securities law grounds, which blocks LTV from accepting tenders of Grumman stock, pending a trial on the merits of the case.

October 15—LTV appeals Judge Mishler's ruling.

October 18—More than 1,000 employees join in the Long Island Project Pride Parade. Pro-Grumman momentum is now in high gear.

October 30—On Bethpage Grumman Appreciation Day, community leaders present the company with petitions signed by local citizens opposing the proposed takeover.

November 13—The Appeals Court unanimously upholds Judge Mishler's decision.

November 16—LTV withdraws its takeover bid.

November 19—5,000 employees and the corporation's board of directors attend a victory celebration in Hangar 3. The event is broadcast live to all other Grumman locations.

A foreman's comment told the story: "We knew we had a tremendous backlog of loyalty in our ranks but the workers went far beyond anything ever expected. All we had to do was call a 3:30 meeting and inform the employees once— just once—with the facts and they showed us the meaning of things like ingenuity and spirit. It was all so spontaneous. We lost no time circling the wagons and readying ourselves to resist the takeover invaders. The employees went so far as to retain their own independent legal counsel and intervene in the lawsuit."

Weyman B. (Sandy) Jones, vice president, public affairs,

for Grumman, had his own summary: "Sometimes the amateurs do it best."

Was Jones's professional confidence fortified by the results of the seven-week LTV experience? "Not exactly," he said. "We had a sobering learning lesson a few years later when we decided to have our 55th Annual Report to stockholders in the form of a tabloid newspaper rather than in the form of a magazine-type brochure. Actually, most people seemed to like the new approach. But some financial analysts thought it was a house organ and they pitched it. A few traditionalists didn't care for it at all. To me, the format conveyed the sense of a lot of things going on within the company. Anyway, after the one-year experiment we went back to the traditional brochure style."

Jones then added: "But that experience of employees taking their support message to the skies will long be remembered as the kind of encouragement we needed when the chips were down."

# Hilton Trains Its Upper Management

Communications skills should be acquired by employees at all levels of the organization— managers as well as their assistants, directors of departments plus their assistants, and those in top positions in accounting, law, finance, strategic planning, marketing, engineering, and all across the board.

"Nothing is taken for granted in our shop," says James R. Galbraith, senior vice president of corporate affairs at Hilton Hotels Corporation, headquartered in Beverly Hills, California. Training is all-encompassing in the hospitality industry, Galbraith stresses. Not only do the doorman, the bellboy, and the reservations clerk have to know what to do and say but their supervisors and all employees have to be on the ball in the daily hubbub of a "we-never-close" business.

A communications seminar was the centerpiece of a recent Hilton effort. In announcing the seminar concept to upper echelon colleagues, Galbraith explained as follows:

> Businessmen—whether corporate policy makers or hotel general managers—are no longer permitted to function in a closed environment. With pressure from regulators, special interest groups, media, stockholders and the general public, they must be prepared to effectively respond to outside stimulation.
>
> Many of these pressures are transmitted to the company by representatives of the news media. Technological improvements in electronic journalism and more aggressive news gathering have combined to offer even greater challenges to business executives.
>
> How can executives handle their responsibilities in a more open society and in this tougher news climate? Clearly, executives must be *informed*. Beyond that, executives must be *trained* to skillfully deal with information and events in a manner beneficial to the company. To assist in meeting these objectives, we are conducting a program to upgrade key Hilton executives' knowledge and communication skills.

The Hilton Communications Seminar will involve these elements:

1. Executives will be given insights into the news process and sensitized to how the news is gathered and how it is reported. They will learn how to make the process work to Hilton's advantage.
2. Communications skills will be measurably improved through intensive training workshops.
3. Training will enhance executives' skills in dealing with media interviews and spoken presentations at special forums.

The Communications Seminar will include key corporate staff, regional senior vice presidents, and general managers. Once the first phase is complete, we will design the regional seminars for our managers.

We are scheduling two workshops, each of which will be comprised of two days of training from 8 AM to 5 PM.

The training sessions will be gruelling and rewarding. Regardless of the amount of speaking experience, participants will find a sharp improvement in their own communications skills. Working newspersons will put the attendees through simulated media situations. With the use of videotape playbacks and instructive discussions, participants will learn techniques to improve their oral skills—thus ensuring that media opportunities are turned into media successes. We are structuring the seminar so that principles and techniques learned in the television setting are easily transferable to all kinds of spokesmanship opportunities, including platform speaking.

The seminar will cover crisis management as well as softer interview situations such as with travel writers or feature reporters.

The workshops will be held in the Beverly Hilton Hotel under the direction of Leonard H. Roller, Inc. Leonard Roller and his team have conducted training workshops for many of the top companies in the nation.

In advance of your scheduled workshop, you will be supplied a packet of training materials. I know you will find the workshop to be instructive and rewarding. The printed program for Hilton's inhouse training for high-level personnel indicated the blue-chip nature of the program.

The keynote speaker was Barron Hilton, chairman and president of the prestigious hotel chain. Among the other speakers were Peter Drucker, educator and author, and John E. Cox, Jr., president of the Foundation for American Communications, and his assistant, Douglas Ramsey.

## Cox's speech contained the following advice:

Becoming a source, declaring yourself a source, getting in a Rolodex file.... The next time journalists think about trying to do a story on the hotel industry, they'll think about you. Teach your staff to look for opportunities. Speak more from the perspective of a consumer. Speak simply. Seize the initiative.

## Ramsey had the following to say:

It is important that you understand that most people in the news business are honest and ethical and very professional but that the pressures put on them demand that they get the story.

We urge that every company have a policy for dealing with the media and that not only the general manager and the public relations people know that policy—not only that you have a designated spokesman or spokeswoman and people who can fill in for that person when he or she is not available—but that your entire staff understand that you have a policy for dealing with the press—and I urge that it be a policy of openness and accessibility, a policy not allowing "no comment" so that, when something does happen that makes it necessary for you to be able to tell your story to the press, somebody can be reached immediately to serve as your spokesman. That kind of policy pays off.

I think Bill Edwards at the Washington Hilton certainly is a fine example of how that helps when he had the electrical switchboard explosion and all the difficulties that followed. His way of dealing with the press was open and resulted in a very smooth conclusion as far as the press was concerned.

It is the reporter's job to get the story. That much of a Lou Grant scenario is true. The reporter gets the story; he moves on. He goes to do something else. He doesn't get the story; he's stonewalled; his sources are not forthcoming; he keeps digging and he digs until he finds the story one way or another. It may not be the accurate story but if the source won't talk, he gets it from someone else, someone else who will speak for you.

The primary source for news about you should be you. The days of stonewalling, I hope, are rapidly disappearing. Openness and honesty are absolutely necessary in dealing with reporters.

So, have a policy, be accessible, tell the truth, be in charge.

Will you be treated fairly if you take this approach? Not always. There are no guarantees; there are some ignorant journalists. I suppose there are even some malevolent journalists but I'm persuaded there are many more conscientious, talented people with high ethical principles working in journalism than there have been at any time in the past. Ethics are now a great concern in the profession.

The Hilton Hotels Corporation's experiment showed that the workshops were notably stimulating as attendees asked questions and "talked back." "Even the brass" in the organization showed an eagerness to learn.

Do efforts such as the Hilton endeavor spillover to rank-and-file employees down the line? There may not be a direct effect but there is an indirect spillover on two counts:

1. Employees at all levels like to see their employer portrayed favorably on the nightly news. They like to be able to say, "That's my company, being forthright and professional all the way."

2. Some—maybe even many—of today's nonexecutive employees will someday advance to positions of greater responsibility and will need understanding and skills not only for internal communictions but also for dealing with the external media.

# Union Pacific Bucks a Trend

Annual reports, as encouraged by the Securities and Exchange Commission and as published by all corporations listed on the New York Stock Exchange, American Stock Exchange, and NASDAQ, have often become such costly products that many organizations are asking, "How can we cut down on the expense?"

Who gets annual reports? Stockholders head the list of recipients, which also includes bankers, financial analysts, financial writers, and community VIPs. In addition, some corporations mail their reports to legislators, suppliers, and even to competitors. Rank-and-file employees are almost always left off the mailing list, unless they are stockholders.

In light of this situation, Richard W. Anthony, vice president of corporate relations for Union Pacific Corporation, merits recognition. He reports, "We are one of very few companies sending annual reports to all employees, stockholders or not, along with a covering letter from an appropriate affiliated company's chief operating officer." Union Pacific's annual report mailing list is substantial: 79,000 stockholders and 37,000 employees. The annual reports are attractive and of blue-chip quality—and expensive, to be sure.

Understandably, most companies regard their annual reports as their most important single communication of the year. This annual formality is a report card that is a summary of stewardship; a demonstration of strengths and weaknesses; a review of operations; and an overall appraisal. Then why do companies refrain from distributing copies to employees either through the mail or at the workplace? The most frequently expressed pros and cons include the following:

1. Most of the cost elements are already scheduled once the annual report is ready for production. As long as it's ready to go on the press, why not print additional copies for employees that will have a low per-unit cost since overhead costs have already been paid for? The additional cost for employee copies (increase in paper usage and a little more press time) should be analyzed.

2. Distribution costs for employee mailings will be brutal, especially postage. "Let's send something simpler and cheaper to employees" is often the compromise.

3. Annual reports, prepared mainly for investors and financial professionals, are complicated and may not be readily understood by some employees.

4. A simplified version is often sent to employees, with abundant pictures and easy-to-understand charts and graphs.

Generally speaking, the case for inclusion of employees is often lost before it is presented. In contrast to earlier, free-wheeling days when companies tried to outdo each other with slick, expensive, multicolor books, the more current rationale is to "do a good job for the main audience, stockholders, and find some other effective way to tune in employees."

Popular compromises include having management people in divisional operations communicate "the state of the company" to their employees—by whatever audio or visual or printed media available.

Union Pacific, it should be added, not only distributes its annual reports to all employees but also provides corollary information in *Info* and *Cycler* newsletters, and in a quarterly, *Update,* which is specially published for management and professional employees and which was recently named by a national professional society as the "best internal newsletter in the nation."

# Jobholders Meet at Pitney Bowes

Anecdotes abound at Pitney Bowes Company, world leader in the manufacture of postage meters. They start with Arthur Pitney, a temperamental, reclusive inventor whose tongue wasn't too partial to the flavor of postage stamps. Then there's Walter Bowes, a gregarious, party-going salesman who teamed up with Pitney in 1920 for the purpose of automating the affixing of two-cent stamps—that's what first-class mail cost in 1920—to envelopes.

There is also Walter Wheeler, for whom Walter Wheeler Drive in Stamford, Connecticut, was named. The six-foot-six Wheeler, an early employee, was "hero material." Rhodes scholar, Harvard football star, World War I submarine officer, and—most important—the man who sold Congress on the idea of a system for metered mail, Wheeler arrived at the top in Pitney Bowes after an 18-month meteoric rise through the New York office. Once established in the high halls of management, he was largely responsible for the formation of the corporate environment that is still a dominant force today and that is credited with helping to establish Pitney Bowes in several lists of "the 10 best companies in the U.S. to work for."

Today's 21,000 Pitney Bowes employees are eager to give credit to their company's longtime policies for low absenteeism, low turnover, and high productivity. More specifically, worker-management communications channels are regarded as an important part of the environment.

Can a company in a high-tech business thrive on old-fashioned roots? "As long as productivity and morale are served and as long as practices are updated" seems to be the prevailing answer.

Can a company specialize in sharing its material progress

with employees? Pitney Bowes not only can but also does share with its employees. It is credited for establishing the nation's first formal profit-sharing plan. Pitney Bowes is also acknowledged as being the first corporation to offer fully paid insurance for employees.

Two Pitney Bowes special projects are these:

1. It has annual "jobholders' meetings"—in addition to the usual stockholders' meetings—at which all employees, in Stamford and beyond, meet with corporate officers in order to have an opportunity to share views and ask questions.

2. It has a unique Council of Personnel Relations, which meets bimonthly to air ideas, to defuse tensions, and, to attempt to resolve conflicting points of view between various organizational levels.

These jobholders' meetings are not always tranquil sessions. When the unique program was launched in 1947, they were initially held only for staff members at Stamford, but now they are held annually at all locations, requiring top officers to visit the field for the purpose.

"Most companies—including ours—do a good job at meeting with those who invest their money," says Mike Quigley, central region vice president in Chicago. "What we at Pitney Bowes are doing is reporting, in person, to people who invest their time and talent and enthusiasm—the employees."

One expression of philosophy in particular stands out today at Stamford headquarters, demonstrating the company's attitude as voiced in 1979 by Fred T. Allen, board chairman and president. Allen said, "It is axiomatic that human relationships need to be nourished by communication, and that human harmony exists only so long as the partners in a relationship get from it what they want. It is probably not love that makes the world go around but rath-

er those mutually supportive alliances through which partners recognize their dependence on each other for the
achievement of shared and private goals."

# Ralston Purina Cooks up 700 Million Twinkies

What happens when a corporation ventures into new fields and acquires new companies along with their plants, products, and employees? The acquisitive corporation's employees are bound to be very curious about what has happened and what it will mean.

Change, per se, is unsettling to most people. Particularly when a company diversifies its operation through a purchase of another company, all affected employees are concerned and often even threatened about the short- and long-term significance of the development. Employees in such a situation naturally expect their managements to communicate promptly and provide them with appropriate information.

By and large, American corporations across the board do an effective job once a major acquisition is ready to be announced. In management's planning of strategies for explanatory communications, employees are obviously the primary constituency. Attention is also given to outside print and electronic media, to stockholders, to financial analysts, to customers, to suppliers, and to communities. In some cases, acquiring and acquired companies will jointly prepare information programs scheduled to last six months or longer.

Ralston Purina Company of St. Louis, a century-old manufacturer of animal feeds and breakfast cereals, created a stir in 1984 when it purchased Continental Baking Company—the largest baker in the U.S.—from ITT for $700 million. Purina also created news in 1986 when it purchased Eveready and Energizer Batteries from Union Carbide Corporation for $1.4 billion, another blockbuster transaction.

In both instances Purina employees were naturally concerned about economic issues and about developments that might affect their jobs. However, there was a particular curiosity that surfaced early in the Continental Baking proceedings, best described as "How about them Twinkies?" Purina employees were curious about Twinkies but not about Continental Baking Company's Wonder Bread, which came onto the market in unsliced form in 1920 and in sliced form in 1930. Nor did they show particular interest in Hostess cupcakes or Hostess "Sno Balls." It was Twinkies causing the curiosity.

So Purina accommodated employees' interest about Continental Baking in general and Twinkies in particular by publishing an article in its attractive employee magazine.

"Approximately 700 million Twinkies are sold annually," the magazine boasted, unnecessarily adding, "700 million is a lot of Twinkies." The magazine explained that the world-famous creme-filled little sponge cakes were developed in 1930 by a bakery plant manager in Chicago, James C. Dewar, who had always been disheartened by noting that the company's sponge cake pans sat idle for most of the year except during strawberry season when shortcake was produced to go with the strawberries.

So it was James C. Dewar, the Purina magazine explained, who came up with the sweet suggestion, "Let's take a yellow sponge mix and give it a nice filling—creme, not cream—and let's make it a year-around item and sell it on a two-to-a-pack basis for a nickel." Depression-era prices indeed.

The name, Twinkies, had occurred to Dewar during a trip to St. Louis when he noticed "Twinkle Toe Shoes" on a billboard. It wasn't much of a jump to Twinkies—and the rest is history. In the fifties, Twinkies were featured during commercials on the Howdy Doody TV show. In the sixties and seventies, TV's Archie Bunker insisted on Twinkies in his lunchbox. Thus was a morsel of Americana born and nurtured.

And now, Purina employees don't need to ask any more. If a sweet tooth beckons, there are vending machines nearby.

# G + W Magazine Dazzles Readers

Using spectacular graphics and sheer showmanship, Gulf + Western Industries, Inc., achieves a dazzling impact with its new corporate magazine for employees, entitled *One*. Among G + W operating affiliates are Paramount Pictures Corporation, Prentice-Hall, Inc., Simon & Schuster, Inc., and Madison Square Garden Corporation. Naturally, such celebrated organizations expect appropriate razzle dazzle in the way they are portrayed in print by their parent company.

As a quarterly magazine for employees, *One* is as attractive in content as it is in style, aptly symbolizing the star-studded conglomerate that rose to fame from the mundane role of an auto parts manufacturer in 1958.

Nestled into the rainbows of two of the magazine's recent editions, a few unusual pieces of information have appeared.

At the front of the first quarterly issue of 1985 issue was a warm welcome from Martin S. Davis, chairman and CEO, saying, "Welcome to the new corporate magazine for employees, which is symbolic of our company today. Though our business family encompasses many individual units with their own well-established names, we are ONE company. From this unity we derive special strengths and opportunities. Probably no other company has a more far-ranging roster of talent than we do."

On the contents page, the following information is provided: The company has sales exceeding $4 billion, up from $8.4 million during the start-up year of 1958, and 1985 has some 60,000 employees and about 50,000 shareholders.

Keep those 60,000 employees in mind.

Jumping to an equally colorful issue for the first quarter

of the following year, 1986, one encounters Martin S. Davis again, whose tune is a bit different in a post-restructuring era. "Today (early 1986) we have approximately 19,000 employees. Before restructuring we had more than 100,000 employees."

Indeed, 19,000 and 60,000 and 100,000 are surely different numbers—especially within the 1985-1986 period.

But G + W was surely not the only belt-tightening practitioner of restructuring during the era. Perhaps significantly, G + W wasn't at all bashful about listing its proud numbers on the contents page of the inside front cover in 1985 but it somehow managed not to include a comparable tidbit the following year.

Do one's little indiscretions rise to haunt one? Can a magazine editor always envision tomorrow's consequence as he sets routine facts in type today?

This should be added: The new (1986) Martin S. Davis did a nice job of bailing out. In his inside-cover editorial, he mentioned that a business writer asked how the changes at Gulf + Western have affected working relationships within the company. The response was simple: "We are developing more of a team mentality, taking diverse personalities, putting them together, and seeing them pull together more effectively.

"Before the company's restructuring, we had more than 100,000 employees, and the majority worked in production facilities. Much of the company's investment was in the plants where they worked and the equipment they used.

"Today, we have approximately 19,000 employees. The majority are involved either in the administration and delivery of services or in creative endeavors. Day-to-day responsibilities today involve efforts that are essentially mental. In short, our people and the result of their thinking and creativity—what the legal world calls intellectual property—are our principal assets. Our sales and earnings derive from people working with people.

"In that environment, the ability of individuals to get the most from their colleagues as well as from themselves becomes perhaps our greatest challenge. Open communication, the free exchange of ideas and viewpoints, and mutual respect assume added importance in our daily behavior.

"Gulf + Western is deeply dependent on individual performance, but even in the most singular of endeavors there are contributions from other sources. 'I' is the smallest pronoun in the English language. 'We' evidences significantly more dimension. To achieve what we need to achieve requires that we work together as 'we.'"

# Allstate Insurance Boasts 36 Publications

Allstate Insurance Company provides another model to emulate in any overall appraisal of internal public relations. Here are a few reasons:

1. The company, with an annual revenue of more than $8 billion, has an amazing total of 36 publications nationwide.

2. The company has recently won a Silver Anvil award from the Public Relations Society of America and a Gold Quill award from the International Association of Business Communicators plus citations from the International Television Association and the Publicity Club of Chicago—all for internal communications.

3. The company has actually been fortifying its broad array of internal communications as a basic strategy during an era when its success has been phenomenal in contrast with the less successful results posted by the insurance industry generally.

4. The company's aggressive and comprehensive communications program has been growing since 1982 when an innovative chairman and CEO named Donald F. Craib, Jr., made internal exchange of information a way of life. He even has a Communications Board, which includes all the top officers of the company.

Allstate has 15,000 of its 48,000 employees in sales and sales-support responsibilities, offering personal lines of insurance—such as homeowners, automobile, life, and casualty—directly to customers plus a smaller segment of activity handled by independent brokers. High on its priority list, the company stresses the importance of employee training, understanding, and support.

In a survey conducted shortly after Craib took over the helm, employees made known the subjects they wanted covered in Allstate's various publications. Edward L. Morgan, assistant vice president of corporate relations, remembers that "employees told us 'don't give us recipes anymore. We don't care if some other employee does decoupage at home. Tell me how I can get ahead. Assure me that I am going to have a job a year from now.'"

The survey told editors that its senior agents wanted more information about industry subjects and about what was going on in state legislatures. The younger agents said, "Tell us what the older guys are doing and how they do it."

Morgan remembers, "Shortly after Sears Roebuck, our parent, bought Dean Witter and Coldwell Banker, there were some financial deregulation problems emerging in Washington, D.C. We were able to provide a lot of information for employees ahead of time. And when we suggested employees might want to consider sending their reactions to Congressmen, no delay was involved."

Morgan adds, "The survey pointed out that we didn't have much viewership for our videotape programs. After experimenting we found that tapes work best in a meeting format when we can provide the chairman of a meeting with sufficient background information. It was important, we found, to enable the meeting chairman to be comfortable and to lead a discussion after the videotape was used."

With so many publications at the corporate level at Northbrook, Illinois, and at 26 widely dispersed regional locations, it is necessary for editors to have training and support. Morgan explains, "We keep sending out a lot of material to help them do a better job. We coach them on how to choose photos and how to write headlines. We've got a news network to make sure everyone is informed. We even provide a library for each editor in the field."

Morgan added, "In our various publications, we don't

simply report what has happened. What's going to happen is also worth exploring. We try to help our people prepare for opportunity and change."

# General Motors Lays out Its Plans

General Motors Corporation, the largest company in the world, consistently underlines its positive attitude toward employees and the importance of effective internal communications.

Roger B. Smith, GM chairman, has characterized his 700,000 worldwide employees as the most valuable asset of the corporation. It is no wonder then that Smith places internal communications high on his list of corporate priorities.

The importance of management's attitude is stressed here again. As demonstrated earlier in the *Handbook* (see Chapter 21), communications programs depend directly on management's understanding and support. Here is what Roger Smith has to say on the subject:

GMC
Inter-Organization Memorandum

Subject: Employee Communications
To: General Managers of Divisions
    General Operating Officers
    Group Executives
    Staff Executives
    Heads of Staff Sections

Effective two-way communications between management and employees is critical for success in our highly competitive worldwide business.

The need for employee understanding, involvement and cooperation has never been greater—and a broad base of information about the business is fundamental to the achievement of all our goals. More than that, GM has an obligation to keep its employees informed about important matters that affect the business and their own livelihood.

Two-way information-sharing can improve decision making and work performance by facilitating the making of decisions at the lowest possible levels by employees who know the most about getting the job done right. In turn, this increased participation can contribute to higher levels of employee satisfaction and quality of work life. We need ideas and suggestions from all employees about how to operate more efficiently—at every level of the business. Good communications also can promote better employee understanding and consequent support for the corporation's positions on key public issues.

The best means of communicating is by regular face-to-face exchange of information. But employee publications, bulletin board postings, letters to employee homes, and other media should be used to supplement management-employee meetings and other forms of face-to-face communications.

Although local news is of primary interest to employees, local communications must also include priority corporate information. Surveys of GM employees have shown a high degree of interest in many corporate activities, such as technological developments, new products, financial performance, government actions, worldwide competition and foreign affiliations, future plans, and other key aspects of the business. Guidelines for optimum management/employee communications at each GM location are attached.

Effective employee communications are essential to General Motors and each of you is urged to give to this important activity your full support and cooperation.

(signed) R.B. Smith
Chairman

Chairman Smith followed up on his memorandum by instructing three appropriate vice presidents to formulate a detailed series of *guidelines* to ensure that the CEO's wishes would prevail out in the company's widespread divisional plants and offices. It was a "given" that corporate communications programs would thrive if for no other reason than their visibility, but it was another matter to establish guidelines that required the myriad of GM decentralized segments to plan and implement communications efforts wherever the GM flag flies.

The guidelines, themselves, are interesting in that they spell out some of the prioritized subjects for employee-management communications. And the public relations people at GM outposts take them seriously. One young writer on the public relations staff remarked, "Even though they are fairly long, I've memorized them." The guidelines follow:

General Motors Corporation
Inter-Organization Memorandum

Subject: Guidelines for Employee Communications

To: General Managers of Divisions
    Plant Managers
    General Operating Officers
    Group Executives
    Staff Executives
    Heads of Staff Sections

The Employee Communications Section of the Public Relations Staff is responsible for coordinating corporate-wide employee communication efforts. Included are development of corporate print information, audio-visual materials, and other services designed to help General Motors staffs, divisions, and plants maintain effective programs of information-sharing with all employees. These activities are developed in cooperation with the Industrial Relations and Personnel Administration and Development Staffs. This memorandum discusses recommended standards and outlines guidelines concerning priority subjects for employee-management communications.

*Recommend Standards*

To maintain a satisfactory level of employee communication throughout the Corporation, basic standards have been developed based on programs already in operation at many locations. The recommendations are that each location:

1. Establish a formal, organized program of regular communication with all employees involving key information about the business and its effect on employees.

2. Establish regular, frequent printed communications for all employees.

3. Encourage regular meetings between management and employees. At least twice a year, management should provide all employees with a review of the state of the business (from both corporate and local viewpoints), as well as discussion of management problems, goals, and outlook, plus what is expected from employees. Employee questions should be encouraged, with answers ideally being given at the meetings or through other communication channels as soon as practical.

4. Make effective use of the supervisory structure to provide for two-way communication. All supervisors should understand the importance of communicating key information to subordinate supervisors and to employees in their work groups. Top management at all GM locations should make sure that supervisors have a regular flow of information to discuss with their employees. Weekly newsletters and regular meetings with all supervisors to exchange information are recommended. Also, supervisors have a responsibility to receive and transmit upward through organizational channels pertainent employee opinions, problem areas, and ideas for improvement.

5. Conduct periodic surveys to evaluate the effectiveness of employee communications and to provide direction for continuing improvements.

*General Guidelines*

- The local Employee Communications Coordinator (or Manager) is the key to a successful program. He or she should have the responsibility for organizing and managing a planned, systematic program involving various channels of communications. Included are printed materials, bulletin boards, employee meetings, and audiovisual materials produced both locally and at the corporate level. To insure a successful program, local communicators should have the full support and cooperation of top management, as well as timely access to essentially all management information of the types listed on the next page.

- Managers and supervisors should be encouraged to share with employees all information that is useful for increasing employee understanding of, and contributions to, the operation of the business. Only truly confidential information should be withheld.

- Employee communications should serve the information needs of both management and employees. Special care should be given to maintaining a reasonable balance in coverage of hourly and salaried activities to demonstrate management's desire to communicate with *all* employees on an ongoing basis.

- It is good practice to communicate the bad news as well as the good news to avoid negative effects of rumors and misinformation and to maintain management credibility with employees. It also is good practice to respond promptly to rumors or negative information about the local organization or GM that would be of concern to employees.

- It is imperative that important information be communicated to employees prior to or simultaneously with its release to the news media.

- Make prompt and effective use of corporate information materials and special services made available by the Public Relations Staff. (See attached list.) All of these materials are approved for release to employees and the public unless specifically restricted.

- Expand or rewrite corporation information whenever possible to reflect local interests as a means of increasing its impact on local employees.

### Priority Corporate Information

To help coordinate corporate-wide information-sharing, a list of priority subjects for employee communications is developed each year and made available to Employee Communications Coordinators. These cover a variety such as:

- Product quality.
- GM's worldwide competitive challenge.
- GM technological leadership.
- GM product leadership; selling GM products.
- Facts about GM's business—special emphasis on economic factors.
- Government actions affecting GM.
- GM's response to social, safety, and environmental problems.
- Benefits of being a GM employee.

### Priority Local Information

The corporate priorities provide a base for development of local priorities. In addition, special attention should be given to the exchange of local information with employees on other subjects, such as:

- Plans, goals, and problems of the local organization.
- Performance levels—production output, absenteeism, quality, reject rates, progress in meeting established goals.
- Work schedules.
- Reports on quality of work life and employee participation groups with emphasis on achievements through teamwork of employees, management, and unions.
- Other local projects involving joint efforts of management and unions.

- Competitive problems, such as: how local plant won or lost contracts for business.

- Expansion or modification of physical facilities, improvement of equipment—what these changes mean to employees.

- Action or events which require special employee understanding—layoffs, reduction in production levels, or changes in overtime needs.

- Plant safety—basic rules, reports on accidents and how employees can help.

- Personnel matters—benefit programs, job opportunities, training and development opportunities, employment levels.

- Role of the local unit in community relations—how its management and employees contribute.

- Significant, interesting news about employees at work.

*Handling of Confidential or Sensitive Corporate Information*

While an open climate of information-sharing is desirable to satisfy both the needs of the business and of our employees, it is important to safeguard the security of certain types of confidential information. This would include information which, if available to competitors or to the general public, would be advantageous to competitors or detrimental to GM, its shareholders, or its employees.

Whenever there is a question concerning the release of information to employees, the matter should be reviewed with the appropriate plant, division, or corporation staff executive. The GM Public Relations Staff also is available to assist in the clearance of informational material.

(signed) William P. MacKinnon     (signed) John W. McNulty
    Vice President                          Vice President
    Personnel Administration              Public Relations
    and Development Staff                  Staff

                      (signed) Alfred S. Warren, Jr.
                                Vice President
                                Industrial Relations Staff

cc:  Public Relations Directors
     Personnel Directors
     Employee Communications Coordinators (or Managers)
     Employee Publication Editors

In addition to the chairman's statement and the guidelines, there was third document: a summary of *sources of information* to enable divisional communicators, often far away from Detroit, to always have access to the vast array of information available for their use. Divisional communicators can never honestly say, "I don't know where to reach for the information I need."

The sources of information follow:

*GM Public Relations Sources of Information Approved For Communication*

| | |
|---|---|
| *GM Daily Newsline* | Available every workday at 8:30 AM, with updates as information breaks. Content: Brief news items about GM, the industry, and the economy. Format: three-minute recorded message on 8-346-3136; hard copy via GM computer, type user number and your password, then EXE NEWS. Contact: 8-346-2005 |
| *News releases* | Copies of GM news releases are available through the Public Relations Regional Offices, or News Relations in Detroit. Contact: 8-346-2028. |
| *Issue Update* | Sent every two or three weeks to all plant managers, general managers, sales offices, GM Employee Communications Coordinators, and GM Editors. Content: brief quotations or statements by top GM executives on current issues. Purpose: to provide executives with ready information for internal or external communications. Contact: 8-346-2018. |
| *PR Computer* | Available from GM Public Relations Regional Offices and Divisional Public Relations Offices. Computer-stored information including: news releases, position statements, executive speeches, testimony, responses to news media. Updated daily. Contact: 8-346-2057. |
| *Public Affairs Newsletter* | Published monthly for GM executives. Content: in-depth feature articles on current public issues. Contact: 8-346-2055. |
| *Executive Speech* | Speeches of top GM Executives. Contact: 8-346-2043. |

| | |
|---|---|
| *News for Editors* | GM Employee Communications Coordinators and GM Editors receive regular mailings of information. Contact your unit's ECC, or 8-346-2018. |
| *Stockholder Relations* | Information on matters of interest to GM stockholders, such as the annual and quarterly reports and proxy statements. Contact: 8-346-2075. |
| *Field Speakers Bureau* | Scripts and visuals for bureau talks Bureau updated regularly. Current topics are government regulation, auto robotics, and a broad view of GM potential for the future. Contact: 8-346-2067. |
| *PR Library* | The GM Public Relations Library provides access to information from references, periodicals, and GM published material. It also can obtain information through its affiliation with national library associations. Contact: 8-346-2051. |

To sum up: This is how a vast, decentralized company communicates with employees and how corporate assistance is available in providing ideas and information for use at all locations.

But what about GM's centralized, corporation communications for employees, those heavyweight, high-impact communications with all the whistles and bells? To be sure, GM does not neglect corporate communications for employees. At the forefront in the corporate effort is *GM Today,* a monthly newspaper that the 168-person corporate public relations staff calls "the flagship of our fleet."

*GM Today* has a monthly press run of 635,000 copies, which are mailed to U.S. employees at their home addresses. It is not surprising that GM's employees' circulation list is easily number one in the world among company-sponsored newspapers. This employee newspaper is a professionally written and professionally edited model that is the envy of industrial editors everywhere.

The guiding force behind *GM Today* has been and continues to be Alvie L. Smith, who in recent years has had the title of director of corporate communications under the leadership of John W. McNulty, vice president of the public relations staff. Significantly, Alvie Smith was honored as a Fellow of the International Association of Business Communicators in 1986.

What does Alvie Smith do? With occasional help of outside agencies specializing in feedback, Smith—to use his words— is always "testing, testing, testing; listening, listening, listening." Suffice it to say, Alvie Smith both preaches evaluation and practices it intensely.

*GM Today* was started in 1973 as a full-sized, 8-1/2 x 11 monthly newspaper which went to a tabloid format in 1982. The professional standards of *GM Today* parallel those of the *New York Times*.

Serving a company and an industry that is perpetually involved in some aspect of the Great American Debate, *GM Today* is mainly reportorial but it also takes the position of stating where the company stands on major economic, social, and political issues. Employees want to know—directly from the primary source of information—about seat belt legislation, air bags, fuel economics, foreign competition, labor viewpoints, share of the market, robots, quality control, safety standards.

That's the arena for *GM Today*.

# PART 6

# Public Relations for Health Care Facilities

David B. Williams

# Chapter 34

# Hospital Marketing

A few years ago, it would have been extraordinary to begin a discussion of hospital public relations with a chapter on marketing. Many hospital administrators, board members, physicians, and even public relations practitioners would have considered it offensive. Some may still bristle at the word.

But consider this: In just three years, 1983 to 1986, hospital advertising expenditures exploded from $50 million to $500 million per year. "The health-care industry has suddenly gone for the hard sell," according to *Time* magazine. "To fill a growing number of empty beds and to stand out amid increased competition, hospitals and clinics have started embracing modern marketing techniques."

Thanks to advances in medicine, hospital stays are shorter and many procedures that formerly required admission can now be performed on an outpatient basis. Third-party reimbursers press for shorter stays to control costs. Patients themselves are exercising more choice, which means that hospitals must compete more actively for these health-care shoppers. Now there are health maintenance organizations, multihospital conglomerates, ambulatory health care centers, and long-term skilled care facilities also delivering health care. (Although the focus of this and subsequent chapters is the hospital, the subject matter discussed also applies to public relations practitioners who serve these other types of health care organizations.)

Today, some degree of marketing is essential to a

hospital's success, in some cases even survival. And the hospital public relations staff—be it one person or a department—plays a key role in the successful hospital's marketing program.

The first step in dispelling any lingering prejudice against the word "marketing" is to understand what it means in the hospital context. Marketing isn't synonymous with hucksterism or ambulance chasing. Essentially, marketing is the process by which the providers of goods or services determine which are in greatest demand so they can produce more of them, and which are in least demand so they can produce less of them. The hospital is a quintessential service provider, so marketing is a necessary hospital management function.

Good marketing seeks to achieve the best match between the supply of goods and services and the demand for them. Hospitals provide the most vital services that human beings can need. Hospitals are also enormously expensive to operate, for both the individual patient and for society, which shares the burden through taxes and insurance premiums. Empty hospital beds and underutilized equipment and staff are costly to patients and to society. By helping to adjust the hospital's facilities and services to best meet the community's true health-care needs, marketing benefits the patient and society.

If this positive view of marketing doesn't convince the doubters, then consider the other side of the coin. In step with rising costs, health care has come under rising scrutiny, criticism, and regulation. Hospitals are the most visible institutional representatives of the health-care system. If hospitals do not respond effectively to the public's needs and concerns, they will be subjected to ever greater scrutiny, criticism, and regulation.

Marketing seeks to match what the hospital provides and what the public wants. Hospitals with responsive, effective marketing programs will enjoy enhanced public acceptance and support; those that neglect or disdain marketing will not.

The good news is that many hospitals have been practicing various forms of marketing for a long time. They just haven't thought of these activities as "marketing." Once hospital management understands that it needs a comprehensive marketing plan, it often doesn't have to start from scratch. It simply needs to recognize the marketing functions it is already performing, identify and plug the gaps, and pull everything together into an effective, integrated plan.

The role of hospital public relations has been enhanced by the recognition of marketing as a needed, even urgent, management function. Public relations practice has always involved several basics of marketing: defining needs, identifying target audiences, communicating with those audiences, and measuring the response. The following case studies illustrate the intrinsic role of public relations in hospital marketing.

## Case Study: Small Hospital, Big Problems

Murray County Memorial Hospital (MCMH) in Chatsworth, Georgia, faced a crisis. The rural, 42-bed, non-profit facility had experienced several years of operating losses (as much as $1.2 million in the previous year), declining census, and an apparent lack of community support. In March 1985, the board directed the administrator to assess the hospital's options: sell out, shut down, operate as a satellite of a larger hospital, accept management by a for-profit chain, or make another try at reversing MCMH's declining fortunes.

Data available from the local health services agency revealed that more county residents were being hospitalized outside the county than at MCMH. Hamilton Medical Center in a neighboring county was admitting a third more Murray County patients than Murray County's own hospital.

Ken Williams & Associates, an Atlanta public relations and marketing firm, was retained to research, plan, and execute a comprehensive PR/marketing program. The process began with a survey to determine why county residents weren't supporting their own hospital.

The study polled 0.8 percent of county residents and revealed that: 91 percent had a physician but 52 percent chose physicians outside the county; 54 percent had been admitted to a hospital within the past three years, but 60 percent of those admissions were at MCMH's leading competitor in the next county; 93 percent would go back to the same hospital again; 18.5 percent had negative feelings toward MCMH, 38 percent had never used MCMH, and 53.7 percent were unfamiliar with MCMH's services.

The campaign's objectives were then established: to portray MCMH as the community's total health-care facility, especially in the event of an emergency; to increase community awareness of MCMH services; and to build positive perceptions regarding the hospital among county residents. The campaign was titled "Let's Save Our Hospital." This slogan highlighted the basic problem, that MCMH was on the brink of closing, and linked the hospital's interests with those of county residents—MCMH was "their" hospital.

The campaign was launched at a special meeting of the Chamber of Commerce on July 25. Campaign components included: weekly newspaper and radio stories; a series of community forums; billboard and newspaper advertising and public-service announcements; window posters, bumper stickers, and buttons; open houses for community groups, meetings with business leaders, and a speakers bureau; hospital tours for 147 school classes (every student in the county); marketing consultations and workshops for county physicians and a series of direct-mail pieces featuring those physicians; patient information booklets and newsletters; and patient satisfaction surveys by physicians.

The campaign began in July and continued through November. Effectiveness was measured by results. During the six months from June through November, both admissions and census increased, contrary to national trends. After several years of operating in the red, 1985 was a profitable year for MCMH. The cost of the campaign was $35,000—a very low price to pay for turning a $1.2 million loss into a profit in less than a year!

## Case Study: Adding Style to Substance

Baptist Medical Center Princeton in Birmingham, Alabama, had somewhat different marketing problems. At 524 beds, it wasn't small, and it shared Birmingham with six other major hospitals. But a study in January 1984 placed Princeton last in terms of association with the words "hospital" and "hospital of choice." Patient loyalty was high, but more than half of current patients were older than 45. Princeton had the image of the small Baptist hospital it had been 60 years ago. For the few who thought of Princeton at all, it was an old hospital for older people.

Based on this research, an image-communications plan was designed with two objectives: to increase awareness of Princeton as a major medical center, combining the highest medical technology with a human touch of genuine compassion, by 100 percent compared to the first survey, and to increase physician referrals by 100 percent by the end of the year.

Other Birmingham hospitals had conducted short-term programs and ad campaigns, but none had attempted to completely change the perceptions of its publics. In approving the program, the board and senior management recognized that a consistent and continuing effort was essential. To maximize chances for success, research wasn't limited to external publics but included critical internal publics such as employees and physicians.

The program's first step was to create a new name and graphic identity for BMC Princeton. J. H. Lewis Advertising, Inc., was retained to handle the graphics design and advertising phases of the campaign. Testing resulted in a new logo with a high-tech look. The new name, The Princeton Network, conveys the fact that the facility is an entire network of sophisticated tertiary-care services: heart institute, cancer center, dialysis center, pulmonary center, laser center, etc.

But, while proclaiming its advanced, high-tech capabilities, Princeton also wanted to preserve the caring image for which it was already known. To convey this, the chosen positioning line became "Uniting People and Progress."

The new graphic identity was established both externally and internally. Even the hospital's 1,700 employees were mobilized with a complete line of Princeton Network clothing, pens, etc.

The *Princeton Network Magazine* was published and distributed to 170,000 households on a quarterly basis. A physician referral and information line was opened. A print and broadcast advertising campaign supported the new image message. A brochure cataloging Princeton's major services was produced as a fulfillment piece for mail and phone inquiries.

Nine months after the program began, survey results showed that Princeton had risen from last place to second place as a hospital of choice. Public awareness had grown by 200 percent from the initial survey. Physician referrals grew by 150 percent during the same nine months, and referral patients indicated 95 percent satisfaction with the service.

## The Position of Public Relations

Now that hospital boards and chief executives are consciously thinking in terms of marketing, they naturally look to the public relations staff for more goal-oriented communication. Indeed, for the small hospital the public relations function may represent virtually the whole marketing vehicle. In the larger hospital, however, public relations must function within the larger marketing program, which may include development and planning, advertising, community relations, publications, and allied activities.

If the hospital is to achieve its marketing goals, none of these activities can work in isolation. Effective marketing requires the careful coordination of all communication functions, which means management leadership to ensure that public relations, advertising, publications, and community relations programs support common goals and speak with one voice.

Public relations clearly has a large direct or supporting role to play in all these areas. But public relations is particularly vital because it deals with the news media. Advertising and publications can present their messages for the public to accept or ignore. But the news media aren't a passive audience. The news media have their own publics to serve, and reporters have no obligation to support the hospital's marketing plan. News media relations therefore represent the potential "loose cannon on deck," and the public relations staff must be alert and skillful in serving two masters—the hospital and the news media (see Chapter 36).

Having discussed the importance of hospital marketing in what is often called the "Age of Marketing," the remainder of this chapter must be necessarily abbreviated. This volume being a public relations handbook, attention will be focused on those aspects of hospital marketing that are most pertinent to the public relations function.

## The Marketing Plan

The foundation of the hospital marketing program is the marketing plan. The marketing plan is a subordinate to, and an essential element of, the hospital's long-range plan. If the hospital doesn't have a long-range plan, it should. The marketing plan tells you how to get where you want to go. If you don't have a long-range plan that defines where you want to go, then a marketing plan is a compass without a needle.

A key concept in marketing is "positioning." Positioning addresses the question, "What does this hospital want to be known for?" As a health-care provider, every hospital must be prepared to serve the immediate medical needs of every patient who arrives at admission. But no hospital can be all things to all people.

The small hospital in a rural community must necessarily refer patients in need of rare or highly sophisticated treatment to specialized centers. Even very large hospitals find it advantageous to concentrate on a selective range of advanced health-care services. These hospitals usually exist in multifacility markets where it is far more efficient and financially prudent to divide, rather than duplicate, responsibility for supporting high-cost, high-tech equipment and scarce specialists.

Some small, struggling hospitals in highly competitive, multifacility markets have managed to keep their doors open by concentrating on one type of care that may be burdensome or uneconomic at neighboring facilities: long-term geriatric care, drug and alcohol rehabilitation, hospice care for the terminally ill. These facilities are the ultimate practitioners and beneficiaries of successful market positioning.

The marketing plan, built on the concept of positioning, is the unifying guide that helps boards and administrators, planners, public relations, publications, and advertising to act together in mutual support of the same objectives.

## Marketing Research

The two case studies given earlier in this chapter are good examples of the proper use of research in planning marketing programs. The public relations practitioner appreciates the importance of objective research to the hospital's marketing strategy—and how useful that research will be to the public relations program. There is no subsitute for valid measures of consumer attitudes. Knowledge may be expensive, but lack of knowledge can cost even more in failed programs and wasted funds. The public relations practitioner should be a strong advocate for an adequate research budget.

If the hospital lacks a specialized marketing staff, the public relations practitioner may be called upon to plan and interpret consumer research. It is easy to generate data, especially bad data. Interpreting data correctly for management is far more difficult. If you don't possess real expertise, it will be far wiser to hire qualified professional help.

If consumer research is a new activity for the hospital, it is also wise to begin small with limited, well-defined objectives. Expensive research projects should produce original data—information you can't obtain anywhere else. A lot of basic data has already been collected by industry associations and government agencies and is available at no cost or for a modest fee.

In planning consumer research, be clear about its purpose. The research project must have well-defined objectives. Sometimes more than one purpose can be served by a specific research project. Public relations and advertising may both benefit from the same data. But multiple objectives must be recognized when the research is designed in order to ensure full value to each intended user.

Above all, consumer research must be objective. While comments or complaints from patients and hospital staff are useful, they do not represent a reliable measure of public attitudes. Nor do they measure the attitudes of target groups that are not yet using the hospital's services.

Hiring a research firm is perhaps the most critical aspect of launching a consumer research project. A bad decision at this stage can't be redressed later. Don't depend on one recommendation. Ask around. Examine several firms in detail. Check references. Assess their track records—client lists, prior experience in the health-care field, credentials of the top people.

Consumer research, like the marketing plan, can't be considered a one-time effort. While it is useful to know what the public thinks right now, it is even more important to identify *changes* in consumer attitudes. Once undertaken, consumer research should become a regular part of the public relations program and the overall marketing effort.

The public, or selected publics, aren't the only target groups to which research should be addressed. Physicians, nurses, and other hospital staff have attitudes that also have a large impact on the hospital's success. Research can also improve the effectiveness of staff recruiting and fundraising programs.

## Marketing Positioning

The beginning of the marketing plan is a clear statement of the hospital's market positioning—what it wants to be known for. "Good medicine" isn't an adequate positioning concept for marketing purposes because it is the elemental purpose of every hospital and doesn't help to differentiate your hospital from any others—to position your hospital in the market.

Of course, if yours is the only hospital in the county, recognizing this circumstance may be all the positioning statement you need. As the most accessible source of hospital services in the area, you can concentrate on building community appreciation and maintaining a general reputation for quality care (as in the case study of Murray County Memorial).

Today, however, a large majority of the population lives in metropolitan areas where a choice of hospitals is available. There may even be a perceived excess of facilities. Having a mission that differentiates your hospital from all the others, and communicating that mission to the public, is important.

Unless you are building and staffing a hospital from scratch, you can't simply think up what you want to be known for. You have to build on what you already are (as in the case study of BMC Princeton).

The discussion of marketing research preceded this section because many hospitals already have at least the seed of a market position. They are known for something, however diffused this impression may be. If you are called Children's Hospital, you need go no further. If not, you need to assess and define what you are, or what you realistically could be, and objective research is a useful check on wishful thinking.

What does your hospital offer that others don't? What's bigger or better? Do you have more specialists in a particular field? Do you provide a particular type of service to more patients, or at lower cost? Does your location have special advantages—transportation access, a pleasant environment, proximity to some attraction? The answer will help to differentiate your hospital from others.

Having defined the strengths and weaknesses of your hospital, you can write an explicit positioning statement. Public relations, publications, advertising, and a graphics design system can then communicate this identity in chorus.

Once adopted, your hospital's positioning statement shouldn't remain a management secret. All elements of the staff should be able to respond immediately and with the same answer to the question, "What is this hospital known for?"

It is worth repeating that a hospital's positioning statement isn't simply pulled out of the blue. Market positioning isn't merely a promotional gimmick. It fulfills the hospital's responsibility to inform the public—its potential patients—about what if offers and what it does best.

The public relations practitioner will appreciate one additional consideration. The simpler a message is, the easier it is to communicate.

After identifying everything about your hospital that you are proud of, it is tempting to overload the positioning statement (and, perhaps, even to exaggerate the special caliber of some services, as if calling them top-notch will make them so). Resist temptation. Reduce and refine your positioning statement to essentials. It should go without saying that all your hospital's services are good. You only need to emphasize what is different or best.

To make choices, remember the purpose of the exercise: to differentiate your hospital from, not equate it with, others. If you really are strong in two or more areas, and another hospital can claim equal strength in one of them, then focus on the strengths you don't share.

## Advertising

Advertising, like marketing itself, is a relatively new field of endeavor for many hospitals. And, like research, advertising requires expertise.

Advertising has grown into one of the world's largest industries for a simple reason: It works. Advertising is a communications too, and today's hospital needs to communicate more than ever before. Public relations is another communications tool, and public relations can do some jobs better than advertising can. But advertising is uniquely suited to deliver specific types of information to target audiences. Above all, advertising content and placement can be completely controlled by the advertiser. And, when well executed, advertising is often the least expensive means to communicate on a cost-per-audience-member basis.

One key to effective advertising is to think in terms of advertising campaigns, not individual advertisements. Like reputations, advertising impressions build over time. Everyone in the target audience isn't watching Channel 6 at 7:01 PM on Wednesday night, or reading the "Living" section of the Sunday newspaper that particular week. And most who do see the ad won't retain a strong impression the first time unless they have an immediate need for the offered service.

There is a form of one-time advertising that more and more hospitals are using quite effectively: the annual report, presented in a newspaper's regular pages or as an insert (usually on Sunday). Such a report, well designed and illustrated, can catch and hold greater reader interest than ordinary advertising, lets the hospital tell its whole story including mission, philosophy, and plans for the future, and can address health-care issues of particular local concern from the hospital's point of view.

Advertising can be very expensive if used ineffectively. Results depend on clearly defining the audience to be reached and astutely selecting the media that will deliver your advertising message to that audience. Then there is the question of the message itself. Writing ad copy that "pulls" is an art. Good ad copy catches more attention and thus delivers many more impressions than bad copy.

All these considerations mean that, when advertising is called for, it pays to hire professional help. The rules for hiring a research firm apply equally well to advertising agencies: examine several candidates, with particular attention to credentials, references, client satisfaction, and previous experience. A good advertising agency isn't just a clerical service to do the dogwork of placements, contracts, and bill paying; it's an expert collaborator that can make a valuable contribution to the planning and execution of the hospital's marketing plan.

## Conclusion

Hospital marketing is no longer the novelty it was a few years ago. Today, as the case histories illustrate, marketing is a fact of life even for the small, isolated hospital that once assumed its mere existence would ensure patronage. Marketing is all the more necessary for the large hospital in a competitive environment.

Hospital boards and administrators have been discomfited by the abrupt shift from the good old days to the Age of Marketing. Public relations practitioners have also had to adjust. Before, the hospital public relations staff had the central, even the exclusive, role of managing internal and external communications. Now, as one part of the overall marketing function, public relations has to become a team player.

Yet the change isn't necessarily bad. If public relations is only one player on a team, it's also a key player on a team that is increasingly important to the hospital. Research that might not have been funded for public relations alone is now deemed essential for marketing purposes. And each newly adopted objective in the marketing plan means additional assignments (and bigger budgets) for public relations.

All things considered, marketing has brought new challenges and increased significance to the role of hospital public relations.

# Chapter 35

# The Public Relations Function

Having established that public relations is a crucial element in the hospital's marketing effort, what does it take to ensure that the public relations function will perform effectively?

**Informed utilization.** Management must appreciate what public relations is and what it can and cannot do for the hospital. Public relations is a communications tool. Perhaps the first duty of a public relations director is to educate the board, chief executive, and other decision makers about how to use this tool well.

**Marketing strategy.** If the public relations staff is to communicate effectively with the hospital's several publics, it needs the clear direction provided by a marketing plan. If you don't know what message you are supposed to communicate, or you are given several contradictory messages, or the desired recipients of the message aren't clearly identified, communication will be garbled.

**An adequate budget.** There's no such thing as a free lunch. If those who hold the purse strings want public relations to perform well, they have to provide adequate funding. A marketing plan also helps to build a realistic budget, because the cost of implementing each of the plan's public relations objectives has to be considered during the planning process.

**A management role.** The public relations director

should be a member of the hospital's management team and a participant in the decision-making process. Public relations can achieve its full potential only when public relations considerations are included in the planning process; after decisions are made, it may be too late to avoid pitfalls or take advantage of potential opportunities. The public relations director also has an important advisory role, counseling management on the attitudes and needs of the hospital's various publics.

**Capable staff.** Public relations, like many other hospital functions, is a specialist's job. Able and knowledgeable public relations practitioners are needed to do the job well.

## The Public Relations Director

As a member of the hospital management team, the public relations director has three roles: counseling, marketing, and communicating. Each of these roles has both internal and external dimensions, since hospital staff, volunteers, and current patients, as well as various segments of the general populace, must be counted among the hospital's several publics.

**Counseling.** The public relations director is the hospital's in-house public relations counsel. In this role, he or she should determine and interpret the views and interests of the hospital's publics to management and recommend suitable actions. As a participant in the planning process, he can advise management on the effects that proposed actions may have on public attitudes. When a potentially adverse decision is unavoidable, he can suggest ways to prepare the affected publics and moderate the expected reaction.

It's often said that communication is a two-way street. It is easy to fall into the conceptual trap of thinking that public relations "puts out" information. But an equally important function of public relations is to "take in" information. Indeed, "take in" must precede "put out" in effective public relations.

The other specialists on the hospital's management team naturally view proposed actions from the perspective of their specialty: administration, finance, personnel, medical services, etc. The public relations director is important in the decision-making process because, among all these specialists, he or she is one who naturally views proposed actions in terms of public perception.

The public views hospitals, whether tax-supported or private, as community resources. Fairly or unfairly, a hospital's actions are therefore subjected to a higher degree of scrutiny than some other institutions or businesses. The counsel of a savvy public relations professional can spare management from any number of needless headaches that may strike when decisions are made without considering their impact on all the hospital's publics.

**Marketing.** A common definition of public relations is goal-oriented communication. The public relations director needs to understand his hospital's marketing plan, and particularly its desired market positioning, because these provide the basis for defining and revising public relations goals. In the marketing context, public relations is a marketing tool, so the public relations director should have a role in preparing the marketing plan. Again, if public relations is to achieve its full potential, public relations input is needed during the planning process.

The public relations director should work closely with the hospital's planning, development, and/or marketing directors to conduct market research. This research provides the public relations staff with information it needs

Mount Carmel Health of Columbus, Ohio, a member of the Holy Cross Health System, produces *The Spirit of Life,* thematic quarterlies distributed to its 3,000 employees, community leaders, financial contributors, the news media, patients, religious leaders, and friends of the hospital. The photographs on this and following pages are reproduced, with permission, from the Fall 1985 edition on "Growing Old: The Best Is Yet to Be." In this photograph, Boen Hallum, 67, recovered from triple bypass surgery at the Mount Carmel Medical Center, is shown in his backyard crowded with grape arbors, where he likes to "sit and think."

In recognition of the special needs of the 65-and-older population, Mount Carmel Health has established its GoldenCare PLUS program, which includes redeemable coupons for health care, a lounge for its cardholders, personal advisors, discounts on meals, physician referral services, free blood-pressure checks, a newsletter, and health enhancement educational services. This intergenerational photograph captures the spirit of Mount Carmel's goal in gerontological medicine: not to discover an elixer of youth but to eliminate diseases that hinder the quality of life for the elderly.

Sister Laurent, CSC, is a discharge planning volunteer at Mount Carmel, having stepped back from her full-time duties in pastoral care. She spends each day, from 8:30 AM to 3:00 PM or so, planning and placing phone calls to every elderly patient who has been discharged from Mount Carmel. She also goes visiting in areas of the hospital where she feels employees rarely have an opportunity to visit with a Sister. "I go to Laundry, and back into Maintenance—I go all over. I'm a free-lancer . . . . I feel wanted and I hope I help them feel wanted. I hope they feel that somebody in Holy Cross knows they are down there working on the mangles, or with the boilers, and appreciates them for the work they do," she states.

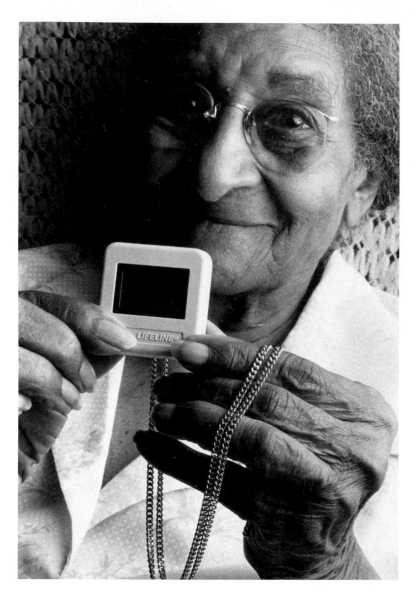

Marie Banner at 96 is a survivor, having lived through 18 presidents, five wars, and the Great Depression. She was born on December 15, 1888, in Frankfort, Kentucky, one of nine children. She first came to Mount Carmel in 1916 to have a cyst in her womb removed. Now, Mrs. Banner is on Lifeline, a system that links her to the emergency care of Mount Carmel on a 24-hour-a-day basis. She is shown holding a small portable button linked to a monitoring system at the Mount Carmel East Emergency Room. "I feel so safe. I know, if I touch that button, I'm going to get some kind of answer," Mrs. Banner was quoted as saying.

The caption in *The Spirit of Life* reads: "Clowns, clowns and more clowns have surrounded Thelma Holmes, Mount Carmel East Hospital volunteer, for more than 25 years. A retired school teacher and seasoned ventriloquist, Thelma has been entertaining school children and senior citizens with her clown puppet shows. 'I like to make people laugh,' says Thelma. 'I get great satisfaction knowing I can make a person's life brighter with the happy faces of my puppets.'"

And this is Gertrude Holbrook, 85, also a hospital volunteer featured in *The Spirit of Life.* "Music is my life," Gertrude was quoted as saying, "I particularly favor religious and classical arrangements." With an interest in music since early childhood, Gertrude at age 16 became the protegé of the first woman to play with the John Phillip Sousa Band. Since then she has been a featured soloist with church choirs and choral societies and has worked with a professional organist, performing before senior citizen groups and at nursing homes.

Two more volunteers at Mount Carmel East Hospital are Brooks and Meggie Westfall, depicted here with their respective favorite pastimes, beekeeping and quilting. Both share in each other's hobbies, experiencing joy and excitement of collecting honey and delicately stitching together a quilt. Now retired, they are busy pursuing their hobbies and doing volunteer work at the hospital.

Joe Ianarina, since retiring as a wine sales representative, volunteers his time at Mount Carmel East Hospital. "I love the fellowship and good friendship associated with volunteering," says Joe. "God has blessed me with a wonderful life, and as a volunteer, I can help those who are less fortunate." Joe also loves to golf and bowl, which he has been enjoying in his retirement—or rather, semiretirement, as he is a consultant or "wine master" with a local distributing firm.

to design and execute programs that support the hospital's marketing strategy.

In smaller or less sophisticated hsopitals, public relations may still be the only available vehicle for many marketing functions. In this circumstance, the public relations director needn't sit back and ignore what is happening in the industry. In the absence of a formal marketing program, the public relations staff can add marketing concepts to its thinking and programs. Goal-oriented communication can't begin until the goals are defined, and marketing considerations can help to select and refine public relations goals.

**Communicating.** Before anything else, the public relations director is, of course, a communicator. Effective communications has many requirements. One of the most important is knowledge. A hospital is a highly complex operation, and medicine is an advanced science. The hospital public relations director must be intimately familiar with his institution and its services. He or she must also be well informed on a multitude of health-care issues that affect the individual patient and the hospital's relationship with the community it serves.

A word of caution is in order here. The hospital public relations spokesman often needs to deal with medical issues. Any communication content that might be construed as a medical advice must be checked and cleared with qualified medical practitioners. Physicians are one of the smallest but also one of the most vital of the hospital's publics. Few things upset physicians more than a layman assuming the mantle of medical expertise.

## Hospital Publics

The hospital's potential publics, both internal and external, are many. These publics include those with whom the hospital already has a relationship and those with whom the hospital desires a relationship. Those that already have a relationship can play a very substantial role in helping the hospital communicate with its desired publics.

**Internal publics.** The hospital's internal publics represent a great number of people. The typical hospital may have three to five employees per bed, plus volunteers, auxiliaries, social workers, and others. Each bed may represent 20 or 30 patients per year, and each patient may draw several visitors to the hospital.

The hospital public relations staff should therefore pay serious attention to these internal publics. All these internal publics have relatives, neighbors, and friends. If they know and support the hospital's mission and the marketing position, they will help to build the hospital's image and convey its communication goals to many others.

Communication methods for these internal publics include a patient handbook as well as literature and displays for visitors, and an employee handbook and publication. There are also many programs and activities that can be adopted to enhance internal communication and general organization spirit. Internal public relations techniques in the hospital aren't significantly different than in comparable businesses and institutions, and guidance can be found elsewhere in this volume.

There is one internal public that is unique to hospitals. The hospital's physicians are not only an important target public themselves, but they can be enormously helpful. The public relations director should strive to establish a close and cooperative working relationship with these valuable resource people. Good communication with physicians means soliciting their guidance on medical issues, keeping them informed of public relations plans, and calling upon them when a professionally qualified medical spokesman is needed.

**External publics.** The hospital's marketing plan is the basis for defining external publics as potential users of the hospital's medical services. Methods for communicating with these publics are discussed in the following chapters. The public relations staff may also be called upon from time to time to assist in communication with some publics that aren't of concern as potential patients. Public relations should participate in developing the "case for support" and communications for fund-raising programs, for example. Then there is what might be termed "political action" programs to communicate hospital needs and concerns to regulatory bodies and legislators.

Serving in the public relations function for a hospital can be personally rewarding above and beyond comparable communications jobs in other fields. Hospitals—and the people who work in them—are providing the most essential services that human beings require. The public relations function plays only a supporting role in these services, but that's true of public relations for any enterprise. In helping the hospital fulfill its mission, you are performing a job worth doing.

# Chapter 36

# News Media Relations

Laymen sometimes think that public relations begins and ends with news media relations. While the news media provide major channels of communication to the hospital's publics, there are also many ways to communicate directly with desired audiences. The news media are middlemen, and the public relations message is inevitably reshaped and interpreted to a greater or lesser degree before reaching the audience. In considering external public relations, it's worth emphasizing that the news media are enormously important, but they are only one segment of the available communications spectrum—and not always the most efficient in achieving a particular communication goal.

The hospital public relations practitioner enjoys a distinct advantage over colleagues in some other fields. The news media have a seemingly insatiable appetite for health-related news. Virtually every newspaper has a medical columnist, every television station has a health reporter, every talk show presents a steady stream of health experts. The hospital public relations practitioner has something the news media want. To supply that demand in a professional manner is what remains to be done.

There is one important restriction on this otherwise mutually beneficial relationship. The news media want stories, but the hospital has an obligation to ensure the rights and privacy of its patients. Some of the most compelling stories involve patients. In these circumstances, the public relations staff must serve as mediator, enlisting the patient's cooperation, spelling out the ground rules, and providing the news media with the information it genuinely needs to report the story. In the final analysis, however, the patient's wishes are paramount and the hospital public relations staff must serve the patient rather than the press.

## The Hospital Press Policy

Considering all the rights, legal requirements, and sensitivities involved with patient information, a formal policy on press relations should be adopted. The American Hospital Association and other trade groups have developed sample hospital press policies.

State law specifies patient information that the hospital is required to make public. In the interest of protecting the hospital from legal liability, any other information must be considered privileged until the patient's permission is obtained. (A waiver in the admission form is prudent but does not provide absolute protection for the hospital.) The public relations staff needs to work with the hospital's legal counsel to develop a press policy that facilitates communication while protecting patient and hospital interests.

Copies of the press policy should be provided to every employee. Normally, employees will refer press inquiries to the public relations office. Hospitals operate around the clock, however, and a public relations staffer may not always be available. Employees who are on duty during off-hours—emergency room personnel, for example—should be particularly familiar with the press policy.

Inform the press, too, about your hospital's press policy. It won't necessarily guarantee that reporters will observe the policy, but they will at least know about the rules that you have to play by.

Good news media relations are based on mutual trust, respect, and cooperation. These considerations apply equally to the public relations practitioner and the news reporter.

As the hospital's designated representative to the news media, you must strive to provide reliable information in a timely manner and useful form. Conversely, the reporter must use your information fairly and accurately and work with you, rather than around you, to obtain any additional information that may be needed.

In general, every press inquiry should be answered promptly and as fully as necessary. If there is a reason why you can't answer a particular question, explain why. Candor, cooperation, and professional courtesy help to build a good working relationship with the press.

## Patient Information

Normally, the name, age, gender, address, marital status, and occupation of each patient can be released. Information about the patient's illness or injury should not be released without the patient's permission. If the patient is unconscious or unable to speak, the permission of the legal next of kin is necessary. For minors, or those who may otherwise be incompetent, permission is needed from a parent or legal guardian. (If, however, the physician believes that publicity might be detrimental to the patient's health, information should be withheld regardless of the patient's consent.)

When consent has been given, the general *condition* of the patient, but not the medical *prognosis,* may be described. Only the physician is qualified to assess the possible outcome of a patient's specific illness or injury and its treatment. The following terms are in general use to describe a patient's condition:

*Good:* Vital signs normal and stable, patient conscious and comfortable.

*Fair:* Vital signs normal and stable, patient conscious but suffering a degree of distress.

*Serious:* Vital signs ranging beyond normal limits and may be unstable, patient experiencing serious distress.

*Critical:* Unstable and abnormal vital signs, serious distress, patient may be unconscious. (It can also be noted that a patient arrived at the hospital in an unconscious state.)

*Dead:* When the next of kin has been notified, or family members have not been reached after a reasonable time, the death can be considered a matter of public record. The *cause* of death can only be released by the patient's physician with approval by the next of kin or legal guardian.

The hospital can also indicate the general nature of an injury: burns, fractured limb, head or internal injuries, gunshot wound, etc. However, the severity or medical details of injuries cannot be characterized except on the basis of a physician's diagnosis.

Some injuries, whose nature could fuel speculation about the patient or those associated with the patient, should not be discussed. These include possible child abuse, possible alcohol or drug abuse, and diagnoses that might suggest abuse, possible sexual assault, or any statements that suggest a wound was received as the result of a criminal act or possible suicide attempt. All of these situations require a conclusion that only authorized medical and legal authorities can make.

A matter of public record is a matter that the hospital is required to report to the coroner, police, public health agencies, and similar public authorities. These differ from state to state, and the hospital's legal counsel can identify the authorities to which reports must be made. As far as the public relations function is concerned, requests for information on a matter of public record that exceed the limited types described must be referred to the appropriate authority.

It is also necessary to obtain the attending physician's permission before releasing his or her name. Releasing the physician's name is inappropriate, however, if the physician's specialty might suggest too much about the nature of the patient's medical treatment.

If a newsworthy person's hospital stay is expected to last some time, the public relations staff should consult with the physician to arrange for the release of a daily bulletin. This will free the physician from press inquiries while assuring that he or she is the source for all information regarding the patient's progress. Some celebrities and public officials have their own press spokesmen. In such cases, the hospital should defer to the patient's representative.

Once a patient is released, the hospital can no longer provide information to the news media. All press inquiries are directed to the patient, next of kin or legal guardian, or personal spokesman.

## Making News

Press inquiries occur unexpectedly and must be dealt with in terms of an appropriate guiding policy. When soliciting press interest, however, planning should guide the process. Public relations is goal-oriented communication. The first question to ask when you have news to release is: What objective will this story serve? If you can't find an appropriate objective in the marketing plan, consider how the news item might be recast to serve an objective. It's a rare story that doesn't contain some angle that serves a current communication goal.

Don't simply announce new equipment or medical services; emphasize those aspects that support the hospital's market positioning. People stories, both hospital personnel and patients, can emphasize the hospital's growing medical stature, community roots, or caring philosophy.

When releasing news items, know who handles each type of story at each newspaper and broadcasting station and direct your story to the right person. As the hospital's press representative, you expect the press to direct its inquiries to you; editors and reporters assigned to cover health, science, business, etc., want appropriate stories directed to them. If nothing else, sending the story to the right news specialist may save it from being delayed or lost in the wrong person's in-basket.

Most stories can be handled with a news release and, perhaps, a follow-up phone call. Some simple news items that are particularly time-dependent, such as the death announcement of a newsworthy person, must necessarily be handled by phone (in this particular case, after informing the family).

A few, really significant stories can be given special-event treatment. In this case, you will be inviting the press to the hospital. You need to plan for press involvement in the activity. Suitable space should be reserved for television cameras, for example, and press microphones have to be accommodated on podiums. It might be appropriate to provide a backdrop with the hospital's logo in a low-traffic area where still photographers can set up shots and television crews can tape brief interviews without disrupting the program.

The most special of special events is the news conference. A poorly directed news conference is a mine field of potential disasters. News conferences should be limited to really significant news that can't be handled well in a more controlled format. News conferences require detailed preparations. Speakers have to be able to handle themselves well before the press and must be ready to field any question with skill.

And alas, after all the preparations, if the topic or timing is wrong, no one shows and you are left writhing with embarrassment. The public relations practitioner who lacks prior news conference experience should attend and study a few news conferences and get all the advice he can from peers and news media acquaintances before venturing upon such an enterprise.

## Press Kits

Reporters like to have ample background information when they write a story. The best way to fill this need is to prepare (and regularly update) a standard press kit about the hospital. A special event or news conference should be supported with special handouts: news releases, fact sheets, biographical sketches, and illustrations related to the particular event. These can be added to the hospital's regular press kit for distribution at the event.

The standard press kit begins with a listing of the staff members who are authorized to serve as press spokesmen. The kit should include a fact sheet that provides the hospital's vital statistics: location, affiliation, number of beds, medical services, and treatment specialties. This can be accompanied by a historical sketch or chronology of important events in the hospital's past. A copy of the hospital's mission statement and current annual report will round out the institutional background.

The kit should also provide personnel information: a list of the board, senior management, and physicians affiliated with the hospital. A selection of photos can include general views of the facilities and portraits of the board chairman, the chief executive, the head of medical staff, etc.

The hospital's press kit should be provided to all the local news media and reporters who cover hospital news. It will then be available, on file, whenever they need background information for a particular story. And the press kit itself serves a public relations function—it presents an image of the hospital to the news people who will be telling your story.

# Chapter 37

# Communicating Directly
# With the Public

More and more hospitals are pursuing public relations, marketing, and medical service goals through programs conducted outside the hospital's walls. These programs include health education and "wellness classes," mobile testing services, poison prevention and other safety awareness campaigns, exhibits at public events, telephone information or "hotline" services, and a plethora of similar activities that take the hospital to the public.

In fact, so many hospitals and other agencies are sponsoring community health and safety programs that the first step in creating a new program is to determine whether it duplicates another sponsor's existing program. The proposed activity should also meet a valid community need and serve the hospital's own communication goals.

One way to generate ideas for medical service programs is to consider an extension of existing "in-house" services into the community. A survey of emergency room, outpatient clinic, and ambulatory service personnel may produce suggestions for needed educational or testing programs that can be developed from existing resources and staff.

## Case Study: Mobile Healthwatch Unit

St. Vincent Medical Center in Toledo, Ohio, wanted to develop a health promotion program that would be unique to its market area and could be fully operational in six to eight months—with a $70,000 budget limit. Competing services and literature were reviewed, consumers were surveyed by telephone and focus groups, and meetings were held with organizations operating health promotion services.

The program objectives were then refined: free the program from the Medical Center's inner-city location to reach as many people as possible throughout a multicounty service area; make the program accessible to everyone (no fee or registration requirements); give the program a person-to-person, "high-touch" character; support the image and marketing strategies of the Center; and reach key publics— Catholics, senior citizens, and suburban and regional residents, especially families.

Clearly, a mobile program would be ideal. Consultation with hospitals operating mobile programs revealed that many were somewhat rigid in their capabililties, so St. Vincent decided upon an open van configuration that would maximize flexibility. First-year goals were set at visiting at least 40 sites in the five-county region, involving at least a hundred St. Vincent employees as volunteers, reaching at least 5,000 people with health information, and staying within budget.

With a $70,000 budget and vans costing $50,000, St. Vincent went looking for a cosponsor and found WTVG-TV, the local NBC affiliate. The station provided funds to buy the van, the hospital operates it, and both share the community visibility and goodwill. Having a television station as a cosponsor also guarantees some heavyweight promotional assistance, though it also naturally reduces competing stations to studied indifference.

An experienced nurse educator was hired as program manager, with particular attention to her personality and community contacts because the van had to be staffed with volunteers. She and a committee assessed the most often used health screenings and made choices based on ease of administration and ability to identify key risk factors. She also developed health information that could be inexpensively printed on cards, aprons in the hospital's logo color for volunteers to wear, and promotional shopping bags and balloons for patrons.

Volunteers were sought internally among employees, auxiliary members, retirees, and nursing school alumni; 462 signed up. The manager then solicited the Sight Center, Cancer Society, and other community agencies to provide materials for the van and assist with screenings.

Initial concern about how to publicize the Healthwatch Unit's availability without expensive advertising evaporated after the van was booked into three big shopping malls and the cosponsoring television station promoted it. People saw it and wanted it at schools, fairs, businesses, senior citizen centers, day camps, golf tournaments, and marathons.

The unit visited 164 sites in the first 10 months, provided 20,100 screenings (with 2,000 abnormal results, in many cases leading to medical treatment), and distributed 100,000 health information pieces. And target audiences were reached: 27 senior centers, 18 Catholic churches and schools, and sites in all suburban areas and the surrounding six-county region.

## Case Study: Goal-Oriented CPR Training

RHD Memorial Medical Center in Dallas, Texas, announced its goal to train one person in each household within its service area in cardiopulmonary resuscitation techniques. This is a fine thing for a hospital to do, but why this particular program for this particular hospital?

In addition to improving the medical center's image as an organization truly concerned with the well-being of the community, the program had these more specific communication objectives: to strengthen name recognition (the hospital has had four different names and logos in its 20 year history), to attract people to the campus to increase awareness of new facilities, and to link the center with heart-health messages to set the stage for an announcement that RHD Memorial would begin performing open-heart surgery.

Project LifeSaver was packaged to attract the person who aspires to be prepared and confident in an emergency. In addition to regular news media releases, a LifeSaver brochure was distribute to schools, businesses, and churches. Two issues of the hospital's external quarterly publication promoted the program, as did the hospital's community calendar distributed through a local bank's checking account statements and physician's offices. A LifeSaver teeshirt was given to all CPR-certified employees and all heart rehabilitation patients.

After six months, when some 300 persons had completed the free, three-hour training course, a print ad campaign was conducted with direct-mail support targeted to the hospital's immediate neighborhood. This was so effective that 500 additional people signed up, and the ads had to be pulled to allow the education coordinator and 50 volunteer nurse instructors to catch up.

Almost 2,000 inquiries were received, indicating that the 800 trainees were only a fraction of those who had received a favorable impression of RHD Memorial. The program also began to promote itself by word of mouth; 33 percent said they heard about the course from a friend.

Aside from providing a free health-care training program to its community and benefiting from the general goodwill this engenders, RHD Memorial achieved two specific communication goals by adopting this specific community program: It attracted 800 people to see its new six-story building and renovation at firsthand, and it associated the hospital with heart overtones in preparation for the introduction of open-heart surgery.

## Speakers and Experts

The news media are an imperfect transmitter of information between the hospital and its publics. Fortunately, there are also many ways to tell the hospital's story directly. A speakers bureau is one obvious way to talk directly to community audiences. Your chief executive, medical department heads, or other staff members can also be groomed to serve as expert guests on public affairs programs and talk shows when the topic involves health care, medical costs, legislation, and other hospital-related matters.

A speakers bureau could be a passive operation, providing speakers for groups when and if they ask; but an active program fits the concept of goal-oriented communication. Even smaller communities have a number of civic and service clubs that meet weekly and therefore have a constant demand for speakers. Then there are church groups, PTAs, the Chamber of Commerce, and fraternal associations. The hospital public relations staff can seek out such groups.

Many local radio and television stations produce community-affairs programs. These are excellent opportunities for the hospital's chief executive or medical head to talk about issues in greater depth and broader terms than news reporting allows. Local programs often feature segments on proper exercise, diet, and similar good-health topics; some of the medical staff's specialists would make appropriate guest experts for these.

Not everyone possesses public speaking skills or on-air confidence. Developing an active speakers program should include a "talent search" among potential hospital representatives and some helpful coaching. Playing back recorded speeches will help speakers polish their delivery. Videotaping mock interviews can help to put beginners at ease before the staring glass eye of the television camera.

The smaller newspapers, weekly "shoppers," and other

publications in the hospital's market area may be amenable to publishing a regular weekly or monthly column bylined by an appropriate hospital staff member. The broad field of health and medicine certainly offers enough topics, and the appearance of such a column demonstrates the hospital's active concern for a healthy and well-informed public.

All of these activities serve to identify your hospital as a useful information resource. More specifically, they also allow you to select the subjects you wish to address according to your communication goals and to speak directly to the audience in your own words.

## Publications

Hospital publications distributed directly to selected publics are yet another means to pursue goal-oriented communication. These days, residents in competitive hospital markets aren't surprised to find hospital newsletters in their mailboxes along with the supermarket mailers. These monthly or quarterly hospital publications appear to offer informative health-related news and features—and most of the space is indeed devoted to just that. But every article is keyed in some way to the hospital's communication goals.

The lead story in one typical hospital quarterly publication is headlined, "Women alcoholics: Are they different from alcoholic men?" The text provides many relevant facts about alcohol abuse by women, then notes that the hospital's Stress Center offers a separate women's group to deal with chemical dependency problems.

The next article, "Estrogen, calcium allied against osteoporosis," isn't tied to a hospital service but features comments by an OB/GYN physician on the hospital staff. On the same page is an announcement of the hospital's expanded no-smoking policy—concluding with a plug for the hospital's Smoke Stoppers classes.

A self-evaluation quiz lets readers rate the health aspects of their lifestyles. It the reader scores poorly in any of the three categories, a doctor's appointment is recommended and the phone number of the hospital's Physician Referral Service is provided. The quiz's questions also echo the hospital's wide array of "wellness classes." A course catalog and registration form are included as an insert.

From a public relations point of view, this publication serves many purposes: Most people don't think about hospitals until they need one, and the publication reminds them that the hospital is there, ready to serve them. The publication's design and production quality project an image of the hospital's quality of care. The articles are genuinely informative and create an impression of the hospital as the reader's partner in good health. And every single article, announcement, and quiz is a goal-oriented communication, directing the reader's attention to the hospital's many services and treatment specialties.

Publications, whether elaborate periodicals or simple pamphlets, can serve many of the hospital's external and internal communication needs. Externally, mail distribution allows you to target chosen publics as closely as you can refine the mailing lists. "Please take one" items in the hospital's visitor areas, outpatient clinics, physicians' offices, and other places will be picked up by a self-selected audience of those who are interested in the offered information.

Considering the institutional complexity of hospitals, publications and printed items can proliferate, along with cost. The public relations staff has an additional concern: Is the content of all these items consistent with the hospital's market positioning and communication goals? Costs and communicative confusion can be controlled with a periodic publications audit, during which all printed materials are identified, collected, and evaluated.

The evaluation includes such concerns as continued need; duplication of content in whole or part with other items; appropriateness of quality and design to intended purpose and audience; conformity of content with the hospital's market positioning and communication goals; and consistency with the hospital's overall graphics design system.

Publication quality is an important consideration because it reflects the hospital's image as a quality care provider. At the same time, considering the level of public concern for health-care costs, quality shouldn't be so opulent that it suggests needless extravagance.

Writing style should also be assessed against the item's intended audience. Younger readers need writing that is appropriate for their reading level. The general level of literacy skills in the hospital's market population should also be considered, as well as the prevalence of languages other than English.

To be cost effective, each of the hospital's publications needs to be carefully controlled in both content and distribution. Each published item's communication goal should be clearly defined and the intended audience clearly identified. Then content and distribution can be sharpened to achieve cost-effective, goal-achieving communication.

## Community Education

Another way to take the hospital to the public is through a more active pursuit of the hospital's potential role as a health-care educator rather than simply health-care provider.

Classes providing information, training, and support in achieving health goals are now a widespread phenomenon. One large midwestern hospital offers such classes at 13 locations around its city. During the first quarter of one year, the curriculum included:

*Fitness:* Ta'i Ch'i, Yoga, fitness assessment, determination of body fat percentage, rowing to fitness, cross-country skiing.

*Family life:* Breastfeeding your baby, caring for your newborn, Caesarean birthing, childhood first aid, grandparents update, infant home monitoring, maternal physical fitness, sibling preparation, fitness during pregnancy, preparation for childbirth, parents again: a childbirth refresher.

*Safety:* CPR, effective babysitting, latch-key kids, smoke stoppers.

*Wellness:* Weight control, breast self-examination, successful behavior change, wellness assessment, wellness over 60.

*Stress:* Stress management techniques, biofeedback stress assessment, mind-power sports, stress management for high school students, troubled sleepers.

*Medical:* Understanding cholesterol and HDL levels, facial cosmetic and reconstructive surgery, women's lifestyle and gender-related diseases.

*Support:* Eating disorders, the recently bereaved.

This type of community education program is a major operation within the hospital's organizational structure, and public relations will play only a supporting role in creating and administering such a program. However, public relations should be very alert to the fact that the hundreds of thousands of local residents who pass through such courses each year are another public with which the hospital has direct contact. The public relations staff should assess this opportunity and consider ways to achieve communication goals through these class sessions.

Nonetheless, as in the case of Dallas' RHD Memorial already described, and the following example, the public relations staff can play a major role in creating and conducting a community education or training program.

## Case Study: Education Through Entertainment

Health maintenance organizations like Kaiser Permanente in Cleveland, Ohio, take "an ounce of prevention is worth a pound of cure" as their credo. Kaiser had therefore developed an extensive health education program for teens, expectant parents, older and younger adults, and groups characterized by specific risk factors. School-age children were one group not yet fully served, although research indicated that health interest and attitudes can be strongly affected by a well-designed presentation, particularly if that presentation is entertaining.

Kaiser decided to create a school-age program with these objectives: 1) to produce a one-hour theatrical performance for grades K-6, utilizing humor and audience participation, 2) to provide support materials for students and teachers to help integrate the show's concepts into the classroom and home environment, 3) to provide the program free to any school or community group in the greater Cleveland area, and 4) to book a minimum of 60 performances during the first school year.

Ten subject areas were selected for appropriateness and the degree to which children can make choices that will affect their health. The messages would be presented by puppet "beasts" ranging from one to six feet in size. The educational objectives and Kaiser's desire for high quality led to consultations with experts in children's theater, health care, and education, as well as technical theatrical experts: a puppeteer, stage set designer, sound engineer, etc. A professional director and four actors were hired to stage the show.

The public affairs department developed a program brochure, a videotape, photos, and a media kit to promote the show. A teachers kit included three preshow posters, 20 postshow posters to reinforce health messages, an evaluation form, and a study guide providing discussion questions and activities for the classroom. A student take-home packet included a color postcard of the cast and characters, a toothbrush, and a newspaper featuring health facts, puzzles, and contests to reinforce health messages solicit student feedback.

All of the show scripts and printed materials were reviewed by physicians and educators for accuracy, appropriateness, and instructional approach. The development budget was $30,000 and the budget for support materials, salaries, and operating costs for the first four months of the school years was $34,000.

In late September, after seven months of development and six weeks of rehearsal, "Professor F. T. W. Bodywise and His Traveling Menagerie" was unveiled in two preview showings at The Cleveland Play House for Kaiser employees, physicians and their families, and representatives of area school systems. A presentation was also made to school superintendents. Reply cards were provided and phone numbers publicized so that schools could book performances or obtain more information. Within a few days, performances were booked through December. With the show on the road, news media were contacted, and all three local network affiliates aired segments of the show and its student audiences.

Prior to each performance, the public affairs department sent out news releases to newspapers covering the school's area. The show is also publicized through Kaiser's own publications directed to members, subscribing companies, and employees. Since the first performance, the show has received weekly print publicity as well as extensive coverage on "PM Magazine" and several cable networks.

By January, the show was completely booked through the end of the school year. More than 125 performances reached 77 schools, 30,000 students, and 1,500 adults. A waiting list for the next school year numbered 110 schools. Research conducted four months after a presentation indicates that students maintained a high recall rate for the "beasts" and their health messages.

## Special Observances

Annual health-related observance weeks provide a regular opportunity to create public relations programs tied to subject of the observance. Not to be missed are the hospital's own cardinal anniversaries. Some amount of drum beating and celebrating are expected for an institution's 50th or 100th anniversary. The public relations staff will usually have responsibility for such events and can make extra efforts to turn a routine commemoration into goal-oriented communication to both internal and external publics.

Swedish Covenant Hospital in Chicago, for example, used the opportunity of its centennial year to develop a comprehensive public relations effort that spanned the entire anniversary year. A 52-page commemorative booklet printed on heavy, high-gloss stock presented the Swedish Covenant story in photos and text under the themes "Looking Backward," "View of the Present," and "Looking Ahead." Fund-raising for new facilities, community relations events, and employee activities were all organized to tie into the celebration.

The hospital is located in a multiethnic area of the city, and its market positioning, "continuity of health for our neighborhood of nations," was communicated to the public through community events, including a two-day Centennial Festival that attracted 12,000 local residents to the hospital's park. The festival featured entertainment and food, a health fair, and a "birthday party" for everyone born at Swedish Covenant. The "neighborhood of nations" concept was dramatized by a march of hospital medical staff, employees, and friends dressed in native styles and carrying the flags of their national origins. A centennial banner was prominently displayed near the intersection at which the hospital is located to inform all who passed by that Swedish Covenant had been serving the community for 100 years.

Another program tied to the centennial and the "neighborhood of nations" concept was "100 Days of Health," a three-month series of free health screenings, community education seminars, and programs featuring the heritage and entertainments of individual nations cosponsored with local ethnic associations.

A centennial recognition honored board members, medical staff officers, administrators, and directors of nursing of the past and present, all of whom received certificates and medallion paperweights. Concluding the year's festivities was a Twelfth Night Party to thank employees for their help during the anniversary year.

Annual observance weeks and institutional anniversaries often inspire the usual range of ho-hum activities. The public relations practitioner's challenge is to develop creative new approaches to mark conventional observances, and to elevate them from mere observances to goal-oriented communication.

# Chapter 38

# Crisis Public Relations

The hospital, the community facility where life so often begins and ends, is a natural locus of crisis events and consequent news media attention. The admission of a newsworthy patient, a serious change in such a patient's condition, or the performance of a dramatic or high-risk procedure, can bring reporters swarming. The public relations staff needs to be informed of such events so that news media needs can be served as fully as possible while honoring the rights and wishes of the patient.

## Case Study: An Anonymous Celebrity

David was born in September 1971 with severe combined deficiency. This left him defenseless against germs and required him to live in a sterile environment, which became known as "the bubble." From the first story shortly after his birth, David was a celebrity. Everything that happened to him was news, but his last name remained unknown because his parents requested anonymity.

In September 1983, a treatment for David's condition, bone marrow transplant using special cells to prevent rejection, became reality. The public affairs office of the Baylor College of Medicine had already released more information about David than for the usual patient, and there was no doubt that the new treatment would be major news.

The adopted crisis communication plan included these objectives: 1) maintain secrecy regarding the treatment plans, 2) control an accurate flow of information to the news media about David's treatment and progress, 3) gain total cooperation by David and his parents, 4) release daily information from a single source, David's physician, and convey it to the news media only by designated spokesmen to ensure accuracy and consistency, 5) provide as much information as possible while preserving patient confidentiality, 6) gain the total dedication of the public affairs staff to the task, which would include night and weekend duty.

The public affairs office was informed of David's planned treatment in late August. Details were discussed with David's physician and the others who would be involved. About 25 local, national, and international news organizations were expected to cover the story; the actual number eventually grew to 52.

While the usual birthday news release was distributed, procedures were planned and materials prepared. Two staff members were assigned primary responsibility for the project, and two others were designated as spokespersons in the event of greater media interest. Press packets, excluding the news release and treatment photos, were assembled on the day before the treatment.

The procedure was performed at 3 AM on October 21 with two photographers and the primary spokespersons present. The press packets were completed by 11:00 AM, and by 12:30 PM the news media were informed of the treatment and of a 2:30 PM briefing. Treatment photos and videotapes were distributed at the first briefing, and a second briefing to update David's condition was held at 9:00 AM the next day.

Each news organization that wished to receive new information as it became available was asked to sign a call list at the initial briefings. Beginning October 24, brief daily condition reports from David's physician were relayed when requested.

On January 16, changes in David's condition made it necessary to implement the call list. A press conference was held 10 days later, when David's physician gave an encouraging report. Regular media calls began as David's condition worsened. When his removal from the isolation unit was announced, condition reports were made available at 1:00 PM each day.

The public affairs staff was placed on alert when it became necessary to put David on an artificial respirator. His death was announced on the evening of February 22. Specifics were provided from a quickly prepared press release by the four spokesmen. Arriving reporters were given interviews at the hospital and college by two spokesmen, while the other two handled phone inquiries. A briefing was held the next morning to discuss causes of death.

The David Center was announced on March 22. The 3,000 get-well and sympathy cards were answered by David's parents in a project coordinated by the public affairs office.

Throughout the program, local and national news reports were monitored daily. Final assessment of the program found that: 1) the news media had no prior knowledge that treatment would occur, 2) the program was controlled and the media were informed as fully as possible of David's progress, 3) there was full cooperation from David and his parents, without which the program could not have succeeded, 4) only a few instances were found when (especially after David died) information came from sources other than the public affairs staff, 5) statements were consistent, inaccurate reporting was corrected, and misinterpretations were clarified, and 6) David's last name has never been reported.

## Planning for Disaster

In David's case, the Baylor staff could estimate likely news media interest and could prepare a specific course of action and supporting materials to deal with a planned treatment. Quite another situation is presented by an unexpected disaster, natural or manmade, that floods the hospital with emergency patients, frantic loved ones, and reporters who want the story before you even know what it is.

Sooner or later, such a situation can occur at any hospital. If the crisis isn't to become a public relations disaster as well, the hospital's crisis medical services plan needs to be supported by a crisis public relations plan. Like the general press policy, the crisis plan should be known to each staff member and employee who might be approached by a reporter when an emergency strikes. With today's mobile radio and television units, the news gatherers can arrive at admission as quickly as the patients. There is no time to brief personnel when the moment strikes. Familiarize personnel with the plan, post it in likely locations, and include it in the procedures manual.

The first item in the plan is a call list of designated hospital representatives with their home and other alternate phone numbers. The duty staff should know where to locate the public relations director at all times. A personal beeper is the ultimate solution to this problem. An alternate spokesman is designated to assume information control when the primary spokesman is not available or is delayed in arriving.

The crisis public relations plan should provide frontline employees with three basic instructions: respond courteously, inform the reporter that you are not authorized to speak for the hospital, and transfer the reporter to a person who is. Designated representatives should then be listed with telephone numbers in order of choice, so that if the first representative is occupied at that moment, the next can be called.

If practical, it is more efficient to separate designated representatives into two groups, those who will handle press information and those who can handle calls from victims' families and friends. The two types of callers want different types of information, and dividing the functions allows the press specialists to deal with news media demands more quickly and effectively.

Also if practical, the designated press spokesmen can be divided into those who will remain at their phones and those who will work out front, dealing in person with arriving reporters and camera crews. Crisis plan instructions for the security staff will ease the situation for the public relations practitioner who is taking phone calls while reporters are wandering the halls and receiving areas.

In a crisis, the hospital public relations practitioner has the same problem as the reporters—finding out just what is happening. In a serious, fast-breaking situation, it is essential to name one person as controller to monitor developments, verify information, and brief other authorized spokesmen on any changes.

The crisis communication plan should provide some detailed instructions on how designated spokesmen should respond to expected questions. It is impossible to anticipate every type of disaster that might occur, but some are more likely than others for a particular hospital. Every community is subject to major fires, gas explosions, and similar events that may strike a school, business, or place of amusement. If your facility is in the vicinity of a major airport, large industrial works, mines, or in tornado country or an active earthquake zone, these can be specified.

List each likely disaster, or class of events, and provide appropriate instructions according to the legal and ethical considerations that might affect the type of information you provide to the news media. The rules regarding the release of individual patient information apply in a mass-casualty crisis, too. But the press will also want to know the number of victims being treated, the general nature and seriousness of injuries, and what special measures the hospital is taking to cope with the emergency. Reporters will also want to interview victims.

It is vital, of course, to prevent reporters or family members from adding to the bustle and confusion of the emergency room and treatment areas, where they could distract the medical personnel and make it more difficult to deal with patients. When preparing the crisis plan, the public relations and security staff should designate a news media center and a family center in the hospital. When crisis strikes, security personnel can then bring reporters to the news center, where their needs can be serviced most effectively.

The press center should be separated from the treatment areas and the location chosen for families of the victims to gather. In selecting the press area, consider such factors as convenient access (with, perhaps, nearby parking for news vehicles where they won't interfere with emergency vehicles), adequate space for reporters and equipment, and sufficient electrical outlets and telephones. The telephones should be designated for press use so reporters won't go in search of other phones that may be needed by hospital personnel to deal with the emergency.

One person should be designated as press center spokesman, and that person should provide updates for the reporters as frequently as possible. All information should be carefully verified before release. In a disaster, no information is better than wrong information. Particular care must, of course, be taken in compiling survivor and fatality lists. In the latter case, it is sufficient to report only the number until next of kin can be notified. Except for protected patient information, it is best to confirm *known* facts, even if they might reflect poorly on the hospital, since reporters will get the story eventually.

News people won't like being penned up "away from the action." It is therefore very helpful in maintaining control and serving press needs to bring some key figures—the hospital's chief executive, appropriate medical department heads, the emergency room's supervising nurse, for example—to the press center for occasional briefings. Providing this access will help to curtail reporters' attempts to reach these people on their own.

News crews will be eager to get some action scenes on tape or film and talk to victims. This access should be provided but carefully controlled so as not to disturb medical services or violate patient privacy. If circumstances make a news pool advisable, let the reporters decide who will comprise this limited group. Patients who are willing and able to be interviewed can be brought to the press room, or the press brought to them on an individual basis, depending on the situation. Patient information release forms must, of course, be signed in either case.

The hospital switchboard is a critical factor in crisis management. The switchboard operators need to know the crisis information procedure, since they have to direct press telephone calls to the proper staff. A serious disaster can swamp the switchboard with incoming calls, so the telephone system needs to be analyzed with regard to how this may affect the ability of reporters to make calls from the press room. When the names of admitted patients are known, reporters may also try to call them for comments. These calls shouldn't be put through when attending physicians do not want patients to be disturbed.

In addition to the security personnel, two other groups can be of great help in a crisis: the chaplain's service and the hospital's medical social workers. On-duty representatives of these services, and off-duty volunteers who can be called in, can deal with the families and friends of patients while the public relations staff handles press relations. The hospital's medical emergency plan, and the public relations plan within it, should specify and coordinate the responsibilities of all departments in meeting the needs of a crisis situation.

The hospital's medical emergency plan should be shared with the local police department, fire department, civil defense, and similar agencies. The public relations staff should also provide an outline of its crisis communications plan to the local news media. Reporters are more likely to cooperate during a crisis if they are already familiar with the procedures that will be followed. Constructive suggestions by reporters may also produce improvements that will make the plan more effective when it is put to the test.

# Case Studies

The case studies presented in this section are award winners in the 1985 and 1986 competitions of the Public Relations Society of America (PRSA) and International Association of Business Communicators (IABC). PRSA conducts an annual competition, called the Silver Anvil Awards, to recognize excellent public relations programs conducted by companies, organizations, institutions, and government agencies to encourage superior public relations performance. IABC's Gold Quill Awards program spotlights professional communicators whose entries are issues-based and well executed and display return on their investment in communication: results.

# Operation Home Free

The Trailways Corporation sought a community-service program that would have significant impact in the more than 12,000 U.S. cities in which it operates. It wanted a program that would benefit all socioeconomic groups, address a specific and timely social issue, and would be directly related to the service the company performs without creating additional operating costs.

It was learned from the International Association of Chiefs of Police (IACP) that more than 1.5 million youths are listed as missing each year. Many of this group are runaways who would return home if they had the means to do so without having to ask their parents for help.

Trailways devised Operation: Home Free, utilizing its existing routes and service (thus not adding to existing operational costs) to offer free transportation to runaways. It worked with IACP as verification centers for runaway youths. Any youngster identified as a runaway by an officer of the court would be eligible for a free ride to his or her hometown. The program would be voluntary in that the child would have to consent to the trip and the family would be notified by IACP.

To launch the program, Trailways held a press conference in New York City on June 7, 1984. Posters were distributed throughout the Trailways network and by the IACP through its member departments in 13,000 cities and towns across America. A public-service radio announcement was issued, a billboard campaign was launched with space donated by the Eighth Street Outdoor Billboard Association and distribution was handled by the Amusement Game Manufacturers Association. There were ticket inserts to alert Trailways passengers of the program, an employee communication program, and press releases. A letter was also sent to social-service agencies to alert them to the program.

Since June 7, 1984, more than 10 runaways have utilized the program daily. By Christmas 1984, more than 2,000 children had been reunited with their families as a result of the program. Trailways has received numerous public service awards, each generating more press contacts. More than 250 million consumer impressions were made through newspaper and television during the first six months of the program.

On December 10, 1984, the Trailways Corporation was named the first member of the transportation industry to receive a "C Flag" from President Reagan's office for Private Sector Initiatives for the Operation: Home Free program. This honor was publicized.

(This public relations program, submitted by the Trailways Corporation, Dallas, Texas, received a Silver Anvil Award in the Community Relations, Business, category of the 1985 Public Relations Society of America (PRSA) competition. Excerpted with permission from PRSA.)

# Art Sunday at JCPenney

With an image as a middle-income, basic-goods retailer established during its 82-year history, JCPenney sought to alter its position to become a more fashionable, upper-middle-income department-store chain. The change of image was to be done through designer fashions, advertising, and modernization of its major stores.

In 1984 the company's five Dallas stores were targeted for a $20-million modernization program. The challenge was to communicate the new image and attract the newly targeted "department-store shopper" in the high-fashion, overdeveloped Dallas retail market.

A public relations/special events campaign was sought to introduce the "new" JCPenney to the Dallas/Fort Worth Metroplex, especially to the "upwardly mobile young professionals with an income of $26,000 plus." The objectives were as follows: to communicate JCPenney's image change through editorial coverage; to attract at least 500 "upscale" shoppers into the featured modernized store; and to secure a sales gain in the targeted modernized stores greater than in the company as a whole and in other modernized stores without campaigns.

The arts were pinpointed as a major concern of upscale Dallas. Therefore, *Art Sunday at JCPenney* was conceptualized: a series of four arts festival/benefits in four modernized stores on four Sundays in July/August 1984, benefiting four different arts-fundraising organizations.

Hundreds of performers and visual artists, key celebrities, refreshments, and a "Fashion in Art" fashion show would be featured. A total budget of $94,000 was established for the four shopping areas, with the public relations firm of Callas, Foster & Sweeney assisting in media contact. Staffing was to consist of one public relations professional, a temporary assistant, help from the sales-promotion manager, and organized help from the stores and arts volunteers.

The major components of the project were as follows:

- *Beneficiaries.* Appropriate beneficiaries in each market area were approached to host an Art Sunday, with JCPenney donating $10,000-$15,000 per group plus operating capital and ticket proceeds. The beneficiaries were to provide an upscale membership audience, all arts entertainment, concessions, catering, labor, and help with publicity.

- *Cosponsors.* Additional sponsors were sought, which included *The Dallas Morning News*, which designed, printed, and donated $10,000-$15,000 worth of invitations, postcard mailers, posters, and ad slicks. It also donated one ad per Sunday. Three shopping malls provided funding, ads, and props.

- *Advertising.* Three-quarter-page ads were run the week before each Sunday in the *News* and other local dailies. Thousands of hand-addressed invitations and postcards were mailed, and posters were distributed by the beneficiaries. Advertising costs came to approximately $9,947.

- *Publicity.* JCPenney developed comprehensive publicity plans. Series of releases and PSAs were targeted to appropriate contacts. Hors d'oeuvres on artist's palates were hand-delivered to the press on the first Sunday.

A tight schedule of Sundays was established to maximize media attention, and special care was taken to avoid the Republican convention and the Olympics. Meetings were held with store management to win and maintain enthusiasm. Highlights of the events are as follows:

- *Northpark*, July 29, benefiting the 500 Inc., a prestigious group of 3,000 young professionals. Special guest was Tony Bennett and the Southwest premier of his paintings. There were 20 performing groups—from ballet dancers and symphony trios to breakdancers—plus the Fashion as Art designer show. Champagne and hors d'oeuvres were served. Some 1,200 attended.

- *Red Bird*, August 5, benefiting Mountain View College Fine Arts Division Scholarship Fund, strongest cultural force in the area. There were more than 200 performers throughout the store and on center stage. Around 700 attended this "family atmosphere" event.

- *Irving*, August 12, "Free to Public" fundraiser gala benefiting Irving Cultural Affairs Council. There were 150-plus entertainers, concession stands, a Fashion as Art show, and a Irving Symphony concert. The attendance came to around 5,000.

- *Six Flags*, August 26, a free fundraiser benefiting the Arlington Fine Arts Council. Featured were 150-plus entertainers, booths of visual arts, concessions in the afternoon, and champagne/hors d'oeuvres in the evening with Miss USA Suzi Humphries and "Fashion as Art." Attendance totaled 3,000.

The initial objectives were met as follows:

1. Publicity totaled 6,826 column inches, 136 broadcast minutes, 19.9 million impressions; substantial publicity in society and business sections of major Dallas/Forth Worth papers; national UPI wire story in 100 papers, major spreads in lifestyle sections, TV and radio stories.

2. Nearly 10,000 "upscale" shoppers attended the Art Sundays. Dallas is now number one in more expensive label-line fashions for JCPenney nationally. The modernized stores had an increase of twice the rate in October of new bankcard business, indicated possible new upscale shoppers.

3. Sales increased 39, 59, and 100 percent in August, September, and October, respectively, in the modernized stores. They also had a 33 percent greater sales increase rate their first month after construction than the average rate of the 40 stores modernized (but with no comparable event their first month).

(This public relations program, submitted by JCPenney Company, Dallas/Fort Worth District, Dallas, Texas, received a Silver Anvil Award in Special Events and Observances, Business, category of the 1985 Public Relations Society of America (PRSA) competition. Excerpted with permission from PRSA.)

# Pharmacists Against Drug Abuse (PADA)

McNeil Pharmaceutical, a Johnson & Johnson company, as a leading voice in the pharmaceutical industry, is a strong proponent of the responsible use of both prescription and nonprescription drugs. At a special White House briefing by First Lady Nancy Reagan on drug abuse and the family, McNeil Pharmaceutical made a commitment to initiate an antidrug program to educate parents on the dangers of illicit drug use by children.

Research revealed that despite a growing national concern for the drug abuse problem among youths, little accurate information on the health hazards of the most commonly abused "gateway" drugs—marijuana, alcohol, and cocaine—was available to parents.

Meetings were held with state and federal officials, appropriate private-sector groups, and national drug-abuse parents groups, providing Clarke & Company Public Relations with an excellent base on which to build a program. The objects of the program were as follows:

1. To provide the public with widely available, accurate information that addressed the gateway drugs, the signs of drug abuse, health hazards, and steps to take with the child involved in drugs. The information was to be available through a widely recognized community resource in towns throughout the country.

2. To encourage parents to become involved in recognizing drug-abuse problems not only in their families but in the community as well through the formation of parents-support groups.

3. To establish McNeil Pharmaceutical as an industry leader committed to halting the drug abuse program in the United States.

4. To select a theme: "Pharmacists Against Drug Abuse." A brochure entitled "The Kinds of Drugs Kids Are Getting Into" was published.

In addition to the development of a theme and logo and publication of the brochure, other steps included the following:

- Creation of a pharmacy kit—poster, door decal, pocket-saver, and brochure easel.

- Production of public-service campaign via print, radio, and television.

- Development of pharmacy speakers' training kit of slides and speeches.

- Contact of key constituents for support and input: ACTION, PRIDE, chain-drug store associations, state pharmaceutical associations, parents groups, and local, state, and federal drug officials.

- Gaining of endorsement for PADA from First Lady Nancy Reagan in the form of a letter in each of the pharmacy kits.

- Distribution of 55,000 pharmacy kits across the country.

- Launching of PADA test in New England and collecting and analyzing initial test results.

- Launching of national PADA program at media conferences, beamed by satellite, plus utilization of AT&T Teleconference network for eight additional media conferences.

- Implementation of PADA pharmacist-training program.

The results of the PADA program were as follows:

1. Ongoing distribution of over 20 million PADA brochures through pharmacists nationwide.

2. Ongoing requests from 4,000 civic, social, school, and religious groups nationwide for over several million brochures for distribution to their memberships.

3. Sharp increase in calls to PRIDE and the National Federation of Parents for Drug Free Youth since the national launch.

4. Formation of more than 300 new parents' groups.

5. Media coverage of more than 75 million impressions, from the largest dailies to the smallest neighborhood weeklies.

6. Expansion of PADA to Europe, South America, and the U.S. Military Overseas Armed Forces.

(This public relations program, submitted by McNeil Pharmaceutical, Spring House, Pennsylvania, received a Silver Anvil Award in the Public Service, Business, category of the 1985 Public Relations Society of America (PRSA) competition. Excerpted with permission from PRSA.)

# Virginia's Tips for the Physically Disabled Traveler

Research conducted by the Virginia Division of Tourism (VDT) showed progress in the field of travel for the disabled, including devices for the deaf used by major travel organizations, availability of rental cars with hand controls, transportation systems with wheelchair accessibility, and a wide range of programs offered by attractions.

A poll of 50 state tourism agencies revealed that many had developed access guides but none had developed a comprehensive public-awareness program that incorporated planning tips to reach disabled travelers.

The marketing opportunity was defined to reach the travel-market segment called "the physically handicapped" with news of opportunities for travel in Virginia. The goal was to increase awareness of Virginia as a primary vacation destination for physically disabled travelers and to increase the number of visitors throughout the state.

To meet the challenge, VDT set two objectives: 1) to stress the importance of advanced planning to disabled travelers and 2) to make it convenient for them to vacation in Virginia by offering information about accessible attractions and a resource bank of advocacy groups, which they could contact if emergencies should arise during their visits to Virginia.

In September 1984 a public relations program was proposed to reach disabled travelers in Virginia's established key markets. VDT developed a budget, gained support of Virginia's disabled community leaders, selected geographic markets, developed a media plan, selected and trained spokespersons, and developed evaluation tools to measure response to the program.

A budget of $15,000 was set to cover travel expenses and collateral materials, and all phases of the program were implemented from October 1984 through March 1985. All accessible Virginia attractions were contacted. Virginia's Advocacy Office for the

Developmentally Disabled provided materials for inclusion in the booklet, "Tips for the Physically Disabled Traveler."

Geographic target markets were selected. Disabled travelers in major major areas were reached through television and radio talk shows with audience levels of more than 50,000. A news release describing the program was sent to all daily newspapers in the continental U.S., and in Canada and Mexico. There were articles in VDT newsletters, which were sent to Virginia travel-industry leaders and bus-tour operators through the United States.

As the only state or city tourism agency invited, VDT participated in a panel of experts on disabled travelers at the U.S. Travel and Tourism Administration's "State/City's Day" in Washington, D.C., on February 6, 1985.

Media coverage included the following:

- Appearances on 17 national news and talk shows in Tampa and Miami, Florida; Altoona and Johnstown, Pennsylvania; Greensboro and Raleigh, North Carolina; Cleveland, Cincinnati, and Youngstown, Ohio; Detroit, Michigan; Louisville, Kentucky; and Albany, New York; with total viewership of 2,860,000.

- Ten radio talk-show appearances in the cities of Miami, Tampa, Louisville, Johnstown, and Detroit, for a total estimated audience level of 1,234,000.

- Coverage by newspapers with combined total circulation of 1,342,143. This coverage was in the states of Virginia, Illinois, North Carolina, Ohio, Arizona, New Jersey, Wisconsin, Florida, Pennsylvania, Texas, and Hawaii, as well as Canada and Mexico.

(This public relations program, submitted by the Virginia Division of Tourism, Richmond, Virginia, received a Silver Anvil Award in the Marketing Communication (Non-Products and Services), Government, category of the 1985 Public Relations Society of America (PRSA) competition. Excerpted with permission from PRSA.)

# Shaping a Positive Consumer Climate

Concerned about the emergence of new values that made an unfavorable impact on the purchase of meat and meat products, the National Live Stock & Meat Board (Meat Board) commissioned studies by Yankelovich, Skelly and White, Inc. (YSW) in 1981 and 1983.

By 1983, it appeared that the reduction in meat consumption seen in 1981 was leveling off and the market climate appeared more favorable for meat-industry messages. The exceptions to the positive trend were processed meats (ham, bacon, sausage, and luncheon meats), which were perceived as too high in fat, salt, cholesterol, and additives.

The Meat Board formed a Processed Meat Committee to deal with these issues and retained Daniel J. Edelman, Inc., to develop a public relations strategy that would defend and expand usage of processed meats. A program was implemented in August 1983.

With the Meat Board staff, the agency adopted a consumer-segmentation model suggested by the YSW data and developed target media and communication strategies for each. Three of the segments—meat lovers, creative cooks, and price-driven—were presumed to already like meat, and the objective was to prevent further erosion by providing new recipes and serving suggestions. Although the two less-favorable groups—active life style and health oriented—comprised only 33 percent of the total consumer public, they were the opinion leaders, with high incomes and influence on the media and the general public. The objective was to reassure this latter group that processed meats could be an appropriate part of a normal, healthful diet and that trendy, fit, slim people included processed meats in their diets.

The following steps were taken:

- The negative "processed"was replaced by the acronym NEAT meat (meat that is nutritious, easy, appealing, and tasty). Where not appropriate, they are referred to as deli-meats, a return to old-fashioned flavor, or as charcuterie, an upscale term for deli meats.

- The national media was invited to CHARCUTERIE in New York City. All deli meats were reintroduced under this upscale umbrella, inviting the media to sample Oragami Hors d' Oeuvres, Sandwich Salads, Star-Spangled Sausages, the Entertaining Ham, a Do-It-Yourself Deli, and Breakfast-on-the Go.

- CHARCUTERIE press kits were distributed to national media and NEAT meat press kits to newspaper food editors nationwide.

- Interviews were arranged in 10 top ADI markets for a fitness expert promoting exercise and proper diet, including deli meats.

- A fitness expert and nutritionist was featured on a radio release to 190 stations for seven weeks during National Meat Week.

- Restaurant futurist George Lang was retained to describe the fun, fantasy, and flavor of deli meats. In interviews on television and radio and in print, he predicted a sausage renaissance and return to "momma food": ham, bacon, and sausage.

- Arrangements were made for features to carry upscale, fun, and fantasy messages or the diet/health messages on network, syndicated, and cable TV.

- Processed Meat Committee was kept current with the objectives and successes of their program.

- Visuals and strategies were developed for revenue development.

The results were as follows:

In the first 18 months of the program 800 million positive consumer impressions were generated.

National media coverage reached all publics through *PM Magazine*, NBC Today (twice), Alive & Well, Associated Press, King

Features (twice), *Christian Science Monitor, Family Weekly,* NEA, and others.

The "Creative Cook" segment of women's service magazines were targeted with recipes and full-color photographs, reaching some 215 million readers of magazines that included *Parents* (twice), *Woman's Day, Redbook,* and *McCalls* (five times).

Positive nutrition messages were targeted at the "Active Life Style and Health Oriented" readers of *Woman's Day, Co-ED & Forecast, Redbook, Good Housekeeping, Mademoiselle,* and *Glamour,* with readership totaling 60 million.

Upscale recipes and features were sent and used in *Food & Wine, Cuisine,* and *Country Living,* with combined circulation of 13 million.

A spokesperson for the Processed Meat Committee summarized the project as follows: "A formal review of the first 18 months of the Meat Board program to increase consumer acceptance of processed meats has been most encouraging. Not only have my expectations from the start of the program been exceeded, but our success has shown me that there is a receptive audience for our message among those that communicate with our target audience."

(This public relations program, submitted by the National Live Stock & Meat Board, Chicago, Illinois, with Daniel J. Edelman, Inc., Chicago, received a Silver Anvil Award in the Marketing Communication (Established Products and Services), Trade Associations, category of the 1985 Public Relations Society of America (PRSA) competition. Excerpted with permission from PRSA.)

# The Vietnam Veterans
# Memorial Fund: Removing the Stain

In the summer of 1983, officials of the Vietnam Veterans Memorial Fund (VVMF) learned that WDFV-TV of Washington, D.C., had assigned an investigative reporter to look into allegations of financial improprieties and mismanagment in VVMF. The Fund, begun in 1979, had raised more than $9 million from the public to build a memorial to those who served in the Vietnam War.

The reporter on the assignment, Carlton Sherwood, was a decorated Vietnam veteran and winner of a Pulitzer Prize and a Peabody Award. The VVMF officials, however, were concerned because Sherwood had not contacted them.

Therefore, VVMP President Jan Scruggs contacted Sherwood in July 1983. After several conversations with the reporter, Scruggs became apprehensive about the direction in which the investigation was going. The design for the memorial had been chosen following a long, difficult fight and after what was believed to be the world's largest design contest. Permission to build the memorial came only after the VVMF agreed to a compromise design that included the addition of a statue and flagpole. Having gone through enough controversy, the Fund asked Hartz/Meek International (HMI) to provide public relations counsel.

Research conducted by HMI revealed that although Sherwood had impressive credentials, journalists and others familiar with his work did not respect him and that he was opposed to the memorial design and was allied with its opponents. Moreover, VVMF had just been audited, without problems, by the Internal Revenue Service and its own special-audit committee.

With this information, HMI outlined the following plan of action:

- A VVMF meeting with WDVM News Director David Pearce to advise him of the two audits of the fund books.

- A contingency plan for VVMF to refute all allegations when and if Sherwood's investigations was aired by the station.

- A major publicity effort for VVMF until Veterans Day 1984, at which time the statue would be unveiled and the Memorial turned over to the National Park Service.

- Involvement of legal counsel.

On November 7, 1983, WDVM-TV aired the first of what was to be a four-part series by Sherwood on VVMF, which included numerous unsubstantiated charges and innuendos.

The Washington media was informed that Scruggs was available for interviews to counter the WDVM-TV charges. A press conference was called by VVMF on the day following the third part of the television series. As part of the HMI rebuttal plan, Senators Warner (R-VA) and Mathias (R-MD), the sponsors of the legislation that enabled the memorial to be constructed on government property, issued strong statements in support of VVMF.

At the press conference, Scruggs offered to open VVMF books for an audit if WDVM-TV would pay for it. The television station accepted the offer and canceled the final Sherwood report. Within a month, WDVM-TV notified VVMF that it was backing out of the audit and Sherwood left the station in a dispute over another VVMF story with more allegations against VVMF. The station refused to substantiate the charges or apologize. The General Accounting Office was then asked and agreed to conduct a complete audit of the fund.

HMI began a major effort to gain positive publicity for VVMF, which included the following:

- Publicizing completion of the lifesize clay model of the statue.

- A lobbying effort to get the Department of Defense (DOD) to include the memorial in the State Funeral of the Vietnam Unknown Soldier on Memorial Day 1984, after DOD had refused to cooperate with VVMF. (As a result a plan was adopted that permitted the cortege to stop at the memorial, an event that was covered live for two hours by all three networks and CNN.)

- Work with the U.S. Postal Service to get a commemorative stamp honoring the memorial and publicizing the stamp.

- Major coverage of the VVMF ceremony at the memorial prior to the interment of the Vietnam unknown.

When word leaked out that the GAO audit would give the fund a clear bill of health, HMI recommended that a news conference be held by Senators Warner and Mathias on the day the GAO report was to be issued. The press conference was held and covered by some 40 members of the media. HMI also drafted an apology for WDVM-TV use and carried on negotiations with top station executives.

Since money spent on public relations was among the VVMF expenditures attacked by Sherwood, expenditure for this activity was limited to less than $30,000 from July 1983 to November 1984.

HMI's efforts to remove the stain on VVMF culminated on November 7, 1984, when News Director David Pearce read the apology to VVMF on prime-time evening newscasts. In addition, VDVM-TV made a $50,000 contribution to the fund.

HMI completed its program of projecting VVMF positively by handling the statue-unveiling ceremony on November 9, 1984, and the final dedication and conveyance of the memorial to the U.S. National Park Service. Almost 500 news-media credentials were issued for the weekend's events, which included the First-Day Ceremony of the U.S. Postal Service stamp featuring the memorial. President Reagan accepted the memorial from Jan Scruggs before more than 100,000 cheering Vietnam veterans and friends gathered on the mall on Veterans Day, November 11, 1984.

(This public relations program, submitted by the Vietnam Veterans Memorial Fund with Hartz/Meek International, Washington, D.C., received a Silver Anvil Award in the Emergency Public Relations category of the 1985 Public Relations Society of America (PRSA) competition. Excerpted with permission from PRSA.)

# Fiber Factor Program

Inasmuch as fiber-depleted diets in the Western Hemisphere had been associated with heart disease, colon cancer, obesity, diabetes, and hypertension, Quaker Oats Company recognized a potential opportunity in the marketing of foods high in complex carbohydrates and dietary fiber.

Research programs initiated by Quaker with university scientists showed that there are two types of dietary fibers: water-soluble and water-insoluble. Oats are a good source of water-soluble fiber, which is effective in reducing cholesterol and blood pressure and in regulating blood glucose. A new product, Quaker Oat Bran, was shown to be an even more concentrated source of water-soluble fiber than oats. Both products could be recommended to individuals with high cholesterol levels and/or diabetes as well as to persons in healthful dietary regimes.

In 1983, Quaker surveyed 135,000 cardiologists, internists, nutritionists, and dietitians to determine their interest in learning about the latest research findings on dietary fiber. An 8 percent positive response was received, surpassing the 3 percent that had been projected.

The company also surveyed 100 food media representatives to determine their interest in the subject. These editors indicated positive interest in information that was responsibly presented, communicated in lay terms, and delivered in publishable segments. A survey of consumers to determine their understanding of the food sources and health benefits of dietary fiber indicated limited knowledge but high interest in products positioned for healthy eating.

With their research results, Quaker developed a public relations campaign, the Fiber Factor Program, to meet the following objective: educate medical/health professionals on the health benefits of oat fiber and generate their endorsement of the product messages among their patients. Quaker then extended the

Fiber Factor Program to food opinion leaders to educate consumers on the health benefits of oat fiber and the versatility and nutritional value of oats and oat bran as recipe ingredients for healthy diets. In conjunction with Myers CommuniCounsel and Marian Tripp Communications, Quaker's Consumer Affairs Center developed and executed the program—from mid-1983 through 1984—within a $250,000 budget.

The program was executed as follows:

1. Dr. James W. Anderson, professor of medicine and clinical nutrition at the University of Kentucky and a pioneer in dietary fiber research, was retained as Quaker's spokesperson for the Fiber Factor Program.

2. Workshops on high-fiber diets were conducted by Dr. Anderson for a total of 500 dietitians in four cities—Boston, Chicago, San Francisco, and Houston. As a result of these workshops, Quaker continues to receive an average of 25 requests monthly for collateral materials and products for distribution by dietitians at community nutrition fairs and hospital seminars.

3. A series of *Fiber Factor Newsletters*, written by medical researchers in the field of dietary fiber and produced by Quaker, was distributed to 11,000 professionals who requested to be on the mailing list, which has since grown by more than 18 percent.

4. Quaker exhibited at the annual meeting of the American Dietetic Association, reaching 10,000 attending dietitians with information about the health benefits of water-soluble dietary fiber. As a result, Quaker was asked by the California Dietetic Association to sponsor its statewide media tour on fiber and health eating, the first time the CDA had sought corporate sponsorship.

5. Quaker arranged speaking engagements for Dr. Anderson at medical conventions, at which he reached more than 1,000 physicians with his latest fiber research findings.

6. Local media interviews with Dr. Anderson resulted in reaching 4.9 million consumers.

7. A series of five recipe pamphlets featuring Quaker Oats and Oat Bran were distributed in quantity, free of charge, to physicians and dietitians for patient use. An initial printing of 100,000 was followed by a second printing of 200,000 to fulfill requests from the medical/health community.

8. The Fiber Factor Program was introduced to food editors at a breakfast meeting on dietary fiber at the Newspaper Food Editors Conference, resulting in 35 major newspaper feature stories that included oats and/or oat bran recipes.

9. A 13-part series of syndicated feature columns was developed for food editors, formatted for easy communication. The series is carried exclusively by newspapers in 104 markets, with a combined circulation of 7 million.

10. Magazine food editors were targeted for features and 15 placements were achieved, including *Family Circle* and *Saturday Evening Post*. The combined magazine circulation was 12 million.

11. A consumer newsletter, *The Oat Report*, was distributed to 3,000 USDA county home extension agents responsible for the dissemination of information to consumers through radio programs, newspaper columns, and workshops.

12. An issue of *Quaker Quotes*, an educator lesson package for use in junior and senior high schools, featuring dietary fiber, was distributed to 55,000 educators and used as a lesson plan for 6 million home economics students.

13. The Fiber Factor Program was featured in *Quaker's CAC* (Consumer Affairs Center) *News and Views*, a newsletter distributed to supermarket consumer affairs directors, who often share the information with customers.

The Fiber Factor Program met all its objectives:

1. Physicians and dietitians learned more about the health benefits of Quaker Oats and Oat Bran, endorsing that information to their patients by distributing 1.5 million Quaker recipe pamphlets.

2. National publicity regarding dietary fiber reached an audience of 100 million.

3. Three newsletters targeted to food opinion leaders resulted in an additional 7 million consumer impressions.

(This public relations program, submitted by the Quaker Oats Company, Chicago, Illinois, with Myers CommuniCounsel, New York, New York, and Marion Trip Communications, Chicago, received the Silver Anvil Award in the Special Public Relations category of the 1985 Public Relations Society of America (PRSA) competition. Excerpted with permission from PRSA.)

# Monsanto Plant Community Communications Program

In the aftermath of the Union Carbide tragedy in Bhopal, India, and subsequent accidents in the U.S., the Monsanto Company faced a challenge to communicate effectively with the communities in which it operates chemical plants. To move out of a defensive posture, Monsanto developed a model communications program that could be run in any of the 50 cities in which it operates. The program was launched in two cities—Springfield, Massachusetts, and Cincinnati, Ohio—and implemented during a three-month period.

The objectives were twofold: 1) to build confidence among key audiences (neighbors around the plant site, local government and civic leaders, business executives, and educators) in plant-site communities about the safety of Monsanto chemical facilities, and 2) to position Monsanto as a responsible contributor to the community's economy and quality of life.

Safety procedures were reviewed in all plants before any public relations activities were started. A companywide task force was appointed to study the issue, and several recommendations were made and implemented—including a sizable reduction in hazardous gases stored at plant sites. Community leaders were informed of all hazardous materials handled at the Monsanto plants, with "Material Safety Data Sheets" (lists of all these materials) made available to city governments, fire departments, and other appropriate agencies.

Then the public relations activities began, including media tours, speeches, special community events and projects, interviews for the media, publicity support for Monsanto plant contributions to community programs, and media training for plant executives.

More than 16 special activities were carried out in the two communities which included the following:

1. *Emergency action card.* These cards, developed in conjunc-

tion with local poison control centers, contained first aid information and emergency telephone numbers, plus the message: "Monsanto—Where Safety Comes First." More than 120,000 cards were distributed to homes and school districts in the two cities.

2. *School bus safety project.* Working with Cincinnati public television station WCET, Monsanto produced a 15-minute movie on bus safety for children, plus a parent/child workbook. The film was shown to more than 120 school districts, and more than 60,000 copies of the workbook were distributed.

3. *Safety drill.* In this publicized drill, "victims" were transported to area hospitals by helicopter and local fire departments practiced emergency procedures.

4. *Fire department fund drive.* In Springfield, Monsanto spearheaded a $100,000 fund drive to purchase special equipment for the fire department to use in fighting toxic spills and chemical fires.

5. *Community clean-up.* Monsanto provided funds in both cities to clean up parks and local rivers.

6. *Cultural activities.* Monsanto was the primary sponsor of 17 plays written by local playwrights and produced by the Cincinnati Commission on Arts. In Springfield, it sponsored "Sundays in the Park," a series of four plays presented outdoors during the summer.

7. *Employee salute.* A banquet was held at the Monsanto plant in Springfield—and attended by local civic and government leaders—to honor plant employees who made major contributions to the community through voluntary work.

A follow-up survey after three months of activities by an independent research firm, Opinion Research Corporation, revealed increases in positive opinion among those who saw the activities in both Springfield and Cincinnati, as follows:

• Opinion leaders and members of the general public said they would be receptive to a new Monsanto chemical plant in their community (from 46 to 58 percent).

- Residents in both cities became more aware that Monsanto had an emergency plan (from 40 to 65 percent in Springfield; from 74 to 85 percent in Cincinnati).

- There was more agreement among Springfield residents that Monsanto is concerned about employee health and safety (from 69 to 83 percent); enjoys good community relations (from 66 to 81 percent); is a good company to work for (from 71 to 84 percent); makes corporate resources available to the community (from 34 to 60 percent); and makes the community a better place to live (from 47 to 65 percent).

- Increased numbers of residents in Cincinnati agreed that Monsanto helps to make the area a better place to live (from 59 to 69 percent); enjoys good community relations (from 64 to 73 percent); is professional and well managed (from 67 to 76 percent); and is a research leader and imaginative in developing new products (from 73 to 85 percent).

Elements of the program were adopted in many of Monsanto's other plant communities.

(This public relations program, submitted by Monsanto Company, St. Louis, Missouri, with Fleishman, Hillard, Inc., St. Louis, received a Silver Anvil Award in the Institutional Program, Business, category in the 1986 competition of the Public Relations Society of America (PRSA). Excerpted with permission from PRSA.)

# Comet Halley: Once in a Lifetime

Facing the challenge of informing the public about scientific developments with only half of that public having shown high interest in the sciences and with public knowledge of science limited—the American Chemical Society (ACS) recognized an opportunity presented by the return of Halley's Comet.

The return of the comet in 1985-86 after 76 years to the inner solar system gave the ACS an opportunity to tell the public how remote-sensing analytical chemistry is essential in the study of comets and that the secrets comets have to share are nearly all chemical in nature. A bit of astronomy, biology, history, and physics could also be taught.

The planning, begun in 1983, focused on producing entertaining and informative materials on the significance of Halley's Comet for the public at large, with focus on the student population. The decision was made to wed science and show business by creating a multimedia presentation, and from this book a book aimed at nontechnical readers. ACS received a proposal from Dr. Mark Littman, then director of the Hansen Planetarium of Salt Lake County, Utah, for a program costing $103,526. The ACS was to provide $37,196 for a joint venture with Hansen.

The ACS would provide staff time and cover incidental expenses for the program, entitled "Comet Halley: Once in a Lifetime," but major funding had to be raised from outside sources. Pledges were obtained from the Bushnell Division of Bausch & Lomb, the Planetary Society, American Association for the Advancement of Science, and American Astronomical Society. Dr. Littman resigned from Hansen Planetarium before the script was completed, and Hansen pulled out of the project, with the Planetary Society consequently withdrawing from its pledge of $10,000.

The ACS switched production to the UNIVERSE Planetarium, Richmond, Virginia, while maintaining good relations with Hansen. With the funding base reduced, UNIVERSE had to commit more of its resources in the project than originally planned and under these circumstances insisted on final approval of the show. Changes included cutting the script from 60 to 43 minutes, deleting some of the scientific information. Howard K. Smith recorded the principal narrator's part pro bono.

Distribution of "Comet Halley: Once in a Lifetime" to planetariums worldwide began in January 1986. Collateral printed matter accompanied the show. The nontechnical book, also titled *Comet Halley: Once in a Lifetime*, an expansion of the script by Dr. Littman and Dr. Donald Yeomans, jet propulsion laboratory astronomer, was published in 1985. Video and filmstrips were prepared, using Dr. Littmann's original hour-long script, and marketed by Educational Images, Ltd., Elmira, New York.

The ACS project was made known through AP Newsfeature, news releases, *Science 85* magazine, and the ACS annual technical research report.

Despite the adversities, the project exceeded objectives. The Planetarium show was presented by 370 institutions, many reporting record attendances. Sale of filmstrip kits totaled 132, and of videocassettes, 73. Book sales totaled 4,500, becoming the fastest selling book in ACS history. The book also won various awards.

(This public relations program, submitted by the American Chemical Society, received a Silver Anvil Award in the Institutional Programs, Nonprofit Organizations, in the 1986 competition of the Public Relations Society of America (PRSA) Excerpted with permission from PRSA.)

# Tang March Across America for MADD

To boost lagging sales of regular Tang, breakfast beverage crystals that had been a General Foods product since 1959, and to promote new Sugar Free Tang, General Foods retained Richard Weiner, Inc., to develop a public relations program targeted to GF's market—mothers. The result was the creation of the Tang March Across America for MADD, the first coast-to-coast walk for mothers and all citizens concerned about the future of the American family.

The stage had been set in May 1984 when Sugar Free Tang was test-marketed in Phoenix, Arizona, and Tang sponsored a 10-kilometer Mother's Day Run to benefit MADD (Mothers Against Drunk Driving). Studies were conducted to reveal that female heads of household perceived MADD as an effective organization dealing with an issue of importance to women. Evaluation of previous MADD events showed that media and public support could be expected on national and local levels.

Planning began in March 1985 and included General Foods marketing and public relations departments; the ad agency, Young and Rubicam; the PR agency, Richard Weiner, Inc.; and MADD executives.

The objectives of the program were as follows:

- To increase sales of Tang and Sugar Free Tang.

- To link Tang and MADD in a way that showed that the brands cared for the safety and well-being of the American family.

- To provide widespread awareness for Tang through extensive media coverage.

- To excite the trade about Tang and Sugar Free Tang.

The Walkers Club of America (WCA) was retained to coordinate the 4,205-mile march, which was routed to pass through 15 of the top 40 ADI markets. The 115-mile march would begin in Los Angeles on August 17 and conclude in Washington, D.C., on December 9.

A massive coupon campaign was staged, allowing a 10-cent donation to MADD for each coupon redeemed, up to $100,000, making Tang MADD's largest corporate contributor. Guidelines on organizing a local MADD march were sent to the 39 participating chapters along the route. A special event—a five-mile walk through the city—was designed for use in the 39 markets.

MADD's national president, chapter presidents, WCA members, and one mother were all trained as spokespeople for media interviews along the march route to discuss Tang/Sugar Free Tang's commitment to MADD and importance of redeeming the coupon.

The media program included the following: features about the march in such magazines as *Family Circle*, *Good Housekeeping*, and *Glamour*; a videotape featuring MADD's founder, Candy Lightner, explaining the program which was prepared for Tang's annual sales meeting; a press conference in New York City—with Governor Mario Cuomo and Mayor Ed Koch, joining Ms. Lightner—to announce the program, resulting in widespread media coverage. Throughout the month of March, network coverage of the impending march was strong.

When the march started from the steps of Los Angeles City Hall, participants included Mayor Tom Bradley (in a "Tang for MADD" T-shirt) and celebrities Henry Winkler, Kate Jackson, and Jamie Lee Curtis. During the march, more than 60 government officials and celebrities participated.

A series of press releases, media alerts, and TV and radio PSAs was sent to local media in each market beginning six weeks prior to that city's event. Radio promotions including Tang/MADD T-shirt giveaways were established with 17 stations. Nationally syndicated consumer columnists were contacted early to announce the coupon program. Visual identification of the Tang march included signage, two vans donated by General Motors Corporation providing further ID, banners hung at event ceremonies and carried by lead walkers, T-shirts, sweatshirts, umbrellas, poster, visors, and balloons. Tang and Sugar-Free Tang product sampling was set up at each march site.

The Tang march is considered among the most successful General Foods PR campaigns ever executed. It also met the objectives of MADD. The Tang brand experienced a 6 percent increase in sales to supermarkets during the March period, compared to minus 6 percent for the same months the previous year, representing a 12 percent increase in sales. As there had been no Tang advertising during the march period, the sales gain was attributed entirely to the PR campaign, which garnered more than 325 million consumer impressions. Some 47 newspapers placed news of the march on its front pages. AP and UPI carried stories on its wires. Many local television stations had the march as their lead stories. Mailings to the trade press also resulted in spreading news of the event.

(This public relations program, submitted by General Foods Corporation, White Plains, New York, with Richard Weiner, Inc., New York, received a Silver Anvil Award in the Special Events and Observances (7 Days or More), Business, category in the 1985 competition of the Public Relations Society of America (PRSA). Excerpted with permission from PRSA.)

# Stabilizing the U.S. Dollar

Faced with the staggering problem caused by the strength of the U.S. dollar in the world marketplace, which had led to a decrease in its revenues, Eastman Kodak Company's corporate communications division proposed a public relations program that would make an impact on this complex international issue.

Although the company knew that the strength of the U.S. dollar abroad hurt Kodak's competitive position, it did not know what forces would bring it down. The company, therefore, arranged fact-finding meetings with President Reagan, high-level administration officials, and key national economic and trade groups. Kodak funded a $150,000 study by the American Enterprise Institute of the relationship between the strength of the dollar and federal budget deficits. Reports were also solicited on foreign economic policies from Kodak offices in five major industrial countries. Positions on the dollar and the deficit were analyzed at other major companies.

Research revealed a direct relationship between the high interest rates required to finance federal budget deficits and the overvalued dollar. Kodak believed a public affairs program could play a major role in persuading the government to pass legislation to eliminate federal budget deficit and intervene in currency exchange markets to stabilize the overhauled dollar.

Kodak developed a 12-month communications program to reach members of Congress, the administration, and others in a position to influence economic policy. The message was that the overvalued dollar and escalating budget deficits were so damaging to American manufacturers that a decisive action was needed. The major elements of the program were as follows:

- A mailing to Kodak's 180,000 shareowners that received national media attention and endorsements from members of Congress.

- Testimony by Chairman Colby Chandler to the Senate Finance Committee plus speeches by Chandler to Chicago's Economic Club and the Conference Board.

- A "white paper" on the dollar and the deficit for targeted distribution.

- Development of a supportive network of business/trade organizations.

- Distribution of a slide/tape talk to stimulate support from civic leaders.

- A grassroots "Write to Congress" campaign in all 50 states.

- Visits by Kodak executives to members of Congress and cabinet members.

- Consultations with U.S. Senators Moynihan, Baucus, and Bradley on their dollar stabilization bills.

- Recruitment of support by Treasury Secretary Baker and Vice President Bush.

Media coverage of many of the activities was arranged, resulting in a widely published AP feature and several stories in the *Washington Post*.

Kodaks' campaign played a direct role in changing the attitudes of government and set the stage for two historic events: the September 1985 "Group of Five" communiqué pledging the five major industrial powers to dollar stabilization and passage of the Gramm-Rudman-Hollings Act, designed to wipe out federal budget deficits by 1991.

(This public relations program, submitted by Eastman Kodak Company, Rochester, New York, received a Silver Anvil Award in the Public Affairs, Business, category in the 1986 competition of the Public Relations Society of America (PRSA). Excerpted with permission from PRSA.)

# San Jose/Cleveland Ballet *Nutcracker*

When the San Jose City Center Ballet/Cleveland Ballet decided to launch its cultural co-venture by presenting the *Nutcracker*, there were obstacles to overcome in San Jose. Eleven other *Nutcrackers* had already been scheduled for the Bay Area's 1985 Christmas season; the San Jose presentation was set for Thanksgiving weekend, which was weeks earlier than the other *Nutcracker* performances; many San Jose area consumers were already loyal to other *Nutcrackers*; the San Francisco media were snobbish about covering San Jose cultural events; the Cleveland Ballet had little name recognition in the Bay Area; the San Jose media were also cynical about the co-venture.

There were two tasks to be accomplished; selling the new concept of a co-venture to a critical press and creating a new audience for the Cleveland Ballet *Nutcracker*, and *Nutcracker* week.

The first phase involved sending a direct-mail piece announcing the *Nutcracker* to a master cultural list created by PRX, having one of the major San Jose market shopping centers base its Christmas catalog on the Cleveland *Nutcracker*, and announcements in the *San Francisco Chronicle* and *San Jose Mercury News* that urged early ticket sales.

To sell the co-venture, PRX persuaded Bay Area media to send cultural reporters to Cleveland to witness the Cleveland Ballet performances firsthand, held press events introducing Cleveland Ballet's president and artistic director. To draw in the community, local auditions for roles in the ballet were conducted. Mayor George Voinovich of Cleveland was invited to join Major Tom McEnery of San Jose at the opening night performance, and both mayors were in attendance as visual proof of the co-venture.

To establish the market, the following steps were taken: Apple Computer founder Steve Wozniak was approached to donate money for a ballet dance institute for children; an opening night gala performance was promoted; corporate sales targeted Silicon

Valley; sponsors were solicited for a special benefit performance; community organizations were contacted to support the co-venture.

The event was promoted through press kits featuring local children in the production and California natives who were members of the Cleveland Ballet Company, a press tour that had PRX staffers dressed as various *Nutcracker* characters, and print ad and radio/TV PSAs that highlighted testimonials from dance critics.

During Nutcracker Week, these events took place: a red-carpet media event on the arrival of the Cleveland Ballet Company at the San Jose Airport; a "Welcome Cleveland" press conference that featured Apple Computer's Wozniak, announcing a $250,000 grant to the co-venture; a media event on the arrival of Major Voinovich and his family to San Jose; AT&T's corporate contribution of a private preperformance reception for the mayors and gala attendees on opening night.

The Cleveland *Nutcracker* was a success, with the inaugural performances achieving 98.6 percent sellout, well over the 75 percent objective. Fundraising amounting to $350,000, exceeding the objective of $273,000, with an additional $67,000 in in-kind services from Residence Inn hotels and United Airlines.

Media coverage totaled 50 million gross impressions, with heavy coverage by both the San Francisco and San Jose press. The co-venture was established as a visible method of bringing first-class ballet to the community.

(This public relations program, submitted by the San Jose City Center Ballet, San Jose, California, with PRX, Inc., Cupertino, California, received a Silver Anvil Award in the Marketing Communication (New Services), Nonprofit Organization, category in the 1986 competition of the Public Relations Society of America (PRSA). Excerpted with permission from PRSA.)

# Child Support Enforcement Campaign

With 80 percent of parents ordered to pay child support in Illinois paying less than the required amount or paying nothing at all, the Illinois Department of Public Aid (IDPA) wanted to help correct this situation. Added to the child support enforcement laws that enabled the Illinois Department of Public Aid to collect back child support from delinquent parents was new legislation that extended IDPA's program to parents who are not on public assistance.

Because the IDPA could already readily reach the welfare family through a computerized system, the department wanted to reach families not on public assistance as a preventive effort that would help keep abandoned families from having to go on assistance. To meet the challenge, the IDPA needed to educate nonassistance parents of the strengthened child support enforcement program. For the program to be successful, it would need to inspire action.

Distancing itself from the animosity inherent in most delinquent support situations, the marketing campaign directed parents' attention to the real issue—the children. The program focused on the rights of the child, stressing that the birthright of a child is to be supported by *both* parents, regardless of the circumstances.

The nonassistance parent was to be reached through the media, through social service and advocacy organizations, and by word of mouth in daily life. A budget of $166,000 was set for an eight-month effort.

May 30 was set for the official launch of the program by Governor James Thompson. In the 90-day period prior to introduction, radio PSAs were produced. Consent was obtained from Oprah Winfrey to narrate a documentary film telling the story of the endorsement program through the experiences of five women and their children, with Governor Thompson serving as co-narrator.

Press materials were readied and spokespersons were trained to assist IDPA administrations in describing the program and directing people to an 800 telephone number that promised them action.

The program was introduced at a May 30th luncheon, to which 200 guests were invited—including press representatives, public affairs directors, and presidents and program chairmen of social service, advocacy, and women's organizations. The dias was shared by the governor; the director of public aid, Gregory Coler; and a bipartisan group of legislators who had been instrumental in passing child support enforcement legislation.

A media blitz in Chicago and downstate followed: 25 interviews by Director Coler, reaching more than 4.3 million residents; other placements in media, having a total circulation of more than 3.6 million; and 180 billboards and more than 4,000 bus cards. Copies of the film and videotape were shown by organizations and by IDPA and on cable television and public affairs programs.

Monthly applications for child support assistance increased—from 353 before the campaign to 721. More than 13,000 calls have come in to the Action line, with the majority from nonassistance parents. Child support collections by the state increased 23 percent in the second half of 1985 as compared with the same period in 1984.

The child support enforcement program aimed at the nonassistance parent is a preventive program with a financial motivation: Every time a parent and one child are kept off the welfare rolls the state saves a minimum of $3,000 annually. The program's impact in human terms—reduced anxiety, improvements in parent-child relationship, independence, and degree of financial security—cannot be measured.

(This public relations program, submitted by the Illinois Department of Public Aid, Springfield, Illinois, with Public Communications, Inc., Chicago, received a Silver Anvil Award in the Marketing Communication (Established Services), Government, category in the 1986 competition of the Public Relations Society of America (PRSA). Excerpted with permission from PRSA.)

# Pace Pre-IPO Investor Relations Program

Pace Membership Warehouse, Inc., founded in 1983, was considering a public offering of its common stock in mid-1985, so it contacted Fleishman-Hillard in early 1984. Problems included little understanding of the warehouse concept by Wall Street security analysts and investors, and the fact that the company had yet to show any net earnings, so that the offering would have to be priced on the basis of future prospects.

The investor relations program developed was divided into three components: 1) printed corporate communications, including a pre-IPO annual report; 2) personal and group meetings with key security analysts and their money manager counterparts; and 3) financial and general media coverage of the company.

It was decided to position PACE as the company within the warehouse membership industry having the best long-term growth prospects because of its management, inventory and management information systems, market demographics, and ability to compete with other market entrants. PACE also carried the industry's largest selection of brand-name merchandise. The objectives of the program were as follows:

- Positioning PACE as the eventual industry leader to key security analysts and major institutional investors.

- Securing favorable national media coverage that would introduce PACE to investors nationally.

- An IPO priced at the maximum multiple of anticipated earnings while enabling PACE to offer the maximum number of shares to the public.

Although it is highly unusual for privately held companies to provide annual reports to the public, PACE prepared a report that provided descriptions of the company, financial results to date, and future growth prospects for public distribution. A financial community presentation with accompanying color slides explained the warehouse concept and PACE's approach to the business. Presentations at meetings included the annual Montgomery Securities Conference in San Francisco. There were also meetings with key retailing industry analysts in New York City, Boston, Chicago, Denver, Los Angeles, Minneapolis, and San Francisco.

Contact with the financial community resulted in wide knowledge of PACE on the part of security analysts and their money manager counterparts. Media coverage prior to the IPO included *Business Week, Nation's Business, Dun's, USA Today,* and the *Los Angeles Times* and other trade media on Wall Street.

On June 20, 1985, PACE offered one million shares more than had previously been expected to be sold by the company's underwriters. Of the shares sold, approximately 75 percent were purchased by institutional investors, many of which had visited with PACE prior to the IPO.

In the period immediately following the IPO, PACE common stock consistently traded above the offering price and reached a high of $21.50 per share in mid-July on the NASDAQ National Market System.

(This public relations program, submitted by PACE Membership Warehouse, Inc., Denver, Colorado, with Fleishman-Hillard, Inc., St. Louis, Missouri, received a Silver Anvil Award in the Investor Relations, Initial Public Offerings, category in the 1986 competition of the Public Relations Society of America (PRSA). Excerpted with permission from PRSA.)

# Think. Don't Drink

## Problem and Opportunity

America's number one killer of teenagers is highway crashes. Alcohol is a major factor. In fact, the life expectancy is increasing for every age group of the U.S. except that of the 15-24 year olds. The leading cause of death for this group is drunk driving.

On the strength of these startling facts, the Advertising Federation of Greater Hampton Roads selected teenage alcohol abuse as the subject of its 1984 public service campaign. The federation is a nonprofit professional organization dedicated to raising the standards of advertising and to fostering meritorious movements for the general good of the organization and the community. Its 100 members are engaged in the buying, selling, or creating of advertising, and in public relations and marketing activities.

By accepting chairmanship of the project, I was responsible for organizing a committee to plan the research; to solicit creative, production, media, and business participation; to direct the implementation and to document the results of the campaign. With no budget, the campaign was an entirely volunteer effort, relying on the donation of all necessary elements and providing an opportunity for the Ad Federation to contribute its time and talent to an effort that will have a positive impact on the community, while creating awareness of the organization and its members.

## Goals and Objectives

Research of the subject revealed the following: 1) Most kids have tried alcohol—over 95 percent will have tried alcohol before they become high school seniors. 2) We probably cannot be totally successful in scaring kids away from drinking since teenagers do not really believe that drinking and driving might kill them; they believe they are immortal, that it cannot happen to them. 3) Kids are drinking at younger ages; they need messages that will influence their decisions before they consider drinking and driving. 4) While we teach kids to drive, we neither really tell them they have a choice in whether or not to drink, nor teach them how to drink if they choose to do so. 5) The youth of today generally have more money, more mobility, more temptation, and less constructive work to do than the youth of 30, 40, or 50 years ago, and there have been major social changes in which all people, including young people, do not obey laws just because they are laws.

Our responsibility then was to explain to teenagers *why* drinking laws should be obeyed, preferably before they get into the criminal justice system; to explain *why* overdrinking is socially unacceptable and thereby provide an opportunity for responsible decision making and to provide encouragement and support for that decision.

Our objectives were 1) to increase awareness of the physical, legal, and social problems attendant to alcohol misuse; 2) to provide information about the effects of alcohol; 3) to influence attitudes about drinking and about drinking and driving; 4) to increase responsible decision making about alcohol use; 5) to change attitudes and behavior regarding alcohol abuse, and 6) to raise the consciousness of parents, teachers, law enforcement officials, the media, and other community and business groups, as well as our youth about the problem.

## Implementation

While strongly inclined to take a positive peer pressure approach, several possible themes and ad messages were tested in a focus group conducted at a local high school. This was felt to be a key step in the development of a campaign that would "talk a teenagers' language" without "turning them off." While the two themes tested equally well, "Think. Don't Just Drink" was selected since it better enabled us to meet our awareness and educational objectives.

Under the direction of volunteer creative director, Bill Campbell of Barker Campbell & Farley, the theme "Think. Don't Just Drink" was developed to convey the following: 1) You don't have to drink. 2) If you do drink, learn what you are dealing with. Be a thinking drinker. 3) Do not in any case, drink and drive.

Five ads for use in student newspapers were designed to address the physical, legal, and social problems that result from alcohol misuse. Original lyrics and music were created for use in three 60-second radio spots, and a TV PSA was produced in a music/video style. All materials tied into an educational poster and brochure placed in schools, libraries, and activity centers, and distributed by traffic court judges and treatment and prevention specialists. To further support the campaign, bumper stickers, buttons, and T-shirts, all sought-after items by this age group, were produced. The campaign also utilized outdoor billboards and transit advertising for dramatic, long-running, out-of-home reinforcement.

The campaign was announced at a January 1984 press conference attended by more than 150 community and business representatives, prevention and treatment specialists, and school officials in addition to the media. A young man who had been the victim of a drunk driving accident was the guest speaker. The event was covered by the three Hampton Roads network TV affiliates, two local TV stations, six radio stations, and both area newspapers. The mayors, or their representatives, of each of the seven area cities were present to proclaim February Special Teen Alcohol Awareness Month, and press kits and campaign materials were distributed.

Special promotions have included display booths at malls and special events and two dozen presentations made regionally, throughout the state and nationally. Nine states have requested and been supplied with information about the campaign.

## Results and Evaluation

Success was measured in part by the amount of support received from various groups. Alcohol and treatment specialists have stated that it is the most comprehensive they have seen to date, that the content is accurate, the approach, honest and realistic, and the materials of a quality rarely if ever seen in a public service campaign on this subject. Area task forces on drinking and driving have contributed $18,600 for production of materials.

Public sector support has been outstanding with nine departments of the Commonwealth of Virginia now contributing funds for production of materials for statewide dissemination. State police cars will carry "Think. Don't Just Drink" bumper stickers. The National Clearinghouse for Alcohol Information is considering national distribution of the materials.

Area businesses were responsible for the donation of $3,600 for production of materials; creative and production services additionally donated to date are valued at $250,000; virtually every member of the Ad Federation contributed to the implementation or creation of the campaign in some manner, and the Hampton Roads naval community—the world's largest—had enthusiastically distributed the campaign to its 446,800 members as well as reporting the campaign on the Navy News Network. So many individuals and groups have contributed in so many ways that it has truly become a community effort.

Marketing consultant Dr. Myron Glassman and Continental Research, a Hampton Roads marketing research firm, have conducted pretest and posttest surveys. Results indicate a high level of responsiveness to the theme and measurable increases in knowledge of two alcohol related facts. From a humanistic perspective, if the campaign saves one life, statistical differences not withstanding, it will have been a resounding success.

As a result of this campaign, the Advertising Federation of Greater Hampton Roads has received recognition from local, state, and national groups and organizations. It has been awarded the G. D. Crain, Jr., Memorial Award for Public Service, and First Place, Group III, AAF Public Service Award, the highest honors bestowed by the American Advertising Federation for public service.

The National Institute on Alcohol Abuse and Alcoholism has recognized our work, reported in their *Technology Transfer Newsletter* and is working with us and the National Clearinghouse on the national rollout.

## Cost

Creative, production, marketing, media, and corporate contributions to date total $400,000, in addition to the countless hours contributed by dozens of volunteers.

(This public relations program, submitted by Laura Rose Zambardi, Creative Displays, Ltd., Norfolk, Virginia, received an Award of Excellence in the Public Service Communication category in the 1985 Gold Quill Awards Program of the International Association of Business Communicators (IABC). Reprinted with permission from the 1985 edition of IABC's *No Secrets*.)

# Communications Program To Battle Steel Imports

## Problem and Opportunity

On January 24, 1985, Bethlehem Steel and the United Steelworkers (USWA) filed a petition with the U.S. International Trade Commission (ITC) seeking quotas on imported steel. This action followed a year in which the industry suffered huge losses and massive layoffs due to foreign imports.

## Goals and Objectives

Since the ultimate decision on import relief would be made by President Reagan in an election year, industry officials and Burson-Marsteller (B-M) agreed that the communications program should position the import crisis in context of the presidential campaign. With this in mind, B-M identified the following objectives:

1. To correct negative perceptions of the industry.

2. To convince the president's advisors of strong public support for quotas in key steel and electoral states thereby forcing President Reagan to grant effective import relief.

3. To position a favorable presidential decision as an asset to reelection prospects.

At any time, decisions could have gone against Bethlehem and the USWA and ended the effort. Flexibility was essential and proved invaluable as the program maintained its focus but always anticipated the events.

## Implementation

- *Utilizing opinion research.* The USWA accepted a B-M recommmendation that formal opinion polls be conducted in nine major steel states—states that controlled 162 electoral votes and were vital to President Reagan's reelection. As suspected from preliminary research, the final results revealed overwhelming support for the Bethlehem/USWA positions.

The polling results were used to shape messages for spokespersons, themes for issue advertising and direct mail appeals to USWA members. In addition, results were released widely to illustrate support for the Bethlehem/USWA position and were given to political pollsters with both presidential campaigns urging them to address the issue.

Media outlets in the key states received hand-delivered copies of the state-specific polls as well as a composite poll for the nine states from local USWA officials to heighten awareness of the poll results.

Copies of the composite poll and national release were distributed to political reporters, columnists, and television news and public affairs programs immediately before the Republican convention. The same materials were delivered to hundreds of national reporters and assignment editors as well as media from the nine target states.

Copies of the state specific polls were delivered by B-M to appropriate state delegations at the convention. Media covering those delegations were encouraged to discuss the issue with delegates.

The account team wrote and distributed testimony and accompanying news releases for USWA appearance before the Republican platform committee and arranged interviews for USWA spokespersons in conjunction with the hearings.

In addition, a heavily attended news conference at the Republican convention was arranged to announce the outcome of a meeting between USWA representatives and Senator Paul Laxalt, chairman of President Reagan's campaign. Press kits were assembled and distributed to attendees. B-M planned interviews for USWA representatives throughout the convention with reporters from steel states.

- *Spokesperson placement—national and regional.* ITC review of the Bethlehem/USWA petition involved five dates for hearings and decisions leading to a final White House decision in late September. For each date, B-M wrote and distributed news advisories and releases, planned and orchestrated news conferences—including a two-city tele-news conference—and arranged interviews for Bethlehem/USWA spokespersons, including Bethlehem's chairman and the USWA president. Press kits were developed to include either testimony or reaction statements.

A media tour program in key steel and electoral states helped build on the awareness of the poll data and broaden political support in those states. B-M identified and trained spokespersons, selected and contacted media outlets, booked interviews, accompanied spokespersons, conducted follow-up mailings to all interviewers and collected stories for distribution to both presidential campaign staffs.

At every stage of the program, B-M developed and placed opinion articles by key supporters, including Lynn Williams, USWA president, and Jay Rockefeller, former governor of West Virginia.

- *Developing Allies.* To expand the base of support for the Bethlehem/USWA position, B-M worked closely with Local Officials for Fair Trade (LOFT), headed by the mayor of Pittsburgh, Pennsylvania. A day-long lobbying and media event in Washington was organized to support the Bethlehem/USWA petition and steel import legislation. B-M handled all arrangements from the initial mailgram notification to LOFT members to the news conference and all lobbying appointments for the 80-plus local officials attending.

## Results

On September 18, 1984, the administration announced that it would negotiate voluntary restraints limiting imports to 18.5 percent of the domestic market. Considering President Reagan's much publicized free trade policies, the decision was widely regarded within and outside the industry as a major victory.

- *International trade story coverage.* In a year in which many industries sought import relief, the Bethlehem/USWA petition was cited in virtually every international trade story—print and electronic.

- *National media coverage.* All television networks, major wire services, major business magazines, and "national" newspapers repeatedly reported the Bethlehem/USWA story at key intervals in the ITC process, at the LOFT lobbying event, at the Republican convention, and at the release of the state polls.

- *Interview/feature coverage.* Stories appeared in/on the *Wall Street Journal,* the *New York Times,* the *Washington Post, Business Week, Forbes, Fortune,* "Good Morning America," "Moneyline," plus numerous local newspapers and electronic outlets, frequently based on interviews of Bethlehem and/or USWA spokespersons.

- *Media tour results.* The 16-week media tour by Bethlehem and USWA spokespersons results in over 150 print and electronic interviews in 40 markets throughout the key steel and electoral states. The interviews stimulated ongoing coverage of the steel import issue and resulted in dozens of additional stories.

- *Local and regional media coverage.* This included opinion articles; release of the polls in the nine target states; the LOFT meeting in Washington; coverage of the USWA delegation at the Republican convention; and coverage of the LOFT advertising program.

## Cost

The entire communications program was carried out for approximately $275,000, including out-of-pocket expenses, but excluding the costs associated with the opinion polling.

(This public relations program, submitted by Timothy G. Brosnahan, Burson-Marsteller, Washington, D.C., received an Award of Excellence in the Public Affairs and Government Relations category in the 1985 Gold Quill Awards Program of the International Association of Business Communicators (IABC). Reprinted with permission from the 1985 edition of IABC's *No Secrets.*)

# Presenting an Undiscovered Gem

## Problem and Opportunity

Dow B. Hickam, Inc., an $8 million, Houston-based pharmaceutical manufacturer, was little known to the Southwest or national investment communities when it became a public company in April 1984. It was competing with more than 600 other new public companies for the attention of Wall Street that year, and at a time when the pharmaceutical industry was losing investor support. When the company retained Tracy-Locke/BBDO Public Relations for investor relations counsel, it had a limited budget for investor relations and no communications systems in place.

## Goals and Objectives

In eight months, Tracy-Locke/BBDO Public Relations sought to create an investor relations program that would accomplish three objectives: 1) build awareness of the company among regional business media, national pharmaceutical, and special situation analysts, stockbrokers, market makers, and shareholders; 2) build a following among analysts, market makers, and media; and 3) sustain stock prices in a market generally unfavorable for drug companies and new public issues.

## Implementation

*Research and planning.* To craft an investor relations program that would be targeted and positioned strategically, Tracy-Locke/BBDO Public Relations acted as follows:

- Analyzed annual reports from other pharmaceutical companies to position Dow B. Hickam, Inc., within the industry and to aid in designing company publications.

- Analyzed research reports and financial publications and learned drug companies were suffering from soaring research costs and generic competition.

- Interviewed senior management at the company, toured manufacturing facilities, accompanied sales representatives on hospital in-service presentations and studied product literature and product development research to determine the company's standing in the pharmaceutical industry and key points to emphasize in discussing the company with the financial press and investment community.

- Learned that Dow B. Hickam does not struggle with the chief problems other pharmaceutical companies have (it does no research and its products have no generic competition), and that despite its small size, the company has a national marketing force, an unusual marketing strategy, and one of the nation's few aerosol manufacturing facilities for pharmaceutical products.

- Compared Dow B. Hickam's earnings record against the national industry and learned that the company is growing five times faster.

- Identified key pharmaceutical and special situation security analysts, particularly those who recently had completed research reports on pharmaceutical companies.

- Identified current and potential market makers for company stock.

- Targeted key financial writers in the state who could help build regional recognition for the company.

- Analyzed the locations of the company's major shareholders and of current and potential market makers to identify target cities for media relations efforts and meetings with the investment community.

- Developed an investor relations plan outlining tactics for building regional recognition for the company and plotting communications efforts through 1985.

*Positioning.* Tracy-Locke/BBDO Public Relations capitalized on Dow B. Hickam, Inc.'s lack of recognition by depicting the company as an "undiscovered gem" investors are always eager to find.

The investor relations program was designed to distinguish the company from the industry as a whole by emphasizing its earnings record and its immunity to the problems other pharmaceuticals have. The program also highlighted the unusual marketing and manufacturing capabilities of a company the size of Dow B. Hickam, Inc.

*Execution.* Within eight months, Tracy-Locke, BBDO Public Relations:

- Mailed query cards to more than 1,000 individuals on the composite mailing lists to determine their interest in receiving information on the company and followed the query with more than 200 phone calls to investment firms to determine key individuals receiving the communications and their interest in the company.

- Wrote and distributed a background kit—demonstrating the company's successful earnings record, marketing, and manufacturing capabilities and management department—to analysts, media, and others seeking information.

- Prepared background materials tailored to the investment audience.

- Distributed a promotional brochure inviting target audiences to "highlight" the company's progress. The brochure included an inscribed highlighter pen, announcement of the company's listing on the NASDAQ national market, and a chart of the company's earnings record.

- Prepared earnings releases and all SEC-required communications.

- Arranged for the company to be listed in regional stock listings in state publications and in industry listings in national publications.

- Arranged interviews with key business writers in Houston and Dallas.

- Recycled press coverage to target audiences regionally and nationally.

- Scheduled seven meetings for corporate management with investment communities in Austin/San Antonio, Dallas, Houston, New Orleans, Minneapolis, and Chicago.

## Results and Evaluation

The eight months of the investor relations program in 1984 met and surpassed all objectives.

*Awareness.* Media coverage in key publications consistently portrayed Dow B. Hickam, Inc., as a growth company with unusual potential in the industry. Interviews with the chief executive officer appeared in the *Houston Post, Houston Business Journal, Houston Chronicle, Dallas/Fort Worth Business Journal, Dallas Morning News and Financial Trend* and ran on the state wire of United Press International. *Texas Business* magazine conducted an interview for publication in April 1985, and *Pharmaceutical Executive* magazine, which highlights successful industry leaders, management techniques, and market trends, requested an article on the company's marketing strategy for publication in 1985.

*Stock following recommendation.* Company stock was cited on a national list of 10 "growth stocks" by the editor of *Growth Stock Outlook* and given a grade of A by *Financial World* magazine. The number of market makers in the company's stock doubled from four to eight between May and December 1984. One research report was published on the company, two more were planned, and five analysts in California, Minnesota, and Texas were actively following the stock by January 1985. More than 300 requests for more information on the company were received from security analysts, stockbrokers, investors, and the financial media.

*Stock prices.* The company's stock, which opened at $8 in April 1984, recently rose to $13.25. Dow B. Hickam, Inc., was one of the state's top performers in a generally poor market for initial public offerings.

## Cost

One half-time professional conducted the program with a budget of approximately $40,000.

(This public relations project, submitted by Jean L. Farinelli and Timothy Palmer, Tracey Locke/BBDO Public Relations, Dallas, Texas, received an Award of Excellence in Financial Relations, Business, category in the 1985 Gold Quill Awards Program of the International Association of Business Communicators (IABC). Reprinted with permission from the 1985 edition of IABC's *No Secrets*.)

# Los Angeles Department of Water and Power Seat-Belt Campaign

## Problem and Opportunity

To remind employees that wearing seat belts can save lives and help prevent serious injuries, the Los Angeles Department of Water and Power (DWP) became the first department in the city to initiate a comprehensive seat-belt safety campaign geared at encouraging its more than 10,500 employees to wear seat belts both on and off the job.

Each year in the United States more than 20,000 deaths and more than one million injuries are attributable to motor vehicle accidents. Such accidents are the number one cause of on-the-job fatalities and account for two out of three deaths among workers off the job. Lost work days from minor to moderate injuries resulting from motor vehicle accidents range from two and one-half to 37 days, respectively. Studies conducted by the National Safety Council have shown that wearing seat belts can reduce accident fatalities by 57 percent and by as much as 90 percent for children under the age of four.

## Goals and Objectives

Six-seat belt-safety goals were set as follows:

1. To increase awareness of the importance of wearing seat belts through educational materials, displays, and personal testimonials.

2. To increase seat-belt usage by 35 percent among employees on the job during the first month of the campaign and by 50 percent by December 31, 1984.

3. To instill a desire in employees to use seat belts in DWP vehicles at all times.

4. To expand the seat-belt/occupant-restraint ethic to employees off the job and to their families and friends.

5. To reduce the number of injuries and fatalities likely to happen to employees resulting from vehicle accidents.

6. To reduce the number of lost work days as a result of minor to moderate injuries sustained from motor vehicle accidents.

## Implementation

Seat-belt usage among employees was encouraged through a variety of mediums including employee publications; safety meeting briefings; displays and exhibits; video programs; bulletin board posters; safety films; handout materials; informational brochures; and news media coverage including print, radio, and television.

A number of employee publications, including a weekly newsletter, bimonthly magazine, and quarterly safety newsletter, carried extensive coverage of the seat-belt safety campaign. DWP safety engineers were also available to employees at various locations to stress the importance of wearing seat belts and to reinforce the DWP's seat-belt policies. Throughout the campaign, news releases were distributed to local media to reinforce the message to employees and their families in the home.

Employees were also given a variety of informational materials, including seat-belt safety brochures, buttons, balloons, key chains, and bumper stickers as a reminder to "buckle up." What remained of a wrecked DWP vehicle whose driver survived a head-on crash because he was wearing his seat belt was displayed at various locations.

## Results and Evaluation

Favorable employee response, media cooperation, and an increase in seat-belt usage were key indicators that the program objectives were reached.

1. Approximately 6,000 bumper stickers, 4,000 buttons, 1,000 brochures, and more than 10,000 key chains and pamphlets were distributed to employees. In addition, more than 1,000 employees viewed two seat-belt-safety video programs.

2. Prior to the seat-belt campaign, usage among employees was approximately 15 percent. During the first month after the campaign, seat-belt usage increased to 33 percent. Usage was up to 40 percent by November 30 and had reached approximately 55 percent compliance by December 31, 1984.

3. Widespread coverage in various community newspapers and local media reinforced the message to employees and their families and friends.

4. The number of major injuries sustained in motor vehicle accidents in the period between October 1 and December 31, 1984, was reduced by 7 percent as compared to the same three-month period in 1983.

5. There was a corresponding decrease of 6 percent in the number of lost work days incurred by employees as the result of injuries sustained in vehicle accidents.

## Cost

Within an overall safety budget for the DWP, combined total costs for the seat-belt-safety campaign was about $15,000, excluding internal labor. Most costs were incurred for outside services, including video production, art services, and printing.

(This public relations program, submitted by Steve Hinderer, Los Angeles Department of Water and Power, Los Angeles, California, received an Award of Excellence in the Special Events, Internal Audience, category in the 1985 Gold Quill Awards Program of the International Association of Business Communicators (IABC). Reprinted with Permission from IABC's 1985 edition of *No Secrets*.)

# Fort St. Vrain: Nuclear Nightmare or Communications Opportunity?

## Background

Located 35 miles north of Denver, Colorado, Fort St. Vrain is the nation's only high-temperature, gas-cooled commercial nuclear reactor. It was built as part of the Atomic Energy Commission's Power Demonstration Program and is operated by Public Service Company of Colorado, the largest electric utility in Colorado.

## Problem and Opportunity

In 1984, the plant suffered through its worst operating year since it began commercial operation in 1979. It was taken out of service for scheduled refueling and maintenance in January and returned to service in June, two and a half months late. However, the plant was again shut down a few weeks later for repairs, necessitated by excessive moisture in the plant's unique helium-gas cooling system. Plagued by mounting problems, the plant never regained operational status in 1984.

Regulatory problems, coupled with the operational difficulties at the plant, resulted in a wide variety of potential concerns for more than a dozen interested audiences. This entry, therefore, is a description of communications strategy carried out by Public Service Company to deal with a volatile and complex "bottom line" issue.

## Communications Objectives

The goal of Public Service Company's communications efforts, with respect to its Fort St. Vrain nuclear power plant, was basically to convince important constituencies that the company was prudently managed and committed to the best interest of its customers.

The persuasion program sought to accomplish the following: to demonstrate that Fort St. Vrain had been crucial in meeting the power needs of Colorado, particularly in the hot summer months when demand for electricity reaches a peak; to show that Public Service Company was keenly interested in protecting customer interests and secured various concessions and agreements with the plant's builder, so that customers' financial exposure was minimized; to explain management's commitment to correcting all problems that exist at the plant; to reaffirm the company's confidence in the high-temperature, gas-cooled reactor technology; to provide factual, complete, and accurate information on Fort St. Vrain, correcting any misinformation in a timely and responsible manner; to demonstrate that Fort St. Vrain represents pioneer technology that holds great promise for the future and is the only nuclear power plant of its kind in the country; to emphasize that the company's investment in the plant is miniscule, when compared to the billion-dollar investments typically made by other nuclear utilities in water-cooled plants; and to focus on the fact that while Fort St. Vrain represents a crucial generating capability, it nevertheless is a very small percentage of the company's overall generating strength.

## Audiences

The various audiences for the company's Fort St. Vrain communications efforts included customers; the power plant's "neighbors"; news media; shareholders; employees; Colorado state legislature; Colorado Public Utilities Commission; financial constituencies; Nuclear Regulatory Commission; special interest and consumer groups; and various nuclear and electric utility industry groups.

## Program Implementation

Fort St. Vrain, like most nuclear power plants, generated a high degree of media attention in 1984. During the year, the company's media relations staff handled more than 400 media inquiries from the local and national news media, specifically about the plant. In addition, the media relations department initiated numerous news stories to provide straightforward and frequent information to key publics through the media.

Other related media relations programs included executive media training, news media tours, and trade media activity.

## Financial Relations

Because of the high level of awareness Fort St. Vrain has among shareholders and various financial constituencies, it was imperative to maintain a steady flow of accurate information to those key audiences including the use of regional shareholder meetings; shareholder publications; broker/securities analyst meetings; correspondence with financial community; and financial news releases.

## General Public/Special Interest Group Relations

Because Fort St. Vrain is the only nuclear power plant in Colorado, it has historically received a great deal of attention from local community and special interest groups. This, coupled with the plant's questionable performance in 1984, served to generate an even greater interest in Fort St. Vrain. Effective communications with specific public groups became even more important through a volunteer speakers bureau, Fort St. Vrain Information Center, miscellaneous inquiries, and Fort St. Vrain neighbors.

## Government/Regulatory Relations

In 1984 a concerted effort was made by Public Service Company to keep key legislators and their political constituencies informed about the issues facing Fort St. Vrain. Through the use of effective verbal and written communications, Public Service Company was successful in keeping the plant a "nonissue" with the legislature during 1984. No special meetings, white papers, or discussions were necessary.

In addition, the company's rates and regulations division worked closely with the Colorado Public Utilities Commission on a variety of Fort St. Vrain related items, including an extensive viability study on the plant, which was conducted by an independent consultant.

Regulators, legislators, and their staff members toured the plant at the company's invitation during the year for background information and to give them a hands-on status report.

## Employee Relations

To hinder the rumor-making process, to maintain employee morale, and to let employees know their knowledge of the plant's operational problems was important to management, a strategic employee communications program was in effect in 1984. The program included establishing a daily communications with employees and the company's bimonthly newsletter, *News Lines*.

## Evaluation

Through a coordinated strategic communications program directed by multiple constituencies, Public Service Company's Public Affairs Division has been able to successfully manage a potentially disastrous situation. The evidence of that success is clear and unmistakable. News media reportage on the issue is fair, factual, and unhysterical. Employees are well informed and confident that their company has the nuclear plant problem well in hand. Professional investors and individual shareholders understand the situation and maintain their confidence in management's ability to deal with it. Regulators have no doubt that the company will communicate forcefully and effectively in its own defense and will not permit the politicization or exaggeration of the issue. Legislators are not motivated to turn the troubles at the nuclear plant into a short-term issue because the exploitationist possibilities have been minimized through maximum disclosure of information.

The utility's customers have not rallied to so called consumer interest groups or activist organizations to "protest" the difficulties at the plant. On the contrary, empirical research shows high customer regard for the company's credibility and a distinct recognition of the company's communications efforts. In short, by any measure the utility's communications and public relations programs have minimized hostile or negative public opinion, reinforced opinion that the company has the managerial competence with which to deal with the problem, and, most importantly, given executive and operational personnel an orderly, calm and rational public atmosphere in which to solve their problems.

707

In terms of specific evaluative measures of this program's effectiveness, the following can be cited:

- *News media coverage.* More than 400 media inquiries on Fort St. Vrain were handled by the company's media relations department. Of the numerous stories generated by the plant during the year, more than 99 percent were balanced and accurate.

- *Residential area survey.* A survey of residents living in close proximity of Fort St. Vrain was commissioned during 1984 to determine their attitudes and plant awareness. The survey showed 70 percent of the residents indicated they have all the information they need on the plant. (This was up 34 percent from the 36 percent figure in 1981.)

- *Shareholder support.* Reactions generated at the company's 1984 annual meeting, at the regional shareholder meeting, and through the company's shareholder services department all indicated strong support for Public Service Company management and policies.

- *Stock price.* Direct and consistent communications with the financial community proved successful in maintaining a stable stock price, which remained between $17 and 18 a share during the year.

- *General public/customer attitudes.* Despite the extensive news coverage of Fort St. Vrain's operational problems, the candid and effective communications program did not result in any changes in general public or customer attitudes. A survey conducted among customers in December 1984 showed Public Service Company superior to any other utility in its job of trying to satisfy customers. In addition, more than 95 percent of the respondents gave the company a positive response in the company's efforts to provide service.

(This public relations program, submitted by Mark E. Severts, Public Service Company of Colorado, Denver, Colorado, received an Award of Excellence in the Multiple Audience Programs or Campaigns category in the 1985 Gold Quill Awards Program of the International Association of Business Communicators (IABC). Reprinted with permission from IABC's 1985 edition of *No Secrets.*)

# RCA "Plan for Health"

## Problem and Opportunity

RCA wanted to reduce inefficient hospital use, give employees information they needed to use the health care system more effectively, and thereby stabilize rising costs. In addition to introducing a number of new procedures employees must learn, the program would be enforced by a 30 percent reduction in medical coverage for care that was not certified. Other new concepts—alternative treatment facilities, outpatient testing and surgery, second opinions, etc.—also needed to be communicated. The program required separate identities for RCA and NBC.

## Goals and Objectives

The goals were as follows:

- To sell plan participants and those who would introduce the plan to them in a positive, upbeat, easy-to-understand, and professional manner.

- To give plan participants different levels of information in different ways. Because some employees and dependents would not attend employee meetings, to design alternative communication vehicles as stand-alones.

- To provide a series of ongoing vehicles to reinforce and continue focusing attention on the plan.

- To ensure a two-way flow of communications. The success of a precertification concept is based on the immediacy of reaction to health care questions and needs.

## Implementation

The program was implemented in three stages: preannouncement, announcement, reinforcement.

**Preannouncement.** (beginning six weeks before announcement).

*Program name/logo.* RCA (NBC) "Plan for Health" meant 1) company identification: something positive the company was doing; 2) a strategy; 3) a plan for *health*, not for sickness: a new idea.

*Program slogan.* "Just think of it!" meant 1) inventiveness, ingenuity of concept; 2) ease of use, nothing complicated.

*Newsletters.* Two newsletters distributed a month apart provided basic information on 1) employee attitudes about health care concerns and 2) the company's growing health care costs and how they were paid.

*Facilitator training.* Two sessions a month apart educated benefits personnel who would later conduct employee meetings on 1) the company's philosophy and approach and 2) role-playing techniques using actual communication materials.

*Posters.* Two posters two weeks before and in conjunction with employee meetings.

*Introductory brochures.* An eight-page brochure was distributed two weeks before meetings. It presented an overview of health care costs and how they had prompted the precertification approach. By filling out and returning a tear-off card at the back of the brochure employees received the assurance that specific questions would be addressed at meetings, as well as a free "thinking cap."

**Announcement** (beginning one month before effective date).

*Video.* A 20-minute video was the focus of employee meetings. Nine scenarios illustrated how the plan works, each with an upbeat, humorous tone. Actors' faces never appeared on camera so employees could identify with "everyman." Scenes were punctuated by an original jingle and commentary by a nurse coordinator who represented the person with whom employees would speak when they dialed a toll-free number.

*Program brochure.* An in-depth explanation of the program was presented in a full-color, 16-page brochure. Photos from the video reiterated major points. A soundsheet, a reformatted videotrack, was saddle-stitched into the brochure. A pocket held separate transition rules.

*Q&A/IBM-PC slides.* For use by meeting facilitators, a series of slides was created, answering frequently asked questions gathered from H/L tear-off cards, and introducing a menu-driven IBM-PC program that would be installed at each location.

**Reinforcement** (after enrollment was completed).

*Hotline.* With the third party administrator, any easy-to-remember toll-free number was introduced, 1-800-1985.

*IBM-PC software.* While the client used its internal staff to write and implement the program, J&H designed the initial format and suggested content, including SPDs on demand and plan quizzes.

*Claims kit.* An easy-to-use claims kit was distributed, including a one-page precertification claims form with self-contained envelope.

## Results and evaluation

Immediate and positive management and employee reaction to the program was witnessed by the following:

- The percentage return of employee comments and questions on tear-off cards from the introductory brochure.

- "Plan for Health" hats being worn by employees and their dependents.

- Applause and even standing ovations following the video presentation.

- An immediate influx of calls on the toll-free information number. The hundreds of daily phone calls are positive and handled smoothly.

- Management voiced its very positive satisfaction with the program.

## Cost

The entire campaign cost approximately $12 per employee.

(This public relations project, submitted by Johnson & Higgins Communications, New York, received an Award of Excellence in the Employee Benefits Communication category in the 1985 Gold Quill Awards Program of the International Association of Business Communicators (IABC). Reprinted with permission from the 1985 edition of IABC's *No Secrets.*)

# Monthly Mutual Funds Postcards

## Problem and Opportunity

There are more than 70,000 securities brokers in the U.S. today, and many have a hundred or more clients. The bigger customers are worth the time and money a broker may devote to frequent contacts, while smaller customers often are not. Yet, it is certainly in a broker's best interests to contact everyone in his or her "book" as often as possible.

And because many brokers sell mutual funds, it is in the best interests of the Investment Company Institute—the national association for the mutual funds industry—to help them.

## Goals and Objectives

With that in mind, we set out to create a series of eye-catching mailers that could keep brokers' costs and labor at a minimum. Each had to be a generic sales pitch for mutual funds, highlighting features representative of most or all of the industry. And each, we decided, had to be inviting enough that a broker's client or prospective client could not resist reading it.

Our answer: colorful monthly postcards, which were inexpensive to produce and mail and which would get our message across in very few words.

Based on comments received in mid-1983, when we tested several cards with brokers around the country, we estimated potential sales of each monthly card at approximately 10,000 and set that as our goal.

## Implementation

That estimate proved very conservative. When we launched the program in September 1983 with an order form covering the last quarter of the year, the whopping response we got told us the project was a winner. The very first card made available for brokers to use with clients and prospects—for October 1983—was more popular than we ever imagined, and more than 120,000 copies were sold.

I quickly put together some rough ideas for the 1984 series, then met with freelance artist, Loel Barr. As she brought the concepts to life with cartoon art, I worked out the word-plays to be used in the message sections. When our joint efforts had been approved by the powers that be at the Institute, we walked down the street to the National Association of Securities Dealers—which offers advisory opinions on all sales literature related to mutual funds—and sought their comments. They had very few recommendations; in fact, they said they liked the cards and that so long as we stayed away from using performance results, we'd have no trouble getting quick approvals. (Performance results vary from fund to fund and, therefore, cannot be reliably shown in a generic context.)

Within a few weeks, Loel went to final art as I hand-lettered the copy for the backsides, and we were off to the presses with the first three cards of 1984 in plenty of time to exploit the seasonal tie-ins.

Offering the cards three at a time, through order forms sent before each calendar quarter, worked well for us. Had we offered a year's crop all at once, we would have lost the flexibility to make changes, and had we sent a new order form each month we would have tripled our mailing responsibilities. (Orders were shipped by our in-house mailroom.)

Our order forms allowed brokers to purchase as many or as few of each card as they wished. Although we did not require prepayment, about a third of all customers sent checks with their orders.

## Results and Evaluation

Total sales for 1984 were more than a quarter of a million postcards. The March card—featuring Individual Retirement Accounts—became our all-time bestseller, with more than 340,000 copies purchased. *USA Today* ran a piece about that card in its Money section, and we received a lot of very complimentary letters and phone calls from brokers around the country. One told us he had mailed 10 cards as an experiment. They resulted in nine interviews and seven sales!

Throughout the year, we continued to receive overwhelmingly favorable responses—and many, many repeat customers. A typical individual order requested 100 cards, but there were several for more than 1,000. In only one month were fewer than 25,000 cards sold; May, with 24,000. The series continued into 1985, and some of the designs—beginning with the December 1984 card—are being put to double-duty, as wall posters for brokers' offices.

All in all, the postcards have been viewed as a significant breakthrough in an industry where for years the watchwords have been "Money isn't funny," and have proven to be a cost-effective and time-effective answer for brokers who want to reach as many clients and prospects as they can.

## Cost

The Investment Company Institute is a nonprofit organization, so this project was run on a break-even basis. Art ran $350 per card. Printing was about seven cents per card for the first 10,000, with relatively small breaks thereafter. Shipping costs varied, of course, with the sizes of the orders involved.

We figured our total costs at approximately eight cents per card, and that's what we charged for the cards throughout 1984. So for 21 cents—eight cents for each card and 13 cents for each stamp—a broker could add her own signature to a unique monthly message and reach an investor who might have otherwise been ignored.

(This public relations program, submitted by Randy Cepuch, Capital Research & Management Co., Los Angeles, California, received an Award of Merit in the Member Relations Programs or Campaigns category in the 1985 Gold Quill Awards Program of the International Association of Business Communicators (IABC). Reprinted with permission from IABC's 1985 edition of *No Secrets.*)

# Lucky To Know You

## Problem and Opportunity

Requests from the new president of Hospital Care Corporation (HCC) to develop a "Pride Program" and the human resources area to restructure new employee orientation stimulated the development of "Lucky to Know You," an orientation program for both current and new employees of HCC.

The existing employee orientation program was a fragmented program that had been conducted by numerous trainers over the years. The program was out of date, unmotivating, and lacked consistency and continuity. Supervisors did not support the program and, overall, it was a lost opportunity.

A number of significant changes needed to be communicated to employees: HCC had merged with three other Blue Cross plans and no formal educational materials had been developed about the new organization. Three health maintenance plans (HMPs) had been developed, adding a new dimension to the business and more new employees. The goals of the organization were changing but most employees were not included in the planning process and few were aware of the direction of the company. The marketplace was changing dramatically and with it, the position of the Blue Cross plans. Finally, the potential of another merger was pending, bringing about many insecurities and questions.

The right timing and commitment from the top were the essential ingredients needed to launch a major communications effort. The orientation program was selected as the vehicle to educate employees about all aspects of HCC. The program had to be motivating, consistent, and unifying. Most importantly, it had to convey the feeling of pride in working for HCC and promote the corporate goal of providing quality service to subscribers.

## Goals and Objectives

Planning of the project was developed by an HCC task force of communications and training staff members and Creative Media

717

Development, Inc. The group analyzed the existing environment of HCC; evaluated the audience; assessed the needs and identified the key issues; established goals and objectives; and determined the scope, content, and format of the project. The following goals of the program were established:

1. Provide a consistent, uniform orientation program for new employees in all areas of HCC and a base of information for current employees.

2. Educate HCC employees about all aspects of the corporation: its history, products, goals, structure, and the business.

3. Promote pride in HCC through increased knowledge and understanding of the corporation and the employees' role in it.

4. Provide employees with information and inspiration to speak knowledgeably and positively as public representatives of HCC.

5. Support the corporate goal of hiring top quality people and providing the training necessary for them to do their jobs effectively.

6. Promote the feeling that employees are joining/working for an innovative leader in the health care field, with strong leadership that is working to meet the challenges of the changing environment.

7. Humanize the claims process.

8. Provide a framework in which employees can understand their role, how their job relates to department and corporate goals and how their work impacts the overall accomplishments of HCC.

9. Reinforce HCC's primary corporate goals of involving everyone in marketing, providing quality service, and utilizing resources cost effectively.

10. Encourage employees to share the vision of the company

and to participate in accomplishing goals both individually and as a contributing team member.

11. Explain the structure of the company, its many parts, and how they all relate to make the whole of HCC.

12. Promote a caring environment where the individual is respected and challenged personally and professionally.

## Implementation

A modular approach was selected as the framework for communicating the massive amount of information in a digestible manner. The program was divided into seven segments with each main topic including an audiovisual module, complemented by print material and discussion. A three-projector format was selected for the audiovisual presentation, assuring uniformity and consistency of the message, while providing a vehicle for creatively delivering the information. In addition, the slide format is easy to update as situations change within the company. The show was transferred to videotape for maximum portability and use in the smaller regional offices.

Production began with candid interviews with 37 employees, ranging from the president to clerks. The interviews were taped and transcribed and comments used for content and quotes in the AV modules.

After several unsuccessful attempts at adapting an existing marketing theme, a totally new approach was taken resulting in the theme, "Lucky to Know You." This takes a look at HCC from a subscriber's point of view—how lucky a subscriber is to know HCC in a time of need. This approach also worked internally for employees—how lucky HCC is to know all its employees, for without them the successes of the corporation would not be possible. This provided the unifying theme and expressed the feeling we wanted to project throughout the program.

Creative treatment for the content was developed, followed by scripts and visualization for each module.

• The opening module introduces the overall theme of the program, "Lucky to Know You" and conveys the feeling of the corporation, its goals, and values, and brings the human element into the business.

- The history module traces the story of HCC from its inception to the changing environment of current years.

- The product profile module provides information on the products HCC markets in a straightforward manner. In order to effectively describe the claims process, the claim form becomes a person (which it actually represents) and takes the claim from the accident featured in the opening scene through the process at HCC.

- The corporate structure module gives a complete organizational profile of the corporation from geographic and functional viewpoints. Using the analogy of the Rubic's cube, the module shows how all the parts of HCC fit together to make the whole and how individuals fit into the organization. A takeoff on the "Twilight Zone" (the Confusion Zone) is used to open and close the module, giving structure as the solution to chaos and confusion.

- In the goals module, an analogy of the goals of an athlete and the goals of HCC is used to depict the importance of the planning process, individual contribution, striving for excellence, and the pride felt in achieving goals.

- The expectations module is a direct account of what HCC expects from employees and what employees can expect from HCC, focusing on the corporation's self-management philosophy.

- The finale brings all the elements together through a subscriber who is feeling "Lucky to Know You."

A two-day training session was held for staff members who served as facilitators and a facilitator's guide was developed to assist with the presentations.

## Results and Evaluation

Evaluation forms were completed by current employees at the group sessions and by new employees after attending the orientation seminar.

Of the 1,500 employees, 1,105, or 74 percent, viewed the program during the first round of meetings. Ninety-one percent completed the evaluation forms. The results of the evaluation were extremely positive, indicating the program had achieved the goals that it set out to accomplish:

- 91 percent liked or strongly liked the program.

- 86 percent thought the right amount of information was included.

- 81 percent felt the program increased their pride in working for HCC.

Comments focused on the professional quality of the production, the availability of information, and the direct approach of presenting it. The theme "Lucky to Know You" was received enthusiastically and more than 100 employees ordered cassette tapes of the song at their own expense. Many comments praised the creative concepts used in the AV modules.

## Cost

A major portion of the project was handled internally by the HCC staff members in the communications and training department. External production costs were approximately $65,000, including audiovisual production, original score of music and lyrics, and design and printing of materials.

(This public relations program, submitted by Susan Hamilton, Mercer-Meidinger, Inc., Washington, D.C., received an Award of Excellence in the Employee/Dealer Training or Orientation category in the 1985 Gold Quill Awards Program of the International Association of Business Communicators (IABC). Reprinted with permission from IABC's 1985 edition of *No Secrets*.)

# People Skills for Today's Managers

## Problem and Opportunity

By definition, good face-to-face communication requires managers who understand the necessity for and subtleties of good interpersonal communication. Until now, there has been no effective training packages that a company could administer to its managers to train them in this critical skill. What has been available has been specific programs in such skills as making speeches, listening, writing better memos, and the like.

Because we at Towers, Perrin, Forster & Crosby, Inc. (TPF&C) inevitably find that managers are named by employees as their preferred information source, we developed a train-the-trainer communication package that any of our clients could successfully administer to their managers. The result is "People Skills for Today's Manager" (PSTM), a unique communication training package to improve a manager's face-to-face communication efforts.

## Goals and Objectives

The goals and objectives we faced in developing PSTM were essentially the following:

- We wanted a simple-to-understand model of the manager's communication responsibility.

- We wanted to develop an interactive package that gave workshop participants plenty of practice in understanding the model and how they could use it daily in their jobs.

- We wanted to develop a cost-effective package that clients could deliver without our help once we had trained their trainers.

- We also wanted a package that we could deliver ourselves for smaller clients who did not have trainers or who simply did not want to do the training themselves.

Our approach was to develop a simple package in a word processing system that our own local offices could produce by means of demand printing.

Pricing is on a case-by-case basis because the package can be modified according to clients' needs. The package itself consists of a trainer's guide with detailed commentary and step-by-step instructions. It also includes 35mm slides or xerographic masters for transparencies that the client can produce on any office copier. Each participant receives a complimentary participant's manual.

## Implementation

Four widely experienced TPF&C consultants with both training and communication backgrounds contributed individual modules to the final package. We developed the prototype package for an automotive company and then ran a train-the-trainer session in early November for the 25 line managers they chose to serve as trainers for their 1,200 division managers and supervisors.

The primary constraint was the time that such a massive training effort represented. Client management agreed that their employee participation program would be enhanced by training their managers in effective communication process. Conversely, they worried that effort could be seriously impeded, or even crippled, if they ignored their manager's face-to-face communication efforts.

## Results and Evaluation

The formal and informal feedback has been outstanding. In each copy of the participant's manual there is an evaluation form, which the participant directs to his or her senior management evaluating the training and advising them as to how senior management can support the supervisor or manager as a face-to-face communicator. All of these evaluation forms are passed along to each senior staff manager as a continuing reminder.

The real importance of PSTM is that is is the first comprehensive communication skills training effort for managers. With participative management and improved face-to-face communication so mutually dependent, we believe that PSTM truly represents an employee communication breakthrough for the 1980s.


(This public relations program, submitted by Roger D'Aprix, Towers, Perrin, Forster & Crosby, New York, received an Award of Excellence in the Communication Training Programs for Noncommunication Personnel category in the 1985 Gold Quill Awards Program of the International Association of Business Communicators (IABC). Reprinted with permission from IABC's 1985 edition of *No Secrets*.)

# CPAs Assist Cobbs Creek Community

## Problem and Opportunity

On May 13, 1985, fire raged out of control in West Philadelphia during the siege on the radical group MOVE, leaving 61 homes destroyed and 250 people homeless. The MOVE confrontation and devastating fire transformed a pleasant, tree-lined, row-house neighborhood into what looked like a bombed-out war zone.

Only in such a tragedy do we begin to realize that our lives are intricately entangled in reams of paper such as birth certificates, marriage licenses, social security cards, driver licenses, tax forms, bank statements, insurance policies, and school diplomas.

We knew that CPA assistance could be invaluable in combating the paperwork maze, so we put our professional skills on the line and volunteered to give one CPA's services to each family to help with the reconstruction of records. The Philadelphia Bar Association joined us and the CPA/lawyer team concept was launched.

## Goals and Objectives

Our prime objectives were as follows:

- To help the 61 households and 250 persons affected by the fire reconstruct their lives and records to where they were prior to the fire.

- To mobilize and train CPA volunteers to service the accounting, tax, and record reconstruction needs of the displaced residents.

Within 24 hours after the tragedy our plan was in order to provide a CPA/lawyer team to each affected household, the city had accepted the offer and volunteers had been identified to participate.

A special newsletter, "Update Reports," was created to communicate with the team members and let them know how to process forms, get duplicate copies of records, and keep up to date on what utilities and taxes had been abated.

## Implementation

Task forces were set up to monitor the progress of the teams and work with the city and other organizations to get answers to common questions. Several times in this cooperative effort, philosophical differences arose between the bar association and the CPA state society regarding promoting media attention and publicity.

Before the letter to the mayor was delivered and the offer of assistance accepted, the bar association wanted to call a news conference to coincide with live TV evening news coverage. The bar association felt that the public's perception of lawyers was often negative, and that this genuine public service project illustrated their professional and personal contributions to community needs.

We felt strongly that helping people was the priority. We were concerned that a "media blitz" would confuse our motives and associate our efforts with an attempt to gain publicity rather than our true desire to help people in need. Our strategy prevailed.

The role of the volunteer CPA was to help in reconstructing records, submitting forms, preparing loan applications, valuing assets, determining inventories, assessing casualty property losses, and amending tax returns. A seminar was held to introduce the team to the families and let them know the kinds of services that could be provided free of charge by the volunteers.

One of the challenges of the project was data collection. People moved three and four times within a one-month period, changing addresses, phone numbers, and our records. We made personal calls to get current information, computerized our list and mailing labels, and set up charts showing the CPA, lawyer, family with old addresses and current address and phone numbers.

A case study illustrates the type of services provided by CPAs. Assistance was provided in reconstructing records for a widow and her family. This involved getting duplicate copies of the deed to the home, Blue Cross cards, automobile and homeowners' policies, and bank statements, and tracking down the account number for the deceased husband's pension.

While help with the paperwork maze was valued, the personal touches most appreciated were the effort in trying to replace some of the personal mementos destroyed, including contacting the photographer to get copies of the twin daughters' high school graduation photos, securing a copy of the son's high school diplomas and trying to get another class ring. The family also lost a pet in the fire, so the CPA firm plans to give the family a dog when the family's new home is completed.

## Results and Evaluation

This was an ongoing project from May 14 through November 30, 1985, when the record reconstruction was completed and requests for replacement tax forms filed. The teams completed family contact forms advising us of their progress, and phone calls were made to touch base periodically and answer their specific questions. The "Update Reports" were published as new information came to light, and the task force first met regularly to report progress on key issues.

In August, PICPA devoted a two-page photo feature in our magazine, *Pennsylvania CPA Journal,* telling our members about this project and giving the volunteers' recognition for their involvement.

We have been pleased to be a part of the massive relief effort that has reached out to the Cobbs Creek Community on a "people helping people" basis. Our one-on-one approach has shown that people do care and are willing to share their professional skills with those in need.

## Cost

A budget was not established for this project. However, the PICPA leadership felt strongly that there was a need for CPA assistance. Approximately 1,100 hours of professional services and staff assistance in excess of 600 hours was provided by the association. Mailing and duplication costs were $2,700.

(This public relations program, submitted by Patricia A. Walker, Pennsylvania Institute of CPAs, Philadelphia, Pennsylvania, received an Award of Excellence in the Community Relations category in the 1986 Gold Quill Awards Program of the International Association of Business Communicators (IABC). Reprinted with permission from IABC's 1986 edition of *No Secrets*.)

# Book It! National Reading Incentive Program

## Problem and Opportunity

In the last quarter of 1982, President Ronald Reagan and then Secretary of Education Terrel Bell issued a challenge to corporations and companies nationwide to become involved with private sector initiatives. Soon after that, in 1983, the Library of Congress issued its now famous report, *Becoming a Nation of Readers.* The report identified reading as a major problem area in our schools and the country in general. It also suggested ways in which the problem could be solved. Other reports on illiteracy placed the total U.S. adult illiterates at 27 million. Another 45 million adults were considered functionally illiterate—barely able to function on the simplest levels in our society. Lastly, a report on schoolchildren's eating habits was published in 1983, which stated that kids' favorite foods were pizza, hamburger, and steak, in that order.

Pizza Hut president, Arthur G. Gunther—whose own son had found reading nearly impossible due to an eye disorder—decided that there was something that Pizza Hut could do about all of the above related problems. Gunther was not certain how to go about it, but he wanted to establish a nationwide program to reward students with free pizza for reading above and beyond their normal assignments. He saw this problem as an opportunity for Pizza Hut to "make a difference."

## Goals and Objectives

In summer 1984, Gunther and the then regional marketing supervisor, Sharon Knight, a Pizza Hut employee based in Kansas City, began making the rounds in Washington, D.C. They visited with the White House Office for Private Sector Initiatives; Secretary of Education William Bennett; Sam Sava of the National Association of Elementary School Principals; Albert Shanker of the American Federation of Teachers (AFT); Mary Futrell of the National Education Association (NEA); and the leaders of every other education association and organization that would see them. Their mission was to obtain support for the program and every single one pledged that support.

It was recommended by these organizations that Pizza Hut conduct a test of the program, and Kansas was chosen since Pizza Hut's corporate headquarters is based in Wichita, Kansas. Sharon Knight was chosen to conduct the test. Knight went to educators in the state—teachers, principals, librarians, superintendents, the PTA, the NEA, and AFT, and others—to ask how the program should be structured. The result was a program designed by educators for educators. In brief, the consulting group said that the program needed to:

- Be easy to administrate. Teachers have enough work already.

- Be adaptable for any class or student.

- Provide immediate positive reinforcement.

- Include parental involvement.

In addition to those goals for the actual design of the program, Pizza Hut decided that we wanted to enroll every student possible statewide, conduct the test in February and March 1985, and based on results of the test, be ready to implement the program nationwide in the 1985-86 school year with a start date of October 1. When Gunther told educators his plan, they said it couldn't be done: "You're talking about education. We don't move that fast." Gunther replied, "No, we're talking about the business of education, and business moves that fast every day. We will do it."

## Implementation

With assistance from Valentine-Radford Advertising in Kansas City and several staff members at the Pizza Hut Home Office, program components were designed and printed. John Hanna of the Kansas State Department of Education offered to help distribute materials, and by the end of the two-month test, 137,000 children statewide had participated. The results of the test, garnered from a teachers' survey indicated that it met all of the prerequisites and more. It also had a strong positive effect on the students in amount of reading accomplished, interaction with peers, other class studies, and more. Most importantly, 97 percent of the teachers said that they would participate again if the program were continued. Pizza Hut decided to go nationwide with the program and asked its franchises for their support. One-half of all Pizza Hut restaurants are franchisee owned and operated, meaning franchisees control nearly 2,300 restaurants. Their support was crucial to the program. We needed a reply two weeks after we sent the letter asking for support. All but one franchisee— representing nine restaurants—chose to participate.

Next, we had to design the national program. By now, the government and public affairs department had been given responsibility for the project. The project team consisted of Art Gunther; Sharon Knight; Larry Whitt, vice president of government and public affairs; Mike Jenkins, corporate public relations manager and BOOK IT! director; Deborah Franklin, BOOK IT! coordinator; and Boris Weinstein of Marc & Co. in Pittsburgh, Pennsylvania, who was responsible for national public relations and counsel.

Adapted from the Kansas test, the program was to run five months: October and November 1985, skipping December for the holidays, and January, February, and March 1986. Teachers would be given a wallchart to plot students' progress, honor diplomas for principals to award, Pizza Award certificates, teacher merit award bookmarks, and full program rules and guidelines.

Superintendents and school board presidents nationwide were mailed registration packets—32,000 in all—and asked to sign up their schools. The original deadline date was set at June 10; however, by this date only 2 million students had been enrolled. Our projections were 6 million when we began the program, so we extended the cutoff to August 10. In July, we had to estimate how many students we would have enrolled because the printing needed to begin in order to have everything ready by October 1. We decided to print for 7.1 million students and we reached that mark on August 7. We estimate that we had to turn away up to another 2 million kids for lack of materials.

The program materials were sent out to the schools in September. At the same time, a training program began in all of our 4,480 restaurants nationwide to explain about BOOK IT! and how it was not a promotion, but a public service program. The training materials, including an implementation manual and filmstrip, were studied by all employees and everyone was cautioned against any selling or commercialism. The filmstrip included role playing, and this really set the tone for the entire in-restaurant program activities.

Once in the teachers' hand, the program followed these general guidelines:

- Teachers signed up kids and assigned individual reading goals according to each child's ability and reading level.

- The students signed up for the program on the wall chart.

- Students read toward their goals and submitted oral or written book reports.

- Parents were sent a letter and reading verification form and urged to become involved with the program.

- Students reaching their monthly goals received immediate positive reinforcement in the Pizza award certificates.

- Students went to their local Pizza Hut restaurants and were awarded a four-color BOOK IT! button and their free pizza. Each award was treated as a miniawards banquet.

- Students who achieved their goal for three consecutive months received a teacher merit award bookmark.

- If all students reached their goal in four of five months, the entire class received a pizza party.

## Research and Cost

Professor John Boulmetis at the University of Rhode Island agreed to conduct simple research on the program's benefits and deficiencies. Teacher surveys were sent to 23,000 participating teachers—a 10 percent sampling. He received more than 5,000 replies and the findings showed that BOOK IT! motivates children to read more and also improves reading skills. The average number of books read per student from before to during the program increased by 300 percent. Reading levels improved by 52.6 percent, and reading enjoyment increased by 77.5 percent. Students' attitudes toward learning improved by 56 percent.

The 1985-86 program included 7.1 million children in 233,000 classrooms nationwide and cost $50 million in free pizza and $2.7 million in administrative costs—i.e., printing, distribution, and staff.

(This public relations project, submitted by Michael J. Jenkins, Pizza Hut, Inc., Wichita, Kansas, received an Award of Merit in the Public Service Communication category in the 1986 Gold Quill Awards Program of the International Association of Business Communicators (IABC). Reprinted with permission from IABC's 1986 edition of *No Secrets.*)

# Woodland Park Zoo Bonds

## Problem and Opportunity

During the first half of 1985 a specially appointed zoo commission, established by the mayor of Seattle and the King County executive board, completed a year-long study on the future of Seattle's Woodland Park Zoo. It was concluded by the blue ribbon commission that the zoo would require a major capital construction program to become the community and tourism resource it could be. The same report concluded that the timing was critical for this program because many facilities constructed at the zoo dated back to the 1930s and had deteriorated to the point where routine maintenance could no longer support them. The health and well being of the animals were considered to be the main reason for significantly upgrading their habitats.

The zoo commission also took note of the fact that voters had twice rejected capital construction bonds for Woodland Park over the past 15 years. Due to this lack of voter support, the zoo's master development plan was proceeding with no progress. On consultation, the city of Seattle with King Country decided a $31.5 million bond measure should be placed on the November 6 election ballot. An organization called "Citizens for a Better Zoo" was formed, and Livingston and Company was appointed its pro bono agency.

## Goals and Objectives

The goals of the campaign were to secure passage of the $31.5 million bond issue and to bring positive attention to the community value of the Woodland Park Zoo for the zoo's strategic marketing support. Livingston and Company conducted focus group research along with a limited quantitative survey to determine voter attitudes and perceptions regarding the bond issue for the zoo. It found that the voters were more concerned with the zoo as an educational resource for their and the community's children, with a secondary interest in the zoo as a tourism, job-generating attraction. The major conclusion reached by the research was that voter apathy in getting out the vote in an off-year election would be the major difficulty faced by the campaign. In the state of Washington, a bond issue must receive a 60 percent approval vote from a turnout equal to at least 40 percent of the most recent general election.

From the research, it was decided to undertake a strategy calling attention to the community value of having a "world-class" zoo. It was also decided to develop campaign materials that could economically build on existing support groups.

## Implementation

To accomplish the task, Livingston Public Relations developed a community group slide show and script, a fact sheet, a brochure, posters, bumper stickers, information kits, and a paid advertising radio spot. The campaign began approximately six weeks prior to the election. The slide show went on circuit to over 30 different community groups. The fact sheet was also mailed to existing zoo supporters who had previously contributed to zoo activities. At the same time, information kits for all King County print and electronic media were distributed as backgrounders. The top 100 employers in the country also received employee information kits designed for use in employee communications.

Approximately four weeks prior to election day, posters and the promotional brochure were distributed. Both political parties agreed to include the zoo brochure in their respective political mailings. Approximately $250,000 brochures were distributed in this manner.

The posters, which featured mezzotint "head"shots of a gorilla, bear, leopard, and an albataross, were designed so they could be attached to the sticks of yard signs of candidates. Volunteers distributed more than 15,000 signs. In addition, zoo supporters donned gorilla and bear suits and distributed several thousand additional brochures at major companies and at college and professional sporting events.

About two weeks before election day, the campaign chairman reported that the yard signs were being "stolen" by collectors. This unique circumstance was the focus of a major publicity push for eleventh hour support. Releases were sent to major print and electronic media commenting on the sign thefts. As a result, the *Seattle Post Intelligence* ran a front page story on the zoo signs exactly one week prior to election day. The same day, the *Seattle Times* ran a major piece, and every major radio station, and two network affiliate television stations picked up the story and gave it major coverage. A late poll showed this effort raised zoo bond awareness and approval to the highest ratings achieved during the campaign.

For the final five days of the campaign, a humorous radio advertising program ran that helped keep the visibility of the issue at extremely high levels.

## Results and Evaluation

The Woodland Park Zoo Bond issue passed with a 67 percent approval rate from a voter turnout approaching nearly 50 percent of all eligible voters. The fund-raising efforts brought in a $5,000 surplus, including a significant donation made by donors who wanted to help defray the cost of replacing stolen signs.

The zoo posters themselves have become collector's items and the Woodland Park Zoo plans to use its small remaining supply for future fund-raising events.

Above all, the people of Seattle and King County will have one of the finest zoos in the world, and the animals will have the best environment a zoo can provide.

## Cost

Approximate cost of the campaign was $70,000.

(This public relations project, submitted by J. Richard Skinner, Holland America Line-WesTours, Inc., Seattle, Washington, received an Award of Excellence, in the Public Affairs and Government Relations category in the 1986 Gold Quill Awards Program of the International Association of Business Communicators (IABC). Reprinted with permission from the IABC's 1986 edition of *No Secrets.*)

# Case IH Farm Radio Broadcaster Relations

## Problem and Opportunity

In early 1985, Tenneco, Inc., purchased International Harvester's agricultural equipment division and merged it with Tenneco's own J I Case affiliate. Farm broadcasters were identified as a major component of the farm media that needed attention from the new organization.

J I Case—now known as Case IH—had never before launched a concentrated public relations program to reach its farm audience through farm radio broadcasters. Now was an opportune time to begin a strong media relations program for farm radio broadcasters, many of whom are members of the National Association of Farm Broadcasters (NAFB).

## Goals and Objectives

Of course, the ultimate goal of this program was to reach farm audiences through public relations messages disseminated via farm radio broadcasts. Farm radio programs reach a highly targeted audience—one very important to Case IH. Image-enhancing messages and general news about the success of the new Case IH organization were important topics to bring to farm radio listeners.

A second goal was to effectively provide the farm radio broadcaster with interviews and information that may otherwise have been difficult for each individual broadcaster to obtain.

Outside of interviewing a local Case IH dealer, catching a company representative at a farm show, or arranging for a telephone interview, most of these farm broadcasters would not have had the opportunity to get detailed information and interviews from company representatives. Budgetary constraints generally prevent these broadcasters from traveling to company-sponsored meetings.

## Implementation

Every November, NAFB members meet in Kansas City for the group's annual convention. Since this event overlaps with the annual Future Farmers of America convention, many broadcasters make it a working session to interview representatives of the agricultural industry. Thus, this was a natural place to begin a media relations effort aimed at this audience.

Approximately 170 NAFB members were sent an advance mailgram alerting them that Case IH was hosting an interview suite during the convention.

At any given time, at least two representatives were available to speak on:

- Corporate matters (such as the merger).
- The Case IH dealer organization.
- General agricultural topics.
- The Case IH product line.

To announce the interview suite location, posters were placed at strategic positions around the hotel where the NAFB convention was being held. Agency personnel also handed out pocket-sized cards to NAFB members during registration.

A package of prerecorded audiocassette tapes was prepared as a "take home" item. This kit included four tapes and transcripts. A business reply card was enclosed to report usage of the material.

Topics of general farm interest were selected, and special care was taken to keep the message noncommercial. In fact, Case IH was mentioned only in the identification of the company expert featured on the tape. Subjects were:

- Rollover protection structures for tractors.
- Highway light safety.
- Off-season equipment maintenance.
- Farm equipment leasing.

The tapes were divided into two sections. The first featured a professional news announcer actually interviewing the Case IH authorities—in short, a finished package that could be used "as is" by farm broadcasters. The second section was the Case IH representative's responses, with "dead air" where the interviewer had talked. This allowed broadcasters to easily insert their own "lead in" to the interviews.

This package was handed out at the interview suite and later mailed to the rest of the NAFB membership.

## Results and Evaluation

A total of 29 radio stations and five agricultural radio networks visited the interview suite. (Demand on the representatives' time was so great that the suite was extended to a second day.) These broadcasters represented virtually all major farm regions of the United States. More than 560,000 farm households were reached via the convention interviews.

So far, an additional 25 stations have returned business reply cards from our mailing of the audio interview package. This represents an additional 145,000 farm households reached. As of late January, we are still receiving cards from broadcasters. Most of the reply cards indicate that all four interviews were broadcast.

From comments made personally at the interview suite, and from the reply cards, farm broadcasters indicated appreciation for the opportunity to air comments from Case IH representatives. "Keep them coming," "Very well done," "Well produced," "Very informative": these are some of the reply card comments we received. Our goal of improving media relations with farm broadcasters got a strong initial boost. And, we reached a minimum of some 700,000 farm households throughout the United States.

(This public relations project, submitted by Gregory D. Leaf, Bozell, Jacobs, Kenyon & Eckhardt Public Relations, Chicago, Illinois, received an Award of Excellence in the Media Relations category in the 1986 Gold Quill Awards Program of the International Association of Business Communicators (IABC). Reprinted with permission from IABC's 1986 edition of *No Secrets*.)

# Floating Point Systems Investor Relations Program

## Problem and Opportunity

Following the loss of a major contract to a competitor in February 1984, Floating Point stock fell from $30 1/2 to $12 1/2 in a matter of days. Several articles appeared in the press questioning the company's technological leadership and hinting that most of the company's best executives had defected to the competition. An independent survey commissioned in late 1984 yielded the following information:

1. Floating point was viewed as having "stale" technology and no viable plan for meeting and beating competition in an increasingly crowded marketplace.

2. The company was viewed as having an unstable management team.

3. The company was criticized for catering to sophisticated, technically oriented investors and analysts at the expense of individual investors.

4. Shareholders had little or no sense of the company's long-term priorities and strategies.

## Goals and Objectives

1. Improve the quality of shareowner communications, principally through the annual report and quarterlies; and, in particular, to demonstrate the company's strengths in the four areas of shareholder concern outlined earlier.

2. Initiate and maintain relations with as many new (report writing) analysts as possible to remove the vulnerability associated with having only a few analysts following the stock.

3. Orient the company's financial communications and contact with analysts to reaffirm FPS's role as the leader in its scientific computing niche.

4. Improve and standardize the company's financial reporting to analysts to ensure all investors are working from the same set of assumptions.

5. Reduce the wide variations of analysts' estimates to help eliminate vulnerability to "earnings surprises."

6. Improve internal support of the investor relations function among vice presidents and directors. (Because of its virtual monopoly in scientific computing, the company could afford to be exceptionally conservative in communicating goals, strategies, and expectations. In the face of increasing competition, however, my objectives required us to be more aggressive in communicating the company's strengths and expectations. Such a major shift in policy would require the full support of all senior officers and the board, which had historically been very conservative in these matters.)

7. Increase daily trading volume to help reduce upside and downside swings of stock on relatively light sell and purchase volume.

8. Reduce size of average institutional holding to help limit vulnerability to institutional selling.

9. Reduce overall institutional holding to help limit vulnerability to institutional selling.

10. Increase price/earnings ratio from 9 to at least the computer industry average (15).

## Results and Evaluation

1. A totally new approach in the annual and quarterly reports prompted Touche Ross, our auditor, to praise our particularly enlightened approach to sharing important, but not legally required, information with our investors. The annual report was cited for its effectiveness by the National Association of Investment Clubs and won the Financial World Award for best high tech annual report in 1985.

2. In fiscal 1985, 51 research reports were published on Floating Point Systems, compared with 23 in the previous

year—a 122 percent increase. This coverage is far in excess of what most companies of our size ($128 million) could reasonably expect. This is particularly noteworthy considering it was well known that earnings would be down in fiscal 1985.

3. A slide presentation was developed for seminars and financial forums throughout the United States and Europe to define the industry, the market, how we serve it and our long-range goals and aspirations. Research reports showed these messages were effectively conveyed.

4. A highly detailed revenue analysis sheet was developed for quarterly distribution to ensure equal access to financial data.

5. An analyst estimate consensus sheet was developed to help "shepherd" errant analysts into a tighter range of estimates more in line with our own expectations.

6. Formal quarterly board reports were initiated to ensure cooperation and support from FPS management of our more aggressive investor relations program.

7. Despite a stock buy-back program, which reduced shares outstanding by 12 percent, the company still enjoyed a 20 percent increase in trading volume in fiscal 1985.

8. Vulnerability to institutional holders was reduced by spreading the stock among more holders. Average holding of each institutional investor declined by 6 percent.

9. Individual investor ownership of Floating Point increased from 22 to 40 percent during the year.

10. At the beginning of the year, the company's stock price was $17 1/4, accompanied by a price/earnings ratio of 9. By the end of the year, the stock price was $31 1/4 with a P/E of 18 (compared with a computer industry average of 15). The stock and P/E advances were achieved during a year of absolutely flat earnings.

(This public relations program, submitted by Austin W. Mayer, Floating Point Systems, Portland, Oregon, received an Award of Excellence in the Investor Relations category in the 1986 Gold Quill Awards Program of the International Association of Business Communicators (IABC). Reprinted with permission from IABC's 1986 edition of *No Secrets.*)

# Oxylights

## Objectives and Results

Oxylights[SM] is a special events light-and sound attraction designed to showcase a community-minded company and its regional headquarters building in support of a program promoting off-season tourism in Niagara Falls, New York. The community is economically depressed, and the tourist season has traditionally focused on the short summer vacation period when visitors come to view one of the world's most famous natural wonders, Niagara Falls.

Oxylights is an innovative and unique art form combining music and lights on a "canvas" seven stories high and equally wide. The computerized color palette is formed by 49 "cells" featuring red, green, yellow, and blue lights—nearly 1,600 bulbs.

## Problem and Opportunity

The economy of Niagara Falls, New York, is closely linked to tourism. The demise of industry and business in the area and a subsequent population decrease (from 102,000 to only 71,000) has made the success of tourism even more critical. Most tourists visit the area during the traditional summer vacation season, extending only from Memorial Day through Labor Day. The off-season slump, especially during the winter months, has a severe negative impact on the local economy.

Five years ago, the chamber of commerce initiated a largely volunteer effort designed to boost off-season tourism through a series of events under the umbrella of a winter holiday program called a "Festival of Lights." Running from Thanksgiving through the Christmas season, the festival attracted 1.8 million visitors during its first four years. OxyChem has supported the festival since its inception, sponsoring special exhibits, donating services and encouraging employee participation.

Our Canadian neighbors, just across the Niagara River, recognized the potential the festival presented and jumped in with their own events, exhibits, promotions, etc., in direct competition for the limited tourist dollar. Because of this it became clear that something major needed to be done if the U.S. festival was not to become a weak second to the Canadian show.

## Goals and Objectives

For the Fifth Annual (1985) Festival of Lights, OxyChem management answered the desperate call of the U.S. Festival Committee and the Niagara Falls Chamber of Commerce. It was determined that OxyChem was the only employer in Niagara Falls, New York, willing to develop something significant enough to refocus tourist and media attention from the Canadian event back to the American festival. Even though time, funding, and manpower were extremely limited, a major program was undertaken—first to develop the concept and then to complete and promote it in time for the festival. The need was clear and management reacted by broadening its scope of support and assistance to reach for an even greater audience—an estimated 100 million people residing within a 400-mile radius of Niagara Falls. Management supported the public relations department proposal for something unique, appealing to all age groups and that could be expanded in the future—promoting repeat visits because of the changes. Thus, Oxylights was born. Oxylights and the festival were seen as special communications vehicles uniquely suited to project the OxyChem name as a company deeply committed to, as well as deeply involved in, the affairs of those communities in which it has plant operations.

While the Festival of Lights continues to have three major objectives—1) to increase community pride through volunteerism; 2) to generate positive publicity for Niagara Falls, and 3) to stimulate the local winter tourism economy—OxyChem sponsored Oxylights in support of all these objectives with the further, company-oriented goal of increasing public awareness of the contribution that Occidental and its 2,000 western New York employees and their families make on a year-round basis to the area's economy and quality of life.

## Implementation

The Oxylights concept was initiated with the public relations director who was assigned responsibility for its development and implementation in cooperation with representatives of the Festival of Lights Committee, the chamber of commerce, and private suppliers and vendors. Public relations also had responsibility for developing and managing a promotion and publicity program in support of OxyLights. The goal for the 1985 program was to have significant impact on the region with planning for national exposure in 1986 and thereafter.

The single, over-riding problem involved in converting the public relations concept for this major special event vehicle into reality was the simple fact that no one to the company's knowledge—or to the knowledge of experts in the field of electronic music—had ever designed and constructed a light-and-sound synthesizer system in the proposed form or on the proposed scale. Another concern was the limited time period in which to complete the project—May to the start of the Festival of Lights (November 23).

The goal required something meaningful that would be remembered, that people would talk about to their friends and neighbors, and that would be difficult (if not impossible) to duplicate. The decision was made to convert the side of the Occidental Chemical Center office building into a seven-story "canvas" on which to paint or stage a computer-driven program of lights and sound. The company is referred to as Oxy and public relations coined the name "Oxylights," which has been registered as a Service Mark (SM). With the support and encouragement of OxyChem management, public relations successfully brought all the elements together and the first public showing of OxyLights went on as scheduled November 21 before an invitation-only preview audience of 400 two days before the official opening of the Fifth Annual Festival of Lights. During the period between concept and reality, public relations was in almost daily contact with such diverse elements of the Oxylights program as the holder of a Ph.D. in music commissioned to create an original work titled "First Album for Oxylights," computer programmers, system designers, photographers, writers, an art director, a video production firm, electricians, a sound system expert, an assortment of volunteer chamber of commerce and festival committee representatives, and local media.

## Results, Evaluation, and Cost

The 1985 Festival of Lights attracted a record attendance—estimated at more than three quarters of a million people. This was about 50 percent of the total of the four prior years' attendance. This result was achieved despite the fact that the Niagara-Buffalo area experienced the heaviest snowfall on record (68 + inches) during the month of December—even more than the famous blizzard of 1977. (The festival ran from November 23 to January 5.) Local festival officials have been quick to credit OxyLights with helping establish the attendance mark.

The TV clips supplied by OxyChem to local media outlets were used frequently and widely. Press kits were mailed to more than 200 daily and weekly newspapers in a three-state area, plus parts of Eastern Canada. A mat service was used to distribute OxyLights features to other print outlets—dailies and weeklies. To date, the clips and known TV uses brought the Oxylights and festival story to the major part of the targeted population markets.

The company and its employees have received numerous compliments; the print media reports have recorded favorable comments from festival visitors who have singled out OxyLights for special mention; additionally, we have received letters of thanks from public officials as well as private citizens. Occidental is working with the survey department, School of Management, State University of New York at Buffalo to complete a community survey to further determine the impact of OxyLights.

Preliminary planning is already under way on how to improve and further use Oxylights as an integral part of OxyChem communications and community relations efforts. The program was budgeted at $75,000.

(This public relations program, submitted by Michael David Reichgut, Occidental Chemical Corporation, Niagara Falls, New York, received an Award of Excellence in the Special Events, External, category in the 1986 Gold Quill Awards Program of the International Association of Business Communicators (IABC). Reprinted with permission from IABC's 1986 edition of *No Secrets*.)

# Excellence Program

## Problem and Opportunity

In 1985 National Mutual Life Association launched an Australia-wide multimillion dollar advertising program introducing the theme "For the most important person in the world. You."

National Mutual's new market positioning was to be a company that provides exceptional, individual, quality service. The key to the success of the positioning was, and is, the quality of effort made by our staff. Tapping into this huge reservoir was our opportunity.

With the Excellence Program, our aims, which paralleled our objectives set out in the next section, were:

- To encourage individual commitment to one's job, and by extension to National Mutual.

- To help make our "exceptional service" market stance a reality.

## Goals and Objectives

The Excellence Program, implemented Australia-wide throughout 1985 at National Mutual Life Association, had long-term objectives:

1. To raise awareness of and give recognition to individual members of staff and to the value of their work.

2. To support the new market positioning of "exceptional service from National Mutual" by raising awareness internally of the importance of excellent, individual effort.

Motivating staff through genuine recognition of appropriate effort seemed one way to go, and the Excellence Program was developed. The base of the program is the Excellence Awards for which over 2,500 staff are eligible. Each quarter 13 or 14 silver level awards are made for individual, outstanding, and excellent efforts in that quarter. The yearly total is 54. From these, 13 gold level winners are selected, and from the latter the Managing Director's Award. Anyone of our 5,000 people in Australia (staff, sales agents, managers, executives) can send in a nomination to the branch judging panels. However, very top management and agents may not be nominated.

The very processes of operating the awards, promoting the program, and celebrating the winners are fundamental in achieving our aims, and each step automatically enhances both objectives simultaneously. A description of the prizes is essentially at this point so the communications strategy and challenges can be seen in perspective. The prizes fully incorporate our objectives. They include:

- A letter of congratulations from the branch manager, given by him personally when he advises the winner of his or her good fortune.

- A celebration tea to which are invited the nominator and the appropriate senior managers.

- A beautiful and distinctive framed certificate.

- A personal letter from the managing director.

- Attendance, with partner, at the annual, three-day Excellence Conference at a five-star hotel in Melbourne.

- Eligibility for the Gold Excellence Award.

The 13 annual gold winners' prizes are a handcrafted trophy and attendance, with partners, at another conference in Hawaii.

The Managing Director's Award is a personal, functional trophy, a perpetual trophy held by the branch of the winner, and an extension of the Hawaii trip to the West coast of the United States.

In all our material we had to be sensitive to three issues:

1. We did not want the prizes to outweigh individual achievement. We had, and have, to keep promoting excellence itself and the desire to recognize it.

2. Although Hawaii is a glittering prize, only 13 of our 2,500 Australian staff can win. The Melbourne Conference for the 54 silver winners had to be the focus, with Hawaii as extra icing.

3. With head office and Victoria branch based in Melbourne, we had to made a hometown conference appealing.

## Implementation

A unique symbol was developed that conveyed a message of striving and energy and that could be used in color or black and white. The designer was the Melbourne firm of Ian Murray and Associates.

It was determined at the outset that all paperwork would be top standard and that senior executives and management would be fully involved, beginning with the launch.

1. The program was launched by a senior manager at a series of small meetings in each branch and at the head office.

2. Each member of the staff received a "Meet the Challenge" folder containing a full-color, glossy, A4 brochure on the Excellence Program and an A4 full-color promotional poster.

3. Excellence program coordinators and a judging panel were established in each branch.

4. Supplies of A4, glossy, color nomination forms were distributed to the personnel division at each branch and head office

Three weeks before the end of the quarter, a circular goes out to each staff member reminding him or her of the nomination deadlines and conditions. This circular, of course, not only acts as a reminder but doubles as a general promotion item.

After the judging, the branch excellence coordinator ensures the proper follow through, including letters, teas, and certificates. The A4, full-color, glossy, six-page *Excellence Quarterly* published five weeks after the quarter closes highlights the winners and their achievements.

We consider all of the above items functional promotion. Nonetheless, we have also carried out traditional promotional activities. This included using the house journal, posters, and bookmarks.

The three-day conference for the silver award winners was held at the Melbourne Hilton from December 1 to 3. The underlying theme of excellence pervaded all aspects—the venue, program, entertainment, speakers, printed materials, and giveaways.

## Evaluation

Although a formal attitude survey will not be taken until later, we have many preliminary signals that show the program is a success.

1. National Mutual executives and senior managers not only support the program but continue to participate happily and fully.

2. The budget was approved for next year.

3. Nominations keep increasing by volume and in the range of nominator and nominee.

4. The excellence theme has become a part of the company culture.

5. Two of our overseas branches have voluntarily started their own programs, seeking our guidance.

6. Smaller pseudo "Excellence Awards" are popping up in many areas.

## Cost

The annual budget, the bulk of it for the two conferences, was $190,000, and we stayed within that.

(This public relations program, submitted by Susan Roberts, National Mutual Life Association, Melbourne, Victoria, Australia, received an Award of Excellence in the Other Internal or Multiple Audience Programs and Campaigns category of the 1986 Gold Quill Awards Program of the International Association of Business Communicators (IABC). Reprinted with permission from IABC's 1986 edition of *No Secrets*.)

# Organizing for Communication
# At Tampa Electric

## Summary and Background

In mid-1983, the senior management of Tampa Electric Company (TECO) took action on what had become a serious problem. Public confidence in the company was eroding as rates rose. And employee morale was sinking as a result. Meantime, management had grown increasingly dissatisfied with the efforts of TECO's small public affairs staff to provide counsel and professional support to handle the problem.

A nationally known consultant with a background in electric utilities was hired. And after many interviews inside the company and much analysis of survey data, the consultant reported these conclusions:

1. TECO's communication effort must shift from reactive to proactive.

2. While the department had some very capable people, staff turnover was high and would get higher if there wasn't a change in leadership.

3. Management should elevate the department head position to a vice president, should hire a highly qualified person to fill the position, and should give that person the resources to get things turned around.

Late in the year, after screening more than 400 applicants, the company named as its new vice president-corporate communications, a former international chairman of the International Association of Business Communicators with an extensive background in electric utility communications. The new vice president joined the company at the start of 1984 and was given the charge and the resources to organize the company for effective communication. This involved virtually starting from scratch.

Some immediate changes were made in staffing, programs, and operating procedures. But developing TECO's new corporate communications department was an evolutionary process "completed" (to the extent that such development ever is completed) toward the end of 1985.

It was an extensive effort involving, among other things:

1. Cancellation of a large-scale public-image advertising campaign as potentially counterproductive.

2. Mobilization of all departments and employees for a total communications effort involving caring for customers and pride in the company.

3. Conversion of the two-element Public Affairs Department (public relations and advertising) into the four-section Corporate Communications Department (Public and Employee Communications, Financial Communications, Community Relations and Educational Services, and Communications Services).

4. Addition over time of 20 employees, including 6 additions to the force and 14 transfers from other departments along with responsibilities for community relations, educational services, investor relations, graphics, and video production.

5. Replacement of an internship program with the company's second largest cooperative education program, bringing two six-person student teams from the University of South Florida into full-time employment in the department.

6. Development of an issues management system regarding as one of the best in the industry.

7. Creation of the company's leading-edge office automation and computerization effort, serving as the model for development in other departments systemwide.

8. Formulation of a wide range of communication-based corporate doctrine, including a new statement of purpose for Tampa Electric's holding company, TECO Energy, Inc.; new mission statements for the operating companies; a comprehensive policy on communications, a communica-

tion-centered model for the corporate business plan; a philosophy of communications for the company; and standards of excellence for the Corporate Communications Department.

9. Implementation of a professional development program, stressing knowledge of company operations as well as communication techniques and encouraging participation in professional associations such as IABC.

10. Development of a computerized project management system along with a network of interdepartmental communication to assure smooth flow of information and coordination of work effort.

11. Total overhaul of the company's communications media, both internal and external, with publications scrapped, consolidated, or started up and a shift of emphasis toward electronic communications as well as greater use of line and staff managers as communicators.

12. Creation of ongoing processes by which efforts are evaluated and results measured.

The results of this two-year effort have been quite positive with the communication staff function now operating at the center of the management decision-making process. Morale in the department is high and much recognition has come to the department in the form of commendations from senior management, compliments from client departments, and awards from professional groups.

Two of the most pleasing results, though, are these:

1. The downward trend in public favorability toward the company, as measured by opinion surveys, has been reversed, making the biggest jump (18 percent) in the experience of the research firm.

2. Corporate communications largely has succeeded in "giving away" responsibility for communication results, with departments throughout the company now feeling a sense of ownership.

(This public relations program, submitted by Tom Ruddell, Tampa Electric Company, Tampa, Florida, received an Award of Excellence in the Communication Plans and Proposals Category in the 1986 Gold Quill Awards Program of the International Association of Business Communicators (IABC). Reprinted with permission from IABC's 1986 edition of *No Secrets*.)

# A Common Sense Guide: Employee Print Communications

## Problem and Opportunity

This entry was produced for personnel directors (PDs) at individual Hyatt Hotel locations: Each PD is responsible for producing his/her hotel employee handbook and hotel employee newsletter (as well as other occasional print pieces such as invitations, payroll stuffers, etc.).

An audit of handbooks and newsletters produced by the PDs had shown that while quality level varied greatly, many of the publications were unacceptable due to incomplete explanations of company policy in handbooks, newsletters without any meaningful content, inappropriate and outdated clip art illustrations, etc. The (generally) low quality was attributed to the fact that the primary responsibilities of PDs were hiring/firing, orienting/training, and benefits administrations; employee communications (in which PDs typically had no formal training) were assigned a low priority.

The major opportunity was to upgrade the level of hotel-produced publications. This was considered an important opportunity by the client (Hyatt Hotels Corporation) because:

- Hyatt recognizes that employee morale and performance are critical in maintaining Hyatt's excellent reputation in an increasingly competitive industry.

- Hyatt has, for the last three years, been committed to upgrading the PD function from a quasiclerical role to a truly professional managerial one.

## Goals and Objectives

An obvious means of accomplishing the goal of producing higher quality hotel communications would have been to create "corporate-approved" prototype designs for each type of publication and then require PDs to use those designs. This "solution" was not feasible because Hyatt Hotels prides itself on its decentralized operating philosophy and because it encourages creative autonomy at the hotel level.

Instead, the client sent the goal of producing a guide that would assist the PDs in making their own creative and production decisions. Specific objectives were:

- To introduce the concepts and methods of design and production.

- To set some minimal standards.

- To suggest acceptable designs by providing attractive, usable examples.

The creative challenge was to balance the amount of general information about print (principles, definitions, technical information) with specific suggestions and standards. The client agreed to a proposed structure of four sections.

- Overview approach: the general information.

- Handbook model: step-by-step application of principles covered in the first section.

- Newsletter method: guidelines and suggestions (since the needs of individual hotels varied widely).

- Appendix tools: glossary, reproducible artwork, etc.

## Implementation

There was never any doubt that the medium for this project would be print. A ring-binder format would enable additions/deletions (primarily in the Handbook and Appendix sections) to be easily made.

After agreeing on a basic structure, we presented a preliminary pagination of the book, which was approved by the client. We then began outlining individual topics to determine where (and how much) detail was most appropriate.

We quickly realized that in order to introduce our examples in a persuasive way, we would have to actually design those examples first. So we (temporarily) abandoned the writing of the text and began to deal with the real problems posed by the need to create an attractive, intelligent economical handbook design. Tissues and comps of a handbook using an alphabet as the visual device were presented to the client for review. Client-requested changes were made at both stages.

Simultaneously, we wrote a draft of the hotel facts that would accompany the alphabet characters. These also underwent several revisions, according to client directions and our own perceptions of what facts could be quantified by individual PDs. Finally, we went back to writing the guide itself. Several drafts were tested for clarity with nondesign personnel.

Then we designed the guide and gave it its present name. Sample pages were typeset and the format revised to accommodate specific needs. Mechanicals were produced and (endlessly) explained to the printer; many pages had double sets of printer's instructions.

## Results and Evaluation

Quality level of hotel publications, primarily newsletters, has risen dramatically. Many PDs have incorporated several of the content suggestions into their newsletters. Some inspired PDs are networking minifeature ideas.

Experience with handbooks has been limited since hotels only produce new handbooks when the inventory is fully depleted. However, the PDs who have used (or are using) the guide for producing new handbooks are enthusiastic: They now call the client to get feedback and advice. And the client is delighted that they now share a common print vocabulary.

Perhaps most interesting was the initial response from several PDs who called the client to complain that the guide was much more than they expected ("too much information"). Our client advised them to take the guide home, read it through completely once, and then call back. Each PD had the same, more considered reaction: "I understand it and I can use it."

## Cost

The client set a budget of $50,000 ± 20 percent, which included writing, design, and production of 200 copies of *A Common Sense Guide* as well as the "internal" writing and design necessary to create the handbook and newsletter examples. The amount of time to fully produce the guide was not specified. Total cost was $60,000 and time was 14 months.

(This public relations program, submitted by Nancy E. Nicholson, Multivision International, Chicago, Illinois, received an Award of Excellence in the Communication Training category in the 1986 Gold Quill Awards Program of the International Association of Business Communicators (IABC). Reprinted with permission from IABC's 1986 edition of *No Secrets*.)

# Annual Lectures, 1981—1986

## Foundation for Public Relations
## Research and Education

Presented on the following pages are the annual lectures of the Foundation for Public Relations Research and Education from 1981 through 1986, delivered by distinguished public relations practitioners. The lectures all deal with the past, present, and future of public relations. Since it was established in 1956 by a group of senior public relations practitioners, the Foundation has pioneered many significant achievements that have had a marked impact on the conduct and acceptance of professional public relations. The Foundation conducts an annual program of scholarships, research grants, achievement awards, and student competitions. It publishes the *Public Relations Review,* a scholarly quarterly journal of public relations research and opinion. The lectures presented here are reprinted with permission from the Foundation's Board of Trustees.

# Public Relations and Business Schools

By Kerryn King

...You don't see change as you come to work each day. Your desk is the same. The people are the same. Sometimes even the newspaper headlines are the same. But when you look back over many years, you see that things really have changed.

...Who would have predicted that... PR practitioners [would] influence corporate policy and the public debate on issues? Things aren't perfect. Too often we still see public relations people pigeonholed. We see them looked on as practitioners of a narrow, sometimes mysterious specialty, like alchemy, incapable of moving into operations.

But in looking back, I feel a little like Martin Luther King, Jr., when he surveyed the Civil Rights movement. He said: "We're not where we want to be. We're not where we're going to be. But we're better off than we were!"...

In heaven, the British are the cops, the French are the chefs, the Swiss are the organizers, and the Italians are the lovers. In hell, the British are the chefs, the French are the cops, the Swiss are the lovers—and the Italians are the organizers!

It is the same in a corporation. How many times have we seen a man or woman who is perfect in one role become ineffective in another? Sometimes it is not the job that changes—it is the times. Thus, a CEO whose range or talents and knowledge was perfect for 1961 may find those same skills sadly lacking in 1981. In fact, I will make precisely that argument today. I will argue that the 1980s will make dramatic, unprecedented demands for new capabilities, not only from CEOs but from those at many levels of corporate management.

I will argue that many of these skills will be in public relations/public affairs. I will argue that the present generation of corporate managers is not being properly prepared to meet these demands. And I will propose some solutions.

## Some Background

But first, a little background: Corporations have had to struggle for a long time to overcome the stereotyped image portrayed by Victorian novels.

"Do other men for they would do you," Dickens wrote once. "That's the true business precept."

"Corporation,"Ambrose Bierce defined: "An ingenious device for obtaining individual profit without individual responsibility."

Stereotypes always distort. But this one was partly justified: "The public be damned," Vanderbilt said.

There *were* robber barons in nineteenth-century American business. Ida Tarbell didn't make them up. And there *were* meat packers who cared more for a side of beef than they did for the men working in their plants. Upton Sinclair made a point.

Today, although there are still some around, it is clear that the era of the buccaneering businessman has ended. Recently, for example, the Business Roundtable issued a statement on corporate responsibility. "The long-term viability of the business sector," it said, "is linked to its responsibility to the society of which it is a part."

Is this just lip service? Are businessmen simply putting a veneer on practices no more "responsible" than they were in the days of Charles Dickens? I think not. The change is real.

I see it at Texaco. For years, Texaco's policy was one of low profile. Our theory was: It's the spouting whale that gets the harpoon. If a TV reporter called, asking for an interview, we just said no.

While we went to great pains to deal with the consumer, we almost ignored the organized consumer groups. We had a knee-jerk reaction. We felt they were all bad.

## Change in Atmosphere

Now, we reach out to consumer groups and young people. We try to anticipate their thinking. We try to find a common ground for assistance and cooperation. We also reach out to reporters. We hold press conferences and open houses. We train our executives to deal with the media. Such openness characterizes more and more of American business.

What happened? Did businessmen—and we are still too often men—suddenly develop a social conscience? Did hearts miraculously thaw after having remained frozen for hundreds of years? No.

I suppose the enormous growth of business and government regulation played a role in this change. Events like Watergate brought a heightened awareness of the effects—and dangers—of an indifference to public standards. One major force has been the pernicious growth of television viewing by all segments of the public.

Two years ago, when I was in this city speaking to the Headline Club, I made that point.

"Today, about 60 million of us watch television every night. About a third or our adults average four or more hours a day. A preschool child watches an average of 54 hours a week. . . . It has produced a civilization in which Captain Kangaroo gets an honorary doctorate from one college and where. . .when asked how to spell 'relief' most children in one survey answered 'R-o-l-a-i-d-s.'"

Television. It has subjected all of us to something unparalleled in history.

And it is just beginning. The next 20 years will see the cable revolution. "The hardware," said *The Wall Street Journal* last month, "is far along; more than 21 percent of the nation's 80 million TV households are wired up, and the figure may reach 40 percent by the end of the decade, with perhaps 100 channels to choose from."

Not everyone agrees on the effect this revolution will produce. There's a new AT&T book, *Information in Society*, in which Thomas Chase outlines the possibility that cable could fragment and paralyze the United States. He quotes Alvin Toffler: "There comes a time when choice, rather than freeing the individual, becomes so complex, difficult, and costly, that it turns into its opposite."

My view is that the corporation of the twenty-first century will find great opportunities for reaching its employees, shareholders, customers, and the general public, through a proliferation of cable. That is why I argued before that the demand on the CEO of 1981 is "unprecedented." That is why I argue that many of the skills are found in our area—the role of communicator.

## "This Area"

There is some debate about exactly what to call this area of responsibility.

Public Relations? To some that smacks too much of glad handling.

Public Affairs? That seems too narrowly governmental.

External Relations? That's too vague.

I was amused by the suggestion I heard at one recent discussion: "Let's, " somebody said, "just call it 'this area!'" Whatever we call it, it's clear that "this area"is increasing in importance— and it's clear to more than just PRSA [Public Relations Society of America] members.

Thus, Harvard Business School Professor Stephen Greyser pointed to a survey of senior market research executives. They listed "effective corporate communications" as one of the "four principal challenges confronting marketing people in the 1980s."

Thus, the Conference Board, in its new report, *Managerial Competence: The Public Affairs Aspect* opines: "The increasingly intricate and sensitive connections between business and society occupy a major portion of the time and attention of corporate chief executive officers and. . . an increasingly important aspect of the duties of other managers."

Thus, Joe Nolan of Monsanto writes in the April/May issue of *Public Opinion*: "The most formidable management challenge of the 1980s will be managing the new business environment. The decisive issues will be external rather than internal, social or political rather than economic."

"Increasingly," wrote Frank Murphy of United Technologies, "corporate chief executives find themselves spending their time, effort, and energy communicating with their constituencies. Skill in public affairs/publications will be demanded more and more of corporate chiefs in the years ahead as the corporation fulfills a broader role in society."

General Electric's Bob Fegley put it this way: "The world economy has become highly politicized. Costs are inflated, expenditures are mandated, inefficiencies are imposed, markets are created and destroyed by decisions made in the presidiums and legislatures of the world. If the business manager fails to learn how to anticipate and influence these public policy decisions, he is going to find his life full of unpleasant—and unmanageable—surprises."

One question I asked in a survey was concrete: "What percentage of the CEO's time will be devoted to public relations/public affairs?"

Here are some answers:

- "Various studies have indicated that 50 percent or more of the chief executive officer's time is devoted to external relations. That trend will continue. . . ." (*Frank Lebart*, John Hancock)

- "One-third of the total." (*Joe Nolan*)

- "In our case—more than 50 percent. Generally 35 to 40 percent." (*Jim Bowling,* Philip Morris)

Let's say the range is 20 to 50 percent. The need exists. But are the new managers—the managers of the future—being trained to deal with these challenges? Not really.

One of the most perceptive people writing about "this area"has been Fran Steckmest of Shell Oil. He has outlined the barriers within corporations to creating what he calls the "public business executive."

There is the self-screening. If you have an articulate, extroverted young man or woman capable of the "rough and tumble of the public arena, he may become a trial lawyer, politician—or standup comic."

There is also a barrier in the way corporations select managerial talent. Companies promote initially on the basis of how well an employee performs in the narrow specialty for which he was hired.

"Further barriers exist throughout the corporate executive career span," Fran writes. He mentions the emphasis on training in managerial skills—not public policy skills.

Corporations tend to move their younger executives around. This makes it difficult for them to develop the community involvement which might provide such extracurricular training.

At Texaco, it is not unusual for a manager to move from White Plains, New York, to Houston, Texas, to Port Arthur, Texas, to Casper, Wyoming—all within a 10- to 15-year period.

How likely is he or she to become active in United Way, or become a precinct captain for a local political party when the next year might produce a move clear across the country?

How does a corporate manager gain the knowledge of public affairs he needs to meet the challenge of the eighties? How can he learn to express his views on these matters? To incorporate such a concern for them into his daily planning? How can he learn that "this area" is not only one which involves the CEO but one which involves every regional manager, everyone involved in any way with the preparation of product—in short, everyone with any corporate responsibility at all? How does one learn these lessons? As Oscar Hammerstein put it once: "You've got to be carefully taught."

Now, let's not overstate the case. It's not as if there is no teaching of public relations.

## Foundation/Business School Project

This year I've spent considerable time and energy on a project called the Foundation/Business Schools Project. We've met with university professors and with leaders in public relations. We're trying to identify the steps business schools could take to provide an overview of this newly critical area.

I've learned a lot. You don't sit down with Howard Chase or John Bell or Kal Druck or Alma Triner or Don Wright without learning something. And, last month, as the group gathered again, we went over our findings.

The educators sat on one side of the table. The—is *practitioners* the right word?—sat on the other. Although we had our differences, we agreed far more than we disagreed.

There are educational and training programs that prepare corporate managers to do a better job in public relations/public affairs. Companies like IBM, GM, Coca Cola, and Shell Oil have some that are in-house. The Public Affairs Council and the U.S. Chamber of Commerce provide seminars and workshops. Then there's Bob Lind of Washington Campus and Lee Preston of the University of Maryland—two innovators on the Capitol scene. And issue management aspects of PR are beginning to appear in advance management courses in some of our colleges and universities. "In making proposals for the business school syllabus," a number of our committee members insisted, "we must be careful not to reinvent the wheel." That's true.

Rogene Buchholz, at the University of Texas at Dallas, has done a number of studies of the teaching of business environment and public policy in the business schools. Professor Buchholz's work shows that business schools are aware of the need to examine the relationships of business and society. In his survey of over 400 schools—all members of the American Assembly of Collegiate Schools of Business—over 80 percent reported separate courses dealing with "public policy."

But the study also revealed that not a single one had "public relations" or "public affairs" in a course title. And even descriptive summaries omitted these elusive words. The closest in nomenclature was "public policy." But, public *policy* is not public *relations*. It's one thing to study how the changing American interest in environmental matters affected Hooker Chemical at Love Canal. It's another matter to learn the *techniques*—which we. . . have spent our lives perfecting—to avoid the consequences of a Love Canal, or to deal openly with it should such an incident arise in our companies.

How do you assess public reaction to a policy decision? How do you do it ethically? How do you handle disclosure when there has been an ethical lapse? How do you handle a perfectly moral decision, but one with grave implications for your community—a plant closing, for example?

To expect a student to be adept at these matters simply by studying public policy is like expecting your child to become a good pilot simply by studying aerodynamics. If you want to be a pilot, you've got to fly the plane!

Our Foundation/Business School Project asked Don Wright of the University of Georgia to investigate the teaching of public relations in the business schools. He studied 12 institutions. His finding: "Few, if any, business schools require public relations course work of their students."

Wright looked at Berkeley, Chicago, Columbia, Cornell, Emory, Harvard, Michigan, NYU, Penn (Wharton), USC, Stanford, and UCLA.

"Public relations is not being taught at these schools—at least not in the sense of having any course that stands alone," he reported to us last month.

Moreover, he pointed out that, of these major universities studied, only USC offered an Accrediting Council on Education in Journalism and Mass Communications (ACEJMC) accredited public relations sequence in a journalism/communications school.

Finally, Wright reported, "Most institutions had never considered having such a course." There were many obstacles listed when interviewers "discussed the prospect of developing a course in public relations/public policy."

What obstacles? "Well," some said, "does public relations have academic content? Is there a textbook that could meet business school standards?"

"If we added a required public relations course what would we omit? Would students enroll if it was an elective?" Others asked: "How do we find qualified teachers?"

USC wondered whether such a course would only "replicate" courses taught in the journalism school. And there are other obstacles that emerged only by implication. As Wright put it: "Despite successful development at a few major universities, public relations education today still lacks the respect accorded other professional training programs." He says diplomatically what Bob McCuen of duPont put more bluntly in his answer to my survey: "My impression is that business school professors think PR is infra dig."

In the light of that suspicion, we would be making a great mistake to do what might occur to us first: "Package" a public relations course and try to sell it intact to the faculty and curriculum committees at major business schools. Such an effort would provoke resentment, some of it justified.

## Some Solutions

...I believe that we must assist in the preparation of materials that business schools might find useful. They cannot be or will not do it themselves—at least not soon. Of the various approaches suggested by our Foundation/Business Schools task force, I favor four.

1.  We should prepare what some educators call "modules"— overview units which can be worked into existing public policy courses, or other appropriate parts of the curriculum.

2.  For those business schools located at universities with American Association for Education in Journalism accredited public relations sequences, we should encourage an overview course in the journalism school.

3.  We should prepare and distribute more complete bibliographies, which demonstrate the existence of a scholarly body of knowledge within public relations.

4.  We should identify those business schools willing to use case studies of public relations problems and cooperate with them in preparing such studies.

...I believe educators in our business schools look at public policy too narrowly. They look at it primarily as legislation, regulation, and enforcement. Thus, for the newly minted MBA, dealing with public policy is a job for the lobbyist or government relations strategist.

But public policy does not begin in Washington or Albany or Sacramento or Springfield. It begins in communities, towns, and cities, all over America. Business must be sensitive to changes in public opinion everywhere. It must pick up these changes early. Very big organizations must have a scanner going all the time. Once these scanners pick up change, the company must be prepared to take action.

Thus, public policy—and public relations—should not be the

province of a narrowly specialized group. It must be broad enough to review constantly those issues that can impact the company concerning its operations, its products, its reputation, and its profits.

For that reason, public relations in the broadest sense—even if we have to find another name for it—must become part of the business executive's understanding.

He or she must know that just as there is a place for the marketing manager, the research head, and the financial and legal departments, there is also a public relations/public affairs group that deals with issue detection and issue management. Furthermore, that group must have CEO-delegated authority to act on its findings.

I believe recognition of these opinions is growing. . . . I believe that if we cooperate constructively with the many willing and dedicated business school educators, these schools will work to fill the vacuum which now exists.

And when they do, imagine the qualities which will emerge in tomorrow's CEO.

- Picture a man or woman whose use of the English language is graceful. Who is comfortable with reporters and knows to look at the little red light when he's in front of a TV camera.

- Picture a CEO whose understanding of "this area" goes deeper than appearances.

- Picture a CEO who looks for trends before they are obvious—and knows how to respond and influence them.

Sounds like a CEO who came out of PR? Precisely.

If institutions that train our future corporate leaders wish to maintain their roles as shapers of American society, they must provide as a minimum an overview of public relations/public affairs.

As Ned Gerrity, of ITT, put it: "MBA graduates need not necessarily take a public relations course, but they should be adequately prepared to communicate, both within and outside a business organization."

In my own view, the need is clear. The question is: Who will satisfy it? Traditionally, the business schools have done an excellent job in preparing graduates for traditional business functions. They now have a new challenge: To meet the needs of a new business era. I hope they will seize on it—and, with the success such a program will engender, our entire society will be enabled to work more closely, more smoothly, and more effectively toward the achievement of our mutual and universal needs.

(This is the 1981 Foundation Lecture, presented on November 8, 1981, prior to the Public Relations Society of America (PRSA) Annual Convention in Chicago, Illinois. The late Kerryn King was Senior Vice President Public Affairs of Texaco, Inc. He was president of PRSA in 1979. Mr. King died on May 23, 1986.)

# The Revolution in Communications Technology: Implications for the Public Relations Profession

Betsy Plank

. . . We shelve Alexander Graham Bell neatly as the inventor of the telephone. Period. What our textbooks seldom, if ever, record is that he also invented something called the photophone—an instrument for transmitting sounds by vibrations in a beam of light. Today, that concept is one of the four key technologies of the Information Age—photonics: glass fibers, carrying information as pulses of light, generated by laser beams. The progeny of his genius—lightwave technology—is already in place in countless communities. Soon it will be linking cities along the Washington-Boston corridor, carrying up to 80,000 telephone calls in strands of glass in a cable which is about the diameter of my finger. It is indicative of the incredible pace of telecommunications technology which is telescoping time and space, doing so with astonishing efficiency and catapulting us into the Information Age.

The first of the other three technologies is microelectronics, which began with the invention by three Bell Laboratories scientists in 1947 of the transistor. Today the equivalent of hundreds of thousands of transistors work intelligently on one silicon chip. Photographers have an irresistible urge to show it side by side with a fingernail or a corn flake.

Another key technology of the Information Age is digital systems—the language of one and zero with which computers talk to one another.

The transportation system is photonics—that vision of Mr. Bell of more than 100 years ago.

And with these three hardware technologies comes the fourth—the software, which tells the other three what to do.

To "gee-whiz" on the wonders of telecommunications technology would be redundant. First of all, the literature on the subject is overwhelming. It is also inescapable. It has captured the mass media and advertising, business, and other specialized publications.

Most assuredly it multiplies geometrically on my desk. I have learned to read without undue panic about femtoseconds, kilobits, and transponders.

## The Information Age

The subject of the Information Age and telecommunications technologies have also captured the agenda of countless meetings. Indeed, the ubiquitous subject of the 70s—the social responsibility of business—has been replaced by the Information Age in one or more of its guises. It's also topping the charts of the security analysts. In a survey of 567 analysts reported this year, 69 percent rated telecommunications as the industry with the highest growth potential for the next five years.

There is widespread infatuation today with such here-and-now applications and future visions as:

- Electronic newspapers—more than 100 already have electronic systems or are putting them in place.

- The marriage of computer with the telephone, enabling people to work, shop, go to school, access libraries, bank, get a doctor's diagnosis without ever leaving home.

- Assurance of home security and energy use and savings by remote control.

- Ability to carry a data display terminal in your briefcase.

- Car telephones, which are becoming as commonplace as the one on your desk.

- Communications services customized to your precise needs.

- Instant opinion polling.

- Computers that are user-friendly, speaking our language instead of insisting that we speak theirs.

Or, to move into the Twilight Zone of perhaps:

- Direct communications with animals.

- Man/machine symbiosis—linking the mind with the computer for instant learning or storing the knowledge of one individual in a computer to pass along to another.

The possibilities transcend imagination. It is no wonder that Philip Meyer, futurist at the University of North Carolina, wryly commented, "Maybe our legs will wither and heads will grow like the genius-villains in old sci-fi comics!"

The changes for our society are almost as fundamental as that. Message movement is replacing people movement.

Is the public-at-large accepting the new communications technologies? When the price is right, the embrace is instant. The younger generation is mainlining computers. Research tracking public attitudes last year reported faith in technology in creating jobs, benefits, and solutions. But there's an equal concern out there about technology creating an inhuman world.

Consider that we are in the midst of massive change from an industrial society to an information-based society. Fifty percent of our work force is now in the business of the collection and dissemination of information. Raj Reddy of Carnegie Mellon predicts that in 30 years only three million people will be employed in manufacturing. By the end of this year, the number of computers—large and small—will exceed the world's population.

Management guru Peter Drucker has declared, "Knowledge, during the last few decades, has become the central capital . . . and the crucial resource of the economy . . . Knowledge has actually become the primary industry."

John LeGates, of Harvard, says, "The Information Age is the substitution of information for our other basic resources such as energy, materials, capital, and labor."

That's economic revolution. But it goes beyond the economy alone. The Information Age—and the technological expulsion that is powering it—is literally changing the nature of the human environment. That's social revolution.

Ian Ross, president of Bell Laboratories, has asserted, "The Industrial Revolution extended our muscles. The Communications

Revolution will extend our minds."

In his recent book on the subject, Frederick Williams, professor of the Annenberg School of Communications at the University of Southern California, reached further in writing, "The electronic environment is instantaneously changeable. It can directly link more human minds, minds with ideas, and minds with machines than any communications means we have developed in our 36,000-year spoken or 6,000-year written heritage. It is permeating, energizing, stultifying, mesmerizing, trivializing, delighting, and dulling . . . We create it and we can control it."

What does all this portend for the public relations professional? Let's consider a few of the answers.

## Changes in Work Habits

First, it portends changes in our daily work habits. For many of us, these changes are already in process.

- We use computer terminals to write, edit, send messages, access information. There are even computer programs that presumably improve writing styles.

- We have such data banks and libraries as Nexis, Dow-Jones, and the New York Times literally at the reach and tips of our fingers.

- We can hold staff meetings, confer with clients, conduct nationwide briefings and press events via teleconferencing.

- We're using electronic mail and programming our calendars by computer.

We can—increasingly—employ communications technology to manage the hardware of our business faster, better, more efficiently, more effectively.

Second, there will be opportunities for the professional agenda of public relations people. Among them will be:

- Improvements in our research capabilities. We're already seeing how new technologies can be applied to issues scanning. We'll extend that to turnaround research to narrow the frustrating gap between surveys and results, which has so often distorted our planning in the past.

- New media for our messages. Electronic media to reach employees at their work locations. Satellites. Cable. Home video playbacks. (In my company today, we're offering company video program to managers who use one-half inch tapes for home viewing. We now have more than 100 on our distribution list—a modest 1 percent among the management group, but we know that trajectory will be straight up in the near future. The special dividends are viewing time at home instead of work and the sharing of company messages with families.)

- The ability to customize messages to specific audiences. That's textbook axiom in public relations, of course. But the potential now is to bypass traditional media and literally reach precise audiences—share owners, customers, specific publics—with messages exactly tailored to their interests, their incomes, and to all the demographic factors vital to your strategy. The critical difference will be that the individual will gain control over the selection of the information you transmit and its time of delivery.

- Improved opportunities for the measurement of the effectiveness of our work.

- One giant potential for an entirely new area of public relations attention: getting employees to accept new technology. The electronic office will inevitably meet resistance. It's a radical change in work habits. Its introduction, its acceptance—(Drucker calls it "attitude training competence of people")—those are new objectives that public relations people can address for their organizations and their clients.

We are a very creative, very resourceful breed. We will capture the new communications technologies and make them our own. They are a candy store for us—exciting, rewarding, with promise to help improve our craft, expand our effectiveness and influence.

But while the sugar plums dance merrily in our heads, I implore you to look with me for a moment beyond that tempting counter, beyond the carpentry of our craft. And here I seek to tread on sacred water, with all the obvious risk and presumption that it infers.

I trace my heritage in this profession to our founding fathers—to Alexander Hamilton and his *Federalist Papers*, to Thomas Jefferson, and Sam Adams—who were consummate practitioners of the art of persuasion and public relations. I take perverse joy in knowing that many of them stood by anxiously one night, hovering over a printer's shoulder as he produced the declarative document for this nation.

## Some Concerns

And so, I am concerned about some of the implications of the Information Age for our unique and sometimes fragile society. I am concerned about the potential for instant feedback that may threaten time to nurture the American genius for compromise and consensus.

I am concerned about the changes that could result when opportunities for human encounter—in the marketplace, in the workplace—are diminished or altered. Does a move back to cottage industries in an electronic era bode ill or well for us? It's estimated that by the mid-nineties more than 10 million people will be working from their homes. Will we need new institutions to provide human contact and avoid isolation from dialogue and debate?

I am concerned about the possibility of the information poor/information rich classes of society. If information is the most valued commodity of the future, will a concentration of that power dangerously rupture our national stability?

I am concerned about privacy in an environment where machines are corruptible. (That has an Orwellian sound to it!) As one observer recently commented: "Information users must be advocates of the free and orderly flow of truthful information." Does this echo the PRSA Code? Should our Code be reexamined to take into account new technologies, new media?

I am concerned about the impact on language and writing skills that will be the likely trade-offs to the necessity of becoming computer literate. In a recent conversation with Ken Phillips, vice president of telecommunications policy and planning at Citicorp—an unusual combination of psychologist and physicist—he said that language and writing are key to the way we solve problems and computer literacy could alter that process dramatically.

I am concerned about overload in an information-intensive society. The critical question is not one of quantity so much as it is of handling information efficiently and well. Who sets priorities? What information gets attention? Alvin Toffler has also pointed out, "There comes a time when choice, rather than freeing the individual, becomes so complex, difficult and costly that it turns into the opposite. There comes a time, in short, when choice turns into overchoice and freedom into unfreedom."

Is Toffler right about the tyranny of too much choice, too much information?

The operative word in this litany is "concern" not doomsday prophecy, but a caring apprehension. My concern is to have these subjects addressed, the alternatives inventoried to avoid these risks and others.

Emily Coleman, of AT&T Corporate Planning, summed it up in blunt fashion: "No one is really doing it yet. The futurist positions are polarized on the subject. Either everything is going to hell in a handbasket or everything will be resolved by technology."

Someplace between those two poles lies a middle ground for thoughtful, objective, pragmatic examination.

Who takes that initiative?

Do these concerns and that initiative have implications for the public relations profession?

The Assembly of this Society (PRSA) has adopted a statement about the nature of public relations. Its preamble states: "Public relations helps our complex, pluralistic society to reach decisions and function more effectively by contributing to mutual understanding among groups and institutions."

## Taking the Initiative

If we accept and believe that, then in an environment that is changing radically, in which no institution will remain untouched, in which some may be replaced, is not the initiative one which we—this professional society, this Foundation—can be responsible for?

How does one begin so awesome a task? In my philosophy, one simply begins. Now.

One could, for example, under the aegis of the foundation, bring together a symposium of interested, knowledgeable people from the disciplines of public relations and the social sciences to begin to study the impacts and implications for new communications technologies—the Information Age—on the future of American society. The positive objective would be to minimize human dislocations in the progress toward a changing social environment, a new order. On a mega scale, it's issue identification: the management of change.

I am convinced that such a forum and a sharing of its results would help to generate the national dialogue so urgently needed. And surely dialogue is our business and our genius!

I am spurred by two fundamental, passionate convictions:

First, while the Information Age and its new technologies will radically change our society, our work habits, our individual lives, it can, most assuredly, improve the value and quality of human life in this republic beyond our present line of vision and imagination.

The second conviction I hold with equal passion: The public relations profession is uniquely qualified to be a catalyst, a steward, an architect in that enterprise and magnificent destiny.

Who else, if not we?

(This is the 1982 Foundation Lecture presented prior to the Public Relations Society of America (PRSA) 1982 Convention in San Francisco. Betsy Ann Plank is Assistant Vice President, Corporate Communications, Illinois Bell, Chicago. She served as president of PRSA in 1973.)

# Public Relations and the Very Human Art of Management

By Robert L. Fegley

... I got my first big break in public relations 28 years ago by writing testimony for General Electric's chief executive officer, Ralph Cordiner. His subject three decades ago: the impact of the electronic revolution .... So I owe my happy career of writing for GE chairmen to this frequently announced revolution .... It will undoubtedly have far-reaching social, economic, and political implications, though they've been somewhat long in coming.

Few other subjects have so completely dominated the business and professional press in recent years. Alvin Toffler has managed to milk another book out of it, and the "communications revolution" has replaced "social responsibility" as a hot topic for symposiums and learned conferences. AT&T is all broken up about it, and the stocks of all the little would-be competitors in telecommunications brought Wall Street to a feeding frenzy. The banks and the brokerage houses are engaged in an epic battle for the financial turf, brought on by computerized money.

We are warned that people stuck with precomputer skills—like PR people—had better get with it, or else. School systems are going broke trying to buy computers for their kindergartens. The younger generation has mastered the joystick and is now moving out of video games and into computer hacking. Mom and Dad are buying home computers, hoping the instruction book will tell them what possible use they can get out of them; nobody wants to be caught computer illiterate. And the old folks are settling down before their TV sets to choose the day's entertainment from a bewildering choice of 60 stations.

So the age of the computers is clearly upon us. But after all that fanfare, perhaps it would be worthwhile to try to put it in perspective. A little counterrevolution, you might say.

For one thing—an important thing—you just don't see our clients, the top executives of business, government, universities, or elsewhere, moving computers into their offices. Why is that?

## Not a Numbers Game

They will all admit that the new electronic machinery is going to be necessary to their operations in one way or another—stepping up the efficiency of the office, making new services possible, revolutionizing the business from one end to the other. But as far as they're concerned, that's staff work. Most chief executives seem to be resisting the idea that they, themselves, need a computer terminal to get their work done. And the reason for that is quite simple: they don't. Management was, is, and always will be an intensely human activity, not a numbers game.

Many computer enthusiasts have suggested that management will now become a matter of developing and using what they call "management information systems" punching in the variables, taking readouts, and making the fairly obvious choices. Chimpanzee work, once you get the hang of it.

We've had these dreams before. I remember, in the 1950s, when General Electric was indoctrinating its managers in the "universal principles of management," our Chairman, Ralph Cordiner, authorized what was called the Measurements Project. About six years were spent in developing numerical indices by which general managers were to be measured and motivated in the eight key result areas: profitability, market position, productivity, product leadership, personnel development, employee attitudes, public responsibility, and balance between short-range and long-range goals. Now, all these are essential aspects of balanced managerial performance, and in fact a fellow who was closely associated with this measurements project, Fred Borch, ultimately succeeded Ralph Cordiner as CEO. But the effort to manage the company by means of numerical indices was a dismal failure. Managers ducked and dodged around the system—laughing all the way. Cordiner quietly dropped it and Fred Borch never tried to revive it when he became chairman in the '60s. And the reason is that these men, experienced and intelligent executives, were obliged to acknowledge that while a good manager keeps his eyes on the key ratios, management cannot be reduced to numbers.

## A Political Activity

In the words of Alex Pollock, a banker who has written good

material on the subject, "Executive management is naturally a *political* activity, dealing with people who have strong capabilities, strong personalities, and a strong will to power. These people are the managers within the organization, the managers of the competitors, the managers of the customers, and the managers of the suppliers, not to mention politicians and regulators." Thus the manager is managing what Pollock calls "a network of power relationships."

Traditionally, business executives have focused most of their time and attention on internal matters. But in the past decade, they have found that they have to spend more time—as much as 40 percent in the case of large corporations—trying to influence people who represent the outside forces: the political, economic, and cultural institutions and interest groups that create the climate in which the enterprise is going to flourish or fade away.

They are out pitching presentations to security analysts. They're down in Washington testifying or buttering up their Congressmen. They're holding press conferences. They're lecturing to college students. They're pleading with regulatory agencies. They're trying to calm down environmentalists and religious activists. Or they're working with their staffs late at night to prepare for these occasions.

Is that going to change in the electronic age?

## Eyeball to Eyeball

Well, some of these messages might be delivered by videoconferencing or by cassette, but believe me, remote hookups can never match the eyeball-to-eyeball effectiveness of personal persuasion. Something is lost in the translation.

Security analysts want to take the measure of the man or woman who is managing the company, and you can't do that by remote control. Do you really believe that the bourbon-and-branch-water meetings by which business is done in Washington will ever be replaced by electronic screens?

Computer terminals and videoconferencing machinery will probably find their way into the executive suite, much as television sets and wet bars have—as status symbols to impress the lower orders. They will even be *used* as they become familiar pieces of furniture. But they will be peripheral to the essential work of management, which is to manage a network of power relationships that determine the success of the enterprise.

## Creating the Message

After all, the new electronic machinery is designed to transmit and manipulate data. But data is not wisdom. Garbage in— garbage out. The new media will carry the message faster and farther than ever. But the message—whether it's delivered in person or through print or electronics—must be arrived at through the process of human thought and experience. The message must be created, discussed, refined, articulated, and made persuasive if it's going to have any effect on human affairs. It can be done only by human minds working with the one social invention that distinguishes the human species from all others—language.

And that is why I am convinced that the talents long associated with public relations people—literary, political, intuitional—are not going to become obsolete in a high-tech era. To the contrary, as the speed, range, and intricacy of communications increases, top management in all fields is going to find it necessary to hire more public relations professionals to help in the management of complex external relationships.

Most of these PR people will probably be engaged in what have been the traditional services of our craft: media relations, investor relations, the writing of brochures, annual reports, and company magazines. Many will specialize in the provision of services associated with the new electronic technology. But the heart of public relations work, and to me its highest aspiration, is to counsel and assist our chief executives in their work of managing the enterprise.

## CEOs Wear Two Hats

It took me quite a few years of working with chief executives to realize that these people have at least two distinct functions, two hats to wear. One function is to make the managerial decisions required to run a successful organization. They have plenty of help on this one. Executive committees. Boards of directors. Task forces. Computers. The whole hierarchy of management is structured to help chief executives make the necessary managerial decisions, and public relations officers today are part of that process, usually at the highest level.

But the other assignment—and this is the one I want to dwell on—is *personal leadership* of a very human enterprise. The chief executives must hold forth the vision and set the moral tone. They must manage the relationships and somehow turn a chaos of clashing wills into a unified, purposeful, achieving enterprise. They are personally responsible for whatever happens to the organization.

This is a very lonely and vulnerable position. And curiously, organizations are very seldom set up to help their leaders to lead.

Here, it seems to me, is where public relations people can be uniquely valuable. Usually the exercise of leadership involves spokesmanship—speaking to or speaking for the organization. And since chief executives are usually very busy people, they need someone to help them in the preparation of speeches, testimony, TV appearances, board reports, published pieces, press interviews—all the instruments of leadership through spokesmanship.

These needs have multiplied in recent years, as CEO's have had to go public to cope with outside pressures. The market for speech writers has burst open, and so has the ceiling on pay for this kind of work, because there never seem to be enough really good candidates to fill the demand.

## Some Career Advice

These Foundation lectures are supposed to bear a few nuggets of accumulated wisdom, like flies in amber, so let me offer some career advice on writing speeches for top executives.

The first question to be faced is whether you want to get into it at all. It does represent a different career path from the administrative path that most commonly leads to top management. Somebody aiming for the top of the hierarchy should get into management early and develop momentum. But for those who prefer writing to administration or selling, speech writing can get you close to the top—financially and otherwise—as a counselor and assistant to the chief.

Certain talents are necessary, of course: creative writing talent, the ability to take on virtually any subject in the world, and the flexibility to collaborate with another person—he [or she] being in the driver's seat.

Perhaps the most important, quite frankly, is to face up to your own ego needs. Some people like to be up front, and some prefer to work behind the scenes. Some want to be kings and others want to be kingmakers. This job imposes some more-or-less built-in conditions. Writing is a lonely business that requires quiet and isolation, and speech writers tend to be loners. You can't let yourself get excited by the game of company politics, or feel hurt if others achieve more fancy titles and overt symbols of power. Believe me, the person working with the chief executive has his hands on the levers of power. He can quietly but unmistakably leave his imprint on the world.

Assuming you want to get into it, you quickly find that speechwriting is only part of the job. The old term "ghostwriting" is closer to it, because in addition to speechwriting—writing for the ear in a colloquial, informal manner—you'll be writing for the eye, anywhere from ghostwritten books to op-ed columns, signed articles, book reviews, and testimony for the record. And if your chief is naturally eloquent, he won't always work from finished manuscripts. Reg Jones, CEO of General Electric and a political activist in the 1970s, often improvised from well-researched notes we called "thought starters."

Even more valuable than the writing skills, according to Jones, is the intellectual work of taking the idea of a wide variety of staff experts and outside sources, and synthesizing them into a clear and coherent presentation. The chief economist has one approach to the issue. The financial officer has another. The Washington Office has its own highly political perspective. And of course the CEO sees the issue in the light of his strategic objectives. Somebody has to make sense out of the discussion and put it all together in a persuasive presentation. That's the function of the writer. Sometimes it's more like negotiating a cease-fire than creating a work of art, but if you've won the confidence of the

CEO, you can put aside the politics of the situation and concentrate on developing the strongest possible presentation.

## From Writer to Counselor

Winning the confidence of the CEO: that's the key to success in this kind of work. It doesn't happen all at once. But over time, if the chemistry is right, the interplay between the two minds becomes almost as close as a good marriage—each one anticipating or understanding the other without a work spoken.

This is how good speechwriters become, in time, counselors to their clients. Chief executives today need more than a wordsmith. They need someone to orchestrate their appearances, develop and articulate their themes, build their media connections, research their chosen issues, develop their positions, and help them to express themselves persuasively. They need counsel on trends and problems among their various constituencies. They need someone to share their doubts and dreams while policy is being formed. This is much like the services that politicians expect from their political advisors. Today, with outside pressures building up to gale force on all institutions, that kind of service is required by chief executives everywhere, in business, public agencies, universities, hospitals, not-for-profit organizations, whatever.

## PR in the Electronic Era

Circling back to the opening theme, we must recognize that the electronic age is at hand. My successors in this kind of work will be using word processors instead of typewriters. They'll have a terminal in the office and another at home so that more of their research can be done by tapping directly into data bases. They'll stay one step ahead of the boss in understanding the new communications media. Public relations people can't afford to fall behind in a generation that learns to interact with computers in grade school.

But the advent of this new machinery does not change the intensely personal art of management. The chief executive's most pressing task, tomorrow as today, will be to manage an ever-shifting network of internal and external relationships.

This kind of work cannot be reduced to numbers. It is political, social, psychological, intricately involved with the nuances of language. And to help them get it done, management will be turning to the PR people—those eclectic, hard-to-categorize, intellectually adventurous lovers of language who choose to be engaged in a profession that may never be satisfactorily defined. The reason for that, I think, is that each of us defines it for himself, through the exercise of his individual talents. And we hope that, in the process, we can build something that will outlast us.

In the construction practices of ancient Rome, when the scaffolding was taken down from a completed arch of stone, beneath it stood the Roman engineer. If, as a result of his incompetence, the arch did not hold—he was the first to know. It is no wonder that so many Roman arches have survived for 2,000 years.

To my colleagues and successors in public relations, I can only urge that whatever you build with your talents, build it so that you can stand beneath it with pride and confidence.

(This is the 1983 Foundation Lecture, presented on October 23, 1983, prior to the Public Relations Society of America Annual Convention in New York, New York. Robert L. Fegley is Retired Staff Executive, Chief Executive Officer Communications, General Electric Company.)

# Public Relations/Public Affairs in the New Managerial Revolution: Ascendancy, Growth, and Responsibility

By Andrew B. Gollner, Ph.D.

I see a profound transformation taking place in the focus, substance, and position of public relations in our society. My objective . . . is to outline the causes of this transformation and to identify how your profession can be *energized* rather than *victimized* by the changes that surround us. More specifically, I will discuss the impact of growing interdependence on our profession.

. . . To ensure that we start from a common position, let me refer you to the Oxford English Dictionary. It defines *dependence* as the relation of having existence contingent on or conditioned by the existence of something else. *Interdependence is* defined as *mutual dependence* or to depend on each other mutually.

If we examine carefully the recent evolution of our society and our world system, we'll find that among the myriad of societal events, changes, and trends, there is one that is particularly significant—namely, the growth of domestic and global interdependence. Gone are the days when developments in one sector of our economy were immune from developments elsewhere. Gone are the days when the boundary line between private and public responsibility could be easily drawn. Gone are the days when superpowers could pursue domestic or international policy objectives without concern for the actions of small or middle powers.

The processes of industrialization and technology are relentlessly reducing the capacity of organizations and nations to remain islands unto themselves. Whether it is a government trying to control inflation or to generate jobs, whether it is a corporation trying to increase its profits or enter new markets, external hands seem to weigh increasingly heavily on the steering mechanisms of most of our major institutions. In this new environment, corporate or any other organizational decision-making is more and more *externally driven*.

In the coming years, the crowding in of external issues will exhibit particularly strong *international dimensions*. As illustrations of this we need only to cite the emergence of OPEC, the development of Japan into a global economic force, the increasing competitiveness of newly industrializing states, or the growing impact of Third World indebtedness.

Whoever would have thought 20 years ago, for example, that Brazil's inability to balance its books could have a severe impact on American financial institutions? The level of wages in Southeast Asia 20 years ago was but a curiosity to a few and was seen as a sad but distant reality. Today, those low wages pose a profound economic challenge to the industrial centers of Canada, the United States, and Western Europe.

The most apocalyptic and tragic illustration of interdependence is that the very survival of our planet rests on a delicate balance of terror, based on the threat of mutual annihilation by the world's two superpowers. Interdependence is not only a horizontal phenomenon, bringing organizations or nations into closer interplay with each other. An important additional aspect of it is that economics, politics, and social and technological forces themselves are more and more intertwined, and economic performance, or the pursuit of profit, is increasingly sensitive to the influence of sociopolitical issues or trends.

## Interdependence: From a Threat to an Opportunity

As we move through this decade and beyond, our political-economic welfare will be largely determined by how our leaders respond to the challenge of interdependence. Should we see it as a threat or an opportunity? Should we see it as a force to guard against or a force to be harnessed? Should we allow interdependence to happen *to* us or should we make it happen *for* us?

I believe that these simple questions bring us to the very crossroads of our political-economic future. And the resolution of these questions will be of particularly great significance for the public relations/public affairs profession.

We in Canada, during the past 10 years or so have pursued a course that by and large and especially with respect to relations with the United States, viewed interdependence as a threat. Many of our key policy choices were driven by a defensive posture—e.g., the National Energy Program, the Foreign Investment Review Agency, the conduct of federal/provincial relations, and the establishment of a host of domestic or external regulatory agencies.

There is a growing recognition in our country today that this defensive approach produces a bitter harvest indeed. Resisting rather than harnessing the forces of interdependence has hindered competitiveness and innovation. We are burdened today with a large government deficit, with excessively high unemployment, and with a productivity record that is second to that of just about every industrialized nation in the world.

Canadians are not alone in recognizing that the Achilles' heel of their system is the incapacity of harness interdependence, but the news from up north is not all gloom and doom. Canadians are moving into a new era, as signaled by the recent change in our federal government, and I suggest that our country is worth keeping a keen eye on in the months and years to come.

In sharp contrast to the past, more and more voices suggest that we should not look on interdependence as a threat but as the engine of our rejuvenation. This philosophy, not yet clearly articulated, and certain to falter on occasion, will significantly change the way that we manage our relations with our neighbors and with groups within our society.

## Leadership in the New Managerial Revolution

Discarding the mistakes of the past will not automatically hand us the key to the future. Interdependence must be *made* to work if it is to work *for* us rather than *against* us. A new managerial revolution does not rise from the ashes of our past like some Phoenix—it must be carefully designed, groomed, and nurtured.

To succeed in harnessing interdependence, we need to develop skills and understanding hitherto unknown to most of us. Harnessing interdependence, above all, will require a new type of leadership and new decision-making systems. Since this is critical to my argument, a brief elaboration is in order here.

In some areas of business and government, the discarding of mistaken ways has been followed *not* by the application of a new system of skills and knowledge, but by the resurrection of some ancient political-economic relics. To use the colorful language of one of my country's great thinkers, Marshall McLuhan, some of our policy innovators today are driving into the future using a rear-view mirror.

To bring this down to the level of our own profession, it seems clear that during the past year or so, some organizations have cut back on their public relations/public affairs activities and have resorted to a more traditional managerial mode. Such managerial neoconservatism may provide some short-term financial gains—but inevitably this will also become the source of serious long-term pain.

Harnessing interdependence is not the same thing as *laissez faire*. It does not call for a diminishing concern with the sociopolitical dimensions of economic pursuit. Harnessing the forces of interdependence does *not* mean that we should abrogate leadership and tag along wherever external market forces may take us. On the contrary, the forces of interdependence place a very high premium on leadership and on the active and responsible participation of managers in the shaping of their organizations' sociopolitical environment.

## What Is the Essence of Leadership?

Leadership, as James MacGregor Burns tells us is " . . . an aspect of power, but it is also a separate and vital process in itself."[1] Power is exercised first and foremost to achieve the goals of power wielders. Leadership, on the other hand, is exercised to achieve the goals of both leaders and followers simultaneously. The ability to motivate and rally followers to achieve their own needs is a key element of leadership. And to succeed in this endeavor, two skills are particularly vital.

First, successful leadership requires the capacity to understand and communicate, as clearly as possible, the hidden hopes, aspirations, and concerns of followers. Second, successful leadership requires the capacity to transform those hopes and aspirations into concrete actions or policies.

But the mere knowledge of what the public wants is not a sufficiently strong platform for leadership. Trust is an additional and vital ingredient, and it must be present if followers are to believe in and act on the proposals of their leaders. In short, trust, credibility, and information are all vital to successful leadership.

Realizing the purposes of both leaders and followers is but another way of expressing the essence of interdependence. Clearly, leadership and interdependence are congruent categories. The successful management of the latter is a critical function of the former.

Modern organizations are increasingly buffeted by the decisional waves of others. External issues will continue to crowd in on traditional management domains. Sociopolitical forces will continue to exercise a powerful but no doubt different influence on economic matters. For these reasons, the leaders of our major institutions will have no choice but to become much more knowledgeable about and trusted by those groups and organizations that bear significantly on them.[2]

Knowing in advance the game plans of our adversaries or competitors is not in itself a sufficient response to the challenge of interdependence. Subscribing to the best and most sophisticated environmental scanning systems will not by itself increase organizational effectiveness.

To reduce the levels of planning uncertainty, to reduce the chances of costly surprises, to make things happen for us rather than to us, requires that we actively *participate in* the policy-making processes of particularly those groups/organizations that have the largest potential impact on our organization's bottom line.

In short, rather than turning inwards, rather than going back to the old basics, rather than minding one's own business, the forces of interdependence will relentlessly pull us in the opposite direction. Active participation in the shaping of the critical external decisions that make up our organization's life-support system is not a *moral* imperative. Such participation and leadership will become, in fact, an indispensable ingredient of successful management in the '80s and beyond. In short, anticipating, monitoring, and controlling the consequences of interdependence—this is the stuff of modern leadership and management responsibility, and this places a special onus on the public relations/public affairs profession.

## Future Growth of Public Relations/Public Affairs

The forces we've outlined here have provided our field with both a unique opportunity and an awesome responsibility. For what is the explicit mandate of our profession? (And you will note I use the singular of profession). The recent task force report of the PRSA indentifies the all-encompassing function of public relations as that of helping "an organization and its publics adapt mutually."[3]

Well now, to use President Regan's celebrated phrase—here we go again.

In its examination of the stature and role of public relations, the PRSA task force isolated three specific emphases or strands that make up the field of public relations. These are, in abbreviated forms:

1. To master the publics of an organization.

2. To block and parry external events and initiatives.

3. To achieve mutual adaptations, to develop relationships of mutual benefit to all parties involved.

Of these three public relations approaches the PRSA task force has identified the third as being the most appropriate emphasis for the world of the 1980s. To enshrine this emphasis at the core of the profession, the task force recommended that it should be formally established that the role of public relations is to achieve, "adaptation between the organization and its publics for their mutual benefit." They suggest, that this should be the basic "premise of educational and informational activity by all organizations in the field and by individual practitioners. Specialized functions and skills can be identified as specialties within that framework."[4]

I wholeheartedly endorse this approach, for clearly, it is the one that is most compatible with the realities of interdependence, and with the leadership style that I highlighted earlier. But what of public affairs? Doesn't it differ from public relations? Is it simply a less offensive, more publicly palatable term than public relations? Or is it an entirely different, perhaps more sophisticated beast?

In my own survey of Canada's top 500 firms, 93 percent of the respondents agreed that public affairs involves a *[two-way]* exchange of signals between an organization and its environment based on *mutual benefit*.[5] Dr. James Post of Boston University, a well-known U.S. authority in the field of public affairs, emphasizes that "public affairs is a boundary-spanning function, with one foot firmly planted in the organization, the other in the social and political environment."[6] These conceptualizations of public affairs do not differ from the directions outlined by the PRSA 1981 Task Force Report, or from the PRSA Long-Range Planning Report of 1978.

The question of how to distinguish public affairs from public relations, in spite of the above commonalities, is a frequent topic of discussion at professional gatherings. I personally find these questions increasingly tedious and irrelevant. In 1979, for example, an extensive study of the public relations field concluded that nomenclature will be the number one problem of the field in the '80s.[7] If this is so then our field is indeed in dire straights. I submit that of the many challenges facing us today, the one involving nomenclature should be put far down on the list so that we can get on with our work.

In short, the direction or emphasis established for public relations by the previously mentioned PRSA Task Force Report (a report, which I may add was endorsed by the Canadian Public Relations Society) is indistinguishable from the mandate of public affairs. If there are competing or contrasting approaches these are, and should be, at the margins. The fundamental mission of each is identical and is central to the new managerial revolution.

## Some Concluding Comments

As the 1970s unfolded, we have witnessed in Canada as well as in the U.S. a sharp increase in the formal utilization of public relations/public affairs mechanisms by public and private organizations alike. In both of our countries, for example, more than half of currently existing public affairs units are less than 10 years old. As surveys show, the existence of these new units and their growing sophistication is largely the product of expanding interdependence. Since the growth of interdependence is to be enduring, the broad prospects for our profession are very positive indeed.

From a generally marginal, informal, individualistic, and noninstitutionalized type of activity, public relations/public affairs is fast becoming a formalized, mainstream element of organizational decision-making. Our ascendance is not part of a fad but is, rather, a long-term phenomenon.

In spite of this positive environment for our professional growth, important challenges remain. I would like to conclude my remarks to you by pointing to six areas that are, from my vantage point, particularly significant.

1. The central mandate of our profession must be continuously reinforced and reemphasized. To achieve mutual adaptations, to help organizations and their publics to adapt to each other, this is our professional mission in life. This is what public relations/public affairs is all about, and we should not hesitate to wear our heart on our sleeves.

   Of course, we have often run into people who hotly contest the wisdom of formulating an all-encompassing definition of our role. I have personally faced not inconsiderable opposition from some of my academic colleagues on this point. Some of them have argued with all the fury that academic politics can muster that we must curb the tendency to define the central principle of public affairs because, as they put it, this simply affirms the *status quo* and narrows the possibilities of application.

   Well, my own response to this should be fairly obvious by now. Curbing the tendency to conceptualize the essence of our profession is simply a mask aimed at covering up our subjective and frequently cavalier approach to the field. Curbing the tendency towards conceptualization has all of the hallmarks of voodoo scholarship, and it stands as one of the most serious barriers to the advance of our field.

   Without a clearly articulated and accepted central mission, our profession will flounder in the wind, unable to establish for itself a solid theoretical base or a commonly accepted educational support system. The credibility of our claim to be useful and responsible players in the new managerial revolution will be severely curtailed.

2. A second challenge is to improve our abilities to tap and to channel relevant external information back into our organizations. In the past, our efforts have been mainly directed at producing information and getting our messages out. In the future, we'll have to be better listeners and perhaps speak a little bit less.

3. In placing greater emphasis on the information inside of our profession, we must be particularly mindful of our role as *translators*. If incoming messages do not reach relevant internal targets within our organization, if they are incomprehensible to their recipients or not fully diffused into the mainstream of organizational decision-making, the contribution of public relation/public affairs to organizational effectiveness will be suboptimal.

4. Related to the above point is the need to increase the functional multilingualism of our members. Our clout, contribution, and status as a profession will grow only as we learn to master the operational languages of finance, marketing, human resources, and so on. The ability to convey to operating managers messages in their own language, and a more intimate knowledge of the diverse operating cultures within our organization, will greatly contribute to the ascendance of our profession.

5. If public relations/public affairs is to live up to its billing as the leading edge of interdependence management, its practitioners must have a much closer and systematic grip on the pulse beat of social change. *Knowledge of public issues,* and of *Issues management processes* is, therefore, an increasingly significant tributary of the overall public relations approach.

6. And finally, if public relations/public affairs is to grow up to assume its rightful place in the new managerial revolution, it must become a full partner in strategic decision-making processes.

In the age of interdependence, our profession plays much the same role for an organization as does the central nervous system in the human body. In both cases, if the linkages with the central decision-making unit are weak, operations are going to be impaired. In short, public relations/public affairs considerations cannot be kept at arms length from bottom-line management.

These six areas of growth and ascendance for public relations/ public affairs are by no means the only dynamic, or expanding frontiers of our field. They are singled out from an otherwise complex and multilayered discipline as key instruments that may, if properly utilized, significantly enhance our effectiveness in the pursuit of our basic mission.

The ascendance of public relations/public affairs in the new managerial revolution will be ensured if, and only if, we can demonstrate with concrete actions our capacity to help organizations and their publics to adapt to each other.

(This is the 1984 Foundation Lecture, presented on October 14, 1984, prior to the Public Relations Society of America Annual Convention in Denver, Colorado. Andrew B. Gollner, Ph.D., is Associate Professor, Department of Political Science, Concordia University, Montreal, Canada.)

### References

1. Burns, James MacGregor. *Leadership.* New York: Harper and Row, 1978: 18.
2. Gollner, A. B. *Social Change and Corporate Strategy.* Stamford: Issue Action Publications, 1983.
3. Task Force on the Stature and Role of Public Relations. Report and recommendations. *Public Relations Journal.* March 1981: 30.
4. *Ibid:* 36.
5. Gollner, A. B. *Public Relations in Canada: A Survey.* Montreal: School of Community and Public Affairs, Concordia University, 1984.
6. Post, James. Public affairs: its role. Nagelschmidt, J. S., ed. *The Public Affairs Handbook.* Washington: ANACOM, 1982: 23.
7. *The Gallagher Report,* October 8, 1979.

# Thinking Leadership

## By Lee Thayer

Recently, we've been hearing more and more about "leadership." In an era in which we seem to know more and more about less and less, this should perhaps not be remarkable.

The famous Austrian psychologist, Otto Rank, who was an early associate of Freud, observed that we already have too much "truth," more than we could possibly use. Whether these recent truths we've been hearing about constitute but one more instance of adding to the broth but not to the stock remains to be seen.

What we can safely observe is that the making of theories about any aspect of human behavior whatsoever depends not on the size of the lode of "truth" that is being mined, but rather on the size of the market *for* such theories. What the recent flurry of talk about "leadership" tells us is not that we are finally closing in on the secrets of leadership, but that there is a vigorous and growing market for talk *about* leadership.

We might perhaps be endangering our civilization in some unknown way by trying to apply one or more of these newfound "truths" about leadership in our political and social affairs were it not for the little piece of wisdom captured in the following Spanish proverb: "To talk of bulls is not the same as to be in the bull ring." To talk about or to read about leadership is not the same thing as leadership.

So we may be safe on that score. The average manager today knows more *about* leadership than Hannibal, Hitler, and Henry Ford knew among them. But knowing about how something is done is not the same as doing it.

The only immediate danger I can see from this growing market for new and better "truths" about leadership is that, unchecked, we will one day have more analysts and commentators on leadership than we will have leaders. If you think that's ominous, try to imagine some of those analysts and commentators actually in charge. The most honored of our current writers on leadership did not, in nearly 500 pages of print, find space to consider the possibility that entrepreneurial activity might be a form of leadership.

So should we be concerning ourselves at all about the idea of leadership? Yes. I think not only that we should, but that we have to. The question is not whether, but *how*.

I'd like first to share some thoughts with you about *how* we should perhaps be thinking about leadership when we think about it. And second, to share some thoughts with you about *what* we should be thinking about when we think about leadership.

## What It Tells About Ourselves

Spinoza once said, "What Peter tells me about Paul tells me more about Peter than it does about Paul." In the same way, perhaps, the real lesson in all of this recent talk about leadership may be not what it tells us about leadership, but what it tells us about ourselves.

For example, many Americans have come to believe that there is, or ought to be, a quick fix for any problem or shortcoming. So we end up making a lot of things sound much easier than they actually are. The same mentality that supports a multibillion-dollar fast-food industry also makes a best-seller of the *One-Minute Manager*. Don't bother us with the details, that mentality says: What we want is the recipe for success. Like many television commercials, much of what we hear and read about leadership these days offers us the expectation that we can provide just that.

One of the main differences between what Machiavelli had to say about leadership and what we currently hear about leadership is that Machiavelli assumed that the leader had to be wise. We assume only that he or she be able to afford the book or the consulting fee. Americans spend 10 million dollars a day on cosmetics, all with great expectations. Add to that much of what we spend on books about leadership.

Another example: We Americans are also into what Carlyle called "hero-worship"—now become celebrity worship. So it seems natural to us that a leader has to be some *person*, and that leadership is what some *person* says or does.

So we overlook the fact that we are "led" by words and by ideas and by images and by beliefs, that we are "led" by public opinion, by fad and by fashion, that we are "led" by folklore and by habit and by the conventional wisdom, that we are "led" by the politics of the situation, by our friends and by the media, by our presumed wants and needs and desires, and that we are, finally, "led" not so much by what's possible as by what's available or what's expedient. And are we not also "led" by our ignorances, by what we know "that just ain't so"?

Our cultural bias is to believe that leadership redirects the course of history. What we are not told is that "the course of history" leads people far more frequently than do leaders. Whatever the case, the leader is an interventionist—one who would have things other than they are, or other than they are likely to be. And what we are not told is that people who do this are probably not going to be liked for doing it, even if it were to bring universal benefit.

We're "led" to believe that leaders can lead where followers can't or won't follow. But the kinds of leaders that are possible depend on the kinds of followers that are ready, willing, and able to follow. Those internal forces that push and pull most people most of the time also determine the kinds of leaders that are even possible.

So the current outpouring of observations on leadership is indeed valuable. But not so much for what those observations purport to tell us about leadership as what they can tell us about the predispositions of our culture—something we need to be very much aware of if we are to think seriously about leadership.

## Cultural Predispositions

Let me offer briefly just a few more observations on the kinds of cultural predispositions we need to think about.

There is, first, our unwillingness to separate the facts of power from the facts of leadership. What Lee Iacocca was presumed to have accomplished at Chrysler was not separable from his almost dictatorial position. So what shall we talk about: such a person's "leadership"? Or the reach and the depth of his power? What good might it do middle managers to read everything that has ever been written on leadership if they do not have the power to make happen what they want to happen? The kind of leadership most of our current commentators talk about is the kind you can exercise only if you first accede to a position of power—meaning simply that you are in a position with respect to others, and in respect to resources and other kinds of wherewithal, such that you can make happen what you want to happen. Are those who are presently telling us all about leadership telling us this?

Second, our predisposition to hero- and celebrity-worship has "led" many of those who write about leadership to focus almost exclusively on those who enjoy high levels of authority or visibility.

This bright-lights syndrome—this penchant for wanting to attribute even the most trivial conditions of our lives to those in the highest positions of authority—has "led" many of those who propose to tell us about leadership these days to ignore another pertinent fact: that is that leadership—perhaps the real leadership in a society such as our own—is something that happens every day in our homes and our schools and on our street corners and in our coffee klatches and at every level of every institution and organization in the country. How parents "lead" their children has in the aggregate more bearing on what kind of society we're going to be living in [in the] next generation than perhaps anything Mr. Reagan might do or say. Everybody is always being led, or misled, in *some* direction, every minute of every day.

Most of what constitutes leadership in our society is so mundane that it does not interest those who have stars in their eyes. There are many small companies—like Johnsonville Sausage Company in Sheboygan, Wisconsin—that are just as "excellent" as IBM. And I've worked for both. But if you want to write a bestseller you have to people it with celebrities. So we end up with the impression that our leadership comes primarily if not exclusively from those who are media celebrities. This is very wrong.

Third, we are as a people very confused about what a leader's function in a democracy such as ours should be. Given our tendency toward a radical egalitarianism, we seem to want to believe not only that all people are equal, but that all ideas and all truths are equal. So some of our experts on leadership tell us that the leader's task is to intuit what the followers want, and to help them get it. There is a Sufi saying that describes how many Americans feel about leadership: "Tell me what you want me to do," they say. "And if it's what I want to do anyway, I'll do it."

The fact that more and more Americans are growing up as spoiled adolescents weighs heavily on how we think about leadership in our society. The thing which seems to correlate best with the health and vitality and longevity of people everywhere is not leisure and comfort and labor-saving devices and entertainment." It is meaningful work.

And making work meaningful in a culture where work foremost is just a means to buy leisure and entertainment is a task of considerable dimensions. If we thought of a leader as a person who would not default himself or herself and who would not permit those around him or her to default themselves, would we find this characterization in the flood of current recipes?

Listen to the words of the great British eighteenth-century statesman, Edmund Burke. Does this sound like what we are hearing about leadership today?

> Certainly, Gentlemen, it ought to be the happiness and glory of a representative to live in the strictest union, the closest correspondence, and the most unreserved communication with his constituents. Their wishes ought to have great weight with him; their opinions high respect; their business unremitted attention. It is his duty to sacrifice his repose, his pleasure, his satisfaction to theirs—and above all, ever, to prefer their interest to his own.
>
> But his unbiased opinion, his mature judgment, his enlightened conscience, he ought not to sacrifice to you, to any man, or to any set of men living. These he does not derive from your pleasure—no, nor from the law and constitution . . . .
>
> Your representative owes you, not his industry only, but his judgment; and he betrays, instead of serving you, if he sacrifices it to your opinion.

I leave it to you to judge whether or not Burke could get elected to any office in twentieth-century America.

Fourth, our cultural drive to scientize everything has "led" us to be much more literal about many things than the people of most other cultures—past and present. So our observers tell us that leadership is something that leaders *do*, rather than something that leaders *are*. In most other human cultures, an understood prerequisite for leadership is wisdom. Since wisdom cannot be measured and quantified, we gloss it. You don't have to be wise to buy a copy of the *One-Minute Manager.* You simply have to be willing to part with the 15 bucks, or less, believing that for that amount of money you can buy a reasonable substitute for wisdom. We get mainly recipes for how to *do* leadership. Little is said about the fact that the kind of creature the leader *is* makes a greater impact than what the leader *does.*

On the other hand, perhaps wisdom (in our Western civilization, at least) has nothing to do with it. The correlation between eminence in various fields of endeavor and intelligence is practically zero—0.14 if you have a special affection for standardized partial regression coefficients. This means not only that 86 out of 100 of those in authority in the Western world get there in spite of their intelligence, but that it may even be possible in our civilization that a person can be too intelligent to attract the allegiance of followers. Or that intelligence may be a handicap in a leader.[1]

If you find that amusing, you will be equally pleased to know that the relationship between leadership and education in our culture is even worse—almost inverse. Presumably, then, the practical advice that our older leaders would be offering your aspirants is 1) don't try to lead when you've been intelligent and 2) education and leadership don't mix. I've not seen much such advice in best-sellers on the subject.

One final observation: Our attempt to "scientize" everything has "led" us to believe that the way things happen in the world is a good bit tidier than they actually are. We're convinced that everything that happens has a "cause," and that if we cannot explain something simply, then we do not know what we are talking about.

So we oversimplify. Our search for "the" cause of this or that may be misleading. There is a saying amongst historians that goes something like this: "Most things don't happen at all, and all the rest happen at the wrong time. But a clever historian can correct all these defects." Like every Monday-morning quarterback, a clever historian—or leadership theorist—can tell us precisely why this or that happened.

D'Arcy Thompson, one of our great twentieth-century biologists, made a cogent parting observation on this cause-and-effect thinking in our culture: Things are the way they are, he said, because they got to be that way. But we keep a *deus ex machina* up *our* sleeves: We say the leader did it.

We need to think about how we think about cause and how our way of thinking about cause affects our thinking about leadership. Consider this: When the first Japanese motorcycles were marketed in the U.S., the only U.S. manufacturer left was Harley-Davidson. In that year, Harley sold about 10,000 motorcycles. Last year, some 20 years later, Harley sold 33,000 odd motorcycles. To whom or to what do we attribute that "success"? How much of Chrysler's success was due to *its* Japanese competitors? Or the changed economy? Or what GM did or didn't do?

There are two other twists on this:

One is that we pretend that what happened had to happen that way. But things happen the way they did, and we have no test of what the outcome would have been had they happened in some other way: We don't *know* that things would have been worse had something else happened, nor do we *know* that the way things happened is better than the way things might have happened. We don't *know*, for example, that, if Euclid Finkelheimer had succeeded to the Chrysler throne, he wouldn't have done even better than did Iaccoca. There's no test of that.

The other little twist on all this is that 8 out of 10 new products fail—almost without regard to how they are researched or promoted. So we may want to consider the possibility that 8 out of 10 would-be leaders also fail. Are the two products that do turn out to be successful the "best" of the 10? Or the "best" for us or for mankind or for the quality of human life in some future generation? If the answer to this must be "no, not necessarily," then the answer to the question of whether our present-day leaders constitute an adequate model for thinking about leadership must be the same.

People accede to the positions of power and authority for all kinds of reasons other than their abilities as true leaders. What it comes down to is this: Do we want to think about leadership the way we do because we happen to have the people we have in positions of power and authority? Or would we have different kinds of people in those positions of power and authority if we thought about leadership differently?

## Headship Versus Leadership

All the preceding comments are intended to bear on those two crucial questions for thinking about leadership.

What I would like to do now is to offer some ideas about how we might view leadership differently if we were to take some of the implications of those comments and examples seriously.

First, there is something very provocative in a look at how traditional and so-called modern societies differ on this matter of leadership. Many traditional societies have no concept of leadership at all, and others only a vague sort of notion about headship, which differs remarkably from what we talk about when we talk about leadership in our culture.

The difference is this: In a traditional society, the future is known. The function of the head or the chief is to do what has to be done to make sure that things turn out the way they're supposed to.

In a traditional society, both the leader and the follower are stewards—stewards of a way of being in the world that must be preserved. In a traditional society, the head or the chief is selected by his fellows as the best person available to *conserve* the present and future truths of that society. In a "modern" society, such as ours, the leader's function is to change things, to lead people in the direction of *his* ideas about what things should be like.

This is a remarkable shift. That we have identified leaders with a change in the status quo is full of implications for thinking leadership.

But what I want to draw your attention to here is even more important. It is that, in either case, the leader is a *moral* agent. That's a small "m," meaning simply that what leaders do bears on the goodness and badness of human life. The leaders who are selected or permitted to exercise themselves on behalf of followers will do things that will have good or bad consequences for those followers' lives, and the followers are, therefore, as morally obligated as the leader.

We are seemingly timid on this point. I don't think we should be—or can afford to be.

Second, each of us is ever and always either leading others, or being led. Leadership is not something that only the boss engages in when he talks; it is also something that every employee engages in when she or he listens. Because it has to do with *how* one listens, with *how* one takes others into account. It has to do with what one thinks one is doing when one commits a social act, or fails to do so.

What this means is that we need to do a much better job of leading—*and* of being lead. We need to be much more astute—especially in our kind of culture—at discerning those who enhance our humanity, and those who demean it. The best training for moral leadership inheres in learning how to follow well only those who are worth following—for one's own good, and for the good of one's community and one's society.

Third, the morally conscious leader (and the morally conscious follower—without whom the former is either without portfolio or merely the person who exercises power over the other—) is one who knows that what moves or constrains people lies in the *meaning* of things, and not in the things themselves. So the tools of the true leader's trade are not those of position. They are not those of power or authority or credentials. They are words, and what can be done with words to create the kinds of worlds which others may advantageously inhabit with their minds.

The best single book that has ever been written on leadership, in my opinion, is entitled, in French, *Citadelle*,[2] which means, roughly, our consciousness. That is our real habitat. The things of the world may have a kind of material existence. But we are stuck with dealing with them as we understand them, as we imagine them, in terms of what they *mean* to us.

The author's intent was to suggest that the leader must first build the place where people dwell—in their consciousness of the world. His job is to help them see and understand themselves and the world in a way that would be a long-range benefit to them as people, so that they might better lead themselves.

Fourth, the leader's task is to help others to think greatly of themselves and what they do. Not to tell them they're great when they're not, for this is pure charlatanism—but to help them or require them to undertake the discipline of mind or of body that would be necessary to do really great things, to be worthwhile, to be a net positive contribution to human society.

So their leader is one who sees himself or herself engaged in a great human drama. A great human drama to make the best of everything, to perfect oneself and all around one in such a way that all who come after will be benefited. And he asks, or requires, others to play their own special role in that human drama, by making the best of themselves and everything around them.

Fifth, the true leader differs not so much in terms of what he or she does, but in terms of how he or she *thinks about what needs to be done.*

The true leader *thinks* differently. Or maybe the difference is that the true leader is the one who thinks at all. Thomas Edison once said, "Five percent of the people think. Ten percent of the people think they think; and the other 85 percent would rather die than think!"

One of the many ways in which true leaders think differently is this: They know that what we refer to as human "motivation," and that what drives all the social machinery, comes down to two very simple questions: Who's responsible? And for what?

One of the notable differences between the Japanese and the American ways of doing business in manufacturing organizations is that the Japanese worker understands that he or she is *morally* responsible for the diligence, the safety, and the quality which he or she gives to one's work. And the Japanese manager accedes to higher positions in the organization not because he or she is a better "manager," in the Western sense of that term, but because he or she is capable of assuming more responsibility for the *human* wants and needs of those with whom one works. The Japanese supervisor is elevated because he or she demonstrated a capacity for being responsible for the *meaning* of others' lives at work.

We have an expression which goes, "Rank has its privileges." The Japanese version might be something like, "Rank has its responsibilities." That's quite a difference. Nor is any Americanized version of Quality Circles going to accomplish the same thing. Because the difference is in the way people think about things, in the way they posture themselves and grab hold of the world.

So the true leader is the ultimate human strategist. He asks the difficult and the onerous questions—of himself and of all of those around him. And then, because he would think greatly of himself and of all those others, *he defines or redefines who's responsible. And for what.*

If this turns out good for people and for humanity, then he was a good leader. If it turns out bad, he was bad.

But if it turns out bad for us, that would merely reflect an inadequacy on our part, as followers, to discern the good leader from the bad. Our complicity as followers for the quality of our leaders cannot be forsworn.

We're not going to learn much about leadership until we begin to learn that leadership is not something that someone does for us, but something that we have to do for each other.

## Implications for the PR Practitioner

So. What are some of the implications of all this for the public relations practitioner?

First, there is the need to acknowledge that the indispensable machinery of our society is *everyday leadership*, and that everyday leaders have no voice. A free and democratic society doesn't have one big hero. It has hundreds of thousands of little heroes. The publicity releases may come from the loci of big business and big government and big bucks. But when it ceases to be the little guy who makes America great, then our greatness will be no more. I can't tell you what to do about this. But you need to think about it.

Second, we all need to understand that *all* leadership and *all* followship are in basis a matter of morality. We're all in the business of making the future. Those people and those ideas and those images of the future we follow are leading us *somewhere*. And in casting our lot as followers with other rather than another, we are casting our destiny, both as individuals and as a people. Leadership and followership are weapons that can be even more powerful than of all of our armaments—because they are the seed bed of the future. They are not the stuff of holocausts. But they are what lead us toward, or away from, human greatness, human calamity.

Third, we need to figure out how to teach people to be intelligent and moral followers. An intelligent and conscientious follower will always we a good leader, so we can go about making good leaders by making good followers. The real danger is always stupid followership, as history has given us ample evidence. Because a bad leader is no leader if there are none who will follow. If we want our leaders to be the instrument of our destiny, then we must be the instrument of theirs. Public relations practitioners could lead the way in changing our whole way of thinking about leadership and followership in this respect.

Fourth, those who are in a position to explain things to others are, wittingly or not, those who most influence the world in which we live—past, present, and future. It is the stories people tell us that influence our lives. Big stories, little stories. Stories about what happened, and why, about what is going on, and why, about what causes what, about what should be done about what. In this sense, public relations practitioners are storytellers. You may even tell us stories about leaders, or about leadership. If you do, and whatever else the story may be about, you will be telling us how you understand leadership, how you think about it. So you need to think hard about what you want to mean by leadership, and about the kind of leadership we need to revitalize and energize this society of ours. For how we think about leadership will determine the kinds of leaders we are going to have.

Fifth, I believe we need a national and ongoing dialogue about what kinds of leaders we want and need in America and for America, and about what all of us followers have to do—and have to be—in order to discern and enable those kinds of leaders. No one is in a better position to bring this fruitfully to the national consciousness than the public relations practitioner.

Finally, whatever else we may say of leadership, the bottom line is that the leader "reads" the world differently than do others. Perhaps we could say that he or she "reads" the world more intelligently, or is better informed. Or is able to inform himself or herself better with respect to what is going on in the world that bears on what *should* be going on, that bears on making the right things happen. The vital leadership role in the future, in human organizations of every sort, will be provided by those who are equipped to sense what is going on in that organization's environment and in that organization's inner-workings, those who are equipped to "read" these goings-on as they bear on the interests of that organization and its many categories or stakeholders.

That leadership will be provided by those who know how to listen, and to interpret, the human interests and needs of employees, of customers, of suppliers, of investors, of the public at large.

That leadership will be provided by those who are uniquely equipped to *translate* the goings-on of the world for those who make the decisions of the world, and by those who are uniquely equipped to explain those decisions and their human and social implications to everyone who has a stake in the consequences.

This vital information-communication-intelligence-strategic leadership in the future could and perhaps should be provided by today's public relations practitioner. If that is to come to pass, you must first lead others to see you in this more global, vital role. And then you must lead the nation's decision-makers—in business and industry and labor and government and education, in social affairs and the arts and in science and technology—to make those decisions that will further our best and most human interests.

The task is to help others to make the right decisions. That's real leadership. And that is the urgent, profound challenge before you.

This is the 1985 Foundation Lecture, presented on November 10, 1985, prior to the Public Relations Society of America Annual Convention in Detroit, Michigan. Lee Thayer is an internationally acclaimed author and consultant to business and government, and is a professor at the University of Wisconsin-Parkside, Kenosha, Wisconsin.)

### References

1. Simonton, D. K. *Genius, Creativity, and Leadership: Historiometric Inquiries.* Cambridge: Harvard University Press, 1984.
2. Saint-Exupéry, Antoine de. *The Wisdom of the Sands* (translated version). Chicago: University of Chicago Press, 1979 [1950].

# The Social, Economic, and Political Context For the Practice of Public Relations

By Carl S. Sloane

I have been asked to comment . . . on three issues: what changes are occurring socially, economically, politically, and technologically; what impact these changes are having on our private and public institutions; and, finally, what implications these impacts have for public relations professionals operating in a democratic society.

What I would like you to consider by way of response to these issues are the following propositions:

- First, at the *most* fundamental level, very little has changed socially, economically, and politically since time immemorial, nor is it likely to change substantially in the future.

- Second, what changes we do observe in our social, economic, and political institutions are largely the result of technological developments and the interplay of technology on fundamental sociological, economic, and political forces.

- Third, what modern society perceives as a radically changing social, economic, and political environment is not so much the result of radical changes in those forces, but rather the result of a revolution in communications technology; a primary impact of the communications revolution has been to destabilize social, economic, and political forces both here and abroad, and create mismatches between what we might call old and new states.

- Finally, for the next decade and beyond, our history will be explained as a quest to restore social, economic, and political equilibria; and, in that quest, and communications revolution will play as great a role in resolving the problem as it did in creating it. Whether history will judge that role kindly or critically is in some small way in the hands of public relations professionals assembled here in our nation's capital this week.

I would now like to explore each of these four propositions in somewhat greater depth and demonstrate their relationship to one another.

**1. Little has changed or will change socially, economically, and politically.**

The social, economic, and political history of mankind is best explained, I believe, as a continuous and immutable drive by individuals to satisfy their fundamental needs for physical safety, food, and shelter, and, once satisfied at the most basic level, to improve on and control the conditions of their physical environment. The thought, as anyone who has taken Psychology 101 will recognize, is not original with me, and there are a variety of more elaborate models to explain what is essentially the same phenomenon.

The manner in which we have come to organize our private and public social, economic, and political institutions is, I would suggest, ultimately a reflection of this fundamental human drive. That is, individuals have grouped themselves into social, economic, or political units and subjugated their individuality to higher authority whatever they had reason to believe that their needs could be more fully, quickly, or assuredly satisfied through some form of collective action.

Much of mankind's progress can be explained in terms of this fundamental paradigm, and it is no less applicable to twentieth-century society than it was at the dawning of mankind. As one searches, for example, to understand broad patterns of decision making in late twentieth century governmental or corporate institutions, do not look to modern financial theory as an explanatory variable, but rather to the desire of people in positions of decision-making authority to preserve or enhance their personal interests; and most notable among these interests is the matter of safety, food, and shelter, or what we today term "lifestyle."

Man's drive for an improved lifestyle explains not only much of human progress but also most of human strife. Where one segment of society possessed a demonstrably higher standard of living than another—a superior means of satisfying its needs or a superior means of hoarding a limited supply of the means for satisfying such needs—conflict invariably ensued, although a variety of more or less elaborate artifices were devised over time to either mask lifestyle disparities and forestall or moderate conflicts. The Berlin Wall, government control of communications media, Moslem fundamentalism, and even collective bargaining and affirmative action legislation are all modern expressions of efforts either to obfuscate or moderate disparities between societies and political economies.

## 2. The interplay of technology and social, economic, and political forces.

Within the context of universal drives for improved lifestyles, technological development has been the engine of change. Discovery of the means for cultivating food and feed grains transformed a nomadic hunting society to an agrarian one, establishing settlements and towns and laying the groundwork for modern nation-states. Ten thousand years later, a series of technological developments, beginning with the printing press and extending to the steam engine, made possible the mass production and consumption of manufactured goods, tranforming society from agrarian to industrial, and from rural to urban.

Each of these technologically driven revolutions in our societal, economic, and political institutions has its own modern idiom in what some have termed the postindustrial revolution, the transformation of an industrially based society to a knowledge- or information-based society.

Let us examine just a few important examples. In the social realm, we see a variety of technologically induced changes, the longer-term significance of which we have yet to either fully appreciate or fathom. First is "the pill," a simple, cost-effective and readily available birth-control device that has changed gender roles and life experiences in ways that affect values, attitudes, and behavior of women *and* men. Second, are advances in medical technology—antibiotics, vaccines, medical imaging, and surgical techniques—which have extended average life spans beyond previously unimagined limits and, in so doing, created an explosion in the elderly segment of our population whose special needs modern society is uniquely ill-equipped to respond to.

In the economic arena, or what we might think of as the social economy, there are comparable examples of technologically induced change. Among such changes, the first I could cite are technological developments in herbicides, pesticides, and genetically engineered seeds. As a result of the so-called Green Revolution, we have for the first time in history the ability to feed the world's population. We have, in fact, succeeded to the point of creating agricultural surplus on a world scale and, in so doing, reversed the United States agricultural trade balance, and created a socioeconomic dilemma of substantial proportions for American, European, and Japanese farmers alike.

Lagging just slightly behind agricultural surplus in point of time is industrial surplus created by advances in manufacturing technology. As a result of the presence and potential of automation, robotization, and computer control technology, society faces a prospect of structural unemployment over the next quarter century of substantial proportions.

Combined with agricultural and industrial advances are a series of technological developments encompassing telecommunications, electronic data processing, and transportation that have combined in one generation to make our domestic economy and those of other nations subservient to a global economy. In this context, one must think not merely in terms of developments that facilitate imports and exports (although these are very important), but also of advances that enhance flows of capital and technology.

Moving on to the political arena, or what we might call the political economy, I would again point to advances in computers and telecommunications, along with nuclear armaments, inertial guidance systems, and missile technology as causally central to current and foreseeable U.S. trade and budget deficits, two of the more pressing issues we face as a nation. Consider the following, admittedly oversimplified perspective on the role played by technology in the major political, economic, and social issues of the day:

> As the partial result of technological developments in nuclear armaments and ballistic missiles, we enter into a military competition with the Soviet Union stimulating massive U.S. defense spending. To conduct this competition while avoiding domestic economic and social crisis, the U.S. government in-

curs massive budget deficits. U.S. budget deficits, in turn, are financed in significant measure by our borrowing capital abroad, the magnitude and timing of which would have been impossible without modern computer and telecommunications technology. Foreign lenders are only too happy to oblige because U.S. domestic prosperity and tranquillity allow foreign manufacturers to sell goods into the U.S. market, thereby avoiding political and social crisis in their own rather depressed domestic economies.

**3. The unique role of advanced communications technology in a changing world and resultant destabilizing effects.**

What I would like to suggest to you now is that what many see as a fundamental discontinuity of past and current social, economic, and political forces is not discontinuity at all. Rather, it is a continuity of man's efforts to improve his lifestyle with technology entering the picture to alter the means by which such ends are achieved individually and collectively through private and public institutions organized primarily for that purpose.

What differences do exist between the past and the present are largely the result of discontinuity in experience and perception— discrepancies brought about by the introduction of advanced communications technology—and I include under the broad heading of advanced communications technology all modern means by which man acquires knowledge of his environment: radio, telephone, television, computer-based information systems, print, media, and jet-age air transportation. Technological advances in each of these and other modes of communication have brought relatively low-cost, highly accurate, and nearly instantaneous global communications within the practical grasp of virtually every community in the world. As a result, information that formerly took centuries, years, or months to convey, now takes weeks, days, hours, or even seconds. Information that previously was vague, dull, and incomplete is now clear, abundant, and powerfully presented in full motion and color. And, most importantly, virtually everyone in the world has access to it.

What has this meant to modern society and what changes is it inducing? First, modern communications technology has, in just a few short years, made a reality of Marshall McLuhan's "global village" and, in so doing, introduced a level of complexity in cross-cultural social, economic, and political interactions and interdependencies that as yet are difficult to even appreciate, so much as understand and respond to effectively.

Protectionist trade legislation, efforts to interdict illicit drugs at our borders or halt their cultivation overseas, summit conferences, international coordination of interest rates and currency exchange values, new legislation to control immigration—all represent means to come to grips with these new and complex realities. The fact that they all represent old remedies for new problems frustrates many of us. The fact that we are unable to devise different responses only serves to underscore the novelty of the "global village" and the type of discontinuity of experience it presents us with.

Second, modern communications technology has illustrated in stark reality for all peoples, here in the U.S. and around the world, the disparity of conditions under which they live; has greatly heightened peoples' expectations for a better life, soon; and has made it increasingly difficult for governments and other institutions of central authority to cloak such disparities in a veil of secrecy, ignorance, or ideology. Unrest in the Middle East; strife in South Africa; export drives in Brazil and elsewhere; the new capitalism of China; stresses within Russian society; urban violence in America; the women's liberation movement; and, yes, even the emergence of Yuppies all bear witness to the universal drive for a better life, irrespective of one's current circumstances.

Lastly, modern communications has greatly enhanced both the speed and the magnitude of technology transfer between communities of interest. Whereas the pace and volume of technological change and its consequent requirements for social, economic, and political change previously was selective in its impact and provided society with a cushion of decades or even centuries for absorption and adaptation, today's society is faced with the challenge of abrupt and comprehensive change. Take, for example, competitive economic advantages achieved by companies and countries through the invention, development, and deployment of new technologies. In the immediate post-World-War-II era it was not unusual to talk in terms of competitive lead times of five years' duration. In the 1960s and 1970s, competitive lead times were reduced to two years and then to one year. Today, it is commonplace for business executives to talk in terms of six months' lead time and, before long, I trust, we will talk of six weeks, six days, and then six minutes.

### 4. Implications for public relations professionals.

As a consequence of such rapid and pervasive technological change, I believe we have entered into what in all probability will be a prolonged period of instability, characterized as a mismatch between old and new states; old values, systems, and behaviors; and a demand for new but as yet ill-defined values, systems, and behaviors. Common to such periods of instability are:

- Intense competition between parties who perceive a momentary opportunity to achieve a sustainable competitive advantage over others, be they segments of society, businesses, or governments.

- The splintering of society into special interest groups acting either to defend their established positions, values, beliefs, and systems or to promote fresh values, systems, and the like which are held to be more congruent with the new state of affairs.

- Concerted efforts by some to halt and then roll back the technological developments that brought about destabilization in the first instance.

- Profound frustration on the part of individuals, groups, and even nations who perceive themselves as relative losers in the new order, often resulting in desperate and violent response.

What does this sociopolitical dynamic portend for public relations professionals? Among other things it means that:

- Issues are going to come at you in rapid-fire fashion.

- They are going to come from nontraditional sources: segments of society, cultures, countries, and competitors that you are unfamiliar with and did not previously count among your recognized constituencies or competition.

- The issues themselves are going to be more novel and complex than those you have previously encountered.

In sum, your job is not going to get easier; no matter how successful you have been in the past, you are going to have to get even better.

Where and how must you get better? I would suggest five points that you may wish to ponder:

1. To be effective, to add value, and to excel in your profession, you will have to get deeper into the substance of issues; you will have to be truly knowledgeable in an expanded range of issues; and you will have to possess sufficient insight to see through the complexities of issues. Form will become an increasingly feeble substitute for substance in the fast-changing, complex environment of tomorrow.

2. You will have to take a longer range view of issues than was previously warranted and have a much clearer and broader sense of longer-term goals and positioning. Otherwise, you will find yourselves operating in a purely reactive mode, entangled in a web of inconsistencies and perceived as narrowly focused and of dubious ethics. And, given the speed, power, and ubiquity of modern communications technology, extracting yourself from such a web will become increasingly difficult.

3. Because mismatches between old and new states invariably produce high degrees of uncertainty and perceived risk, to succeed you will have to excel at *explaining, ameliorating, guiding,* and *educating*—practices that stand in stark contrast to *obfuscating, stonewalling, manipulating,* and *disinforming.*

4. Because your publics are likely to view issues in absolute rather than relative terms, you will have to devise innovative risk communications programs that help people to truly

understand and willingly confront the inherent trade-offs that society faces. And, because interests will conflict, meaningful and timely resolution of issues will hang on your ability to achieve a high level of public involvement and trust.

5. Last, you will have to resolve, in ways that are meaningful, lasting, and intensely personal, the relative merits of controlled versus freely flowing information. Today, more than ever before, we have the technical means to centrally control information flows. What's more, with a perceived need to redress the societal problems that ensue from the mismatch of old and new states, we have a ready-made set of pressures to exercise authority over the timely dispersion of accurate information.

Borrowing on the previously discussed paradigm of self-interest, it is altogether likely that many of you will identify your personal well being and interest as being tied to the control or artful management of information. . . . It strikes me as worthwhile to address a special appeal to those of you who understand that self-interest encompasses tomorrow as well as today. I encourage you to vigorously defend rights of free speech; to take personally your obligations in a free society to ensure abundant flows of accurate and timely information; and to actively combat all efforts, witting and unwitting, that may lead to excessive concentration of, or central control over, the media of mass communications. So long as information is flowing freely, free societies will be well served; old and new states will be brought into congruence sooner and with less conflict. Even if it is information people do not particularly like to hear, at the very least a dialogue will be taking place.

(This is the 1986 Foundation Lecture, presented on November 6, 1986, prior to the Public Relations Society of America Annual Convention in Washington, D.C. Carl S. Sloane is President and Chief Executive Officer, Temple, Barker & Sloane, Inc.)

# APPENDIX III

# Bibliography

This bibliography appears through the courtesy of the Public Relations Society of America (PRSA). It is divided into four sections: I. General; II. Special Interest; III. Bibliographies/ Directories; IV. Periodicals.

# I. General

Aronoff and Baskin. *Public Relations: Profession and Practice.* West 1983. $22.95.

Awad, Joseph. *The Power of Public Relations.* Praeger 1985. $29.95.

Benn, Alec. *The 23 Most Common Mistakes in PR.* AMACON 1982. $17.95.

Bernays, Edward L. *Public Relations.* Univ. Oklahoma Press 1977. $10.95pb.

Bittleston/Shorter. *Book of Business Communications Checklists.* Wiley 1982. $29.95.

Black, Sam. *Public Relations in the 1980s.* Pergamon. $46.00.

Black, Sam and M. Sharpe. *Practical Public Relations.* Prentice-Hall 1983. $16.95. $8.95pb.

Brough, B. *Publicity and Public Relations Guide for Business.* Oasis Press, 1287 Lawrence Station Rd., Sunnyvale, CA 95089. 1985. $33.95.

Cantor, Bill (Chester Burger ed.). *Experts in Action: Inside Public Relations.* Longman 1984. $29.95, $17.95pb.

Center/Walsh. *Public Relations Practices: Case Studies.* Prentice-Hall 1985. $19.95.

Cole, R. *Practical Handbook of Public Relations.* Prentice-Hall 1981. $18.95, $8.95pb.

Conner, Dee et al. *Hitting Your Target with PR and Publicity.* PR Enterprise, 3616 N. 36th St., Boise, ID 83703. 1981. $20.00.

*Critical Issues in Public Relations.* Hill and Knowlton, 420 Lexington Av., NYC 10017. 1976. $9.95.

Cullingan/Greene. *Getting Back to the Basics of Public Relations.* Crown 1982. $10.95.

Cutlip and Center. *Effective Public Relations.* Prentice-Hall 1985. $28.95.

Dilenschneider, Robert L. and Dan J. Forrestal. *The Dartnell Public Relations Handbook.* The Dartnell Corporation, 4660 N. Ravenswood Av., Chicago, IL 60640. 1987. $49.95.

Ehrenkranz/Kahn. *Public Relations/Publicity.* Fairchild 1983. $14.50.

Grunig, J. and T. Hunt. *Managing Public Relations.* Holt Rinehart 1984. $29.95.

Helm/Hiebert, *Informing the People: A Public Affairs Handbook.* Longman 1981. $27.95.

Kadon, A. *Successful Public Relations Techniques.* Modern Schools, Box 8, Scottsdale, AZ 85251. 1976. $5.00pb.

Klein and Danzig. *Publicity: How to Make the Media Work for You.* Scribner 1985. $17.95.

Lesly, Phillip. *Lesly's Public Relations Handbook.* Prentice-Hall 1983. $42.50.

Lewis, H. G. *How to Handle Your Own Public Relations.* Nelson-Hall 1976. $19.95pb.

Londgren, R. *Communication by Objectives: A Guide to Productive and Cost-Effective Public Relations and Marketing.* Prentice-Hall 1983. $16.95, $7.95pb.

Lovell, Ronald. *Inside Public Relations.* Allyn & Bacon 1982. $21.95.

Marston, John. *Modern Public Relations.* McGraw-Hill 1979. $14.95.

Marston, John. *The Nature of Public Relations.* McGraw-Hill 1983. $23.95.

Massnick. *Do-It-Yourself PR.* Mascom, 890 Galaxy Bldg., 330 Second Ave. S., Minneapolis, MN 55401. 1982. $4.95pb.

Moore, Frazier. *Public Relations: Principles, Cases, Problems.* Irwin 1981. $26.95.

Nager and Allen. *Public Relations Management by Objectives.* Longman 1983. $29.95.

Newsom and Scott. *This is PR: Realities of Public Relations.* Wadsworth 1984. $27.50.

Nolte, L.W. *Fundamentals of Public Relations.* Pergamon 1979. $16.45.

Nolte and Wilcos. *Effective Publicity: How to Reach the Public.* Wiley 1985.

Norris, James. *Public Relations.* Prentice-Hall 1981. $27.95.

Reilly, R. *Public Relations in Action.* Prentice-Hall 1981. $27.95.

Rogers, Henry. *Rogers' Rules for Success.* St. Martin/Marek 1984. $13.95.

Ross, R. D. *Management of Public Relations.* Krieger 1984. $25.95.

Seitel, Fraser. *The Practice of Public Relations.* Merrill 1984. $25.95.

Simon, R. *Public Relations: Concepts and Practice.* Grid 1984. $36.95.

Simon, R. *Publicity and Public Relations Worktext.* Grid 1982. $18.95pb.

Sperber/Lerbinger. *Manager's Public Relations Handbook.* Addison-Wesley 1983. $25.00.

Steinberg, C. *Creation of Consent: Public Relations in Practice.* Hastings 1975. $6.95.

Stevens, Art. *The Persuasion Explosion.* Acropolis 1985. $12.95.

Voros and Alvarez. *What Happens in Public Relations.* AMACOM 1981. $17.95.

Walsh, Frank. *Public Relations Writer in the Computer Age.* Prentice-Hall 1985. $17.95pb.

Wilcox/Ault/Agee. *Public Relations: Strategies & Tactics.* Harper 1985.

## II. Special Interest

### Biography/Memoirs

Barmash, I. *Always Live Better Than Your Clients: The Fabulous Life and Times of Benjamin Sonnenberg.* Dodd, Mead 1983. $15.95.

*Biographies of the FORTUNE 100 PR Departments Heads.* O'Dwyer Co., 271 Madison Ave., NYC 10016. 1981. $15.00 prepaid.

Hiebert, Ray. *Courtier to the Crowd* (Ivy Lee). Iowa State Univ. Press 1966. $8.95.

Rogers, Henry C. *Walking the Tightrope.* Morrow 1980. $10.95.

### Business/Corporate/Management

Baldridge, L. *Complete Guide to Executive Manners.* Rawnon 1985. $22.95.

Bradshaw and Vogel. *Corporations and Their Critics: Problems of Corporate Social Responsibilities.* McGraw-Hill 1982. $14.95.

Buchholz, R. *Business Environment and Public Policy: Implications for Management.* Prentice-Hall 1982. $24.95.

Budd, J. *Corporate Video in Focus: A Management Guide to Private TV.* Prentice-Hall 1983. $10.95pb.

Burger, Chester. *The Chief Executive: Realities of Corporate Leadership.* CBI Publ. Co., 51 Sleeper St., Boston, MA 02110. 1978. $19.95.

D'Aprix, R. *The Believable Corporation.* AMACOM 1977. $13.95.

Deal and Kennedy. *Corporate Cultures.* Addison-Wesley 1982. $14.95.

Drucker, Peter. *Management: Tasks, Responsibilities, Practices.* Harper 1974. $23.95.

Fallon, W. *AMA Management Handbook.* AMACOM 1983. $69.95.

Grefe, E. *Fighting to Win: Business Political Power.* Harcourt 1981. $35.00.

Henry, K. *Defenders/Shapers of Corporate Image.* Univ. Press, New Haven, CT 1972. $2.95pb.

Lesly, Phillip. *Overcoming Opposition: A Survival Manual for Executives.* Prentice-Hall 1984. $15.95.

Marlow, E. *Managing the Corporate Media Center.* Knowledge Industry Publications, White Plains, NY 1981. $24.95.

Marsteller, Wm. A. *Creative Management.* Crain Books 1981. $19.95.

Neal, Alfred. *Business Power and Public Policy.* Praeger 1982. $11.95pb.

Paluszek, J. *Business and Society: 1976 2000.* AMACOM 1976. $10.00.

Paluszek, J. *Will the Corporation Survive?* Prentice-Hall 1977. $10.95.

Peters and Waterman. *In Search of Excellence.* Harper 1982. $19.95.

Ruch and Goodman. *Image at the Top: Crisis and Renaissance in American Corporate Leadership.* Macmillan 1983. $16.75.

Sethi and Swanson. *Private Enterprises and Public Purpose.* Wiley 1981. $16.95pb.

Spitzer, Carlton. *Raising the Bottom Line: Business Leadership in a Changing Society.* Longman 1982. $24.95.

Steckmest, F. *Corporate Performance: The Key to Public Trust.* McGraw-Hill 1982. $16.95.

Ways, Max. *The Future of Business: Global Issues in the 80s and 90s.* Pergamon Press, Elmsford, NY 10523. 1980. $15.00 hardcover, $6.95pb.

## Communication/Persuasion/Social Science

Abelson and Karlins. *Persuasion.* Springer 1970. $10.95pb.

Bittner, J. *Mass Communication.* Prentice-Hall 1977. $17.95.

Blake and Haroldson. *Taxonomy of Concepts in Communication.* Hastings 1975. $9.95pb.

Boettinger, H. *Moving Mountains.* Macmillan 1975. $4.95pb.

D'Aprix, Roger. *Communicating for Productivity.* Harper 1982. $14.95.

deMare, G. *Communicating at the Top.* Wiley 1979. $19.95.

Didsbury, Howard. *Communications and the Future. World Future Society,* Bethesda, MD. 1984. $14.50pb.

Goldhaber, G. *Organizational Communication.* W. C. Brown Co. 1979. $13.95.

Haigh/Gerbner/Byrne. *Communications in the Twenty-First Century.* Wiley 1981. $24.95.

Hiebert, Ray et al. *Mass Media III.* Longman 1982. $17.95.

Lesly, Philip. *How We Discommunicate.* AMACOM 1979. $13.95.

Lesly, Philip. *Selections from Managing the Human Climate.* Philip Lesly Co., 130 E. Randolph St., Chicago, IL 60601. 1979. $9.00.

Naisbitt, John. *Megatrends.* Warner Books 1982. $15.50.

Reardon, K. *Persuasion: Theory and Context.* Sage Publications 1981. $9.95pb.

Redding, C. *Corporate Manager's Guide to Better Communication.* Scott-Foresman 1984. $7.95pb.

## Community Relations

Yarrington, R. *Community Relations Handbook.* Longman 1983. $24.95, $12.95pb.

## Crisis/Emergency

Bernstein, Alan. *Emergency Public Relations Manual.* Pase Inc. 1982. $75.00.

Newton, C. *Coming to Grips with Crisis.* AMACOM 1981. $20.00pb.

## Design Services

Jones, Gerre. *How to Market Professional Design Services.* McGraw-Hill 1983. $32.50.

Jones, Gerre. *How to Prepare Professional Design Brochures.* McGraw-Hill 1976. $21.95.

Jones, Gerre. *Public Relations for the Design Professional.* McGraw-Hill 1980. $18.50.

## Education/Careers

Bortner, D. *Public Relations for Public Schools.* Schenkman 1983. $18.95, $11.95pb.

*Building Public Confidence in Your Schools.* NSPRA, 1801 N. Moore St., Arlington, VA 22209. 1978. $13.95pb.

*Careers in Public Relations.* Public Relations Society of America (PSRA), 845 Third Ave., NYC 10022. $1.00 prepaid (quantity prices available).

*Design for Public Relations Education.* $3.00 *Status/Trends of Public Relations Education.* $3.00. Fdn. for Public Relations, 415 Lexington, NYC 10017. Prepaid.

*Effective Public Relations for Colleges.* CASE, 11 Dupont Circle, DC 20036. $17.00

Kobre. *Successful Public Relations for Colleges/Universities.* Hastings 1974. $19.95.

*Public Relations in the Community College.* CASE (address above) 1981. $9.50.

*Public Relations Job Finder.* Prentice-Hall 1981. $6.95pb.

Reck. *Changing World of College Relations.* CASE (address above) 1976. $8.50.

Rotman, M. *Opportunities in Public Relations.* National Textbook Co., 4255 W. Touhy, Lincolnwood, IL 60646. 1983. $7.95, $5.95pb.

Topor, R. *Marketing Higher Education* CASE (address above) 1984. $16.50.

Walling, D. *Complete Book of School Public Relations.* Prentice-Hall 1982. $17.50.

West, P. *Education Public Relations.* Sage 1985. $25.00.

Woodress. *Public Relations for Junior Colleges.* Interstate 1976. $3.95pb.

**Employee Relations** (for Employee Publications, see section: Writing/Newsletters)

Burkett, D. *Very Good Management: Guide to Management by Communicating.* Prentice-Hall 1983. $12.95, $6.95pb.

D'Aprix, Roger. *Communicating for Productivity.* Harper 1982. $14.95.

Deutsch. *Human Resources Revolution.* McGraw-Hill 1979. $12.50.

Dunham/Smith. *Organizational Surveys.* Scott Foresman 1979. $7.95.

*Employee Annual Report: Purpose, Format, Content.* Ragan Communications, 407 S. Dearborn, Chicago, IL 60605. 1984. $22.50.

*How to Prepare and Write Your Employee Handbook.* AMACOM 1984. $75.00.

*Inside Organizational Communications.* IABC, 870 Market St., San Francisco, CA 94102. 1981.

Rush/Goodman. *Image at the Top.* (management-employee relationship). MacMillan 1983. $17.00.

**Ethics**

Christians et al. *Media Ethics.* Longman 1983. $24.95, $14.95pb.

Hill, Ivan. *Ethical Basis of Economic Freedom.* Praeger 1980. $12.95pb.

Karp, R. *Corporate Morality and Executive Ethics.* Gin Publishing. 1985.

Litschert and Nicholson. *Corporate Role and Ethical Behavior.* Reinhold 1977. $17.95.

Walton, Clarence, ed. *Ethics of Corporate Conduct.* American Assembly, Columbia Univ. Prentice-Hall 1977. $9.95, $4.95pb.


## Financial

*Effective Public Relations and Communications: A Handbook for Banks.* American Bankers Assn., 1120 Connecticut Av. NW, DC 20036. 1982. $49.90.

Gilden, R. *Meeting the Media.* BMA, 309 W. Washington, Chicago, IL 60606. 1984. $25.00.

Graves, Joseph. *Managing Investor Relations.* Dow Jones-Irwin 1983. $27.50.

Marcus, Bruce. *Competing for Capital in the '80s: An Investor Relations Approach.* Quorum Books, Box 5007, Westport, CT 06881. 1983.

Roalman. *Investor Relations Handbook.* AMACOM 1974. $17.95.

Roalman. *Investor Relations That Work.* AMACOM 1981. $34.95.

*The SEC. The Securities Market and Your Financial Communications.* Hill and Knowlton, Wilson, M.H. *Corporate Investor Relations Function.* UMI Press 1980. $39.95.


## Government/Politics/Public Affairs/Issue Management

Chase, Howard. *Issues Management: Origins of the Future. Issue* Action Publications, 105 Old Long Ridge Rd., Stamford, CT 06903. April 1984. $24.95.

Gilbert. *Public Relations in Local Government.* ICMA, 1140 Connecticut Av., DC 20036. 1975. $19.00.

Gollner, Andrew. *Social Change and Corporate Strategy: The Expanding Role of Public Affairs.* IAP, 105 Old Long Ridge Road, Stamford, CT 06903. 1984. $29.95.

*Government/Press Connection: Press Officers and Their Offices.* Brookings Institution, 1775 Massachusetts Av. NW, DC 20036. 1984. No charge.

Helm/Hieber. *Informing the People: A Public Affairs Handbook.* Longman 1981. $27.95.

Hiebert, R. *Political Image Merchants.* Acropolis, 2400 17th St. NW, DC 20009. 1975. $6.95pb.

*Issues Management Programs: Why They Fail and How to Make Them Work.* Human Resource Network, 2011 Chancellor St., Philadephia, PA 19305. 1984.

*Leveraging the Impact of Public Affairs.* Human Resources Network, 126 Arch St., Philadelphia, PA 19103. 1984. $100.00.

Nagelschmidt, J. *Public Affairs Handbook.* AMACOM 1982. Available from PRSA. $12 Public Affairs Section members, $17/other PRSA members, $24/nonmembers.

*Social Change and Corporate Strategy: The Expanding Role of Public Affairs.* Issues Action Publications (address above) 1983. $29.95.

Trent, Judith and R. Friedenburg. *Political Campaign Communication: Principles and Practices.* Praeger 1984. $13.95pb.

Yorke and Doherty. *Candidate's Handbook for Winning Local Elections.* Harvey Yorke, Box 252, Novato, CA 94948. $19.95.

**Graphics/Photography**

Douglis, Philip. *Pictures for Organization: How and Why They Work as Communication.* Ragan Communications Inc. (address above) 1982. $35.00.

Lefferts, Robert. *Elements of Graphics: How to Prepare Charts/ Graphics for Effective Reports.* Harper 1981. $12.95.

Marsh, P. *Messages That Work: Guide to Communication Design.* Prentice-Hall 1983. $32.95.

Selame. *Developing a Corporate Identity.* Lebhar-Friedman 1980. $19.50.

White, Jan. *Mastering Graphics: Design and Production Made Easy.* Bowker Co., POB 1807, Ann Arbor, MI 48106. 1983. $24.95.

**International**

Currah. *Setting Up a European Public Relations Operation.* Business Books, London. 1975. $19.95.

*Financial and Other Relations in Europe.* Burson-Marsteller, 866 Third Ave., NYC 10022, 1979. $3.00.

Roth, Robert. *International Marketing Communications.* Crain 1982. $22.95.

## Legal

*Association Legal Checklist.* Chamber of Commerce, 1615 H St. NW, DC 20062. 1983. $10.00.

Lamb, R. et al. *Business, Media, and the Law.* N.Y. Univ. Press 1980. $15.00.

Nelson/Teeter. *Law of Mass Communications.* Fdn. Press, 170 Old Country Rd., Mineola, NY 11501. 1982. $19.75.

Sanford, Bruce. *Synopsis of the Law of Libel and the Right of Privacy.* World Almanac, 200 Park Ave., NYC 10166. 1981. $2.20 37-page brochure.

Simon, Morton. *Public Relations Law.* 1969. Fdn. for Public Relations, 415 Lexington Ave., NYC 10017. $20.00 prepaid.

## Libraries

Edsall, M. *Library Promotion Handbook.* Oryx Press, 2214 N. Central Ave., Phoenix, AZ 85004. 1980. $32.50, $25.00pb.

Garvey, M. *Library Public Relations.* Wilson 1980. $14.00.

Harrison, K.C. *Public Relations for Librarians.* Lexington Books 1982. $19.00.

Leerburger, B. *Marketing the Library.* Knowledge Industry Pub., 701 N. Westchester, White Plains, NY 10604. 1981. $24.50.

Rummel, K. and Perica. *Persuasive Public Relations for Libraries.* American Library Assn., Chicago. 1983. $20.00pb.

Usherwood, R. *The Visible Library: Practical PR for Public Libraries.* Oryx Press, (address above) 1981. $24.50.

## Marketing/Research

Breen. *Do-It-Yourself Marketing Research.* McGraw-Hill 1982. $24.95.

DeLozier. *Marketing Communications Process.* McGraw-Hill 1976. $16.50.

Fine, Seymour. *Marketing of Ideas and Social Issues.* Praeger 1981. $23.95.

Goldman, J. *Public Relations in the Marketing Mix.* Crain 1985. $14.95.

Lowery and DeFleur. *Milestones in Mass Communications Research.* Longman 1983. $24.95.

Robinson, Edward. *Public Relations Survey Research.* Irvington 1969. $29.50, $15.95pb.

Stempel and Westley. *Research Methods in Mass Communication.* Prentice-Hall 1981. $20.95.

Udell and Laczniak. *Marketing in an Age of Change.* Wiley 1981. $23.95.

Weinrauch and Piland. *Applied Marketing Principles.* Prentice-Hall 1979. $17.95.

## Media/Press Relations

Bland, M. *Executive's Guide to TV/Radio Appearances.* Knowledge Industry 1980. $14.95.

Blyskal. *PR: How the Public Relations Industry Writes the News.* Morrow 1985. $17.95.

Blythin and Samovar. *Communicating Effectively on Television.* Wadsworth 1985.

Brush. *Private Television Communications: Into the Eighties.* International Television Assn. (address above) 1981. $39.95.

Clifford, Martin. *Complete Guide to Satellite TV.* Tabl 1984. $17.95, $10.95pb.

Corrado, F. *Media for Managers.* Prentice-Hall 1984. $13.95.

*Having Effective Media Interviews.* Brum & Anderson, 425 Lumber Exchange Bldg. Minneapolis, MN 55402. 1984. $15.00.

Hiebert, Ray. *Impact of Mass Media.* Longman 1985.

Hiebert et al. *Mass Media IV.* Longman 1985.

Howard, C. and W. Mathews. *On Deadline: Managing Media Relations.* Longman 1985. $29.95.

Klein, T. and F. Danzig. *Publicity: How to Make the Media Work for You.* Scribner 1985. $18.00.

Klepper, Michael. *Getting Your Message Out: How to Get, Use and Survive Radio & TV Air Time.* Prentice-Hall 1984. $16.95, $9.95pb.

MacDougall, Kent. *Ninety Seconds to Tell It All: Big Business and the News Media.* Dow Jones-Irwin 1982. $14.95.

Martin, Dick. *Executive's Guide to Handling a Press Interview.* Pilot Books, NYC. $3.95pb.

*Media Resource Guide.* Fdn. for American Communications, 3383 Barham Blvd., Los Angeles, CA 90068. 1983. $5.00pb.

Mincer. *Talk Show Book.* Facts on File Inc., 460 Park Ave. S., NYC 10016. 1982. $14.95.

Rossie, C. *Media Resource Guide.* Fdn. for American Communications, (address above) 1983. $5.00pb.

Rowan, Ford. *Broadcast Fairness: Doctrine, Practice, Prospects.* Longman 1984.

Unguarait et al. *Media Now.* Longman 1985.

**Meetings**

*How to Run Better Business Meetings.* Visual Div. 3M, St. Paul, MN 55101. 1979. $11.95.

*Planning, Conducting, Evaluating Workshops.* Learning Concepts, 2501 N. Lamar, Austin, TX. $9.95.

**Museums**

*Museum Public Relations.* AASLH Inc., 708 Berry Road, Nashville, TN 37204. 1985. $21.00.

**Nonprofit/Health/Fund Raising**

Basic Guide to Hospital Public Relations. AHA Inc., POB 99376, Chicago, IL 60693. $33.75.

Bates, D. *Communicating and Moneymaking.* Heladon, Box 2827 GCS, NYC 10017. 1979. $7.50 pb.

Broce. *Fund Raising.* Univ. Oklahoma Press 1979. $17.50.

Connors, Tracy. *Nonprofit Organization Handbook.* McGraw-Hill 1979. $29.95.

Fine, S.H. *Marketing of Ideas and Social Issues.* Praeger 1981. $23.95.

Gaby, P. and D. *Nonprofit Organization Handbook.* Prentice-Hall 1983. $49.95.

Grasty and Sheinkopf. *Successful Fundraising.* Scribners 1982. $17.95.

Harbert and DiGaetani. *Writing for Action: Guide for the Health Care Professional.* Dow Jones-Irwin 1984. $17.50.

*Hospital and the News Media: Guide to Media Relations.* AHA Inc. (address above) $16.00.

Kotler. *Cases and Readings for Nonprofit Organization.* Prentice-Hall 1983. $19.95pb.

Kotler. *Marketing for Nonprofit Organizations.* Prentice-Hall 1982. $26.95.

Kreps and Thornton. *Health Communication: Theory and Practice.* Longman 1984.

Kurtz. *Public Relations and Fund Raising for Hospitals.* Thomas 1980. $23.50.

Lord, James. *Philanthropy and Marketing: New Strategies for Fund Raising.* Third Sector Press 1983. $47.50.

*Marketing Your Hospital: Strategy for Survival.* AHA Inc. (address above). $20.00.

McMillan, Norman. *Marketing Your Hospital.* American Hospital Assn. 1982. $18.75.

Miller, Irwin. *Health Care Survival Curve: Competition and Cooperation in the Marketplace.* Dow Jones-Irwin 1984. $27.50.

Oaks. *Communication by Objective.* Groupwork, Box 258, S. Plainfield, NJ 17080. 1977. $11.00.

*Planning Hospital Health Promotion Service for Business/ Industry.* AHA Inc. (address above). $33.75.

Pray, Francis. *Handbook for Educational Fund Raising.* Jossey-Bass 1982. $25.95.

*Public Relations Guides for Nonprofit Organizations: 1. Planning/ Setting Objectives 2. Using Publicity to Best Advantage 3. Working with Volunteers 4. Making the Most of Special Events 5. Measuring Potential/Evaluating Results 6. Using Standards to Strengthen Public Relations.* 1977. Foundation for Public Relations, 415 Lexington Ave., Suite 1305, NYC 10017. $3.00 each, set of six $14.40 prepaid.

Rados, D. *Marketing for Nonprofit Organizations.* Auburn House 1981. $24.95.

Riggs, Lew. *The Health Care Facility's Public Relations Handbook.* Aspen 1982. $28.50.

Ruffner, R. *Handbook of Publicity and PR for the Nonprofit Organization.* Prentice-Hall 1985. $49.95.

Snook, I.D. *Building a Winning Medical Staff.* Hospital Pub. Co., Chicago 1984. $14.75.

## Police/Fire Departments

Earle, H. Police/Community Relations. Thomas Pub. Co., 2600 S. First St., Springfield, IL 62717. 1980. $16.95.

Garner, G. *The Police Meet the Press*. Thomas Pub. Co. 1984 $29.75.

Mayhall, P. *Police-Community Relations*. Wiley 1985. $27.95.

Radelet, L. *Police & the Community*. MacMillan 1980. $22.95.

*Successful Public Relations*. Natl. Fire Protection Assn., 470 Atlantic Ave., Boston, MA 02110. 1974. $7.00.

## Presentations

Leech, T. *How to Prepare, Stage, and Deliver Winning Presentations*. AMACOM 1983. $39.95.

## Professionals/Consultants/Personal

Betancourt, Hal. *The Advertising Answerbook: Guide for Business and Professional People*. Prentice-Hall 1982. $7.95pb.

Braun, Irwin. *Building a Successful Practice with Advertising*. AMACOM 1981. $24.95.

Gould, J.S. *How to Publicize Yourself, Your Family, and Your Organization*. Prentice-Hall 1983. $15.95, $7.95pb.

Gray, James. *The Winning Image*. AMACOM 1982. $13.95.

Hameroff and Nichols. *How to Guarantee Professional Success*. Consultant's Library, 815 15th St. NW, DC 20005. 1982. $28.00.

Johnson B. *Private Consulting*. Prentice-Hall 1982. $6.95pb.

Kennedy, J.H. *Public Relations for Management Consultants*. Consultants News, Templeton Rd., Fitzwilliam, NH 03447. 1980. $15.00.

Kotler, Philip and Paul Bloom. *Marketing Professional Services*. Prentice-Hall 1984. $31.95

McCaffrey, Mike. *Personal Marketing Strategies: How to Sell Yourself, Your Ideas, and Your Services*. Prentice-Hall 1983. $11.95pb.

Pace/Culbertson. *Successful Public Relations for the Profession*. Professional Publishing Company. 1982. $39.50pb.

Sarnoff, D. *Making the Most of Your Best: A Complete Program for Presenting Yourself and Your Ideas with Confidence and Authority.* Holt, Rinehart 1983. $7.95pb.

## Publicity

Knesel, D. *Free Publicity: A Step by Step Guide.* Sterling 1982. $6.95pb.

*Publicity Handbook.* Brum & Anderson, 425 Lumber Exchange Bldg., Minneapolis, MN 55402. 1984. $39.95.

Quinlan, J. *Industrial Publicity.* Van Nostrand 1983. $19.95.

Wagner. *Publicity Forum.* R. Weiner Inc. 888 7th Av., NYC 10106. 1977. $6.95pb.

Weiner, R. *Professional's Guide to Publicity.* R. Weiner Inc., (address above) 1977. $7.95pb.

Winston, M. *Getting Publicity.* Wiley 1982. $8.50pb.

Yale, David. *Publicity Handbook.* Bantam 1982. $3.50pb.

## Real Estate

*Guide to Effective Public Relations.* National Assn. of Realtors, 430 N. Michigan, Chicago, IL 60611. $2.00pb.

Marcus, B. *Marketing Professional Services in Real Estate.* National Assn. of Realtors (address above). 1981 $18.00pb.

*Home Builders Publicity Manual.* NAHB, 15th & M Sts. NW, DC 20005. 1984. $9.50.

## Religion

Craig. *Christian Communicators Handbook.* Broadman Press, Nashville. $5.95.

*Religious Public Relations Handbook.* 1982. RPRC, 475 Riverside Dr., NYC 10027. $3.50.

Sumrall and Germany. *Religious Publications Handbook.* Seabury Press 1979. $8.95.

Williams, B. *Public Relations Handbook for Your Church.* Judson 1985. $7.95.

## Restaurants/Food Service

Fisher, Wm. P. *Creative Marketing for the Foodservice Industry.* Wiley 1982. $29.95

## Small Business/Retailing/Shopping Centers

Blake and Bly. *How to Promote Your Own Business.* New American Library 1983. $8.95.

Carlson, L. *Publicity/Promotion Handbook: Complete Guide for Small Business.* CBI Co., 51 Sleeper St., Boston, MA 02210. 1982 $21.50.

Hammond. *Public Relations for Small Business.* Gage Ltd. 164 Commander Blvd., Agincourt, Ontario, Canada M1S 3C7. 1982. $7.50pb.

*Public Relations/Publicity: Fundamentals for Shopping Center Professionals.* Intl. Council of Shopping Centers, 665 Fifth Av., NYC 10022. $7.00.

*Retailer's Guide to Public Relations.* NRMA, 867 Sixth Av., NYC 10001. $10.50.

## Special Events

*Leibert. Handbook of Special Events for Nonprofit Organizations.* Assn. Press 1982. $12.95.

## Sports/Recreation/Travel

Bronzan. *Public Relations for Athletic Programs.* Wiley 1976. $22.50.

Eppley. *Improve Your Public Relations.* (parks) NRPA, 1601 N. Kent, Arlington, VA 22209. 1977. $12.95.

Reilly. *Travel/Tourism Marketing Techniques.* Merton House 1980. $14.95.

## Theater

Marshall, S. *Promotion for Theater.* Creative Books 1983. $8.95pb.

## Utilities

Sullivan, F. *Crisis of Confidence, Public Relations and Credibility.* Phoenix 1977. $9.95.

## Writing/Speaking/Stylebooks/Newsletters

Arnold, E.C. *Editing the Organizational Publication.* Ragan Communications (address above) 1982. $25.00.

*Ayer Public Relations/Publicity Stylebook.* IMS Press, 426 Pennsylvania Av., Fort Washinton, PA 19034. 1983. $12.95

Beach, M. *Editing Your Newsletter.* Coast to Coast Books, 2934 NE 16th Av., Portland, OR 97212. 1983. $17.50, $9.95pb + $3.00 postage prepaid.

Bernstein. *The Careful Writer.* Atheneum 1975. $14.95, $9.95pb.

*Broadcast News Stylebook.* Associated Press, NYC. $2.00.

Darrow. *House Journal Editing.* Interstate Co., Danville, IL 61832. 1975. $5.95pb.

Detz, J. *How to Write and Give a Speech.* St. Martin's Press 1985. $5.00pb.

Douglas, G. *Writing for Public Relations.* Merrill 1980. $10.95pb.

*Editing the Organizational Publication.* Ragan Communications (address above). 1984. $25.00.

Excutive Speechmaker. Fdn. for Public Relations, (address above). $5.00.

*F,F, & B: Producing Flyers, Folders and Brochures.* Ragan Communications (address above). 1984. $20.00.

*Guidelines for Report Writers: Complete Manual for On-the-Job Report Writing.* Prentice-Hall 1982. $17.95, $9.95pb.

Hayakawa. *Language in Thought and Action.* Harcourt 1978. $11.95.

Hudson, Howard Penn. *Publishing Newsletters.* Scribners 1982. $16.95.

Jacobi, P. *Writing with Style: The News Story and the Feature.* Ragan Communications (address above) 1982. $15.00pb.

*New York Times Manual of Style/Usage.* McGraw-Hill 1977. $10.00.

Newscom and Carrell. *Writing in Public Relations Practice.* Wadsworth 1985.

*On Graphics: Tips for Editors* (newsletters). 1981. $15.00pb. *How to Conduct a Readership Survey.* 1982. $30.00pb. Ragan Communications (address above).

Pesmen, S. *Writing for the Media.* Crain 1983. $12.95pb.

Reid. *How to Write Company Newsletters.* Rubicon, POB 144, Deming, WA 98244. 1980. $8.00pb.

Reid. *Speaking Well.* McGraw-Hill 1982. $14.95.

Roman and Raphaelson. *Writing That Works.* Harper 1981. $9.95.

Skillin and Gay. *Words Into Type.* Prentice-Hall 1979. $20.95.

Stedman. *Guide to Public Speaking.* Prentice-Hall 1981. $12.95.

*Stylebook/Libel/Manual.* Associated Press, NYC. $2.95.

Tarver. *Effective Speech Writing.* Speech Writing Inst., POB 444, Richmond, VA 23173. 1982. $20.00.

Wales. *Practical Guide to Newsletter Editing/Design.* Iowa Univ. Press 1976. $4.50pb.

## III. Bibliographies/Directories

**Bibliographies**

Norton, Alice. *Public Relations: Guide to Information Sources.* Gale 1970. $40.00.

*Public Relations, the Edw. Bernayses and the American Scene.* Faxon 1978. $25.00.

Public relations bibliographies from PRSA: 1900-1963 $6.00, 1964-1972 $10.00 prepaid.

Annual bibliographies from 1973 on are available from *Public Relations Review,* 7100 Baltimore Blvd. #500, College Park, MD 20740. $5.00 each volume prepaid.

**Media Directories**

Atlanta Publicity Outlets. Box 7057, Atlanta, GA 30308. $49.50.

*Ayer Directory.* IMS Press, 426 Pennsylvania Av., Fort Washington, PA 19034. $99.00.

*Bacon's Media Alerts.* Bacon Publishing Co., 332 S. Michigan, Chicago, IL 60604. $140.00.

Bacon's Publicity Checker: Magazines/Newspapers. Bacon Publishing Co. (address above). $135.00 (2 vols.)

*Black Media in America.* Hall Co., 70 Lincoln, Boston, MA 02111. $50.00.

*Broadcasting Yearbook.* Broadcasting Publications, 1735 DeSales NW, DC 20036. $85.00.

*Burrelle's Media Directories: New York State* $42, *New Jersey* $68,
*Pennsylvania* $38, *New England* $49, *Connecticut* $32, *Maine*
$25, *New Hampshire* $25, *Massachusetts* $44, *Rhode Island* $25,
*Vermont* $25, *New England Talk Show* $30, *Greater Boston* $29.
Burrelle Co., 75 E. Northfield, Livingston, NJ 07039.

*Burrelle's Special Directories: Black Media* $50, *Hispanic Media*
$50, *Women's Media* $50.

*Business/Financial News Correspondents & Contacts.* Larriston,
POB 1351, NYC. $60.00.

*Cable TV Publicity Outlets-Nationwide.* Box 329, Washington
Depot, CT 06794. $125.00.

*California Media.* Box 329, Washington Depot, CT 06794.
$72.00.

*College Alumni Publications.* R. Weiner Inc. (address above) 1980.
$20.00

*East Coast Publicity Directory.* IMS Press (address above).
$77.50.

*Editor and Publisher Yearbook.* 11 W. 19th St., NYC 10011.
$50.00.

*Family Page Directory.* Box 329 Washington Depot, CT 06794.
$60.00.

*Finderbinder.* 4141 Fairmont Ave., San Diego, CA 92105. Local
media directories (15), $70 each with newsletter updates.

*Gebbie Press All-in-One Directory.* Box 1000, New Paltz, NY
12561. $58.00 prepaid.

*Hudson's Newsletter Directory.* 7811 Montrose, Potomac, MD
20854. $60.00.

*Hudson's State Capital News Media Contacts Directory* (address
above). $65.00.

*Hudson's Washington Media Directory.* 7811 Montrose, Potomac,
MD 20854. $90.00.

*Internal Publications Directory* ("house organs"). Natl. Research
Bureau, 310 S. Michigan, Chicago, IL 60604. $111.00.

*Investment Newsletters.* R. Weiner Inc. (address above) 1982.
$35.00.

*Kaufman Editorial Guide.* 2233 Wisconsin Av. NW, DC 20007.
$19.95.

*Mediamatic Calendar of Special Editorial Issues.* Media Distribution Services. 307 W. 36th St., NYC 10018. $95.00.

*Medical/Science News Correspondents.* Larriston Inc., POB 1351, NYC 10025. $60.00.

*Metro California Media.* Box 329, Washington Depot, CT 06794. $72.00.

*Midwest Media Directory.* 176 W. Adams, Chicago, IL 60690. $30.00.

*Military Publications.* R. Weiner Inc. (address above) $15.00.

*National Directory of Newsletters.* Gale Co., Book Tower, Detroit, MI 48226. $78.00.

*National Radio Publicity Directory.* Glenn Inc., 17 E. 48th St., NYC 10017. $150.00.

*New England Media Directory.* 5 Auburn, Framingham, MA 01701. $49.00.

*New York Publicity/Outlets.* Box 329, Washington Depot, CT 06794. $72.00.

*News Bureaus in the U.S.* R. Weiner Inc. (address above) $40.00

*Newsletter Yearbook Directory.* POB 311, Rhinebeck, NY 12572. $60.00.

*Northwest Handbook.* Box 9304, Seattle, WA 98109. Annual. $12.00.

*Philadelphia Publicity Guide.* Fund-Raising Institute, Box 365, Ambler, PA 19002. $31.50.

*Publicity in Chicago.* Chicago Convention Bureau, McCormick Place, Chicago, IL 60616. Free.

*Oxbridge Directory of Newsletters.* 150 Fifth Av., NYC 10011. $75.00.

*Radio Programming Profile.* BF/Communication Inc., Cathy Court, Glen Head, NY 11545. $220.00.

*Radio Programs Source Book.* Broadcast Bureau, 100 Lafayette, Syosset, NY 11791. $64.95.

*Standard Periodical Directory.* Oxbridge Inc., 150 Fifth Av., NYC 10011. $195.00.

*Syndicated Columnists.* R. Weiner Inc. (address above). $30.00.

*Texas Media Guide.* Ampersand Inc. 1103 S. Shepard Dr., Houston, TX 77109. $80.00.

*Television & Cable Factbooks.* TV Digest Inc., 1836 Jefferson Place NW, DC 20036. 2 vols. $173.00.

*TV Contacts* $189.00, *TV News* $141.00 *Radio Contacts* $193.00, *Cable Contacts* $171.00. Larimi Inc., 246 W. 38th St., NYC 10018.

*TV Publicity Outlets-Nationwide.* Box 329, Washington Depot, CT 06794. $125.00.

*Twin Cities Media Directory.* ExecuCom, 425 Lumber Exchange Bldg., Minneapolis, MN 55402. $49.95.

*Working Press of the Nation.* National Research Inc., 310 S. Michigan, Chicago, IL 60604. 5-vol. $241.00 (Volume 5 is employee publications directory).

**International Media Directories**

*Bacon's International.* Bacon Publishing Co. (address above) $155.00.

*Hollis Press & Public Relations Annual.* Contact House, Lower Hampton Rd., Sunbury-on-Thames, Middlesex, England TW16 5HG. $50.00.

*Matthews List* (Canadian media). Box CP 1029, Pointe Claire, Quebec, Canada H9S 4H9. $160.00.

*Media Guides International:* 1. *Newspapers Worldwide* $97.50. 2. *Consumer Magazines Worldwide* $75.00. 3. to 6. *Business/ Professional Publications Asia/Pacific, Europe, Latin America, Middle East & Africa.* $95 each except for Europe $115. Directories International, 150 Fifth Ave., NYC 10011.

*Medios Publicitarios Mexicanos.* Av. Mexico 99, Col. Hipdromo Condesa, Mexico City 06170. $320 (3 vols. covering all Mexican media).

*Ulrich's International Directory.* Bowker Co. (address above). $82.00.

**Other Directories**

*American Society of Journalists & Authors Directory.* 1501 Broadway, NYC 10036. $50.00. (Freelance writers).

*Awards, Honors, Prizes.* Gale Research Co., Book Tower, Detroit, MI 48226. $85.00.

*Chase's Annual Events.* Contemporary Books, 180 N. Michigan, Chicago, IL 60611. $14.95.

*Consultants/Consulting Organizations.* Gale Co. (address above). $95.00.

*Corporate Philanthropy Directory.* Gale Co. (address above). 1984. $245.00.

*Directory of Minority PR Professionals* (150 names). PRSA 1984 Members $5.00, Non-members $10.00 prepaid.

*Encyclopedia of Associations.* Gale Research (address above) $150.00.

*Finding the Right Speaker.* ASAE 1575 Eye St. NW, DC 20005. $20.00.

*FORTUNE 500 Directory.* 250 W. 49th St., NYC 10019. $8.00 prepaid.

*Guide to Black Organizations.* Public Relations Dept., Philip Morris USA, 120 Park Ave., NYC 10017. No charge.

*International Directory of Special Events & Festivals.* Special Events Reports, 213 W. Institute Place, Chicago, IL 60610. $69.00.

*Literary Market Place.* Bowker Co. (address above). $49.95.

*Madison Avenue Handbook.* Glenn Co., 17 E. 48th St., NYC 10017. $30.00.

*National Directory of Speakers on Public Relations Topics.* PRSA 1982. $10.00 PRSA members, $35.00 nonmembers, prepaid.

*National Directory of Corporate Public Affairs.* Columbia Books (address above) $50.00.

*Natl. Trade/Professional Assns.* Columbia Books (address above) $40.00.

*O'Dwyer's Directory of Corporate Communications.* 271 Madison Av., NYC 10016. $90.00.

*O'Dwyer's Directory of Public Relations Executives.* (address above) $70.00.

*O'Dwyer's Directory of Public Relations Firms.* (address above) $90.00.

*Personal Image Consultants.* Editorial Service, 96 State St., NYC 11201. $18.00.

*Professional's Guide to Public Relations Services.* R. Weiner Inc. (address above). 1985. $90.00.

*Public Interest Profiles* (250 activist groups). Fdn. for Public Affairs, 1220 16th St. NW, DC 20036. 1984. $180.00
*Public Relations Directory.* PRSA membership directory. $95.00 to nonmembers.
*Speakers & Lectures: How to Find Them.* Gale Co. (address above) $62.00.

## IV. Periodicals (with annual subscription cost)

*Cable Hotline.* Larimi Inc., 246 W. 38th St., NYC 10018. Monthly. $150.00.
*Case Currents.* CASE, 11 DuPont Circle, DC 20036. $30.00.
*Channels.* POB 600, Exeter, NH 03833-0600. Monthly. $30.00.
*Community Relations Report.* POB X, Bartlesville, OK 74005. Monthly. $85.00.
*Contacts.* Larimi Inc. (address above) Weekly. $197.00.
*Corporate Communications Report.* 112 E. 31st St., NYC 10016. 6 issues/year. $75.00.
*Corporate Public Issues.* 105 Old Long Ridge Road, Stamford, CT 06903. 2/mo. $150.00.
*Corporate Shareholder.* 271 Madison Av., NYC 10016. 22 issues/year. $138.00.
*Investor Relations Newsletter.* 305 Madison Av., NYC 10165. Monthly. $95.00.
*Investor Relations Update.* NIRI 1730 K St. NW, DC 20006. Monthly. $125.00.
*IPRA Review.* Keswick House, 3 Greenway, London, England N20 8EE. Quarterly. $56.00.
*Jack O'Dwyer's Newsletter.* 271 Madison Av., NYC 10016. Weekly. $120.00.
*Media Alerts.* Bacon's Inc., 332 S. Michigan, Chicago, IL 60604. Bimonthly. $120.00.
*Newsletter on Newsletters.* POB 311, Rhinebeck, NY 12572. Weekly. $66.00.
*PR Aids' Party Line.* 330 W. 34th St., NYC 10001. Weekly. $130.00.
*PR Reporter.* Box 600, Exeter, NH 03833. Weekly. $125.00.
*Professional Marketing Report.* POB 32387, DC 20007. Monthly. $85.00.

*Public Affairs Review.* 1220 16th St. NW, DC 20036. Annual. $15.00.

*Public Relations Business.* Larimi, Inc. (address above). Weekly $187.00.

*Public Relations Journal.* PRSA. Monthly. $32.00 to nonmembers.

*Public Relations News.* 127 E. 80th St., NYC 10021. Weekly. $217.00.

*Public Relations Quarterly.* POB 311, Rhinebeck, NY 12572. $16.00.

*Public Relations Review.* 7100 Balto. Blvd. #500, College Pk., MD 20740. 4/yr. $27.00.

*Ragan Report.* Ragan Inc., 407 S. Dearborn, Chicago, IL 60605. Weekly. $129.00.

*Social Science Monitor.* 7100 Balto. Blvd., #500, College Pk., MD 20740. Monthly. $64.00.

*Special Events Report.* 213 W. Institute Pl., Chicago, IL 60610. 24/yr. $320.00.

*Speechwriter's Newsletter.* Ragan Inc. (address above), 24/yr. $128.00.

*Television Index, Inc.* 150 Fifth Av., NYC 10011. Weekly $210.00.

*Video Monitor.* 7100 Baltimore Blvd. #500, College Pk., MD 20740. Monthly. $98.00.

# Index

## A

ABC, 108
Accreditation program, of Public Relations Society of America, 40
Advertising
in corporate public relations, 171
and hospital marketing, 611–613
limits on use of, by professional service firms, 223
Advocacy function, of public relations, 52–53
Agence France Presse, 361
Agriculture, public relations activities in, 56, 60–61
Airline Pilots Association (ALPA), use of teleconferencing by, 519–520
Air pollution, 17–18
Air Transport Association (ATA), 75
Alcoholic spirits, advertising of, 301–302
Allstate Insurance, employee publications of, 587–589
American Bankers Association (ABA), on withholding provision, 202–203
American Chemical Society, publicity program for Halley's comet, 674–675
American Cyanamid Company, 312
American Gas Association, 48
American Hospital Association, on press policy, 621

American Institute of Certified Public Accountants, 57
American Iron and Steel Institute, 308–309
American Medical Association, 57
American Petroleum Institute, 48, 56
American Society of Newspaper Editors, 355
Amoco, publication of style book by, 559–561
Analyst tours, use of, for reaching professional investors, 142
Anheuser-Busch Companies, Inc. internal communications program of, 415, 549–551
*Annual Directory of Syndicated Services*, 262
Annual lectures, Foundation for Public Relations Research and Education, 762–820
Annual meetings, in financial public relations, 138
Annual reports, in financial public relations, 136–138
Annual review, by professional services firm, 249
Antidrunk driving program, of Greater Hampton Roads Advertising Federation, 687–691
Antinuclear activism, 8
Antitrust legislation, enforcement of, 142
AP Newsfeatures, 263
Apprenticeship, learning financial public relations under, 128
AP/UPI Radio Network, 115

847

# E